A Cumulative Index to the *Biographical Dictionary* of *American Sports*

A Cumulative Index to the *Biographical Dictionary of American Sports*

Compiled by David L. Porter

GREENWOOD PRESS

Westport, Connecticut • London

Library of Congress Cataloging-in-Publication Data

Porter, David L.
  A cumulative index to the Biographical dictionary of American
sports / compiled by David L. Porter.
    p.   cm.
  "This cumulative index covers the first five volumes in the
Biographical dictionary of American sports series"—Introd.
  ISBN 0-313-28435-0 (alk. paper)
  1. Athletes—United States—Biography—Dictionaries.
I. Biographical dictionary of American sports. II. Title.
GV697.A1P576 1993
796'.092'2—dc20
[B]   93-18030

British Library Cataloguing in Publication Data is available.

Library of Congress Catalog Card Number: 93-18030
ISBN: 0-313-28435-0

First published in 1993

Greenwood Press, 88 Post Road West, Westport, CT 06881
An imprint of Greenwood Publishing Group, Inc.

Printed in the United States of America

The paper used in this book complies with the
Permanent Paper Standard issued by the National
Information Standards Organization (Z39.48-1984).

10 9 8 7 6 5 4 3 2 1

Contents

Introduction

This cumulative index covers the first five volumes in the <u>Biographical Dictionary of American Sports</u> series. The five volumes, classified by sport and published between 1987 and 1992, provide comprehensive biographical information on over 2,700 of the nation's most extraordinary sports figures. These biographical subjects had excelled at the amateur and/or professional level as athletes, managers, coaches, club officials, league administrators, officials, referees, rules developers, broadcasters, writers, and/or promoters.

All major American sports are included in the <u>Biographical Dictionary</u> series. The first two volumes feature baseball and football, America's most prominent team sports. The first (1987) covers 522 baseball luminaries, while the second (1987) encompasses 529 football notables. The third and fourth volumes include eminent persons from other team, dual, and individual sports. Over 500 prominent figures from auto racing, golf, harness and thoroughbred racing, lacrosse, skiing, soccer, tennis, track and field, and other primarily outdoor sports grace the third volume (1988). The fourth volume (1989) highlights over 550 important subjects from basketball, bowling, boxing, gymnastics, ice hockey, figure and speed skating, swimming and diving, weightlifting, wrestling, and other largely indoor sports. The supplemental volume (1992) comprises over 600 additional entries from all major outdoor and indoor sports, with special emphasis on baseball, football, and basketball personnel. Golf, horse racing, ice hockey, tennis, and track and field also are represent-

ed in that volume. Sportscasters, sportswriters, and sports promoters generally are included in the third or fifth volumes. The criteria for the selection of these athletic figures, along with information about the biographical contributors, appear in the preface of each volume.

This cumulative index cites all entries alphabetically. People are listed before other kinds of entries with the same name. Track star Ralph Boston, for example, appears before Boston, MA academic institutions, athletic clubs or associations, newspapers, sporting events, or sports facilities. Middle initials of persons are provided, if known. Individuals with the same first and last names and middle initial are differentiated by notation of their respective sports in parentheses. Nicknames often follow in quotation marks to assist readers in identifying entries.

Five letter classifications indicate the volume location of a particular entry. The classification letter always precedes the page number (s) for the given entry in that particular volume. The five classifications used in order of appearance are:

B - Baseball volume
F - Football volume
I - Basketball and Other Indoor Sports volume
O - Outdoor Sports volume
S - Supplement volume

The page numbers for entries mentioned in more than one volume are listed in the same sequential order as above (B, F, I, O, S).

The index employs several other guidelines:
1. The page numbers of the <u>main</u> biographical entry for a particular subject are italicized. Baseball player Hank Aaron's main biographical entry, for example, reads as B *1-2*.
2. Magazines and newspapers are italicized.
3. Colleges and universities are listed under their given name. State universities usually are cited as "University of" rather than by their geographical location.
4. The names of formal sports clubs, notably Athletic, Boxing, Canoe, Country, Cricket, Fencing, Golf, Horse Racing, Jockey, Lacrosse, Recreation, Rowing, Soccer, Swim, Tennis, Track, Weightlifting, Wrestling, and Yacht, are capitalized.
5. In most instances, the leagues or associations of professional baseball, football, basketball, ice hockey, lacrosse, soccer, and tennis clubs appear in abbreviated form in parentheses immediately following the club entry.
6. Boxers usually are cited under ring names rather than real given names. The real given names are cross referenced to the ring names. The same system applies to other sports figures who performed under different names than their given names.

7. Women athletes are listed under their last married name, where applicable. The given name and earlier married name (s) are cross referenced to the last married name.

8. Olympic Game entries are indexed under either Olympic Games, Summer or Olympic Games, Winter and are subdivided by years. The geographical locations of particular Olympic Games are cross referenced either to Olympic Games, Summer or Olympic Games, Winter.

9. Some major sporting event entries are subdivided chronologically, with the specific year (s) being underlined. Examples include the Summer and Winter Olympic Games, the All-Star and World Series baseball games, the National Basketball Association playoffs, National Collegiate Athletic Association, National Invitation Tournament, and Amateur Athletic Union basketball championships, the Masters, United States Open, and Professional Golfers Association golf tournaments, the United States National and Wimbledon tennis tournaments, and the Pan American Games and World Track and Field Games. All other major sporting events, including auto racing, thoroughbred racing, ice hockey, soccer, swimming and diving, and wrestling, are not subindexed by year.

No separate divisions are made for the biographical subject entries, their specific sports and places of birth, or the names of contributors for the biographical subject entries. This information already appears in the appendixes of the various volumes.

A William Penn College Professional Development Grant and Shangle research funds helped with reproduction costs and other expenditures. Cynthia Harris furnished adept guidance and made numerous valuable suggestions in the planning and preparation of this index. I am deeply indebted to Perry Lund of the Applied Computer Science Department at William Penn College for taking time out of his very busy schedule to put the entire index into camera-ready form.

Index

Aaron, Henry L. "Hank," **B** *1-2*, 4, 97, 388, 394, 412, 486; **S** 7, 51, 95, 163

Aaron, Tommie L., **B** 1

Abbaticchio, Edward J. "Ed," **B** 28

Abbott, Cleve, **O** 448

Abbott, Margaret, **S** 622

Abbott, Senda Berenson, **I** *1-2*, 13

ABC, *See* American Broadcasting Company

ABC-TV, **S** 350, 356

ABC-TV "Game of the Week," **S** 350

ABC-TV "Monday Night Baseball," **S** 350, 355-56, 358

ABC-TV "Superstars," **O** 533

ABC-TV "Wide World of Sports," **S** 350-51, 356

Abdallah, **O** 15, 174, *586-587*

Abdallah Chief, **O** *587*

Abdul-Jabbar, Kareem, **I** *2-4*, 59, 82, 118-19, 188, 225, 251, 278, 294, 317, 331; **S** 272, 278, 315, 325-26, 347

Abdul-Rahmad, Mahdi, **S** *251-52*

Abe Frank, **S** 531

Abebe Bikila Award, **O** 530

Abel, Clarence "Taffy," **I** 570, **S** *537-38*

Abele, Louis, **I** 626

Abercrombie, Ronald T., **O** *233-34*

Aberdeen, SD baseball club (DL, NoL), **B** 512, 595

Aberdeen, WA baseball club (NWL), **B** 193

Abilene Christian University, **B** 351; **F** 399; **I** 303; **O** 501-02

Ablowich, Edgar, **O** 466

Abrahams, Harold, **O** 530, 552

Abrams, Calvin R. "Cal," **B** 15

Abrams, George, **O** 482

Abramson, Jesse, **F** 309; **O** 565-66

Abruzzese, Raymond "Ray," **S** 478

A Coach's World, **S** 312

AC Spark Plug 500 NASCAR Race, **S** 606

Academic All-American, **I** 278, 328;

S 379, 394, 406, 446, 450, 459
Academic All-Big Ten Conference, **S** 391
Academy Award, **S** 496
Academy of Sport, **F** 571
Ack Ack, **O** 229
Acker, Carl, **O** 283
Acom Stakes, **O** 604
Action, **O** 192
Adamek, Donna, **I** 342
Adams, Alvan L., **I** 303; **S** 327
Adams, Benjamin W. "Ben," **S** 565
Adams, Charles B. "Babe," **B** *2-3*
Adams, Donald L. "Don," **I** 230
Adams, Franklin P., **B** 55
Adams, John, **O** *173-74,* 210
Adams, John "Tree," **F** 53
Adams, O. D., **S** 324
Adams, Platt, **S** *565*
Adams Division, **I** 545
Adcock, Joseph W. "Joe," **B** *3-4*
Adderley, Herbert A. "Herb," **F** *1-2,* 354
Addie, Pauline Betz, **O** *319-20,* 327, 336, 348
Adee, George T., **F** 266
Adelboden, Switzerland Ski Competition, **O** 281
Adel-el-Koree, **S** 533
Adelphi University, **F** 127; **O** 428-29
Adios, **O** 207, 574
Adirondack Bat Company, **S** 192
Admiration, **O** 593, **S** 526-27
Admiring, **O** 192
Adored, **O** 606
ADR Belgian Cycling Team, **S** 618
Adrian, MI baseball club (MISL), **B** 195, 581; **S** 238
Advisory Committee for Women, **I** 611
Advocator, **O** 581
Aero Club, Portland, OR, **I** 614
Affectionately, **O** 192, 612

Affirmed, **O** *569-70,* 592, 606, 610
African Track Team, **O** 497
Agase, Alexander "Alex," **F** 482; **S** *361-62*
Agnes, D., **O** 184
Agnew, Spiro, **S** 516
Aguirre, Mark A., **I** 209, 298; **S** *252-54*
Ahern, James "Jimmy," **F** 378
Ahrens, Arthur, **S** 168
Ahumada, Jorge, **I** 385
Aiken, James "Jim," **F** 409, 617
Aikman, Troy K., **S** 393
Ainge, Daniel R. "Danny," **I** *254-55*
Ainley, Bruce, **O** 319
Ainsmith, Edward W. "Ed," **B** 227
Ainsworth, George, **I** 435
A. J. Voit Award, **S** 455
Akron, OH baseball club (OPL), **F** 597; **S** 42
Akron, OH Firestone basketball club (AAU, NBL), **I** 99; **S** 202, 277, 309
Akron, OH Firestone Swim Club, **I** 606
Akron, OH Goodyear basketball club (AAU, NBL), **I** 34; **S** 262, 277
Akron, OH Indians football club (APFC, Ind.), **F** 183, 456, 476-77; **S** 411, 457
Akron, OH Pros football club (NFL), **F** 259, 477-78, 498
Akron, OH Race Track, **O** 230
Akron, OH Skating Club, **I** 512-13
Ak-Sar-Ben Race Track, Omaha, NE, **O** 602
Al Cervi Basketball Camps, **I** 45
Al Somers Umpire School, **S** 29
Alabama, **O** 206
Alabama A & M University, **F** 565
Alabama Amateur Athlete of the Year, **I** 592
Alabama-Florida League (AlFL), **S**

227
Alabama International Speedway, **O** 41
Alabama Military Institute, **S** 195
Alabama Polytechnic Institute, *See* Auburn University
Alabama Sports Hall of Fame, **B** 508; **F** 147, 282; **S** 208, 228, 395, 415
Alabama Stakes, **O** 225, 597; **S** 534
Alabama State University, **O** 485; **S** 566
Alameda, CA baseball club (CaSL), **B** 259
Alameda, CA Naval Air Station, **F** 467
Alamode, **O** 583
Alan-a-Dale, **O** 183
Alaric, **O** 188
Alaskan League, **B** 16
Alaskas of Brooklyn baseball club, **B** 429
Albany College (OR), **O** 469
Albany, GA baseball club (GFL), **B** 490, 503
Albany, NY baseball club (EL), **B** 170, 240, 306, 377; **S** 126-27, 149, 181
Albany, NY baseball club (IL, NA, NYSL), **B** 90,170, 235, 297, 621; **S** 47, 200, 240
Albany State Teachers College (GA), **I** 313; **O** 448
Albatross, **O** 182, 600
Albert, Frank C. "Frankie," **F** *2-3,* 67, 215
Albert, Howard, **I** 395
Alberto, Carlos, **O** 298
Albion College, **F** 292; **S** 124
Albright, Tenley E., *See* Tenley Albright Gardiner
Albright College, **F** 413
Albritton, David D., **O** 476; **S** *566*
Albuquerque, NM Academy, **I** 486

Albuquerque, NM baseball club (PCL, TL), **B** 58, 209, 544; **S** 2, 90, 109, 185
Alcatraz Island Swim, **I** 585
Alcindor, Lewis F., *See* Kareem Abdul-Jabbar
Alco Reriti Track Club, **O** 451
Alcorn College, **B** 192
Alcott, Amy S., **S** *505-06,* 507, 509
Aldens Soccer Club (FRDSL), **O** 309
Alderman, **O** 573
Aldrich, Charles C. "Ki," **F** *3-4*
Aldridge, Victor E. "Vic," **B** 114
Alex, the Life of a Child, **S** 341
Alexander, Charles C., **S** 248
Alexander, Charles F., **S** 411
Alexander, David Dale, **S** *1-2*
Alexander, Doyle L. , **S** 2
Alexander, Frederick B., **O** *320-21,* 325, 356, 378, 385, 421
Alexander, Grover Cleveland, **B** *4-6,* 74, 93, 213, 325, 335, 345, 420, 612; **S** 42, 111, 144
Alexander, Joseph A., **F** *4-5*
Alexander, Robert, **O** 174
Alexander, Robert A., **O** *174,* 185
Alexander, William A. "Bill," **F** *5-6,* 145, 504
Alexander's Abdallah, **O** 586, 588
Alexandria, LA baseball club (CSL, EvL, TL), **B** 418, 522, 593; **S** 227
Alfa-Romeo Racing Team, **0** 8
Alford, Samuel "Sam," **S** 255
Alford, Stephen T. "Steve," **I** 162; **S** *255-56,* 317
Alford, Toinetta, **O** 393-94
Ali, Muhammad, **I** *353-54,* 383-86, 395, 401, 428, 466; **O** 59, 61; **S** 343, 347, 359, 612, 623
Alice Carneal, **O** 594
Alice Gray, **O** 609
Alkmann, The Netherlands Speed

4

Skating Competition, **O** 313

All-Air Force Boxing Championship, **I** 384

All-America Academic Team, **S** 263

All-America Baseball Team, **I** 105, 295; **O** 537; **S** 89, 94, 114, 138, 146, 204, 402

All-America Basketball Team (AAU), **I** 63-64, 106, 123, 138-39, 148-50, 181, 192-93, 241, 253, 283, 324

All-America Basketball Team (College Men), **I** 3, 5, 7, 10, 16, 23, 25-26, 31, 34-35, 38, 41, 43, 46, 50-51, 56-63, 67, 70-72, 76, 78, 83-88, 90-91, 94, 96-97, 100-01, 104, 108, 113, 116-18, 124, 127, 129, 134-35, 137-38, 142, 146, 148, 150-51, 153, 155, 160, 162-63, 166-67, 169, 180-81, 184, 186-87, 189-94, 196, 198-200, 204, 211-12, 219, 225-27, 237, 239, 241, 244, 249-52, 254, 256, 259, 261, 264, 266-67, 269, 272, 274, 277, 281-83, 293, 295, 297, 299, 301-03, 306, 308, 310-11, 315, 317-18, 322-23, 327, 329, 331, 333; **O** 171; **S** 251-55, 260, 262, 265, 267-68, 270-71, 273, 276, 278, 282, 284-85, 292, 294, 296-98, 302-04, 306, 309, 312, 315-18, 320-31, 333, 362

All-America Basketball Team (College Women), **I** 27, 54-55, 59, 72, 175; **S** 320

All-America Basketball Team (High School Girls), **I** 183, 214

All-America Bowling First Team, **I** 339, 341-43, 347-49, 351

All-America Bowling Second Team, **I** 339, 343, 348-49

All-America Diving Team, **I** 497

All-America Field Hockey Team, **O** 270

All-America Football Conference (AAFC), **F** 2-3, 26, 34, 69-70, 118-19, 165. 179, 184, 188, 203, 215, 229, 268, 272, 283, 318-19, 331, 340, 369, 379, 381, 386, 393, 408-09, 453, 457, 467, 488-89, 549, 559-60, 600, 645, 656-67, 670; **O**, 104; **S** 361, 380-81, 424, 430, 460, 465; championship game of, **F** 70, 203, 215, 409, 453, 457, 559, 656-57

All-America Football Team (college or university), **F** 2, 4-5, 8-9, 11-14, 16, 18, 20, 24, 27, 29, 32-33, 38-39, 41, 43-45, 49-51, 54, 56-59, 62-66, 68, 71-72, 74-79, 81, 83, 86-87, 89-91, 93-94, 98-102, 104, 107, 109, 111-15, 117, 119-22, 125-33, 136-39, 141-42, 144-45, 149-50, 153-54, 157-62, 167-70, 172, 174-78, 181, 184, 186-87, 189, 191-93, 195, 197-201, 204-05, 207, 211-15, 217-18, 220-22, 224-26, 230-31, 235-41, 243, 248-50, 253, 255-56, 258-59, 263, 265, 267, 269-73, 275-79, 281, 286, 291-93, 296-99, 301-03, 305, 307, 310, 314, 318-20, 322-25, 327, 332, 335-38, 340-42, 344, 347, 349-51, 353, 355-59, 361, 364, 367-70, 372, 374, 377-80, 382-83, 386-88, 390-94, 396-97, 401, 403-04, 406-07, 409-10, 412-13, 415-16, 418, 422-23, 425-27, 431, 433, 437-39, 441-43, 448, 451-52, 454, 457-58, 463-65, 468-72, 474-76, 479, 485, 489, 491-92, 495-98, 501-02, 504-05, 509, 512, 514-16, 518, 524-25, 528, 530-33, 535-37, 539-40, 545-53, 555-56, 560, 563-64, 566, 568-69, 571-77, 579-80, 583-85, 587-88, 592, 594-95, 597-99, 602, 604-06, 609-10, 615, 621-

22, 627, 629-30, 633, 637, 641-44, 646-51, 653, 655, 657-61, 664, 668, 670-71; I 39, 67, 80, 113, 116, 163, 660; O 80, 87, 99; S 361-62, 365-71, 373-77, 379-80, 385-86, 388-89, 391-98, 400, 402-17, 419-21, 423-25, 429-31, 433-35, 437-39, 443-49, 452-53, 455-56, 458-67, 470-74, 476-78, 481, 483-85, 487, 489-91, 493-96, 498-501, 546, 580

All-America Golf Team, O 130, 143, 146; S 508, 521

All-America Gymnastic Team, I 526

All-America Hockey Team, I 546, 550, 561, 564-67; S 541

All-America Lacrosse Team,O 234-42, 244-50, 302

All-America Soccer Team, O 236, 301-03, 307-08, 310

All-America Softball Team, I 325; O 262

All-America Swim Team, I 579, 596, 604

All-America Track and Field Team, I 531; O 435, 448, 477, 522, 557, 562, 564; S 467

All-America Volleyball Team, I 676; S 613

All-America Wrestling Team, I 639-40, 642, 654-55, 658, 666

All-American Basketball Association All-Rookie Team, S 296

All-American Basketball Association First Team, I 17, 81, 98; S 273-74, 288, 305

All-American Black Tourists baseball club, F 195

All-American Board of Football, F 358, 504

All-American Bowl football game, F 330

All-American Football League Team,

S 363, 389, 394, 433, 443, 450, 469, 478-79

All-American Gymnastic Classic, I 526

All-American League Baseball Team, S 6, 51, 193, 214

All-American Pro Basketball Club, I 113

All-American Racers, O 12

All-American Track and Field Meet, O 457

All-Army Basketball Team, I 676

All-Army Football Team, I 676

All-Athletic Association of Western Universities Team, S 467

All-Atlantic Coast Conference Team, I 34; S 275, 282, 298, 304, 316, 386, 429, 482

All-Atlantic Coast Conference Silver Anniversary Football Team, S 429

All-Basketball Association of America First Team, I 89, 334-35

All-Big Eight Conference Team, I 303, 323; S 404, 408

All-Big Six Conference Team, I 148, 216; O 427; S 320, 461

All-Big Ten Conference Academic Team, S 451

All-Big Ten Conference Team, I 85, 117, 167, 297, 310-11; S 262, 276, 299, 303, 306, 317, 391, 397-98, 402, 414, 449, 494

All-Black All-Star baseball game, I 102

All-Border Conference Team, S 425, 484

All-Central Conference Basketball Team, I 271

All-Comers Tennis Championships, See U. S. Men's and Women's Tennis Championships through 1911

All-Eastern Intercollegiate Basketball

League, I 84

All-Eastern Professional Basketball League Team, S 267

All-Eastern Team, I 113, 254; S 271, 400, 416, 425, 459-60, 484, 541

All-Eastern Track and Field Games, O 497

All-England Croquet and Lawn Tennis Club Rules, S 560

All-England Field Hockey Team, O 254

All-England Tennis Championships, *See* Wimbledon Tennis Championships

All-Fort Wayne Basketball Team, I 195

All-Ivy League Team, I 286; S 265, 541

All-Kentucky Indiana Athletic Conference Basketball Team, I 88

All-Lone Star Conference Team, I 174

All-Maryland Basketball Team, O 239

All-Maryland Football Team, O 234, 241

All-Maryland Lacrosse Team, O 236, 238-39, 249-50

All-Metropolitan Basketball Team, I 200

All-Mid-America Conference Basketball Team, O 329

All-Midwestern Basketball Team, I 329

All-Midwestern Soccer Team, O 305

All-Military Service Basketball Championship, I 100, 334

All-Missouri Valley Conference Team, I 140, 181; S 268, 440

All-Mountain States Athletic Conference Team, S 396

All-National Basketball Association Defensive Team, I 46-47, 54, 65, 87, 145. 148, 153, 203, 205, 219, 279, 303, 323; S 269, 300, 315, 328

All-National Basketball Association First Team, I 3, 10-11, 19, 24, 26, 46, 51, 58, 62, 82, 86-87, 89, 96, 102, 119, 145-47, 149, 153, 188, 190, 203-04, 212, 237, 241, 251, 263, 270-71, 274, 278, 298, 300, 309, 323, 334-35; S 258, 261, 286, 294, 327

All-National Basketball Association Rookie Team, S 272, 278, 285, 292, 294, 298-99, 328, 331

All-National Basketball Association Second Team, I 3, 10, 24, 33, 44, 46, 51, 59, 61, 78-79, 82-83, 87, 96, 104, 106, 108, 119, 124, 136-37, 145-46, 149, 151, 185, 188, 200, 203-05, 212, 237, 239, 241, 263, 271, 278-79, 298, 308, 319, 323-24, 334; S 261, 275, 282, 294, 306, 327, 330

All-National Basketball Association Third Team, S 315

All-National Basketball League First Team, I 44, 62, 133, 194-95; S 277

All-National Basketball League Second Team, I 133, 194, 266

All-National Collegiate Athletic Association Basketball Tournament Team, I 249

All-National Collegiate Athletic Association Hockey Tournament Team, I 550, 565

All-National Football League Rookie Team, S 391, 414, 487

All-National Football League Team, S 364, 368, 378-79, 383, 386, 391, 406, 413-15, 429-30, 436-38, 440-42, 451, 457-58, 466-67, 469, 474, 485, 487, 495, 499-500, 503; *See* All-Pro Football Team

All-National Hockey League Second

Team, **S** 545

All-National League Baseball Team, **S** 26, 73, 166

All-Nations baseball club, **S** 43, 137, 224

All-North American Soccer Team, **O** 305

All-Ohio Conference Team, **I** 6; **S** 397

All-Pacific Coast Conference Team, **I** 76, 91, 93, 96, 101, 134, 241, 274; **S** 38, 204, 445

All-Pacific Eight Conference Team, **S** 326, 494

All-Pacific Ten Conference Team, **S** 278

All-Pro Football Team, **F** 1-2, 9-11, 14, 16-20, 23, 25-26, 28, 31, 33, 36, 40, 42, 50, 56, 59, 62-63, 67, 69, 71-73, 77, 79-81, 89, 91, 98, 103-04, 106, 111-12, 119, 121-22, 131-32, 140, 142-43, 146, 150, 152, 154, 158, 160-61, 169, 176, 178, 184, 186-87, 193, 202-03, 205, 207, 216-17, 220-24, 226, 229-32, 234, 237-38, 247, 249, 253-54, 256, 258-60, 263-64, 267, 271, 273-75, 278-79, 282, 285-86, 292, 296, 298, 303-04, 307, 309, 312, 315-16, 319, 322-24, 330-32, 334-37, 340-41, 346-49, 351, 357, 361-64, 367, 370-71, 375, 382, 385-87, 389-90, 392, 395-96, 398-400, 408, 414-15, 417, 419-20, 423, 425, 430-31, 434, 437, 441, 445, 448, 451-52, 454, 462, 466-67, 470, 476, 478, 480, 482-83, 490, 496-97, 499, 502-03, 521-22, 525, 535-37, 542, 548-51, 557, 560, 566-67, 569-70, 574, 581, 583, 587-90, 598, 600-01, 605, 608, 610, 613-15, 619, 629, 631, 634-35, 639, 641-43, 645, 647, 650-52, 656-62, 667; **I** 660-61; **O** 554; *See also* All-National Football League Team

All-Pro 300 Auto Race 300, Harrisburg, NC, **O** 41

All-Rochester Pro Basketball Five, **I** 45

All-Rocky Mountain Conference Team, **I** 301, **S** 331

All-Rookie Football Team, **S** 391, 414

All-Service Boxing Championships, **I** 362

All-Service Football Team, **F** 66, 154, 305, 319, 576, 604, 622; **S** 466

All-Service Wrestling Championships, **S** 498

All-Southeastern Conference Academic Team, **S** 399

All-Southeastern Conference Team, **I** 135, 237, 249; **S** 260, 277, 286, 329, 365, 394-95, 399, 412, 431, 452, 463, 478, 504

All-Southern Conference Team, **S** 388, 466

All-Southern Intercollegiate Athletic Conference Team, **S** 441

All-Southwest Conference Team, **I** 205; **S** 54, 96, 423, 428, 450

All-Southwestern Athletic Conference Team, **S** 364, 389

All/Sports Pro Magazine, **I** 45

All-Star Baseball Game, **B** <u>1933</u>, 27, 35, 87, 178, 212, 243, 326, 591, 594; <u>1934</u>, 35, 87, 178, 212, 242, 570, 577, 591; <u>1935</u>, 35, 87, 145, 178, 212, 242, 570, 577, 591; <u>1936</u>, 161, 178, 212, 242; <u>1937</u>, 18, 142, 178, 212, 242, 246, 570, 591; <u>1938</u>, 161, 178, 212, 235-36, 344, 570; <u>1939</u>, 145, 235-36, 344, 570; <u>1940</u>, 145, 570, 616; <u>1941</u>,

130, 157-58; 1966, 57, 157-58, 193; 1967, 35, 57, 157-58, 166, 244; 1968, 57, 157-58; 1969, 9, 57, 157-58; 1970, 35, 57, 157, 160, 166; 1971, 35, 57, 80, 138, 157; 1972, 9, 57, 78, 123, 148, 170; 1973, 9, 29, 51, 57, 89, 136, 148, 185; 1974, 9, 35, 53, 136, 138, 148, 213, 244; 1975, 57, 78, 138, 148, 193, 214, 244; 1976, 78, 103, 138, 185, 357; 1977, 25, 49, 80, 173, 193, 214, 218; 1978, 29, 51, 213-14; 1979, 12, 53, 205, 218; 1980, 8, 103, 114, 175, 185, 217; 1981, 8, 51, 115, 172, 207; 1982, 49, 78, 80, 90, 172, 207, 218; 1983, 172, 206-07, 236; 1984, 153, 172, 207, 236; 1985, 6, 34, 172, 207, 236; 1986, 6, 90, 172, 207, 237; 1987, 6, 51, 96, 172, 206-07; 1988, 2, 49, 207; 1989, 6, 174, 207; 1990, 49, 207; 1991, 7, 49, 141, 206-07

All-Star Baseball Team, I 261

All-Star Canadian Soccer Team, O 511

All-Star Club Lacrosse Team, O 247

All-Star College (North-South) Lacrosse Game, O 235, 238-39, 247, 249

All-Star Football Game, O 104

All-Star Sports Associates, F 345

All-Star Teams: American Negro League, S 189; Associated Press, S 206, 282; John Donaldson Baseball, S 43; Knute Rockne, S 483; United Press International, S 6; West Coast Army, S 394

All-Time Teams: All-American Field Hockey, O 260; American Football League, S 363, 375, 450, 478-79; American Lacrosse, O 242; American Olympic, O 522; Buffalo Bills Silver Anniversary, S 472, 479; Cornell Football, S 394; East, S 476; Football Writers Association of America Midwest Sectional, S 362; George Kirksey, S 443; George Trevor's College Football, S 434; George Trevor's Midwest Sectional, S 424; George Trevor's South Sectional, S 388; Harvard, S 376, 489, 541; Iowa, S 392; Johns Hopkins University Lacrosse, O 234, 237, 239, 249-51; Lacy Lockert's All-American, S 433; Michigan State Football, S 472; Minnesota Vikings, S 490; Negro League All-Star, S 10, 224; New York *Evening World* All-American Football, S 444; Pennsylvania, S 482; Pittsburgh Steelers, S 367, 407; Rose Bowl, S 500; St. Louis Browns, S 32; Southeastern Conference, S 499; Specialists, S 371, 376, 388, 394, 424; University of Pittsburgh, S 482; Walter Camp All-American, S 376; Washington Club Lacrosse Team, O 250-51; Western Conference, S 362; Yale University, S 371

All-Tournament Teams: National Collegiate Athletic Association, S 547; National Invitation Tournament, S 322, 325; World Cup, S 613

All-Utah-Idaho Junior College Conference Basketball Team, I 320

All-West Coast Athletic Conference Basketball Team, I 214-15

All-West Coast Basketball Team, S 18

All-Western Athletic Conference Team, O 480; S 273

All-Western Conference Team, I 129,

167, 191, 234, 272, 312, 329; **S** 333, 392, 443

All-Wisconsin State Conference Team, **S** 279

All-Women's Professional Basketball League Team, **I** 175

All-World Basketball Tournament Team, **I** 195, 325; **S** 277

All-World Volleyball Team, **I** 676

All-World Women's Softball Team, **S** 325

Allegheny College, **I** 158

Allegheny, PA baseball club (AA, IA), **B** 206-07

Allegheny, PA football club, **F** 176

Allen, Aileen, **I** 493

Allen, Forrest C. "Phog," **I** 4-6, 37, 39, 45, 69, 77, 116, 139, 148, 181, 184, 216, 229, 242, 251, 256-57, 281-82; **S** 259, 321

Allen, George H., **F** 6-8, 20-21, 33, 197, 292, 362, 471, 489, 503, 593; **S** 365, 429

Allen, Gerald "Gerry," **F** 304

Allen, John T. "Johnny," **S** 24

Allen, Lisa Marie, **I** 505

Allen, Lucius, **I** 331

Allen, Marcus, **F** 8-9, 494; **S** 468, 473

Allen, Melvin "Mel," **F** 244; **O** 45-46, 49-50, 67, 84; **S** 86, 348-49

Allen, Newton H. "Newt," **B** 6-7

Allen, Richard A. "Dick," **B** 7-8; **S** 135

Allen Fieldhouse, Lawrence, KS, **I** 182

Allen's All-Time College Basketball Team, **I** 77

Allentown, PA baseball club (CL, EIL, EL, PSL), **B** 281, 304, 537, 541; **S** 21

Allentown, PA Crestettes basketball club, **I** 28

Allerdice, Ellen Hansell, **O** 321-22, 405

Allerdice, Louise, **O** 321, 405

Allerdice, Mary T., **O** 321

Allis, Peter, **O** 119, 158

Allison, Robert A. "Bobby," **O** 1-2, 41, 44

Allison, William Robert "Bob," **S** 2-3

Allison, Wilmer L., **O** 322-23, 347, 395, 408, 410, 418; **S** 357

Allison Danzig Cup, **O** 61

Allison Danzig Trophy, **S** 339

Allison Danzig's All-Time Specialists, **S** 371, 376, 388, 394, 424, 431, 489

Alma Ata, USSR Speed Skating Competition, **O** 314

Alma College, **F** 6, 136, 244

Almahurst Farm, **O** 586

Almendares, Cuba baseball club (CUWL), **S** 224

Aloha Bowl football game, **F** 289, **S** 393

Alou, Matteo "Matty," **S** 34

Alouette, **S** 533

Alpental Ski Racing Program, **O** 273

Alphonso XIII of Spain, **O** 212

Alpine, TX baseball club (SpL), **S** 163

Alsah, **O** 615

Alston, Walter E. "Walt," **B** 8-9, 139, 619; **O** 93; **S** 46, 90, 109, 133

Alta, UT Ski Competition, **O** 276

Althea, **S** 530

Altobelli, Joseph S. "Joe," **B** 596

Altoona, PA baseball club, **S** 18

Altoona, PA 200 Auto Race, **O** 22

Altrock, Nicholas "Nick," **B** 227

Altwegg, Jeanette, **I** 506

Alworth, Lance D., **F** 9-10, 312, 335

Alydar, **O** 569-70

Alysheba, **O** 204, 218, 227, 229

Amaker, Thomas,"Tommy "S 295
Amarillo, TX baseball club (TL), S 103, 134
Amateur Athlete, I 670
Amateur Athletic Union, F 50, 510, 597; I 28, 55, 57, 63, 70, 74, 77, 80, 93, 105-07, 111, 123, 125, 138-39, 148-50, 166, 175, 177, 180-81, 184, 188, 192-93, 208-10, 214, 221, 246, 253, 255, 264, 276, 283, 288, 302, 324-27, 333-34, 486, 488, 490-91, 498, 529-30, 576, 603-04, 610, 612, 617-19, 623, 650, 665, 670-71; O 255, 258, 268, 448, 455, 458, 491, 515-17, 546, 556, 558-59; S 262, 289, 331, 367, 594, 598
Amateur Athletic Union All-American Basketball Team, O 262
Amateur Athletic Union All-Star basketball game, I 284
Amateur Athletic Union Basketball Committee, I 125, 269, 326
Amateur Athletic Union Basketball Tournament, I 38, 54-55, 70, 125, 166, 172, 255, 325-26; 1906, 87; 1907, 87, 236; 1908, 87; 1918, 264; 1921, 63; 1923, 63; 1924, 236; 1925, 181; 1926, 63; 1927, 63; 1929, 326; 1932, 192; 1933, 57; 1934, 57, 148; 1935, 148; 1937, 57, 106, 139, 192, 276; 1938, 106, 193, 296; 1939, 106, 139, 193, 283; 1940, 57, 139, 188, 193; 1941, 57, 193; 1942, 106, 193, 283; 1943, 106, 193, 283-84; 1944, 106, 193, 283-84; 1945, 106, 193, 253, 283-84; 1946, 106, 283-84; 1947, 106, 283-84; 1948, 106, 166, 253, 283-84; 1949, 253, 283-84; 1950, 123, 166, 253, 283-84; 1951, 18, 334; 1952, 166, 253, 334; 1953, 253; 1956, 246, 255;

1957, 246, 255, 325; 1958, 255, 325; 1959, 246, 255, 325; 1960, 255, 325; 1961, 202, 246, 255, 325; 1962, 55, 123, 255, 325; 1963, 55, 123, 255, 325; 1964, 55, 123, 255, 325; 1965, 123, 325; 1966, 123, 325; 1967, 123, 325; 1968, 123, 325; 1969, 123; 1970, 246; 1971, 246; 1978, 28; 1979, 28; S 289, 331
Amateur Athletic Union Boxing Championships, I 359, 380-81, 389, 397, 401, 417, 427, 445, 447, 452, 459, 645; S 612
Amateur Athletic Union Cross Country Championships, O 424, 512, 521, 534
Amateur Athletic Union Diving Championships, I 486
Amateur Athletic Union Far Western States Swim Meet, I 610
Amateur Athletic Union Hall of Fame, I 55, 123, 193, 325
Amateur Athletic Union Indoor Diving Championships, I 485-87, 489, 491-93, 495-98
Amateur Athletic Union Indoor Track and Field Championships, O 423-24, 428, 432-33, 437, 440, 447-48, 452, 454, 476, 490, 495, 497-98, 500, 506, 508, 513, 522, 533-34, 538, 546, 555, 559; S 367, 566, 570, 577, 581, 585, 588-89, 595-96; *See also* Track Athletic Congress Championships
Amateur Athletic Union Junior Greco-Roman Wrestling Tournament, I 640
Amateur Athletic Union Junior Gymnastic Championships, I 522, 539
Amateur Athletic Union Junior Olympic Diving Championships, I

491
Amateur Athletic Union Junior Outdoor Swimming Championships, I 599
Amateur Athletic Union Junior Track and Field Championships, S 576, 590
Amateur Athletic Union Marathon Championships, S 583
Amateur Athletic Union Men's Gymnastic Championships, I 521, 523-27, 529-31, 535, 537
Amateur Athletic Union Men's Indoor Swimming Championships, I 578, 587, 591-95, 598, 608-09, 618, 620
Amateur Athletic Union Men's Outdoor Diving Championships, I 485, 487, 489-90, 492-93, 495-98
Amateur Athletic Union Men's Outdoor Swimming Championships, I 576-78, 584, 586-87, 591-95, 598, 600, 603, 605-06, 608-09, 613, 616, 618, 620
Amateur Athletic Union New England Track and Field Championships, S 596
Amateur Athletic Union Outdoor Swimming Championships, S 622
Amateur Athletic Union Outdoor Track and Field Championships, O 171, 423-24, 427-28, 430, 432, 436-38, 440, 442, 445, 447-51, 454, 456-66, 468, 470-73, 475-80, 483-85, 488-92, 494, 496-97, 499-500, 502, 505-06, 508-13, 519-22, 524, 528, 530, 533-35, 538, 542-43, 545-50, 553, 555, 557-60, 562, 564, 566, 568; S 367, 565-68, 570-78, 585-89, 593-97
Amateur Athletic Union Outstanding Wrestler, I 658

Amateur Athletic Union Records Committee, I 177
Amateur Athletic Union Road Racing Championships, S 582-83
Amateur Athletic Union Southern Pacific Association, S 574
Amateur Athletic Union/USA Junior Olympic Program, S 597
Amateur Athletic Union Water Polo Championships, I 489
Amateur Athletic Union Women's Gymnastic Championships, I 529, 531-32, 534
Amateur Athletic Union Women's Indoor Swimming Championships, I 579, 583, 586, 596, 599, 608, 610, 619, 621-22
Amateur Athletic Union Women's Junior Outdoor Swimming Championships, I 622
Amateur Athletic Union Women's Outdoor Swimming Championships, I 575, 579-80, 583, 586, 596, 599, 607-08, 610-11, 613, 619, 621-22
Amateur Athletic Union Women's Track and Field Championships, I 531
Amateur Athletic Union Wrestling Championships, I 359, 637-38, 640, 645, 647, 649-51, 653-59, 662-63, 665; S 608, 616, 624
Amateur Athletic Union Wrestling Committee, I 651-52
Amateur Athletic Union Wrestling Handbook, I 666
Amateur Basketball Association of the United States of America, I 214, 288; S 279, 321
Amateur Basketball Association of the United States of America Women's Games Committee, I 291
Amateur Basketball Association

Officials Committee, **I** 277

Amateur Basketball Hall of Fame, **I** 106

Amateur Bicycle League of America, **O** 316

Amateur Fencers League of America, **I** 669

Amateur Hockey Association of the United States, **I** 549, 552, 555; **S** 537, 543-44

Amateur of the Year Award, **I** 674

Amateur Sports Act, **I** 611

Amateur Sportsman of the Year Award, **S** 627

Amateur Wrestling Athletic Hall of Fame, **I** 647; **S** 609

Amateur Wrestling News, **I** 641

Amberoid, **O** 575

Ambers, "Lou," **I** *354-55,* 356, 364, 435, 483

Ambush, **S** 536

Ameche, Alan D. "The Horse," **F** *10-11,* 165; **S** 378

America, **O** 101

American, **O** 64, 72

American Alliance for Health, Physical Education, Recreation, and Dance, **F** 564; **I** 2; **O** 254

American Association, **B** 109-10, 309, 407, 541, 557, 561, 576; **S** 4-6, 12, 14-15, 17, 21-22, 25, 27, 32-34, 42, 45, 47, 53-54, 58-59, 66, 78-79, 81-82, 84, 86-87, 97, 100, 102, 106, 110-12, 119, 123-24, 126, 131, 135, 143, 145, 149-51, 155, 159, 163, 171, 173-74, 182, 192, 195, 197-98, 200, 204-05, 207-08, 217, 223, 226, 229-31, 233, 237, 239, 245

American Association of Basketball Coaches Hall of Fame, **I** 155-56

American Auto Racing Writers and Broadcasters Hall of Fame, **O** 7, 22-23, 26, 35, 43

American Automobile Association Championships, **O** 32, 35

American Automobile Association Driver of the Year Standings, **O** 6-8, 14, 20, 22-26, 31, 42

American Automobile Association Stock Car Circuit, **O** 22-23, 26, 32, 42

American Baseball Coaches Association, **S** 74

American Baseball Federation, **F** 97

American Basketball Association, **I** 3, 15-17, 19-20, 34-35, 47, 58, 81-82, 95-96, 98, 109-12, 117, 121-22, 142, 148-50, 160, 196, 211, 213, 225-26, 234, 239, 279, 288, 299, 335; **S** 266, 273-74, 286-88, 292-97, 304-05

American Basketball Association All-Rookie Team, **I** 196

American Basketball Association All-Star Games, **I** 58, 81, 142, 196, 299; **S** 273-74

American Basketball Association Championships and Playoffs, **I** 17, 35, 81-82, 98, 110-11, 121, 196, 202-03, 275; **S** 266, 269, 272, 274, 288, 292, 305

American Basketball Association Coach of the Year, **I** 35

American Basketball Association Rookie of the Year, **I** 98, 121, 142, 299

American Basketball League, **F** 48, 97; **I** 14, 21, 30, 32-33, 66, 102, 117, 131, 157, 170-71, 178, 186, 194-95, 198, 222-23, 232-33, 250, 260-61, 268, 273-75, 334; **S** 284, 287-89, 322

American Basketball League All-Star Team, **I** 33, 261

American Basketball League

Championships and Playoffs, **I** 32, 66, 102, 170, 178, 194, 202, 223, 260, 273, 275; **S** 322

American Bowling Congress, **I** 338-41, 343, 348, 350; **S** 194

American Bowling Congress All-Events Tournament, **I** 341, 343, 348

American Bowling Congress Doubles Classic, **I** 340, 344, 348, 351

American Bowling Congress Hall of Fame, **I** 337-39, 341, 343, 345, 348, 350-51

American Bowling Congress Masters Tournament, **I** 337-38, 340-41, 344, 348, 351

American Bowling Congress Singles Classic, **I** 339, 343, 351

American Bowling Congress Team Classic, **I** 339, 344, 348, 351

American Broadcasting Company, **F** 74, 208, 308, 419, 458, 500, 509, 514, 545, 581, 584, 649, 654; **I** 8, 28, 176, 215, 251, 263, 308, 339, 503, 511, 532, 611, 618; **O** 47-48, 59, 67-68, 76, 78, 80, 100, 146, 190, 271, 307-08, 475, 488, 533; **S** 123, 343, 350-51, 357

American Classic Golf Tournament, **I** 124

American College Baseball Coaches, **S** 201

American College of Modern Weightlifting, **I** 627

American College of Physical Education, **I** 264

American Derby, **O** 209, 579, 603; **S** 531

American Eclipse, **O** 101, *570-71,* 609

American Expeditionary Force Basketball Team, **I** 248, 497

American Expeditionary Force Boxing Team, **I** 431, 471

American Farmer, **O** 94-95

American Field Hockey Association, **O** 253

American Flag, **O** 194, 596

American Football Association Cup, **O** 306, 310

American Football Coaches Association, **F** 6, 12, 16, 35, 49, 52, 81, 84, 147, 164, 168, 242, 289, 344, 351, 369, 374, 392, 407, 422, 457, 460, 496-97, 499, 514, 516, 523, 525, 559, 564, 585, 626, 663, 671, 674; **I** 177; **S** 396, 436, 448, 456

American Football Coaches Association Membership Committee, **I** 177

American Football Conference, *See* National Football League

American Football Conference Championship Games, **F** 15, 43, 55, 62-63, 72-73, 77, 163, 180, 191, 196, 199, 222, 230, 235, 237, 246, 258, 286, 296, 321, 330, 333, 335, 384-85, 428, 473, 488, 540, 543, 561-62, 565, 572, 580, 585, 590, 620, 643, 657, 659

American Football: Its History and Development, **S** 498

American Football League, **F** 9-10, 18, 20, 26, 31, 36-37, 42, 50, 55-56, 59, 67, 69, 72-73, 75-76, 91-92, 98, 127-29, 133-34, 152, 165, 178-79, 188, 201-02, 210, 217, 234, 243, 253, 256, 273, 277, 280, 285, 293-94, 314, 318, 320, 332, 349, 367, 376, 381-82, 389, 392, 396, 405, 408, 418, 420, 423, 432, 441, 445, 454, 462, 465, 478-79, 496, 539-40, 543, 545, 560-61, 572-73, 581, 590-91, 609-10, 614-15, 631, 633-34, 638, 658, 660,

662, 668; **O** 67, 87, 105; **S** 335,
363, 375, 377, 379, 389-90, 394,
398, 408, 419, 425-26, 429, 432-
33, 441-43, 450, 457, 463, 467,
469-70, 472, 474-75, 478-79, 486-
87, 492, 496
American Football League All-Star
Games and Teams, **F** 2, 10, 18,
20, 36, 42, 50, 55-56, 59, 69, 73,
76-77, 79, 88, 91-92, 104, 132,
134, 141, 202, 223, 230, 234, 236-
37, 245, 247, 253, 258, 260, 273-
74, 279, 298, 316, 324, 333, 337,
340, 347, 355, 371, 389, 396, 415,
419, 423, 425, 430-31, 434, 437,
441, 445, 452, 454, 462-63, 478,
482-83, 487, 491, 496, 502, 525,
529, 539-40, 543, 545, 554, 557,
566, 569, 581, 583, 585, 591, 610,
614-15, 634, 643, 658, 660, 662;
S 363, 375, 433, 443, 450, 478-79
American Football League
Championship Game and Playoffs,
F 10, 36, 55, 72, 76, 91-92, 128,
133, 202, 210, 354, 376, 389, 396,
419, 432, 540, 572, 590-91, 610,
615, 643, 659; **O** 67; **S** 363, 432,
442, 450, 469, 478-79, 492
American Football League Executive
Council, **S** 126
American Golf Hall of Fame, **O** 164
American Golfer, **O** 164
American Hellenic Educational
Progressive Association Athletic
Hall of Fame, **S** 473
American Hockey Association, **I** 36,
553, 555, 559-60, 570
American Hockey Coaches
Association, **I** 546, 569, 572
American Hockey Coaches
Association Coach of the Year, **I**
569
American Hockey League, **I** 421, 545-

46, 554, 557, 560, 562, 564, 567,
573
American Indian Athletic Hall of
Fame, **O** 499
American International College, **I** 129
American Jockey Club, **O** 177
American Lawn Tennis, **O** 375-76,
383
American League, **B** 24, 55, 110,
123-24, 169, 199, 216, 219, 226,
243, 253, 285, 321-22, 353, 355,
367, 369, 430, 435, 457, 477, 483-
84, 492, 512, 516, 523-24, 529,
550, 586-87, 633, 635-37; **F** 9,
23, 40-41, 84, 100, 162, 208-09,
233, 241, 287-88, 314, 383, 385,
389, 391, 402, 418, 420, 424, 430,
453, 492, 573, 592, 602; **I** 29-30,
61, 64, 113, 213, 236, 261, 268,
295, 332-33, 337, 340; **O** 45-46,
49, 52-53, 57, 60, 67, 73-75, 89-
90, 97-98, 124, 129, 234, 453; **S**
1-3, 5-9, 11-22, 24-25, 27-29, 31-
32, 34-41, 43-60, 63-74, 76-81,
83-84, 86-92, 94-96, 98, 100-15,
118-22, 124-28, 130-42, 145-50,
152-61, 163-68, 170-75, 177, 179-
87, 189-215, 218-19, 221-22, 224-
32, 234-37, 239-48, 254, 264-65,
297, 320-21, 342-44, 346-49, 353-
55, 382, 402, 462, 494
American League All-Star Soccer
Club, **O** 294
American League Championship
Series, **S** 2-3, 7, 9, 12, 15-16, 25,
29, 49-51, 57-58, 71, 87-89, 107-
08, 135-36, 141, 146-48, 153, 177,
214-15, 222, 225, 236-37
American League Playoff Game, 1948,
S 103, 121, 163
American Legion, **F** 225
American Magazine, **O** 122, 161
American Negro League, **I** 143, 332;

S 188-89

American Officials Organization, **F** 486

American Olympic Association, **O** 255

American Olympic Committee, **I** 622, 671

American Outstanding Physical Educator Award, **I** 542

American Physical Education Review, **I** 108

American Professional Football Association, **F** 97, 234, 328, 464, 477, 498, 597; **S** 411-12, 457

American Professional Football Association Championships, **S** 457

American Professional Football Conference, **S** 411

American Quarter Horse Association, **O** 590

American Soccer League, **I** 52; **O** 291-93, 297, 29, 303, 310

American Soccer League All-Star Team, **O** 299

American Soccer League Championships, **O** 291, 305

American Soccer League Most Valuable Player, **O** 291

American Society of Newspaper Editors, **S** 337

American Softball Association, **I** 325; **O** 261-62

American Sports Publishing Company, **I** 670

American Sportscasters Association, **F** 376; **O** 46, 50, 53, 63, 68, 79, 84, 100

American Sportscasters Association Hall of Fame, **O** 46, 50, 53, 68, 79, 84, 100; **S** 343

The American Sportsman, **O** 47, 68

American Stud Book, **O** 180, 227

American Swimming Coaches Association, **I** 585

American Telephone and Telegraph Award, **O** 282

American Telephone and Telegraph National Pro-Am Golf Tournament, **S** 524

American Tennis Association Boys Championships, **O** 323

American Tennis Association Girls Championships, **O** 344

American Tennis Association Men's Championships, **O** 323

American Tennis Association Women's Championships, **O** 344

American Trainers Association, **S** 528

American Trotting Register, **O** 227-28

American Turf Register and Sporting Magazine, **O** 85-86, 94-95

American Women's Sports Federation, **S** 320

America's Cup Yacht Race, **O** 51, 100-03, 185, 266

Amerine, James "Jim," **I** 528

Ames, Knowlton L., **F** 116

Ames, Leon K. "Red," **B** 46, 230; **S** 3-4

AMF Grand Prix Bowling, **I** 347

AMG Gymnastics, **I** 523-24

Amherst College, **B** 92, 206; **F** 238; **I** 177; **S** 337

Amiel, "Jack," **O** 205

Amiziah, Anne, **S** 509

Amling, Warren E., **F** 262-63

Amos Alonzo Stagg Award, **S** 456

Amsterdam, The Netherlands 1928 Summer Olympic Games, *See* Olympic Summer Games, 1928

Amsterdam, NY baseball club (CAL), **B** 62; **S** 172

Amsterdam, NY *News,* **S** 238

Anaconda Race Track, **O** 186

Anaheim Stadium, Anaheim, CA, **S**

44

Anall Stable, **O** 198

Anandale Golf Club, Pasadena, CA, **O** 152

Anchovitz, Charles, *See* Charley White

Andersen, Greta, **I** 587

Anderson, David P. "Dave," **S** *335-36*

Anderson, Edward A. "Eddie," **F** *12-13*, 377

Anderson, Eugene, **S** 333

Anderson, Forrest A. "Fordy," **I** 94

Anderson, George L. "Sparky," **B** *9-10*, 614; **S** 72, 74

Anderson, "Gil," **O** 6

Anderson, Heartley W. "Hunk," **F** 12, *13-15*, 377, 532

Anderson, James O. "Jim," **O** 362

Anderson, John, **O** 164

Anderson, Kenneth A. "Ken," **F** *15-16*, 631

Anderson, Ladell, **I** 94

Anderson, Miller, **I** 485

Anderson, Ottis J., **F** *16-18*

Anderson, Paul E., **I** *625-26*

Anderson, Richard P. "Dick," **F** *18-19*

Anderson, Robert C. "Bobby," **F** 18

Anderson, William, **I** 99

Anderson, William Harold "Andy," **I** *6-7*, **S** 270

Anderson, Willie, **O** *107-08*, 132

Andersson, Frank, **I** 641

Andolsek, Ludwig, **I** 547

Andre, Denise Long Sturdy, **I** *7-9*, 183

Andreas, Lewis P. "Lew," **I** 113

Andretti, Aldo, **O** 2-3

Andretti, Mario G., **O** *2-4*, 11, 19, 29, 38-39; **S** 620

Andretti, Michael M., **S** 620

Andrews Air Force Base Basketball Team, **I** 109

Andrews, Michael J. "Mike," **B** 182

Andries, Dennis, **S** 612

Andros, Plato, **S** 462

Androus, **O** 598

Andy Granatelli Syndicate, **O** 3

Andy Williams Golf Tournament, *See* San Diego Open Golf Tournament

Anet, Robert "Bobby," **I** 91

Angell, Roger, **S** *336-37*, 337, 348, 351

Angelmann, Valentin, **I** 481

Angott, "Sammy," **I** 404, 450, 477

Angsman, Elmer, **S** 381, 438, 491

Anheuser-Busch Budweiser Bowling Team, **I** 340, 350

Anheuser-Busch Golf Classic, **S** 522, 524

Ann Arbor, MI Swim Club, **I** 488-89

Ann Curtis School of Swimming, **I** 587

Annacone, Paul, **O** 370

Annapolis, MD Lacrosse Club, **O** 247

Anson, Adrian C. "Cap," **B** *10-12*, 29, 96, 115, 131, 160, 226, 240, 270, 303-04, 324, 496, 549, 568, 584; **F** 159; **S** 169

Ansonia, CT baseball club (CtL, CtSL), **B** 221; **S** 238

Anthony, Earl R., **I** *337-38*, 349

Antoniolli, Carl, **I** 528

Antuofermi, Vito, **I** 397-98

Antwerp, Belgium Summer Olympic Games, *See* Olympic Summer Games, 1920

Aparicio, Luis E., Jr., **B** *12-13*

Apawamis Golf Club, Rye, NY, **O** 107, 153

Apgar, Gordon, **O** 319

Apostoli, Fred, **I** 370

Appalachain League, **S** 1, 11, 136,

147, 221, 231
Appalachain State Teacher's College,
    F 170
Appel, Kenneth, O 408-09
Applebee, Constance M. K., O 253-
    55; I 1
Applegate, Cameron, F 249
Applegate, Hamilton C., O 600-01
Appleton, Gordon Scott, F 515
Appleton, Peter W. "Pete," B 86
Appleton, William, O 349
Appleton, WI baseball club (ML,
    MWL, WSL), B 220, 279; S 6,
    63
Appling, Lucious B. "Luke," B 13-
    15
Aqueduct Handicap, O 192, 579, 581
Aqueduct Race Track, Ozone Park,
    NY, O 175, 180, 197, 203-04,
    206, 215, 223, 596, 604; S 531
Aranza, O 201
Arbanas, Frederick "Fred," S 363
Arbour, Alger "Al," S 545
Arcaro, George Edward "Eddie," O
    174-77, 178, 189-90, 195, 216-18,
    576-77, 598, 612, 615
Archer, Fred, O 201
Archer, "Freddie," I 404
Archer, James P. "Jimmy," B 46
Archer, "Joey," I 396, 456
Archibald, "Joey," I 389, 406
Archibald, Nathaniel "Nate," I 9-10
Arden Hills Swimming and Tennis
    Club, I 612
Ardsley Golf Club, Ardsley-on-the-
    Hudson, NY, O 133
Arena Football League, F 464
Arena Management Association, I
    240
Argentina National Soccer Team, O
    299
Argentina National Tennis
    Championships, O 343; S 550

Argentina Open Golf Tournament, O
    150
Argentina Polo Club, O 260
Argosy, O 64
Arguello, Alexis, I 452
Arian, Walter, I 512
Ariel, O 571; S 526-27
Arion, O 185
Arizin, Paul J., I 10-11, 100, 103,
    239, 252
Arizmendi, "Baby," I 356, 438
Arizona Boxing Championships, I
    426
Arizona Professional Athlete of the
    Year, O 6
Arizona Sports Hall of Fame, I 80
Arizona State League, S 59
Arizona State Tennis Championships,
    O 418
Arizona State University, B 57, 248,
    276, 409, 437; F 136-37, 290-91,
    294, 324-25, 383, 481, 526, 586-
    87, 663; I 426, 540, 642; O 114,
    438, 532; S 8, 18, 89, 142, 175,
    241, 355-56, 406-07, 422-23, 515,
    621
Arizona State University Hall of
    Fame, F 587
Arizona Western University, F 411; I
    9
Arizona Wranglers football club
    (USFL), F 7, 198, 325, 671; S
    409, 454
Arkansas Agricultural, Mechanical &
    Normal College, See University of
    Arkansas at Pine Bluff
Arkansas baseball club (IL, TL), B 7,
    44, 251; S 34, 174, 217
Arkansas City, KS baseball club
    (KSL), B 336
Arkansas Derby, O 183
Arkansas Intercollegiate Conference, F
    245, 390, 663

Arkansas Motor Coaches basketball club, Little Rock, AR, **I** 57
Arkansas Sports Hall of Fame, **F** 282, 390, 395-96; **I** 55, 57; **O** 153, 441
Arkansas State Teachers College, **B** 299; **F** 663; **S** 388-89
Arkansas State Open Golf Tournament, **O** 152
Arkansas State University, **I** 652
Arkansas Tech University, **F** 390
Arkansas-Texas League, **B** 16
Arkansas Travelers basketball club, **I** 57
Arlberg-Kandahar Alpine Ski Competition, **O** 276, 284
Arledge, Roone P., **O** *44-48,* 76; **S** 350
Arlett, Russell L. "Buzz," **S** *4-5*
Arlington Classic Race, **O** 178, 570, 575
Arlington Handicap, **O** 603
Arlington Park, Arlington, IL, **O** 105, 179, 183, 204, 227, 575
Arlington Park Hall of Fame, **O** 179
Armas, Antonio R. "Tony," **B** 249; **S** 51
Armed, **O** 195, *571-72,* 576; **S** 529
Armenia, **O** 206
Armful, **O** 571
Armour, John, **I** 522
Armour, Thomas D., Sr. "Tommy," **O** *108-09,* 111, 116, 145; **S** 515
Armour, Thomas D., Jr., **O** 109
Armour, William C. "Bill," **B** 155, 415
Armstrong, Deborah "Debbie," **O** *273-74*
Armstrong, "Dollie," **O** 273
Armstrong, Henry "Hank," **I** *355-56,* 404, 459, 483
Armstrong, Hugh, **O** 273
Armstrong, Neil, **F** 566

Armstrong Racing Team, **O** 13
Army, *See* United States Military Academy
Arndon, **O** 207
Arneson, Mark E., **S** 497
Arnold College, **F** 503
Arnold Palmer Golf Academy, **O** 149
Arnsparger, William S. "Bill," **S** 384
Arrivederci, Italy basketball club, **I** 189
Arrow Racing Car, **O** 10
Arrudas Soccer Club, Fall River, MA, **O** 309
Art Ross Cup, **I** 555
Arth, Jeanne, **O** 358
Arthur L. Trester Award, **I** 309, 311
Arts and Letters, **O** 190
Art's Chandelle, **O** 227
Artus, George, **I** 223
Asahi Classic, *See* Fukuoka Marathon
Asbury, Taylor, **S** 528
Ascot Gold Cup, **O** 585, 602
Ascot Park, **O** 20
Ashburn, Don Richie, **B** *15-16,* 74, 406; **S** 220, 355
Ashe, Arthur A., Jr., **O** *323-24,* 341; **S** 341
Ashenfelter, Horace III "Nip," **O** *423-24*
Asheville, NC baseball club (Pil, SAL, SL), **B** 10, 86, 410-11, 525, 530; **S** 33
Ashford, Emmet L., **B** *16-17*
Ashford, Evelyn, *See* Evelyn Ashford Washington
Ashland College, **O** 454
Ashland Oaks, **S** 531
Asian Games, **S** 569
Aspen, CO Ski Competition, **O** 276, 281, 284, 288
Aspromonte, Kenneth J. "Ken," **S** 84
Assault, **O** 571-72; **S** 527

Assembly Hall, Bloomington, IN, **I** 162

Assignee, **O** 224

Assistant Wrestling Coach of the Year, **I** 635

Associated Outlook, **I** 108

Associated Press, **F** 12-13, 18, 51, 53, 59, 72, 77-80, 84, 90, 94, 100, 106, 127, 129-30, 132, 137, 143, 146, 155, 158, 169, 173, 184-85, 192, 197-98, 206, 243, 248, 276-77, 305, 310, 317-18, 335, 338, 344, 353, 357, 367, 378, 399, 402, 415, 444, 452, 457-58, 472, 492, 496-97, 504, 507-08, 526, 528, 530, 537, 545, 554, 560, 570, 575-76, 583, 589, 592-95, 597-99, 614, 621-22, 638, 641, 671; **I** 10, 26, 41, 57, 64, 71, 81, 90, 109, 113, 116, 134, 174, 188, 190, 211, 217, 257, 266, 293, 317, 375; **O** 69, 74, 110, 127, 145, 147, 150, 163, 168, 170, 172, 326-28, 344, 352, 361, 364, 374, 387, 474, 482, 492, 546; **S** 135, 206, 256, 264, 282, 303, 316, 344, 346, 370, 402, 404, 414, 453, 501

Associated Press Athlete of the Decade, **O** 147, 150

Associated Press College All-Time All-American Basketball Team, **I** 64

Associated Press Female Athlete of the Year, **I** 57, 344, 511, 536, 598, 611; **O** 110, 127, 168, 170, 172, 326-28, 344, 352, 361, 364, 374, 387, 482, 546

Associated Press Male Athlete of the First Half Twentieth Century, **I** 188, 211, 375

Associated Press Male Athlete of the Year, **I** 26, 266, 615, 617; **O** 145, 163, 474, 492

Associated Press Poll, **S** 268, 291, 370, 379, 400, 412, 419-21, 428-29, 449, 476, 480

Associated Press Rating and All-American Selection Committee, **I** 81

Associated Press Swimmer of the First Half Century, **I** 620

Association of Intercollegiate Athletics for Women, **I** 27, 175, 258, 284-85, 289, 291, 314; **O** 117, 254, 259, 436, 557; **S** 64, 319-20, 517, 579

Association of Intercollegiate Athletics for Women Award of Merit, **O** 254

Association of Intercollegiate Athletics for Women Basketball Tournament, **I** 25, 175, 258, 284-85, 289, 291, 314; **S** 319

Association of Intercollegiate Athletics for Women Field Hockey Championships, **O** 259

Association of Intercollegiate Athletics for Women Golf Championships, **O** 117; **S** 517

Association of Intercollegiate Athletics for Women Golfer of the Year, **O** 117

Association of Intercollegiate Athletics for Women Swimming and Diving Championships, **S** 64

Association of Intercollegiate Athletics for Women Track and Field Championships, **O** 436, 557; **S** 579

Association of Professional Baseball Players, **B** 27

Association of Tennis Professionals, **O** 324, 341, 365, 399-400

Asteroid, **O** 594

Astley Belt, **O** 560

Astor, Henry, **O** 597

Astoria Stakes, **O** 604

Astro-Bluebonnet Bowl football game, *See* Bluebonnet Bowl football game

Assumption College, **B** 384

Atan, Adil, **I** 665

Atco, GA baseball club, **S** 245

Athens, Greece Summer Olympic Games, *See* Olympic Summer Games, 1896, 1906

Athlete of the Year Award, **S** 72, 263, 488, 505, 584; *See also* Most Valuable Player Award

Athletes for Athletes, **I** 597

Athletes-in-Action, **I** 655; **O** 399

Athletic Association of Western Universities, **F** 114, 201, 256, 369, 566, 631; **S** 454, 461-62, 467-68, 499

The Athletic Congress Track and Field Championships, **S** 579, 584

Athletic Directors Hall of Fame, **I** 321

Athletic Institute, **F** 310; **I** 75

Athletic Journal, **F** 572; **I** 276

Athletic League of North American YMCA's, **I** 125

Athletic Park, Minneapolis, MN, **S** 233

Athletics West Club, **O** 425, 539

Atiyeh, Joseph, **I** 636

Atkins, Douglas L. "Doug," **F** *20-21*

Atkins, Kenneth, **S** 613

Atkins, Pervis, **F** 663

Atkins, Robert, **S** 426

Atkinson, Juliette P., **O** *324-26,* 354, 376-77, 406

Atkinson, Kenneth G., **O** 324

Atlanta All-Events Bowling Tournament, **I** 351

Atlanta Athletic Club, **F** 257

Atlanta Baseball Association, **F** 257

Atlanta baseball club, **F** 604

Atlanta Black Crackers baseball club, **I** 332; **S** 224

Atlanta Braves baseball club (NL), **B** 2, 14, 63, 81, 215-16, 318, 387-88, 409-10, 420-22, 436, 438, 445, 504, 514, 531, 542, 559-60, 588, 595, 608; **F** 230; **I** 261; **O** 57, 93, 102-03; **S** 2, 7, 21, 27, 51, 63, 67, 73, 84, 89-90, 95-96, 107, 109, 125, 132, 134, 138-39, 146, 153, 158, 177, 244

Atlanta *Constitution,* **F** 231; **S** 348

Atlanta Crackers baseball club (SA, SAL, SL), **B** 14, 93, 129, 161, 249, 330, 337, 384, 388, 401, 482, 583, 601; **S** 66, 119, 128, 135, 177, 247, 348

Atlanta Falcons football club (NFL), **F** 19-20, 25, 274, 279, 323, 364-65, 398, 431, 463, 487, 577, 618

Atlanta Flames hockey club (NHL), **I** 545-46; **O** 102

Atlanta Golf Classic, **O** 135

Atlanta Hawks basketball club (NBA), **I** 20, 24, 26, 82, 107, 137-38, 153, 203-04, 247, 260, 279, 311; **O** 102; **S** 251, 269, 288, 329, 331

Atlanta International Speedway, **S** 605

Atlanta *Journal,* **O** 89, 90

Atlanta *Journal/Constitution,* **I** 604-05

Atlanta *Journal* 500 Auto Race, **I** 1

Atlanta Naval Air Station, **F** 480

Atlanta Sports Arena Blues basketball club, **I** 283-84

Atlanta Touchdown Club, **F** 198, 236, 575

Atlanta Track Classic, **O** 541

Atlanta 250 Auto Race, **O** 33

Atlanta University, **S** 616

Atlantic City, NJ Bacharach Giants baseball club (ECL), **B** 190, 290, 334, 338-39, 378, 466, 548, 553;

S 242
Atlantic City, NJ Golf Classic, S 506
Atlantic City, NJ Golf Course, O 152
Atlantic Coast Conference (ACC), F
    111, 157, 170, 197, 303, 320, 453,
    464, 487, 496-97, 543, 584-85,
    588, 640, 650; I 42-43, 58, 71-72,
    152, 189, 198-99, 209, 266, 277,
    280-83; O 537; S 259, 263, 275,
    280, 292, 295, 298, 304, 316, 366,
    382-83, 386, 399-400, 419-21,
    429, 456, 482
Atlantic Coast Conference (ACC)
    Championships, S 280, 282, 295,
    298, 382, 400, 420-21, 456
Atlantic Coast Soccer League, O 299
Atlantic League, B 25, 116; S 97
Atlantic Side baseball club, I 332
Atlantic Ten Conference, S 267-69
Attell, "Abe," I 356-58, 415, 476
Attell, "Monte," I 415
Attleboro, MA baseball club (NEL),
    B 155
Attles, Alvin A., Jr. "Al," I 34; S
    256
Auble, David C. "Dave," I 650
Auburn, NY baseball club (NA,
    NYPL, NYSL), B 313, 326, 598;
    S 47
Auburn University, F 19, 71, 75,
    109, 146-47, 181, 202, 209, 231,
    257, 286-87, 495, 576-78, 599,
    664; I 210, 285, 591-92, 665; S
    257, 368-69, 395, 430, 617
Audley Farm, O 609
Audubon Magazine, O 72
Auerbach, Arnold J. "Red," I 11-13,
    51, 53, 118, 124, 133, 135, 151,
    156, 239, 245, 251, 262, 274, 279;
    S 281, 307
Augsburg College, S 309-10
Augusta, GA baseball club (SAL), B
    98-99, 263
Augusta, GA National Golf Club, I
    403-04; O 136; See also Masters
    Golf Tournament
Augusta, NY baseball club (Pol), B
    406
Augustana College (IL), F 15
Augustana College (SD), S 451
Auker, Eldon L., B 49
Aurora, IL baseball club (WIL), B
    534
Austin, "Doug," O 326
Austin, Henry W. "Bunny," O 322,
    331, 395-96, 410, 418
Austin, "Jeff," O 326
Austin, John, O 326
Austin, "Pam," O 326
Austin, Tracy A., O 326-27, 380
Austin College, F 406
Austin, TX American-Statesman, S
    475
Austin, TX baseball club (TL), B 55,
    421; S 218
Austin, TX Civitan Golf Tournament,
    S 513
Austin, TX Country Club, S 510
Australian Davis Cup Tennis Team, O
    356, 372; S 552, 554, 558, 561
Australian Men's Doubles Tennis
    Championships, O 320
Australian Men's Singles Tennis
    Championships, O 320, 323, 330,
    341, 370, 410; S 561, 563
Australian Olympic Gymnastic Team,
    I 538
Australian Olympic Swim Team, I
    593, 606
Australian Rules football, F 438
Australian Women's Doubles Tennis
    Championships, O 337, 380-81,
    397; S 550
Australian Women's Singles Tennis
    Championships, O 328, 337, 351-
    53, 358, 360, 364, 380, 397; S

550

Austrans, France Cross Country Ski Competition, O 282

Austrian Grand Prix, O 28

Austrian National Soccer Team, O 310

Austrian Olympic Swim Team, I 592

Authors Guild, S 336

Automobile Racing Hall of Fame, O 5-7, 9, 12, 15, 20, 22-26, 34-35, 40, 45

Autoworks 500 NASCAR Race, S 506

Autry, "Gene," F 492; O 62-63, S 58

Autry, Martin "Chick," S 54

Autumn Gold Cup, O 582

AVCO Cup Hockey Playoffs, I 558

Averill, Howard Earl, B 17-18, 142, 553, 577; S 54

Avila, Roberto F. "Bobby," S 118

Avilov, Nikolai, O 475

Avon Futures Tennis Championships, Portland, OR, O 326

Avranches, France Track and Field Meet, O 430

Award of Merit, National Federation of State High Schools Athletic Associations, S 279

Awful, O 230

B Group Hockey Championship, S 543

Babashoff, Shirley F., I 576-77

Babbit, James, I 492

Babcock and Wilcox Soccer Club, Bayonne, NJ, O 294, 310

Babe Didrikson Zaharias Trophy, O 344

Babe Ruth All-Stars, S 242

Babe: The Legend Comes to Life, S 340

Babka, Richard A. "Rick," O 510

Babson Institute, O 529

Baby League, S 535

Bachman, Frank, I 458

Bachrach, William "Bill," I 620

Back of the Year Award, S 402, 448, 467

Bacon, Charles J., Jr. "Charley," O 471; S 596

Bacon, McCoy, F 295

Bacone Indian College, F 103

Badger, Sherwin L., I 509; S 601-02

Badger Swim Club, Larchmont, NY, I 577-78

Badgro, Morris H. "Red," F 23-24; S 458

Baer, Clara G., I 13-14

Baer, Maximillian A. "Max," I 358, 360-61, 429, 458; S 23, 610

Baer, Raymond "Ray," F 194

Baeza, Braulio, O 203, 575

Bagby, James C. J., Sr. "Jim," S 5-6

Bagby, James C. J., Jr., S 6

Bagdon, Edward "Ed," F 126, 413

Bahamas Golf Classic, O 135

Bahamas Olympic Volleyball Team, I 676

Bahamas Stakes, O 225

Bahr, "Casey," O 292

Bahr, "Chris," O 292

Bahr, Matthew D. "Matt," O 292

Bahr, Walter A., O 291-92

Bailey, James, O 435

Bailey, Robert S. "Bob," B 618

Bain, William E. "Bill," S 469

Bainbridge, MD Golf Tournament, S 522

Bainbridge, MD Naval Training Station, F 304

Bainbridge Park, Cleveland, OH, O 175

Baines, Harold D., S 6-7

Baird, Charles, F 669

Baker, Beverly, *See* Beverly Baker Fleitz

Baker, Charles E. "Charlie," **F** 182-83

Baker, E. H., **O** 586

Baker, Hobart A. H., "Hobey," **I** *543-44,* 556, 574

Baker, John Franklin "Home Run," **B** *19-20,* 103, 113, 197, 357, 359; **S** 232

Baker, Johnnie B., Jr. "Dusty," **B** 518; **S** *7,* 244

Baker, "Johnny," **F** 300, 512

Baker, L. H., **F** 231, 379

Baker, Loris, **F** 229

Baker, Sylvia, **S** 549

Baker, Terry W., **F** *24-25*

Baker, Thane, **S** 594

Baker, William P. "Bill," **S** 144

Baker Bowl, Philadelphia, PA, **B** 120, 309

Baker University, **I** 5, 176-77

Baker University Relays, **I** 177

Bakersfield, CA baseball club (CaL), **B** 42, 159; **S** 22

Bakersfield, CA Track and Field Meet, **O** 526

Bakersfield Junior College, **F** 207

Bakken, James L. "Jim," **F** *25-26,* 557; **S** 497

Balancer Gloves Bowling Team, **I** 351

Balboa Law School, **I** 580

Bald Eagle, **O** 222

Baldwin, Charles B. "Lady," **S** 123

Baldwin, Elias J. "Lucky," **S** 526, 531, 534

Baldwin, "Johnny," **I** 397

Baldwin, Marcus E. "Fido," **B** 568, 576

Baldwin-Wallace College, **F** 268, **I** 90, **O** 452-53; **S** 338-39

Ball, Phillip, **B** 45, 243, 456, 558

Ball Four, **S** 133

Ball Players Protective Association, **B** 226

Ball State University, **I** 191-92

Ballantine Classic, **O** 591

Ballard, "Ike," **I** 312

Ballard, Margarette, **O** 321, 405

Ballard, Raymond "Ray," **I** 275

Ballintine, Harriet, **O** 253

Ballot, **O** 211; **S** 533

Ballou, "Win," **S** 52

Balls, H. O., **I** 55, 123

Bally Ache, **O** 225

Ballyhoo Bey, **O** 221, 593

Baltimore American Soccer Club, **O** 303

Baltimore Athletic Club, **O** 237, 240-42

Baltimore baseball club (FL), **B** 34, 241, 459; **S** 48

Baltimore Black Sox baseball club (ANL, ECL), **B** 30, 140, 150, 255, 334, 338-39, 362, 378, 548, 620; **I** 143

Baltimore Bullets basketball club (ABL, BAA), **S** 293, 322

Baltimore Bullets basketball club (NBA), **I** 23, 90, 110, 119, 134-35, 148, 159, 196, 220, 278, 303, 309, 335; **S** 276, 280, 284, 293, 318, 323

Baltimore Cantons Soccer Club, **O** 303

Baltimore City Boxing Championships, **I** 406

Baltimore Claws basketball club (ABA), **I** 142

Baltimore Colts football club (AAFC), **F** 26, 203, 283, 549, 600, 656; **O** 104-05; **S** 460

Baltimore Colts football club (NFL), **F** 11, 26, 42, 55, 68, 104, 111, 127, 146, 162, 165, 199, 203, 246, 258, 264, 274, 292, 298, 303, 325,

348, 352, 363, 370-71, 382, 389,
392-94, 396, 400-01, 405, 411,
418-19, 423, 454, 466-67, 511,
519, 542-44, 553, 556-57, 578,
600, 613-14, 622-23, 633, 656,
670; I 378; O 104-05; S 335,
348, 361, 365, 377-78, 384, 386,
452, 455, 462-63, 465, 504
Baltimore Comets Soccer Club
(NASL), O 303
Baltimore Elite Giants baseball club
(NAL, NNL), B 69, 141, 244,
269-70, 362-63, 599; S 188
Baltimore *Evening Sun,* O 75, 249
Baltimore *Evening Sun* Medal, O
249
Baltimore Hunt, O 95
Baltimore *News-American,* O 248
Baltimore Olympic Club, O 248
Baltimore Orioles baseball club (AA),
B 224, 354, 363, 371, 549, 568;
S 82, 233
Baltimore Orioles baseball club (AL),
B 13-14, 45, 72, 102, 138, 149,
154, 163, 206, 229, 277, 300, 314,
339, 341, 353, 355, 364-65, 367,
372, 391-92, 410-11, 419, 425,
437-38, 440, 455, 475-79, 485,
497, 502, 509, 511, 515, 531, 536,
559, 574, 590, 596-97, 607-08,
614, 623; F 314, 418; I 337; O
234; S 2-3, 11, 15, 17, 19, 25,
35, 47-48, 52, 58, 67, 71, 76, 78-
79, 87, 89, 96, 106, 112-13, 115,
139, 146, 150, 177, 194, 198, 211,
214, 217, 221, 226, 234, 320-21,
348
Baltimore Orioles baseball club (EL),
B 241, 281, 363, 481, 509; S 48
Baltimore Orioles baseball club (IL),
B 19, 155, 194, 232, 261, 279,
293, 328, 373, 384, 494, 597; S
5, 45, 48, 81, 112, 271

Baltimore Orioles baseball club (NL),
B 52, 153, 240, 281, 298-99, 301,
354, 360, 363, 407, 481, 511, 541,
568; S 19, 65, 100, 210, 215
Baltimore Orioles Hall of Fame, B
439
Baltimore Rockets Soccer Club
(ASL), O 303
Baltimore Soccer Club (MISL), O
304
Baltimore Stars baseball club (Negro
Leagues), B 331, 548
Baltimore Stars football club (USFL),
See Philadelphia/Baltimore Stars
football club (USFL)
Baltimore *Sun,* B 389
Baltusrol Golf Course, Springfield,
NJ, O 107, 151
Banach, Edward "Ed," I *635-36,* 659
Banach, Ludwig "Lou," I 635, *636-
37*
Bancroft, David J. "Dave," B *20-21,*
302
Bancroft, Frank C., B 541, 555
Bancroft, Mrs. Thomas, O 579
Bando, Salvatore L. "Sal," B 276; S
8-9, 241, 355
Banker, William "Bill," S 388
Bankhart, Larry H., F 646
Bankhead, Daniel R. "Dan," S 10
Bankhead, Samuel "Sam," S *9-10*
Banks, "Davey," I 65, 170
Banks, Earl, F 334
Banks, Ernest "Ernie," B *21-22,* 609;
O 53; S 53
Banks, "Freddie," I 293
Banks, M. Beal, F 151
Banks, Thomas S., Jr. "Tom," S 370
Banks, William Augustus III "Willie,"
O *424-25*
Banks Business College, I 675
Bannockburn, Scotland Golf
Tournament, S 522

Banquet, **O** 219
Bantam Books, **S** 347
Bantamweight Boxing
    Championships, **I** 370-71, 399-
    400, 406, 430-31, 434, 447, 450,
    468, 478
Barabas, "Al," **F** 350
Barak, Ronald "Ron," **I** 521-22
Barbarians Soccer Club, San
    Francisco, CA, **O** 301
Barbella, "Nick," **I** 392
Barbella, Rocco, *See* Rocky Graziano
Barber, Stewart C. "Stew," **S** 479
Barber, Walter L. "Red," **B** 366; **O**
    48-50, 67, 92; **S** 340, 343, 348-49
Barbizon, **O** 190; **S** 529
Barbuti, Raymond J. "Ray," **O** *426-
    27*
Barcelona, Spain Grand Prix, **O** 9
Barcelona, Spain Gymnastic Invitation
    Meet, **I** 539
Barcelona, Spain Summer Olympic
    Games, *See* Olympic Summer
    Games, 1992
Barclay, "Captain," **I** 440
The Bard, **O** 595
Bardstown, **O** 195
Barishnykov, Mikhail, **S** 626
Barker, Clifford "Cliff," **S** 261, 287
Barkley, Charles W., **S** *257-58,* 269
Barkley, Iran, **S** 612
Barlick, Albert J. "Al," **B** *22-23;* **S**
    122
Barlow, John, **O** 544
Barlow, Thomas B. "Tom," **I** *14-15*
Barnard, Ernest S., **B** *23-24,* 243,
    524
Barnes, Bruce, **O** 368
Barnes, J. H. "Hap," **F** 296
Barnes, James M. "Long Jim," **O**
    109-10, 133-34
Barnes, Joseph "Joe," **F** 209
Barnes, Lee, **O** 440, 462

Barnes, Roscoe C. "Ross," **B** *24-25,*
    270, 371, 603, 628
Barnett, Leonard, **I** 470
Barnett, Richard "Dick," **I** *15,* 133,
    202
Barney, Lemuel J., Jr. "Lem," **S** *364*
Barnhill, John A., **I** 202
Barnholth, Larry, **I** 627
Barnholth, Lewis, **I** 627
Barnie, William H. "Bill," **B** 363
Barnstable, Dale, **S** 261
Barr, George M., **S** *10-11,* 122
Barr, Terry A., **F** 546
Barrasso, Thomas "Tom," **I** *544-45*
Barrera, "Liz," **O** 226, 569
Barres, "Herty," **F** 58
Barrett, Charles H. "Red," **B** 572; **S**
    33
Barrett, Ernie D., **I** 94
Barrett, Roger, **O** 345
Barrick, "Mike," **O** 438
Barrow, Edward G. "Ed," **B** *25-26,* 94,
    259, 408, 415, 492, 494; **S** 181,
    190
Barrow, Joseph L., *See* Joe Louis
Barry, "Jimmy," **I** 434
Barry, John J. "Jack," **B** 19, 103, 357
Barry, Justin "Sam," **I** *15-16*
Barry, Peter "Pete," **I** 21, 66, 170; **S**
    287, 314
Barry, Richard F. II, **I** 16
Barry, Richard F. III "Rick," **I** *16-18,*
    111, 227; **S** 256, 306
Barry Ashbee Trophy, **I** 559
Barry College for Women, **O** 358
Bartell, Richard W. "Dick," **B** *26-27*
Bartfield, "Soldier," **I** 448
Bartkowitz, Jane "Peaches," **S** 550
Bartlesville, OK baseball club (WA),
    B 29; **S** 17
Bartolo, "Sal," **I** 450
Barton, George, **I** 390
Bartow, Gene B., **S** *258-59*

Barwegan, Richard J. "Dick," F 26
Baseball, B 625; O 74; S 336
Baseball Abstracts, B 248
Baseball Chapel, S 349
Baseball Coaches Hall of Fame, I 63
Baseball Complete, S 350
Baseball Digest, B 418
Baseball Players Association of
America, B 124, 186, 285, 318,
367-68, 402-03, 477
Baseball Players Fraternity, B 135,
468
Baseball Stars Series, S 347
Baseball Writers Association of
America, B 133, 151, 246, 283,
300, 316, 409, 431; I 371; O 74,
89, 98; S 77, 88, 107-08, 312,
338, 359
Basgall, Romanus "Monty," B 545
Basilio, Carmen, I 358-59, 387, 456,
477
Basketball Association of America, I
66, 89, 192, 114, 156, 171, 179,
203, 211, 218, 232, 235, 239-40,
261, 270, 334-35; S 264-65, 293,
322
Basketball Association of America
All-Star Game, I 335
Basketball Association of America
All-Time Basketball Team, I 241
Basketball Association of America
Championships and Playoffs, I 89,
102, 114, 179, 235, 261; S 293,
332
Basketball: Building the Complete
Program, S 321
Basketball Committee for Women, I 2
Basketball Congress International, I
276
Basketball Federation of the United
States of America, I 287-88; S
279
Basketball Guide, I 306

Basketball Illustrated, I 168
Basketball Times, I 293
Basketball Writers Association of
America, I 127
Baskin, Weems, O 554
Basloe, Frank, S 259-60
Basloe's Globe Trotters Basketball
Club, S 260
Bass, "Benny," I 363, 494
Bass, Richard L. "Dick," F 363
Bassett, VA baseball club (BSL), B
475
Bastione, Daniel "Dan," I 240
Baston, Albert P. "Bert," F 27, 655
Baston, Frederick, F 27
Batavia, NY baseball club (Pol), B
579
Bateau, O 596
Bates College, I 155
Baton Rouge, LA Open Golf
Tournament, O 113
Battaglia, "Frankie," I 466
Battalino, Chris "Battling," I 417,
438, 451, 468
Battey, Earl J., S 202
Battle, Kenny S 292
Battle Mountain Rodeo, I 265
The Battle of the Network Stars, I 503
Battles, Clifford F. "Cliff," F 28-29,
385-86
Battleship, O 596
Battling Levinsky, See Levinsky,
Battling
Battling Nelson, See Nelson, Battling
Bauer, Henry A. "Hank," B 382, 596
Baugh, Laura Z., O 132
Baugh, Samuel A. "Sammy," F 3,
28, 29-31, 66, 179, 215, 336,
357, 386, 391, 437, 479, 598-99,
608; S 385, 422, 503
Baughan, Maxie C., Jr., S 364-65,
478
Baumholtz, Frank C., S 187-88

Bausch, James A. B. "Jim," O *427-28*, 501
Bavasi, Emil J. "Buzzy," O 81
Bay, "Rick," F 228
Bay City, MI baseball club (MOL, NWL), B 128, 194; S 79
Bay Counties Tennis Championships, O 361, 415
Bay Hill Club and Lodge, Orlando, FL, O 149
Bay Hill Golf Classic, O 149; S 524
Bay Meadows Derby, O 603
Bay Meadows Race Track, O 210; S 532
Bay State Bombadiers basketball club, I 53
Bayi, Filbert, O 489, 532, 567
Baylor, Don E., S *11-12*, 89
Baylor, Elgin G., F 591; I *18-19*, 82, 135, 322
Baylor University, B 343; F 73, 293, 392, 448, 541-42, 548, 663; I 42, 257; S 401, 448, 474, 478
Bayonne, NJ Hall of Fame, O 294
Bayonne, NJ Rovers Soccer Club, O 294
Bayonne, NJ Track and Field Meet, O 460
Beach, James "Jim," F 358
Beachem, Joseph W., F 426
Beacon Hill Athletic Association, O 350, 392
Beacon Park Athletic Association, See Beacon Hill Athletic Association
Beacon Race Course, Hoboken, NJ, O 544, 593
Beadle's Dime Base Ball Player, B 82
Beagle, Ronald G. "Ron," S *365-66*
Beame, Abraham "Abe," O 61
Beamon, Robert "Bob," O *428-29*, 433, 458, 472, 485-87
Beanpot Hockey Tournament, I 561;

S 541
Bear Down Gymnasium, Tucson, AZ, I 80
Beard, Ralph, Sr., S 260
Beard, Ralph, Jr., I 233; S *260-61*, 287
Bearden, Henry Eugene "Gene," S 83
Beasley, Mercer, O 322, 358, 409
Beasley, Terry P., F 577
Beasley, Thomas "Tom," I 402
Beasley, William "Bill," F 378
Beathard, Peter F. "Pete," S 426
Beattie, Robert "Bob," O 281-82
Beatty, James T. "Jim," O *429-30*; S 592
Beaty, Zelmo "Big Z," I *19-20*, 204
Beau Jack, See Jack, Beau
Beaumont, Clarence H. "Ginger," B *27-28*, 95
Beaumont Sword, O 64
Beaumont, TX baseball club (STL, TL), B 222, 261, 263, 356, 418; S 87, 120, 159, 183, 195, 226-27, 245
Beban, Gary J., F *31-32*
Beck, Barry D., I 563
Beck, Lewis W., I 97
Beck International Trophy, O 284
Beckenbauer, Franz, O 298
Becker, Boris, O 370
Becker, Elizabeth, I 494
Beckett, Beverly Baker, See Beverly Baker Beckett Fleitz
Beckley, Jacob P. "Jake," B *28-29*
Beckley, WV baseball club (MAL), B 348
Beckman, Edwin J., I 22
Beckman, John, I *20-22*, 33, 65, 88, 131, 170, 194-95, 223; S 287, 314
Beckner, John G., I *521-22*
Beckner, Richard A., I 521
Beckwith, John, B *29-30*, 189, 515

Bednarik, Charles P. "Chuck," F 32-33

Bedrosian, Stephen W. "Steve," S 160

Bedsole, Harold "Hal," F 370

Bedwell, Harvey G., O 608; S 525-26

Bee, Clair F., I 22-23, 187, 231, 264, 293; S 290

Beeckman, Livingston, O 392, 398-99

Beer, Klaus, O 433

Beers, Paul B., F 401

Beggs, Joseph S., S 127

Begovich, Matthew W. "Matty," I 233

Behave Yourself, S 535

Behind the Mask, S 57

Behr, Karl G., O 362, 378

Behr, Sidney, I 404

Belair Farms, O 184, 585

Belanger, "Frenchy," I 389

Belcher, John, O 573

Beldame Handicap, O 199

Belfray Farm, Middleburg, VA, O 578

Belgian Grand Prix, O 11

Belgian National Soccer Team, O 299

Belgian Olympic Water Polo Team, I 621

Believe It, O 569-70

Bell, David G. "Buddy," B 30-31; S 78

Bell, David R. "Gus," B 30

Bell, De Benneville "Bert," F 34-35, 55, 185, 263, 350, 431, 462, 489, 516, 583, 593

Bell, George, S 225

Bell, Gregory C. "Greg," S 567-68

Bell, James T. "Cool Papa," B 31-32, 127, 223-24, 451, 453, 533, 543, 612

Bell, John A. III, O 579

Bell, Madison A. "Matty," F 35-36, 403, 407; I 67

Bell, R. Berkeley, O 322

Bell, Richard T. "Ricky," F 370

Bell, Robert L. "Bob," F 36-37, 161, 334

Bell, Theopolis "Theo," F 98

Bell, Thomas "Tommy," I 455

Bell Award or Trophy, F 185, 226, 431, 462, 583, 593

Bell Cup Tennis, S 551

Bell Syndicate Newspapers, S 345

Bellamy, Walter J. "Walt," I 23-24, 64, 231

Bellarmine College, S 286, 300

Belle Action, O 191

Bellfounder, O 597

Bellino, Joseph M. "Joe," F 37

Bellisarius, O 219

Belmar, O 224

Belmont, August, Sr., O 177-78, 187-88, 595; S 526, 533

Belmont, August, Jr., O 177

Belmont, Raymond, O 578

Belmont Abbey College, I 197, 200

Belmont Cricket Club, Philadelphia, PA, O 321, 408; S 615

Belmont Futurity Stakes, O 183, 188, 194, 202, 211-12, 569, 607

Belmont Park, Elmont, NY, O 180, 188, 578, 591, 596, 603-04, 606, 611

Belmont Stakes, O 175-76, 185-86, 189, 190, 194, 197-98, 204-05, 211, 213-14, 216, 218, 220, 222-25, 227, 229, 570, 572-73, 577-79, 585, 595-96, 598-99, 601, 604, 606-08, 610-15; S 345, 527, 529, 531, 533, 536

Belo Horizonte, Brazil Soccer Championships, O 291

Beloit College, B 28, 270, 365; F 438; I 286;

Belote, Melissa, See Melissa Belote Hamlin Ripley

Beltmar Drug Soccer Club, O 299

Bemiller, Albert D. "Al," S 479
Ben Brush, O 220
Ben Hogan Award, O 139, 157; S 508
Ben Or, O 209
Benbrook, Albert, F 38, 229
Bench, Johnny L., B 10, 32-33, 146, 409, 486; O 533
Bender, Charles A. "Chief," B 33-34, 112, 255, 287, 333, 359, 450, 579, 588, 612; S 161, 189
Bender, Jules "Julie," I 23
Bendlin, Kurt, O 553
Benger, Thomas, O 597
Benington, John, I 231
Benitez, Wilfred, I 422; S 612
Bennett, Curt A., I 545-46, 549
Bennett, G. C., S 531
Bennett, Harvey A., Sr., I 545
Bennett, Harvey A., Jr., I 546
Bennett, James Gordon, Jr., O 50-51
Bennett, James "Jim," I 546
Bennett, John, I 546
Bennett, Leeman, S 384
Bennett, Lewis "Deerfoot," O 430-31
Bennett, Russell, O 49
Bennett, T. Wesley "Wes," S 261-62
Bennett, William, I 546
Bennett Park, Detroit, MI, B 155, 408, 554-55
Benoit, Joan, See Joan Benoit Samuelson
Benson, Michael Kent, I 162, 169; S 262-63
Benswanger, William "Bill," B 331
Benton, James "Jim," F 39
Benvenuti, Nino, I 396
Benz, Joseph L. "Joe," B 501
Berbick, Trevor, I 353, S 343, 625
Berenson, Senda, O 253; See also Senda Berenson Abbott
Beretta, Fred, I 167

Berg, Edward H., See Harry Greb
Berg, Jack "Kid," I 451
Berg, "Matt," I 653
Berg, Patricia J. "Patty," O 110-11, 159, 172
Berger, Elsie, O 600
Berger, Walter A. "Wally," B 35
Bergere, Clifford "Cliff," O 64
Berkeley, CA Track and Field Meet, O 455, 526
Berkeley, CA Women's City Club, I 595
Berlenbach, Paul C., I 359-60, 372, 463, 475, 645
Berlin, Germany Summer Olympic Games, See Olympic Summer Games, 1936
Berlinger, Barney, I 598
Bermuda National Soccer Team, O 291, 294
Bermuda National Tennis Championships, O 343
Bern, Switzerland Track and Field Meet, O 438, 450, 541
Bernal, Joseph "Joe," I 436
Bernard, George, I 448
Bernard, J. Charles, S 458
Bernardi, Jose, O 298
Bernhard, William H. "Bill," B 322, 524
Berning, Susan Maxwell, S 506
Bernstein, "Jack," I 379, 392
Bernstein, "Phil," I 389
Berra, Dale A., B 3
Berra, Lawrence P. "Yogi," B 33, 35-37, 54, 146-47, 559, 597; O 65; S 92, 172
Berrien, "Captain," F 644
Berry, Charles F. "Charlie," F 39-40; S 477
Berry, David J., F 40-41, 60
Berry, Howard, F 350
Berry, Raymond E., F 41-43, 165,

196, 335, 401, 547
Berry, Robert C. "Bob," **S** 499
Bert Bell Award, **S** 373, 475
Bertelli, Angelo B., **F** *43-44,* 344, 358
Bertha Teague Mid-America Girls Basketball Tournament, **I** 297
Berwanger, John J. "Jay," **F** *44-45,* 564
Besitkas Soccer Club of Turkey, **O** 294
Best Sixth Man Award, NBA, **S** 299-300
Best Sports Stories Award, **S** 337
Best Sportswriting Award, ASNE, **S** 337
Besterman, Henry, *See* Harry Lewis
Bet Twice, **O** 204, 222, 227
Bethany College, **F** 446; **O** 567
Bethel College, **F** 110, 402-03
Bethlehem Steel Soccer Club (ASL), **O** 310
Bethlehem *Times,* **F** 200
Bethune-Cookman College, **S** 267, 441
Betsey Richards, **O** 609
Betsy Rawls Peace Blossom Golf Tournament, **O** 170
Bettencourt, Lawrence J. "Larry," **F** 377
Bettenhausen, Gary, **O** 4
Bettenhausen, Melvin E., Sr. "Tony," **O** *4-5,* 18, 39
Bettenhausen, Melvin E., Jr., **O** 4, 19
Bettenhausen, Merle, **O** 4-5
Bettina, Melio, **I** 367, 482
Betz, Pauline, *See* Pauline Betz Addie
Beverly, IL Country Club, **S** 520
Beverly Hills, CA Speedway, **O** 23
Beverly Hills, CA Tennis Club, **O** 320, 337, 340
Bewitch, **O** 576; **S** 529
Beyond the Seventh Game, **S** 346

Bezdek, Hugo F., **F** *45-46,* 159, 242
Bezic, Sandra, **I** 501
Bi-Continental Cup Competition, **O** 307
Bianchi, Alfred A. "Al," **I** 7
Bias, Leonard "Len," **I** 71
Bibbs, Rainey, **B** 6
Bibby, Charles Henry, **I** 331
Bible, Dana K., **F** 6, *46-47,* 293; **S** 423-24, 438
Bicknell, "Jack," **F** 181
Bicycle World, **O** 375
Biddison, Thomas N. Sr. "Tom," **O** *234*
Bidwill, Charles W., Sr., **F** *47-48,* 113
Bidwill, Charles W., Jr., **F** 48; **S** 370, 425, 438
Bidwill, Violet F., **F** 48
Bidwill, William "Bill," **F** 17, 48; **S** 370, 425
Bieber, Isidor, **O** 192-93
Bierbauer, Louis W. "Lou," **B** 541, 600
Bierman, Bernard W. "Bernie," **F** 27, *48-50,* 174, 300, 413, 433, 554-55, 652-53; **S** 388, 443, 491
Bierman, William, **F** 49
Bierman Field Athletic Building, **F** 49
Big Bill Tilden: The Triumphs and the Tragedy, **S** 341
Big East Conference, **I** 83, 301; **S** 259, 264, 266-67, 305-06, 581, 589
Big East Conference Championships, **S** 267, 581
Big Eight Conference, **F** 18, 61-62, 71, 73, 135-38, 151, 171, 195, 208-09, 219, 288, 423, 443-44, 448, 481, 493-95, 507-08, 518, 524, 537, 546, 570-71, 581-82, 659; **I** 35, 46, 81, 139, 182, 184, 271, 303-04, 323, 328, 639, 641,

644, 652, 654, 659, 663-64; **O** 134, 498; **S** 278, 295, 301-02, 320-21, 324-25, 361-62, 370, 372, 392-93, 403-04, 408-09, 428, 448, 454, 461-62, 470, 473, 480, 490, 496

Big Eight Conference Championships, **O** 498; **S** 321, 324, 408, 461

Big Nine Conference, **F** 215; **S** 361-62, 380, 476, 490, 500

Big Nine Conference Championships, **S** 361-62, 380, 500

Big Nine Conference Scholarship Medal, **S** 362

The Big Out, **S** 347

Big Six or Big Seven Conference, **F** 44, 77-78, 95, 167-68, 288, 301, 360, 362, 364, 373, 392, 480, 515, 584, 605-06, 622, 627, 641, 646, 653; **I** 69-70, 94, 148; **S** 320, 381-82, 474, 580

Big Six or Big Seven Conference Championships, **S** 381

Big Sky Athletic Conference, **I** 224, 276; **S** 486

Big State League, **S** 219

Big Ten Conference, **F** 1, 11, 25, 36, 45, 49, 79, 92, 98-100, 120, 126-27, 133, 136-37, 141, 157, 159, 161, 172-74, 184, 218, 218, 225-28, 289, 297, 307, 314, 322-24, 355-56, 395, 404, 413, 430, 443, 454, 457-58, 482, 525-27, 556, 563, 585, 607, 610, 633, 642-43; **I** 62-63, 73, 79-80, 85, 130, 138, 146, 159, 161-64, 167, 181-82, 186, 191, 206-07, 209, 216-17, 225, 227-28, 234, 236, 239, 259-60, 269, 272, 286, 295, 310-11, 329-30, 485, 527, 584, 594, 612, 618, 635-36, 640, 642, 649, 651; **O** 52, 449, 514; **S** 56, 106, 167, 213, 255, 259, 262-63, 270, 276,

281, 288, 291-92, 295, 299, 303, 306, 310, 317, 361-63, 365, 391, 397-98, 401-03, 405-06, 414, 419-20, 449, 451, 472, 492, 494, 567, 572, 578

Big Ten Conference Championships, **O** 449, 513-15; **S** 213, 262, 292, 303, 309, 317, 398, 401, 414, 449, 572

Big Ten Conference Male Athlete of the Year, **I** 635

Big Ten Conference Medal, **I** 164, 528

Big Three Conference, **F** 269, 342, 541, 563; **I** 131

Big West Conference, **S** 291, 320

Bignotti, George, **O** 13

Biletnikoff, Frederick "Fred," **F** *31-32, 62, 96*, 335

Bill McGowan Umpiring School, **S** 122

Billet, **O** 597

Billings, MT baseball club (PrL), **B** 47, 485

Billy Direct, **O** 574, 580

Billy Kelly, **O** 199, 215, 608; **S** 525-26

Billy Mills Leadership Institute, **I** 499

Bimstein, "Whitey," **I** 355

Bing, David "Dave," **I** *24-25*, 113, 298; **S** 263

Bing Crosby Pro-Am Golf Tournament, **O** 113, 130-34, 143, 166

Bingen, **O** 185

Binghamton, NY baseball club (EL, IA, NYPL, NYSL), **B** 85, 187, 195, 218, 231, 257, 299; **S** 19, 127, 146, 178, 204, 230

Binglin Stables, **O** 194

Biondi, Matthew "Matt," **S** *602-03*

Bird, Larry J., **I** *24-25*, 146, 218-19, 225; **S** 254, 274, 281-82, 300

Bird, "Tex," **O** 563

Birdsong, Otis L., **I** 174
Birkhofer, Ralph J. "Lefty," **S** 62
Birmingham, AL baseball club (SA),
  B 228, 384, 400, 446, 524, 537,
  547, 562, 605; **S** 19, 230
Birmingham, AL baseball club (SL),
  B 37, 80, 179, 181, 277; **S** 51,
  84, 235
Birmingham, AL Barons baseball club
  (CSL), **S** 187
Birmingham, AL Black Barons
  baseball club (NAL, NNL), **B** 127,
  244, 393, 436, 543; **S** 9
Birmingham, AL Bulls hockey club
  (WHA), **I** 562
Birmingham, AL Giants baseball club
  (Negro Leagues), **B** 548-49
Birmingham, AL Golf Classic, **O**
  118; **S** 518-19
Birmingham, AL Quarterback Club, **F**
  198, 236, 287
Birmingham, AL Southern College, **F**
  434
Birmingham, AL Stallions football
  club (USFL), **F** 561
Bi-State League, **S** 102, 221
Bishop, Max F., **B** 232; **S** 13
Bishop, Ralph E., **I** 76
Bishop's Hambletonian, **O** 597
Bismarck, ND baseball club, **B** 132
Bispiel, "Matt," **I** 528
Bit of White, **S** 535
Bivins, "Jimmy," **I** 424
Bjurstedt, Molla, *See* Molla Bjurstedt
  Mallory
Black, Charles T. "Charlie," **I** 5; **S**
  302
Black, Donald P. "Don," **S** 83
Black, E. D., **O** 345
Black Achievement Award, **S** 627
Black Athletes Hall of Fame, **F** 332,
  525; **O** 449, 496
Black Bill, **I** 480

Black Entertainment Network, **S** 364
Black-Eyed Susan, **O** 194
Black Gold, **O** 194
Black Hills, **O** 175
Black Maria, **O** 571
Black Opportunity, **S** 417
Black Sheep, **O** 228
Black Sports Hall of Fame, **S** 598
Black Watch, **O** 267
Black World Series, **S** 9-10, 129, 137,
  242
Blackman, Robert "Bob," **S** 181
Blackmoore, Lennox, **I** 452
Blackwell, Ewell "The Whip," **B** 141,
  381
Blackwell, Nathaniel "Nate," **S** 268
Blades, Francis Raymond "Ray," **B**
  525
Blaik, Earl H. "Red," **F** *51-52,* 130,
  301, 353, 606-07; **O** 426; **S** 377
Blaik, Robert, **F** 52
Blair, Bonnie, **I** 492; **S** *603-04*
Blair, Wren, **I** 573
Blake, Avery F., Sr., **O** 234, *235-36*
Blake, Avery F., Jr., **O** *234-35,* 236
Blake, George, **I** 370, 417
Blake, Thomas "Tom," **I** 439
Blalock, Jane, **S** 506, *506-07*
Blanchard, Felix A., Sr., **F** 52-53
Blanchard, Felix A., Jr. "Doc," **F** *52-*
  54, 78, 117, 129-30, 345, 358-59,
  605-06; **O** 99, 269; **S** 464
Blanchard, Theresa Weld, **I** *499-500*
Bland, Harriet C., **S** 593
Blanda, George F., **F** 25, *54-56,* 74,
  177, 384, 633; **S** 469, 487
Blank, **O** 608
Blankenship, Clifford D. "Cliff," **B**
  400
Blasingame, Donald S. "Don," **S** 34
Blatnik, Jeffery C. "Jeff," **I** *637-38*
Blazejowski, Carol A., **I** *27-28,* 315
Bleibtrey, Ethelda, *See* Ethelda

Bleibtrey MacRobert Schlafke
Bleier, Robert P. "Rocky," S *366-67*
Blenheim II, O 614
Bless Bull, O 222
Blevins, Leon G., I 80
Blinn Junior College, F 514
Blitzen Benz Race Car, O 26
Blockade, O 596
Blockbuster Bowl football game, S 369
Bloebaum, "Buddy," B 485
Blood, Benjamin, I 29
Blood, Ernest A. "Prof," I *28-29,* 253
Blood, Johnny, *See* John V. McNally
Blood, Paul, I 29
Bloom, "Phil," I 365
Bloomer, Shirley J., O 358
Bloomfield, NJ Country Club, O 169
Bloomfield Rams football club (Ind.), F 613
Bloomingdale's Track Club, O 466-67
Bloomington, IL baseball club (3IL), B 229, 558
Bloomsburg, PA baseball club (MtnL), B 509
Blossom Time, O 194
Blount, Melvin C. "Mel," F *56*
Blount, Roy, Jr., F 222
Blozis, Albert C., Jr. "Al," S *367-68*
Blubaugh, Douglas M. "Doug," I *638-39,* 664
Blubaugh, "Jack," I 638-39
Blue, Luzerne A. "Lu," S *12-13*
Blue, Vida R., Jr., B *37-38,* 179; S 9
Blue Grass League, B 84; S 223
Blue Grass Stakes, O 176, 204, 603, 610
Blue-Gray football game, F 18, 33, 133, 164, 279, 523, 583, 600; S 395-96, 399, 466
Blue Larkspur, O 186; S 535

Blue Man, O 205, 222
Blue Paradise, S 534
Blue Ridge College, F 163
Blue Ridge League, S 12, 121, 200
Blue Swords, O 579
Bluebonnet Bowl football game, F 236, 258, 302, 347, 422, 444, 481, 553, 632, 664; S 393, 401, 408, 421, 428, 468
Bluefield, WV baseball club (ApL), B 279, 339, 410, 455; S 11
Bluege, Oswald L. "Ossie," S *13-14*
Bluege, Otto A., S 14
Blunt, "Ted," I 90
Blute, James "Jimmy," O 197
Bluth, Raymond "Ray," I 340, 350
Blyleven, Rik Aalbert "Bert," S *14-15*
Blyth Arena, Squaw Valley, CA, I 569
Blytheville, AR Army baseball club, S 163
B'nai B'rith Hall of Fame, S 343
B'nai B'rith New York Giants Most Valuable Player, S 414
Boand System, F 378
Board of Basketball Officials, I 313
Board of Trade Handicap, O 209
Bob Douglas Hall of Fame, O 449
Bob Hope Desert Golf Classic, O 126, 144; S 516
Bob Jones Trophy, O 139, 148; S 511, 515
Bob Miles, O 206
Bobby Brocato, S 532
Bobby Clarke Trophy, I 559
Boca Raton, FL Golf Club, O 109
Bocchicchio, Felix, I 472
Bodie, Frank S. "Ping," B 65
Bodine, O 586
Bodine, "Geoff," O 42
Bodo, Peter, O 370, 381
The Body Builder, I 662

Boeckmann, Delores "Dee," S *568-69*

Boeheim, James, Jr. "Jim," S *263-64*

Bogash, Louis "Lou," I 372

Boggs, Wade A., S 119

Bogus Hunter, O 583

Boise, ID baseball club (PrL, WTL), B 392; S 128

Boise Junior College, I 148; S 92, 499

Boitano, Brian, I *500-02*

Bok Award, B 359

Boland, William, S 527

Bolanos, Enrique, I 477

Bold Arrangement, O 203

Bold Bidder, O 222

Bold Ego, O 226

Bold Reasoning, O 606

Bold Ruler, O 176, 184, 190, 228, *572-73*, 607, 610

Bold Venture, O 223, 572; S 527

Bolden, Edward "Ed," B 338, 500

Bolero's Orphan, S 529

Bolt, Thomas "Tommy," S *507-08*

Bolton, Joseph "Joe," O 45

Bolton, William Clifton "Cliff," S 45

Bomar, Herbert B. "Buddy," I *338-39*, 341

Bomar, Lynn, F 368

Bombast, O 201

Bond, Thomas H. "Tommy," B *38-39*, 628

Bond Bowl football game, F 155

Bonds, Barry L., B 39

Bonds, Bobby L., B *39-40;* S 31, 148

Bonds, Larry, I 422

Boniface, S *525-26*

Bonner, "Jack," I 461

Bonnets o'Blue, O 583

Bonnie Kelso, O 214

Bonniwell, Roberta, I 530

Bonthron, William R. "Bill," O *431-32*, 445-46

Bonura, Henry J. "Zeke," B 317

Bonus, O 613

Bonventre, Peter, O 59

Booker, James "Pete," B 255

Boone, George, F 16

Boone, Isaac M. "Ike," S 5

Boone, Raymond O. "Ray," S 15

Boone, Robert R. "Bob," S *15-16*, 214

Boone, Rodney, S 15

Booth, Albert, J., Jr. "Albie," F *57-59;* S 489, 501

Booth, Mordecai, O 590

Booth Memorial football game, F 58

Boozer, Robert L. "Bob," F 507; I 23, 231

Bordas, Manuel Casals Y., O 335

Border Conference, F 136-37, 294, 324, 389, 608, 663; I 79; S 291, 422-23, 425, 484

Border League, S 199

Borell, "Joe," I 425

Borg, Bjorn, O 324, 341, 369-70

Borge, Arne, I 620

Borgmann, Bernard "Bennie," I *29-30, 32*, 223

Borman, Lorraine, I 517

Born, Bertram H., I 5

Boros, Julius N., O *111-12*

Boros, Stephen "Steve," B 43

Borotra, Jean, O 322, 362, 389, 395, 404, 460

Borque, Raymond J., I 563

Borries, W. R. "Fred," F 37

Borrow, O 196, 591

Boryla, Vince, I 250

Bosch 200 CART Race, S 620

Bosco, Robert "Robbie," S 396

Bosporus Swim, I 581

Boston, O *573-74*, 583, 594, 602

Boston, Ralph H., O 428, *432-34*

Boston *American*, O 73
Boston Arena, Boston, MA, I 35, 561
Boston Athletic Association, F 64; I
26; S 571, 583
Boston Athletic Association Track and
Field Meet, O 443
Boston baseball club (UA), B 628
Boston Beaneaters baseball club (NL),
S 19, 36, 115, 151-52; *See also*
Boston Red Stockings baseball club
(NL)
Boston Bees baseball club (NL), *See*
Boston Braves baseball club (NL)
Boston Braves baseball club (NL), B
3, 17, 20-21, 28, 35, 59, 62, 103,
131, 133, 145, 154, 160-61, 167,
170, 176, 178, 184, 193, 203, 216-
17, 230, 238-39, 250, 258, 261,
283, 301, 311, 313, 327, 329, 335-
37, 346-48, 356-57, 360-61, 373,
376-77, 384, 387-88, 391, 396,
416, 459, 468, 476, 495, 509-10,
513, 516, 524-25, 534, 550-51,
587-88, 590, 592-93, 617, 636; F
251, 397; I 572; S 11, 33, 41,
69, 104, 110-12, 116-17, 126, 135,
144, 149-50, 186, 203, 207, 220,
223, 228-29
Boston Braves football club (NFL), F
28, 160, 315, 385
Boston Braves hockey club (AHL), I
573
Boston Breakers football club (USFL),
F 198
Boston Brothers baseball club (PL), B
52, 303, 464, 506, 541; S 151,
178
Boston Bruins hockey club (NHL), I
36, 545-47, 555, 563, 571-73; S
540, 544, 546-47
Boston Bulldogs football club (NFL),
S 439
Boston Celtics basketball club (BAA,

NBA), I 2, 9, 11-12, 16, 25-26,
36, 44, 47-48, 51-54, 61, 71, 98,
103-04, 109, 111, 117-18, 123-24,
134-36, 145-47, 150-54, 184, 189-
90, 199, 217-19, 239, 245, 249,
251-52, 261-63, 266, 271, 274,
279, 298, 300, 306, 310, 318, 324;
S 253-54, 264-65, 281-82, 284,
298-300, 307, 325-28, 330-31
Boston College, B 161, 348; F 102,
110, 144-46, 181-82, 287, 309,
344-45, 350, 422, 440, 569, 576; I
52, 560-61, 566; O 558; S 418-
19, 459-60, 477-78, 573
Boston Five Golf Classic, S 505
Boston Garden, Boston, MA, F 239;
I 118, 152-53, 217, 275, 573, 661;
O 520
Boston *Globe*, B 59; F 118, 196,
547; S 339, 546
Boston *Herald*, S 339
Boston hockey club (AHAUS), S 537
Boston *Journal*, S 571
Boston Marathon, I 36; O 451-52,
466-67, 519, 523, 528-29, 537; S
582-83
The Boston Marathon, S 344
Boston Normal School of Gymnastics,
I 1
Boston Patriots football club (AFL,
NFL), F 37, 92, 203, 277, 420,
465; S 375, 419, 442, 463, 478
Boston Pilgrims baseball club (AL),
See Boston Red Sox baseball club
(AL)
Boston *Post*, F 30; S 571
Boston Race Track, O 586
Boston Red Sox baseball club (AL), B
10, 13, 19, 21, 26, 41-42, 58, 64,
76, 81, 84, 87, 91, 93, 95, 104-06,
110, 112-13, 115, 119-20, 123,
129, 135, 149, 152-53, 155, 158,
161, 169, 177-79, 182, 197, 197,

208, 232-33, 241, 245, 251-52,
254, 259, 263, 266, 269, 278-79,
282, 286, 288-89, 291, 293, 300,
328, 339, 341-43, 346-47, 357,
361, 376, 379, 382, 392, 401, 406,
413, 431, 443-44, 446-47, 456,
459, 470-72, 474, 476, 489, 491-
92, 494, 503, 505, 513, 517-18,
523, 529, 536, 544, 547, 558, 571-
72, 575, 577, 581, 587-88, 594-95,
602, 613-16, 624-25, 633-37; **F**
40, 385; **I** 29, 61; **O** 53, 67; **S** 1,
6-7, 11-12, 14, 16-17, 21-22, 24-
25, 31, 36, 39-41, 44, 47, 49, 51-
52, 54, 57, 64, 66-67, 76, 85, 94-
96, 100-01, 111, 124, 126, 128,
135, 142-44, 149, 153-54, 157,
159, 163-66, 172-73, 182, 190,
193-95, 198, 205-06, 213-14, 218,
221-22, 226, 231, 234, 242-43,
245-47, 346, 354
Boston Red Stockings baseball club
(NA), **B** 24, 270, 371, 428, 527,
603, 627-28
Boston Red Stockings baseball club
(NL), **B** 38, 52, 59, 96, 104-05,
154, 160, 256, 281, 301, 303, 336,
347, 360, 389, 419, 428, 464, 506-
07, 537-38, 541, 550, 603-04, 617,
628; **S** 97, 100, 178, 210, 215
Boston Reds baseball club (AA), **B**
52, 59, 160, 225; **S** 100
Boston Redskins football club (NFL),
F 178-79, 282, 385, 393, 472; **S**
422, 474
Boston Tigers hockey club (CAHL), **I**
35
Boston to Washington, DC Long
Distance Walk, **O** 559
Boston University, **B** 101; **O** 296,
529; **S** 339, 500, 571, 583, 596-
97
Boston Wonder Workers Soccer Club,

O 299
Boston Yanks football club (AAFC,
NFL), **F** 30, 112, 453; **I** 154; **S**
401, 405
Boswell, David W. "Dave," **S** 145
Boswell, Thomas M. "Tom," **S** *337,*
351
Bosworth, Brian K., **F** 582
Botafoga of Brazil Soccer Club, **O**
294, 299
Bottomley, James L. "Jim," **B** 8, *40-
41,* 193; **S** 23
Boudreau, Louis, Jr. "Lou," **B** 18,
41-42, 573, 611, 616; **I** 105; **O**
53; **S** 40, 125
Boulmetis, Sam, Sr., **O** *178*
Boulmetis, Sam, Jr., **O** 178
Bounding Home **O** 205
Bourbon Belle, **O** 588
Boussac, Marcel, **O** 615
Bousset, **O** 223
Bouton, James A. "Jim," **B** 186; **S**
133, 359
Bowa, Frank, **B** 42
Bowa, Lawrence R. "Larry," **B** *42-43;*
S 207
Bowa, Paul, **B** 42
Bowden, Donald P. "Don," **S** 581
Bowden, Robert "Bobby," **S** *368-69*
Bowdoin College, **I** 538; **O** 529
Bowen, "Andy," **I** 420
Bowen, George W., **O** 597
Bowerman, Frank E. "Mike," **B** 45
Bowerman, William J. "Bill," **O**
434-35, 470, 518
Bowie Race Track, Bowie, MD, **O**
180, 203
Bowling, **I** 339-341, 343, 348-49,
351
Bowling Brook, **S** 527, 536
Bowling Brook Farm, **S** 536
Bowling Green State University, **F**
526; **I** 6-7, 208, 302; **O** 566; **S**

281
Bowling Proprietor's Association of America, I 341, 349
Bowling Proprietor's Association of America All-Star Tournament, I 341-46, 349-51
Bowling Proprietor's Association of America Doubles Tournament, I 341, 350
Bowling Proprietor's Association of America Open Tournament, I 339, 343-44, 346-47, 351
Bowling Proprietor's Association of America Showboat Invitation Tournament, I 350
Bowling Proprietor's Association of America Team Championship, I 344
Bowling Writers Association of America, I 344
Bowling Writers Association of America Bowler of the Decade, I 337, 347
Bowling Writers Association of America Male Bowler of the Year, I 337-43, 347-49, 351
Bowling Writers Association of America Woman Bowler of the Year, I 342, 344, 347
Bowlium, Chicago, IL, I 346
Bowman, Ralph "Scotty," I 545; S 541, 547
Bowman, Robert J. "Bob," B 396; S 32
Bowrey, William "Bill," O 394
Boxing Hall of Fame, See The Ring's Boxing Hall of Fame
Boxing Writer of the Year Award, I 372
Boxing Writers Association, I 354, 371, 387, 398
Boyd, Dennis R. "Oil Can," S 44
Boyd, Joseph M. "Joe," F 434

Boyd-Rochfort, Cecil, O 602, 613
Boydston, "Max," F 654
Boyer, Cletis L. "Clete," B 43
Boyer, Cloyd V., B 43
Boyer, Kenton L. "Ken," B 43-44; S 23
Boykoff, Harry, I 70
Boylan, "Jack," I 373
Boyle, Michael "Mike," O 35
Boyle's Thirty Acres, Jersey City, NJ, I 431
The Boys of Summer, S 351
Brabham Race Cars, O 12
Braddock, James J. "Jim," I 358, 360-61, 426, 428-29
Braddock, "Johnny," I 404
Braden, Victor "Vic," O 326
Bradenton, FL baseball club (GCL, GCRL), B 251, 439, 542; S 51
Bradenton, FL Explorers baseball club (SPBA), S 153
Bradford, PA baseball club (Pol), B 174, 525
Bradlee, Fred J., F 65, 238
Bradley, Alva, B 24
Bradley, Dominick, I 403
Bradley, Edward, S 534-35
Bradley, Patricia "Pat," S 508-09
Bradley, Ruby, I 480
Bradley, William W. "Bill," I 30-32, 64-65, 133, 137, 220, 260; S 280
Bradley, CA Track and Field Meet, O 559
Bradley University, I 67, 180, 198, 234, 251, 315; O 51, 53
Bradshaw, Mark, I 492
Bradshaw, Terry P., F 59-60, 247, 432, 525
Brady, James "Jim," F 94
Brady, Michael J. "Mike," O 112-113
Brady, William A., I 407
Brae Burn Golf Club, West Newton, MA, O 128

Bragan, Robert R. "Bobby," **B** 619
Bragg, Donald G. "Don," **S** *569-70*
Brahaney, Thomas F. "Tom," **S** *369-71*
Braidburn Golf Club, Madison, NJ, **O** 127
Brain, David L. "Dave," **B** 617
Brainerd, MN 100 Auto Race, **O** 16
Brallier, John K., **F** 41, *60-61*
Bramble, **S** 533
Bramham, William, **B** 561
Branca, Ralph T. J., **S** 221
Branch, Clifford, Jr. "Cliff," **F** *61-62*
Branch Rickey Award, **S** 263
Brand, Dale, **I** 639
Brand, Glen, **I** *639-40*, 660
Brandeis University, **F** 195; **I** 150-51; **S** 339
Brandsten, Ernest M. "Ernie," **I** 486, 496-97
Brandwein, Peter, **O** 62
Branham, George III, **I** 349
Brannum, Clarence, **I** 94
Brasse, Ordell, **F** 519
Brastand, "Pat," **I** 456
Bratkowski, Edmund "Zeke," **F** 55
Brattleboro, VT Outing Club, **O** 279
Bratton, "Johnny," **I** 362, 477
Braun, Carl A., **S** *264-65*
Brauner, Clinton "Clint," **O** 3
Bravy, Galaxy, **O** 215
Braxton, Dwight, **S** 623
Bray, Raymond "Ray," **F** 609
Brazil, Larry, **O** 138
Brazil National Basketball Team, **I** 55-56
Brazil National Soccer team, **O** 299-301, 307
Brazil National Tennis Championships, **O** 343
Brazil Open Golf Tournament, **O** 124
Brazile, Robert L. Jr. "Bob," **F** *62-63*

Breadon, Sam, **B** *44-45*, 202, 260, 473, 525
Breakers Pool, Palm Beach, FL, **I** 623
Brecheen, Harry D. "The Cat," **S** *16-17*, 75
Bredlow, "Chuck," **I** 183
Breeder's Cup Classic, **O** 204, 218, 227, 229
Breeder's Cup Distaff Race, **O** 183
Breeder's Futurity Stakes, **O** 603, 611
Breeder's Stakes, **O** 201
Brenna Hanover, **O** 574
Brennan, Joseph R. "Joe," **I** *32-33*
Brennan, Mary E., *See* Mary Brennan Merrell
Brennan, Peter J. "Pete," **I** 199
Brennan, "Red," **I** 461
Brennan, Terence "Terry," **F** 176; **S** 437
Brennan, William "Bill," **I** 391; **O** 613
Brentwood Golf Club, **O** 120
Breslin, William J., *See* Jack Britton
Bresnahan, Roger P., **B** *45-47*, 569
Bressler, Raymond B. "Rube," **B** 488
Bret Hanover, **O** 574-75
Brett, George H., **B** *47-48*, 115, 370; **S** 237
Brett, John., **B** 47
Brett, Kenneth A. "Ken," **B** 47
Brett, Robert, **B** 47
Brewer, Arthur H., **F** 64
Brewer, Charles "Charlie," **F** *63-65*
Brewer, "Chet," **B** 269
Brewer, James T. "Jim," **S** 90
Brewer, Ronald C. "Ron," **I** 219
Brewers Cup, **O** 209
Brewster, Arthur, **I** 181
Brick Small Soccer League, **O** 297
Bricker, Calvin "Cal," **O** 463
Brickhouse, John B. "Jack," **O** *51-53*
Brickley, Charles E., **F** *65-66*, 299, 379-80, 465, 571

Bridal Flower, S 527
Bridgeman, Ulysses L. "Junior," S 294
Bridgeport, CT baseball club (CtL, EL), B 27, 197, 428, 495, 587; S 191
Bridges, Thomas J. "Tommy," B 48-49
Bridges, William C. "Bill," I 33-34
Bridgewater College, O 521
Briggs, Walter O., B 49-50, 356, 416, 561
Briggs, Walter O. II, B 50
Briggs Stadium, Detroit, MI, B 50, 418
Brigham Young University, B 409; F 139, 289, 371-72, 671-72; I 264, 320-21, 577; O 143, 428, 518; S 145, 254, 395-96
Brighton Beach Swim, I 589
Brighton Cup, S 536
Brighton Derby, O 196
Brighton Junior Stakes, O 578
Brighton Mile, O 196
Brill, Martin "Marty," F 95, 506
Brimsek, Francis C. "Frankie," I 544-45, 546-47, 561, 572-73
Brinker, Maureen Connolly "Mo," O 327-28, 352, 360, 374
Brinley, Geoffrey M., O 392
Brisbane, Arthur, O 91
Brisco, Valerie, See Valerie A. Brisco-Hooks
Brisco-Hooks, Valerie A., O 435-37; S 579
Briscoe, "Bennie," I 397
Bristol Channel Swim, I 581
Bristol, CT baseball club (EL), B 341, 471; S 225, 236
Bristol, TN International Speedway, O 41; S 605
Bristol, VA baseball club (ApL), S 221

Bristol, WV basketball club, S 290
British All-Comers Track and Field Meet, O 465
British Amateur Athletic Association Track and Field Championships, O 460, 483, 489, 504-05
British Amateur Medalist Golf Tournament, O 117, 136, 138, 159, 161-62
British Broadcasting Corporation, O 365
British College of Physical Education, O 253
British Columbia Lions football club (CFL), F 411, 645
British Curtis Cup Team, S 518, 521
British Elite League, I 568
British Empire Track and Field Team, O 465-66
British GI Golf Championship, O 141
British Hard Court Tennis Championships, O 388
British Ladies Amateur Golf Tournament, O 151, 165
British Masters Golf Tournament, O 163-64
British National Epee Team Championship, O 64
British National Soccer Team, O 291, 300-01, 307, 309
British National Tennis Team, O 345, 349, 356, 359, 372, 374, 397, 415; See also Wightman Cup Tennis team
British Open Golf Tournament, O 108-09, 119, 124, 126, 128, 131, 133, 135-36, 140, 144, 149, 153-55, 158-59, 163, 166-67, 169; S 516
British Track and Field Championships, S 567
British Winter Sports Association, O

278
Brito, Eugene "Gene," **F** 297, 329
Britt, "Jimmy," **I** 444
Britton, Helene, **B** 44
Britton, "Jack," **I** *361-62,* 394-95, 421, 474, 476
Broad Bush, **O** 203
Broadmoor Invitational Golf Tournament, **O** 152
Broadway Athletic Club, **I** 387, 434
Broadway Stakes, **O** 211
Broberg, Gustave, Jr. "Gus," **S** *265-66*
Broberg, Peter S. "Pete," **S** 265-66
Brock, "Debbie," **I** 314
Brock, James "Jim," **S** *17-18*
Brock, Louis C. "Lou," **B** *51-52,* 72, 104, 248, 449, 618; **S** 34, 72
Brockton, MA baseball club (NEL), **B** 347, 511
Brodbeck, Emil, **F** 574
Broderick Award, **I** 72, 214-15, 579; **O** 481
Broderick Cup, **I** 72, 176, 214, 290, 608; **O** 481
Brodhead, Lucas, **O** 174
Brodie, John R., **F** *66-67,* 560
Brodie, Walter S. "Steve," **S** *18-19,* 210
Broeg, Robert W. "Bob," **O** 55; **S** *337-38*
Broglio, Ernest G. "Ernie," **B** 51
Brokers Tip, **S** 535
Bromwich, John, **O** 337-38, 390; **S** 552
Bronson, "Jimmy," **I** 465
Bronson Trade School, **I** 429
Bronx Giants baseball club, **S** 248
Bronzan, Robert, **F** 478
Bronze Hugo Award, **O** 69
Brookdale Handicap, **O** 206
Brookdale Stud, **S** 533
Brooke Army Medical Center, **F** 628

Brooke, George, **F** 204
Brookes, Norman "Norm," **O** 362, 366, 372, 421
Brookhattan Soccer Club, **O** 291
Brooklawn Golf Club, **O** 153
Brookline, MA Country Club, **I** 499; **O** 128, 148; **S** 519
Brooklyn Americans basketball club, **I** 30
Brooklyn Arcadians basketball club, **I** 233
Brooklyn Atlantics baseball club (NA), **B** 38, 122, 442-43, 531
Brooklyn baseball club (PL), **B** 307, 429, 568, 592, 600; **S** 100
Brooklyn Bridegrooms baseball club (AA), **B** 78-79, 171, 194, 429, 599; **O** 78
Brooklyn Bridegrooms baseball club (NL), **O** 78; **S** 47-48, 98, 155; *See* Brooklyn Dodgers baseball club (NL)
Brooklyn Bushwicks baseball club (Negro Leagues), **B** 613; **I** 332
Brooklyn Chess Club, **I** 671
Brooklyn Concourse Club, **O** 192
Brooklyn Dodgers baseball club (NL), **B** 3, 8-9, 15, 20, 24, 40, 52, 65, 72, 78, 84-85, 87-88, 97, 113, 117-18, 126, 129, 131, 133-35, 137, 155, 158-59, 161-62, 165, 169, 174, 178, 181, 183, 187, 193-94, 200-01, 208, 216, 224-25, 228-29, 238, 240-41, 245, 249-51, 256-58, 266, 270, 274, 281-82, 293, 298-99, 301-02, 311, 313-15, 326, 330, 332, 335, 337, 344, 347, 353-54, 363, 366, 375-77, 381, 383-84, 396-97, 404, 408, 417-18, 420, 426-27, 459, 466-70, 473-76, 480-82, 493, 495, 511, 516-17, 520-21, 529, 534, 538, 540-41, 556, 565-68, 570, 577, 582-83, 590, 592,

600-02, 614, 621, 626; **F** 130,
498; **I** 165, 274; **O** 48, 59-60, 78,
92-93; **S** 4-5, 10, 13, 23, 32, 38,
45-46, 60-62, 68, 86, 108, 117-18,
127-28, 135, 153-54, 156-57, 162-
64, 173, 177, 180, 183, 188, 207-
08, 221, 228-29, 335, 348, 351,
359

Brooklyn Dodgers Baseball Hall of
Fame, **B** 467

Brooklyn Dodgers basketball club, **I**
32

Brooklyn Dodgers football club
(AAFC, NFL), **F** 23, 28, 83, 170,
189, 215, 281, 319, 361, 381, 452-
53, 579, 658; **O** 296; **S** 380, 413,
439, 448, 457

Brooklyn *Eagle,* **B** 82, 299; **O** 62;
S 335

Brooklyn Eagles baseball club (NNL),
B 141, 150, 548; **I** 143, 332

Brooklyn Eagles football club (Ind.),
F 353

Brooklyn Eckfords baseball club, **B**
464

Brooklyn Enterprise baseball club, **B**
531

Brooklyn Excelsiors baseball club, **B**
122, 128

Brooklyn Feds baseball club (FL), **B**
54, 429, 592; **S** 240

Brooklyn Giants baseball club (Negro
Leagues), **B** 331, 466

Brooklyn Greenpoint basketball club
(MeL), **I** 14

Brooklyn Handicap, **O** 194, 196, 211,
223-24, 573, 580, 582, 584, 58,
591-92, 605; **S** 533

Brooklyn Hispano football club
(ASL), **O** 299-300

Brooklyn Horseman football club
(AFL), **F** 188

Brooklyn Jewels basketball club, **I**

32, 273;

Brooklyn Jockey Club, **O** 212

Brooklyn *Long Island Star,* **B** 82

Brooklyn Robins baseball club (NL),
S 42, 111, 156, 184; *See also*
Brooklyn Dodgers baseball club
(NL)

Brooklyn Royal Giants baseball club
(ECL), **B** 287, 334, 343, 378,
452, 466, 500, 519, 553, 612; **O**
731; **S** 43, 143, 148, 238

Brooklyn Superbas baseball club (NL),
S 47-48, 98, 124, 209, 220; *See
also* Brooklyn Dodgers baseball
club (NL)

Brooklyn Visitation basketball club
(MeL, ABL), **I** 32, 131, 157, 194,
198, 250, 260-61

Brooklyn Wanderers Soccer Club, **O**
293

Brookmeade Stables, **O** 186, 198

Brooks, Herbert P."Herb," **I** *547-49,*
550, 554, 557, 563-64, 567-68,
572; **S** 539, 543, 547

Brooks, Hubert "Hubie," **S** 18

Brooks, James R., **F** 19

Brooks, Steve, **O** *178-79*

Broome County, FL Golf Tournament,
O 126

Brosnan, James P. "Jim," **B** 186

Broten, Aaron, **I** 550, 567

Broten, Neal L., **I** *549-50,* 558, 566-
67

Broten, Paul, **I** 550

Brotherhood of Professional Base Ball
Players, **B** 112, 117, 240, 307,
549, 576, 592; **S** 151, 169

Brotherhood Park, Chicago, IL, **B**
108

Brough, Althea Louise, **S** *549-50;
See also* Althea Louise Brough
Clapp

Brouillard, Louis "Lou," **I** 370, 381,

470, 481
Broun, Heywood C., I 411; O *53-55*, 74, 90
Broun, Heywood Hale, O 54
Brouthers, Dennis J. "Dan," B *52-53*, 160, 240, 554, 604; S 178
Brovelli, Angelo, F 378
Broward Junior College, O 214
Brown, Aaron, *See* The Dixie Kid
Brown, Boyd, O 470
Brown, Charles Edward "Ed," F 55
Brown, David "Dave," S *19-20*
Brown, David E. "Davie," O *292-93*, 310
Brown, Earlene Dennis, S *570-71*
Brown, Edward, O 293, 589
Brown, Ellison M., S 582
Brown, Francis Gordon, Jr., S *371-72*
Brown, Fred "Downtown," I 300
Brown, Herbert "Herb," S 313
Brown, "Ice," I 447
Brown, James N. "Jimmy," F *69-69*, 70, 87, 111, 122, 246, 279, 294, 312, 349, 395, 401, 461, 494, 534; O 10; S 384, 412
Brown, Joe, I *362-63*, 446
Brown, Joe L., S 150
Brown, Johnny Mack, F 625
Brown, Lawrence H. "Larry," I *34-35*, 56, 112, 324; S 301
Brown, Lawrence, Jr. "Larry," F 494; S *372-73*
Brown, "Lew," I 465
Brown, Mordecai P. "Three Finger," B *53-54*, 468, 507, 593; S 98, 161, 226
Brown, Paul E., F 15, *69-70*, 165, 199, 203, 215, 218-19, 229, 272, 339-41, 409, 432, 543, 559, 656-57; S 261, 384, 412-13
Brown, Raymond C. "Tay," F 512; S 495

Brown, Richard "Dick," O 540
Brown, Robert, O 292
Brown, Robert J., F 194
Brown, Robert S. "Bob," F *71*
Brown, Robert W. "Bobby," B *54-55;* S 140, 172
Brown, Roosevelt, Jr. "Rosie," F *71-72*
Brown, Russell, O 293
Brown, Terry L., S 497
Brown, Theotis, Jr., F 17
Brown, Thomas, S 554
Brown, Thomas P., Jr., O 337-38, 365
Brown, Timothy "Tim," S *373-74*, 420
Brown, Walter A., I *35-36*, 217, 245, 306
Brown, Warren, F 95
Brown, William F. "Willie," F *72-73*, 500
Brown, William H., O 101
Brown University, B 500; F 57, 64-65, 85, 163-65, 192, 204, 231, 256, 376, 426, 459, 469, 475-77, 625, 647; I 545-46; O 59, 102, 464, 547-48
Browne, Mary K., O *328-30*, 354, 359, 362, 374, 385, 387, 391, 403, 411, 415-17
Browne, "Nat," O 329
Browner, Ross, F 138, 495; S *374-75*
Brownie, O 223
Browning, David, I 485
Browning, Kurt, I 501
Browning, Louis R. "Pete," B *56-57*
Brown's Gym, New York, NY, I 431
Broyles, John Franklin "Frank," F 6, *73-74*, 206, 516, 581; S 428, 480
Bruce, Ethel Sutton, O 352
Bruce Yohe Memorial Trophy, S 584
Brugnon, Jacques, O 404

Brumbaugh, Carl M., F 600
Brummel, Valery, S 496-97
Brunansky, Thomas A. "Tom," S 206
Brundage, Avery, O 255-56, 268
Brunet, Jean Pierre, I 511
Brunet, Pierre, O 509, 511; S 601
Bruno, Frank, S 625
Brunswick World Invitation Bowling
    Tournament, I 339-40, 343-45,
    347-48
Brush, John T., B 199, 301, 457,
    539; S 194
Brushup, O 613
Bruton, William H. "Billy," B 290; I
    333
Bryan, David, O 593
Bryan, James E. "Jimmy," O 4, 5-6
Bryant, "Clay," S 108
Bryant, "Hallie," I 192
Bryant, Kelvin L., F 518; S 454
Bryant, Paul W. "Bear," F 54, 74-
    75, 81, 121, 198, 281, 302, 369,
    418, 427, 458, 499, 501, 561, 564;
    S 365-66, 368, 379, 382, 384,
    395, 399, 422, 439, 462-63, 477,
    479-80
Bryn Mawr College, B 162; O 253
Bubas, Victor "Vic," I 43; S 535
Bubbling Over, O 194; S 535
Buchanan, O 209
Buchanan, Junious "Buck," F 75-76,
    500
Buchanan, Kenneth "Ken," I 446
Buchanon, Willie J., F 76-77
Bucher, Frank, S 439
Bucholz, Earl, Jr. "Butch," S 556
Buck, Jason O., S 386
Buck, John F. "Jack," F 573; O 55-
    56, 57, 65; S 355, 357
Bucketeers basketball club, I 119-20
Buckeye Conference, S 290
Buckley, Richard D. "Dick," B 493
Bucknell University, B 390; F 267,

    403, 558, 665-66; I 154
Bucknell University Hall of Fame, F
    267
Buckner, James, B 57
Buckner, Robert, B 57
Buckner, William J. "Billy," B 57-
    59; S 142
Buckner, William Quinn, I 162; S
    303
Buckpasser, O 575-76, 577, 579,
    581
Buckwalter, Morris, I 94
Bud Collins' Modern Encyclopedia of
    Tennis, S 339
Bud Lerner, S 526-27
Bud Wilkinson Award, S 279
Budd, Francis J. "Frank," O 438
Budd, Zola, O 540-41
Budd Doble, O 230
Budde, Brad E. "Brad", S 468
Buddhist, O 589
Budge, John, O 330
Budge, John Donald "Don," O 330-
    32, 343, 374, 386, 404, 410, 418;
    S 341, 551, 554
Budge, Lloyd, O 330
Budlong, Clarence R., O 413
Budnitz, Emil A., Jr. "Buzzy," O
    236-37
Budweiser 500 NASCAR Race, O 1;
    S 605
Budweiser 400 NASCAR Race, O 1,
    41
Budweiser GI Joe 200 CART Race, S
    619
Budweiser International Race of
    Champions Series, O 29, 44
Budweiser Million Race, O 229, 591
Bueno, Maria, O 357-58, 363; S 550
Buff, "Johnny," I 400, 431, 440
Buffalo All-Americans football club
    (NFL), F 27, 350, 440-41
Buffalo baseball club (EL, Ind.), B

104, 115-16, 207, 230
Buffalo baseball club (FL), **B** 89, 612
Buffalo baseball club (NL), **B** 52,
   116, 207, 428, 463, 604; **S** 178
Buffalo Bills football club (AAFC), **F**
   3; **S** 391, 424, 429
Buffalo Bills football club (AFL), **F**
   129, 179, 408, 479, 545, 590; **S**
   363, 432, 442, 467, 469, 472, 478-
   79
Buffalo Bills football club (NFL), **F**
   135, 180, 264, 295, 321, 364, 384,
   408, 483, 485, 496-97, 545
Buffalo Bisons baseball club (IA), **B**
   206-07, 221, 604-05
Buffalo Bisons baseball club (IL), **B**
   33, 41, 61, 80, 146, 155, 144-46,
   280, 293, 345, 356, 369, 392, 448,
   501, 509, 557, 565-66, 607; **S**
   165, 177, 189, 195, 200, 227-28,
   234, 240
Buffalo Bisons baseball club (PL), **B**
   265, 358, 604
Buffalo Bisons basketball club (ABL,
   NBL), **I** 44; **S** 283, 289
Buffalo Bisons football club (NFL), **S**
   431
Buffalo Braves basketball club (NBA),
   I 9, 60, 189, 203-04, 244, 271; **S**
   251
Buffalo Classic, **S** 291
Buffalo Colored Giants baseball club
   (Negro Leagues), **B** 287
Buffalo Country Club, **O** 140
Buffalo Germans basketball club, **I** 4;
   S 260, 289
Buffalo Open Bowling Tournament, **I**
   351
Buffalo Orioles basketball club, *See*
   Buffalo Germans basketball club
Buffalo Sabres hockey club (NHL), **I**
   544, 550; **S** 541-42, 545, 547-48
Buffinton, Charles G. "Charlie," **B**

59, 160
Buford, "Chris," **F** 591
Buick Open Golf Tournament, **O** 135
Bulgarian National Gymnastic Team, **I**
   542
Bulgarian National Wrestling Team, **I**
   640, 659, 666
Bulger, "Jack," **I** 474
Bulkeley, Morgan G., **B** *60-61,* 271
Bull, "Billy," **F** 469
Bull Lea, **O** 195, 571, 576
Bundy, Dorothy, *See* Dorothy Bundy
   Cheney
Bundy, May Sutton, **O** 329, *332,*
   336, 347, 354, 377, 415
Bundy, Thomas C. "Tom," **O** *332,*
   336, 347, 372, 421
Bunion Derby, **O** 88
Bunker Hill Day Marathon, **S** 582
Bunn, John W., **I** 5, *36-38,* 256
Bunning, James P. "Jim," **B** *61-62,*
   439
Bunte, Arthur "Art," **I** 94
Buntin, William "Bill," **I** 259
Bunting, **S** 533
Buoniconti, Nicholas "Nick," **S** *375-
   76*
Burbridge's Harry, **O** 594
Burch, William P., **O** 213
Burdette, Selva Lewis, Jr. "Lew," **B**
   62-63, 526
Burfoot, "Amby," **O** 527
Burge, Richard, **I** 420
Burgess, Forrest H. "Smoky," **S** *20-
   21*
Burgess, Thomas W. "Bill," **I** 589
Burghley, Lord, **O** 549
Burgomeister, **O** 191
Burgoo King, **S** 535
Burk, Joseph W. "Joe," **O** *256-57*
Burke, David, **O** 476
Burke, Edward A. "Ed," **O** 476
Burke, John J., Sr., **O** 113

46

Burke, John J., Jr. "Jack," **O** *113-14,* 119

Burke, Michael "Mike," **B** 175, 318

Burke, Mildred, *See* Mildred Burke Younker Wolfe

Burke, Thomas E. "Tom," **S** *571-72,* 592

Burkel, John, **I** 522

Burkemo, Walter "Walt," **O** 410

Burkett, Jesse C., **B** *63-64,* 360; **S** 36

Burleson, Dyrol J., **O** 435, 526

Burleson, Tom L., **I** 280

Burleson College, **F** 428

Burlington, IA baseball club (CA, ML, MOVL, 3IL, WA), **B** 37, 65, 78, 195, 563, 609; **S** 83-84

Burlington, IA Junior College, **S** 273

Burman, "Joe," **I** 431

Burman, "Red," **I** 426

Burnett, Dale, **F** 447

Burnine, Harold, **F** 168

Burning Tree Country Club, **S** 522

Burns, "Frankie," **I** 370, 400, 478

Burns, George H. "Tioga George," **B** *64-65*

Burns, George J., **B** 64, *66-67,* 231; **S** 191

Burns, Isaac, *See* Isaac Murphy

Burns, Martin "Farmer," **I** 643

Burns, "Sleepy Bill," **I** 357

Burns, Thomas "Tommy," **O** 206

Burns, "Tommy," **I** 398, 408-09, 445

Burris, Donald "Don," **F** 77

Burris, Kurt, **F** 77

Burris, Lyle, **F** 77

Burris, Lynn, **F** 77

Burris, Paul "Buddy," **F** *77-79,* 653; **S** 462

Burris, Robert "Bob," **F** 77

Burton, Lewis, **F** 192

Burton, Michael J. "Mike," **I** *576-77*

Burton, Nelson, Sr., **I** 339

Burton, Nelson, Jr. "Bo," **I** *339*

Burton, Ronald "Ron," **F** 458

Busanda, **O** 184-85, 575

Busch, August A., Jr. "Gussie," **B** *67,* 540; **S** 174

Busch Classic NASCAR Race, **S** 605

Busch 500 NASCAR Race, **O** 44

Busch Pole Award, **O** 41; **S** 606

Busch Memorial Stadium, St. Louis, MO, **B** 32, 67; **F** 16; **S** 206

Bush, George H., **S** 65

Bush, Leslie A., "Bullet Joe," **B** 558; **S** *21-22,* 190, 200

Bush, Owen J. "Donie," **B** 129

Busher, **O** 614

Bussey, Dexter M., **F** 546

Busso, "Johnny," **I** 363

But Why Me, **S** 527

Butkus, Richard M. "Dick," **F** 33, *79-80,* 548; **S** 357

Butkus Award, **F** 582

Butler, Jerry O., **S** 383

Butler, John "Jack," **F** *80*

Butler National Golf Course, Chicago, IL, **O** 163

Butler, PA baseball club (MAL), **B** 187

Butler University, **F** 189; **I** 129-30, 236, 302; **O** 245-46

Butte, MT baseball club (MtL, NWL), **B** 353, 407

Butterflies, **O** 188

Butterworth, Frank S., **F** 266

Button, Richard T. "Dick," **I** *502-03,* 504, 507, 510, 513-14; **O** 269

Butts, James Wallace, Jr. "Wally," **F** *81,* 549; **S** 430

Butts, Joseph, **I** 387

Buxton, Angela, **O** 359

Buzhardt, John W., **S** 202

Byng High School, **I** 296-97

Byrd, Harry, **F** 585; **S** 171

Byrne, Brendan, **O** 105

Byrne, Charles, **B** 429

Byrne, Eugene, **F** 178

Byrne, Raymond "Ray," **F** 426

Byron Nelson Award, **O** 116, 166

Byron Nelson Golf Classic, **O** 124, 146, 166; **S** 521

Byron V. Kanaley Award, **I** 208

Cable News Network, **O** 102; **S** 341

Cactus Derby Auto Race, **O** 26

Caesar's Palace, Las Vegas, NV, **I** 397, 423, 430, 527, 535; **S** 625-26

Caesar's Palace Gymnastic Invitation Meet, **I** 527, 535

Caffey, Lee Roy, **F** 104, 430

Cagle, Christian K. "Chris," **F** 57, *83-84,* 301

Cahill, Mabel E., **O** *333-34,* 376

Cahill, Ronald "Ronnie," **F** 12

Cain, C. J., **I** 345

Cain, James L. "Johnny," **F** 625

Cain Hay Stable, **O** 322

Cairnes, J. J., **O** 392

Cairney, Ralph, **I** 76

Calder Trophy, **I** 544-46, 553, 560; **S** 538, 542

Calderon, Ivan P., **S** 172

Calderwood, Ethel, **O** 513

Caldwell, Charles W., Jr. "Charlie," **F** *84-85,* 309, 505

Caledonian Games, **O** 469

Calgary, Canada Winter Olympic Games, *See* Olympic Winter Games, 1988

Calgary, Canada Flames hockey club (NHL), **I** 566-67; **S** 543

Calgary Stampeders football club (CFL), **F** 3, 179, 293-94, 397, 448; **S** 399

Calhoun, George, **S** 440-41

Calhoun, Lee Q., **I** 671; **O** *437-38,* 479; **S** 572, 583

Caliente, Mexico Race Track, **O** 175, 217; **S** 531

California All-Stars football club, **O** 87

California Alpine Ski Championships, **O** 286

California Amateur Golf Championships, **O** 143; **S** 517

California Angels baseball club (AL), **B** 4, 39, 58, 63, 70, 138-39, 159, 167, 201, 251, 277-78, 284, 305, 312, 329, 341-42, 449, 472, 478, 497-98, 526, 543-45, 560, 608, 614; **F** 287, 492; **I** 213; **O** 62; **S** 11, 15-16, 18, 25, 35, 44, 49, 51, 53, 58, 72, 84, 87-88, 90, 104, 106, 131, 135, 138, 167, 171, 175, 203-04, 214-15, 222, 241

California Angels Booster Club, **S** 16

California Angels Owners Trophy, **S** 44

California Boys Tennis Championships, **O** 330

California Collegiate Athletic Association, **F** 76, 115, 198, 206, 376, 408; **S** 405

California Dreams basketball club (WPBL), **I** 259

California 500 Auto Race, **O** 18-19, 37, 39

California Golden Seals hockey club (NHL), **I** 573

California Golf Hall of Fame, **O** 140, 142

California Intercollegiate Track and Field Championships, **O** 568

California Interscholastic Federation, **F** 129, 276; **I** 214, 583, 613

California Junior College Basketball Championships, **I** 292; **S** 310

California League, **B** 89; **S** 22, 30, 34, 48, 59, 84, 90, 92, 96, 131, 134, 237

California Polytechnic University, **F** 198, 376, 478; **S** 206

California Relays, **S** 590

California Sportscaster of the Year Award, **O** 63, 93

California Stakes, **O** 612

California Stars basketball club, **I** 215

California State Boxing Championships, **I** 447

California State League, **S** 80, 161

California State Tennis Championships, **O** 353, 361

California State University, Fresno, **I** 292

California State University, Hayward, **B** 405

California State University, Long Beach, **I** 59, 95, 292-93, 493, 531, 616

California State University, Long Beach Hall of Fame, **I** 617

California State University, Los Angeles, **S** 50

California State University, Northridge, **F** 161; **I** 525; **O** 62, 436; **S** 579

California State Volleyball Championships, **I** 676

California State Wrestling Championships, **I** 658, 660

California Surf Soccer Club (NASL), **O** 303, 305, 311

California Tennis Club, **O** 371

California Winter League, **S** 20

Callahan, James J. "Jimmy," **B** 581

Callahan, "Tim," **I** 434

Callaway, Jeanna, **O** 590-91

Callaway, John, **O** 590-91

Callison, John W. "Johnny," **S** 22-23

Callura, "Jackie," **I** 406

Calnan, George C., **I** *669-70*

Calumet Farms, Lexington, KY, **O** 175, 179, 190, 195, 569-72, 576-77, 606, 614; **S** 528-29

Calverley, Ernest A. "Ernie," **I** 155

Cambria, Joseph, **B** 227; **S** 158, 246

Cambria County, PA Hall of Fame, **S** 611

Cambridge, MA Skating Club, **I** 515

Cambridge, MA Track and Field Meet, **O** 479

Cambridge, MD baseball club (ESL), **S** 149

Cambridge University, **O** 258

Camden Handicap, **O** 598

Camden Stakes, **O** 592

Cameron, David, **S** 544

Cameron, Edward, **S** 295

Cameron, G. Don, **O** 578

Camilli, Adolf L. "Dolf," **B** 366, 467; **S** *23-24*

Camilli, Douglas J. "Doug," **S** 24

Camp, Walter C., **F** 4, 27, 38-39, 51, 63, 66, *85-87,* 109, 115, 158, 177-78, 200, 204, 217, 221, 226, 231, 239-40, 251, 254-55, 259-61, 265-66, 269, 286, 298-99, 342, 359, 379-80, 403, 410, 426, 437-38, 440, 463-65, 469, 473-75, 477, 497-99, 504, 530-31, 540, 551, 563, 568, 597, 602, 627, 634, 644, 649; **O** 398; **S** 376, 397, 417, 419, 444, 473, 477, 498, 546

Camp Foundation, **F** 497, 499

Camp Grant, **F** 601

Camp Lejeune, NC Marines, **S** 262. 461

Camp Lewis Army, **F** 46

Camp MacArthur Army, **F** 148

Camp Pendleton Marines, **F** 348

Camp Perry, VA, **S** 578

Camp Rucker, **F** 526

Camp Trophy, **F** 11, 53, 100, 121, 130, 138, 320, 337, 344, 437, 473, 568, 585, 605, 649

Camp of Champions, Watertown, WI,
I 654

Campanella, Roy, B 9, *69-70,* 146,
213, 256, 270, 311, 362, 467; S
188

Campanis, Alexander S. "Alex," B 97

Campbell, Clarence, I 552

Campbell, David C., S 376-77

Campbell, Earl C., F *87-88,* 104,
139-40, 483, 509, 547

Campbell, Frank, S 23

Campbell, "Frankie," I 358

Campbell, Hardy, O 592

Campbell, John B., O 614

Campbell, Milton G. "Milt," O 477,
493; S *572-73*

Campbell, Oliver S. "Ollie," O *334-
35,* 398

Campbell, "Tonie," S 584

Campbell College, I 332

Campbell University, B 444-45

Campi, "Eddie," I 478

Canadeo, Anthony R. "Tony," F *88-
89,* 329

Canadian Alpine Ski Championships,
O 286

Canadian-American (Can-Am)
Challenge Cup Auto Races, O 12,
28; S 619

Canadian-American Hockey League, I
35, 240

Canadian-American League, S 29,
108, 172, 199

Canadian-American Ski Competition,
O 275

Canadian Auto Championship, O 8

Canadian Broadcasting Company, S
352

Canadian Cricket Club, S 615

Canadian East-West All-Star football
game, F 297

Canadian Figure Skating
Championship, I 501-02

Canadian Football League, F 3, 50,
129, 179, 199, 209, 218-19, 224,
293-94, 297, 325, 329, 389, 397,
411, 448, 478, 508, 515, 535, 560,
593, 622, 633, 642, 645, 656, 662;
O 395, 397, 448-49, 453, 463,
466, 489, 572

Canadian Football League
Championship Game, F 199

Canadian Girls Singles Tennis
Championships, S 551

Canadian International Championship
Stakes, O 607

Canadian Lacrosse League, O 242

Canadian National Basketball Team, I
28, 250

Canadian National Lacrosse Team, O
245

Canadian National Soccer Team, O
293, 297, 300-01, 305, 310

Canadian National Swim Team, I 577

Canadian Olympic Gymnastic Team, I
535

Canadian Olympic Hockey Team, I
555, 565, 568

Canadian Olympic Rowing Team, I
623

Canadian Olympic Wrestling Team, I
651, 660, 662

Canadian Open Golf Tournament, O
108, 116, 119, 124, 126, 130, 138-
39, 149, 158, 163, 167, 169; S
516, 519

Canadian Tennis Championships, O
325-26, 339, 349, 420

Canadian Track and Field
Championships, O 268, 464, 470,
504-05, 534

Canadian Women's Amateur Golf
Tournament, O 165

Canadian Women's Open Golf
Tournament, O 129; S 512

Canadian Wrestling Championships, I

206

Candelaria, John R., **S** *24-25*

Candlestick Park, San Francisco, CA, **B** 351, 380; **S** 84, 139

Candor, **O** 181

Candy Spots, **O** 218

Canham, Donald "Don," **F** 443, 526

Canisius College, **I** 43, 199

Cann, Howard G., **I** 23, *38;* **S** 323

Cannes, France Tennis Championships, **O** 387

Cannon, John J. "Jack," **F** *89-90*

Cannon, William A. "Billy," **F** *90-91;* **S** 469

Cannonade, **O** 222

Canterbury Club, Cleveland, OH, **O** 150

Cantillon, Joseph "Joe," **B** 400, 580

Canton, OH baseball club (CL, MAL, OPL, TSL), **B** 330, 360, 383, 635; **S** 387, 411-12

Canton, OH Bulldogs football club (Ind., APFA, NFL), **F** 102-03, 231, 259, 262, 359, 464, 498, 505, 510, 597, 647; **S** 387, 411-12

Canton, OH Professionals football club, **S** 387, 411

Cantwell, William J., **F** 556

Canzoneri, "Tony," **I** 354, *363-64,* 436, 451-52, 459, 468

Cap and Bells, **S** 533

Cap d'Agle, France Tennis Championships, **O** 353

Capilla, Joaquin, **I** 485

Capital Center, Landover, MD, **I** 309

Capital Health Center, New York, NY, **I** 346

Caponi, Donna Young, **S** *509-10*

Caponi, Harry, **S** 509

Caponi, "Tony," **I** 448

Capote, **S** 530

Cappelletti, Gino R., **F** *92*

Cappelletti, John R., **F** *92-94,* 460;

S 414

Captain's Cup, **F** 554

Caray, Harry C., **O** 53, 55, *56-58,* 65; **S** 348-49

Caray, Harry "Skip," **O** 57

Carbo, Bernardo "Bernie," **B** 115

Carbondale, PA basketball club (PSL, TCL), **I** 88, 250, 273

Cardigan Bay, **O** 182

Cardozo School of Law, **I** 289

Carew, Rodney C. "Rod," **B** *70-71,* 115

Carey, Max G., **B** *71-72,* 534

Carey, Richard J. "Rick," **I** *577-78,* 605

Carey, Robert "Bob," **F** 413

Cariboo, "Chief," **I** 358

Carideo, Francis F. "Frank," **F** *94-95,* 532

Carille, Mary, **O** 369

Carlen, James "Jim," **F** 509

Carleton College, **I** 62

Carlisle, **O** 191

Carlisle Indian School, **B** 33; **F** 125, 175, 230, 299, 402, 469, 477, 596-97, 635-36, 644; **S** 396-97, 502

Carlos, John W., **O** 516, 543, 551

Carlson, Henry C. "Doc," **I** *38-40,* 168; **S** 271

Carlton, Steven N. "Steve," **B** 67, *72-74,* 474; **S** 76, 160, 174, 354

Carlton Stakes, **O** 588; **S** 533

Carmichael, Lee Harold, **F** *96-97,* 220, 295, 335

Carnegie Tech University, **B** 581; **F** 3, 12, 14, 94, 200, 213-14, 391, 437, 506, 528, 532; **S** 482, 485

Carner, Donald, **O** 114

Carner, JoAnne Gunderson, **O** *114-15*

Carnera, Primo, **F** 602; **I** 358, 429, 462

Carnesecca, Luigi "Lou," **I** 247; **S**

266-67
Carnevale, Bernard L. "Ben," I 40
Carnoustie, Scotland Golf Course, O 151
Carolina Association, S 231
Carolina Clippers football club, S 447
Carolina Cougars basketball club (ABA), I 34-35, 58, 117; S 305
Carolina 500 Auto Race, O 1
Carolina Golf Hall of Fame, O 152
Carolina League, S 15, 24, 51, 67, 78, 106, 118, 136, 147, 170, 193, 216, 239, 242
Carolina Open Golf Tournament, O 150
Carpenter, Robert "Bobby," I *550-51, 566*
Carpenter, Robert R. M., Jr. "Bob," B *74-75;* S 277
Carpenter, Robert M. III "Ruly," B 75
Carpenter, Walker G., F 231
Carpenter, William S., Jr. "Bill," S *377-78*
Carpentier, Georges, I 374-75, 377, 391, 405, 412, 416, 425, 428, 448, 453, 465, 471
Carr, Austin G., I *40-42,* 60, 226
Carr, Henry, O *438-39,* 542
Carr, Joseph F. "Joe," F *97-98,* 154, 281, 380-81, 452, 549; S 457
Carr, "Nate," I 652
Carr, Roger D., F 296
Carr, Sabin W., O *439-40*
Carr, William A. "Bill," O *440-42,* 575
Carrasquel, Alfonso C. "Alex," B 12
Carrier Dome, Syracuse, NY, S 264
Carrigan, William F. "Bill," B 208
Carrol, Frank, I 505
Carroll, James S. "Grumpy," F 277, 458
Carroll, Joe Barry, I 266

Carroll, Joseph "Joe," I 502
Carroll College, F 35, 109
Carrora, Guiseppe, *See* Johnny Dundee
Carson, James "Jimmy," I 556; S *538-39*
Carson-Newman College, F 46-47
Carter, Anthony, F *98-99,* 527
Carter, Donald J. "Don," I 337, *339-41,* 350
Carter, Gary E., B *75-76,* 311
Carter, "Jack," I 440
Carter, James Earl, Jr. "Jimmy," I 591-92, 611, 654
Carter, "Jimmy," I 477
Carter, Richard, B 186
Carter, Rubin, I 396
Carter Handicap, O 223, 584
Cartier Field, South Bend, IN, F 416; S 486
Cartmell, Nathaniel J. "Nat," O 557
Cartwright, Alexander J., Jr., B *77-78*
Caruso, Michael "Mike," I 647
Caruthers, Robert L. "Bob," B *78-79,* 194
Carver-Hawkeye Arena, Iowa City, IA, I 642
Casals, Rosemary, O *335-36,* 352, 363
Casals, Victoria, O 335
Casanova, Thomas H. III "Tommy," F *100-01*
Casares, Ricardo "Rick," S *378-79*
Case, Everett N., I *42-43,* 280, 312, 321; S 263
Case Institute of Technology, *See* Case Western Reserve University
Case Western Reserve University, F 456, 520, 543; I 513, 574
Caserio, Fred, I 423
Casey, Bernard T. "Bernie," S 427
Casey, Edward L., S 490

Casey, Hugh T., **B** 467
Cash, Norman D. "Norm," **B** *79-80*
Casino, "Jimmy," **I** 467
Casper, David J. "Dave," **S** *379-80*
Casper, William E. "Billy," Jr., **O**
    115-16, 139
Casper Rule, **S** 379
Cass Club of Detroit baseball club, **B**
    206
Cassady, Howard "Hopalong," **F** *99-*
    100, 241, 454
Cassiano, Richard "Dick," **F** 214
Cassidy, Charles, **S** 431
Cassidy, George, **O** 180
Cassidy, James, **O** 179
Cassidy, "Mars," **O** 179
Cassidy, Marshall W., **O** *179-81*
Cassidy, Wendell, **O** 180
Cassilas, Tony S., **F** 582
Castianirah, **O** 608
Castle Forbes, **O** 184
Castle Rock 150 Auto Race, **O** 16
Castleman, Benjamin "Ben," **O** 606
Castleton Farms, Lexington, KY, **O**
    575, 578, 593
Castro, Fidel, **S** 222
Cata-Pole 500 Auto Race, **O** 533
Catalina Island Swim, **I** 581
Catawba College, **F** 403
Catchings, Harvey L., **S** 294
Catholic University of America, **F**
    319
Catlin, Mark S., **F** 159
Cator, Sylio, **O** 465
Caugus, PR baseball club (PRWL), **S**
    113
Caulkins, Amy, **I** 579
Caulkins, Timothy "Tim," **I** 579
Caulkins, Tracy, **I** *578-80,* 607; **S**
    607
Causwell, Duane, **S** 268
Cauthen, Steve, **O** 203, 570
Cavalcade, **O** 186

The Cavalcade of Basketball, **S** 498
Cavanaugh, Francis W. "Frank," **F**
    101-02, 254; **S** 483
Cavanaugh, John L., **F** 507
Cavaretta, Philip J. "Phil," **B** *80-81*
Caveat, **O** 222
Cawley, Evonne Goolagong, *See*
    Evonne Goolagong
Cayton, William, **S** 625
Cayuga, **S** 536
CBC-Radio-TV "Hockey Night in
    Canada," **S** 352
CBS, *See* Columbia Broadcasting
    System
CBS-Radio "Game of the Week," **S**
    357
CBS-TV "The NFL Today," **S** 357
Ceasar, Leonard, **I** 362
Cedar Rapids, IA baseball club (ML,
    MOVL), **B** 514, 563; **S** 174
Cedar Rapids, IA baseball club (3IL),
    B 41, 102, 354, 469, 624
Cedeno, Cesar, **S** *25-26*
Celebrity Billiards, **I** 677
Cella, Louis, **S** 531
Cellular One Ping Golf Tournament,
    O 137; **S** 518
Celt, **S** 533
Centel Golf Classic, **S** 508
Centenary College, **F** 277, 373, 434,
    539
Centennial Gold Medallion, **O** 191
Centerville, MD baseball club (ESL),
    S 163
Centinela Golf Classic, **S** 508
Central Association, **S** 201
Central Brewery Soccer Club, St.
    Louis, MO, **O** 299
Central Conference, **I** 271
Central Hockey League, **I** 553, 556
Central Hockey League All-Star First
    Team, **I** 566
Central Hockey League All-Star

Second Team, I 566

Central Hockey League Player of the Year, I 566

Central Hockey League Rookie of the Year, I 566

Central Intercollegiate Athletic Association, F 72, 183, 312, 334, 539; I 90, 201; O 520; S 416

Central League, S 24, 179, 198

Central Michigan University, O 62

Central Missouri State University, I 5; S 259

Central Park, New York, NY, O 333, 411, 530

Central Pennsylvania League, S 101

Central State College, OH, S 244

Central State Teachers College, OK, S 556

Central State University, S 313

Centre College, F 35, 373, 402-03; I 67; S 494

Century Club, S 72

Cepeda, Orlando M. "Baby Bull," B 81-82, 97; S 7, 157

Cepeda, Peruchio, B 81

Cerdan, Marcel, I 418, 483

Cerritos Junior College, F 206, 667

Cervantes, Antonio, I 452

Cervi, Alfred N. "Al," F 215; I 43-45, 132

Cey, Ronald C. "Ron," B 209, 518; S 7, 26-27, 114, 185

Chabot, Lorne, S 537

Chabot, Norman W., F 64

Chace, Malcolm G., O 420

Chacornac, S 533

Chadwick, Florence M., I 580-81

Chadwick, Henry, B 82-83, 122, 128

Chadwick, Lester, B 391

Chadwick, William L. "Bill," I 551-52

Challenge Tennis Round, See United States Tennis Championships

Chalmers Award, B 135, 156, 322, 539; S 191

Chamberlain, Elton P. "Icebox," S 115

Chamberlain, Wilton N. "Wilt," I 4-5, 12, 24, 45-48, 58, 96, 100-01, 103-04, 111, 136, 161, 172, 199, 243, 251-52, 262, 294, 302, 308-09, 315, 322; S 256, 302, 306, 359

Chamberlin, Berlin Guy, F 102-03, 646; S 412

Chambers, Jerome P. "Jerry," I 94

Chambliss, Carroll Christopher "Chris," B 441; S 27-28

Chamonix, France Alpine Ski Competition, O 288

Chamonix France Winter Olympic Games, See Olympic Winter Games, 1924

Champagne Stakes, O 194, 206, 211, 213, 220, 224, 569, 575, 578-79, 581, 606-07, 610

Champaign, IL Police Benevolent Association, S 603

The Champion Athletics, S 342

Champion Handicap Horse of the Year, O 571, 612

Champion Player of the Year, I 215

Champion Spark Plug Busch Grand National Race, S 605

Champion Spark Plug 400 NASCAR Race, O 28; S 605

Champion Stakes, O 219, 588, 605

Champions Golf Club, Houston, TX, O 119

Championship Auto Racing Teams Driving Championships, O 29, 34; S 619-20

Championship Auto Racing Teams Tour, O 28-29; S 619-20

Chance, Frank L., B 83-84, 89, 170, 255, 311, 507, 556-57, 611; S

165, 223, 342, 345

Chance Sun, **O** 601

Chandler, Albert B. "Happy," **B** *84-85,* 162, 201, 426; **S** 232

Chandler, Donald G. "Don," **F** *103-04*

Chandler, Spurgeon F. "Spud," **B** *85-86,* 490

Chandler, Wesley S. "Wes," **F** *104-05*

Chandler, William S., **I** 206

Chaney, Donald "Don," **I** 118, 174, 278

Chaney, George H. "K. O.," **I** *364-65,* 415, 469

Chaney, John, **S** *267-68*

Chaos, **O** 219

Chapa, Rudy, **O** 528

Chapdelaine, Ovila, *See* Jack Delaney

Chapman, Harry C. "Tub," **B** 86

Chapman, John C., **B** 531

Chapman, John M. "Colonel," **O** 264

Chapman, Raymond J. "Ray," **B** 393, 508; **S** *28-29*

Chapman, Robert, **I** 277

Chapman, William Benjamin "Ben," **B** *86-87,* 606

Chapman College, **B** 16; **O** 262, 311; **S** 310

Chappuis, Robert R. "Bob," **F** 120; **S** *380-81*

Charentus, **O** 206

Chariots of Fire, **O** 531

Charity, "Ron," **O** 323

Charity Golf Classic, **S** 513-14

Charles, Ezzard M., **I** *365-66,* 424, 437, 472; **O** 52

Charles Comiskey All-Stars Baseball Team, **S** 198

Charles Edward, **O** 196

Charles Pond Palaesium, Champaign, IL, **I** 534

Charles Town Race Track, **O** 214

Charleston, Oscar M., **B** 31, *87-89,* 223, 290, 362, 453, 548-49

Charleston, SC baseball club (SAL, SL, WCL), **B** 129, 600; **S** 24, 219

Charlestown, WV baseball club (AA, EL, IL), **B** 284, 295, 439; **S** 24, 150, 216

Charlie Bartlett Award, **O** 116, 139

Charlie McAdam, **O** 178

Charlotte, NC baseball club (Pil, SA, SAL, SL), **B** 231, 411, 630; **S** 1, 3, 152

Charlotte, NC 500 Auto Race, **O** 1

Charlotte, NC Hornets basketball club (NBA), **I** 289

Charlotte, NC Motor Speedway, **O** 41; **S** 604

Charlotte, NC Open Golf Tournament, **O** 142

Charlotte, NC World 600 Auto Race, **O** 13

Charlton, Andrew, **I** 620

Charlton Athletic Soccer Club of England, **O** 294

Charlton Mill Soccer Club, **O** 299

Chase, Charles A., **O** 398

Chase, Harold H. "Hal," **B** *89-90,* 135, 253, 331; **O** 54, 74; **S** 52, 248

Chateaugay, **O** 612

Chatham, Canada baseball club (CnL), **B** 121

Chattanooga, TN baseball club (SA, SAL, SL), **B** 129, 227-28, 261, 279, 295, 326, 400, 490; **F** 402; **S** 3, 93, 154, 194, 198, 225

Chattanooga, TN basketball club, **I** 65-66

Chattanooga, TN Black Lookouts baseball club (NSL), **B** 436

Chattanooga, TN *Times,* **F** 118

Chavoor, Sherman "Sherm," **I** 576,

612-13, 617
Checkmate, O 209
Cheeks, Maurice E., S *268-69*
Cheeseborough, Chandra, O 436
Chelsea, MA Dreadnaughts baseball
  club, S 150
Cheney, Dorothy Bundy, O 332,
  336-37, 347
Cheney State University, S 267-68
Chenier, Philip "Phil," I 224
Cherry, J. Blair, F 340, 367
Cherry Hills Country Club, Denver,
  CO, O 126; S 512-13
Cherry Point Marines, F 433
Chesapeake Lacrosse Club, O 240
Chesapeake Stakes, O 198
Chesapeake Trial, O 576
Chesbro, John D. "Jack," B *90-92,*
  95, 352, 408, 454, 547
Chesney, Stanley "Stan," O 293
Chester, "Lew," I 465
Chester, Raymond T., F 296
Chestnut Hill Lawn Tennis Club, O
  321, 405
Chestnut Hill Lawn Tennis Club Open
  Championships, O 321
Chestnut Oaks, O 200
Chevrolet World Championship of
  Women's Golf, O 137
Chevy Chase Country Club, S 522
Cheyenne *Eagle,* O 66
Chiapucci, Claudio, S 618
Chicago *American,* F 95; O 73; S
  357
Chicago American Eagles Soccer
  Club, O 303
Chicago American Gears basketball
  club (NBL), S 277
Chicago American Giants baseball
  club (NNL), B 29, 32, 88, 127,
  144, 150, 188-90, 192, 244, 255,
  286, 333-34, 339, 342, 378, 452,
  466, 483, 500, 520, 533, 543, 548-

49, 599, 620; S 19, 43, 99, 129,
  137, 143, 168, 224
Chicago Athletic Association, F 159;
  O 455, 459, 462, 483, 487
Chicago Auto Race, O 6
Chicago baseball club (UA), B 347
Chicago Bears football club (NFL), F
  7, 14, 20, 26, 28, 31, 39, 45, 48,
  55, 79-80, 103, 112, 140, 143,
  152, 155, 170-71, 182, 185-87,
  191, 196, 205, 207, 217, 233-35,
  237, 241, 254, 263, 267, 274, 277,
  281-82, 286, 304, 308-09, 312,
  315, 323, 341, 344, 346, 357, 359-
  62, 372, 381, 388, 393, 414-15,
  417, 424, 451, 461-62, 472, 480,
  496, 499, 510, 517, 524, 538, 548,
  554, 566, 573-74, 576, 589, 596,
  601-02, 608-09, 633, 641, 651; I
  261; O 52, 87, 554; S 361, 378-
  79, 399, 415, 419, 425, 429, 436,
  439, 445-46, 458, 460-61, 474,
  481, 484-85, 491, 503
Chicago Bears Alumni Association, F
  254
Chicago Blackhawks hockey club
  (NHL), I 547, 553-54, 560, 562,
  564, 570-73; S 344, 537-38
Chicago Black Sox scandal, B 90, 93-
  94, 103, 108, 135, 173, 231, 275-
  76, 322-23, 501, 574, 638
Chicago Blitz football club (USFL),
  F 7, 195; S 451
Chicago Bricklayers Soccer Club, O
  306
Chicago Brown Bombers baseball club
  (Negro Leagues), B 144; F 478
Chicago Bruins basketball club (ABL),
  F 48; I 30, 131, 222-23, 261
Chicago Bulls basketball club (NBA),
  F 280; I 24, 50, 96, 98, 153, 160,
  224, 252, 260, 266, 303, 315; O
  52; S 258, 269, 285, 301, 304

Chicago Bulls football club (AFL), F 26

Chicago Cardinals football club (NFL), F 4, 12, 31, 48, 103, 113, 121, 152, 176, 214, 237, 284, 315, 327, 329, 332, 344, 359, 387, 421, 424-25, 454-55, 491, 511, 536, 551, 575, 578, 598-99, 604-05, 652; I 264; O 427; S 344, 381, 436-39, 466-67, 481, 488-89, 491

Chicago City Amateur Golf Tournament, O 121

Chicago City Tennis Championships, O 368

Chicago Coliseum, Chicago, IL, I 470

Chicago Colts baseball club (NL), F 159; See Chicago White Stockings baseball club (NL)

Chicago Columbia Giants baseball club, S 238

Chicago Cubs baseball club (NL), B 4-5, 15, 21-22, 26-28, 39-42, 45-46, 49, 51, 54, 58, 62, 65, 80, 83-84, 87, 92, 95, 101, 108, 112, 119, 129, 133, 138, 140, 143, 145, 156-57, 162, 170, 181, 183-84, 193, 197, 200, 203, 219, 228-30, 235-36, 242, 246, 250-51, 255, 261, 274, 291, 302, 306, 309-11, 315-16, 325-26, 330, 332, 343-46, 352, 354, 356-57, 372, 377, 387, 389, 401, 417, 419-20, 438-39, 457, 468, 475-76, 484-85, 489, 499, 501-02, 504, 507-09, 511, 513, 520, 536-37, 542, 544, 556-57, 562, 566, 571, 573, 579, 586-87, 593-94, 607-11, 614, 619, 621, 629; F 152, 212, 234, 453; I 93, 236; O 45, 52-53, 57-58, 65, 73, 93; S 20, 22-23, 27, 33, 49, 61, 70-71, 83, 85, 88-89, 92-94, 96, 98, 104, 107, 110-11, 114-15, 130, 134-35, 142, 144, 148, 153-56, 159, 161-62, 164, 167, 173-74, 177, 183-84, 187-88, 190-91, 196-97, 203, 205, 207, 213, 218-21, 223, 227-29, 245, 248, 342-43, 349, 399

Chicago Daily News, B 261

Chicago Daily News Relays, O 433

Chicago Defender, B 189

Chicago District Golf Tournament, S 521

Chicago Duffy Florals basketball club, I 85

Chicago Evening-American, B 346; I 80

Chicago Examiner, O 73; S 342

Chicago Gears basketball club (NBL), I 44, 194, 209, 211

Chicago Giles Post American Legion basketball team, I 267

Chicago Golden Gloves Tournament, I 423, 482

Chicago Gunthers baseball club, S 125

Chicago Herald-Examiner, F 118; S 342

Chicago hockey club (AHA), I 560

Chicago Hornets football club (AAFC), F 179; S 380-81

Chicago Inter-Ocean, O 72-73

Chicago Kathryn's Bowling Team, I 338, 341

Chicago LaSalle Hotel Cavaliers basketball club (AAU), I 208

Chicago Leland Giants baseball club (Negro Leagues), B 29, 188-89, 255, 334, 612; S 143, 168

Chicago Majors basketball club (ABA), I 239

Chicago Marathon, O 529

Chicago Metropolitan Striders Track Club, S 597

Chicago Open Bowling Tournament, I

351

Chicago Owls football club (CoL), F 323

Chicago Packers basketball club (NBA), I 23, 33

Chicago Pirates baseball club (PL), B 107, 160, 307, 496; S 169

Chicago Pro-Am Golf Tournament, S 515

Chicago *Record*, S 345

Chicago Relays, O 454, 521

Chicago Rockets football club (AAFC), F 43, 203, 268, 393; S 361

Chicago Rosenburg-Avery basketball club (AAU), I 105

Chicago Savoy Big Five basketball club, I 267

Chicago Sparta Soccer Club, O 303

Chicago Sports Hall of Fame, F 670

Chicago Sportswriters Association, F 550; O 53

Chicago Springs baseball club (WL), B 496

Chicago Stadium, Chicago, IL, F 417; S 317, 436

Chicago Stags basketball club (BAA, NBA), I 51, 86, 235, 239, 334-35

Chicago Staleys football club (NFL), F 601

Chicago Sting Soccer Club (NASL), O 304

Chicago State University, S 597

Chicago *Times*, S 341

Chicago *Today*, I 80; O 52

Chicago *Tribune*, B 324, 527, 629; F 12, 77, 99-100, 155, 159, 172, 226, 249, 275, 277, 308, 413, 506, 533, 551, 554, 574, 576, 596, 599; I 159; O 52-53, 63, 73, 84, 103-04, 549; S 342, 345

Chicago *Tribune* Silver Football Trophy, F 413, 554; S 361, 402, 443, 458, 476

Chicago Whales baseball club (FL), B 54, 556; S 85

Chicago White Sox baseball club (AL), B 7-8, 12-14, 34, 39, 44, 74, 79-80, 84, 87, 89-93, 96, 102-03, 107-10, 120, 135-38, 151-52, 158-59, 161, 163, 167-68, 170, 173-74, 181, 183, 189, 191, 193, 196, 220, 222, 243, 245, 253, 259, 265, 275-76, 284, 292, 295, 300, 306, 311-12, 314, 317, 329, 332, 338, 340, 334-44, 381, 406, 448, 459, 468, 488-90, 499, 501, 505, 509, 511, 513, 523, 536, 547, 554, 563, 565, 574, 582, 584, 586-87, 602, 608, 626, 631, 634; F 40, 208, 420, 602; I 64, 236, 261, 357; O 52-53, 57, 73, 104; S 6, 13, 20, 22, 41, 43-44, 52, 54-55, 58, 64, 66-68, 79, 90, 98, 101, 106-07, 112-13, 117-19, 126, 140, 144-45, 160, 163-65, 169, 172, 175, 177, 184, 187, 192, 197, 199, 202, 204-05, 208, 219, 227, 231-32, 235, 241-43, 245, 247-48, 342-44, 349

Chicago White Stockings baseball club (NA, NL), B 11, 24, 60, 78-79, 83, 86, 115-16, 131, 160, 226, 240, 256, 262, 270-71, 302-03, 324, 350, 369, 371, 399, 401, 493, 496, 527, 531, 549, 568, 584, 603, 628; S 69-70, 97, 151, 168, 209, 215

Chicago Winds football club (WFL), S 463-64

Chicago Women's District Golf Tournament, O 129

Chicago Zephyrs basketball club (NBA), S 276, 284, 306-07

Chicago's *American*, I 80

Chicagoan Stakes, O 575

Chickahominy, **O** 200
Chickasaw Golf Club, **O** 142
Chickasha, OK baseball club (SSL),
　B 490
Chickerneo, John, **F** 214
Chico, CA Race Track, **O** 586
Chico State University, **F** 262
The Chief, **O** 216
Childs, Clarence A. "Cupid," **B** 63,
　92-93; **S** 36
Chilean National Soccer Team, **O** 300
Chilhowee, **O** 194
Chillicothe, OH baseball club (OSL),
　B 547
Chin, Tiffany, **S** 626, 628
Chinese National Gymnastic Team, **I**
　542
Chip, George, **I** 376, 390-91, 416
Choynski, Joseph "Joe," **I** *366-67,*
　368, 407, 473
Christensen, "Chris," **I** 396
Christian, David W. "Dave," **S** *539-
　40*
Christian, Gordon G., **S** 539
Christian, Roger A., **I** 569, 573; **S**
　539
Christian, William D. "Billy," **I** 569,
　573; **S** 539
Christiana, Norway Lawn Tennis
　Club, **O** 373
Christiansen, John L. "Jack," **F** *105,*
　337
Christie, Walter, **O** 469
Christie Race Car, **O** 26
Christman, Marquette J. "Mark," **S**
　382
Christman, Paul J., **F** 6, 48, 113,
　167-68; **O** 67; **S** *381-82,* 426,
　438, 491
Christman Award, **F** 26
Christoforidis, Anton, **I** 423
Christy Walsh's "25 Year All-
　American Team," **S** 490

Chrysler Invitation Golf Classic, **O**
　144
Chrysler Plymouth Golf Classic, **S**
　505
Chuckovits, Charles "Chuck," **I** 6; **S**
　269-70
Church, George M., **O** 378
Churchill Downs, Louisville, KY, **O**
　178-79, 183, 195-97, 206, 209,
　601, 607; **S** 535; *See also*
　Kentucky Derby
Churicha Cup Gymnastic
　Championship, **I** 523, 535
Chuvalo, George, **I** 383
Chylak, Nestor L., Jr., **S** *29-30*
Ciccarelli, Dino **I** 549
Cicotte, Edward V. "Eddie," **B** *93-94,*
　108, 501; **S** 184
Cincinnati baseball club (UA), **B** 217,
　349, 481
Cincinnati Bengals football club
　(AFL, NFL), **F** 15-16, 70, 77,
　101, 105, 152, 224, 228, 295, 303,
　363, 397-98, 490, 495, 631-32,
　662; **O** 543; **S** 374-75, 383, 411,
　491-92
Cincinnati Buckeyes baseball club
　(NAL), **B** 282
Cincinnati *Commercial-Gazette,* **B**
　285
Cincinnati *Enquirer,* **B** 541; **S** 345
Cincinnati Red Stockings baseball
　club (AA), **B** 303, 368, 407, 600,
　605; **S** 97
Cincinnati Red Stockings baseball
　club (1869-1870), **B** 371, 443,
　531, 627
Cincinnati Reds baseball club (NL), **B**
　3-4, 10, 25, 27, 29-33, 35, 40, 43,
　49, 54, 66, 78, 87, 89, 93, 103,
　107-09, 117, 121, 125, 128-29,
　135, 141, 145, 153-54, 161, 163,
　168, 171, 182, 185, 191, 193, 199,

215-16, 226, 230-21, 237, 241-42, 247, 250, 258, 261, 265-66, 268, 271, 275, 285, 296, 301-03, 307-08, 311-12, 324-26, 335, 342, 347-49, 351, 361, 366, 368-69, 371, 373, 381, 384-86, 389-93, 398-99, 405-07, 416-17, 438, 440-41, 449, 459, 464, 474, 476-78, 485-89, 493, 505, 509, 511, 513, 530-31, 544, 547, 556-57, 567, 576, 584, 586, 588, 590, 593, 600, 603-05, 613-14, 634, 636; F 230, 289, 420, 597; I 312; O 48, 67; S 4-5, 7, 10, 20, 24, 26, 28, 33, 35, 42, 45, 49, 52, 59, 62, 64-66, 70-77, 84, 89, 92, 97, 104, 106, 108, 115-17, 127, 130, 144, 146, 154-55, 160-61, 165-66, 170, 175, 183-84, 187, 194, 210, 216, 219, 222-23, 228-29, 232, 245, 346, 356

Cincinnati Reds football club (NFL), O 427

Cincinnati Royals basketball club (NBA), I 9, 52, 114, 184-86, 251-52, 308, 311, 315, 319; S 265, 273, 284, 292

Cincinnati Stingers hockey club (WHA), I 554

Cincinnati Tennis Club, O 406

Cincinnati Tigers baseball club (Negro Leagues), B 213

Cinema, S 559

Circuit de la Sarthe Cycling Race, S 617

The Citadel, F 127, 576; I 280

Citation, O 176, 179, 195, *576-78,* 598-99, 607, 610-11; S 529

Citizen's Advisory Committee on Fitness of American Youth, I 326

Citizens Savings Bank, *See* Helms Athletic Foundation

Citizens Stakes, O 595

Citrus Bowl football game, S 400

City and Suburban Stakes, O 71

City College of New York, B 198; F 4, 195; I 23, 42, 67, 128, 131-32, 157, 171, 179, 273, 371, 381-82, 664-66; O 71; S 339-40, 351

City Park, New Orleans, LA, O 211

Civic Arena, Pittsburgh, PA, S 308

Clabby, "Jimmy," I 377

Claiborne, Jerry, S *382-83*

Claiborne Farms, Paris, KY, O 222, 572-73, 576, 580, 584-85, 592, 601-03, 605, 607, 611, 615

Clancy, "Gil," I 395

Clapp, Althea Louise Brough, O *337-38,* 344, 348-49, 358-59

Claremont, CA Track and Field Meet, O 455

Clarendon Junior College, I 54

Clark, Clarence, O 338, 402

Clark, David "Dave," I 482

Clark, Donald M., I 574

Clark, Dwight E., S *383-84*

Clark, Earl H. "Dutch," F *106-08,* 480

Clark, "Elky," I 417

Clark, Jack, S *30-31,* 109

Clark, James "Jim," F 421

Clark, Joseph S. "Joe," O *338-39,* 392, 398, 402

Clark, Robert H. "Bob," O 501

Clark, Sharon Stouder, I *581-82*

Clark College, B 548

Clark Handicap, O 209, 225

Clark Our New Thread Soccer Club, Newark, NJ, O 297

Clarke, Fred C., B 3, 28, 91, *94-96,* 113, 158, 447; S 225, 233

Clarke, Joshua B., B 94

Clarke, Ronald "Ron," O 498

Clarkson, Arthur H. "Dad," B 96

Clarkson, John G., B *96-97,* 420, 568

Clarkson, Walter H. "Bill," B 96

Clarkson College of Technology, **I** 290; **O** 71

Clary, Jack T., **F** 70

Classique, **O** 206

Claxton, Tracy, **I** 285

Clay, Cassius M., *See* Muhammad Ali

Clay, Ezekiel F., **O** 588-89, 597

Clayton, Derek, **O** 528

Clayton, Mark J., **F** 384

Cleary, Robert B. "Bob," **I** 568; **S** 541

Cleary, William J., Jr. "Bill," **I** 568; **S** *540-41*

Cleburne, TX baseball club (NTL), **B** 529

Clelland, "Odie," **O** 203

Clemens, W. Roger, **B** 74

Clemente, Roberto W. "Bob," **B** *97-98*, 205-06; **S** 22, 30, 157, 347

Clemson Hall of Fame, **F** 423, 640

Clemson University, **F** 91, 108, 110, 151, 208, 257, 281, 344, 347, 422, 518, 522, 640; **I** 99; **O** 43; **S** 383, 399-400, 418, 420-21

Cleveland, Grover, **I** 461

Cleveland All-Star Hockey Team, **I** 574

Cleveland Arena, Cleveland, OH, **I** 540; **S** 281

Cleveland baseball club (PL), **B** 57, 144; **S** 215

Cleveland Blues baseball club (AA), **B** 291, 360, 511, 524, 584

Cleveland Broncos baseball club (AL), *See* Cleveland Indians baseball club (AL)

Cleveland Broncos baseball club (NL), *See* Cleveland Spiders baseball club (NL)

Cleveland Browns baseball club (NNL), **B** 343; **S** 238

Cleveland Browns football club (AAFC), **F** 2, 69-70, 76, 165, 203, 215, 229, 272, 340, 408-09, 453, 457, 559, 60, 656; **O** 104

Cleveland Browns football club (NFL), **F** 20, 25, 42, 68, 70, 100, 104, 111, 121, 129-31, 133, 146, 157, 163, 165, 169, 180, 184, 190, 198-99, 203, 215-16, 222-23, 229, 236, 246, 264, 271, 276-77, 279, 291, 296, 311-12, 323, 331, 333, 340-41, 354, 362, 364, 367, 370, 385, 395, 397, 399, 405, 408-09, 427, 432, 447, 473, 481-83, 488, 493, 519-20, 542, 559, 566, 568, 575, 610, 617, 633, 649, 656-57, 659; **I** 117, 261; **O** 104; **S** 361, 384, 391, 412-13, 426, 429, 449, 452, 455, 463, 466, 495, 572

Cleveland Buckeyes baseball club (NAL), **B** 127, 282

Cleveland Bulldogs football club (NFL), **F** 194, 456

Cleveland Cavaliers basketball club (NBA), **I** 41-42, 87, 303, 327-28; **S** 280-81

Cleveland Chiropractor College, **I** 149

Cleveland Cubs baseball club, **S** 224

Cleveland Forest City baseball club (NA), **B** 389, 603

Cleveland Forest City baseball club (NL), *See* Cleveland Spiders baseball club (NL)

Cleveland Giants baseball club (Negro Leagues), **B** 144

Cleveland Golf Tournament, **O** 329

Cleveland Graphite Bearings Soccer Club, **O** 303

Cleveland Indians baseball club (AL), **B** 4, 14, 17-18, 23-24, 30-31, 39, 41, 65, 79, 87, 102-03, 110, 118, 126, 133-34, 151-52, 162-63, 167, 169, 175-79, 184-85, 208, 222, 228, 241-43, 258, 262, 274-75,

279-80, 283-84, 288-89, 291-93,
306, 316, 322, 328-29, 337-38,
346, 357, 361, 381-82, 385, 393-
94, 408, 410, 413, 417-19, 422,
435-36, 441-42, 444-45, 449, 455,
469-70, 478, 490, 508, 513, 523-
26, 529, 535-36, 540, 563, 565-66,
573-75, 577, 584, 606-08, 614,
616, 625, 630-31, 635-36; **F** 209,
391; **I** 268, 572; **O** 46, 124, 453;
S 5-6, 8, 11, 15, 21, 27-29, 48-49,
52, 54, 63-64, 67-69, 76-78, 81,
83-84, 86, 101-03, 106-07, 112,
118, 120, 128, 140, 147-48, 152,
156, 159, 165, 169-71, 174, 182,
186, 192, 201, 208, 211, 222, 229,
231, 234, 247, 347
Cleveland Indians football club
    (AAFC, NFL), **F** 27, 66, 103,
    231-32, 259, 359, 373, 456; **I** 39;
    S 411, 457
Cleveland Indians Hall of Fame, **B**
    118; **S** 103
Cleveland Napoleons baseball club
    (AL), **S** 37, 124, 165; *See also*
    Cleveland Indians baseball club
    (AL)
Cleveland Nationals baseball club
    (NL), **S** 47; *See also* Cleveland
    Spiders baseball club (NL)
Cleveland Naval Reserve basketball
    club, **I** 264
Cleveland *News,* **O** 89
Cleveland Panthers football club
    (AFL), **S** 457
Cleveland Pipers basketball club
    (ABL, NIBL), **I** 15, 117, 186, 202,
    274-75
Cleveland *Press,* **B** 292
Cleveland Rams football club (NFL),
    39, 46, 107, 210, 361, 393, 488,
    639, 656; **O** 296
Cleveland Rebels basketball club

(BAA), **I** 66; **S** 322
Cleveland Rosenblums basketball club
    (ABL), **I** 66, 88, 113, 170, 223,
    260
Cleveland Skating Club, **I** 512
Cleveland Spiders baseball club (NL),
    B 59, 63-64, 92-93, 96, 136, 171,
    217, 240, 349, 359-60, 363, 407,
    454, 522-23, 538, 585, 598, 600,
    635-36; **S** 36, 215-16
Cleveland Sports Hall of Fame, **F**
    198; **O** 556
Cleveland State University, **I** 202
Cleveland Tate Stars baseball club
    (Negro Leagues), **B** 243
Cleveland Touchdown Club, **F** 111,
    203, 337
Cleveland Track Club, **O** 500
Cleveland White Horses basketball
    club (NBL), **I** 194; **S** 293
Clifford, "Jack," **I** 444
Clift, Harlond B., **S** *31-32*
Cline, Timothy "Tim," **I** 176
Clinton, James "Jimmy," **I** 222
Clinton, IA baseball club (CA, 3IL),
    B 401; **S** 68
Closterman, Nona, **O** 354
Clothier, William J. "Bill," **O** *339-
    40,* 371-72, 412, 421-22
Clothier, William J. II, **O** 339
Clotworthy, Robert L., **I** *485-86,*
    497
Clyde Van Dusen, **O** 202, 596
C. Markland Kelly Award, **O** 238
CNN, See Cable News Network
Coach & Athlete, **F** 149; **I** 276
Coach of the Year Award, **I** 18, 38,
    56, 201, 259, 267-68, 282, 290,
    295, 305, 307, 310, 312, 320-21,
    369, 382-84, 393, 395-96, 400,
    402, 419, 428, 430, 437, 448, 454,
    456, 461, 468-69, 543
The Coach Sports Extra, **I** 44

Coaches All-America football game, F 76, 279, 303, 347, 433, 586, 633, 643; S 370, 395-96, 406, 499

Coaches Hall of Fame, I 39

Coaching Club American Oaks, O 194, 604

Coaching Club, New York, NY, O 51

Coakley, Andrew J. "Andy," B 450, 579

Coaldale Club, F 259

Coalinga Junior College, F 662

Coaltown, O 176, 195; S 529

Coan, Elroy Bert, S 408

Coastal, O 610

Cobb, John, S 270-71

Cobb, Tyrus R. "Ty," B 2, 13, 32, 47, 51, 98-100, 110, 121, 155, 163, 185, 208, 211, 247-48, 250, 261, 267, 275-76, 281-82, 286-87, 296, 299, 322, 325, 333, 342, 398, 400, 408, 415-16, 451, 471, 486-87, 516, 529, 554, 572-73, 581, 597, 605-06, 618; I 543; O 89-90; S 12-13, 81, 98, 126, 168, 191, 232

Cobleskill Agricultural College, O 191

Cobleskill baseball club (NYSL), B 131

Coca Cola 500 NASCAR Race, O 1, 44; S 604

Coca Cola 600 NASCAR Race, S 606

Cochems, Edward B. "Eddie," F 108-09; S 434

Cochet, Henri, O 322, 362, 385, 404, 410

Cochran, Barbara Ann, I 274-75

Cochran, Linda, I 274-75

Cochran, Marilyn, I 274-75

Cochran, Richard, I 510

Cochran, Robert, I 274-75

Cochran, Welker, I 673

Cochrane, John "Red," I 393, 483

Cochrane, Gordon S. "Mickey," B 33, 50, 100-02, 146, 219, 359, 374, 401, 584; O 74; S 59, 183

Cockrell, Donald "Don," I 437

Cocoa, FL baseball club (FECL, FSL), B 76, 594; S 67, 136

Codex, S 530

Cody, Joshua C. "Josh," F 109-10, 368

Coe, Sebastian, O 532

Coe, William Wesley, Jr., O 524

Coe, W. R., O 201

Coe College, S 281

Coetzee, Gerrie, I 466

Coffey, Earl, S 556

Coffeyville Junior College, F 518

Cogan, Kevin, S 619

Coghlan, Eamon, O 532

Cohalen, Neil, I 171

Cohane, Timothy "Tim," S 371

Cohen, Joel H., O 394

Cohen, Lester, I 39

Cohen, Tiffany, I 582-83

Cohesion, O 214

Cohoes, NY basketball club (NYSL), I 223

Colavito, Rocco D. "Rocky," B 102-03, 316, 370; S 3, 106-07

Colbert, "Mike," I 397

Colby College, B 112

Coleman, Derrick, S 264

Coleman, Donald "Don," F 126, 413

Coleman, Georgia, I 487, 496

Coleman, Joseph "Joe," I 114

Coleman, Vincent M. "Vince," B 618

Colen, Marvin, I 264

Coles, Nathaniel, O 570

Cole's American Giants baseball club (Negro Leagues), B 533

Colgate Dinah Shore Golf Tournament, S 509

Colgate Dinah Shore Winners Circle, O 168

Colgate Hall of Fame Classic, O 135, 166

Colgate University, F 4, 68, 185, 242, 313, 468, 477, 620, 627, 646-47; I 114, 248, 318, 372; S 263-64, 416-17, 483

Colima, "Bert," I 372

Colin, O 208, 211, *578;* S 533-34

Coliseum, Chicago, IL, F 649

The Coliseum, Corvallis, OR, I 97

College All-American basketball club, I 113

College All-Star basketball game, I 40, 61, 94, 182, 194, 209, 212, 241, 273, 276, 305, 321

College All-Star football game, F 1-2, 12, 16, 26, 30, 33, 40, 49-50, 63, 67-68, 76, 79, 81, 101, 118, 122, 129, 133, 143, 145, 148, 151, 155, 170, 176, 210, 215-16, 236-38, 249, 268, 273, 275, 277, 279, 283, 296, 305, 308, 320, 340, 344, 346-47, 362, 364, 367, 378, 393, 395, 414, 423, 430-31, 433, 460, 464, 466, 482, 491-92, 514, 533, 542, 550, 554, 556, 558, 566, 568, 574, 576-77, 586-87, 596, 599, 604, 610, 629, 633, 643, 650, 653, 656, 658, 660, 664, 670, 674; O 104; S 361, 365, 370, 381, 390, 429, 439, 443, 461-63, 465-66, 474, 478, 481, 491, 504

College All-Time All-America Basketball Team, I 113

College and Pro Football Newsweekly, F 247, 449, 634

College Baseball Championships (Pre-NCAA), S 444-45

College Baseball Coaches Association, F 286; S 38

College Baseball World Series, F 404, 453

College Basketball Hall of Fame, *See* Helms Athletic Foundation Hall of Fame or Naismith Memorial Basketball Hall of Fame

College Basketball Coach of the Century, I 256

College Basketball Coach of the Decade, I 202, 321

College Basketball Coach of the Year, I 5, 35, 38, 40, 56, 89, 94, 116, 127, 140, 174, 191, 193, 197-98, 202, 209, 216-17, 256-58, 280-81, 285, 291, 293, 296, 301, 320-21, 331

College Basketball Player of the Year, I 10, 26, 35, 38, 41, 59, 77, 90, 98-99, 113, 153, 159, 185-88, 190, 205, 211, 214-15, 220, 236, 260, 266, 286, 294, 300, 303, 317, 328, 330

College Basketball Referee of the Year, I 81, 209

College Basketball Rookie of the Year, I 152

College Basketball Rules Committee, I 221, 235, 269, 283

College Commissioners Basketball Tournament, S 262

College Diving Coach of the Year, I 497

College Football Championships (Pre-NCAA), I 433-34, 444, 477, 502

College Football Eastern Championships, S 486

College Hockey Coach of the Year, *See* Spencer Penrose Award

College Humor, F 261

College of Emporia, *See* Emporia Teachers College

College of Idaho, I 18, 236

College of St. Thomas, I 390

College of the Holy Cross, S 284,

335, 448, 461; *See also* Holy Cross College

College of the Pacific, **S** 554

College of William and Mary, **F** 118, 155, 175; **I** 11, 40, 590; **S** 172, 419-20, 466

College of Wooster, **F** 564; **I** 264-65

College Park, MD Track and Field Meet, **O** 500

College Swimming Coach of the Year, **I** 585

College World Series, *See* NCAA College World Series

Collegiate Basketball Officials Association, **I** 172, 277, 316

Collegiate Guide, **I** 84

Collett, George H., **O** 164

Collett, Glenna, *See* Glenna Collett Vare

Collett, Wayne C., **O** 458

Collier, Blanton L., **F** 199; **S** *384-85*, 452

Collier, Joseph "Joe," **F** 479

Collier's, **B** 169; **F** 145, 172, 275, 469, 504, 575, 641; **I** 134, 168, 195; **O** 62, 64, 72, 91, 383, 517, 531; **S** 349, 453

Collier's All-World Basketball Team, **I** 195

Colliers Encylopedia, **S** 340

Collins, Arthur, Sr., **S** 338-39

Collins, Arthur, Jr. "Bud," **O** 381, 394, 408; **S** *338-39,* 346

Collins, Edward T., Sr. "Eddie," **B** 19, *103-04,* 108, 119, 157, 162, 196, 357-59; **S** 248

Collins, Edward T., Jr., **B** 104

Collins, Gary J., **F** *110-11*

Collins, Harry Warren, **B** 456

Collins, Herman, **S** 194

Collins, James A. "Rip," **B** 8, 593; **S** 291

Collins, James J. "Jimmy," **B** 91,
104-05, 161, 506-07, 550; **S** 23, 115

Collins, John, **I** 577-78

Collins, John F. "Shano," **S** 126

Collins, Raymond W. "Ray," **B** 208

Collinsworth, Anthony Cris, **F** 15

Cologne, Germany Track and Field Meet, **O** 541

Colonel Tenny, **O** 206

Colonial Club, Fort Worth, TX, **O** 169

Colonial League, **I** 156

Colonial National Invitation Golf Tournament, **S** 523

Colorado College, **F** 62; **I** 128, 510, 514; **S** 351, 593

Colorado College Athlete of the Year, **F** 62

Colorado Rockies hockey club (NHL), **I** 551, 563; **S** 544

Colorado School of Mines, **F** 107

Colorado Sports Hall of Fame, **F** 18, 106; **I** 511

Colorado Springs, CO baseball club (PCL, WL), **S** 78, 241

Colorado Springs *Gazette,* **O** 90

Colorado State University, **F** 363; **I** 37; **O** 500-01

Colored World Baseball Championship, **S** 238

Columbia baseball club, **S** 56

Columbia Broadcasting System, **F** 60, 271, 278, 304, 376, 458, 491, 567; **I** 58, 124, 234, 289, 503, 523, 539; **O** 45, 48-49, 56, 67-68, 70, 75-76, 93, 99, 168, 308, 342, 408; **S** 239, 248, 339, 352, 355, 357, 475

Columbia College, **F** 12, 188

Columbia Saving Gold Classic, **O** 118

Columbia, SC baseball club (SAL, SL), **B** 3, 218, 312, 478, 589, 605

Columbia 300 Bowling Tournament, **I** 344

Columbia University, **B** 103, 210, 358, 591; **F** 23, 28, 54, 130, 220, 251, 270, 316, 350-51, 356-57, 468, 491, 540, 644; **I** 73, 84, 89-90, 128-29, 193, 222, 233, 250, 256, 286, 288, 305, 307, 628, 666; **O** 46, 60-61, 64, 70, 99-100, 246, 296, 307, 334-35, 374, 385, 426, 467; **S** 371, 404-05, 417, 431, 434

Columbus, GA baseball club (SAL, SL), **B** 8, 517; **S** 119

Columbus Giants (Chicago) baseball club (Negro Leagues), **B** 286

Columbus Handicap, **O** 215

Columbus, OH baseball club (WL), **B** 121, 579

Columbus, OH Buckeyes baseball club (NNL), **B** 303, 334, 349, 553; **S** 238

Columbus, OH Clippers baseball club (IL), **B** 39, 54, 425, 447, 530; **S** 75, 243

Columbus, OH *Dispatch*, **B** 23

Columbus, OH Elite Giants baseball club (NNL), **B** 269; **S** 238

Columbus, OH Open Golf Tournament, **O** 129

Columbus, OH Panhandles football club (NFL), **F** 97

Columbus, OH Red Birds baseball club (AA), **B** 113, 177, 297, 365, 373, 429, 485, 517, 557, 561, 600; **F** 97; **S** 17, 32-33, 42, 59, 110, 143, 149, 200

Columbus, OH Tigers football club (NFL), **I** 660; **S** 457

Columbus, OH Touchdown Club, **F** 127, 236, 457, 547, 568; **I** 256

Colvin, "Jack," **I** 106

Colwell, Paul, **I** 344

Comanche, **O** 220

Combs, Earle B., **B** *105-07,* 269

Come Back With Me, **S** 516-17

Comeback Player of the Year Award, **S** 25, 61, 94-95, 175, 203, 222, 225, 244, 294, 327, 463

Comeback Swimmer of the Year Award, **I** 596

Comiskey, Charles A. "Charlie," **B** 94, *107-08,* 137, 160-61, 189, 243, 275-76, 343, 347, 496, 524, 576, 586-87; **S** 98, 101, 198, 342

Comiskey, J. Louis, **B** 108

Comiskey Park, Chicago, IL, **B** 7, 108-10, 119, 213, 374, 574, 584, 594; **I** 643; **S** 247

Commando, **O** 578; **S** 533

Commemorative Seniors Golf Tournament, **O** 140

Commission on Olympic Sports, **I** 611

Committee for National Basketball Rules Interpretation, **I** 276

Commonweal, **B** 391

Commonwealth Stadium, Lexington, KY, **I** 110

Compton Junior College, **F** 365, 467, 516; **O** 456, 476; **S** 442

Compute, **S** 536

Concord, NC baseball club (NCSL), **S** 108

Concord, NC Race Track, **S** 605

Concordia College, **B** 72

Concordia Country Club, Little Rock, AR, **O** 152

Concordia Junior College, **S** 200

Concordia Seminary, **S** 200

Concordia Turnverein Society, **I** 525

Coneff, Thomas P. "Tom," **O** 479, 487

Conerly, Charles A., Jr. "Charley," **F** 600, 621; **S** *385-86,* 464

Conerly, Perian, **S** 386

Coney Island Derby, **O** 588
Coney Island Jockey Club Futurity
    Stakes, **O** 177
Congressional Country Club,
    Rockvine, MD, **S** 522
Conlan, John B. "Jocko," **B** *109;* **S**
    340
Conlan, Joseph, **B** 109
Conlan, Shane P., **F** 460
Conley, "Frankie," **I** 370, 379
Conley, Thomas A. "Tom," **F** 532
Conn, "Jackie," **I** 367
Conn, William D., Jr. "Billy," **I**
    367-68, 370, 409, 423, 429, 481-
    82; **S** 343
Connaught Cup, **O** 201
Connaughton, Harry, **F** 350
Connecticut Falcons softball club, **O**
    262
Connecticut League, **S** 238, 324
Connecticut State Boxing
    Championships, **I** 450
Connecticut State League, **B** 117,
    309, 428
Connelly, Daniel "Dan," **I** 526
Conner, Bart, **I** *522-24*
Conner, "Nick," **S** 296
Connie Mack Stadium, Philadelphia,
    PA, **S** 23
Connolly, "Eddie," **I** 420
Connolly, Harold V. "Hal," **S** *573-
74*
Connolly, Maureen "Mo," **S** 550,
    553-54; *See also* Maureen
    Connolly Brinker
Connolly, Olga F., **S** 573
Connolly, "Pat," **O** 557
Connolly, Thomas H., Sr. "Tom," **B**
    109-11
Connor, George S., **F** 26, *111-12,*
    176, 249, 345
Connor, Joseph F. "Joe," **B** 111
Connor, Roger, **B** *111-12,* 429; **S**

150, 233
Connor, OK Junior College, **S** 291
Connors, Gloria T., **O** 340
Connors, James S. "Jimmy," **O** 323,
    340-43, 369-70
Conquistador Cielo, **O** 222
Conrad, Bobby Joe, **S** 426
Conradt, Jody, **S** 320
Conroy, **S** 533
Conroy, Anthony J. "Tony," **I** 555
Constellation, **O** 85
Continental Basketball Association, **I**
    324; **S** 299
Continental Basketball League, **I** 96
Continental Broadcasting Company, **O**
    52
Continental Cup, **O** 328
Continental Football League, **F** 471,
    561, 631
Continental League, **B** 427, 473
Converse Basketball Yearbook, **I** 137,
    218, 295
Converse Rubber Company, **I** 10,
    134-36, 202, 212, 218, 291, 295,
    303
Conway, George, **O** 613
Conzelman, James G. "Jimmy," **F**
    48, *112-13,* 455; **I** 60; **S** 438
Coogan Award, **S** 459
Coogan's Bluff, New York, **S** 342
Cook, Fred H. III, **F** 296
Cooke, Elwood T., **O** 343
Cooke, Sarah Palfrey Fabyan, *See*
    Sarah Palfrey Fabyan Cooke
    Danzig
Cookesville, TN Universal Plastics
    basketball club, **I** 325
Coolidge, Calvin, **O** 164
Coolidge, Thornton, **I** 515
Cooling, Willis, **I** 486-87
Coombus, John W. "Jack," **B** *112-
15,* 120, 208, 287, 450
Coombes, Harry A., **I** 159

Cooney, "Gerry," I 401; S 623
Cooper, Arley Wilbur, B *113-14*
Cooper, Artis Wayne, I 160
Cooper, Cecil C., B *114-15;* S 193
Cooper, Charles H. "Chuck," I 12
Cooper, Charles T. "Tarzan," I *48-49,* 69
Cooper, "Chatty," O 354
Cooper, Christin, O 273
Cooper, Cynthia, I 214
Cooper, Earl P., O *6-7*
Cooper, Fred, I 645
Cooper, George, I 440
Cooper, Harry "Light-Horse," O *116-17*
Cooper, John, B 114
Cooper, Morton C. "Mort," B 45; S *32-33,* 33, 127
Cooper, Sydney J., O 116
Cooper, Sylvester, B 114
Cooper, William Walker, B 45, 381; S 32, *33-34*
Cooper-Monaco Race Car, O 28
Cooper Union College, I 305
Coor's Classic Cycling, S 617
Cope, Myron, B 174
Copeland, Lillian, S *574-75*
Copenhagen, Denmark Track and Field Meet, O 489
Copernica, O 604
Copper Bowl football game, F 396
Copper Mountain, CO Alpine Ski Competition, O 273
Coquette, O 214
Coral Ridge Country Club, Fort Lauderdale, FL, S 523
Corbett, James J. "Jim," I 366, *368-69,* 376, 382, 395, 407-08, 428, 432, 467, 644; O 469
Corbett, Young, I 369, 434
Corbett, Young III, I 357, *369-70,* 381, 435, 444, 475
Corbin, E. A. "Spike," I 172-73

Corbus, William "Bill," F *113-14*
Corcoran, Fred, O 111, 145
Corcoran, Lawrence J. "Larry," B 11, *115-16*
Corcoran, Thomas W. "Tommy," B *116-18*
Cordele, GA baseball club (GFL), B 72
Cordileone, Lou A., F 600
Cormier, Vernon, I 438
Cornell College (IA), I 646; O 446; S 616
Cornell University, B 169, 182; F 51, 63, 65, 85, 144, 192, 204, 231, 240, 342-43, 379, 426, 468, 551, 558, 584, 607, 635, 669; I 129, 222, 286, 650; O 61-62, 70, 246, 366, 462, 479-80; S 263, 365, 393-94, 416, 431, 477, 562
Corning, NY baseball club, S 98
Corning, NY Golf Classic, S 508
Cornwall Lacrosse Club, O 242
Corpus Christi, TX baseball club (GCL), S 471
Corpus Christi, TX Naval Air Station, F 621
Correction, S 536
Corridon, Marie L., I 587
Corrigan, "Ed," O 209
Corrigan, Edward, S 526
Corrigan Stable, O 209
Cortina d'Ampezzo, Italy Winter Olympic Games, *See* Olympic Winter Games, 1956
Coryell, Donald D. "Don," F *114-15,* 190, 206, 248, 408, 659; S 370, 405
Corzine, David J. "Dave," I 98
Cosell, Howard W., F 500; O 47-48, *58-60,* 80, 553; S 350, 356, 359
Cosmopolitan, B 592; O 64, 91
Cosmopolitan Club's Medal, I 391
Costa Rica Golf Cup, O 124

Costa Rica National Soccer Team, O 299

Costas, Robert Q. "Bob," S 353

Costello, Frank, O 506

Costello, Lawrence R. "Larry," I 49-51, 104, 112-13; S 307

Costello, Paul V., O 263

Cote, Aubert, I 651

Cote, Gerald, S 582

Cothron, Paige, F 621

Cotton, Norman "Norm," I 167

Cotton, Thomas Henry, O 155, 167

Cotton Bowl Athletic Association, S 494

Cotton Bowl Basketball Tournament, Dallas, TX, I 107

Cotton Bowl, Dallas, TX, F 449; O 83; S 343

Cotton Bowl football game, F 3, 5-6, 30, 35, 47, 68, 74, 110, 128-29, 138-39, 147, 170-71, 181, 236, 246, 286-87, 305, 316, 318, 341, 344, 346, 367, 369, 377-78, 383, 394, 397, 403, 422, 431, 434, 444, 458, 516, 519, 534, 550, 558, 561, 567-68, 592, 594, 600, 617, 647; S 373, 393, 400-01, 418, 428, 456, 463, 498

Cotton States League, S 5, 131, 187, 233

Cougar, O 229

Cougar II, O 228-29

Cougar Hall of Honor, F 665

Coughlin, T. Walker "Lefty," I 113

Coulon, Emil "Pop," I 370

Coulon, "Johnny," I 370-71, 478

Counselor Wernberg, O 206

Counsil, Roger, I 539

Counsilman, Brian, I 584

Counsilman, James E. "Doc," I 583-85, 594, 601, 603, 618

Count Arthur, O 223

Count Fleet, O 205, 578-79

Count Turf, O 205, 579

Countdown to Super Bowl, S 335

Countess Adios, O 207

Countess Vivian, O 207

Country Life, O 383

Country McCloske, See John McCleester

Counts, Mel G., I 97, 101, 135

Coupe Internationale des Aviation Prize, O 50

Court, Margaret Smith, O 381, 386

Courtney, Peter, I 369

Courtney, Thomas W. "Tom," O 442-43

Courtship, O 206

Cousins, Robin, I 518-19

Cousy, Robert J. "Bob," I 12, 36, 43, 51-52, 107, 111, 124, 150, 154, 190, 201, 239, 251-52, 262, 274, 278, 298

Coveleski, Harry F., B 119

Coveleski, Stanley A. "Stan," B 118-19

Coventry, O 197

Covington, KY baseball club (ApL, KL), B 328; S 136

Cowan, Catherine A., See Catherine Cowan Rush

Cowan, Hector W. "Hec," F 115-17

Cowdin Stakes, O 581

Cowens, David W., "Dave," I 53-54, 124, 169, 279

Cowle, Osborne, S 265

Cowler, "Tom," I 376

Cowperthwait, Charles, O 133

Cox, Forrest "Frosty," I 5, 256

Cox, Frederick W. "Fred," F 25

Cox, Robert, O 133

Cox, William D. "Bill," B 74, 323

Cox, William R. "Billy," B 467; S 180

Coy, Edwin H. "Ted," F 117-18, 298-99, 406

Cozens, Ernest B., **F** 552

Cozza, Carmen, **F** 526

CPC International Golf Tournament, **O** 168; **S** 518-19

CRA Auto Circuit Race, **O** 38

Crabbe, Clarence L. "Buster," **I** *585-86*

Craft, William, **O** 609

Craig, Jack, **S** 354

Craig, Ralph C., **O** *443-44,* 483

Cram, "Steve," **O** 531-32

Cramer, Roger M. "Doc," **B** *119-20*

Crampton, Bruce, **O** 125

Crandall, Clifford, **I** 97

Crandall, James Otis "Doc," **B** 610

Cravath, Clifford C. "Gavvy," **B** *121-22;* **S** 144

Crawford, Frederick "Fred," **F** 626

Crawford, Jack, **O** 331, *395-96,* 410, 418; **S** 552

Crawford, Jerry, **B** 372

Crawford, Joan A. "Jodie," **I** *54-55,* 123

Crawford, Marianne, *See* Marianne Crawford Stanley

Crawford, Robert, **I** 54

Crawford, Samuel E. "Sam," **B** *121-22,* 247, 281, 287, 299, 554, 572

Crawford, Willie M., **B** 594

Crawford Plate, **O** 219

Crawfordsville, IN baseball club (CIL), **B** 195

Crawley, Marion L., **I** 321

Crazy Legs, All-American, **S** 496

Creacy, A. Dewey, **B** 6

Cream, Arnold R., *See* Joe Walcott

Creamer, Robert W., **B** 572; **S** *339-40*

Crease Lacrosse Club, **O** 240

Creedon, "Dan," **I** 432

Creekmur, Louis "Lou," **F** *118-19*

Creighton, James "Jim," **B** *122-23*

Creighton University, **B** 214; **F** 254, 360, 533; **I** 126-27, 247-48, 268, 278; **S** 276

Creighton University Hall of Fame, **I** 127

Creme Fraiche, **O** 222

Crenshaw, Ben D., **S** *510-11,* 514

Creosate, **O** 209

Crescent Athletic Club, **O** 109, 233, 239, 329

Crescent Athletic Club Invitation Tennis Championships, **O** 378

Crespi, Frank A. "Creepy," **B** 381

Cresta Bobsled Competition, **O** 258

Crestar Farm Fresh Golf Classic, **S** 518-19

Cribb, "Tom," **I** 439-40

Cribbs, Claire, **S** *271-72*

Cribbs, Joe S., **F** 19

Crickmore, **O** 589

Criger, Louis "Lou," **B** 91

Criminal Type, **S** 530

Cripes Bakery basketball club (AAU), **I** 276

Criqui, Eugene, **I** 379, 415

Crisler, Herbert O. "Fritz," **F** 6, *119-20,* 243, 413, 442-43, 551; **S** 380, 500

Crisler Arena, Ann Arbor, MI, **F** 120

Crispin, **O** 184

Criss, Charles W., Jr., **S** 291

Croker, Richard, **O** 219

Cromwell, Dean, **O** *444-45,* 465, 568; **S** 590

Crone, Raymond H. "Ray," **B** 503

Cronin, John J., **B** 45

Cronin, Joseph "Joe," **B** 35, *123-24,* 179, 225-26, 232, 267, 446, 635; **S** 14

Cronkite, Walter, **O** 76

Crosby, Bing, **B** 206; **O** 194

Crosby, John G. Jr., **I** 528

Crosley, Powel, Jr., **B** *124-26,* 366, 441

Crosley Field, Cincinnati, OH, **B** 593
Cross, Amos C., **B** 126
Cross, Frank A. "Mickey," **B** 126
Cross, Lafayette N. "Lave," **B** *126-27,* 600
Cross, Leach, **I** 476
Cross, Montford M. "Monte," **B** 156
Crow, John David, Sr., **F** 74, *120-21*
Crow, John David, Jr., **F** 121
Crow, Lindon, **F** 578
Crowder, "Eddie," **F** 18, 61
Crowe, George D., **I** 312
Crowley, James H. "Sleepy Jim," **F** 121, *187-90,* 344, 353; **S** 400, 440; *See also* Four Horsemen
Cruiserweight Boxing Championships, **I** 466
Crum, Denzil E. "Denny," **I** *55-56,* 331; **S** 263
Crump, Diane, **O** 214
Crusader, **O** 194, 585, 596
Crutcher, Hazel Walker, **I** *56-57*
Crutchfield, John W. "Jimmie," **B** 31, *127,* 435
Cruz, Carlos, **I** 446
Cruz, Cirilo "Tommy," **S** 34
Cruz, Hector L. "Heity," **S** 34
Cruz, Jose, **S** *34-35*
Crystal Plunge Club, San Francisco, CA, **I** 585
Csonka, Lawrence R. "Larry," **F** *122-23,* 333, 349, 535; **S** 335, 441
Cuban Baseball Hall of Fame, **B** 148; **S** 36, 224
Cuban Giants baseball club (Negro Leagues), **B** 195, 222; **F** 183; **S** 238
Cuban Grand National Race, **O** 198
Cuban National Soccer Team, **O** 299-300
Cuban Stars baseball club (ECL), **B** 147; **S** 137, 222, 224

Cuban Winter Baseball League, **B** 6, 88, 132, 141, 148, 213, 244, 255, 270, 273, 282-83, 287, 290, 331, 333, 338, 342, 378, 435, 452, 466, 519-20, 533, 543, 553, 599, 612, 619-20; **S** 118, 137, 143, 168, 188, 224
Cuban X Giants baseball club, **S** 238
Cuccinello, Anthony F. "Tony," **B** 250; **S** 112
Cudgel, **S** 525-26
Cuellar, Miguel A. "Mike," **S** *35-36*
Cuevas, Pipino, **S** 612
Cuff, Ward, **F** 447
Cuhel, Frank J., **O** 549
Cuisinier, F. "Bo," **F** 416
Cullen, Hugh Roy, **O** 77
Cullom Field, West Point, NY, **F** 200
Cullop, Henry Nicholas "Nick," **B** 456
Culmone, Joseph "Joe," **O** 217
Culp, Curley, **F** 325
Culpepper, David, **S** 244
Culver City, CA Auto Race, **O** 7
Culver City, CA Swim Team, **I** 582
Culverhouse, Hugh F., **F** 288
Cum Posey's All-American team, **S** 189
Cumberland College, **F** 175, 257
Cumiskey, Frank J., **I** *524-25*
Cummings, "Jumbo," **I** 386
Cummings, Robert Terrell "Terry," **I** 209; **S** 278
Cummings, William A. "Candy," **B** *127-28*
Cuneo, Ann Curtis, **I** 579, *586-87*
Cuneo, Gordon, **I** 587
Cunningham, Gary, **I** 56
Cunningham, Glenn V., **O** 431-32, *445-47,* 526; **S** 580
Cunningham, Joseph R. "Joe," **O** 56
Cunningham, Robert "Bob," **I** 199
Cunningham, Samuel L. "Sam," **F**

370
Cunningham, William "Bill," F 30
Cunningham, William J. "Billy," I
    57-59, 104, 112, 249, 278
Cupit, Jacky, O 112
Cuppy, George J., "Nig," B 63; S
    36-37
Curci, "Fran," F 572
Curl Brothers, O 197
Curran, James "Jimmy," O 440
Current Biography, I 587
Curry, Bruce, S 612
Curry, Denise M., I 59
Curry, Robin, I 508
Curry Veterans football club, O 296
Curt Gowdy Broadcasting Company,
    O 68
Curtis, Ann, See Ann Curtis Cuneo
Curtis, Charles, S 525
Curtis, F., O 582
Curtis, Glenn, I 321
Curtis, Harriott, S 511
Curtis, Isaac F., F 15
Curtis, James Michael, S 386-87
Curtis, "Kid," I 457
Curtis, Margaret, S 511-12
Curtis, William, O 553
Curtis Cup, O 110-11, 114, 117,
    151, 159
Curtis Cup Team, S 517-18, 521
Curtis Trophy, S 511
Curtis Turner Award, O 13
Curzon Cup, O 258
Cus D'Amato's Boxing School,
    Catskills, NY, S 625
Cusack, Jack, S 387-88
Cushing, OK baseball club (OKSL),
    B 267
Cushman, J. F., O 592
Cut n'Run, S 341
Cutler, David "Dave," F 55
Cuyler, Hazen S. "Kiki," B 128-29,
    536, 626

Cvercko, Andrew "Andy," F 458
Cy Young Award, S 35, 49, 93, 125,
    132, 145, 160
Czechoslovakian National Hockey
    Team, I 548, 565, 568-69
Czechoslovakian National Soccer
    Team, O 294, 300, 310

Dacey, "Bill," I 373
Dade, Harold, I 447
Dado, "Speedy," I 389, 438
Dahlen, William F. "Bill," B 131-32
Dahlia, O 229
Dahlstrom, Carl S. "Cully," O 553,
    570-71
Daiei, Japan Volleyball Team, S 613
Daily, Hugh I. "One-Arm," B 347
Daily America, O 220
Daily Princetonian, S 341
Dakota League, S 233
Dale Frost, O 207
Daley, Arthur J., F 66, 346, 351,
    354; I 171; O 60-61; S 335, 569
Daley, Robert, O 61
Daley, "Steve," O 52
Daley, William E. "Bill," F 120, 555
Dallas baseball club (TL), B 5, 55-56,
    230, 236, 254, 351, 420, 472, 602;
    F 40, 402; S 55, 131, 239
Dallas Chapparals basketball club
    (ABA), I 109
Dallas Civitan Women's Open Golf
    Tournament, O 129
Dallas Cowboys football club (NFL),
    F 1, 9, 16, 42, 59, 67, 96-97, 122,
    140, 143, 149-51, 171, 210, 223,
    245, 264, 273-74, 276, 285, 303,
    316, 322, 331, 333, 341, 347, 354,
    364, 371, 397, 400, 405, 408, 423-
    24, 432, 462-63, 466, 487-88, 529,
    558, 565, 568-70, 581, 586, 590,
    605, 614, 631, 640-41, 650; I
    249; O 80-81, 468; S 268, 383,

386, 427-28, 441, 452, 455, 467-68, 475, 478, 500
Dallas Cowboys Ring of Honor, **F** 274, 347
Dallas Cowboys Weekly, **S** 475
Dallas Diamonds basketball club (WPBL, WABA), **I** 175-76
Dallas Indoor Track and Field Meet, **O** 436
Dallas Mavericks basketball club (NBA), **I** 41, 224, 234; **S** 253, 255-56, 301
Dallas *News,* **F** 30
Dallas Race Track, Dallas, GA, **O** 30
Dallas Sidekicks Soccer Club (MISL), **O** 295
Dallas Southwest All-Star football game, **F** 3
Dallas Texans football club (AFL), **F** 36, 55, 76, 133, 253, 280, 382, 572, 610; **S** 363, 389, 450, 465, 469
Dallas Texans football club (NFL), **F** 148, 493, 670
Dallas Tornado Soccer Club (NASL), **F** 280; **O** 308
Dallas University, **S** 494
Dallas-Fort Worth baseball club (TL), **S** 58, 71
Dalma, Rush, **I** 447
Dalmation, **S** 526-27
Dalrymple, Abner F., **B** 496
Dalrymple, Clayton E. "Clay," **B** 379
Dalrymple, Gerald "Jerry," **S** *388-89*
Dalton, Harry, **B** 596; **S** 9
Dalton, Judy Tegart, **O** 335
Dalton, Ralph, **I** 300
Daly, Charles D., **F** *125-26,* 200, 300, 440; **S** 253
Daly, "Jack," **I** 420
Daly, Maurice, **I** 673
Daly, Thomas P. "Tom," **B** 117
Daly, William C. "Bill," **O** 187-88,

205, 212
D'Amato, Constantine "Cus," **I** 449; **S** 625
D'Ambrosio, Louis J., *See* Lou Amber
Damascus, **O** 218, *579-80,* 581-82
Dame Pattie, **O** 266
Damrosch, **O** 201
D'Annunzio, Louis, **S** 56
Dan Patch, **O** *580-81,* 587
Dancer, Harold, **O** 181
Dancer, Ronald, **O** 181
Dancer, Stanley F., **O** *181-82,* 191
Dancer, Vernon, **O** 191
Dancer's Crown, **O** 182
Dancer's Image, **O** 183, 225, 599
Dandridge, Raymond "Ray," **B** *132-33,* 543
Dandridge, Robert L., Jr. "Bob," **S** *272-73*
Dandy, Donald "Don," **O** 396
Danek, Ludwick, **O** 510
Daniel, Daniel "Dan," **F** 606; **I** *371-72,* 382
Daniel, Elizabeth Ann, **O** *117-18;* **S** 517
Daniell, Averill, **S** 439-40
Daniels, Charles M., **I** *587-88*
Daniels, Clemon, Jr., **S** *389-90*
Daniels, Melvin J. "Mel," **S** *273-74*
Daniels, "Terry," **I** 386
Danny Thomas Memphis Open Golf Tournament, **O** 163
Danowski, Edward F. "Ed," **F** 353, 447; **S** *390-91*
Dante, James "Jim," **O** 120
Dantley, Adrian D., **I** *59-61,* 79; **S** 253
Danville, IL baseball club (ML, 3IL), **B** 115, 145, 489; **O** 293
Danville, VA baseball club (CrL), **B** 87, 351; **S** 239
Danzer, Emmerich, **I** 519

Danzig, Allison, F 154, 230, 452, 468, 598; O *61-62*, 407, 492; S 371, 376, 388, 393-94, 424, 431, 489

Danzig, Sarah Palfrey Fabyan Cooke, O 319, 331, *343-44*, 348, 360, 374, 415

Danzig Connection, O 204, 222

Dapper Dan Golf Tournament, O 127

Dapper Dan Hall of Fame, I 39

Dapper Dan Man of the Year Award, F 460

Darben, Althea Gibson, O 323, *344-45*, 358, 360, 375

Darby Creek Road, O 570

Darby Daisies baseball club (Negro Leagues), B 127, 290; I 332

Darcy, "Les," I 465

Darden, Oliver, I 259

Dares, J., O 218

Dark, Alvin R. "Al," B 81, *133-34*, 175, 379; F 618;

Dark Secret, O 184

Dark Star, O 189, 599

Darley, *See* Lexington

Darley Arabian, O 590, 596

Darleymey, *See* Lexington

Darlington, SC International Raceway, O 30, 41; S 605

Darrow, James K. "Jimmy," I 7

Dartmouth College, B 175, 348, 468, 510; F 4, 51, 57-58, 64-65, 101-02, 113, 192, 194, 231, 254, 426, 468, 544, 563, 644; I 85, 99, 128-29, 154, 197, 200, 222, 241, 485, 561, 568-69, 660; O 266, 276, 279, 286-87, 317-18, 445, 462-63, 471, 506; S 181, 208, 219, 265, 393, 405, 416, 431, 483

Darwin, Bernard, S 520

Dash for Cash, I 530

Daubert, Jacob E., Jr. "Jake," B *134-35*

Daugherty, Bradley L. "Brad," I 328

Daugherty, Hugh Duffy, F *126-27*, 136, 404

Daughters, Raymond "Ray," I 598-99

Dauss, George A. "Hooks," B *135-36*

Dauthuille, Laurent, I 418

Dauvray Cup, S 152

Davenport, IA baseball club (NWL, 3IL), B 61, 316, 368; S 28, 219

Davenport, IA Track and Field Meet, O 529

Davenport, Willie D., O *447-48*, 478, 497

Davey, "Chuck," I 393

Davey O'Brien Quarterback Award, S 396, 487

Davidson, Owen, O 363

Davidson, Sven, S 554

Davidson College, I 71, 169; S 139, 447

Davies, John, I 543

Davies, Laura, O 114

Davies, Lynn, O 433

Davies, Robert E. "Bob," F 215; I 23, 44, *61-62*, 114, 132, 261, 318

Davies, William "Willie," I 480

Davis, Al "Bummy," I 364

Davis, Allen "Al," F 9, *127-28*, 179-80, 211, 479, 517, 562; S 389

Davis, Alvin G., S 18

Davis, Anthony, F 370

Davis, Clarence E., F 370

Davis, Curtis B. "Curt," B 396

Davis, David, S 590

Davis, Dwight F., O 339, *345-46*, 383, 412-14, 422; S 560

Davis, Ernest "Ernie," F 122, *128-29*, 349, 370, 395, 534; S 398

Davis, Floyd, O 32

Davis, George S., B *136-37*, 171

Davis, Glenn A. "Mr. Outside," I *449-50*

Davis, Glenn W., F 52-53, 78, *129-31*, 345, 358, 577, 605-06; O 99; S 413, 464

Davis, Harry H. "Jasper," S *37*

Davis, Herman Thomas "Tommy," B *137-38;* I 327

Davis, Howard E. Jr., I 452

Davis, Jack W., O 437-38

Davis, Jefferson, I 413

Davis, John H., I *626-27,* 631, 633

Davis, Muriel, *See* Muriel Davis Grossfeld

Davis, Otis C., O *450-51*

Davis, Parke H., F 94, 115, 158, 172, 218, 231, 240, 265, 403, 426, 440, 468, 531, 668; S 477

Davis, Richard H., F 603

Davis, Richard, Jr. "Rick," O *294-95*

Davis, Steven "Steve," S 263

Davis, Virgil L. "Spud," B 588

Davis, Walter, B 533

Davis, Walter P. "Walt," S *274-75*

Davis, William D. "Willie," F *131-32*, 354, 500

Davis, William H. "Willie," B *138-39*

Davis, William R., O 608

Davis, Willis E., O 391

Davis, Wilton, F 663

Davis and Elkins College, S 290

Davis Cup, O 69, 322-23, 330-31, 339, 342, 345-47, 355-56, 362, 365-66, 368, 370, 372, 384, 390, 394-96, 399, 401, 404, 407-08, 410, 412-14, 416-18, 420-21; S 501, 552, 558-59, 561, 563

Davis Cup Committee, S 559

Davison, Clarence, O 175

Davos, Switzerland hockey club, I 548, 567

Davos, Switzerland Speed Skating Competition, O 316-17

Dawkins, John E., Jr. "Johnny," S 295

Dawkins, Peter M. "Pete," F *132-33*, 310; S 377

Dawson, Andre F., B *140*

Dawson, "Buck," I 610

Dawson, "Freddie," I 477

Dawson, Joseph "Joe," O 24

Dawson, Leonard R. "Lenny," F *133-34*, 572, 591

Day, Eagle, F 621

Day, Edward P., Sr. "Ned," I 338, *341-42*

Day, Edward P., Jr., I 341-42

Day, John, S 150-51

Day, Leon, B *141-42*

Day, "Pat," O 227

Day Boat, O 101

A Day in the Bleachers, S 347

Dayton, OH baseball club (CL, ISL, MAL, OSL), B 184, 237, 250, 360, 577; S 4, 24, 200, 228

Dayton, OH Rens basketball club (NBL), S 283-84

Dayton, OH Triangles football club (APFC, NFL), F 425; S 411

Daytona Beach, FL baseball club (FSL), B 102, 412; S 2, 114

Daytona Beach, FL Race Track and International Speedway, O 8, 23, 25-26, 31, 35, 41; S 605-06, 620

Daytona 500 NASCAR Race, O 10, 27, 29-30, 41, 44; S 605-06

Daytona 100 Card Race, S 620

Daytona 24 Hour Auto Race, O 10, 13, 33

DCAA Basketball Tournament, I 44

De Anza Junior College, I 500

de Balzac, Bernard, I 465

De Berg, Steven L. "Steve," F 672

De Bernardi, Forrest S., I *63-64*

De Busschere, David A. "Dave," I 31, *64-65*, 121, 133, 148, 220

De Jesus, Ivan, B 42; S 142

De Lamielleure, Joseph "Joe," S *391-92*

de la Pena, S 626

De La Rose, O 222

de Leeuw, Dianne, I 504

De Leon, Carlos, I 466

De Maestri, Joseph P. "Joe," B 382

De Mar, Clarence H., O *451-52,* 519

De Marco, "Tony," I 359

De Mont, Richard J. "Rick," I 577

De Moss, Elwood B. "Bingo," B 88, *144,* 189, 549; S 189

De Neri basketball club (EL), I 20-21; S 314

De Palma, Ralph, O *7-8*

De Paolo, Peter, O *8-9*

De Paul University, F 12; I 6-7, 43, 116, 164, 208-11; S 252-53, 333

De Pauw University, B 200; 430; F 358; O 526

De Spirito, Anthony "Tony," O 208

de Varona, David "Dave," I 610

de Varona, Donna E., *See* Donna de Varona Pinto

De Windt, Harold "Hal," F *557*

De Witt, Charles, S 201

De Witt, John R., F 269

De Witt, William O. "Bill," S 201

Dead Ahead, O 222

Dean, Everett S., I *62-63,* 191

Dean, Jay H. "Dizzy," B 18, 45, *142-43,* 213, 246, 290, 553; F 29; I 332; O 63, 67, 77; S 76, 99, 125, 183

Dean, Paul D. "Daffy," B 142; I 332

Debernard Danielle, O 275

Debutante Stakes, O 225

Decathlon Athletic Club, Bloomington, IN, I 544; S 492

Decatur, IL baseball club (3IL, ML), B 230, 330; S 134

Decatur, IL Staleys football club (NFL), F 102-03, 112, 152, 234, 601; S 45

Decker, John B., O 586

Decker, Mary, *See* Mary Decker Slaney

Decorated, S 532

Dedeaux, Raoul M. "Rod," B 9; S *37-38,* 56, 75

Dee, John "Johnny," I 41

Dee, Larry, O 389

Defensive Lineman of the Week Award, S 403

Defensive Player of the Year Award, S 295, 367, 386, 406, 410, 504

Defiance Club of Philadelphia baseball club, B 540-41

Deford, Alexandria, S 341

Deford, Frank, S *340-41*

Dehnert, Henry "Dutch," I 21, 32, *65-66,* 131, 158, 170, 195; S 287, 314

Deibel, Arthur F. "Art," S 477

Del Greco, Albert L. "Al," F 571

Del Isola, John J., F 447

Del Mar 100 Auto Race, O 20

del Sarta, Andrea, O 283

Delahanty, Edward J. "Ed," B *143-44,* 238, 591; S 19

Delahanty, Frank G., B 143, 591

Delahanty, James C. "Jim," B 143, 591

Delahanty, Joseph N. "Joe," B 143, 591

Delahanty, Thomas J. "Tom," B 143, 591

Delahoussaye, Eddie, O *182-83*

Deland, Lorin F., F 64, 86, 425

Delaney, "Cal," I 365

Delaney, "Jack," I 360, 372, 428, 463

Delaney, Joe A., F 670

Delaney, Robert "Bob," S 349

Delaware Field Club Tennis Championships, O 321, 405

Delaware Sports Hall of Fame, S 122

Delaware State College, **S** 416

Delaware Valley College, **F** 471

Delhi, **S** 533

Deliberator, **O** 221

Dell Publications, **I** 209

Della Gorra, **O** 593

Dellinger, William S. "Bill," **O** 435, 518, 527

Delmarie, **O** 579

Delmonica Hanover, **O** 207

Delmont, "Al," **I** 365

Delp, Grover C. "Bud," **O** 610

Delph, Marvin, **I** 219

Delta Bowl football game, **F** 118, 621; **S** 385, 464

Delta State University, **I** 258, 284, 289-90, 314-15

Delta State University Hall of Fame, **I** 290

Demaret, James N. "Jimmy," **O** 113, *118-19,* 139, 141

Demijohn, **O** 192

Demings, "Doug," **I** 397

Dempsey, "Bernie," **I** 373

Dempsey, "Jack," **I** 373

Dempsey, "Nonpareil Jack," **I** 372-73, 377-78, 460

Dempsey, Thomas J. "Tom," **F** 135

Dempsey, William H. "Jack," **I** *373-75,* 376, 380, 382, 391, 405, 412-13, 453, 462, 471, 476-79; **O** 60, 63, 90, 205

Denison, IA High School, **I** 183

Denison, TX baseball club (WA), **B** 260

Denison University, **F** 210, 251; **S** 619

Denmark National Soccer Team, **O** 310

Denmark Olympic Swim Team, **I** 587

Denmark Olympic Wrestling Team, **I** 662

Dennis, Earlene, *See* Earlene Dennis Brown

Denny, Jeremiah D. "Jerry," **S** 119

Denny, John A., **S** 160

Dent, "Phil," **O** 363

Dent, Russell E. "Bucky," **B** 441

Denver Ambrose basketball club (AAU), **I** 106

Denver American Legion basketball club (AAU), **I** 106

Denver Antler's Hotel basketball club, **I** 276

Denver Athletic Club, **F** 101

Denver baseball club (WL), **B** 2, 556, 595; **S** 126, 215

Denver Bears baseball club (AA), **B** 140, 236, 385, 421, 446; **S** 57, 87, 171

Denver Broncos football club (AFL, NFL), **F** 17-18, 43, 72, 92, 134, 163, 196, 246, 253, 295, 331, 334, 349, 363, 367, 408, 424, 428, 442, 488, 547, 560, 562, 565, 569, 589-90, 650; **S** 405-06, 409-10, 428-29, 451, 455, 464, 472, 475

Denver Gold football club (USFL), **S** 455, 464

Denver Golf Club, **O** 152

Denver Murphy-Mahoney basketball club (AAU), **I** 106

Denver *News,* **O** 90

Denver Nuggets basketball club (AAU, ABA, NBA), **I** 35, 78-79, 96, 106, 139, 142-43, 193, 196, 210, 270, 279, 299-300; **S** 275, 285, 299, 305

Denver Open Bowling Tournament, **I** 343

Denver Open Golf Tournament, **S** 523

Denver *Post,* **B** 269

Denver Rockets basketball club (ABA), **I** 34-35, 111, 121, 202; **S** 305

Denver Safeways basketball club

(AAU), I 106, 139, 192-93, 276
Denver Spurs hockey club (WHL), I 546
Dernier, Robert E. "Bob," S 134
Derringer, Samuel Paul "Duke," B 144-46, 336; S 228
Des Instructeurs Trophy, S 544
Des Moines Aquatics Club, I 577
Des Moines Area Community College, I 9
Des Moines baseball club (NWL, WL), S 32, 53, 110, 156, 233
Des Moines Blade, B 25
Des Moines Daily News, B 25
Des Moines East High School, I 183
Des Moines Leader, B 25
Des Moines Swim Federation, I 577
Des Moines 300 Auto Race, O 24
Desert Wine, O 580
Desjardins, Ulise J. "Pete," I 486-87
Desmond, "Connie," O 45, 92
Determine, S 5
Detmer, Tyrus "Ty," S 396
Detroit Athletic Club, B 554
Detroit baseball club (WL), B 579
Detroit Black Sox baseball club (NAL), B 533
Detroit College of Law, B 415
Detroit Eagles basketball club (NBL), I 66, 91-92; S 293, 309
Detroit Free Press, S 344
Detroit Golf Club, O 157
Detroit Grand Prix CART Race, S 619-20
Detroit Junior Wings hockey club, I 558
Detroit Lions football club (NFL), F 3, 14, 31, 39, 55, 68, 92, 100, 105-07, 119, 135, 140, 147-48, 155, 199, 203, 216, 238, 249, 293-94, 297, 307-08, 320, 323, 332, 336, 341, 346, 356, 366, 373, 387, 393, 395, 400, 405, 409, 448-49,
454-55, 480, 490-92, 521, 528-29, 543, 546, 549, 566, 574, 578, 589, 609, 628-29, 642, 647, 657, 660-61, 672; O 450, 501; S 364-65, 390, 415, 432, 436, 467, 469, 478
Detroit Lions Hall of Fame, F 119
Detroit News, F 194; S 344
Detroit Panthers football club (NFL), F 113; I 660-61
Detroit Pistons basketball club (NBA), I 2, 23-24, 26, 61, 64, 86, 92, 98, 134-35, 142, 147, 151, 153, 169, 189, 200-01, 249, 277-78, 298, 309, 311, 334; S 253, 263, 269, 276, 280, 285, 301, 304, 313, 326-27
Detroit Press, F 38
Detroit Quarterback (Touchdown) Club, F 337, 413
Detroit Red Wings hockey club (NHL), I 547, 554, 558, 560, 562-63, 569, 571, 573; S 538-39
Detroit Senators baseball club (Negro Leagues), B 32
Detroit Stars baseball club (NNL), B 132, 144, 255, 342, 378, 533, 553; S 43, 129, 168, 224
Detroit Tigers baseball club (AL), B 2, 10, 14, 17, 25, 27, 46, 49-50, 61, 65, 79-80, 86, 93, 99-102, 110, 112-14, 119, 121, 125, 136, 142, 145, 151, 154-56, 163, 169, 174, 176-77, 181, 185, 193, 211-12, 219-20, 222, 230, 237, 245-48, 250, 254-55, 262-64, 266-67, 276-77, 279, 281-82, 287-88, 296-97, 300, 311, 316, 323, 327, 329-30, 333-35, 337, 342, 344, 348, 356, 376, 385, 388, 396, 401, 406, 408, 415, 418-19, 421, 433, 445-46, 448-49, 456, 476, 497, 503, 510, 513-14, 529, 532, 554-55, 557, 561, 565, 567, 572-74, 581-84,

588, 593, 605-06, 614, 617-18, 624, 634; F 289; O 45, 71, 129, 137; S 1-2, 12-13, 44, 46, 50-52, 55-57, 65, 68, 83, 86-87, 101, 106-07, 110-11, 115-16, 124-26, 131-32, 145-46, 153, 155, 159, 161, 164, 167-68, 172, 177, 181, 183, 186, 190, 195, 198, 201, 211-12, 214-15, 218, 224-28, 234, 236, 243, 245-47, 344, 348-49, 494-95

The Detroit Tigers, S 344

The Detroit Tigers: An Illustrated History, S 344

Detroit *Times,* S 344

Detroit Wolverines baseball club (NL), B 52, 207, 240, 307, 406, 554, 604-05; S 47, 123, 178

Detroit Wolverines football club (NFL), F 194

Detroit Wolves baseball club (EWL), B 31, 453, 543, 599

Devaney, Robert S. "Bob," F 71, *135-36,* 443-44, 507; S 403-04, 411

Devil Diver, O 175

Devil's Bag, O 222, 611

Devine, Aubrey A., F 29, 511; S *392*

Devine, "Bing," B 73; O 55

Devine, Daniel J. "Dan," F *136-39,* 149, 324; S 496

Devine, Thomas "Tommy," F 338

Devore, Joshua D. "Josh," B 230

Dew Drop, O 201

Dexter, O 230

Dexter Pavilion, Chicago, IL, I 643

Deyna Kaz, O 304

Di Biasi, Klaus, I 442, 491, 497

Di Gennaro, Frank, *See* Frankie Genaro

Di Nardo, "Larry," F 458

Dial American Cup Gymnastic Championship, I 539

Diamond Sculls, O 256, 263

Diamond X Oilers of Tulsa basketball club (AAU), S 331

Dias, Niege, O 35

Diavala, O 184

Dice, O 184

Dick Siebert Field, Minneapolis, MN, S 201

Dickerman, Leo L., S 42

Dickerson, Eric D., F *139-40,* 628; S 469

Dickey, George W., B 147

Dickey, Richard L. "Dick," I 43

Dickey, William M. "Bill," B 33, 36, *146-47,* 213, 490; S 91

Dickinson, Frank G., F 94, 452, 513, 532, 598

Dickinson, Richard, S 616

Dickinson College, B 33; F 267, 313; O 417; S 397

Dickinson System, F 57-58, 188, 193, 353, 378, 416, 452, 513; S 388, 400, 424, 483

Dickson, Murry M., S *38-39*

Diddle, Edgar A., Sr. "Ed," I *66-68,* 116

Didrikson, Mildred E. "Babe," *See* Mildred E. Didrikson Zaharias

Die-Hard 500 NASCAR Race, S 605

Diegel, Leo, O *119-20*

Dierdorf, Daniel L. "Dan," F *141,* 527; S 356, 370

Dietz, Michael "Mike," I 629

Dietz, William "Lone Star," F 472

Dietzel, Paul, F 91, 211

Digger Phelps and Notre Dame Basketball, S 312

Dihigo, Martin, B *147-48,* 453, 482, 543

Dike, IA High School, I 183

Dillard, William Harrison, F 395; O *452-53,* 552; S 577

Dillon, "Jack," I *375-76,* 416, 424

Dilweg, Lavern R., F *142;* S 441
DiMaggio, Dominic P. "Dom," B 148, *536,* 591; S *39-40*
DiMaggio, Joseph P. "Joe," B 106, *148-50,* 213, 258, 296, 298, 346, 374, 516, 520, 553, 591, 597; F 614; O 46, 60; S 39-40, 86, 95, 102, 158, 335, 352
DiMaggio, Vincent P. "Vince," B 148, 591; S 39
Diminutive, O 206
Dinneen, William H. "Bill," B 91; S *40-42*
Dinsmore, "Duke," O 20
Diomed, O 583, 608-09
Diplomat Club, Hollywood, FL, O 143
Directly, O 221
Disastrous Night, O 611
Disch, William, S 74
Dischinger, Donas, S 295
Dischinger, Terry G., I 23, 231, 272; S *295-96*
Dismukes, William "Bill," B 549
Disney World on Ice, I 518
Distillers Stakes, O 209
Distinguished American Award, National Football Foundation, S 378, 417
Distinguished National Journalism Medal, University of Missouri, S 338
Distinguished Service Award, University of Nebraska, S 475
Ditka, Michael K. "Mike," F 37, *142-43,* 566
Ditson, Henry A., B 682
Divine Comedy, O 229
Dixiana Stakes, O 209, 213
Dixie Kid, The, I *376-77,* 473
Dixie Basketball Classic, I 127, 209
Dixie Bowl football game, F 118, 403

Dixie Football Classic, S 494
Dixie 400 Auto Race, O 27
Dixie Junior College, I 320
Dixon, C. P., O 372
Dixon, George, I 357, 434
Dixon, Herbert A. "Rap," B *150-51*
Dixon, Medina, I 285
Doak, William L. "Bill," B *42-43*
Dobbins, O 219-20
Dobbs, Glenn, F 78, 215
Dobbs, Robert C. "Bobby," F 78; I 377
Dobie, Gilmour "Gil," F *144,* 468; S 431
Doble, "Bud," O 586
Dobler, Conrad F., S 370
Doby, Lawrence E. "Larry," B *151-52,* 362, 543, 573-74, 619
Dr. Fager, O 579-80, *581-82*
Doctor Rice, O 224
Dodd, Robert L. "Bobby," F 6, 73, *145,* 444, 460; S 478
Dodd Award, F 460
Dodds, Gilbert L. "Gil," O *453-54*
Dodge City, KS Junior College, S 372
Dodge Stock Car Racing Team, O 17, 27
Dodger Stadium, Los Angeles, CA, B 159, 427, 618; O 92; S 142, 244
Doeg, Doris, O 347
Doeg, Eric, O 347
Doeg, John T. G. H., O 62, 322, *347-48,* 368, 395, 404; S 501
Doeg, May, O 347
Doeg, Violet Sutton, O 347
Doeg, William "Bill," O 347
Doerr, Robert P. "Bobby," B *152-53,* 536; S 64, 198
Doggett, "Jerry," O 77, 92
Doherty, Hugh L., O 354
Doherty, Lawrie, O 354
Doherty, Reginald F. "Reggie," O

346, 412, 414, 420
Dohoney, Donald "Don," F 413
Dolan, James "Jimmy," O 70
Dolan, Patrick H. "Pat," B 323
Dole Rex Award, I 94
Dolgan, Robert, S 103
Dolly Spanker, S 533
Dombrot, Irwin, I 132
Dominant, O 211
Dominican Republic baseball club, S 189
Dominican Republic Baseball League, B 16, 26, 224, 378-79, 435
Domino, O 219; S 531, 533
Domino's Pizza Pocono 500 Auto Race, O 3
Domres, Martin F. "Marty," F 296
Don de Oro, O 188
Don Quixote, O 593
Donaldson, John, S 43-44
Donato, "Sam," O 591
Donelli, Aldo T. "Buff," O 295-97, S 500
Donerail, O 198
Donlin, Michael J. "Mike," B 153-54, 255, 301
Donna, TX baseball club S 54
Donohue, Mark, O 21, 28
Donohue, Terrance "Terry," F 501; S 392-93
Donohue-Penske Auto Racing Team, O 20
Donovan, Ann, I 285
Donovan, Arthur "Art," F 145-46, 165, 348, 519
Donovan, Arthur B., F 145; I 378
Donovan, Arthur J., Jr., I 378
Donovan, Michael J. "Mike," I 377-78, 390, 464
Donovan, Patrick J. "Patsy," B 153-54, 255, 301
Donovan, William E. "Bill," B 155-56, 282; S 161

Dooley, Vincent J. "Vince," F 146-47, 535
Dooley, William "Bill," F 146
Dorais, Charles E. "Gus," F 89, 126, 148-49, 245, 504-05
Doral-Eastern Open Golf Tournament, O 124, 163; S 516, 520
Dorian, O 188
Dorothy Poynton Aquatics Club, Los Angeles, CA, I 496
Dorsett, Anthony D. "Tony," F 149-50, 630; S 449
Dorsey, James E. "Jim," S 214
Dos Passos, John, O 402
Dotson, William "Bill," I 646
Doty, Floretta, See Floretta Doty McCutcheon
Double Jay, O 590
Doubleday, Abner, B 78, 528; O 99
Doug Sanders International Junior Golf Championship, S 516
Dougherty, "Jack," I 425
Dougherty, Nathan W., F 150-51
Dougherty, Patrick H., B 286; S 143
Douglas, Bobby E., I 657
Douglas, Findlay, O 161
Douglas, James "Buster," S 626
Douglas, James E. I., O 297
Douglas, James E. I., Jr., O 297
Douglas, Phillip B. "Phil," B 323
Douglas, Robert L. "Bob," I 49, 68-69
Douglas, Sherman, S 264
Dover, DE baseball club (ESL), B 101, 489
Dover, DE Downs, O 215
Dover, DE Race Track, O 30
Dover, Sail, S 508
Dow Chemical Company basketball club (AAU), I 276
Dowler, Boyd H., F 96, 151-52
Dowler, Walter, F 151
Down Play, S 527

Downey, Glenn, S 373
Downey, William B., I 394
Downing, Alphonso E. "Al," B 43; I 333
Downing, Brian J., S 44-45
Downing, Richard, O 574-75
Downtown Athletic Club, New York, NY, I 361, 442
Doyle, "Jimmy," I 455
Doyle, "Kathy," I 214
Doyle, Lawrence J. "Larry," B 53, 117, 156-57, 259; S 248
Doyle, Richard "Skip," S 463
Doyle, William Carl, B 49
Dozier, William H., Jr. "D. J.," F 93, 394, 460
Drahos, Nicholas "Nick," S 393-94
Drake, Bruce, I 69-71, 166
Drake, Dale, O 22
Drake, Elvin "Ducky," O 478
Drake Relays, F 171; O 475, 502, 513, 521, 536; S 343
Drake Relays Hall of Fame, O 550; S 368
Drake University, F 262, 368, 478
Draper, Foy, O 496
Drayton, Otis Paul, O 438
Drenth, Jeff, O 530
Dressen, Charles W. "Chuck," B 8-10, 145; S 45-46
Drew, Harold, F 621
Drew, Howard P., O 443, 455
Drew, John E., S 329
Drexler, Clyde, I 174
Dreyfuss, Barney, B 114, 157-58, 457, 569, 581
Dreyfuss, Samuel, B 158
Driesell, Charles G. "Lefty," I 71-72; S 298
Driessen, Daniel "Dan," B 544
Driscoll, John L. "Paddy," F 103, 152-53, 241
Drobny, Jaroslav, O 355, 379, 390; S 554
Dromo, John, I 56
Druid Hills Golf Club, Atlanta, GA, O 152; S 522
Drulis, Charles "Chuck," F 657
Drury, Morley E., F 153-54, 299
Drury College, S 229
Dryden, Charles, B 84; S 341-42
Dryden, Kenneth W. "Ken," I 544
Drysdale, Ann Meyers, I 72-73
Drysdale, Clifford "Cliff," O 324
Drysdale, Donald S. "Don," B 9, 158-60, 315, 544, 618; I 73; S 160, 167, 355
Drysdale, Scott, B 158
du Maurier Golf Classic, S 509, 514
duPont, Margaret Osborne, O 337-38, 343, 348-49, 359, 374, 401; S 550
duPont, Mrs. Allaire, O 592
Du Quoin Auto Race, O 17, 32, 42
Du-Well Athletic Club, Norwich, CT, I 450
Dubenion, Elbert, S 432
Dublin, GA baseball club (GFL), 595
Dubuque College, F 148
Dubuque, IA baseball club (ML, MOVL, NWL, 3IL), B 107, 173, 241, 284, 463, 563
Dubuque, IA Telegraph-Herald, O 104
Dudley, James "Jimmy," S 192
Dudley, William M. "Bill," F 154-56, 511
Dudley Cup, O 365
Duenna, O 182
Duer, Alva O., I 73-75
Duesenberg Special Racing Car, O 8, 23
Duffy, Frank T., S 120
Duffy, Hugh, B 160-61, 256, 280, 298, 347, 568, 617; S 115
Duguay, Ronald "Ron," I 568

Duke of Kent, O 389
Duke of Magenta, S 536
Duke Rodney, O 191
Duke Stadium, Durham, NC, F 626
Duke University, B 74, 113, 518; F
    214, 30, 303, 327, 350, 361, 452-
    53, 561, 595, 607, 625-26; I 25,
    56, 71, 101, 104-05, 210, 225,
    259, 282, 406, 596-97, 638, 658-
    59; O 425, 537-38; S 251, 280,
    292, 295, 312, 386, 455-56; See
    also Trinity College
Duke University Sports Hall of Fame,
    S 293, 456
Dukes, Walter, I 43, 180, 261
Duluth, MN baseball club (MWL,
    NoL), B 20, 136, 262
Duluth, MN Eskimoes football club
    (NFL), F 315, 374, 424
Duluth, MN Northern Hardware
    hockey club, I 574; S 546
Duluth, MN Sports Hall of Fame, B
    21
Duluth, MN-Superior, WI baseball
    club (NoL), S 57, 81
Dumas, Charles E. "Charley," O
    455-56
Dumont Network, O 46-47
Dunbar, Louis, I 174
Duncan, George, O 128
Dundee, Angelo, I 422
Dundee, "Johnny," I 365, 378-79,
    392, 394-95, 407, 411, 415, 454,
    469, 576
Dundee, "Joe," I 381, 470, 474
Dundee, "Vince," I 367, 481
Dundee hockey club (British Elite
    League), I 568
Dunfield, Sonya, I 503
Dunhill Cup Team, S 520
Dunkel, Richard "Dick," F 338
Dunkel System, F 595
Dunkhorst, E, I 366

Dunlap, Frederick C. "Fred," B 221;
    S 46-47
Dunlop, Alfred, O 320
Dunlop Phoenix International Golf
    Tournament, I 126, 143-44
Dunn, James C., B 23-24, 524
Dunn, John J., B 232, 241, 494; S
    47-48
Dunn, John J., Jr. "Jack," S 48
Dunn, John J. III "Jack," S 48
Dunn, Velma C., I 496
Dunn, William "Willie," O 133
Dunne, Finley Peter, S 341
Dunphy, Donald "Don," O 67; S
    342-43
Dupas, Ralph, I 396
Duper, Mark S., F 384
Duquesne University, B 452-53; F
    188, 214, 510; I 67, 124, 180,
    187; O 296; S 284, 308
Duquesne University Hall of Fame, O
    296
Duran, Roberto, I 397-98, 422; S
    612
Durelle, Yvon, I 442
Durgan, "Jeff," O 297-98
Durham, Diane, I 535
Durham, Hugh, S 329
Durham, NC baseball club (CrL,
    NCL, Pil), B 229, 405, 446, 515;
    F 453; S 67, 106, 135, 228
Durham, NC Open Bowling
    Tournament, I 351
Duroc, O 570
Durocher, Leo E. "The Lip," B 9, 85,
    133, 145, 161-62, 366, 393, 432,
    467, 570, 607; S 25, 45-46, 61,
    88, 154, 164, 208
Durr, Francoise, O 358
Durrance, Richard, O 275-77
Durst, Cedric M., B 489
Dustwhirl, O 614
Dutcher, James "Jim," I 95

Dutra, "Mortie," O 120
Dutra, Olin, O *120-21*
Duvall, Edith M. McGuire, O *457-58*, 550
Dwight, James "Jimmy," O 338, *349-51*, 391-93, 398, 402
Dwyer, Michael F., O 206, 219, 588-89, 592, 597; S 533
Dwyer, Philip J., O 206, 219, 588-89, 592, 597; S 533
Dwyer, William, O 223
Dwyer Handicap, O 194, 198
Dwyer Stakes, O 197-98, 579, 585, 596, 599, 615
Dyche, Schubert R., I 301
Dye, Patrick "Pat," F 287; S 394-95
Dye, William H. "Tippy," I 134, 295
Dyer, Edwin H. "Eddie," B 381, 517, 525
Dyer, Hector M. "Hec," O 568
Dykes, James J. "Jimmy," B 14, *162-63*, 208, 343, 401; S 68, 107, 235

E. A. Diddle Arena, Bowling Green, KY, I 68
Eagen, Edward P. F. "Eddie," I *379-80*
Eagen, "Joe," I 463
Eagle Race Car, O 11-12
Eagleson, Allen, S 543
Earlham College, I 307
Early Bird, O 175
Earnhardt, Ralph, S 604
Earnhardt, Ralph Dale, O 41; S *604-05*
Easley, Kenny, F *157-58*; S 393
East Central State University (OK), I 296
East Carolina League, S 19, 153
East Carolina University, S 395
East Dixie League, S 17, 207, 245
East Germany Swim Meet, I 618

East Germany Swim Team, I 579, 583, 592, 609
East Lake Golf Course, Atlanta, GA, O 135
East Los Angeles Junior College, S 83
East New York Club, O 192
East Stroudsburg State College, O 307
East Texas League, S 235
East-West All-Star Baseball Game (Negro Leagues), B 7, 69, 88, 127, 141, 147, 150-51, 192, 213, 224, 244, 269, 273, 331, 339, 362, 483, 520, 533, 543, 548, 599, 620; S 10, 99, 189
East-West All-Star Basketball Game, S 297; *See also* National Basketball Association All-Star Game
East-West All-Star Football Game, Columbus, OH, F 410
East-West Shrine All-Star Football Game, San Francisco, CA, F 1-2, 42, 49, 67, 76, 90, 101, 127, 138, 141-43, 151, 155, 161, 164, 176, 186, 207, 249, 267, 272-73, 275, 297, 313, 321, 347, 362, 370, 401, 410, 412, 416, 453, 461, 479, 482, 492, 499, 514, 523, 533, 536, 566, 574, 586, 588, 610, 633, 642-43, 651-52, 657, 664; O 52; S 94, 393, 40, 423, 425, 443, 450, 458, 462, 474, 476, 481, 491, 493
Easter, Luscious Luke, B 331, 453
Easter Stockings, O 609
Eastern Amateur Golf Tournament, S 519, 521
Eastern Amateur Hockey League, I 547, 552, 564
Eastern Association of Officials, F 58
Eastern Basketball League, I 150, 178, 243, 250, 333

Eastern Basketball League Championships and Playoffs, **I** 150, 178

Eastern College Basketball Association, **I** 287

Eastern College Gymnastic League, **I** 528

Eastern Collegiate Athletic Conference, **I** 210, 232, 248, 277, 287, 316

Eastern Collegiate Athletic Conference Basketball Tournament, **I** 40, 287; **S** 325

Eastern Collegiate Athletic Conference Hockey Tournament, **I** 561

Eastern Colored League, **I** 143, 332; **S** 19-20, 188, 238, 242

Eastern Colored League Championships, **S** 242

Eastern Football Coach of the Year, **O** 296

Eastern Golden Gloves Tournament, **I** 395

Eastern Intercollegiate Athletic Association, **F** 558

Eastern Intercollegiate Basketball League, **I** 84, 222, 232, 316

Eastern Intercollegiate Football Association, **I** 248

Eastern Intercollegiate League, **S** 219, 297

Eastern Intercollegiate League Championships, **S** 219, 297

Eastern Intercollegiate Wrestling Association, **I** 647

Eastern Interstate League, **S** 238

Eastern Interstate League Championships, **S** 238

Eastern Kentucky State University, **B** 105-07; **F** 480

Eastern Lawn Tennis Association, **O** 411, 413

Eastern League, **B** 22, 26, 384, 597; **I** 20, 65, 102; **S** 16, 19, 21, 29, 37, 41, 48, 81, 83, 104, 118, 126-27, 146, 149-50, 163, 165, 181, 183, 191, 193-94, 201-02, 204, 208, 213, 216, 225, 230, 236, 242-43, 287, 314

Eastern League Basketball Championships and Playoffs, **I** 65, 102; **S** 287, 314

Eastern Massachusetts Board of Approved Officials, **I** 137

Eastern Michigan University, **I** 95; **O** 478

Eastern Olympic Boxing Championships, **I** 401

Eastern Open Golf Tournament, **S** 505

Eastern Pro Basketball League, **S** 267

Eastern Professional League, **I** 573

Eastern Rowing Sprints, **O** 256

Eastern Senior Figure Skating Championships, **S** 628

Eastern Shore League, **S** 60, 68, 149, 163

Eastern Sports Network, **F** 547, 671; **I** 215, 217, 234, 288, 541, 638; **S** 56, 175, 352

Eastern States Figure Skating Championships, **I** 502, 504, 506

Eastern United States Alpine Ski Championships, **O** 276, 284

Eastern Washington State College, **O** 36

Eastern Women's Amateur Golf Tournament, **O** 114

Easton, William "Bill," **F** 524

Easton, MD baseball club (ESL), **B** 20, 197, 574

Eastman, Benjamin B. "Ben," **O** 440-41, 466

Eastman Award, **S** 254

Eastment Business College, **I** 670

Eau Claire, WI baseball club (MWL,

NoL), **B** 1, 228, 279, 485, 559; **S** 115

Eau Gallie, **O** 219

Ebbets, Charles H., **B** 135, *165-66*, 426, 429, 568

Ebbets Field, Brooklyn, NY, **B** 3, 165, 257, 366, 412, 427, 429, 467; **I** 22, 360, 400; **O** 49, 59, 310; **S** 61, 229

Ebling basketball club **I** 305

Ebony, **F** 539; **S** 407

Echevarria, Guillermo, **I** 576

Eckersall, Walter H., **F** 38, 142, *158-60*, 244, 262, 406, 468, 551, 668; **S** 485

Eckersley, Dennis L., **S** *48-50*

Eckert, Claudia, **I** 496

Eckert, William D. "Bill," **B** *166-67*, 175, 318, 356, 367, 426, 504

Eckman, Arthur, **S** 356

Eclipse, **O** 570

Eclipse Award, **O** 203-04, 222, 226-27, 229, 569, 591, 606, 610-11; **S** 530

Eclipse Stakes, **O** 578, 597

Eddie Sachs Award, **O** 36

Eddy, Nicholas M. "Nick," **F** 277, 458

Ederle, Gertrude C., **I** 494, 581, *588-90*, 623

Edgar, J. Douglas, **O** 133

Edgemore Handicap, **O** 192

Edgerson, Booker T., **S** 478

Edgerton Saber, **F** 440

Edgewater Country Club, Chicago, IL, **O** 121

Edinboro University, **S** 611

Edison Junior College, **S** 523

Edison, NJ Open Bowling Tournament, **I** 351

Edith Cavell, **O** 596

Edmonton, Canada baseball club (WCaL), **B** 249, 376, 613

Edmonton, Canada Eskimoes football club (CFL), **F** 55, 515, 622, 633, 642; **S** 395

Edmonton, Canada Oilers hockey club (WHA, NHL), **I** 554, 557, 563, 566-67; **S** 538

Edmundson, Clarence S. "Hec," **I** 75-77

Edmundson Field House, Seattle, WA, **I** 76

Edmundson Pavilion, Kansas City, MO, **I** 199

The Education of a Tennis Player, **S** 339

Edward J. Neil Memorial Award, **I** 387, 398, 423-24, 477

Edwards, Albert G. "Turk," **F** *160*, 385

Edwards, "Billy," **I** 466

Edwards, Donald L. "Don," **I** 550

Edwards, George, **I** 646

Edwards, Harry, **O** 272

Edwards, Henry P. "Hank," **B** 280

Edwards, Kenneth, **S** 330

Edwards, Leroy, **I** 195; **S** *276-77*

Edwards, R. Lavell, **S** *395-96*

Edwards, Thomas L. "Tom," **F** 194

Edwards, Tonya, **I** 291

Edwards, William "Bill," **F** 90, 193, 265

Edwin Forest, **O** 174

Egan, Aloysius J. "Wish," **B** 418

Egyptian National Soccer Club, **O** 301

Eichelberger, Edward "Ed," **I** 647

Eichenlaub, Ray J., **F** 505

18 Caret, **O** 206

Eintracht Soccer Club (GAL), **O** 291

Eisenhower, David, **S** 337

Eisenhower, Dwight D., **F** 52; **I** 326, 380; **O** 516; **S** 498

Ekwanck Golf Club, Ekwanck, VT, **O** 148

El Centro Junior College, **S** 80

El Dorado, AR Leon Oil Company basketball club, **I** 57

El Ouafi, Boughera, **O** 520

El Toro Marines football club, **F** 28, 268

El Touni, Khadr, **I** 628, 633

Elberfield, Norman A. "Kid," **B** 278

Elder, Jack, **F** 90, 94, 532

Elementary Futurity Stakes, **O** 576

Elewonibi, Mohammad, **S** 396

Elgin National Road Race, **O** 7, 26

Elias, "Eddie," **I** 344

Elixir, **O** 178

Elizabeth, **O** 586

Elizabeth II of England, **O** 357, 607

Elizabethtown College, **S** 62

Elk City, OK High School, **I** 297

Ellard, Henry, **S** 469

Ellendale State College, **F** 490

Eller, Carl L., **F** *161*, 451; **S** 450

Ellinger, Charles F., Sr., "Charlie," **O** *237-38*

Elliott, Chalmers "Bump," **S** 380

Elliott, Frank, **O** 22

Elliott, Herbert "Herb," **O** 527

Elliott, James "Jim," **O** 120; **S** 570, 581

Elliott, Peter R. "Pete," **S** 380

Elliott, Robert *L.* "Bob," **B** *167*

Elliott, Sean M., **S** *277-78*

Elliott, William "Bill," **S** *605-06*

Ellis, "Jimmy," **I** 386

Ellis, Kathleen, **I** 582

Ellsworth, Rex C., **O** 612

Ellsworth Ranch, Chino, CA, **O** 612

Elmendorf Farm, Lexington, KY, **O** 604-05

Elmira, NY baseball club (EL, NYPL, NYSL, PoL), **B** 7, 258, 364, 377, 403, 595; **S** 32, 128, 143, 159, 201

Elmore, Leonard J. "Lenny," **I** 71; **S** 298

Elon College, **S** 304

Elson, Robert "Bob," **O** 52; **S** *343-44*

Elway, "Jack," **F** 161

Elway, John A., **F** *161-63*

Ely, NV baseball club, **S** 197

Elyria Club, **F** 456

Elysian Field, Hoboken, NJ, **B** 77, 627; **O** 101

Elysian Rink, Duluth, MN, **I** 574

Emerson, Nathaniel, **O** 421

Emerson, Roy, **O** 324, 341; **S** 555-56

Emerson Piano baseball club (CmA), **B** 47

Emery, Walter, **I** 70

Emery Edge Trophy, **I** 559

Emeryville, CA Race Track, **O** 211

Emmelmann, Kirsten, **O** 436

Emmy Award, **I** 503

Emory University, **O** 135; **S** 348

Emperor, **O** 201

Empire City Track, **O** 26, 20, 206

Employers Casualty Company, Dallas, TX, **O** 171

Emporia Athletic Association, **O** 450

Emporia, KS baseball club (WL), **B** 336

Emporia State Teachers College, **I** 268; **O** 485

Emporium Stakes, **O** 588

Emslie, Robert D. "Bob," **B** 310

Enberg, Richard A. "Dick," **I** 197; **O** *62-63*

Endacott, Paul, **I** 77

Ender, Cornelia, **I** 575

Engel, George, **I** 416, 421

Engle, Charles A. "Rip," **F** *163-64*, 401, 459, 556

Engleman, Howard, **S** 302

Englert, Terrie, **I** 535

English, Alexander "Alex," **I** *77-79,*

143

English, William "Bill," I 90

English Channel Swim, I 581, 585, 589, 602

English Derby, O 201

English National Soccer Team, *See* British National Soccer Team

English Soccer League, O 303

Englund, Eugene "Gene," I 85

Enich, Michael "Mike," F 13

Enke, Fred A., I *79-80*

Enke, Fred W., I 80

Ennia Challenge Cup, S 628

Ennis, Delmer "Del," B *168*

Enright, James E., "Jim," I *80-81*

Ensor, Lavelle "Buddy," O 193

Epperson, "Charlie," I 85

Epperson, Lee, I 437

Epsom Derby, O 609

Epsom Gold Cup, O 201

Equipoise, O 198, 230-31, 572, 613

Equipoise Mile Race, O 615

Eric, O 604

Erickson, Keith R., I 101; S 251

Erickson, Scott G. III, S 145

Erie Athletic Association, Kearny, NJ, O 293, 310

Erie, PA baseball club (CL), B 34

Erins Isle, O 229

Erne, Frank, I 387-88, 420, 434

Errand King, O 178

Errard's Guide, O 200

Erskine, Carl D., B 467

Erskine College, F 560

Ertle, "Johnny," I 478

Eruzione, Michael A. "Mike," I 548, 567

Erving, Julius W. II "Dr. J," I *81-82*, 96, 148, 196; S 257-58, 269, 284

Erwin, TN baseball club (ApL), S 231

ESPN "Baseball Tonight," S 346

Eschenbrenner, William "Bill," O 163

Eschevarria, "Joe", I 455

Escoba, O 211, 582

Escobar, Sixto, I 406

Eskilstuna, Sweden Speed Skating Competition, O 316

Espirit de Court, O 419

Esposito, "Al," O 117

Esquire, I 168; O 64; S 337, 349, 351, 546

Essex Country Club, Manchester, MA, O 133

Estep, Michael "Mike," O 381

Etcheverry, Samuel "Sam," S 426

Eternal, O 608

Ethan Allen, O 230

Eugene, OR baseball club (PCL), B 42, 502; S 16, 118

Eugene, OR Track and Field Meet, O 541

Eureka College, F 414

Europa Cup Skiing Circuit, O 273, 275, 280-81, 284, 287

European All-Star Soccer Club, O 295

European Armed Forces Track and Field Championships, S 568

European Boxing Union, I 442

European Cross Country Championships, O 512

European Figure Skating Championships, I 502, 515, 519

European Junior Cross Country Skiing Championships, O 282

European Professional Bicycle Sprint Championships, O 264

European Ryder Cup Team, S 514

European Track and Field Championships, O 512

Evangeline League, S 227

Evans, Charles, Jr. "Chick," O *121-22*

Evans, Darrell W., S 7, *50-51*, 95

Evans Dwight M., S *51-52*

Evans, Eleanor, S 50

Evans, Janet, I 583; S 602, *606-08*

Evans, "Jimmy," I 359

Evans, Lee E., O *458-59*

Evans, Raymond "Ray," I 5; S 409

Evans, Richard, O 371; S 50

Evans, William G. "Billy," B 110, *169*; F 551; S 199

Evanston, IL Golf Club, S 515

Evansville College, I 193-94

Evansville, IN baseball club (AA, KL, NWL, 3IL), B 49, 222, 308, 488, 525, 554, 631; S 15, 96, 145, 179, 211

Evashevski, Forest J. Sr., F 243, 297

Eve Challenge Golf Tournament, O 168

Eveleth, MN High School, I 546-47, 559, 564-65, 567, 572

Eveleth, MN Junior College, I 559, 572

Eveleth, MN Rangers hockey club, I 559

Evensen, Bernt, O 315, 318

Evered, Mrs., O 354

Everett, Kelso, O 592

Everglades Handicap, O 576

Everglades Stakes, O 575

Everly, IA High School, I 8

Evers, John J. "Johnny," B 84, *169-70*, 311, 416, 507, 556-57, 611; S 161-62, 223, 345

Evert, Christine M., *See* Christine Evert-Lloyd

Evert, Jeanne, O 352

Evert-Lloyd, Christine M., O 335, 341, *351-53*, 363, 379, 381, 396-97

Everybody's Al-American, S 341

Evonne, S 339

E. W. King Stable, O 178

Ewbank, Wilbur C. "Weeb," F 11, *164-65*, 218, 320

Ewell, Harold N. "Barney," O 453; S *576-77*, 590

Ewing, "Cal," B 569

Ewing, Patrick A. "Pat," I *82-84*, 283, 300-01, 304

Ewing, William B. "Buck," B *170-71*; S 150

Ewry, Raymond C. "Ray," O *459*; S 567

Exceller, O 229, 606

Excelsior Stakes, O 209

Exclusive Nature, O 569

Executive of the Year, S 88, 399, 475

Exendine, Albert A., S *396-97*

Expectation Stakes, O 219

Experimental Free Handicap, O 614

Exterminator, O 194-96, 199, 202, *582*, 597; S 531

Eyser, George, I *525-26*

Faber, Urban C. "Red," B *173-74*

Fabius, O 176, 190; S 529

Fabre, Leon, I 663

Fabyan, Sarah Palfrey, *See* Sarah Palfrey Fabyan Cooke Danzig

Face, Elroy L. "Roy," B *174-75*; S 217, 243

Fadeev, Alexsandr, I 501

Fagan, Clifford B. "Cliff," S *278-79*

Fager, Dr. Charles, O 581

Faggs, Heriwentha Mae, *See* Heriwentha Faggs Starr

Fahlvist, Bengt, I 665

Fahr, Otto, I 600

Fain, Ferris R., B 406; S *52-53*

Fain, Oscar, S 52

Fair Empress, O 582

Fair Grounds, New Orleans, LA, O 182, 225; S 527

Fair Grounds, St. Louis, MO, S 531

Fair Play, O 211, 578, 595

Fairbanks, Charles "Chuck," F 481, 581

Faireno, O 184

Fairly, Carl, S 53

Fairly, Ronald R. "Ron," B 618; S 53-54

Fairmont Athletic Club, New York, NY, I 421

Fairmont Normal School, F 668

Fairmont Park, Philadelphia, PA, B 155

Fairy Jane, O 597

Fairy Manhurst, O 579

Faith Baptist Bible College, I 8

Faithless, O 201

Faldo, Nicholas A. "Nick," S 519

Falk, Bibb A., S 54-55, 74

Falk, Chester E. "Chet," S 54

Falkenberg, Robert "Bob," O 355, 365; S 553-54

Fall, David A., I 498

Fall River, MA baseball club (NEL), B 239-40, 321; S 69

Fall River, MA District Soccer League, O 309

Fall River, MA Marksman football club (ACSL), O 299

Fall River, MA Soccer Club (ASL, NLNE), O 297, 305, 309

Falls, Joseph F. "Joe," S 344-45

Falsetto, O 209

Falstaff Team Trophy, O 13

Falstaff's Bowling Team, St. Louis, MO, I 341, 348

Family Circle Tennis Championships, Hilton Head, SC, O 326

Family Style, S 530

Fanatorium Majors Bowling Team, I 344

Fanning, William James "Jim," B 614

Far Western Conference, F 377, 409, 539, 564; I 276

Faraway Farm, Lexington, KY, O 596, 614

Fargo, ND baseball club (NoL), B 382; S 233

Farley, Richard L. "Dick," S 317

Farma Way, S 530

Farmer, Larry, I 56; S 259

Farmer, "Tommy," I 447

Farmer's Herald, St. Johnsbury, VT, O 85

Farmer's Library and Monthly Journal of Agriculture, O 95

Farnham, Canada baseball club (ProL), S 9-10

Farnum, Mark, F 477

Farquhar, Marion Jones, O 325, 353-55, 363, 376-77, 383

Farr, Miller, Jr., S 426

Farr, "Tommy," I 361, 429

Farrar, Sidney D. "Sid," B 507

Farrell, Charles A. "Duke," B 160

Farrell, Frank, B 89, 91; O 196, 201

Farrell, John J. "Johnny," O 122-24

Farrington, "Kip," S 541

Fashion, O 574, 583, 602

Fashion Race Course, O 230

Fashion Stakes, O 194, 604

Fassi, Carlo, I 504, 506, 510

Fastnet Yacht Race, Ireland, O 103

Father Joseph, I 417

Fatheree, Jess, F 599

Faurot, Donald B. "Don," F 138, 167-69, 584; S 381

Faurot Field, Columbia, MO, F 168

Fator, Laverne, O 183-84, 193

Faultless, O 195

Fay, William "Bill," F 275

Fayetteville, NC baseball club (TSL), S 20

Fazio, George, O 153

FBO Studios, O 87

Fears, Thomas J. "Tom," F 169, 332, 617

Feathers, William Beattie, F 169-70,

576

Featherstone, Glen, **S** 540

Featherweight Boxing Championship, **I** 355-57, 363-64, 369, 378-81, 387,394-95, 406, 415, 417, 434, 438-39, 447, 450, 459, 461-62, 468

Federal, **O** 593

Federal City College, **I** 152

Federal Express St. Jude Golf Classic, **S** 519

Federal League, **B** 26, 29, 34, 117, 323, 550, 556; **O** 97; **S** 48, 85, 98, 240

Federal Shipyard Soccer Club, Kearny, NJ, **O** 306

Federation Cup Tennis Championships, **O** 326, 335, 352, 357, 364, 380, 396; **S** 551

Federation Internationale de Ski Championships, **O** 276, 281-82, 284-85

Federation Internationale de Ski Congress, **O** 279

Federation Internationale des E'ches, **I** 672

Federation of International Gymnastics, **I** 533

Fee, "Ray," **I** 417

Feeney, Charles S. "Chub," **B** *175,* 318

Feigay, Paul, **I** 503

Feigner, "Eddie," **O** *257-58*

Fejer, Ferenc, **I** 631

Felaschi, Nello, **F** 447

Feldman, "Abe," **I** 426

Feldman, "Lew," **I** 438

Fell, "Jim," **I** 373

Feller, Robert W. A. "Bob," **B** 18, 152, 167, 169, *176-77,* 213, 227, 242, 493, 520, 605; **I** 572; **S** 64, 76, 83, 120, 186, 201, 203

Fellowship of Christian Athletes, **F**

73, 96, 228, 335, 413, 444, 548, 569; **I** 664; **S** 262-63, 406, 453

Fenelon, **O** 184, 223

Fenimore, Robert D. "Bob," **F** *170-72*

Fensky, Charles "Chuck," **O** 446

Fenway Park, Boston, MA, **B** 110, 149, 152, 161, 182, 197, 472, 492, 616,635; **F** 385; **I** 661; **O** 67; **S** 44, 111, 163, 195

Ferdenzi, "Til," **S** 192

Ferdinand, **O** 204, 218, 227, 229

Ferguson, Cathy J., **I** 582

Ferguson, Joe C., Jr., **F** 206

Ferguson, Kent, **I** 492

Ferguson, Robert "Bob," **F** 129; **S** *397-98*

Ferguson, Robert V. "Bob," **B** 111

Ferida, **S** 536

Fernandez, Ignacio, **I** 417

Fernandez, Jorge, **I** 396

Ferns, "Rube," **I** 464, 473

Ferrari Sports Car, **O** 11

Ferraro, Charles "Charlie," **O** 192

Ferrell, Barbara A., **S** *577-78*

Ferrell, George, **B** 177

Ferrell, Marvin, **B** 177

Ferrell, Richard B. "Rick," **B** *177-78*

Ferrell, Wesley C., **B** 169, 177, *178-79,* 490, 566

Ferries, Charles "Chuck," **O** 288

Ferris, Daniel J. "Dan," **I** *670-71*

Ferry, Daniel J. "Danny," **S** *279-81,* 295

Ferry, Robert D., Sr., **S** 279-80

Ferry, Robert D., Jr., **S** 280

Fesler, Wesley E. "Wes," **F** *172-74,* 289; **S** 402

Feustel, Louis, **O** 199, 595

Fiat Race Car, **O** 26

Field Hockey Coach of the Year, **O** 260

Fieldale, VA baseball club (BSL), **S**

102

Fields, "Jackie," I 370, *380-81*, 413, 459, 470

Fields, Judson "Jud," B 453

Fiesta Bowl football game, F 8, 149, 162, 221, 291, 325, 383, 444, 460, 501, 527, 547, 582, 634; S 393, 396, 406, 420, 487

Fiesta Bowl Mile Race, O 533

Fiete, Sandra, I 255

FIFA World All-Star Soccer Game, O 295

"Fight of the Week," S 349

"Fighter of the Year Award," S 613; *See also* Edward J. Neil Award

Fighting Back, S 367

Fighting Fox, O 223

Fighting Nick Bob, I 392

Fighting Spirit, S 420

Fignon, Laurent, S 618

Figure Skating Hall of Fame, I 500, 509, 513, 516

Figure Skating Judges School, Lake Placid, NY, I 500

Fiji National Soccer Team, O 301

Fikotova, Olga, *See* Olga Connolly

Filigrante, S 536

FINA, See International Swimming Federation

Finch, Larry, S 259

Fincher, William E. "Bill," F *175*

Findlay College, I 75

Fingers, Roland G. "Rollie," B *179-80*

Fink, Jule, O 180, 222

Fink, Louis, I 476

Finkelstein, Jacob, *See* "Jackie" Fields

Finks, James E. "Jim," S *398-99*

Finland National Gymnastic Team, I 542

Finland National Hockey Team, I 548

Finland National Soccer Team, O 301

Finland Olympic Wrestling Team, I 662-63

Finley, Charles O. "Charley," B 37, 134, *180-82*, 186, 271-72, 277, 318, 614; S 68, 89, 106, 241-42, 343-44

Finnegan, "Chris," I 384

Finnegan, "Jack," I 407

Finnegan, Kevin, I 397

Finneran, Sharon E., I 611

Finneran, William "Bill," B 373

Firecracker 400 Auto Race, Daytona Beach, FL, O 27-28, 30, 44

Fireman of the Year Award, S 49, 139, 167

Firestone Tire and Rubber Company, O 26

Firestone Tournament of Champions, I 337, 343-44

Firethorn, O 601

Fireways, O 587

Firpo, Luis A., I 374, 412, 477; O 63

First German Soccer Club, Newark, NJ, O 296

First Special Race, O 593

First Union 400 NASCAR Race, S 605

Fischer, "Eddie" P., O 325, 413

Fischer, Robert J. "Bobby," I *671-72*

Fischer, William "Bill," F *175-76*, 231, 249, 345

Fiscus, Lawson, F *176-77*

Fiscus, Newell, F 177

Fiscus, Ross, F 177

Fish, Hamilton, F *177-78*

Fish, Jenny, O 364

Fisher, Harry A., I *84-85*

Fisher, Paul, I 39

Fisher, Raymond L. "Ray," B 323, 476

Fisher, Young, I 372

Fishwick, Diana L., O 165; S 521

Fisk, Carlton E., B *182-83*

Fiske, William M. L. III "Billy," **O** *258-59*, 318

Fiske Memorial Trophy, **O** 258

Fitch, Billy C. "Bill," **I** 9; **S** *281-82*

Fitchburg Business College, **S** 582

Fitipaldi, Emerson, **S** 619

Fitz Gerald, Edward R. "Ed," **B** 448

Fitzgerald, "Ed," **F** 614; **I** 555

Fitzgerald, Raymond, **S** 346

Fitzgerald, Roy, **O** 400

Fitzgerald, GA baseball club (GFL), **B** 595

Fitz Herbert, **S** 526-27

Fitzsimmons, Frederick L. "Freddie," **B** *183-84*, 467, 553; **I** 62

Fitzsimmons, James "Jimmy," **O** 185

Fitzsimmons, James E., **O** *184-85*, 208, 223, 572, 585, 598, 601, 605

Fitzsimmons, John, **O** 185

Fitzsimmons, Lowell "Cotton," **I** 107

Fitzsimmons, Robert L. "Bob," **I** 369, 373, 407-08, 445, 457, 460

Five Seasons, **S** 336, 348

Flaherty, Raymond "Ray," **F** *178-79*, 385-86, 645

Flam, Herbert "Herb," **O** 554

Flambino, **O** 601

Flamboyant, **O** 191

Flamingo Stakes, **O** 222, 225, 575-76, 598, 606, 610

Flanagan, John J., **O** *459-60*, 489, 491, 524

Flanagan, William "Hoot," **S** 439

Flanders, **O** 210

Flanley, George, **B** 122

Flannery, "Doc," **O** 587

Flannery Cup Lacrosse Club, **O** 239

Flash Stakes, **O** 224-25

Flatbush Stakes, **O** 221, 578, 604

Flatley, Paul R., **F** 458

Fleet City Navy football club, **S** 460

Fleet City Training Base, **F** 670

Fleetfoot, **O** 583

Fleischer, Nathaniel "Nat," **I** 357, 371, *381-82*, 400, 410, 432, 450, 644, 649

Fleischman, Julius, **B** 199

Fleitz, Beverly Baker Beckett, **O** 357-58; **S** *549-50*

Fleitz, John, **S** 549-50

Fleming, Marvin "Marv," **F** 292

Fleming, Peggy, *See* Peggy Fleming Jenkings

Fleming, Peter, **O** 369-70

Flesch, William "Bill," **I** 338

Fletcher, Arthur "Art," **B** 269; **S** 55

Fletcher, Robert "Bobby," **F** 241

Flick, Elmer H., **B** *184-85*, 322, 524

Flint, MI baseball club (MOL), **B** 317; **F** 510

Flippen, J. C., **O** 45

Flirtilla, **O** 608

Flood, Aaron Ross, **S** *608-09*

Flood, Curtis C. "Curt," **B** 67, *185-87*, 449; **O** 58, 61

Flood, John, **S** 608

Flora Temple, **O** 230, *583-84*

Florence, **O** 589

Florence State Teachers College, *See* University of North Alabama

Flores, **O** 585

Flores, Ramon, **I** 363

Flores, Thomas R. "Tom," **F** *179-80*

Florida Agricultural & Mechanical University, **B** 140, 369; **F** 312, 501; **I** 173; **O** 344, 468

Florida Amateur Athlete of the Year, **F** 104

Florida Aquatics Swim Team, **I** 596

Florida Association of Broadcasters, **O** 49

Florida Citrus Golf Classic, **O** 135

Florida Derby, **O** 225, 598, 610-11

Florida East Coast Golf Tournament, **S** 521

Florida Intercollegiate Ladies Golf

Tournament, **S** 506

Florida International University, **S** 508

Florida International University Hall of Fame, **S** 508

Florida Junior College Golf Championship, **S** 523

Florida Sports Hall of Fame, **F** 105, 226; **O** 2, 49; **S** 516

Florida State Golf Tournament, **S** 521

Florida State League, **S** 1-2, 15, 34, 51, 67, 93, 114, 136, 140, 205, 217, 236, 244

Florida State Swim Championships, **I** 591

Florida State University, **F** 50, 206, 288; **I** 53, 189; **O** 126; **S** 108, 369, 406-07, 459

Florissant Valley Community College, **O** 301

Flowers, Bruce, **I** 451

Flowers, Theodore "Tiger," **I** 372, 394, 474

Floyd, Eric A. "Sleepy," **I** 83, 266, 283

Floyd, Raymond L. "Ray," **O** *125-26*

Flutie, Douglas R. "Doug," **F** *180-82*

Flying Dutchman Class, **O** 103

Flying Ebony, **O** 216

Flying Outriggers, **O** 278

Flying Paster, **O** 610

Flynn, "Jim," **I** 376, 448

Flyweight Boxing Championships, **I** 389, 400, 417, 431, 435 , 447, 450, 480-81

Fogarty, "Jack," **I** 373

Fogg, May P., **O** 270

Fohl, Leo A. "Lee," **B** 145, 625

Folley, Zora, **I** 384, 527

Follis, Charles W., **F** *182-83*

Fondy, Dee V., **B** 312

Fonseca, Lewis A. "Lew," **B** 14; **S**

101

Foolish Pleasure, **O** 604

Football crisis (1905-06), **F** 86

Football Digest, **F** 119; **S** 191

Football Immortals, **S** *498*

Football News, **F** 62, 137, 332, 413, 457, 581, 671; **S** 393, 419

Football Roundup, **F** 461, 635

Football Rules Committee, **S** 502

Football Thesaurus, **F** 595

Football World, **F** 12

Football Writers Association of America, **F** 18, 38, 109, 150, 153-54, 158, 172, 176, 199, 230, 248, 261, 265, 277, 344, 349, 351, 374, 406, 415-16, 439, 457, 460, 468, 495, 497, 499, 512, 514, 525, 530, 570, 575, 598, 621, 630, 671; **I** 372; **O** 61; **S** 362, 396, 419

Football Writers Association of America Distinguished Service Award, **O** 61

Football Writers Association of New York, **O** 62

Forbes, Harry, **I** 434

Forbes, J. Malcolm, **O** *185-86*

Forbes Farm, Milton, MA, **O** 185

Forbes Field, Pittsburgh, PA, **B** 97, 158, 213, 453, 530, 581; **F** 580; **S** 219, 486

Ford, Christopher J. "Chris," **I** 169

Ford, "Danny," **S** *399-400*

Ford, Douglas M. "Doug," Sr., **O** *125-26*

Ford, Edward C. "Whitey," **B** *187-88*, 375, 470, 485, 497; **S** 74

Ford, Gerald R., **F** 280, 414; **I** 611; **O** 435

Ford, Henry, **I** 433; **O** *9-10*, 26

Ford, Leonard G., Jr. "Len," **F** 70, *183-84*, 409

Ford, Michael, **O** 125

Ford, Phil J., Jr., **I** 282; **S** *282-83*

Ford, William Clay, **F** 529

Ford Athletic Club Soccer Club, **O** 293

Ford C. Frick Award, **O** 50; **S** 344, 350, 358

Ford Model-T Race Car, **O** 10

Ford Motor Company, **O** 8-11, 22, 27, 44

Fordham Ram, **O** 60

Fordham University, **B** 175, 202, 426, 539; **F** 39-40, 73, 102, 168, 188, 214, 318, 344, 350, 352-53, 378-79, 387, 407, 644, 661; **I** 67, 132, 180; **O** 60, 71, 92, 385, 442; **S** 148-49, 266, 311, 339-40, 390-91, 400-01, 452, 477, 587

Forego, **O** *584-85*

Foreman, Earl, **I** 17

Foreman, Francis I. "Frank," **B** 450

Foreman, George, **I** 353, *382-83,* 386, 442, 462

Foreman, Walter E. "Chuck," **F** *184-85,* 485

Forest, **S** 531

Forest Hills Tennis Championships, *See* United States Outdoor Tennis Championships

Forester Magazine, **O** 89

Forli, **O** 611

Formula Atlantic Cars, **S** 619

Formula 500 Auto Race Circuit, **O** 37

Forsythe, Dorothy Hamill, **I** *503-05,* 516, 518

Fort Belvoir, VA football club, **F** 127

Fort Benning, GA basketball club, **I** 254

Fort Benning, GA football club, **F** 186-87, 639

Fort Green Park, Brooklyn, NY, **O** 324

Fort Knox, KY football club, **F** 464

Fort Lauderdale, FL baseball club (FIL, FSL), **B** 233, 387

Fort Lauderdale, FL Soccer Club (NASL), **O** 298

Fort Monmouth, NJ football club, **S** 405

Fort Ord, CA football club, **F** 332

Fort Pierce football club, **F** 358

Fort Scott Community College, **F** 219

Fort Sill, OK football club, **F** 622

Fort Smith, AR baseball club (WA), **B** 233, 236, 387, 583

Fort Union, VA Military Academy, **S** 487

Fort Wayne, IN baseball club (CL, ISL, WA, WeIL, WL), **B** 217, 237, 308, 408, 454; **S** 82, 238

Fort Wayne, IN Hoosiers basketball club (ABL), **I** 30, 32, 222-23, 250

Fort Wayne IN Kekiongas baseball club (NA), **B** 388-89, 603

Fort Wayne, IN Knights of Columbus baseball club, **S** 287

Fort Wayne, IN Zollner Pistons basketball club (ABL, NBA), **I** 11, 45, 86, 105, 110, 132-34, 194-95, 239, 270; **S** 270, 277, 293

Fort Worth, TX baseball club (AA, TL), **B** 9, 174, 258, 261, 313, 420, 456, 609, 614, 618; **S** 131, 245

Fort Worth, TX Women's International Golf Tournament, **O** 172

Fort Worth, TX Wonders baseball club (Negro Leagues), **B** 500

Fortmann, Daniel J. "Danny," **F** *185-86*

Fortunato, Joseph F. "Joe," **F** *186-87*

Forty Niner, **O** 222

Forward Pass, **O** 222

Fosbury, Richard D. "Dick," **O** *460-61*

Foss, Frank K., **O** *461-62*

Foster, Andrew "Rube," **B** 29, 88, 144, *188-90*, 192, 243-44, 255, 286, 342, 452, 549, 612; **S** 19-20, 43, 129, 137, 143, 168, 224

Foster, Brendan, **O** 489

Foster, Charles W., **O** 447

Foster, George A., **B** *190-91*, 544

Foster, Gregory "Greg," **O** 507; **S** 118

Foster, Harold E. "Bud," **I** 85, 206

Foster, "Pop," **I** 435

Foster, Robert, **S** 623

Foster, Robert W. "Bob," **I** *383-85*, 386

Foster, Stephen, **O** 584

Foster, William "Bill," **I** 179

Foster, "Willie," **B** 30, *192*

Foster Hewitt Award, **S** 353

Fothergill, Dorothy "Dotty," **I** *342-43*

Fountain of Youth Stakes, **O** 610-11

Four Horsemen, **F** 95, 121, 187-90, 200, 338, 381, 424, 505-06, 627, 645-46; **S** 440

Four States Area Hall of Fame, **I** 57

Fourie, Pierre, **I** 385

Fournet, Sidney "Sid," **F** 599

Fournier, John F. "Jack," **B** *193*; **S** 201

Foust, Lawrence M. "Larry," **I** *85-86*, 180

Fouts, Daniel F. "Dan," **F** 105, *190-91*, 248, 291, 295, 384, 632

Fouts, Robert, **F** 190

Foutz, David L. "Dave," **B** *194-95*

Fowler, John W. "Bud," **B** *195-96*

Fowler, Larry, **F** 126

Fox, "Billy," **I** 418, 424

Fox, Jacob Nelson, **B** 13, *196-97*; **S** 106, 220

Fox, "Jimmy," **I** 415

Fox, Michael "Mike," **O** 295

Fox Cities, WI baseball club (ML, 3IL), **B** 339, 364, 455, 595

Fox Point, RI Soccer Hall of Fame, **O** 309

Foxx, James E. "Jimmie," **B** 101, *197-98*, 222, 242, 267, 290, 359, 376, 401, 432, 471, 634-35; **S** 1, 81, 155

Foy, Joseph A. "Joe," **B** 431

Foyt, Anthony J., Sr., **O** 10

Foyt, Anthony J., Jr. "A.J.," **O** *10-11*, 21, 28, 34, 36, 38; **S** 614

Francis, Samuel H. "Sam," **F** 263

Francis H. Burr Scholarship, **S** 501

Franck, George H., **F** 555

Franco, Edmund "Ed," **F** 39, 188, 353; **S** *400-01*

Frank, Arthura A., **F** 191-92

Frank, Clinton E. "Clint," **F** *191-93*

Frank, Stanley, **I** 51

Frank G. Dickinson System, **F** 388, 400, 424, 483

Frank Gibbons Good Guy Award, **S** 78

Frank Gill, **O** 211

Frank Haggerty Award, **S** 323

Frank J. Cumiskey Hall of Fame, *See* National Gymnastics Judges Association Hall of Fame

Frank Selke Trophy, **S** 539, 544

Frankford Yellow Jackets football club (NFL), **F** 34, 103, 350, 403, 646; **S** 425, 439

Frankfurt, Germany Gymnastic Meet, **I** 525

Frankian, Malcolm, **S** 290

Franklin, Benjamin "Ben," **I** *590-91*; **O** 136

Franklin, Ronald "Ronnie," **O** 610

Franklin and Marshall College, **B** 318

Franklin Athletic Club, Cleveland, OH, **F** 468

Franklin College of Indiana, **I** 312; **S**

255

Franklin Field, Philadelphia, PA, **F** 468; **O** 488, 495

Franklin Hill Country Club, **O** 159

Franklin, PA baseball club (TSL), **B** 345

Franklin, PA football club, **F** 61

Franks, Herman L., **B** 81

Fraser, Alexa Stirling, **S** *512*

Fraser, Dawn, **I** 575, 582

Fraser, Donald W. "Don," **O** 277

Fraser, Gretchen C., **O** *277-78,* 284

Fraser, John, **O** 504

Fraser, Neale A., **O** 349

Fraser, Ronald "Ron," **S** *55-56,* 75

Fraser, Steven H. "Steve," **I** 638, *640-41*

Fraser, William A., **O** 277

Fraser, William P. "Willie," **S** 55-56

Fratianne, Linda S., **I** *505-06*

Frazee, Harry H., **B** 492; **S** 111, 190

Frazer, Lee, **O** 31

Frazer, William, **O** 325

Frazier, George, **I** 416

Frazier, Joseph "Joe," **I** 383-84, *385-86*; **O** 533

Frazier, Marvis, **I** 386; **S** 625

Frazier, Walter II "Walt," **I** 15, 21, *86-87,* 133, 194, 220

Fred Haskins Trophy, **S** 510

Fred Hannon, **O** 178

Fred Hutchinson Award, **B** 48, 284

Frederick, Jane W., **O** 481

Frederick C. Miller Award, **O** 344

Frederick, MD baseball club (BRL), **B** 577

Freedman, Andrew, **B** *198-99,* 355; **S** 342

Freedom Bowl football game, **F** 289, 356; **S** 393, 402

Freehan, William A. "Bill," **S** *56-57*

Freehold Raceway, Freehold, NJ, **O** 181

Freeland, **O** 209, 595

Freeman, Ronald J. II "Ron," **O** 438

Freeman, "Tommy," **I** 381, 470, 481

Freese, Eugene L. "Gene," **S** 22

Fregosi, James L. "Jim," **B** 497; **S** 44, *57-58*

Freitas, Antonio, Jr. "Tony," **S** *58-59*

French, Lawrence H. "Larry," **B** *200*

French Amateur Golf Tournament, **O** 165

French Chef, **O** 182

French Grand Prix, **O** 8, 11, 25

French National Alpine Ski Championships, **O** 274

French National Basketball Team, **I** 88

French National Soccer Team, **O** 301

French National Tennis Team, **O** 404

French Olympic Swim Team, **I** 586

French Olympic Water Polo Team, **I** 621

French Open Golf Tournament, **O** 69, 108, 148, 156

French Open Men's Doubles Tennis Championships, **O** 368, 407-08; **S** 561

French Open Men's Singles Tennis Championships, **O** 330, 341-42, 355, 384, 407; **S** 556

French Open Mixed Doubles Tennis Championships, **O** 369

French Open Women's Doubles Tennis Championships, **O** 337, 348, 352, 357-58, 360, 364, 381, 387, 397

French Open Women's Singles Tennis Championships, **O** 328-29, 344, 349, 351, 353, 357-59, 364, 380, 387; **S** 550

French Sporting Club, New York, NY, **S** 626

Freshman of the Year, **S** 302

Fresno, CA Auto Race, **O** 7

Fresno, CA City College, **F** 179; **S** 130

Fresno, CA Giants baseball club (CaL), **B** 39, 191; **S** 30, 92, 131, 134

Fresno, CA Pacific College, **B** 460

Fresno, CA Relays, **S** 590

Fresno, CA State University, **O** 556; **S** 71, 320; *See also* California State University at Fresno

Frey, Benjamin R. "Bennie," **B** 237

The Friar, **S** 536

Friar Rock, **S** 526-27

Frick, Ford C., **B** *200-02*, 206, 216, 382, 476; **S** 232, 344, 350, 358

Frickey, Herman, **F** 555

Friddle, Carlyle, **I** 312

Frieden, Diane, **I** 255

Friedman, Benjamin "Benny," **F** 95, *193-95*, 442; **O** 63-64

Friedman, Max H. "Marty," **I** *87-88*, 273

Friedricks, Robert, *See* Ed "Strangler" Lewis

Friend, Robert B. "Bob," **S** *59-60*

Frietas, Robert, **B** 561

Frisch, Frank F. "Frankie," **B** 45, *202-03*, 260, 302, 387

Frisinger, Jesse, **B** 34

Fritz, John, **I** 646

Frizette, **S** 537

Frnka, Henry, **F** 77

Fromme, Arthur H. "Art," **B** 230; **S** 4

Frontier Conference, **F** 589

Fruenczy, "Alex," **O** 499

Frush, "Danny," **I** 415

Fry, Evelyn, **O** 359

Fry, Ida, **O** 359

Fry, John Hayden, Jr., **S** *401-02*

Fry, Lester, **O** 359

Fry, Shirley, **I** 550; *See also* Shirley Fry Irvin

Fryar, Irving D., **F** *195-96*

Ftorek, Robin B., "Robbie," **I** *553-55*, 566

Fuchs, James E. "Jim," **O** 509

Fukuoka, Japan Marathon, **O** 523, 528, 536

Fulks, Joseph E. "Joe," **I** *88-89*, 102, 239

Fuller, Jay, **I** 386

Fuller, Peter, **O** 225

Fuller, Steven "Steve," **S** 383

Fuller, William **I** 440; **S** 360, 367

Fullerton, Hugh, Sr., **S** *345-46*

Fullerton, Hugh, Jr., **S** 346

Fullerton, CA Aquatics Swim Club, **S** 607

Fulljames, George, **I** 373

Fullmer, "Don," **I** 386, 396

Fullmer, "Gene," **I** 359, *386-87*, 455-56

Fuqua, Ivan W., **O** 466

Furey, James "Jim," **I** 21, 65; **S** 314

Furillo, Carl A., **B** 9, 467; **S** *60-61*, 162

Furlane, "Nicky," **I** 452

Furman University, **F** 175; **I** 113, 625; **O** 117; **S** 318

Furuhashi, Hironoshin, **I** 603

Fusina, Chuck A., **S** 454

Futch, Edward, **S** 623

Futurity Stakes, **O** 221, 224, 578, 598-99, 611; **S** 533

Gable, Daniel M. "Dan," **I** 635, *641-43*, 652, 662, 666

Gabriel, Roman L., Jr., **F** 96, *197-98*, 285, 640

Gadsden, AL baseball club (SEL), **B** 87

Gaedel, Edward C. "Eddie," **B** 574

Gaetjens, Joseph, **O** 291

Gaffney, John H., **B** 310

Gahr, Marlies, **O** 436

Gain, Robert "Bob," F 74, *198-99*

Gainer, Delos C. "Del," B 112

Gaines, Ambrose IV "Rowdy," I *591-93*, 605

Gaines, Clarence E. "Bighouse," I *89-91*

Gaines, Reginald, I 91

Gainor, "Al," I 426

Gaiters, Robert "Bob," F 663

Galan, August J. "Augie," S *61-62*

Galbraith, Clinton "Clint," O 600

Galbreath, Daniel M. "Dan," B *205-06*

Galbreath, John W., B *205-06*; F 289; O 612

Galbreath Farm, Lexington, KY, O 612

Gale, Lauren H., I *91-92*

Galehouse, Dennis W. "Denny," S 163

Galesburg, IL baseball club (CIL, ItML), B 4, 195

Galicia Soccer Club, O 300

Gallagher, David D. "Dave," F 527

Gallagher, Edward C. "Ed," I 653, 662; S 608, *609-10*

Gallagher, John "Taps," I 50

Gallagher, Richard "Dick," F 361

Gallagher, "Rudy," S 314

Gallant Bloom, S 527

Gallant Fox, O 184, 215-16, *585-86*, 597, 601

Gallant Man, O 190, 217-18, 573, 603; S 532

Gallatin, Harry J. "The Horse," I *92-93*, 107, 201

Gallico, Paul W., O *63-64*

Gallow, Austin "Rusty," O 256

Galore, S 536

Galveston, TX Anicos basketball club (AAU), I 283

Galveston, TX baseball club (TL), B 406, 456; S 17

Galvin, James F. "Pud," B *206-07*, 604

Gambee, David P. "Dave," I 97

Gamble, Oscar C., B 441; S 22

Gambrill, Donald "Don," I 497

Game and Gossip, F 118

"The Game for All America," S 349

Gammons, Betty, S 347

Gammons, Donald, S 347

Gammons, Edward, Jr., S 347

Gammons, Peter, S *346-47*

Gammoudi, Mohamed, O 498

Gandil, Charles A. "Chick," B 193

Gannett News Service, F 671

Gannon University, S 308

Gans, "Joe" B., I *387-88*, 421, 425, 434, 444, 453, 474, 480

Gant, Harvey, S 605

Gant, John, I 312

Gant, Joseph, *See* Joe B. Gans

Garagiola, Joseph H. "Joe," B 36; O 46, 55, 57, *64-66*, 68, 93; S *353-54*

Garber, Henry Eugene Gene," S *62-63*

Garbisch, Edgar W. "Ed," F *199-201*

Garcia, Ceferino, I 356, 370, 466

Garcia, Edward Miguel "Mike," B 242; S *63-64*, 83

Garden State Park, O 178

Garden State Stakes, O 190, 607

Gardena, CA Auto Race, O 6

Gardiner, Tenley Albright, I *506-07*, 511, 515

Gardner, C. D., O 356

Gardner, George, I 456-57

Gardner, James H. "The Fox," I *93-95*

Gardner, "Jimmy," I 376, 416

Gardner, Robert "Bob," O 439

Gardner, William Lawrence "Larry," B *208*, 280; S 232

Gardner-Webb Junior College, I 97

Garland, Charles "Chuck," **O** 417

Garman Award, **F** 72

Garmisch-Partenkirchen, Germany Winter Olympic Games, *See* Olympic Winter Games, 1936

Garner, Charles, **O** 186

Garner, David, **O** 186

Garner, Guy, **O** 186

Garner, Harry, **O** 186

Garner, Jeffrey "Jeff," **O** 186

Garner, John Mack, **O** *186-87*, 193

Garner, Lambert, **O** 186

Garner, Wayne, **O** 186

Garner, "Willie," **O** 186

Garrett, Michael L. "Mike," **F** *201-02*, 369

Garrett, William "Bill," **I** 192

Garrison, Edward Henry "Snapper," **O** *187*, 200, 205, 209, 219; **S** 527

Garrison, "Jimmy," **I** 356

Garrison, Walter B. "Walt," **F** 273, 331

Garry, R. L., **O** 201

Garsh, Harry, **I** 389

Garver, Ned F., **S** 227

Garvey, Steven P. "Steve," **B** 9, *209-10*, 518, 545; **S** 7, 26, 114, 185

Garza, Josele, **O** 39

Gassaway, Charles C. "Charlie," **S** 107

Gastineau, Marcus D. "Mark," **F** 589

Gaston, Nathaniel Milton "Milt," **S** 200

Gastonia, NC baseball club (WCL), **B** 425

Gate Dancer, **O** 183, 226-27

Gates, William "Pop," **S** *283-84*

Gatewood, William "Bill," **B** 31

Gato Del Sol, **O** 183

Gator Bowl football game, **F** 50, 74, 77-78, 147, 170, 219, 221, 349, 355, 381, 423, 509, 534, 553, 577, 581, 584, 632; **S** 365, 382, 399-

400, 421, 459, 474

Gatski, Frank, **F** *202-04*

Gatzos, Steve, **I** 551

Gault, Willie J., **S** 584

Gautama, **S** 527

Gavilan, Kid, **I** 359, 404, 477

Gavitt, David "Dave," **I** 154

Gavle, Belgium Track and Field Meet, **O** 442

Gavrilenko, Yevgeny, **O** 503

Gay Vic, **O** 267

Gaylord, "Chuck," **I** 526-27

Gaylord, Mitchell J. "Mitch," **I** *526-27*

Gazelle Stakes, **O** 224

Geary baseball club of Philadelphia, **B** 399

Geddes, Jane, **S** 506

Gedeon, Elmer Joseph "Joe," **B** 456; **S** 126

Geers, Edward "Pop," **S** 534

Geertsen, John, **O** 143

Gehrig, Henry Louis "Lou," **B** 29, 49, 106-07, 147, 210-11, 213, 222, 242, *267-69*, 331, 382, 388, 471, 503, 600; **I** 366, 392; **O** 64, 74-75; **S** 7, 127, 146, 152, 340

Gehringer, Charles L. "Charlie," **B** *211-12*, 242, 356, 573

Geisha, **O** 599

Gelbert, Charles M. "Charlie," **F** 204

Gelbert, Charles S., Jr. "Charlie," **F** *204-05*

Gelinas, Martin, **S** 538

Genaro, "Frankie," **I** *389*, 417, 480

General Assembly, **O** 607

Geneva College, **F** 277, 373, 434; **I** 179

Geneva Cup Singles Tennis Championships, **O** 416

Geneva, NY baseball club (NYPL), **B** 372, 485; **S** 166, 216

Geneva, OH baseball club (Ind.), **B**

326

Gentleman's Quarterly, S 337

Genuine Risk, O 211

George, Ed Don, I 661

George IV of England, O 596

George, George, I 628

George, James D. "Jim," I 628

George, Peter Tony, I *627-28*

George, Walter G., O 479, 487, 505, 543

George, William "Bill," F 187, *205*

George Barr's National League Umpiring School, S 122

George C. Calnan Memorial Trophy, I 669

George Foster Peabody Award, O 48, 65, 68

George Fox College, S 33

George Halas Award, S 367, 406, 427

George Kessler, O 598

George Kinney, S 533

George M. Patchen, O 584

George Peabody College for Teachers, I 324

George Smith, O 199

George Washington Golf Classic, S 513-14

George Washington University, B 227, 365; F 345-46; I 11; O 398

George Woolf Memorial Award, O 179

George Young Memorial Award, I 337, 343, 349

Georgetown College of Kentucky, S 384

Georgetown University, B 293, 602; F 231, 344-45, 350, 403, 440, 488, 510; I 56, 82-83, 152, 174, 250, 256, 276-77, 282-83, 300-01, 305, 309; O 558-59; S 259, 264, 293, 310, 367, 397, 434-35, 460, 580

Georgetown University Track and

Field Invitation Meet, O 559

Georgia Amateur Athlete of the Year, I 604-05

Georgia-Florida League, S 219, 246-47

Georgia Football Athletic Hall of Fame, F 175

Georgia Institute of Technology, B 380; F 5-6, 73, 94, 145, 147, 167, 175, 189, 199, 230-31, 257, 287, 338, 345, 504, 506, 561, 604, 618; I 152, 223, 282; O 135, 464; S 365, 381, 478, 617

Georgia Institute of Technology Hall of Fame, F 257

Georgia Military College, F 81

Georgia Navy Pre-Flight Skyscrapers football club, F 237, 576

Georgia Sports Hall of Fame, F 145, 147; 284; O 449, 539; S 516

Georgia Swimmer of the Year, I 604

Geran, "Gerry," S 537

Gerber, James "Jim," I 7

Gerber, Robert "Bob," I 6

Gergen, Joseph "Joe," O 475

German-American Soccer League (GAL), O 291, 300, 309

German-American Soccer League Championships, O 309

German Hungarians of New York Soccer Club, O 291, 309

German Junior Alpine Ski Championships, O 276

German National Soccer Team, O 299

German Olympic Swim Team, I 600

German Open Golf Tournament, O 156

German Ramblers basketball club, *See* Buffalo Germans basketball club

Germantown Cricket Club, O 338, 403

Gerry, Martha Farish, O 584

Gerry Farm, Mill Neck, NY, O 584-85

Gerschweiler, Hans, I 502

Gerulaitis, Vitas, O 369, 380, 387, 397

Gervin, George "Iceman," I *95-96*

Gestring, Marjorie, I 487, 496

Gettysburg College, B 450; I 62

Gettysburg, PA baseball club (BRL), B 162

Ghezzi, Victor "Vic," O 141; S *512-13*

Giachetti, Richie, I 401

Giamatti, Angelo Bartlett, S *64-65*, 239-40

Giard, Joseph O. "Joe," S 200

Gibbons, James "Jim," I 652

Gibbons, Michael J., Sr. "Mike," I *389-90*

Gibbons, Michael J., Jr., I 390

Gibbons, Thomas J. "Tommy," I *390-91*, 412-13

Gibbons, William, O 583

Gibbs, Jerry D., F 622

Gibbs, Joe J., F *206-07*

Gibson, Althea, S 550; *See also* Althea Gibson Darben

Gibson, "Billy," I 421

Gibson, George, F 416; S 425

Gibson, George C., B 581

Gibson, J. L. "Doc," S 545-46

Gibson, "Jerry," B 213

Gibson, Joshua "Josh," B 31, 88, 127, *213-14*, 223, 244, 269, 290, 331, 362-63, 453; S 83

Gibson, Kirk H., S 49, 109

Gibson, Robert "Bob," B *214-15*, 445; F 507; S 212, 354

Gibson, Samuel B. "Sam," S 197

Gibson, Vincent "Vince," S 372

Gibson, William "Billy," F 380-81

Giegengack, Robert "Bob," O 438

Giel, Paul R., F 174; S 201, *402-03*

Gifford, Frank N., F 33, *207-08*, 348, 578; O 47; S 350, 356

Gilbert, Elias, S 572

Gilbert, "Jerry," O 407

Gilbert, Lawrence W. "Larry," B 524

Gilbert, Louis M. "Lou," F 194

Gilbert, Walter J. "Walt," B 250

Giles, George, B 6

Giles, Warren C., B 125, 175, *215-16*, 441

Giles, William Y. "Bill," B 75, 215

Gilkerson's Union Giants baseball club, S 224

Gill, Armony T. "Slats," I *96-97*

Gill, Cynthia, I 485

Gill, Turner H., Jr., F *208-09*

Gillette Razor Company, S 343

Gilliam, Armon L., I 293

Gilliam, James W. "Jim," B 9, 270; S 188

Gillick, Patrick "Pat," S 25

Gillies, Frederick, F 103

Gilliland, G. E., B 561

Gillman, Sidney "Sid," F 127, *210-11*, 367, 382, 432, 525-26; S 442

Gilmer, Harry, F 529, 595, 600

Gilmore, Artis, I *96-97*; S 327

Gimrack, O 101

Ginay, John, I 664

Giordano, Rafelle C., *See* Young Corbett III

Giosa, "Eddie," I 441

Gipp, George, F 12-13, 90, 94, *211-13*, 245, 359, 377, 433, 506, 539, 595, 601

Girard College, S 37

Girones, Jose, I 438

Giudice, Ross, I 231

Give All, O 196

Givens, Robin, S 625

Gjovik, Norway Speed Skating Competition, O 317

Glabby, "Jimmy," I 390

Gladman, Marjorie K., O 409

Glamack, George G., F 215; I 44, *98-100*, 132

Glamocli, Gjuro Gregorvitch, *See* George G. Glamack

Glasgow, Scotland Celtics Soccer Club, O 293, 299-300

Glasgow, Scotland Rangers Soccer Club, O 293

Glassboro State College, I 651

Glassboro State College Hall of Fame, I 651

Glass Bowl football game, F 210

Glasscock, John W. "Jack," B *216-17*; S 47

Glassgow, Willis A. "Bill," F 416

Gleason, Harry G., S 66

Gleason, William J. "Kid," S *65-66*

Gledhill, Keith, O 409-10

Glen Campbell Golf Classic, O 135

Glen Garden Country Club, Fort Worth, TX, O 131

Glen Lakes Country Club, Dallas, TX, O 162

Glen Riddle Farm, O 178

Glen View Golf Course, Golf, IL, O 107

Glencoe, O 602

Glencoe Athletic Club, New York, NY, I 305

Glendale Junior College, O 568

Glenville State College, S 290

Glickman, Martin "Marty," O 315

Glisson, Gordon, O 217

Globe, AZ baseball club (ASL), S 59

Gloucester, MA Race Track, O 194

Glover, Michael "Mike," I 361

Glover, Richard, F 136, 444, 495; I 90; S *403-04*

Glumdalclitch, *See* Peytona

Glyndon, MD Lacrosse Club, O 245

Goal Magazine, S 548

Gobert, A. H., O 362

Godfrey, George, I 366

Godolphin Arabian, O 590, 608

Godoy, Arturo, I 429

Goheen, Francis Xavier "Moose," I *555-56*

Gola, Thomas J. "Tom," I 43, *100-01*, 103, 135, 180, 199, 252

Gold Coast Indy CART Race, S 619-20

Gold Coast Suns baseball club (SPBA), S 26, 84-85

Gold Glove Award, S 16, 26, 51, 57-58, 72, 76, 96, 112, 153, 157, 171, 193, 196, 207, 213, 225, 236-37, 239, 354

Gold Key Award, I 156, 240

Gold Medal Award, S 410

Goldberg, "Benny," I 447

Goldberg, Marshall, F 48, 113, *213-14*; S 381

Golden Act, O 610

Golden Anniversary Award, I 127

Golden Bay Soccer Club, San Francisco, CA (NASL), O 307

Golden Broom, O 196, 199-200

Golden Bu, O 175

Golden Chance Farm, O 590

Golden Gate Fields, Albany, CA, O 217, 577

Golden Gate Park, San Francisco, CA, O 335, 348, 361, 371-72, 374; S 552

Golden Gaters Tennis Team (WIT), S 298

Golden Gloves Boxing Championships, O 52, 63, 104, 217; S 612, 625; *See also* Amateur Athletic Union Boxing Championships

Golden Glow Award, I 45

Golden Hawk Farm, O 205

Golden Key World Sprint, O 317

Golden Lights Golf Tournament, **O** 118

Golden Maxim Farm, St. Matthews, KY, **O** 198

Golden State Warriors basketball club (NBA), **I** 8, 16-18, 34, 46, 58, 100, 102-03, 111, 147, 150, 160-61, 186, 204, 224, 231, 252, 260, 266, 275, 302, 324; **S** 251, 256, 283, 285, 294, 299, 306-08, 313, 315, 328

Golden Submarine Race Car, **O** 26

Golden West Broadcasters, **F** 492

Golden West College Pool, **I** 575

Golden West Invitation Track and Field Meet, **O** 541

Goldenberg, Charles "Buckets," **F** 329

Goldman, "Sammy," **I** 363-64

Goldsmith, Alden, **O** *586*

Goldsmith, Fred E., **B** 116

Goldsmith Maid, **O** 174, 586

Goldsmith Sporting Goods Company, **O** 172

Goldstein, "Abe," **I** 431

Goldstein, "Ruby," **I** 392, 395, 435

Goldstein, Walter, *See* Walter Miller

Golf, **O** 69

Golf Digest, **O** 124, 126, 152, 166-67; **S** 337, 509, 517

Golf Digest Comeback Player of the Year, **O** 167

Golf Digest LPGA Founders Cup Award, **S** 517

Golf Digest Rookie of the Year, **O** 124

Golf Hall of Fame, **O** 120, 127, 132, 150, 154, 158, 162; **S** 516

Golf Magazine, **O** 116; **S** 505, 508

Golf Magazine Player of the Year, **O** 116

Golf World, **O** 69

Golf Writers Association of America, **O** 69, 116, 132, 139, 143; **S** 519-20

Golf Writers Association of America Player of the Year, **O** 115-16, 143

Gomez, Vernon L. "Lefty," **B** *217-18,* 490, 553; **S** 462

Gone West, **O** 222

Gonfalon, **S** 526-27

Gonsalves, William A. "Billy," **O** *298-300,* 310

Gonzaga University, **F** 88-89, 148, 178

Gonzales, Richard A. "Pancho," **O** *355-56,* 390, 407-08; **S** 553-54

Gonzalez, Jose Luis, **O** 532

Gonzalez, Miguel A. "Mike," **B** 231

Good Enough to Dream, **S** 352

Good Guy Award, **O** 191

Good Hands Equestrian Award, **O** 267

Good Housekeeping, **O** 64

Goodbody, Manliffe F., **O** 419

Goode, John M., **O** 199

Goodell, Brian S., **I** *593-94*

Gooden, Dwight E., **S** 76

Goodman, "Izzie," **I** 675

Goodman, "Jimmy," **I** 416

Goodman, John "Johnny," **O** 138, 155

Goodman, Joseph "Joe," **O** 215

Goodman, William D. "Billy," **B** 300; **S** *66-67*

Goodreault, Eugene "Gene," **F** 344

Goodrich, Gail C., Jr., **I** *101-02,* 210, 260, 331; **S** 251

Goodrich, "Jimmy," **I** *391-92,* 411

Goodson, James Edward "Ed," **S** 244

Goodwill Games, **I** 215, 658; **O** 103, 425, 481, 486, 503-04, 558; **S** 296, 584, 603, 607-08

Goody's 500 Auto Race, Martinsville, VA, **O** 41

Goolagong, Evonne, **O** 352, 381; **S** 339

Goose, Roscoe, **O** 198

Goose's Gang Bowling Team, **I** 351

Gordien, Fortune E., **O** 510; **S** *578*

Gordon, Bridgette, **I** 291

Gordon, John "Jackie," **I** 573

Gordon, Joseph L. "Joe," **B** 346, 381, 469, 583; **S** 33, *67-68*, 107

Gordon, Malcom K., **I** 543, *556-57*

Gordon, Sidney "Sid," **S** *68-69*

Gore, Arthur W., **O** 334, 414

Gore, George F. "Piano Legs," **B** 496; **S** *69-70*

Gore, Irwin, **I** 338

Gore, William "Bill," **I** 362

Goslin, Leon A. "Goose," **B** *218-19*, 226, 376, 453

Goss, Eleanor, **O** 389

Goss, "Woody," **I** 385

Gossage, Richard M. "Goose," **B** *220*; **S** 216

Gotch, Frank A., **I** *643-44*

Gotham Bowl football game, **F** 71, 136

Gotham Stakes, **O** 579

Gottfried, Brian, **O** 324

Gottleib, Edward "Eddie," **B** 331; **I** 14, *102-03*, 178, 252

Gotzis, Austria Track and Field Meet, **O** 481

Goucher College, **O** 254

Gould, Alan, **F** 192

Goullet, Alfred, **O** 264

Gourdin, Edward O. "Ned," **O** 463, 465

Gourdine, Simon, **S** 240

Governali, Paul V., **F** 350; **S** *404-05*

Governor of Florida Award, **O** 13

Governor's Trophy, **O** 28

Gowdy, Curtis "Curt," **O** 63, 65, *66-69*, 84, 100; **S** 348, 353

Goyette, Cynthia L., **I** 582

Graceland College, **O** 474-75

Gradishar, Randy C., **S** *405-06*

Graebner, Carol C., **S** 550

Graebner, Clark E., **O** 324; **S** 561

Graef, "Jed," **I** 485

Graf, "Steffi," **O** 352, 379-80, 397

Grafton, WV YMCA Basketball Team, **S** 290

Graham, "Bushy," **I** 389, 417

Graham, Charles H. "Charlie," **B** 259

Graham, Earnest, **I** 71

Graham, Frank, **B** 20; **F** 115

Graham, Louis K. "Lou," **O** 126

Graham, Michael, **I** 300

Graham, Otto E., Jr., **F** 2, 70, 203, *214-16*, 362, 409, 447, 559, 566, 627

Graham, William "Billy," **I** 359

Grambling College, **F** 72, 75-76, 131, 139, 295, 499-501; **I** 247; **O** 438

Gramercy Park Gymnasium, New York, NY, **I** 449

Grand Award of Sports, **I** 615

Grand Canyon College, **S** 327

Grand Circuit Harness Racing, **O** 182, 191, 207

Grand Forks, ND baseball club (NoL), **B** 530

Grand National Auto Racing Championships, **O** 17, 29-30

Grand National Tabogganing Championships, **O** 258

Grand Prix de l'Academy des Sports, Paris, France, **I** 616

Grand Prix, Lima, Peru, **S** 620

Grand Prix Tennis, **O** 365, 370

Grand Rapids, MI baseball club (MISL, WL), **B** 78, 121, 229, 579, 601

Grand Rapids, MI Hornets basketball club, **I** 99

Grand Street Boys Athletic Club, New York, NY, **S** 594

Grand Union Hotel Stakes, **O** 578,

595, 598

Grand Union Prize Race, O 206

Grange, Harold E. "Red," F 98, 152, 178, *216-18*, 234, 243, 299, 360, 381, 392, 417, 424, 601, 646, 669-70, 674; O 87-88

Grant, Bryan M., Jr. "Bitsy," O 410, 418; S 556

Grant, Charles "Charlie," B 255

Grant, Chester "Chet," F 595

Grant, Edward L. "Eddie," B 230-31; S 4

Grant, Frank, B 221

Grant, Harold P. "Bud," F 185, *218-19*; S 399

Grant, James T. "Mudcat," B 179

Grant, Wylie, O 377

Grant Field, Atlanta, GA, F 231

Grantham, George F. "Boots," B 114; S *70-71*

Grantland Rice Memorial Award, O 61, 96

Granville, O 184, 223, 585

Grattan, S 526-27

Graves, Adam, S 538

Graves, "Tubby," I 76

Gravesend Track, Brooklyn, NY, O 211; S 533

Gray, Clinton, O 525

Gray, Clyde, S 612

Gray, "Dolly," F 13

Gray, "Jack," I 205

Gray, Leonard, I 292

Gray, Melvin D. "Mel," F *219-20*

Gray, Ted G., B 503

Gray, William "Bill," F 211

Gray, William "Bill," O 163

Gray, Wyndol, I 7

Grayson, "Harry," F 221, 439

Grayson, Mark, I 97

Grayson, Robert H. "Bobby," F 24, *220-21*, 300, 513

Graziano, "Rocky," I *392-94*, 482-83

Graziano, "Tommy Rocky," I 393

Great American Stakes, O 224-25, 569

Great and Greatest Bowling Tournament, I 342

Great Britain National Basketball Team, I 281

Great Britain National Polo Team, O 260

Great Britain Olympic Wrestling Team, I 651

Great Chesire Stakes, O 201

Great Falls, MT baseball club (MtSL, PrL), B 556; S 30

Great Lakes Bowl football game, F 74, 198

Great Lakes Naval Training Station basketball club, I 61, 99, 130

Great Lakes Naval Training Station football club, F 69, 112, 152, 165, 218, 233, 327, 345, 409, 555, 559, 627; S 384, 461, 480

Great Lakes Naval Training Station Track and Field Team, S 588

Great Long Island Stakes, O 597

Great Metropolitan Stakes, O 201

Great Plains Wrestling Tournament, I 657

Great State Post Stakes, O 594

Great Trial Stakes, O 578

Greater Buffalo Open Bowling Tournament, I 349

Greater Greensboro, NC Open Golf Tournament, O 124, 127, 158, 167; S 516

Greater Hartford, CT Open Golf Tournament, O 126, 163

Greater Jacksonville, FL Open Golf Tournament, O 124-26

Greater New York Irish-American Athletic Association, O 466

Greater St. Louis Hall of Fame, I 127

The Greatest Giants of Them All, S

347

Greb, "Harry," **I** 355, 376, 390-91, *394-95*, 416, 428, 471, 475

Greco-Roman Style Wrestling, **S** 624

Green, David "Dave," **I** 422

Green, Dorothy, **O** 329

Green, George, **I** 460

Green, George Dallas, **B** 230; **S** 134

Green, Hubert M. II, **O** *126-27*, 164

Green, Hugh D., **F** *221-22*; **S** 480

Green, "Jerry," **F** 529

Green, Katherine Rawls "Kathy," **I** *487-88*, 494, 496

Green, Leroy, **I** 384

Green, Sidney, **I** 293

Green, Sihugo "Si," **S** *284-85*

Green, Woodrow, Jr. "Woody," **F** 325; **S** *406-07*

Green Bay baseball club (3IL, WSL), **B** 138, 264; **S** 162

Green Bay Bobcats hockey club, **I** 565

Green Bay Packers football club (NFL), **F** 1, 12, 28, 30, 33, 55, 68-69, 76-78, 89, 92, 97-98, 102, 104, 107, 131, 133, 136-38, 142-43, 148, 151-52, 170, 184, 188, 197, 199, 222-24, 256, 258, 260, 267, 271, 275, 278, 281-83, 291-92, 303, 315, 321-23, 328-29, 346, 351-55, 361, 372, 374-75, 392-93, 417, 430, 480, 487, 495-96, 502, 517, 529, 555, 567, 572, 575, 585, 587-88, 591, 599, 602, 607-08, 615, 618, 639, 651-53, 662; **O** 80, 104; **S** 363-64, 375, 381, 384, 390, 401, 408, 426, 429-30, 436, 439-41, 452, 458, 463, 469, 474, 486, 491, 503

Green Bay Packers Hall of Fame, **F** 89, 152, 267, 271, 282, 284, 568, 662

Green Mountain Maid, **O** 584

Green Speed, **O** 191

Greenalgh, John, **O** 544

Greenberg, Henry B. "Hank," **B** *221-23*, 563; **S** 56, 69

Greenberg, "Steve," **S** 56

Greenbriar Golf Classic, White Sulphur Springs, WV, **O** 158

Greenbriar Pool, White Sulphur Springs, WV, **I** 623

Greene, Charles E. "Charlie," **O** *471-72*

Greene, Charles E. "Mean Joe," **F** *222-23*, 247; **S** 407

Greene, Frank, **F** 200

Greenlee, William A. "Gus," **B** 88, *223-24*, 290, 436, 453; **I** 426

Greenlee Field, Pittsburgh, PA, **B** 88, 223

Greensboro Junior College, **O** 29

Greensboro, NC baseball club (CrL, Pil), **B** 179, 376, 403; **S** 136, 147

Greensburg, PA Athletic Association football club, **F** 176-77, 665

Greensburg, PA baseball club (PSA), **B** 114; **S** 113

Greentree Stables, **O** 175, 178, 198; **S** 534

Greenville, MI baseball club (MISL), **B** 195

Greenville, MS baseball club (EDL), **S** 207

Greenville, SC baseball club (ECaL, EDL, SAL, WCL), **B** 115, 313, 497, 574, 583; **S** 17, 51, 108, 153

Greenville, TN baseball club (ApL), **S** 1

Greenville, TX baseball club (ETL), **B** 387

Greenwade, Thomas "Tom," **B** 374

Greenwood, David K., **S** *285-86*

Greenwood, Joseph, **S** 285

Greenwood, L. C., **S** 285, *407-08*

Greenwood, SC baseball club (EDL, WCL), **B** 8, 409

Greer, Harold E. "Hal," **I** 58, *103-04*; **S** 291

Greer, Lurlyne E., *See* Lurlyne Greer Rogers

Greer, Ralph, **I** 253

Gregg, Alvis Forrest, Sr., **F** *223-24*, 354, 397, 662

Gregg, Alvis Forrest, Jr., **F** 224, 662

Gregor, Gary W., **I** 279

Grekin, Norman "Norm," **I** 100, 180

Grelle, James E. "Jim," **O** 526

Grenada, **S** 536

Grenoble, France Speed Skating Competition, **O** 317

Grenoble, France Winter Olympic Games, *See* Olympic Winter Games, 1968

Gretel, **O** 266

Gretz, Teresa Shank, **I** 258

Gretzky, Wayne, **S** 538

Grey Cup Championship football game, **F** 218

Grey Lag, **S** 526-27

Grey Lap Handicap, **O** 178

Greyhound, **O** *586-87*

Grich, Robert M. "Bobby," **S** 44, *71-72*

Grier, Roosevelt "Rosey," **F** *224-25*, 298, 397, 441, 503

Griese, Robert A. "Bob," **F** 122, *225-26*, 333, 384, 404-05, 524, 642; **O** 538

Griffey, George Kenneth, Sr. "Ken," **B** 544; **S** *72-73*

Griffey, George Kenneth, Jr. "Ken," **S** 73

Griffin, Archie M., **F** *226-28*, 412; **S** 263

Griffin, "Corn," **I** 360

Griffin, Gilroye, **S** 240

Griffin, "Hank," **I** 407

Griffin, Henry F. "Harry," **O** *187-89*

Griffin, Michael J. "Mike," **B** 224-25

Griffin, Peck, **O** 362

Griffing, Glynn, **F** 622

Griffith, Calvin R., Sr. "Cal," **B** 225, 227-28, 305; **S** 13-14

Griffith, Clark C. "The Old Fox," **B** 11, 91-92, 160-61, *225-28*, 245, 304, 321, 331, 400, 408, 430, 470, 524, 554, 606; **S** 13-14, 231

Griffith, Delorez Florence, *See* Delorez Florence Griffith-Joyner

Griffith, Emile A., **I** *395-96*

Griffith, "Johnny," **I** 361

Griffith-Joyner, Delorez Florence, **S** *579-80*

Griffith Stadium, Washington, DC, **B** 213, 318, 453-54; **S** 212

Griffo, Young, **I** 420

Grim, "Joe," **I** 377

Grimek, John C., **I** 629

Grimes, Burleigh A., **B** *228-29*; **S** 117

Grimm, Charles J. "Charlie," **B** 29, 41, 114, *229-30*, 246, 573; **S** 70

Grimsley, Will H., **O** *69-70*

Grimstead, Oscar "Swede," **I** 21

Grimtrae Stud Farm, **O** 575, 613

Grinnell College, **O** 549

Groat, Richard M. "Dick," **I** *104-05*; **S** 239

Grogan, James D. "Jimmy," **I** 514

Groh, Henry K. "Heinie," **B** 66, *230-31*, 302, 332; **S** 4

Groh, Lewis C. "Lew," **B** 231

Gromek, Stephen J. "Steve," **S** 215

Gros, Yvonne, **O** *259-60*

Gross Medical School, Denver, CO, **I** 229

Grosse Point, MI Auto Race, **O** 9

Grossfeld, Abraham I. "Abie," **I** *527-28*, 529

Grossfeld, Muriel Davis, **I** *528-29*

Grote, Gerald W. "Jerry," **S** 244

Grout, "Jack," **O** 146

Grove, Robert M. "Lefty," **B** 101, *231-33*, 241, 359, 401, 437, 444, 453, 468, 634-35; **O** 74; **S** 99, 183, 242

Grove City College, **F** 40, 60-61

Groza, Alex J., **I** 166, 212, 233, 257; **O** 261, *286-87*

Groza, Frank, **I** 286

Groza, John, **I** 286

Groza, Louis R. "Lou," **F** 25, 55, 70, *229*, 409, 633; **S** 286, 362

Gruber, Kelly W., **S** 74

Gruenig, Robert F. "Bob," **I** *105-06*

Grumman Flyers basketball club, **S** 283

Gruner, G. A., **B** 576

Guerin, Oliver Eric, **O** *189*, 599

Guerin, Richard V. "Richie," **I** *106-07*

Guernsey, Frank, **S** 557

Guerrero, Roberto, **O** 37

Guglielmi, Ralph V., **F** 338

Guida, Louis "Lou," **O** 600

Guidry, Ronald A. "Ron," **B** *233-34*

Guiffi, Ignazio P., *See* Harry Jeffra

Guilford College, **B** 177

The Guinness Book of Records, **I** 626

Gulch, **O** 218

Guldahl, Ralph, **O** *127-28*, 155

Gulf Coast League, **S** 15, 51, 174, 217, 237, 471

Gulf States Conference, **F** 53, 59, 557

Gulf States League, **S** 428

Gulfstream Park Handicap, **O** 603

Gulick, Luther H., **I** *107-08*

Gullett, Donald E. "Don," **S** *73-74*

Gulotta, Peter, *See* Pete Herman

Gun Fire, **O** 175

Gunderson, JoAnne, *See* JoAnne Gunderson Carner

Gunsel, Austin, **F** 516

Gunter, Nancy Richey, **S** *550-51*, 563

Guokas, Matthew G., Jr. "Matt," **I** 112

Gurney, Daniel S. "Dan," **O** *11-12*, 19, 25, 28

Gushikin, Koji, **I** 541

Gustafson, Clifford "Cliff," **S** *74-75*

Gustav, King of Sweden, **F** 597

Gustavson, Linda L., **I** 612

Gustine, Frank W. "Frankie," **B** 589

Gutenko, John, *See* Kid Williams

Guthrie, Janet, **O** *12-14*

Gutterson, Albert L. "Al," **O** *462-63*

Gutzler, "Don," **I** 539

Guy, William Ray, **F** *229-30*

Guy Abbey, **O** 586

Guy Lafleur Trophy, **S** 544

Guyon, Joseph N. "Joe," **F** 175, *230-32*

Haas, George W. "Mule," **B** 163

Haas, Robert, **O** 381

Haas, Walter J., **B** 181

Habbi, Emmali, **I** 639

Hack, Stanley C. "Stan," **B** 49, *235-36*

Hackensack, NJ High School, **I** 29

Hackenschmidt, George, **I** 643-44

Hackett, Harold H., **O** 320, *356-57*, 372, 414

Hackett, Robert W. "Bobby," **I** 593

Hackett, William C., **S** 362

Hackney, Elmore, **F** 452

Haddix, Benjamin, **S** 75

Haddix, Fred, **S** 75

Haddix, Harvey, Sr., **S** 75

Haddix, Harvey, Jr. "The Kitten," **S** *75-76*

Haddock, George S., **B** 160

Haden, Patrick C. "Pat," **F** 228, 370

Hadl, John W., **F** 285; **S** *408-09*

Hadley, Arthur T., **F** 270, 540

Hadley, Irving D. "Bump," **B** 101

Hadley, Kent W., **B** 382

Haegg, Gundar, **O** 454, 521

HAF, *See* Helms Athletic Foundation

Hafey, Charles J. "Chick," **B** 40, *236-37*

Hagan, Clifford O. "Cliff," **I** *108-10*, 113, 244-45, 257

Hagen, Joseph F., *See* Philadelphia Jack O'Brien

Hagen, Walter C. B., **O** 89, 108-09, 119, *128-29*, 133-34, 150, 153-55, 159, 164; **S** 515, 517

Hagenbocher, Erich, **I** 677

Hager, "Bobby," **I** 447

Hagerstown, MD baseball club (Pil), **S** 3

Haggen, James Ben Ali, **O** 206, 597-98, 604

Haggerty, George W. "Horse," **I** 170; **S** *287-88*, 314

Hagler, Marvin "Marvelous," **I** *397-98*, 423; **S** 612

Hagne, Ian, **I** 419

Hague, James "Jimmy," **F** 173

Hahn, Charles Archibald "Archie," **F** 262; **O** *463-64*

Hahn, Donald P. "Don," **O** *238*

Hahn, Frank G. "Noodles," **S** 76-77

Hahn, Lloyd, **O** 454, 548

Hahnenkamm Combined Ski Championships, **O** 275, 288

Hail to Reason, **O** 192, 226

Haines, George, **I** 614-15

Haines, Jesse J. "Pop," **B** 5, *237-38*

Hairston, Harold "Happy," **I** 101

Hairston, Wanda, **I** 314

Haiti National Soccer Team, **O** 298, 301

Halas, George S., Sr., **F** 14, 20, 48, 55, 79, 102, 112, 143, 152, 170, 186, 217, 219, *233-35*, 254, 263, 282, 308, 315, 341, 357, 361, 414, 417, 499, 524, 538, 543, 574, 601-02, 608; **I** 30, 223, 261; **O** 87; **S** 45, 484

Halas, George S., Jr., **F** 233

Halas, Walter, **F** 188

Halas Award, **F** 135, 222, 419, 524

Hale, Samuel D. "Sammy," **S** 190

Hale, William Bruce, **I** 16-17

Half Time, **O** 589

Halimon, Shaler, **I** 315

Hall, Albert W. "Al," **S** 573

Hall, Bob "Showboat," **I** 173

Hall, Dean, **S** 611

Hall, Ervin "Erv," **O** 447

Hall, Gary W., **I** 584, *594-95*

Hall, Henry, **I** 474

Hall, Kenneth "Ken," **F** 546

Hall, Miriam, **O** 332

Hall, Val G., **O** 335

Hall, Walter Merrill, **O** 356

Hall of Fame football game, **F** 553; **S** 382-83

Hall of Fame of the National Association of Intercollegiate Athletics, **O** 550

Hall of Fame of the Trotter, **O** 182, 191, 207

Hallman, William W. "Bill," **B** 600

Hallowell, N. P., **O** 420

Halma, **O** 589

Halter, H. H., **S** 381

Ham, Jack R., **F** *235-36*, 460

Hamas, Steven "Steve," **I** 428; **S** *610-11*

Hambletonian, **O** 174, 185, 586, *587-88*, 597

The Hambletonian, **O** 182, 191

Hambletonian 10, *See* Hambletonian

Hamburg, **O** 589, 614

Hamburg Place, Lexington, KY, **O** 600, 608

Hamey, Roy, **B** 75

Hamill, Dorothy S., *See* Dorothy

Hamill Forsythe

Hamilton, Brutus, O 563; S *580-81*

Hamilton, Leon, S 2

Hamilton, Milo, O 53

Hamilton, Scott, I 500-01, *507-08*

Hamilton, Thomas J. "Tom," S *409-10*

Hamilton, William R. "Billy,", B 143, *238-39*, 617; S 152

Hamilton, Canada baseball club (IL), S 19

Hamilton, Canada Tiger-Cats football club (CFL), F 55, 325, 389

Hamilton College, F 644

Hamilton County Athletic Hall of Fame, O 408

Hamilton Grange Lawn Tennis Club, Washington Heights, NY, O 411

Hamlin, Melissa Belote, *See* Melissa Belote Hamlin Ripley

Hamline, MN Race Track, O 580

Hamline University, I 212

Hamm, Edward B. "Ed," O *464-65*

Hammon, Clifford, S 534

Hammon, Marion, F 407

Hammond, IN Buccaneers basketball club (NBL), I 99, 195

Hammond, IN Caesar All-Americans basketball club (NBL), S 270

Hammond, IN Pros football club (NFL), F 27, 476-77; I 264

Hammond, IN Tigers football club (Ind.), F 234

Hamon, Arthur, S 331

Hampden Park, Springfield, MA, F 63

Hampton, VA Gulls hockey club (AHL), I 562

Hampton, VA Institute, I 201; S 417

Hamsho, Mustafa, I 397

Hanburger, Christian, Jr. "Chris," S *410*

Hancock, A. B. "Bull," O 603

Hancock, Seth, O 611

Hancock Junior College, F 376

Handicap Horse of the Year, O 615

Handicap Triple Crown, O 196, 211

Handle With Care, O 191

Handler, Philip "Phil," F 315, 455; S 438

Handley, Louis de Breda, I 622-23

Hanes 500 NASCAR Race, S 605

Hanford, Carl, O 592

Hanford, Ira, S 527

Hangsen, Walter "Walt," O 28

Hanifan, James M. F. "Jim," F 141; S 370

Hanika, Sylvia, O 353

Hankins, G. V., O 206

Hankinson, Melvin "Mel," I 315

Hanley, Richard "Dick," F 268

Hanlon, Edward H. "Ned," B 117, *239-41*, 283, 299, 301, 363, 481; S 19, 220

Hanna, W. B., F 125, 468

Hannah, John A., F 75, *236-37*

Hannegan, Robert "Bob," B 45

Hannibal, MO baseball club (CA), B 29; S 201

Hannigan, J., O 597

Hannum, Alexander M. "Alex," I 16, 50, *110-12*

Hano, Arnold, B 278; S *347-48*

Hanover, O 206, *588-89*, 592

Hanover, PA baseball club (BRL, CbL), B 66, 326

Hanover Shoe Farm, O 207, 574

Hanrahan, "Billy," I 398

Hanratty, Terrence H. "Terry," F 458, 592

Hansell, Ellen, *See* Ellen Hansell Allerdice

Hansen, Erika, S 608

Hanson, Harold "Hal," F 416; S 425, 484

Hanson, Victor A. "Vic," I *112-14*

Hantze, Karen, *See* Karen Hantze Susman

Happy Gal, O 184

Haras Fresnay le Bufford, O 615

Harbett, E. J., O 358

Harbett, "Slim," S 557-58

Harbor Junior College, F 408; I 144

Harbor View Farm, Ocala, FL, O 569

Hard, Darlene R., O 344, *357-58*; S 550

Hard, Ruth, O 357

Hard Turk, O 605

Harder, Marlin M. "Pat," F 48, 113, *237-38*; S 381, 438, 476, 491

Harder, Melvin L. "Mel," B *241-42*, 630

Hardin, Glenn F., O *465-66*

Hardin, William F., O 466

Hardin-Simmons University, F 31, 608, 663; S 291, 484

Harding, "Hallie," B 6

Harding, "Jessie," O 321

Harding, Warren G., O 109

Hardwick, Huntington R. "Tack," F 66, *238-39*

Hardwick, R. Mary, O 375

Hardwick, William B. "Billy," I 342, *343*

Hardy, Carol Ann Mann, O *129-30*

Hardy, Derek, O 117

Hardy, Kevin, F 277

Hardy's Pitch-N-Putt Golf Course, Dallas, TX, O 113

Hare, Thomas Truxton, F 38, *239-40*; S 371

Hargrove, Dudley Michael "Mike," S *77-78*

Harlan, Julian W., F 231

Harlan, KY baseball club (ApL), B 431

Harlem Commonwealth Arena, New York, NY, I 68

Harlem Globetrotters basketball club,

F 463; I 46, 48, 68, 102, 119-20, 156, 158, 172-73, 176, 190, 209, 250-51, 267, 293-94, 329; S 93, 260, 284, 288, 294

Harlem Magicians basketball club, I 119-20, 293-94

Harlem Renaissance Casino Ballroom, New York, NY, I 49, 68-69, 143

Harlem Yankees basketball club, S 283

Harley, Charles W. "Chick," F *241-42*

Harlon Hill Trophy, S 415-16

Harlow, Richard C. "Dick," F 173, *242-43*, 627

Harlow, Robert E. "Bob," O 157

Harmon, Claude, O 113

Harmon, Eugene "Gene," F 243

Harmon, Harold, F 243

Harmon, James "Jim," I 646

Harmon, Louis "Lou," F 243

Harmon, Mark, F 244

Harmon, Merle, S 350

Harmon, Richard "Rick," I 94

Harmon, Thomas D. "Tom," F 99, 120, *243-44*, 660, 669

Harold, S 536

Harold M. Gore Award, I 306

Harness Horse of the Year, O 191, 207, 574-75, 600

Harp, Richard "Dick," I 5

Harper, Derek R., S 292

Harper, Donald D. "Don," I 485

Harper, Jesse C., F *244-45*, 377, 504-05

Harper, John, O 595

Harper, Willie M., S *410-11*

Harper Junior College, S 103

Harper's, S 337

Harper's Bazaar, S 95

Harper's Weekly, F 469, 603; O 383

Harrah, Colbert D. "Toby," S *78-79*

Harrah, Dennis W., S 469

Harrell, John, I 665

Harrelson, Kenneth S. "Ken," B 182

Harridge, William H. "Bill," B 110, 219, *242-43*; S 41

Harriman, W. Averill, O 197, 276-77

Harriman Cup, O 276, 288

Harrington, John, I 567

Harris, Anthony Spencer, S *79-80*

Harris, Chalmer Luman, B 12

Harris, Charles, S *557*

Harris, Clifford A. "Cliff," F *245-46*

Harris, "Danny," O 503-04

Harris, David S. "Dave," B 49

Harris, Donna Marie, I 541

Harris, E. Victor "Vic," B *243-44*, 453

Harris, Franco, F 17, 59, 150, *246-47*, 394, 432, 460; S 367

Harris, Frederick H. "Fred," O *278-79*

Harris, George, I 617

Harris, James L. "Jamie," F 190, 295, 500, 618

Harris, Jerome "Whitey," I 340

Harris, Joseph "Joe," B 65

Harris, Lusia, *See* Lusia Harris Stewart

Harris, Mrs. Alan H., O 321

Harris, "Sam," I 433-34

Harris, Stanley R. "Bucky," B 226, *244-45*, 469, 535, 606; S 14, 131

Harris, "Steve," I 266

Harris, Waldo E., O 435

Harris Hill, Baltimore, MD, O 279

Harrisburg, PA baseball club (AtA, EIL, PSL, TSL), B 221, 239, 509, 617; S 194

Harrisburg, PA basketball club (ABL, EBL), I 66, 243

Harrisburg, PA Colored Giants baseball club (ECL), B 451, 548; I 143

Harrisburg, PA Giants baseball club (ANL), B 30, 150

Harrisburg, PA Hilldale baseball club (ECL), B 88

Harrison, Carter H., I 388

Harrison, Dwight W., F 408

Harrison, Ernest J. "Dutch," O *130-31*

Harrison, Lester "Les," I *114-15*; S 283

Harrison Soccer Club, O 293

Harriss, William J. B. "Slim," B 500

Harroun, Raymond "Ray," O 24

Harry Bassett, O 595; S 530-33

Harshman, David, I 117

Harshman, Marvin "Marv," I *115-17*

Hart, "Alex," I 365

Hart, "Bud," O 358

Hart, Doris, O *358-59*, 360, 375, 394, 401; S 550

Hart, Eugene "Sugar," I 397

Hart, Gaetan, I 452

Hart, James R. "Jim," B 11

Hart, James W. "Jim," F 141, *247-48*; S 426

Hart, Leon J., F 176, *248-50*, 345

Hart, Marvin, I *398*, 457

Hart, Tommy L., S 414

Hart Trophy, I 561

Hartack, William J., Jr. "Willie," O *189-90*, 217, 225

Harter, Richard "Dick," S 311

Harter, "Steve," I 376

Hartford, CT baseball club (EL, NECSL), B 64, 160-61, 210, 222, 258, 266, 279, 358, 525

Hartford, CT baseball club (NL), B 38, 128, 271, 531, 628

Hartford, CT Dark Blues baseball club (NA), B 60, 128

Hartford, CT Times, O 81

Hartford, CT Whalers hockey club (WHA, NHL), I 544, 551, 554, 558, 567, 569-70, 573; S 542

Hartley, "Pete," **I** 365

Hartman, "Jack," **I** 140

Hartnett, Charles L. "Gabby," **B** 146, 230, *245-46*, 562

Hartsel, Tully F. "Topsy," **B** 255

Hartsgrove, Le Ann, **I** 540

Hartung, James "Jim," **I** 533

Hartwick College, **S** 105

Hartwig, Rex, **O** 394, 407

Hartwig Award, **F** 142

Harvard Athletic Association News, **F** 204

Harvard Cup, **O** 391

Harvard Stadium, Cambridge, MA, **F** 426; **O** 548; **S** 585

Harvard University, **B** 39, 161, 166, 298, 357, 560; **F** 35, 57-58, 61, 63-66, 84-86, 116-17, 125-26, 173, 177-78, 192-93, 204, 238-40, 242, 250-51, 255, 261, 265-66, 269-70, 299, 302, 311, 343, 368, 373, 376, 379-80, 402, 425-26, 465, 469, 474-77, 571, 597, 636, 669; **I** 67, 128, 176-77, 222, 313, 380, 502-03, 506-07, 514, 538-39, 543, 556, 590, 593, 602, 606, 533-34; **O** 53, 70, 77, 91, 135, 237, 243, 253, 260, 296, 338, 345, 347, 349, 392, 412-14, 416, 419-22, 452, 495, 512; **S** 280, 336, 358, 371, 376, 397, 433, 444, 458, 489-90, 501-02, 540-41, 546, 571, 601

Harvard-Yale Tennis Team, **S** 501

Harvard-Yale Track Team, **O** 439

Harvey, Beatrix Loughran, **I** *509*

Harvey, Charles, **S** 610

Harvey, Harold Douglas "Doug," **S** *80*

Harvey, Harold Wollen, **S** 80

Harvey, "Len," **I** 426

Harvey, Philip "Phil," **O** 283

Harvey, Raymond, **I** 509

Harwell, William Earnest "Ernie," **S** *348-49*, 349

Hary, Armin, **O** 538

Haselrig, Bruce, **S** 611

Haselrig, Carlton L., **S** *611-12*

Hashizume, Shiro, **I** 603-04

Haskell Institute, **F** 35, 446, 469, 596

Haskell Invitation Race, **O** 204, 227

Hassett, William J. "Billy," **I** 250

Hastings, **O** 188

Hastings College, **F** 443

Hastings, MI baseball club, **S** 123

Hastings, NE baseball club (NSL), **B** 94

Hasty House Farm, **O** 173

Hasty Road, **O** 173, 176

Hattiesburg, MS baseball club (CSL), **B** 456; **S** 5

Hatton, Grady E., **S** 54

Haughton, Percy D., **F** 125, 178, 238, *250-51*, 299, 302, 379; **S** 376

Haughton, Peter, **O** 191

Haughton, Robert "Cammie," **O** 191

Haughton, Thomas "Tom," **O** 191

Haughton, William, Sr. "Billy," **O** 181, *190-91*

Haughton, William, Jr., **O** 191

Haugsrud, Ole, **F** 315

Hauser, George W., **F** 655

Hauser, Joseph J. "Joe," **B** 279; **S** *80-81*

Hauser, Peter "Pete," **S** 397

Havana, Cuba baseball club (CUWL), **S** 224

Havana, Cuba Golf and Tennis Club, **O** 484

Havana, Cuba Race Track, **O** 183

Havana, Cuba Sugar Kings baseball club (IL), **S** 35

Haverford College, **O** 377; **S** 220

Haverhill, MA baseball club (NEL), **B** 239, 347, 357, 506, 549

Haverly, La Verne, **I** 340

Havlicek, John J. "Hondo,", **I** 67, *117-18*, 124, 136, 161, 186, 231, 296

Havre de Grace, MD Race Track, **O** 576

Hawaii Islanders baseball club (PCL), **S** 355-56

Hawaiian Ladies Open Golf Tournament, **S** 518

Hawaiian Open Golf Tournament, **O** 126, 135

The Hawaiians football club (WFL), **F** 264

Hawerchuk, Dale, **S** 542

Hawker, Peter, **O** 86

Hawkes, John B., **O** 362, 38

Hawkeye Wrestling Club, Iowa City, IA, **I** 635

Hawkins, Benjamin C. "Ben," **F** 325

Hawkins, Cornelius L. "Connie," **I** 101, 295; **S** *288-89*

Hawkins, "Del," **I** 387

Hawkins, Hersey R., Jr., **I** 251

Hawkins, "Larry," **I** 259

Hawkins, Lemuel "Hawk," **B** 6

Hawksworth Farm, **O** 610

Hawley, "Sandy," **O** 203

Hawthorne Gold Cup, **O** 603

Hawthorne Race Track, Chicago, IL, **O** 196

Hay, Ralph, **S** 387, *411*

Haycraft, Kenneth "Ken," **F** 416; **S** 425, 484

Hayden, "Ted," **O** 564

Hayes, Arthur S., **O** 370

Hayes, Elvin E., **I** 104, *118-19*, 121, 174, 224; **S** 313

Hayes, John J. "Johnny," **O** *466-67*

Hayes, Robert L. "Bob," **O** 439, *467-69*

Hayes, Thomas Woodrow "Woody," **F** 99-100, 164, 210, 227-28, *251-52*, 290, 454, 457-58, 526, 585; **S** 171, 365-66, 397-400, 405-06, 435

Hayes, William "Billy," **S** 598

Haynes, Abner, **F** *253*

Haynes, Herbert, **O** 590

Haynes, Joseph "Joe," **I** 119

Haynes, Marques O., **F** 463; **I** *119-20*, 173, 267, 294; **S** 294

Haynes, Michael D. "Mike," **F** 325

Haynes, Wendell, **I** 119

Haynie, Sandra, **O** 381; **S** *513-14*

Hayward, William L. "Bill," **O** 434, *469-70*, 545

Hayward Award, **I** 97

Hayward Field, Eugene, OR, **O** 519

Hayward Relays, **O** 434, 470

Haywood, Spencer, **I** *120-22*, 169

Hazleton, "Bob," **I** 385

Hazleton, PA baseball club, **F** 573

Hazzard, Walter R., Jr., **I** 101, 210, 327, 331; *See also* Mahdi Abdul-Rahmad

Hazzard, Wilton, **F** 30, 213, 317

He Did, **O** 198

Head, Donald C. "Don," **I** 565

Head, John L., **I** 55, *122-23*, 284, 324

Head Play, **O** 198

Headliners Club Award, **O** 82

Healdsburg, CA Track and Field Meet, **O** 524

Healey, Edward F., Jr. "Ed," **F** *254*

Healy, J. Simon, **O** 582

Healy football club, White Plains, NY, **O** 299-300

Heap, Joseph "Joe," **F** 338

Hearn, "Chick," **I** 249

Hearn, William "Tiny," **I** 223

Hearns, Thomas "Tommy," **I** 356, 397, 422-23; **S** *612-13*

Hearst, William Randolph, **O** 72, 90; **S** 342

The Heart of the Order, **S** 337

Heath, "Rod," O 366
Heathcote, "Jud," I 146
Heather Broom, O 216
Heavenly Body, O 222
Heavenly Cause, O 222
"Heavenly Twins," S 587-88
Heavenly Valley, CA Alpine Skiing
Competition, O 275
Heavyweight Boxing Championship,
I 353-54, 358-61, 365-69, 372,
374-77, 380, 382-86, 390-91, 394-
95, 398-99, 401-03, 405-09, 412,
414, 418-19, 424, 426-30, 437-40,
442-43, 445, 449, 453, 457, 462,
465-67, 471-72, 474-79
Hecker, Guy J., S 81-82
Hedberg, Anders, I 568
Heenan, John C., I 398-99, 403, 443
Heeney, "Tom," I 372, 471
Heep, Daniel W. "Danny," B 497
Heerenveen, The Netherlands Speed
Skating Competition, O 313
Heffelfinger, William W. "Pudge," F
38, 116, 254-55, 260, 262, 425,
530, 654; S 444
Heffernan, "Ed," F 378
Hefferon, Charles, O 467
Hegan, James E. "Jim," S 82-83
Hegan, James Michael "Mike," S 83
Heida, Anton, I 529-30
Heidelberg Soccer Club, O 295-96
Heiden, Elizabeth L. "Beth," O 313,
315
Heiden, Eric A., O 313-14, 315
Heiden, Nancy T., O 313
Heilmann, Harry E., B 246-48, 512,
565, 572
Hein, Melvin J. "Mel," F 255-56,
417, 447, 608; S 503
Heineman, G. H., I 530
Heinemann, A. J., B 524
Heinrich, Ignace, O 492
Heinsohn, Thomas W. "Tom," I

12,123-25, 159-60, 201; S 284,
307
Heintz, George, Jr., I 669
Heinz, Louis, I 665
Heinz, W. C., I 365
Heinz Southern 500 NASCAR Race,
S 605
Heisman, John W., F 5, 108, 115,
150, 158, 175, 230-31, 240, 256-
57, 259, 530; S 423-24
Heisman Memorial Trophy, F 2, 8,
11, 13, 24, 31-33, 37, 43-45, 51,
53, 74, 79, 84, 87, 91, 93, 100,
121-22, 128-30, 132, 136, 149,
162, 174, 181-82, 184, 191, 201,
209, 222, 225-26, 243, 248, 257,
271-72, 276, 286-87, 289-90, 302,
308, 310-11, 314, 320, 337, 339,
344-45, 355-57, 364-65, 369, 383,
391, 412, 431, 437, 444, 448, 454,
458, 473, 481, 490, 507, 509, 518,
534, 545-46, 549, 554, 560, 564,
568, 570, 577, 582, 592, 605-06,
609, 622, 629-30, 649, 660; S
373-74, 385, 395-97, 399, 402,
404-05, 414, 420, 431, 445, 448-
49, 468-69, 473, 487
Heiss, Carol E., See Carol Heiss
Jenkins
Heiss, Nancy, I 511
Heldman, "Carrie," S 551
Heldman, Gladys Medalie, S 551-52,
554, 558
Heldman, Julie, S 551
Heldman, Julius, S 551
Helen Stephens Olympic Coeds basketball club, O 547
Helena, AL baseball club (CSL), B
537
Helena, MT baseball club (MtSL), B
556
Helfer, "Al," O 48
Helioscope, O 178

Hellickson, Russell O. "Russ," I 654
Hellwig, Helena, O 325, 333, 377, 406
Helmet, O 211
Helms, Thomas "Tommy", F 337
Helms Athletic Foundation, F 2, 65, 83, 94, 115, 127, 130, 145, 153, 158, 190, 230, 240, 248, 261, 265, 269, 338, 374, 426, 439-40, 468, 475, 530, 554, 637; I 7, 10-11, 37-38, 64, 70, 77, 99, 113, 129, 137-38, 211-12, 227, 272, 301, 581, 662; O 5-6, 9, 12, 15, 20, 23-26, 35, 40, 43, 61, 128, 132, 146, 161, 172, 319, 325, 343, 374, 445-46, 456, 496, 522, 545, 550, 561; S 261, 263, 265, 271, 273, 276, 297, 316, 322, 433-34, 445, 458, 461, 476
Helms Athletic Foundation Achievement Award, I 64, 128, 166, 581
Helms Athletic Foundation Amateur Athlete of the Year, O 319, 374
Helms Athletic Foundation All-Time All-American Basketball Team, I 77, 188, 205, 211, 272
Helms Athletic Foundation Hall of Fame, F 3, 6, 12, 31, 35, 45-47, 49, 52, 54, 81, 84, 86, 90, 94, 102, 107, 109, 112, 114-15, 117, 120, 126, 131, 144-45, 148, 153-54, 168, 172, 175, 187, 193, 199, 212, 214, 218, 221, 240-42, 244, 256-57, 259, 261, 265, 269, 272, 282, 292, 297-98, 301-02, 313, 318-20, 337, 342, 344, 351, 360, 369, 374, 377, 380, 392-93, 402, 406, 411, 414-15, 423, 425-26, 429, 435, 438-39, 443, 446, 452, 455, 464-65, 471-72, 476, 491, 503-04, 528, 530, 540, 549-50, 553, 559, 564, 574, 580, 584, 594, 598, 626-27, 629, 636-37, 642, 646-48, 652, 655, 663, 668, 674; I 7, 11, 37, 40, 55, 57, 70, 75-76, 80, 84-85, 94, 106, 113, 123, 127, 140, 155-56, 182, 185, 191, 193, 202, 207, 218, 221, 231, 235, 243, 246, 253-56, 264, 269, 271, 273, 276, 284, 302, 306, 321, 323, 325-26, 334, 496, 525, 611, 614, 623, 645, 648, 651-52, 670; O 5-6, 9, 12, 15, 20, 23-26, 35, 40, 43, 61, 128, 132, 146, 148, 161, 172, 343, 445-46, 456, 496, 522, 545, 550, 561; S 251, 262, 265-66, 271, 276-77, 291, 293, 297, 309, 316, 318, 322-23, 328, 331, 334, 366, 368, 371, 376, 382, 386, 388, 394, 414-16, 418, 421, 431, 436, 453, 456-57, 465, 476-77, 483, 490, 500, 521, 594, 609, 617
Helms Athletic Foundation North American Athlete of the Year, O 325
Helms Athletic Foundation Poll, I 37-38, 77, 79, 130, 138, 159, 167, 188, 227, 234, 236, 254, 256, 272, 301, 330; S 271, 461, 476
Helser, Brenda M., I 587
Helsinki, Finland Summer Olympic Games, See Olympic Summer Games, 1952
Helsinki, Finland Track and Field Meet, O 430, 504, 521
Hemenway, Mary, I 1
Hemenway Gymnasium, Cambridge, MA, I 538
Henagar Business College, I 320
Hencken, John F., I 595-96
Henderson, Eli "Cam," S 290-91
Henderson, Rickey H., B 248-49, 618; S 614
Henderson State University, S 133
Hendrick, Brian, S 83

Hendrick, George A., Jr., **S** *83-85*
Hendrick, Harvey L., **B** 237, 309
Hendrick, "Rick," **O** 42
Hendricks, Theodore P. "Ted," **F** *258*
Hendrickson, "Gud," **I** 567
Hendrix, Claude R., **S** *85*
Hendrix College, **F** 390
Henie, Sonja, **I** 515
Henley British Royal Regatta, **O** 256, 263
Henley United States Single Sculls Competition, **O** 263
Henne, Jan M., **I** 613
Hennessey, John F., **O** 368, 408
Hennessey, Thomas "Tom," **I** 340
Henning, Lorne, **I** 549
Henrich, Thomas D. "Tommy," **B** 169, 258, 470; **S** *85-87*, 102
Henrietta, **O** 51
Henrion Golf Classic, **O** 118
Henrotin, Sylvia, **O** 391
Henry, Wilbur F. "Fats," **F** 200, *259-60*, 359; **S** 412
Henry Archy, **O** 609
Henry of Navarre, **O** 188, 220; **S** 533
Henschel, George, **I** 222
Henson, Louis "Lou," **S** *291-92*
Hepbron, George T., **I** *125-26*, 306
Hepburn, Ralph, **O** 17
Herber, Arnold "Arnie," **F** *260-61*, 329; **S** 474
Herford, "Al," **I** 387
Hering Award, **F** 276
Heritage Golf Classic, **O** 126, 134-35, 143; **S** 524
Heritage Stakes, **O** 610
Herman, Floyd C. "Babe," **B** 193, *249-50*, 567
Herman, Lee, **I** 97
Herman, "Pete," **I** *399-400*, 431, 478
Herman, William J. "Billy," **B** 168, *250-51*, 366, 467
The Herman Hickman Reader, **S** 413

Hernandez, John, **B** 251
Hernandez, Keith, **B** *251-52*, 530; **S** 53, 84
Herrerias, Rene, **I** 231
Herrman, Garry, **B** 285, 550, 556
Hershey, PA Country Club, **O** 150
Hershiser, Orel L. IV, **S** 109
Hertz, John D., **O** 196
Hertz, Mrs. John D., **O** 587, 596
Hervey, John, **O** 578
Herzog, Charles L. "Buck," **B** 53
Herzog, Dorrel N. E. "Whitey," **B** 622; **S** 30, 84, *87-88*, 109, 136, 206, 217-18, 237
Hess, Leon, **O** 105
Heston, William M., Sr. "Willie," **F** *261-63*, 668-69
Heston, William M., Jr., **F** 173, 262
Heusser, Edward B. "Ed," **S** 62
Hewitt, Robert "Bob," **O** 324
Hewitt, William E. "Bill," **F** *263-64*, 417
Heydler, John A., **B** 201, 253, 340, 374
Heyliger, Victor "Vic," **I** 570-71
Heyman, Arthur B. "Art," **F** 67; **S** *292-93*
Hialeah Park, Miami, FL, **O** 178, 190, 193, 205, 221, 223, 603
Hibbs, Jesse J., **F** 299
Hibiscus Stakes, **O** 225, 603
Hickcox, Charles B. "Charlie," **I** 584
Hickerson, Robert Gene, **S** *412-13*
Hickey, "Dan," **I** 359
Hickey, Edgar S. "Ed," **I** *126-27*, 180, 269
Hickman, Herman M., Jr., **S** *413-14*
Hickok, William O. "Bill," **F** 469
Hickok Award, **B** 382, 477; **F** 33, 419; **I** 340; **O** 10, 143, 150
Hickox, Edward J., **I** *128-29*
Hicks, Helen B., **S** 520-21
Hicks, John, Jr., **S** *414-15*

Higbe, Walter Kirby, **B** 306

Higgenbotham Trophy, **O** 238

Higgins, "Jim," **I** 431

Higgins, Michael F., Jr., "Pinky," **B** 254-55; **S** 243

High All-Star Soccer Game, **O** 307

High Echelon, **O** 192-93

High Gun, **O** 189; **S** 527

High Point, NC baseball club (NCSL, Pil), **B** 388, 588

High Strung, **O** 202

High Voltage, **O** 184

Highland Blade, **O** 580

Highland Golf Club, Pittsburgh, PA, **O** 153

Hildreth, Samuel "Sam," **O** 215; **S** 525, 526-27

Hill, Albert B., **F** 231

Hill, Andrew "Drew," **S** 469

Hill, Calvin, **F** 264-65, 331

Hill, Cleo, **I** 90

Hill, Daniel "Dan," **F** 452, 626

Hill, Donald E. "Don," **S** 18

Hill, Dorothy Poynton, *See* Dorothy Poynton Teuber

Hill, Gail, **O** 176, 195

Hill, George E. B., **I** 515

Hill, Harlon, **S** 415-16

Hill, J. D., **F** 290, 325

Hill, J. Preston "Pete," **B** 255-56

Hill, Jerome, **S** 612

Hill, "Jess," **F** 129; **S** 590

Hill, Lucille E., **O** 253

Hill, Opal Burns, **S** 520-21

Hill, Peter "Pete," **S** 143, 168

Hill, Ralph A., **O** 470, 521

Hill, Richard "Dick," **O** 497

Hill, Thomas L., **O** 447, 497

Hill, Virgil, **S** 613

Hill Award, **F** 665

Hill Prince, **O** 175

Hillerich, John, **B** 57

Hillerich & Bradsby Company, **B** 57, 467

Hillier, Randy G., **S** 545

Hillman, Harry L., Jr., **O** 470-71

Hills, James, **O** 606

Hinault, Bernard, **S** 617

Hinchman, Lewis "Lew," **F** 173

Hinchman, Lionel, **S** 546

Hindeland, Germany Ski Competition, **O** 281

Hindoo, **O** 206, 586, 589, 597; **S** 533

Hindoocraft, **O** 589

Hinds Junior College, **F** 587

Hines, Harold, **I** 70

Hines, James R. "Jim," **O** 458, 471-72, 541

Hines, Paul A., **B** 256

Hinkey, Frank A., **F** 64, 265-67, 343, 603; **S** 371, 376

Hinkey, Louis, **F** 266

Hinkle, Carl C., **F** 407

Hinkle, Paul D. "Tony," **I** 129-30, 236, 313

Hinkle, William Clarke, **F** 267-68, 329, 558; **S** 436

Hinton, Gary, **I** 452

Hiram College, **S** 239

Hirsch, Elroy L. "Crazy Legs," **F** 215, 268-69, 285; **S** 476

Hirsch, Mary, **S** 527-28

Hirsch, Maximillian "Max," **O** 572; **S** 527-28

Hirsch, Walter, **S** 261

Hirsch Jacobs Stakes, **O** 193

Hirschfeld, Emil, **O** 484

Hirshberg, Al, **S** 350

Hirshon, Harold "Hal," **F** 637

His Eminence, **O** 183

History of Colored People, **S** 238

Hitch, Lewis R. "Lew," **I** 94

Hitchcock, Thomas, Sr., **O** 89, 260, 261

Hitchcock, Thomas, Jr., "Tommy," **O**

260-61
Hitchcock, William C. "Billy," **B** 475
Hitler, Adolf, *See* Olympic Summer Games, 1936
Hixson, "Chuck," **F** 577
Hoad, Lewis "Lew," **O** 394, 507; **S** 554
Hobart, Clarence, **O** 333-34, 420-21
Hobart College, **I** 45; **O** 49
Hobey Baker Award, **I** 550
Hoboken, NJ Turnverein, **I** 632
Hobson, Howard A., **I** 91, *130-31;* **S** 297
Hockey Broadcasters Association, **S** 353
Hockey Hall of Fame, **I** 36, 544, 547, 552, 555; **S** 353, 537, 543, 546
Hodapp, Urban John "Johnny," **B** 536
Hodge, Daniel A. "Dan," **I** *644-45,* 660
Hodges, Gilbert R. "Gil," **B** *256-57,* 467, 575; **O** 60; **S** 149
Hodges, Russell "Russ," **S** 348, *349-50*
Hoff, Charles, **O** 462
Hoffman, Jan, **I** 518
Hoffman, Justin, **I** 423
Hoffman, Robert C. "Bob," **I** *629-30,* 632
Hoffman, Zdzislaw, **O** 425
Hofstra University, **B** 515
Hogan, James J. "Jim," **F** *269-70*
Hogan, "One Round," **I** 480
Hogan, William Benjamin "Ben," **O** 89, 112, 118-19, 126, 128, *131-32,* 139, 141, 143, 145, 159; **S** 507, 520
Hogshead, Nancy L., **I** *596-97*
Hogue, Maxine King "Micki," **I** *488-89*
Hohokus Valley Tennis Club, Ridgewood, NJ, **O** 376
Holbrook, "Swede," **I** 97
Holcomb, Stuart K. "Stu," **F** 259
Holiday, **S** 336
Holiday Bowl football game, **F** 139, 372, 671; **S** 402, 473
Holiday Festival Basketball Tournament, New York, NY, **I** 31, 169, 180, 252, 259
Holiday Festival Hockey Tournament, New York, NY, **I** 545-46
Holiday on Ice, **I** 503, 514
Holieway, Jamelle, **F** 582
Holland, Jerome A. "Brud," **S** *416-17*
Holland, Joe, **S** 261, 286
Holland, Stephen "Steve," **I** 593
Holland, William D. "Bill," **B** 612
Hollander, Zander, **S** 339
Hollandia, **O** 267
Hollenback, William M. "Bill," **F** 242, 531; **S** *417-18*
Hollingberry, O. E., **F** 160
Hollingsworth, Albert W. "Al," **B** 588
Hollins, Marion, **S** 520-21
Holly Farms 400 Auto Race, North Wilkesboro, NC, **O** 41
Hollywood Athletic Club, **O** 472
Hollywood Bears football club (PCPFL), **F** 638
Hollywood Derby, **O** 569
Hollywood Gold Cup, **O** 179, 218-19, 228-29, 577, 603, 605
Hollywood Juvenile Stakes, **O** 569
Hollywood Park, Inglewood, CA, **O** 180, 203-04, 218, 227, 229, 591; **S** 532
Hollywood Stars baseball club (PCL), **B** 152, 250, 395, 461, 485, 626; **S** 79, 197, 247
Holm, Eleanor G., *See* Eleanor Holm Whalen
Holman, Allen M., **F** 172
Holman, Nathan "Nat," **I** 21, 23, 32-

33, 65, 88, *131-32,* 157, 170-71, 195; **S** 287, 314

Holmenkollen, Norway Alpine Skiing Competition, **O** 288

Holmes, Earnest L. "Ernie," **S** 407

Holmes, James M., **O** 214

Holmes, James W. "Ducky," **B** 199

Holmes, Larry, **I** 353, 386, *401-02,* 466; **S** 623, 625

Holmes, Thomas "Tommy," **S** 338

Holmes, Thomas F. "Tommy," **B** *257-58*

Holmfirth, **S** 531

Holovak, Michael J. "Mike," **F** 92; **S** *418-19*

Holt, John "Casey," **I** 49, 68

Holtz, Louis L. "Lou," **F** 553; **S** 373, *419-21*

Holtzer, Maurice, **I** 439

Holtzman, Kenneth D. "Ken," **S** *88-89*

Holub, Emil Joe "E. J.," **F** 367

Holub, Richard W. "Dick," **I** 22-23

Holum, Dianne M., **O** 313, *314-15*

Holway, John B., **B** 331; **S** 129

Holy Cross College, **B** 64, 348, 495, 522; **F** 12-13, 101, 111-12, 238, 254; **I** 43, 51, 67, 78, 124, 126, 128, 154, 163; **O** 554

Holyfield, Evander, **S** 626

Holyoke, MA baseball club (EL, NA), **B** 111, 598

Holystone, **O** 596

Holzman, William "Red," **F** 215; **I** 44, 110, *132-34,* 201, 247

Homans, Amy, **I** 1

Home Box Office, **I** 423; **O** 83

Home Sports Entertainment, **S** 358

Homestead, PA Grays baseball club (ANL, EWL, NNL), **B** 30-31, 88, 147-48, 150, 192, 213, 244, 282, 290, 331, 436, 452-53, 553, 599, 612, 620; **S** 9-10, 188

Homewood Field, Baltimore, MD, **O** 249

Honda Golf Classic, **S** 519

Honey Mark, **O** 183

Hong Kong National Soccer Team, **O** 301

Honolulu, HI baseball club (PCL), **B** 329

Honolulu, HI Marathon, **O** 537

Honolulu, HI Swim Meet, **S** 622

Honolulu, HI Town Club, **F** 637

Hook, James "Jim," **O** 408

Hooks, Alvin L., **O** 436-37

Hoop, Jr., **O** 175

Hooper, Harry B., **B** 208, *259-60,* 293, 529; **S** 111-12

Hooper, William U., Jr. "Bill," **O** *238-39*

Hooton, Burt C., **B** 277; **S** 74

Hoover, Herbert C., **F** 380

Hope, Frank, **I** 673

Hope College, **B** 295

Hopeful Stakes, **O** 196, 199, 211, 231, 569, 598, 611

Hopkins, Mrs. E. A., **O** 196

Hopkins, Robert M. "Bob," **I** 328

Hopkins Bulldogs Lacrosse Club, **O** 237

Hopman, Harry, **O** 369, 374, 395

Hoppe, William F. "Willie," **I** *673-74*

Hopps, Janet, **S** 339

Horgan, Dennis, **O** 524

Horizon Hills Country Club, El Paso, TX, **O** 163

Horky, Rita, **I** 123, 255

Horn, Elyard Theodore "Ted," **O** *14-15*

Hornell, NY baseball club (Pol), **B** 137, 618

Hornellsville, NY baseball club (IA), **S** 47

Horner, George R. "Red," **I** 570

Horner, James Robert "Bob," **S** 18, *89-90*

Horning, Clarence E., **F** 647

Hornsby, Rogers "Rajah," **B** 24, 29, 45, 80, 202, *260-61,* 268-70, 276, 290, 345, 404, 567, 611, 621; **S** 95, 231

Hornsby, William, **B** 261

Hornung, Paul V., **F** 104, *270-72,* 307-08, 321-22, 354, 404, 517, 529, 588; **S** 399

Horrell, Edwin C. "Babe," **F** 552, 637

Horse of the Year, **O** 176, 184, 189, 192, 222, 229, 570, 573, 576-77, 579, 581, 584, 591-92, 595-96, 599, 603, 605-08, 610-12, 614-15; **S** 529-30, 532

Horsemen's Benevolent and Protective Association Foundation, **O** 180, 185; **S** 526

Horton, Willie W., **B** 262; **S** 136

Horton Act, **I** 387, 432

Horvath, Leslie "Les," **F** *272-73*

Horvath, Paul, **I** 43

Hoskins, Mark H., **S** 476

Hostak, "Al," **I** 466, 482

Hot N'Nasty, **O** 604

Hot Springs, AR baseball club (CSL), **B** 317

Hotchkiss, George, **S** 277

Hotchkiss, Hazel, *See* Hazel Hotchkiss Wightman

Hotel Wentworth Open Tennis Championships, **O** 339

Houbregs, Robert J. "Bob," **I** *134-35*

Houck, Angela, **S** 603-04

Houck, Michael "Mike," **I** 640, 654

Hough, Charles O. "Charlie," **B** 277; **S** *90-91*

Hough, Mark, **I** 423

Hough, Richard, **S** 90

Houk, Ralph G., **B** *262-63,* 559; **S** 203, 340, 353

Houlgate, "Deke," **F** 598

Hourless, **S** 526-27

House of David baseball club, **B** 34, 227; **O** 171

Houseman, "Lou," **I** 457

Houser, Lemuel C. "Bud," **O** 444, *472-73,* 485, 490

Housley, "Phil," **S** *541-42,* 548

Houston, Kenneth R. "Ken," **F** *273*

Houston Aeros hockey club (WHA), **I** 558

Houston Angels basketball club (WPBL), **I** 290

Houston Astrodome, Houston, TX, **F** 500; **I** 118; **S** 34

Houston Astros baseball club (NL), **B** 36, 76, 138, 162, 196, 201, 216, 252, 254, 380, 388, 391-92, 405, 419, 421-22, 441, 475-76, 491, 497-98, 532, 543-44, 594, 614, 639; **F** 230; **O** 137; **S** 25-26, 34-35, 114, 131-32, 136, 160, 174-76, 182, 230, 244, 355, 358

Houston baseball club (AA), **B** 499, 517, 609

Houston baseball club (TL), **B** 8, 40, 43, 55-56, 142, 236, 310, 381, 387, 396, 529, 557, 583, 595; **S** 17, 32, 38, 149, 218

Houston Champions Invitation Golf Tournament, **O** 126

Houston Colt 45s baseball club (NL), **S** 67, 177, 196-97, 220, 244; *See also* Houston Astros baseball club (NL)

Houston Gamblers football club (USFL), **F** 209, 630; **S** 375, 411

Houston Hurricane Soccer Club (NASL), **O** 308

Houston Oilers football club (AFL), **F** 31, 55, 72, 91, 253, 273, 293-94, 367, 423, 560, 590, 642-43; **S** 363, 426, 432, 442, 469

Houston Oilers football club (NFL), F 63, 87, 135, 140, 180, 191, 210, 222, 230, 236, 273, 291, 295, 335, 519, 556-57, 562, 571-72, 586, 643, 665; S 379, 408, 419

Houston Open Bowling Tournament, I 350-51

Houston Open Golf Tournament, O 113, 125; S 519

Houston Rockets basketball club (NBA), I 3, 18, 26, 61, 79, 118-19, 146-47, 150, 203, 226, 230, 266, 318; S 281-83, 298-99, 313, 326

Houston *Tennis News,* S 551

Hovde, Frederick, F 416

Hovey, Fred H., O 334, 419-20

Hovious, John A., F 621

How Fair, O 194

How Life Imitates the World Series, S 337

How the Weather Was, S 352

How to Train, S 598

Howard, Charles S., O 605

Howard, Elston G., B 609; S *91-92,* 170

Howard, Frank J., F 640; S *421-22*

Howard, Frank O. "Hondo," B *264-65;* S 96, 100

Howard, Kevin, I 423

Howard, Lindsey, O 194

Howard, Maxwell, O 216

Howard Award, F 640

Howard College, F 293; S 368

Howe, Gordon "Gordie," I 558, 569-70

Howe, James, O 85

Howe, Mark S., I *558-59*

Howe, Marty G., O 558

Howell, Bailey E., I *135-36*

Howell, James Lee "Jim," F 331, 353, 447; S 466

Howell, Millard F. "Dixie," F 74, 281, 595; S *422-23,* 439

Howland, Edward M., I 509

Howley, Charles L. "Chuck," F *274,* 331;

Howley, Daniel P. "Dan," S 13

Howton, William "Billy," F *275-76*

Hoy, William E. "Dummy," B *265-66*

Hoyt, Beatrix, O *132-33*

Hoyt, George H., I *136-37*

Hoyt, Waite C., B *266-67,* 269, 456, 612; S 190

Hrniak, Walter J. "Walt," S 51

Huarte, John G., F *276-77,* 458, 577

Huarte, Joseph D., F 276

Hubbard, R. Cal, B 110, 267; F 4, *277-78,* 329, 392

Hubbard, William DeHart, O *473-74,* 549

Hubbell, Carl O., B 46, 183, *267-68,* 552, 583; S 10, 45

Hubert, Allison, O 625

Hudkins, "Ace," I 469, 475

Hudlin, Richard, O 323-24

Hudson, George A., S 554

Hudson, Judy, I 255

Hudson, Louis C. "Lou," I *137-38*

Hudson and Chandler Auto Racing Team, O 24

Hudson County basketball club, O 293

Hudson River League, I 222-23, 273

Hudson River Valley Tennis Championships, O 333

Hudson Stakes, O 595

Hudson Valley League, S 260

Huell, "Mitch," I 635

Huether, Erving "Erv," F 333

Huff, George, B 468; F 637

Hugasian, "Harry," F 533; O 493

Huggins, Miller J., B 46, 106-07, 117, 161, 260, *268-69,* 291, 392, 444, 492; S 22, 42, 55, 199

Hughes, "Harry," **O** 501

Hughes, "Pat," **O** 418

Hughes, Samuel T. "Sammy," **B** *269-70*

Hughes, Thomas O., **B** 547

Hughson, Cecil C. "Tex," **S** 54

Hugo, OK baseball club (TOL), **B** 260

The Huguenot, **S** 533

Hui Macani Swim Club, Honolulu, HI, **I** 600

Hula Bowl football game, **F** 1, 101, 127, 138-39, 141, 143, 147, 149, 221, 236, 297, 347, 364, 372, 396, 412, 423, 473, 481, 548, 571, 586, 633, 635, 642-43, 664; **S** 365, 393, 406, 450, 459, 462, 499

Hulbert, William A., **B** 60, *270-71*

Hulen, "Max," **O** 285

Hulman, Anton, Jr. "Tony," **O** *15-16,* 31

Hulse, William "Bill," **O** 454

Hume, "Redman," **F** 407

Humes, "Larry," **I** 193

Humm, David H., **F** 209

Humphrey, Claude B., **F** *279-80*

Hundley, Rodney C. "Hot Rod," **I** 43

Hundred Guinea Cup, **O** 101-02

Hungarian Business and Tradesman's Club, Cleveland, OH, **I** 348

Hungarian National Gymnastic Team, **I** 542

Hungarian National Soccer Team, **O** 310

Hungarian National Track and Field Team, **O** 429

Hungarian Olympic Swim Team, **I** 587

Hunt, Charles, **S** 552

Hunt, Jacque Carolyn Virgil, **S** 552

Hunt, Joseph R. "Joe," **O** 418; **S** *552-53,* 556

Hunt, Lamar, **F** *280-81;* **O** 341, 365

Hunt, Lee, **S** 259

Hunt, Marianne, **S** 552

Hunt, Oliver Joel, **S** *423-24*

Hunt, Reuben, **S** 552

Hunt, Ronald K. "Ron," **B** 445

Hunt, Toby, **F** 378

Hunt Reynolds Stable, Lexington, KY, **O** 209

Hunter, Francis T. "Frank," **O** 347, 362, 387, 409

Hunter, Harold, **I** 201

Hunter, James A. "Jim," **B** 179, 182, *271-72,* 441

Hunter College, **O** 71

Hunting Park, Philadelphia, PA, **O** 229-30

Huntington, Robert P. Jr., **O** 334-35

Huntington Avenue Grounds, Boston, MA, **B** 636

Huntington Beach, CA Aquatics Club, **I** 575

Huntington, WV baseball club (MAL), **B** 8, 380

Hurd, Dorothy Campbell, **O** 329; **S** 520-21

Hurley, "Jack," **I** 451

Huron, MI baseball club (NoL), **S** 118, 173

Hurry Off, **O** 186; **S** 531

Hurst, Frank O. "Don," **S** 23

Hurst, Timothy C. "Tim," **B** 110

Husing, Edward B. "Ted," **F** 275; **I** 156; **O** 49, *70-71,* 77, 79, 82, 99

Husky Sports Hall of Fame, **I** 135

Husta, Carl L., **I** 222

Husta, "Mickey," **I** 222

Huston, Tillinghast, **B** 492

Hutcheson Stakes, **O** 610-11

Hutchinson, Frederick C. "Fred,", **B** 50, 236

Hutchinson, "Jock," **O** 109, *133-34*

Hutchinson, KS baseball club (WA, WL), **B** 2, 624

Hutson, Donald M. "Don," **F** 39, 74, 92, 151, 256, 260, 275, *281-82*, 329, 395, 417, 595; **S** 422, 439, 474

Hyatt, Charles D. "Chuck," **I** 39, *138-39*

Hydrangea, **O** 211

Hydroplane II, **O** 576

Hyer, Jacob, **I** 402

Hyer, Thomas "Tom," **I** *402-03,* 443

Hyland, "Dick," **I** 444

Hylton, J. R., **O** 609

Hyman, Flora J., **S** *613-14*

Hynes, David "Dave," **I** 567

Hynson, Robert, **O** 375

Iba, Clarence, **I** 139

Iba, Earl, **I** 139

Iba, Henry P. "Hank," **I** 69, 116, 121, *139-40,* 141, 162, 166, 192-93; **S** 321

Iba, Howard, **I** 139

Iba, "Moe," **I** 140

Ice Capades, **I** 36, 503-04, 511, 519

Ice Follies, **I** 36, 500, 506, 511, 513, 516

Iceland National Soccer Team, **O** 291, 301

Icelandic Chess Federation, **I** 672

Icely, Lawrence, **O** 127

Idaho Falls, ID baseball club (PrL), **B** 385

Idaho-Oregon Baseball League, **S** 92

Idalia, **O** 201

Idle Hour Farm, Lexington, KY, **S** 534-35

Idlewild, **O** 594

Igloi, Mihaly, **O** 429; **S** 592

Ignatiev, Ardalion, **S** 581

Ikola, Willard J., **I** 572

Il Messagaro basketball club (ItL), **S** 280

Ildrim, **O** 224-25, 593

Ilion, NY baseball club (NYSL), **S** 3

Illinois Amateur Athletic Union, **S** 597

The Illinois Athlete, **I** 242

Illinois Athlete of the Year, **I** 528

Illinois Athletic Club, **I** 264, 620

Illinois Basketball Classic, **S** 292

Illinois Coaches Association, **O** 53

Illinois Coaches Hall of Fame, **S** 312

Illinois College Conference, **F** 15, 414

Illinois Governor's Council on Health and Fitness, **S** 597

Illinois High School Athletic Association, **I** 242

Illinois Institute of Technology, **I** 272

Illinois Intercollegiate Athletic Conference, **S** 173

Illinois PGA Tournament, **S** 515

Illinois Physical Fitness Committee, **F** 339

Illinois Sports Hall of Fame, **I** 208, 243, 338; **O** 522

Illinois State Athletic Commission, **O** 515

Illinois State Normal School, **I** 242

Illinois State Wrestling Championships, **I** 649, 660

Illinois War Memorial Stadium, Champaign-Urbana, IL, **F** 217

Illinois Wesleyan University, **S** 241

Illustrated Football Annual, **F** 90, 172, 193, 409, 416, 426, 637

I'm Marie, **O** 200

Imbros, **S** 532

Imhoff, Darrall T., **I** 23, 231

Imlay, Talma "Tut," **F** 410

Immaculata College, **I** 258-59, 284, 314

Imp, **O** 225

Impellitiere, Ray, **I** 429

Imperial Valley League, **S** 111

Imported Messenger, *See* Messenger

Inamori Golf Classic, S 518-19
Inchcape, S 526-27
Independence Bowl football game, S 420, 428
Independence, MO baseball club (KOML, SWL), B 374, 626; S 229
Independence Stadium, Shreveport, LA, F 501
Independent Insurance Agent Open Golf Tournament, S 519
Independent Rail Transit Subway Soccer Club, O 306
Indian Creek Country Club, Miami Beach, FL, S 513
Indian of the Year, S 397
Indian Sports Hall of Fame, S 397
Indiana Basketball Hall of Fame, I 281, 311-12, 322
Indiana Central College, S 598
Indiana Collegiate Conference, S 259
Indiana Football Hall of Fame, F 439
Indiana Golden Gloves Tournament, I 482
Indiana High School Athletic Association, I 307
Indiana, PA Normal School, F 60, 510
Indiana Pacers basketball club (ABA, NBA), I 60, 73, 78, 148, 196, 213, 225, 244, 266, 304; S 273-74, 296
Indiana Sports Hall of Fame, I 350; S 437
Indiana State University, B 284; I 25-26, 146, 219, 330, 539; S 274, 300
Indiana University, B 180, 311-12; F 13, 100, 173, 212, 241, 307, 356, 373, 439, 457, 470, 526, 532, 544, 551, 613, 667; I 23, 25, 62, 86, 129-30, 162-63, 191, 195-96, 231, 236-37, 269, 272, 281-82, 296-99, 310-12, 321, 577, 584-85, 594, 601-02, 618, 639, 664-65; O 62; S 255, 262-63, 295, 303, 317, 333, 424, 567-68, 572, 598
Indiana University Natatorium, Indianapolis, IN, I 585
Indiana University of Pennsylvania, I 210
Indiana University Sports Hall of Fame, S 303
Indianapolis ABC's baseball club (NNL), B 88, 127, 144, 342, 362, 466, 548-49; S 43, 129
Indianapolis baseball club (AA), B 14, 25, 35, 79, 102, 145, 191, 246, 322, 337, 345, 369, 382-83, 501, 536-37, 554, 572; S 22, 192, 200, 226, 229, 233
Indianapolis baseball club (FL), B 361, 409, 488
Indianapolis baseball club (NL), B 63, 116, 217, 256, 349, 493
Indianapolis baseball club (WL), B 554; S 123
Indianapolis Clowns baseball club (NNL), B 1, 88, 435-36, 599
Indianapolis Colts football club (NFL), F 325; 487-88
Indianapolis Crawfords baseball club (Negro Leagues), B 88
Indianapolis 500 CART Race, O 2-26, 28-29, 31-40, 42-43; S 614, 619-20
Indianapolis Fairgrounds, O 42
Indianapolis Jets basketball club (BAA), I 89, 99
Indianapolis Motor Speedway, O 2, 6-7, 9, 15-17, 28, 31, 35, 38-40, 43; S 614, 619-20; See also Indianapolis 500 CART Race
Indianapolis Motor Speedway Hall of Fame, O 5-6, 9, 15, 20, 22-26, 35, 40, 43

Indonesian National Soccer Team, **O** 301

Infiniti Golf Tournament of Champions, **S** 514-15

Ingram, William A. "Bill," **F** 410

Ingrid, **O** 211

Inkster, Juli Simpson, **S** 509

Inland Empire Hall of Fame, **O** 194

Inman, Dale, **O** 30

Inman, F. G., **O** 356

Innsbruck, Austria Winter Olympic Games, *See* Winter Olympic Games, 1964, 1976

Inside Sports, **S** 337

Insurance City Open Golf Tournament, **O** 113

Inter-Allied Games, **I** 88, 380; **O** 462

Intercollegiate Association of Amateur Athletics of America, **F** 54, 224, 579; **S** 367, 567, 571, 575-76, 581, 583, 591, 594-95

Intercollegiate Association of Amateur Athletics of America Cross Country Championships, **O** 512; **S** 583

Intercollegiate Association of Amateur Athletics of America Indoor Track and Field Championships, **S** 367, 576, 581, 594

Intercollegiate Association of Amateur Athletics of America Outdoor Track and Field Championships, **O** 423, 426, 439-41, 443, 462, 472-73, 479, 483, 495, 512-13, 558, 566, 568; **S** 367, 567, 571, 575-76, 581, 591, 594-95

Intercollegiate Association of America, **O** 444

Intercollegiate Basketball Association, **I** 207, 269

Intercollegiate Basketball Association Metropolitan Award, **I** 269

Intercollegiate Boxing Championships, **S** 610

Intercollegiate Committee on Athletics, **F** 456

Intercollegiate Football Officials, **O** 426

Intercollegiate League, **I** 221-22

Intercollegiate Tennis Championships, *See* National Collegiate Athletic Association Tennis Championships

Interlachen Country Club, Minneapolis, MN, **O** 110; **S** 444

International Amateur Athletic Federation, **I** 671

International Amateur Basketball Federation, **I** 227, 326

International Amateur Wrestling Federation, **I** 643

International Association, **B** 128; **S** 47, 123, 178, 233

International Association of Approved Basketball Officials, **I** 172, 218, 277, 316; **S** 279

International Association of Approved Basketball Officials Sportorial, **I** 277

International Baseball Association, **S** 56

International Basketball Board, **I** 40

International Basketball Committee, **I** 326

International Basketball Federation of the U. S., **I** 74, 182, 217, 288, 296; **S** 279

International Basketball Federation Rules Committee, **I** 326

International Boxing Council, **I** 449

International Boxing Federation, **I** 401, 452; **S** 623, 625-26

International Cross Country Championships, **O** 523

International Cup Polo, **O** 260

International Federation of Women's Hockey Associations, **O** 259, 270

International Four Ball Golf Tournament, S 515

International Freedom Games Dream Mile, O 489

International Golden Gloves Tournament, I 427

International Gymnast Magazine, I 525

International Hockey Federation, I 36

International Lacrosse Federation, O 237

International Lawn Tennis Federation, O 365

International League, B 22, 26, 117, 483, 516, 547; I 154, 158; S 1, 5, 7, 20-21, 24, 29, 35, 45-46, 48, 51, 60, 63, 68-69, 71, 75, 81, 90-91, 101, 104-05, 108, 112-12, 121, 127-28, 146-47, 149, 159, 165, 167, 172, 177, 189, 191, 195, 197, 199-200, 211-12, 216, 218, 221, 227-28, 230, 234, 240, 243, 354, 546

International Motor Cartist Association, O 38

International News Service, F 12, 90, 189, 515, 528, 551; I 156; S 453

International Olympic Committee, F 598; O 255, 458, 507, 543

International Players Tennis Championships, O 342

International Professional Tennis Players, O 342

International Race of Champions Series, S 605

International Regatta Association, O 256

International Road Race, O 19

International Ski Racers Association, O 282

International Sports Organization Committee, F 310

International Swimming Federation, I 577, 585, 616-17

International Swimming Federation Prize Eminence, I 617

International Swimming Hall of Fame, I 486-87, 490, 496-98, 581, 585, 589, 591, 594, 598, 601, 603-04, 606-07, 610-11, 614-15, 619-23

International Tennis Hall of Fame, O 51, 61, 319-21, 323, 325, 328, 330-32, 334-35, 338-40, 342-45, 348-49, 351, 356-61, 364, 366-68, 371-73, 375, 377-78, 381-82, 384-85, 387-91, 393-94, 396-97, 399-401, 405-06, 408, 410-11, 413-14, 417, 419-20, 422; S 551, 553-55, 557-60

International Track Association, O 458, 488, 527

International Volleyball Association, I 48

International Weightlifting Federation, I 628, 631

International Weightlifting Federation Congress, I 629

International Women's Professional Softball Association, O 262

International Women's Swim Meet, I 579

Interstate League, I 65, 158, 232, 250; S 314

Interstate League Championship and Playoffs, I 223

Inter-State League, S 60, 120, 202

Intra-City Golden Gloves Tournament, I 395

Intrepid, O 266

Inverness Country Club, Toledo, OH, O 135, 145

Inverness Four-Ball Golf Tournament, O 127

Inverness Invitation Golf Tournament, O 113

Inverrary Golf Classic, **O** 135, 144, 163, 167

Inwood Golf Course, **O** 136

Inzell, Germany Speed Skating Competition, **O** 313

Iona College, **I** 106, 578

Iooss, Walter, Jr., **S** 335

Iowa Amateur Athletic Union Wrestling Championships, **I** 647

Iowa baseball club (AA), **B** 37, 220, 421; **S** 6, 84, 112

Iowa Coronets basketball club (WPBL), **I** 8

Iowa Girls High School Basketball Hall of Fame, **I** 9

Iowa High School Athletic Association Hall of Fame, **I** 648, 652

Iowa High School Female Athlete of the Year, **I** 183

Iowa Pre-Flight School, **F** 584, 651-53

Iowa Sports Hall of Fame, **B** 21, 95, 371; **F** 297, 320, 550; **I** 9, 577, 647, 652; **O** 550

Iowa State High School Basketball Tournament, **I** 7-8, 183

Iowa State Teachers College, *See* University of Northern Iowa

Iowa State University, **F** 296, 392; **I** 5, 184, 635, 637, 639-42, 652, 654-56; **S** 361, 428, 448, 480, 609, 624

Iowa State Women's College Championships, **S** 319

Iowa State Wrestling Championships, **I** 639, 641, 645, 647, 651, 666

Iowa Wesleyan College, **I** 255; **S** 114

Iowa Wrestling Hall of Fame, **I** 647-48, 652; **S** 617

Iqual, **O** 572

Iranian Olympic Wrestling Team, **I** 639

Irby, "Jan," **S** 320

Ireland, George, **S** 309

Irish, Edward S. "Ned," **I** 99, *140-42*, 171

Irish-American Athletic Club, **I** 570; **O** 460, 489, 491, 534; **S** 585, 592

Irish-American Soccer Club, **O** 310

Irish National Soccer Team, **O** 297, 301

Irish Open Golf Tournament, **O** 126

Irish Rebellion, **O** 205

Irish Tennis Championships, **O** 333, 377, 392

Irish Track and Field Championships, **O** 460

Iron and Oil League, **S** 42

Iron Liege, **O** 190, 195, 217, 573, 603; **S** 529, 532

Iron Mask, **S** 533

Iron Peg, **O** 222

Ironton, OH Tanks football club (Ind.), **F** 479-80

Iroquois, **O** 201

Irvin, Monford "Monte," **B** 132, 141, *273-74*, 362, 543, 553; **S** 10

Irvin, Shirley Fry, **O** 358, *359-60*

Irvington football club, **O** 242

Irwin, "Al," **S** 485

Irwin, Hale S., **F** 18; **O** *134-35*

Irwin, Michael "Mike," **F** 556

Isbell, Cecil, **F** 89, *283-84*, 329

Iselin, James "Jimmy," **S** 529

Iselin, Mrs. Oliver, **S** 531

Iselin, Philip, **O** 105

Isle of Wight Yacht Competition, **O** 101

Iso-Hollo, Volmari, **O** 423

Isolater, **O** 223

Israel, Melvin Allen, *See* Melvin Allen

Israeli National Basketball Team, **I** 250

Israeli National Soccer Team, **O** 291,

300

Israeli Tennis Center, **S** 563

Issel, Daniel P. "Dan," **F** 15; **I** *142-43;* **S** 286

Italian Grand Prix, **O** 7-8

Italian National Soccer Team, **O** 296, 299, 307, 309

Italian Olympic Track and Field Team, **S** 565

Italian Pro Basketball League, **I** 96, 122, 189, 329; **S** 280, 304

Italian Women's Singles Tennis Championships, **O** 326, 388

Ives, Frank, **I** 673

Ivory Bells, **O** 600

Ivy League, **F** 28, 32, 34, 51, 57-58, 63, 65, 85-86, 119, 125, 144, 163, 173, 177, 192, 195, 204, 238-40, 242, 250-51, 254-57, 264-65, 269, 298-99, 301, 309-10, 316, 338, 342, 350, 356, 376, 379-80, 421, 425-26, 459, 465, 468, 473-77, 540-41, 544, 552, 558, 563, 584, 597, 602-03, 625, 635, 644-45; **I** 30-31, 154, 222, 232, 250, 285, 485, 544, 556; **O** 296; **S** 263, 265, 280, 311, 365, 371, 376, 393-94, 404-05, 413, 416-18, 431, 433-34, 444, 483, 489-90, 501-02, 541

Ivy League Championships, **S** 265, 393, 416-18, 541

Izo, George, **F** 395, 572

J & B Gold Putter Award, **S** 508

Jablonski, Raymond L. "Ray," **B** 43

Jack, "Beau," **I** *403-04,* 477, 483

Jack High, **O** 202

Jack-in-the-Box Track and Field Meet, **O** 532

Jackie Robinson Award, **O** 59

Jackson, Alvin N. "Al," **B** 43

Jackson, Arnold, **O** 548

Jackson, Darrell P., **B** 410

Jackson, Harold, **F** *285-86*

Jackson, Henry, Jr., *See* Henry Armstrong

Jackson, James, **O** 602

Jackson, Joseph J. "Shoeless Joe," **B** 108, *275-76,* 325; **S** 54

Jackson, Keith J., **F** 582

Jackson, Keith M., **F** 58; **O** 47, 59, 80; **S** *350-51*

Jackson, Lawrence C. "Larry," **S** *92-93*

Jackson, Leroy, **F** 395

Jackson, Lloyd, **O** 503

Jackson, Lucious B. "Luke," **I** 104, 315

Jackson, Madeline Manning, *See* Madeline Manning Jackson Mims

Jackson, Mervin P., Jr., "Merv," **I** 94

Jackson, Peter, **I** 368-69, 407

Jackson, Ransom J. "Randy," **S** 54

Jackson, Reginald M. "Reggie," **B** *276-78,* 386, 441, 502; **S** 44, 84, 89, 147, 241, 355

Jackson, "Stu," **S** 301

Jackson, Travis C. "Stonewall," **B** *278-79*

Jackson, Vincent E. "Bo," **F** *286-88*

Jackson, Virgil, **O** 492

Jackson, "Willie," **I** 379, 381

Jackson, "Young Peter," **I** 377, 381

Jackson, MI baseball club (WA), **B** 78

Jackson, MS baseball club (CSL, SEL), **B** 146, 279; **S** 131

Jackson Naval Training Station football team, **F** 584

Jackson State University, **F** 62, 285, 399, 461; **S** 364, 415

Jackson Strode, **S** 585

Jacksonville, FL baseball club (IL), **B** 284, 313, 431, 497, 504, 515; **S** 230, 237

Jacksonville, FL baseball club (SAL, SEL, SL), **B** 1, 337, 384, 421,

460, 622; **S** 230, 237

Jacksonville, FL Bulls football club (USFL), **F** 228, 519

Jacksonville, FL Duval Giants baseball club (Negro Leagues), **B** 338

Jacksonville, FL Open Golf Tournament, *See* Greater Jacksonville, FL Open Golf Tournament

Jacksonville, FL Sharks baseball club (WFL), **F** 258

Jacksonville, IL baseball club (Ind.), **B** 307; **S** 82

Jacksonville University, **I** 97-98, 169

Jacobs, Albert, **O** 192

Jacobs, David, **I** 422

Jacobs, Ethel Dushock, **S** 192-93

Jacobs, Eugene "Gene," **S** 192

Jacobs, Helen Hull, **O** 343, *360-61,* 387

Jacobs, Hirsch, **O** *191-92;* **S** 551

Jacobs, James, **S** 625

Jacobs, "Joe," **I** 389

Jacobs, John, **O** 192

Jacobs, Michael S. "Mike," **I** *405-06*

Jacobs, Patrice, **O** 193

Jacobs, Sidney, **O** 192

Jacobs, William P., **O** 375

Jacobs Blocking Award, **F** 444, 495

Jacobson, Larry P., **F** 444, 495

Jacobson, William C. "Baby Doll," **B** *279-80,* 558

Jacoby, Joe, **F** 388

Jada, **O** 214

Jaeger, Andrea, **O** 379

Jaffee, Irving W., **O** *315-16*

Jager, Thomas "Tom," **S** 602-03

Jaguar XK 120 Auto Race Car, **O** 12

Jaipur, **O** 218

Jamaica Golf Classic, **S** 518

Jamaica National Tennis Championships, **O** 343

Jamaica Race Track, Jamaica, NY, **O**

180, 216, 599, 601; **S** 531

Jamaica Track and Field Invitation Meet, **O** 532

Jamerson, Wilbur, **F** 199

James, Bill, **B** 248

James, Donald E. "Don," **F** *288-89*

James, Jesse Craig, **F** 139

James, Lionel "Little Train," **F** 287

James, William "Bill," **F** 35, 403

James E. Sullivan Memorial Trophy, **I** 215, 317, 487-88, 490-91, 493, 503, 531, 539, 579, 584, 587, 596, 598, 601, 612, 615-17, 630, 641, 654; **O** 138, 268-69, 331, 424, 427, 429, 432, 441, 445, 450, 453-54, 457, 474, 478, 481, 492, 501-03, 521-22, 525, 529, 537, 561, 564; **S** 580, 598, 607

James Gordon Bennett Cup, **O** 50

James J. Walker Award, **S** 359

James Madison University, **I** 72; **O** 303

James Naismith Peach Basket Award, **I** 331

James R. Keene Stables, Lexington, KY, **O** 211

Jameson, Elizabeth "Betty," **O** 111; **S** 521

Jamestown, **O** 202, 613

Jamestown, NY baseball club (NYPL, Pol), **B** 115, 196; **S** 51, 95

Jamieson, Charles D. "Charlie," **B** *280-81;* **O** 54

Jane Blalock Athletic Scholarship Fund, **S** 507

Janiro, "Tony," **I** 404

Janneys, Stuart, **O** 603

Janowicz, Victor F. "Vic," **F** 174, *289-90*

January, Donald "Don," **O** 126, 139, 159

Janus, **O** *589-90*

Japan Bowl football game, **F** 138-39,

147, 149, 221, 286, 356, 412, 481, 548, 571, 588

Japan Central League, S 90

Japanese Baseball League, B 139, 152, 264, 519, 619

Japanese National Gymnastic Team, I 542

Japanese National Soccer Team, O 301

Japanese Olympic Diving Team, I 490

Japanese Olympic Wrestling Team, I 635, 659

Japanese Open Golf Tournament, O 113

Japanese Women's Track and Field Team, S 569

Jarrett, Eleanor Holm, *See* Eleanor Holm Whalen

Jarvis, "Ernie," I 389

Jarvis Field, Cambridge, MA, F 63

Jaskwich, Charles "Chuck," F 532

Jastremski, Chester A. "Chet," I 584

Jaworski, Chester "Chet," I 99, 155; S 322

Jazy, Michel, O 526

Jean Beliveau Trophy, S 544

Jean Bereaud, S 527

Jeanette, "Joe," I 419

Jeannette, Harry E. "Buddy," S *293-94*

Jeannette, PA baseball club (EL), B 114

Jeby, "Ben," I 481

Jefferson, John L., F 105, 191, *290-91,* 325, 352

Jefferson, Lafayette, I 167

Jefferson, Roy L., F *292*

Jefferson Downs, O 591

Jefferson Productions, S 283

Jefferson State Junior College, S 2

Jeffords, Jerome V., *See* Jeff Smith

Jeffra, "Harry," I *406-07*

Jeffries, James J. "Jim," I 366, 369, 382, 395, 398, *407-08,* 409, 453, 457, 460-61, 644; S 345

Jeffries, "Kid," I 369

Jenkings, Peggy Fleming, I *510-11,* 516-17

Jenkins, Carol Heiss, I 507, 510, *511-12,* 513-14

Jenkins, Charles L., Sr. "Charlie," O 442; S *581-82*

Jenkins, Charles L., Jr., S 581

Jenkins, Clarence "Fats," B 519; I 49, 68, *143-44,* 333

Jenkins, Darold W., F 168

Jenkins, David W., I 507, *512-13,* 514

Jenkins, Ferguson A. "Fergie," B 364; S 92, *93-94,* 136

Jenkins, Hayes Alan, I 507, 512, *513-14*

Jenkins, "Lou," I 354, 483

Jenkins, Nancy Sue, I 513

Jenkins, Sara Wilkinson, I 512-13

Jenkins, Thomas "Tom," I 643

Jenner, William Bruce, O *474-76*

Jennings, "Al," I 372

Jennings, Hugh A. "Hughie," B 113, 121, 240-41, *281-82,* 299, 301, 363, 494, 605; S 12

Jennings, William M. "Bill," F 71, 292-93

Jenny, O 593

Jensen, Jack E. "Jackie," S *94-95*

Jensen, Zo Ann Olsen, S 94

Jericho, NY Golf Course, O 151

Jerome, Frankie, I 468

Jerome Park, New York, NY, O 177, 220; S 533

Jerome Stakes, O 225

Jersey City, NJ baseball club (EL), B 93, 466, 555

Jersey City, NJ baseball club (IL), B 154-56, 246, 250, 273, 278, 280,

510, 559, 572, 574; **S** 68, 128, 221, 240

Jersey City, NJ Reds basketball club (SL), **I** 40; **S** 114

Jersey Derby, **O** 192, 225, 581

Jersey Handicap, **O** 604

Jersey Jockey Club Purse, **O** 595

Jesse Owens International Trophy, **I** 492; **O** 425, 482; **S** 618

Jessup, Marion Zinderstein, **O** 387, 415

Jet Pilot, **O** 189

Jethroe, Samuel "Sam," **B** *282-83*

Jewish Athlete of the Year Award, **I** 176

Jewish Sports Hall of Fame, **F** 396

J. G. Taylor Spink Award, **I** 105; **S** 342, 346

J. H. Kiphuth Award, **I** 579

Jim Dandy, **O** 192, 585

Jim Malloy Award, **O** 36

Jim Thorpe Award, **O** 425

Jim Thorpe Memorial Athletic Hall of Fame, **I** 297, 662

Jim Thorpe Trophy, **S** 373, 385, 415

Jimmy Clark Award, **O** 36

Jipcho, Benjamin "Ben," **O** 527

J. M. Murphy Club, New York, NY, **I** 423

Joachim, **O** 226

The Jockey Club Gold Cup, **O** 198, 223, 570, 576-77, 580, 585-86, 591-92, 598, 606, 610, 613-15

The Jockey Club of New York, **O** 50, 180-81, 197, 199, 201, 209, 544

The Jockey Club Purse, **O** 594

The Jockey Club Round Table, **O** 180

The Jockey Club Stakes, **O** 596

The Jockey Club Training Club, **O** 180

Jockey's Guild, **O** 178-79, 205

Jockey's Hall of Fame, **O** 173, 176, 179, 184, 186-87, 200, 202, 206,

208-09, 212, 216, 218, 221, 231

Jocko, **S** 340

Joe and Marilyn, **S** 352

Joe Cotton, **O** 206

Joe Cronin Award, **B** 48

Joe Daniels, **S** 530-33

Joe Hayman, **O** 206

Joe Madden, **S** 527

Joe Patchen, **O** 580

Joesting, Herbert W. "Herb," **F** 416; **S** *424-25,* 484

Johansen, "Wally," **I** 91

Johansson, Ingemar, **I** 449; **O** 59

Johansson, Thomas, **I** 638

John, Thomas E. "Tommy," **B** *283-84;* **S** 226

John A. Morris Track School, **S** 527

John B. Kelly, Sr. Award, **O** 263

John Blount, **O** 583

John Brown College, **S** 389

John Bunn Award, **S** 279

John Carroll University, **F** 542-43; **I** 250, 519

John F. Kennedy College, **S** 319

John Hancock Sun Bowl football game, **S** 393

John Henry, **O** *590-91*

John Henry Handicap, **O** 218

John Henry Lloyd Baseball Park, Atlantic City, NJ, **B** 334

John Lucas Fitness Program, **S** 299

John P. Grier, **O** 197; **S** 533

John R. Wooden Award, **I** 266; **S** 254, 278, 282, 302, 306

John Tudor Cup, **S** 541

John Ward Stable, **O** 221

Johncock, Gordon W., **O** *16-17,* 21, 34

Johnen, **S** 533

Johns Hopkins University, **O** 233-34, 236-39, 242-44, 246, 248-51, 302-03; **S** 96, 502

Johnson, Albert, **O** *193-94*

Johnson, Alexander "Alex," S 136

Johnson, Arnitz "Arnie," I 114

Johnson, Arthur John "Jack," I 366, 406, *408-11,* 418-19, 430, 453, 476-77, 479, 543, 643; O 91

Johnson, Barbara, I 255

Johnson, "Beany," S 46

Johnson, Benjamin "Ben," O 487, 541; S 199

Johnson, Byron Bancroft "Ban," B 24, 26, 107, 110, 137, 199, 226, 242-43, *285-86,* 292, 322, 353, 355, 358, 392, 456-57, 492, 512, 523-24, 529, 636; O 97-98

Johnson, Charles, I 430

Johnson, Charles W. 'Charley," F 248; S *425-27*

Johnson, Cornelius C., O *476-77;* S 566

Johnson, Darrell D., B 619

Johnson, David A. "Davey," S 7, 51, *95-96,* 212-13

Johnson, Dennis W. "DJ," I *144-45;* S 327

Johnson, Derek, O 442

Johnson, Donald "Don," I *343-44*

Johnson, Dujuan, I 452

Johnson, Earvin, Jr. "Magic," I *145-47,* 218, 298; S 300

Johnson, Ed L., S 292

Johnson, Grant "Home Run," B 255, *286-87,* 333, 451; S 168

Johnson, Gus, Jr., I *147-48,* 220

Johnson, Hunter H., O 473

Johnson, Ivan W. "Ching," S 537

Johnson, James Earl, S *427*

Johnson, James William "Jimmy," S *427-28*

Johnson, John Henry, F *293-94*

Johnson, "Junior," O 42

Johnson, Mark, S 544

Johnson, Marques K., I 219; S *294-95*

Johnson, Ollie, I 138

Johnson, Pete, F 228

Johnson, Rafer L., O *477-78;* S 427, 572

Johnson, Robert "Bob," I 94

Johnson, Robert "Bob," I 572; S *543-44*

Johnson, Robert D. "Bob," B 431

Johnson, Robert L. "Indian Bob," B *287-88*

Johnson, Roger, I 80

Johnson, Roy C., B 287

Johnson, Trumaine, F 500

Johnson, Virgil, I *570-71*

Johnson, Vonzell, S 623

Johnson, Wallace F., O 362

Johnson, Walter, O 323

Johnson, Walter P. "The Big Train," B 93, 159, 173-74, 208, 213, 266-67, *288-89,* 293, 332, 337, 342, 361, 400, 417, 420, 465, 493, 516, 558, 606, 612, 625; O 60, 82, 90; S 101, 183, 243

Johnson, William C. "Bill," I *148-49*

Johnson, William D. "Bill," O *279-81*

Johnson, William J. "Judy," B 31, 127, 223, *289-91,* 453

Johnson, William R., O 573-74, 583, 608-09

Johnson City, TN baseball club (ApL), B 233; S 147

Johnson Foundation, F 294

Johnsos, "Luke," F 417

Johnston, David, O 579

Johnston, Donald Neil, I *149-50*

Johnston, James, S 610

Johnston, Wheeler, B 65

Johnston, William M. "Billy," O 356, *361-63,* 372, 378, 385, 403-04, 416-17

Johnstown, O 184, 223

Johnstown, NY baseball club (NYSL), **B** 90

Johnstown, PA baseball club (EL, MAL), **B** 3, 34, 123, 193, 460; **S** 242

Joiner, Charles, Jr. "Charlie," **F** 15, 191, 291, *295,* 500

Joint Basketball Rules Committee, **I** 264

Jolley, Smead P., **S** 5

Joly, Andree, **I** 509, 511; **S** 601

Jonabel Farm, **O** 579

Jones, Barry, **S** 172

Jones, Benjamin A. "Ben," **O** 176, *194-95,* 571, 576, 614; **S** 528-29

Jones, Bertram H. "Bert," **F** 296

Jones, Calvin J., **F** 297

Jones, Charles W., Sr. "Charley," **S** *96-98*

Jones, Charles W., Jr., **S** 97

Jones, Clinton "Clint," **F** 127

Jones, David, **F** 48

Jones, David "Deacon," **F** 224, *297-98,* 441, 640

Jones, "Doug," **I** 384

Jones, Dwight, **I** 174

Jones, "Ed," **S** 517

Jones, Fielder A., **B** 241; **S** *98-99*

Jones, Georgina, **O** 354

Jones, "Gorilla," **I** 466

Jones, Grover W. "Deacon," **S** 34

Jones, Hayes W., **O** 437-38, 447, *478-79*

Jones, Horace Allyn "Jimmy," **O** 195, 571, 576; **S** *528-29*

Jones, Howard H., **F** 23, 153-54, 266, *298-300,* 513, 551; **S** 495

Jones, "Jerry," **S** 428

Jones, John Paul, **O** *479-80,* 548

Jones, K. C., **I** 12, 124, *150-51,* 180, 184, 210, 231, 262; **S** 281

Jones, Lawrence M. "Biff," **F** 83, *300-01,* 440

Jones, Louis W. III, **S** 581

Jones, Marion, *See* Marion Jones Farquhar

Jones, Perry, **O** 365; **S** 553-54, 560

Jones, "Piano Man," **I** 441

Jones, Ralph W., **F** 500

Jones, Robert Clyde "Bobby," **I** 404; **S** 269

Jones, Robert T., Jr. "Bobby," **O** 63, 89, 108-09, 121, 127-28, 131-32, 134, *135-36,* 138, 146, 158, 160, 162, 165, 268; **S** 512

Jones, Rufus Parnelli, **O** 37; **S** *614*

Jones, Samuel "Sam," **I** 12, 124, *151-52,* 199

Jones, Samuel P. "Sam," **B** *291-92;* **S** 325

Jones, Stanley P. "Stan," **S** *428-29*

Jones, Stuart "Slim," **S** *99-100*

Jones, Thomas A. D. "Tad," **F** 298-99, *301-02,* 504

Jones, "Tom," **I** 448, 479

Jones, Wali C. "Wally," **S** 261, 287

Jones, William A. "Dub," **F** 296, 409, 524

Jones, Willie E. "Puddin Head," **B** 75

Jones Stadium, Lubbock, TX, **F** 293

Joplin, MO baseball club (MVL, WA), **B** 374; **S** 87, 110, 190

Jordan, Henry W., **S** *429-30*

Jordan, James Ralph, "Shug," **F** 147, 577; **S** 368, *430-31*

Jordan, Lee Roy, **F** 75, *301-02*

Jordan, Michael J., **I** *152-54,* 283, 304

Jordan Field, Auburn, AL, **S** 141

Joseph, Newton "Newt," **B** 6

Joseph P. Day Cup, **I** 588

Josephson, Lester A. "Les," **F** 363

Joss, Adrian "Addie," **B** *292-93,* 408, 587

Joyce, Donald "Don," **F** 348, 520

Joyce, Joan, **O** *261-62*

Joyce, Kevin F., I 199

Joyce, Robert, S 540

Joyce, William M. "Bill," S *100*

Joyce, "Willie," I 477

Joyner, "Al," Jr., O 481; S 579

Joyner, Jacqueline, *See* Jacqueline Joyner-Kersee

Joyner-Kersee, Jacqueline, O *480-82*

J. P. Allen Award, O 401

Judge, Joseph L. "Joe," B *293-94;* S 127

Judge, "Steve," O 204, 221

Judge Fullerton, O 586

Judger, O 222

Julian, Alvin F. "Doggie," I *154-55*

Julliard School of Music, S 298

Juneau, William "Bill," S 434

Juniata College, F 320

Junior A Hockey Championship, I 558

Junior Champion Stakes, O 198

Junior College Baseball Championships, S 17

Junior College Basketball Championships, S 324

Junior Davis Cup Tennis Team, O 401; S 278

Junior Featherweight Boxing Championships, I 431

Junior Heavyweight Boxing Championships, I 645

Junior Lightweight Boxing Championships, I 363-64, 378-79, 469

Junior Middleweight Boxing Championships, I 396, 422

Junior Olympic Basketball Team, S 262

Junior Olympic Indoor Swim Championships, I 582

Junior Olympic Outdoor Swim Championships, O 577, 582

Junior Olympics, I 670

The Junior Superstars, I 503

Junior Welterweight Boxing Championships, I 446, 452

Jurgensen, Christian A. III "Sonny," F 292, *303-04,* 354, 593; S 482, 497

Jurich, "Jackie," I 447

Jurupa Hills, CA Country Club, O 120

Justice, Charles "Choo Choo," F 78, *304-05,* 558-59, 60

Juvenile Champion Horse, O 598-99, 614

Juvenile Stakes, O 598, 613

Kaat, James L. "Jim," B *295-96;* S 145

KABC Radio-Television, Los Angeles, CA, F 244; I 263

KABE-Radio, Los Angeles, CA, S 350

Kaer, Morton "Mort," F 153

Kaese, Harold, S 346

Kaftan, George A., I 154

Kahanamoku, Duke P., I 586, *597-98,* 600, 620

Kahn, Roger, O 59; S *351-52*

Kai Sang, S 526-27

Kaiser, David "Dave," F 404

Kaiser International Golf Tournament, O 143-44

Kalama, Thelma, I 587

Kalamazoo, MI baseball club (TSL), B 92

Kalamazoo, MI Race Track, O 584

Kalamazoo State Normal College, *See* Western Michigan University

Kaline, Albert W. "Al," B 80, *296-97,* 300, 514; S 44

Kalule, Ayub, I 422

Kameda, Akio, I 452

Kamm, William E. "Willie," S *100-01*

Kane, "Eddie," I 390, 436

Kane, PA baseball club (ISL), B 134

Kankakee, IL baseball club (NA), B 534, 572

Kansas, "Rocky," I 392, *411-12*, 415, 436, 469, 476

Kansas Centennial Hall of Fame, I 5

Kansas City Amateur Sports Hall of Fame, I 75

Kansas City Athletic Club basketball club, I 4, 63, 181

Kansas City Athletics baseball club (AL), B 14, 37, 41, 133, 163, 167, 179, 181, 184, 229, 246, 277, 352, 364, 382, 385, 393, 404, 436, 517, 597, 614; S 8, 39, 50, 67-68, 87, 106-09, 113, 142, 171-72, 186, 195, 227, 237, 247

Kansas City baseball club (FL, WA, WL), B 328, 353, 419

Kansas City Blue Diamonds basketball club, I 313

Kansas City Blues baseball club (AA), B 2, 27, 29, 62, 123, 187, 237-38, 258, 263, 311, 317, 326, 336, 346, 367, 374, 385, 416, 475, 529, 535-36, 571, 600, 624, 626; S 4, 81, 87, 97, 106, 170, 182, 204, 229-31

Kansas City Blues hockey club (CeHL), I 546

Kansas City Chiefs football club (AFL), F 36, 75-76, 179, 201-02, 253, 277, 280, 334, 354, 367, 376, 572, 591, 610; O 67; S 363, 432, 442, 450, 469, 486-87

Kansas City Chiefs football club (NFL), F 36, 55, 75-76, 96, 133-34, 157, 219, 277, 314, 334, 363, 483, 485, 572-73, 591, 593, 610, 665, 670; I 22; S 407, 486-87

Kansas City Chiefs Hall of Fame, F 610; S 450

Kansas City Colts baseball club

(Negro Leagues), B 482

Kansas City Comets Soccer Club (MISL), O 304

Kansas City Cook Paint Company basketball club, I 63-64, 326

Kansas City Country Club, O 165

Kansas City Cowboys baseball club (NL), B 307

Kansas City Cowboys football club (NFL), F 232, 447

Kansas City Giants baseball club (Negro Leagues), I 482

Kansas City Hall of Champions, I 75

Kansas City Healy Motors basketball club, I 106, 193

Kansas City Independent Basketball Tournament, I 149

Kansas City Junior College, I 201

Kansas City Monarchs baseball club (NAL, NNL), B 6, 21, 31, 55-56, 141, 192, 214, 290, 362, 436, 479-80, 482-83, 500, 520, 533, 599, 608-09, 612; S 43, 137, 224, 242

Kansas City-Omaha Kings basketball club (NBA), I 9, 311, 324; S 282-83, 326

Kansas City Pla-Mors hockey club (USHL), I 571

Kansas City Royals Baseball Academy, S 237

Kansas City Royals baseball club (AL), B 38, 42, 47-48, 75, 81, 102-03, 138, 242, 305, 329, 370, 392, 425, 431, 445, 449, 460-61, 497, 502, 575, 619, 622-23; F 288, 383; S 16, 28, 34, 50, 63, 68, 87, 136-37, 170, 193, 214, 225, 237, 355

Kansas City Schmeltzers baseball club (Ind.), B 310

Kansas City Stars baseball club (Negro Leagues), B 32

Kansas City Stars basketball club, I

119

Kansas City Steers basketball club (ABL), I 33

Kansas Conference, I 177

Kansas Conference Coaches Association, I 177

Kansas-Oklahoma-Missouri League, S 11, 229

Kansas Relays, F 62; O 501

Kansas Sports Hall of Fame, B 95; F 525; I 182, 217, 269

Kansas State College, Pittsburg, KS, I 271; O 485

Kansas State Teachers College, Emporia, KS, I 73

Kansas State University, F 209, 373, 481, 515, 531, 627, 663; I 16, 93-94, 109, 257; O 427; S 370, 372, 580, 609

Kapanga, O 592

Kaplan, Louis "Kid," I 392

Kaplowitz, Daniel "Danny," I 23

Kappahu, Helene Madison, I 598-600

Karabachak, Resit, I 659

Karakas, Michael G. "Mike," I 553, 559-60, 570-72

Kareem: Basketball Great, S 347

Karl, George M., S 307

Karolyi, Bela, I 533, 535

Karpov, Anatoly, I 672

Karr, William "Bill," F 417

Karras, Alexander G. "Alex," F 161, 271, 297, 307-08, 517

Karras, Louis "Lou," F 307

Kasko, Edward M. "Eddie," B 43

Katcavage, James R. "Jim," F 397, 503

Kate Smith's Celtics basketball club, I 171, 273

Katie Pease, S 533

Kauai King, O 575, 599

Kauff, Benjamin M. "Benny," B 323, 488

Kaufmann, Carl, O 450-51

Kautsky's Athletic Club basketball club, I 310

Kautz, Wilbert, I 264

Kavanaugh, Kenneth "Ken," F 308-09

Kaw, Edgar L., S 431-32

Kawamoto, Evelyn, I 604

Kazantsev, Vladimir, O 423

Kazmaier, Richard W., Jr. "Dick," F 84, 309-10

KCET-Radio, Los Angeles, CA, O 63

KDKA-Radio, Pittsburgh, PA, S 358

Kealoha, Warren D., I 600-01

Keane, Clifford "Cliff," S 346

Keaney, Frank W., I 155-56; S 322

Keaney, Warner "Flip," I 155

Keaney, Winifred, I 155

Kearney, James L. "Jim," F 591

Kearney, NE baseball club (NeSL), B 195

Kearns, Jack "Doc," I 374, 412-13, 453, 474-75, 479

Kearns, "Soldier," I 424

Kearns, Thomas F., Jr. "Tom," I 199

Kearny Scots-American Soccer Club (ASL), O 299

Keefe, Timothy J. "Tim," B 297-98, 384, 420, 429, 598; S 151

Keefe, William "Bill," F 155

Keeler, O. B., O 136

Keeler, William H. "Willie," B 95, 131, 240, 281, 298-99, 301, 354, 363; S 19, 210

Keenan, Michael "Mike," I 558

Keene, James R., O 196, 578, 592-93; S 533-34

Keene, Thomas "Tom," O 426

Keene Stakes, O 595

Keeneland, Lexington, KY, O 178, 182, 222, 610

Keep Off My Turf, S 387

Keino, "Kip," O 527

Kell, George C., B 297, *299-300*

Keller, Charles E. "Charlie," B 258, 597; S 86, *101-02*

Keller, Harold K. "Hal," S 102

Keller, Patricia J., *See* Patricia Keller McCormick

Kellerman, Ernie J., F 526

Kelley, John "Snooks," I *560-61;* S 543

Kelley, John A., S *582-83*

Kelley, John J., S *583*

Kelley, Joseph J. "Joe," B 240-41, 281, 299, *301,* 568; S 19, 210

Kelley, Lawrence M. "Larry," F *310-11;* S 490

Kelly, Daniel "Dan," S *352-53*

Kelly, Daniel J. "Dan," O 455, 470

Kelly, Donaldson N. "Don," O *239-40*

Kelly, Eugene E. "Gene," F 202

Kelly, George L. "High Pockets," B *302-03,* 488

Kelly, Harold, S 352

Kelly, Hugo, I 414, 416, 448

Kelly, "Jack," I 51

Kelly, James E. "Jim," F 518; S 487

Kelly, "Jimmy," I 468

Kelly, John, I 420; S 353

Kelly, John B., Sr. "Johnny," O *262-64*

Kelly, John B., Jr., O 263

Kelly, John S. "Shipwreck," F 83

Kelly, John, *See* "Nonpareil" Jack Dempsey

Kelly, Leroy, F *311-12;* S 412

Kelly, Mark, F 154

Kelly, Michael J. "King," B 11, 96, *303-04,* 349, 496, 541, 637; S 152

Kelly, Pamela, "Pam," I 315

Kelly, Reynolds J. "Ren," B 302

Kelly, "Rich," I 160

Kelly, Roberto C., S 211

Kelly Post Award, O 244

Kelsall, Keri, I 535

Kelsey, John, B 50

Kelso, O 176, 189, 576, *591-92*

Keltner, Kenneth F. "Ken," S *102-03,* 182

Kemmer, Lloyd, I 228

Kemp, John F. "Jack," S *432-33*

Kemp, Steven F. "Steve," S 38

Kemper Open Golf Tournament, O 124, 167

Kemper Women's Open Golf Tournament, O 168

Kendall College, *See* University of Tulsa

Kendrick, "Pat," I 377

Kenilworth Park, O 608

Kenko Sports Academy, B 258

Kennedy, James Walter, I 8, 42, *156-57;* O 70

Kennedy, John F., F 647-48; O 61

Kennedy, Joseph, O 87

Kennedy, Karol E., S *614-15,* 615

Kennedy, Matthew P. "Pat," I *157-58,* 233

Kennedy, Michael E. III "Peter," S 614, *615*

Kennedy Road, O 228-29

Kennett Award, F 497

Kennewick, WA baseball club (NWL), B 522

Kenosha Club football club (Indep.), F 375

Kenrick, "Jim," I 370

Kensington Stingrays Swim Club, South Bend, IN, I 619

Kent, Charles, O 587

Kent State University, B 425; F 288, 330, 634; I 628; S 146, 420

Kentucky, O 594

Kentucky Athletic Hall of Fame, S 384

Kentucky Basketball Tournament, Lexington, KY, **I** 109
Kentucky Colonels basketball club (ABA), **I** 142, 226; **S** 286
Kentucky Derby, **O** 173, 175-76, 179, 183, 185-86, 189-90, 194-96, 198-99, 202-06, 209, 211, 215-18, 220, 222-7, 229, 232, 569-70, 572-73, 575, 577-79, 582, 584-85, 589, 596, 598-99, 601, 603-04, 606-08, 610-15; **S** 345, 527, 529-36
Kentucky Horse Park, Lexington, KY, **O** 591
Kentucky Jockey Club Stakes, **O** 198, 230-31, 613
Kentucky League, **S** 163, 190
Kentucky Oaks, **O** 199, 609
Kentucky Pride, **O** 195
Kentucky Sports Hall of Fame, **I** 256
Kentucky State University, **F** 656; **I** 202
Kentucky Wesleyan College, **I** 90
Kenyon College, **B** 573; **F** 496; **S** 556
Keogan, George E., **I** *158-59,* 163-64, 208; **S** 309
Keokuk, IA baseball club (ML, 3IL, WL), **B** 195, 382; **S** 354
Keokuk, IA Westerners baseball club (NA), **S** 97
Keough, Harry J., **O** *300-02*
Keough, Hugh, **O** 73
Keough, William, **O** 300
Kerala, **O** 579
Kerkorian, Gary, **F** 533
Kerner, "Ben," **I** 110-11
Kerr, Andrew "Andy," **F** 185, *313,* 636
Kerr, John G. "Red," **I** 96, 113, *159-60,* 199
Kerr, Richard H. "Dickie," **B** 412
Kerr, Travis, **O** 603
Kerr, William W. "Bill," **B** 158

Kerr Stadium, Hamilton, NY, **F** 313
Kerry Patch, **O** 212
Kersee, Robert "Bob," **O** 436, 480-81; **S** 579
Kersee's World Class Track Team, **S** 579
Kessler, Robert "Bob," **I** 167; **S** 333
Ketchel, Stanley "Stan," **I** 390, *413-14,* 416, 445, 448
Key to the Mint, **O** 607
Key West, FL baseball club (FSL), **B** 542
Keyes, Marvin Leroy, **F** *314*
Keystone League, **O** 295
Keystone Ore, **O** 182
Keystone Pioneer, **O** 191
Keystone Race Track, Philadelphia, PA, **F** 511
Kezar Stadium, San Francisco, CA, **F** 378
Khaled, **O** 612
Khozaam, **O** 606
Kid Blackie, *See* William H. "Jack" Dempsey
Kid Chocolate, **I** 417
Kidd, William W. "Billy," **O** *281-82*
Kiecal, Stanislaus, *See* Stanley Ketchel
Kiel Auditorium, St. Louis, MO, **I** 126
Kieran, John F., **B** 107, 390; **F** 95; **I** 458; **O** 60-61, *71-72*
Kiesling, Walter A. "Walt," **F** *314-15*
Kiev, USSR Track and Field Meet, **O** 500
Kight, Lenore, **I** 599
Kiick, James F. "Jim," **F** 122, 333; **S** 335, 441
Kilbane, John P. "Johnny," **I** 357, 364, 379, 411, *415,* 476
Kilfoyle, John F., **B** 523
Kilgrow, Joseph "Joe," **F** 595

Killebrew, Harmon C., **B** 228, *304-05*, 633; **S** 3, 89

Killefer, William L. "Bill," **B** 5; **S** 144

Killy, Jean Claude, **O** 281, 533

Kilmarnock Soccer Club, Scotland, **O** 306

Kilmer, William O. "Billy," **F** 37, 292, 593

Kilmer, William S., **S** 531

Kilmer, Willis S., **O** 582

Kilpatrick, John Reed, **I** 141; **S** *433-34*

Kilrain, "Jake," **I** 467

Kilroy, Francis J. "Bucko," **F** *316*

Kim, Sang Hyun, **I** 452

Kimball, Bruce, **I** 491

Kimball, John, **S** 331

Kimbrough, "Jack," **F** 317

Kimbrough, John A., **F** *316-18*, 434

Kinard, Frank M. "Bruiser," **F** *318-19*, 621

Kinard, William "Billy," **F** 622

Kinchen, James, **S** 612

Kiner, Ralph M., **B** 305, *306-07*, 388, 404, 502; **O** 83; **S** 188, *355*

King, Albert, **I** 71, 160

King, " Becky," **S** 321

King, Bernard, **I** *160-61*

King, Billie Jean Moffitt, **O** 262, 335-36, 358, *363-64*, 375, 381, 386-87, 389; **S** 341, 563-64

King, Charles F. "Silver," **B** *307-08*

King, "Don," **I** 401

King, Elizabeth "Betsy," **S** 508, 518

King, George S., Sr., **I** 45

King, J. Barton, **S** *615-16*

King, James, **S** 526-27

King, Kenneth L. "Kenny," **F** 586

King, Larry, **O** 363-64

King Levinsky, *See* Levinsky, King

King, Maxine J., *See* Maxine King Hogue

King, Nelson, **S** 284

King, Philip "Phil," **F** 108, 343, 438, 603; **S** *434-35*

King, Raymond W. "Ray," **F** 27

King, Robert "Bob," **S** 273-74

King, "Tom," **I** 399

King, William "Dolly," **I** 23, 114-15; **S** 283

"The King and His Court softball club, **O** 257-58

King Features Syndicate, **O** 85, 91

King International Freedom Games Dream Mile, **O** 488

King Louie Open Bowling Tournament, Kansas City, MO, **I** 349

King Ranch, Kingsville, TN, **O** 572; **S** 527

King Tut, **I** 451

Kingdom, Roger, **S** *583-85*

Kingman, **O** 183

Kingman, David A. "Dave," **B** 190; **S** 38, *103-04*

Kings County Tennis Club, Brooklyn, NY, **O** 375-76

King's Courier, **O** 593

King's Plate, **O** 596

Kingscote, "Algy," **O** 362

Kingsport, TN baseball club (ApL), **B** 409

Kingston, **O** 206, *592-93*

Kingston, Canada hockey club (EPL), **I** 573

Kingston, Jamaica Track and Field Meet, **O** 457, 489

Kingston, NY Colonels basketball club (NYSL, ISL, MeL), **I** 20, 29-30, 222-23

Kinnick, Nile C., Jr., **F** 13, *319-20*

Kinnick Stadium, Iowa City, IA, **F** 320

Kinsella, John P., **I** 584, *601-02*

Kinsey, Edward, **O** 348

Kinston, NC baseball club (CrL, VL), B 177, 233; S 78
Kinzig, Lloyd, I 222
Kiphuth, Delancy, I 602
Kiphuth, Robert J. H. "Bob," I 602-03, 606
Kipke, Harry G., F 120, 263; I 312; S 435-36, 458
Kirby, Vernon, O 396
Kirham, Thomas, O 602
Kirin Cup Golf team, S 520
Kirkland, James, S 345
Kirkman, Boone, I 383
Kirksey, George, F 30; S 443
Kirksey, Morris, S 589
Kirrane, John J. "Jack," I 565
Kite, Thomas O., Jr. "Tom," S 510, 514-15, 520
Kittiwak, O 222
Kitty League, S 81, 246
Kitzbuhel, Austria Alpine Ski Competition, O 275, 288
Kiviat, Abel R., O 548; S 585-86
Kizer, Noble E., I 312
Klares, John, I 348
Klaus, Frank, I 376, 414, 415-16, 448
Kleberg, Robert J., O 572; S 527
Klein, Charles H. "Chuck," B 74, 168, 308-09
Klein, Joseph "Joe," B 372
Klein, Joseph "Joe," F 659
Kleine, Joseph W. "Joe," S 254
Kleinhans, Theodore O. "Ted," B 309
Kleinow, John P. "Jack," B 91
Klem, William J. "Bill," B 23, 110, 157, 309-10; S 156, 179, 199, 208, 248
Klemme, IA High School, I 183
Klepper, O 213
Klier, Leo, I 250
KLIF-Radio, Dallas, TX, O 77
Klima, Petr, S 538

Kling, John G. "Johnny," B 310-11
Kluszewski, Theodore B. "Ted," B 125, 311-12
KMOX-Radio, St. Louis, MO, F 17, 141; O 55-57, 65; S 352-53
KMPC-Radio, Los Angeles, CA, F 492; O 62
Knape, Ulrika, I 489
Knapp, Percy, O 334, 338
Knapp, William, Sr. "Willie," O 195-97, 200, 582
Knapp, William, Jr., O 197
Knapp Cup, O 258
Kneip, Philip "Phil," O 237
Knevil, Evil, O 76
Knickerbocker Base Ball Grounds, Hoboken, NJ, O 101
Knickerbocker Club, New York, NY, O 367
Knickerbocker Yacht Club, New York, NY, O 505
Knight, Charles Ray, O 137
Knight, F. D. "Dixie," O 582
Knight, Henry, O 586
Knight, Laura, O 321
Knight, Nancy Lopez Melton, O 136-38
Knight, Robert M. "Bobby," I 23, 63, 161-63, 186, 296-98; S 255-57, 262, 295, 303
Knight's Farm, O 582
Knoehr, Albert, See Abe Attell
Knopp, Martin, I 658
Knostman, Richard W. "Dick," I 94
Knowles, Carl, I 360
Knox, Charles R. "Chuck," F 320-21, 590; S 384
Knox College, I 16; S 483
Knoxville, TN baseball club (SA, SAL, SL), B 27, 167, 262, 333, 369, 438, 446, 495; S 6, 57, 245
Knoxville, TN Track and Field Meet, O 447

Knute Rockne Memorial Trophy, S 429, 452, 499
Koch, "Ben," I 445
Koch, Burton, F 293
Koch, Desmond D., O 510
Koch, Morita, O 436
Koch, William "Bill," O 282-83
Kocsis, Bruce, I 582
Kodak, O 46
Kodak All-American Selection Committee, S 320
Kodak Award, S 404
Kodak Basketball Classic, Rochester, NY, I 115, 154
Kodes, Jan, O 379, 399
Koenig, Mark A., B 309
Kofoed, Jack C., F 65, 204, 269
Kohl, Herbert, S 307
Kohler, Charles, S 526
Kohout, Slarka, I 516
Kok, Ada, I 582
Kokomo, IN baseball club (ML, MOVL), B 81, 137
Kolb, Claudia A., See Claudia Kolb Thomas
Koll, Christopher, I 645
Koll, David, I 645
Koll, Frank H., I 645
Koll, Michael, I 645
Koll, Robert, I 645
Koll, William H. "Bill," I 645-47
Komenich, Milo, I 70
Komives, Howard K. "Butch," I 7
KOMO Radio-TV, Seattle, WA, S 350
Komonenen, David, S 582
Konetchy, Edward J. "Ed," B 312-13
Konno, Ford H., I 603-04
Kono, Tommy T., I 630-31
Konstanty, Casimir James "Jim," S 104-05
Konz, Kenneth "Ken," F 599
Koosman, Jerome M. "Jerry," B 313-14
Kopcha, Joseph "Joe," F 186, 417; S 436-37
Koplilov, Sergei, I 592
Koppe, George, See George Cuppy
Korachuen Stadium, Tokyo, Japan, S 626
Korbut, Olga, I 531
Korean Olympic Diving Team, I 490
Kormann, Peter M., I 528
Kornig, Helmuth, O 530
Kosar, Bernie, S 487
Kosky, "Ed," F 94, 532
Kotz, John, I 85
Koufax, Sanford "Sandy," B 9, 159, 176, 314-16, 380, 497, 544; O 81-82; S 69, 88, 120, 138, 160, 167, 347
Kovacs, Frank, O 331; S 556
Kovalev, Vladimir, I 518
KOWB-Radio, Laramie, WY, O 68
Kozelub, Karel, O 404
Kraak, Charles, S 317
Kraenzlein, Alvin C., O 482-84; S 591-92
Krall, Gerald "Gerry," F 173
Kramer, "Danny," I 365
Kramer, Frank L., O 264-65
Kramer, Gerald L. "Jerry," F 104, 321-22, 354-55
Kramer, John A. "Jack," O 341-43, 355, 365-66, 386, 389, 400, 407; S 341, 552-54, 556
Kramer, John H. "Jack," B 536
Kramer, Ronald J. "Ron," F 322-23
Kramer Tennis Club, O 326
Krapp, Eugene H., B 408
Kratschmer, Guido, O 475
Krause, Edward W. "Moose," I 159, 163-64, 208; S 271
Krause, Henry "Red," O 65
Kreevich, Michael A. "Mike," B 582
Kremer, Remy P. "Ray," S 105-06

Kreuter's Billiard Parlor, New York, NY, I 677
Krichell, Paul B., B 222, 474
Krieger, "Solly," I 481
Kristiansen, Ingrid, O 529
Kroc, Joan B., S 206
Kroc, Ray A., B 134; S 206
Kronk Gymnasium, Detroit, MI, S 612
Krupp, Eric, S 545
Krushelnyski, Michael "Mike," S 538
Krzyzewski, Michael "Mike," S 280, 295-96
KSPO-Radio, San Francisco, CA, S 356
KTLA-Radio, Los Angeles, CA, F 244; O 63
KTTV-TV, Los Angeles, CA, O 62, 92; S 142
Kualheim, Arne, O 435
Kubek, Anthony C. "Tony," O 65, 68; S 230, 353-54
Kubicka, Terry P., I 500
Kubski, "Al," S 71
Kuck, John, O 484-85
Kuechenberg, Robert J. "Bob," F 323-24
Kuechenberg, "Rudy," F 323
Kuenn, Harvey E., Jr., B 316; S 106-07
Kuharich, Joseph "Joe," F 382, 566; S 437-38
Kuhel, Joseph A. "Joe," B 317; S 14
Kuhn, Bowie K., B 16, 175, 182, 186, 317-19, 322, 375, 394, 426; O 61, 103, 272
Kumagae, Ichiya, O 362, 421
Kummer, Clarence, O 193, 197, 596
Kummer, Edward, O 197
Kundla, John A. "Johnny," I 164-65, 241
Kunigk, Clara, O 277

Kurland, Robert A. "Bob," I 70, 113, 140, 165-67
Kurochi, O 196
Kurtsinger, Charles E., O 197-99, 614
Kush, Frank J., F 126, 291, 324-25
Kutis Soccer Club, St. Louis, MO, O 301
Kutner, Malcolm J. "Mal," S 438-39
Kutroff, Clara, O 411
Kutsher's Country Club, Monticello, NY, I 171, 308
Kutz, O 583
Kuznetsov, Vasily, O 477-78
Kyle Rote Football League, S 471
Kyocera Inamari Golf Classic, O 118
Kyriadkides, Stylianos, S 582

La Barba, Fidel, I 389, 417, 435, 468
La Beach, Lloyd, O 453
La Blanche, George, I 373
La Crosse, WI baseball club (WSL), B 312-13
La Crosse, WI State Teachers College, S 279
La Fontaine, Barbara, I 506
La Fontaine, Patrick "Pat," S 544-45
La Gorce Golf Tournament, S 523
La Guardia, Fiorello, I 115
La Jolla, CA Beach and Tennis Club, I 581
La Jolla, CA Golf Club, O 152
La Morte, "Willie," I 480
La Motta, Giacobe "Jake," O 417-18, 455, 483
La Prele Creek Ranch, O 609
La Prevoyante, O 576, 607
La Quinta Country Club, Palm Springs, CA, O 410
La Russa, Anthony, Jr. "Tony," S 58,

107-08

La Russo, Rudolph "Rudy," **I** 154

La Salle University, **I** 43, 86, 100, 109, 150, 179-80, 241; **S** 14

La Starza, Roland, **I** 437

La Verne College, **B** 460; **O** 522

La Vie Claire French Cycling Team, **S** 617

Labatt Open Golf Tournament, **O** 115

Labold Brothers, **O** 223

Lacey, Samuel **S** 291

Lach, Stephen J. "Steve," **F** *327-28,* 616

Lacoste, Jean Rene, **O** 362, 385, 404, 418

Lacrosse Coach of the Year, **O** 236, 240

Lacrosse Hall of Fame, **O** 233, 235-51, 303

Ladd, Ernest "Ernie," **F** 75, 500

Ladd, Peter L., **B** 594

Ladewig, Marion, **I** *344-45*

Ladies Club for Outdoor Sports, **O** 333, 392; **S** 560, 562

Ladies Club for Outdoor Sports Tennis Championships, **O** 333, 392; **S** 562

Ladies Handicap, **O** 206, 220

Ladies Home Journal, **O** 271

Ladies Pro Bowler Tour, **I** 347

Ladies Professional Golf Association, **O** 110-11, 114, 130, 151-52, 168, 172

Ladies Professional Golf Association Championships, **O** 137, 168, 170; **S** 508-10, 513-14

Ladies Professional Golf Association Hall of Fame, **O** 110, 114, 129, 132, 137, 160, 168, 170, 172; **S** 505-06, 509, 514

Ladies Professional Golf Association Hidden Spring Open Golf Tournament, **O** 129

Ladies Professional Golf Association Rookie of the Year, **O** 114, 118, 137

Ladies Profesional Golf Association Tour, **O** 117-18, 130, 151-52, 159, 165, 168, 170, 262; **S** 505-09, 513, 517-19

Ladies Stakes, **O** 224, 597

Ladies Titleholders Golf Tournament, **O** 110, 160

Ladies World Championship of Golf Tournament, **O** 110

The Lady, **O** 593

Lady Byng Trophy, **I** 566, 571

Lady Carling Open Golf Tournament, **O** 129

Lady Fair Lanes Open Bowling Tournament, Houston, TX, **I** 347

Lady Golconda, **O** 584

Lady Greenfield, **O** 209

Lady Kate, **O** 230

Lady Lightfoot, **O** 571, 608

Lady Lindsay, **O** 206

Lady Michelob Golf Tournament, **O** 168

Lady Sterling, **O** 608

Lady Suffolk, **O** 230, *593-94*

Lady Tara Golf Classic, **S** 518-19

Lady's Secret, **S** 530

Laetner, Christian, **S** 295

Lafayette College, **F** 39-40, 155, 204, 343, 392, 421, 425, 551, 579, 668; **I** 99, 313; **S** 477

Lafayette College Athletic Hall of Fame, **O** 39

Lafayette, LA baseball club (TL), **S** 30

Lafayette Stakes, **O** 603

Laguerre, Andre, **S** 340

Laguna, Ismael, **I** 446

Laird, Joseph "Joe," **O** 583

Lajoie, Napoleon "Nap," **B** *321-22,* 507, 524; **S** 72

Lajoie, William R. "Bill," S 236
Lake Charles, LA Bowling Classic, I 347
Lake Erie College, O 330
Lake Forest College, O 329
Lake Forest Park, Chicago, IL, S 169
Lake Placid, NY Speed Skating Competition, O 315
Lake Placid, NY Winter Olympic Games, See Winter Olympic Games, 1932, 1980
Lakeland, FL baseball club (FSL), B 327; S 236
Lakeview-Auburn, IA High School, I 183
Lakeville Golf Club, Great Neck, NY, O 158
Lakewood Farm, O 223
Lally Cup International Lacrosse Series, O 241-42, 245, 247
Lalonde, "Don," I 423
Lamar, Dwight "Bo," S 296-97
Lamar, E. B., Jr., B 189
Lamar University, S 324
Lambeau, Earl L. "Curly," F 89, 187, 219, 260, 328-29, 375, 392, 487, 652; S 440
Lambeau Field, Green Bay, WI, F 329
Lambert, Eugene "Gene," S 556
Lambert, John H. "Jack," F 236, 329-30, 565
Lambert, Ward L. "Piggy," I 167-69, 227-28, 312, 329-30; S 333
Lambert-Chambers, Dorothy Douglas, O 332, 363
Lambert Trophy, F 51, 84, 164, 460, 534, 558, 579; S 377, 499
Lambuth College, I 122
Lamonica, Daryle P., F 55, 179
Lamp, Dennis P., B 51
Lamplighter, O 219
Lancaster, Harry, I 110
Lancaster, PA baseball club (EL, ISL),

B 80, 196, 299, 446
Lancaster, PA Lightning basketball club (CBA), S 299
Lance, John F., I 271
Landaluce, O 606; S 530
Landis, Kenesaw Mountain, B 24, 84, 93, 108, 176-77, 202, 243, 253, 276, 286, 310, 322-24, 331, 376, 396, 401, 492; F 498; O 74-75, 98, 272; S 86, 200, 232
Landis, Lavoy, S 554
Landon, "Alf," O 515
Landry, Thomas W. "Tom," F 42, 143, 210, 219, 279, 331-32, 347, 463, 608, 650; S 428
Landsdowne Ladies Open Singles Handicap Tennis Championships, O 333
Lane, Floyd, I 132
Lane, Frank C., B 43; S 68, 106-07, 171
Lane, H. W. "Bill," S 197
Lane, "Kenny," I 446
Lane, Richard "Dick," "Night Train," F 332-33, 337
Lang, "Chick," O 216
Lang, Millard T., O 302-03
Langdon, David, S 336
Lange, Kent, S 616
Lange, "Les," I 522
Lange, Lowell W., S 616-17
Lange, William A. "Bill," B 11, 83, 302, 324-25, 493, 496
Lange, William "Billy," I 99
Langer, "Ludy," I 620
Langford, "Sam," I 418-19, 478
Langhorne, PA Auto Race, O 5
Langrishe, May, O 333
Langston University, I 119
The Language of Pro Football, S 471
Langway, Rod C., I 561-62
Lanier, Robert J., Jr. "Bob," I 169-

70, 219

Lanier, Willie E., **F** *334-35*

Lanius, **O** 199

Lannin, Joseph J. "Joe," **B** 529

Lansdrop, Robert, **O** 326

Lansford, Alex "Buck," **F** 618

Lansing, MI baseball club (MISL), **B** 195

Lansing, MI Colored Capital All-Americans baseball club (Negro Leagues), **B** 221

Lapchick, Joseph B. "Joe," **I** 11, 21, 23, 49, 65-66, 131, *170-71,* 334; **S** 266, 307

Lapointe, Guy G., **I** 562

Larchmont, NY Golf Club, **O** 153

Lardner, Ringgold W. "Ring," **B** 602; **O** 54-55, *72-74,* 91; **S** 248, 337

Larew, Joseph, **O** 565

Largent, Steve M., **F** 96, 220, 295, *335-36*

Larkin, "Tippy," **I** 404, 477

Larkins, Richard "Dick," **F** 173

Larmer, Steve D., **S** 542

Larned, Edward P., **O** 367

Larned, William A. "Bill," **O** 323, 339, *366-67,* 372, 392-93, 413-14, 419-21

Larranaga, **O** 198

Larsen, Arthur D. "Art," **S** 552, *554-55*

Larsen, Donald J. "Don," **B** 382, 482, 597; **S** 80

Larsen, Gary, **F** 451; **S** 450

Larson, Frank, **F** 27, 49

Larson, "Ojay," **F** 13

Larson, Reed D., **I** *562-64,* 573

Lary, Robert Yale, Sr., **F** *336-37*

Las Colines Country Club, **S** 611

Las Vegas, NV Americans Soccer Club (MISL), **O** 304

Las Vegas, NV baseball club (PCL), **B** 42

Las Vegas, NV Open Bowling Tournament, **I** 351

Las Vegas, NV Quicksilver Soccer Club (NASL), **O** 303

Lash, Donald R. "Don," **O** 446

Lasky, Arthur "Art," **I** 360; **S** 610

Lasorda, Thomas C. "Tom," **B** 9; **S** 26, 90, *108-09,* 114

Late Innings, **S** 336

Latone, Anthony "Tony," **S** *439*

Latonia Park Race Track, Florence, KY, **O** 221

Latrobe, PA *Clipper,* **F** 40

Latrobe, PA Country Club, **O** 149

Latrobe, PA football club, **F** 40-41, 60-61, 603

Lattner, John J. "Johnny," **F** *337-39,* 345

Latzo, "Pete," **I** 428, 474

Lau, Charles S. "Charlie," **B** 47, 370

Lauberhorn, Switzerland Downhill Ski Competition, **O** 280, 288

Laurel Country Club basketball club, **S** 316

Laurel Futurity Stakes, **O** 569, 607, 610

Laurel, MD Park Race Track, **O** 178, 215, 569

Laurel, MS baseball club (CSL), **B** 593

Laurer, Martin, **O** 437

Laurin, Lucien, **O** 607

Lausanne, Switzerland Track and Field Meet, **O** 504

Lavagetto, Harry A. "Cookie," **B** 467

Lavan, John L. "Doc," **B** 456

Lavelle, "Jack," **F** 53

Lavelli, Anthony, Jr. "Tony," **S** *297-98*

Lavelli, Dante B. J., **F** 70, 215, *339-40,* 409, 559-60

Laver, Rodney "Rod," **O** 324, 341; **S** 339, 561

Laverne Hanover, **O** 191

Lavigne, George "Kid," **I** *419-20,* 461, 464, 473

Lavoy, Robert W. "Bob," **I** 68

Law, Vernon S. "Vern," **S** 24

Lawford, Herbert F., **O** 392-93

Lawn Tennis, **O** 383

Lawn Tennis Writers Association of America, **O** 69

Lawrence, Andrea Mead, **O** *283-85*

Lawrence, David, **O** 284; **S** 277

Lawrence, Janice, **I** 315

Lawrence, Leonard, **O** 593

Lawrence College, **F** 438; **I** 15

Lawrence, MA baseball club (EL, NEL), **B** 64, 154, 238

Lawrence Realization Stakes, **O** 198, 206, 220, 575, 596, 604; **S** 534

Lawrin, **O** 175, 195

Lawson, Earl, **S** 72

Lawson's LPGA Open Golf Tournament, **S** 513-14

Lawther, "Johnny," **I** 209

Lawton, Brian, **I** 551

Lawton, OK baseball club (SSL), **B** 279

Layden, Elmer F., **F** *187-90,* 340; **O** 296

Layne, Alan, **F** 341

Layne, "Rex," **I** 437

Layne, "Rob," **F** 341

Layne, Robert L. "Bobby," **F** 147, 216, 331, *340-42,* 404, 600, 629; **S** 426

Lazio of Rome, Italy Soccer Club, **O** 296

Lazy F Ranch, **O** 584

Lazzeri, Anthony M. "Tony," **B** 5, 269, *325-26,* 553

Le Baron, Edward "Eddie," **F** 329, 331

Le Doux, Scott, **I** 466

Le Flore, Ronald "Ron," **S** 243

Le Force, Clyde, **F** 78

Le Grendre, Robert L., **S** 580

Le Mans, 24-Hour Auto Race, **O** 6, 10-11

Le Mars, IA baseball club (ISDL), **B** 472

Le Mond, Gregory J. "Greg," **S** *617-19*

Le Moyne College, **I** 359

Le Moyne-Owen College, **I** 213

Le Tarte, Warren, **B** 561

Lea, Francis, **F** 343

Lea, Gilbert, **F** 343

Lea, Langdon, **F** *342-43*

Leach, Thomas W. "Tommy," **B** *326-27*

Leadville, CO Blues baseball club (Ind.), **B** 194

League of American Wheelmen, **O** 269

League Park, Cleveland, OH, **B** 577

Leahy, Francis W. "Frank," **F** 81, 110, 176, 333, *343-45,* 358, 369, 528; **O** 104; **S** 418, 460, 480

Leahy, Marshall, **F** 516

Leakesville, VA baseball club (BSL), **B** 179

Leamington, **O** 594

Lear, Harold C., Jr. "Hal," **I** 252

Leary, J. Scott, **I** 587

Leavenworth, KS baseball club (WL), **B** 29; **S** 100

Leaver, Linda, **I** 500-01

Lebanon, PA baseball club (NatL), **B** 43

Lebanon Valley College, **F** 313, 558

Leboir Sportsmanship Trophy, **O** 352

Lebrowitz, Barney, *See* Battling Levinsky

Lecomte, **O** 594

Lee, Alfred "Butch," **I** 282

Lee, Gregory S. "Greg," **I** 331

Lee, Samuel "Sammy," **I** *489-90,* 491

Lee, William C. "Bill," S *109-10*

Lee, William "Caveman," I 397

Lee, William E. "Big Bill," F 595; S *439-40*

Leeds, "Arabian," O 590

Leeman, Albert, I 647

Leeman, Gerald G. "Gerry," I *647-48*

Leemans, Alphonse E. "Tuffy," F *345-46,* 447

Leesburg, FL baseball club (FSL), B 179; S 51

Leever, Samuel "Sam," B 95, *327-28*

Legends of Golf Tournament, *See* Liberty Mutual Legends of Golf Tournament

Legere, Mrs. "Ted," S 528

Legion Field, Birmingham, AL, S 368

Legionnaires basketball club (MeL), I 30

Lehane, "Jan," S 563

Lehigh University, F 155, 200, 255; I 647-48; O 28; S 479

Leifield, Albert P. "Lefty," B 95; S *110-11*

Leigh, Eugene "Gene," O 224

Leighton, "Con," O 219

Leiner, Benjamin, *See* Benny Leonard

Leino, "Elmo," I 662

Leiser, William "Bill," F 90

Leith, Lloyd R., I *171-72*

Leland, Frank, B 188

Leland College, F 499-500

Lemm, Walter "Wally," S 426

Lemon, Meadow G. III "Meadowlark," I 119-20, *172-73,* 267

Lemon, Robert G. "Bob," B 32, 242, *328-29,* 490; S 64, 83

Len Eshmont Award, S 427, 499

Lendl, Ivan, O 342, 370, 379

Lenglen, Suzanne, O 88, 329, 338, 359, 361, 373, 385, 387-89

Lenox Open Tennis Championships, O 339

Leonard, "Benny," I 361, 365, 379, 392, 411, 413, 415, *420-22,* 454, 469, 476

Leonard, "Chris," S 287, 314

Leonard, Emil J. "Dutch," B *329-30,* 607

Leonard, Hubert B. "Hub," S 111

Leonard, Joseph P. "Joe," O *17-18,* 37-38

Leonard, Ray Charles "Sugar Ray," I 356, 397, *422-23;* S 612

Leonard, Walter F. "Buck," B 148, 213, 244, 290, *330-32,* 453, 548; S 99

Leonard, William Robert "Bob," I 113, 192; S 317

Leonatus, O 595

Leskovar, William "Bill," F 199

Leslie, Frank, O 268

Leslie, "Jock," I 461

Leslie's Weekly, F 342

Lesnevich, "Gus," I 367, *423-24*

Lester Patrick Award, S 353

Lethbridge, Canada baseball club (PrL), B 140

Lettunich, Martin, O 163

Letzeiser Award, I 69

Leuty, Haskell "Pete," S 331

Leuyendyk, Arie, S 619

Levane, Andrew J. "Fuzzy," F 215; I 44, 132; S 265

Levinsky, "Battling," I 376, 391, *424-25,* 471, 475

Levinsky, "King," I 429

Levy, Marvin D. "Marv," F 466, 566, 631

Lewellen, Verne, S *440-41*

Lewis, "Chris," O 370

Lewis, "Ed," I 97

Lewis, Ed "Strangler," I 644, *648-49,* 661

Lewis, Evan "Strangler," I 648
Lewis, Evelyn, O 485
Lewis, Frederick Carlton "Carl," O 485-87
Lewis, George E. "Duffy," B 208, 259, 529; S 111-12
Lewis, "Gussie," I 400
Lewis, Guy V., I 173-74
Lewis, "Harry," I 360, 425-26
Lewis, James C. "Jimmy," O 240-41
Lewis, John E., I 426
Lewis, John Henry, I 360, 426-27
Lewis, John K. "Buddy," S 14
Lewis, Mayley, S 608
Lewis, Morey, I 557
Lewis, R. S. "Bubbles," B 192
Lewis, "Randy," I 642
Lewis, Ted "Kid," I 361, 390, 454, 476
Lewis, Wilfred, O 402
Lewis, William H., F 64, 476; O 485
Lewis, "Willie," I 377, 390, 414, 425, 448
Lewis and Clark College, I 615
Lewis Cup Soccer Championships, O 291, 299
Lewis E. Teague Memorial Award, I 253
Lewiston, ID baseball club (NWL), B 277
Lewiston, ME baseball club (NEL), B 64, 293
Lexington, O 174, 594
Lexington, KY Colts baseball club (BGL), S 223
Lexington, KY Race Track, O 587
Lexington, NC baseball club (WCL), B 39
Lexington Stakes, O 611
Leyva, Nicolas T. "Nick," S 58
Liangde, "Tan," I 491-92

Liberal Soccer Club, O 299
Liberty, F 437, 637; O 64, 531; S 345
Liberty Bell Race Track, Philadelphia, PA, F 511; O 215
Liberty Bowl football game, F 24, 74, 128, 181, 258, 286-87, 292, 370, 501, 534, 650; S 393, 399
Liberty Mutual Legends of Golf Tournament, O 119, 140
Liberty Radio Network, O 77-78, 82-83, 92
Libertys baseball club, S 233
Libya National Basketball Team, I 277
Liddel, Eric, O 531
Liddle, Donald E. "Don," S 234
Lieb, Frederick G. "Fred," B 572; O 54, 74-75, 90, 98
Liebendorfer, Don E., F 533
Liebermann, Nancy, See Nancy Lieberman-Cline
Liebermann-Cline, Nancy, I 174-76, 285, 315; O 381
Lietzke, Bruce A., S 510
Life, I 531, 606, 611; S 338
Life's Magic, S 530
Liggett, Walter W., F 269
Light Heavyweight Boxing Championships, I 353, 356, 359-60, 367, 372, 375-76, 380, 383-86, 391, 394, 401, 413, 418-19, 423-26, 428, 432, 437, 441-42, 445, 453, 455, 457-59, 463, 465-66, 471, 475, 482
Lightbody, James D., O 423, 487-88
Lightweight Boxing Championships, I 354, 356-57, 368, 379, 387-88, 391-92, 404, 411-13, 418-21, 434-36, 440-41, 444, 446, 450-54, 469, 473-77, 479-80
Lillard, Robert "Bob," I 340
Lilly, Christopher, I 402

Lilly, Robert L. "Bob," F 331, *346-47*
Lima, OH baseball club (OSL), B 45
Lincoln, Abraham, O 99
Lincoln-Mercury Open Golf Tournament, S 509
Lincoln, NE baseball club (NeSL, WL), B 29, 63, 93, 195-96; S 196, 233
Lincoln, NE *Journal-Star,* F 570
Lincoln University of Pennsylvania, B 273; S 416
Lindell Athletic Club, Detroit, MI, F 307
Linden, Andrew, S 620
Linder, Joseph, S *545-46*
Lindgren, Gerald P. "Gerry," O 518
Lindgren, Harold Blaine, O 478
Lindstrom, Charles W. "Chuck," B 332
Lindstrom, Frederick C. "Fred," B 231, *332-33*
Line, James, S 261
Lineman of the Year Award, S 365, 403, 441, 452-53, 499
Linseman, Ken, I 551
Linz, Philip F. "Phil," B 36
Lion d'Or, S 525-26
Lippe, "Al," I 448, 465
Lippencott, Donald F., O 443
Lippincott's, B 592; O 405
Lipscomb, Gene A., F 146, 165, *347-48,* 367, 519
Liquori, Martin W., Jr. "Marty," O 458, *488-89,* 527, 566
Lira, "Ernie," I 426
Liska, "Jerry," F 507
Liston, Charles "Sonny," I 353, *427-28,* 449
Liston, Emile S., I 74, *176-78*
Literary Digest, O 72
Litkenhous, Frank, F 338
Little, Floyd D., F 122, *348-50,* 535

Little, George E., F 194, 669
Little, Larry C., S *441-42*
Little, Louis L. "Lou," F 23, 28, 130, 259, *350-51,* 356; S 404-05
Little, Raymond D., O 320, 354, 356, 421
Little, William Lawson, Jr., O 109, *138-39,* 154
Little All-American College Basketball Team, I 247
Little All-American College Football Team, F 390, 478, 490, 503, 539, 608; S 368
Little Brown Jug (Minnesota-Michigan), F 262, 655
Little Chief, S 526-27
Little Rock, AR baseball club (SA, SL), B 61, 146, 229, 249, 278-79, 401, 529, 601; F 402; S 131
Little Rock, AR Dr. Pepper Bottling Company basketball club, I 57, 253
Little Rock, AR Junior College, I 253
Little Rock, AR Lewis and Norwood Flyers Insurance basketball club, I 57
Little Three Conference, F 173; I 177
Little World Series, Baseball, B 230, 263, 480; S 101
Littler, Eugene A. "Gene," O 115, *139-40;* S 516
Litwack, Harry, I *178-79,* 252
Living Legacy Award, I 581
Livingwell-Provimi 200 Auto Race, O 3
Llangollen Farm, O 228
Lloyd, Christine Evert, *See* Christine M. Evert-Lloyd
Lloyd, Earl F., I 45
Lloyd, John, O 351
Lloyd, John Henry, B 255, 286, 290,

333-34, 342, 451, 466, 519; **S**
43, 137, 143, 168
Lloyd, Lewis K., **I** 289
Lloyd, "Vince," **O** 53
Lo Presti, Samuel "Sam," **I** 572
Loayza, Stanislaus, **I** 392, 451
Lobello, "Si," **I** 23
Lock Haven University, **S** 611
Locke, Gordon C. "Gordie," **F** 299,
551
Locke, Taylor "Tates," **I** 161-62
Lockert, Lacy, **F** 90; **S** 433
Lockhart, Thomas "Tom," **I** 552
Lockman, Carroll W. "Whitey," **S**
196
Lockport, NY baseball club (PoL), **S**
20
Lodi, CA baseball club (CaL), **S** 84
Lodi, CA Open Bowling Tournament,
I 351
Loeffler, Kenneth D. "Ken," **I** 100,
179-81
Lofton, James D., **F** 291, *351-52*
Loftus, John P. "Johnny," **O** *199-
200,* 596
Log Cabin Stable, **O** 197
Logan Squares baseball club, **S** 13
Logan, UT baseball club (UIL), **S** 23
Lohaus, Brad A., **S** 254
Lohrman, William L. "Bill," **S** 24
Loi, Duilio, **I** 446
Lola-Ford Racing Car, **O** 37
Lolich, Frank, **B** 334
Lolich, Michael S. "Mickey," **B**
334-35; **S** 44, 186
Lolich, Ronald J. "Ron," **B** 334
Lollar, John Sherman, **S** *112-13*
Lollipop Ski Competition, **O** 274
Lom, Benjamin "Ben," **F** 6
Lomady, Clara Schroth, **I** *530-31*
Lomax, Neil V., **F** 17
Lombardi, Ernest N. "Ernie," **B** 125,
216, 237, 250, *335-36*

Lombardi, Vincent T. "Vince," **F** 33,
102, 104, 138, 151, 188, 207, 223,
271, 278-79, 323, 328, 331, *352-
55,* 362, 430, 495, 502, 529, 547,
567, 591, 661-62; **S** 372, 400-01
Lombardi Award or Trophy, **F** 136,
138, 236, 355, 495, 537, 547-48,
571, 650; **S** 374, 395, 404, 420,
468, 480
Lon Morris Junior College, **S** 324
Lonborg, Arthur C. "Dutch," **I** 5,
181-82, 256
London Athletic Club, **O** 559
London, Canada baseball club (IL,
MOL), **B** 154, 211
London, England Long Distance Walk,
O 560
London, England Marathon, **O** 529
London, England Summer Olympic
Games, *See* Olympic Summer
Games, 1908, 1948
London, England Track and Field
Meet, **O** 430, 465, 504, 541, 545
London Pastime, **O** 350
London Prize Ring Rules, **I** 369, 399
Lone Star Conference, **F** 399; **I** 174;
S 324
Lone Tree, IA High School, **I** 183
Long, Charles F. II "Chuck," **F** *355-
56*
Long, "Cindy," **I** 8
Long, Dallas C. III, **S** *586-87,* 589
Long, Denise, *See* Denise Long
Andre
Long, Herman C. "Germany," **B**
336-37, 550; **S** 115
Long, Lemuel, **O** 609
Long, Melville H. "Mel," **O** 361,
372-73
Long Beach, CA City Gold Cup, **I**
493
Long Beach, CA Grand Prix CART
Race, **O** 3; **S** 619-20

Long Beach, CA *Press-Telegram*, O 517
Long Beach, CA Relays, O 568
Long Beach City College, O 436; S 310
Long Beach Shore, NJ Athletic Club, S 594
Long Beach State University, S 296, 310
Long Branch, NJ baseball club (NYNJL), S 117
Long Island Athletic Hall of Fame, S 343
Long Island University, B 151; I 22-23, 67, 90, 115, 129, 179, 187, 264; S 347
Longden, "Johnny," O 178, 210, 218, 579
Longfellow, O *594-95*
Longhorn Hall of Fame, F 367, 431, 550
Longhorn Swim Club, Austin, TX, I 592
Longman, "Shorty," F 504
Longo, Tracy, I 214
Longstreet, O 595
Longwood Bowl Tennis Championships, O 322, 362, 366, 420
Longwood Cricket Club, Brookline, MA, O 345, 350, 413, 415, 420
Longwood Tennis Championships, O 347
Look, F 248, 641; I 10; O 52, 93; S 453
Loomis, Frank Joseph "Joe," O 455; S 576
Loos, Roger, S 336
Lopat, Edmund W. "Eddie," S *113-14*, 173
Lopatynski, Edmund, *See* Lopat, Edmund
Lopes, David E. "Davey," B 209; S 26, *114-15*, 185
Lopes, "Joe," I 362
Lopez, Alfonso R. "Al," B *337-38*, 589; S 16, 107, 159, 214
Lopez, "Chief," I 447
Lopez, Domingo, O 137
Lopez, Nancy, *See* Nancy Lopez Melton Knight
Loras College, *See* Columbia College
Lorayne, "Harry," I 187
Lord At War, O 218
Lord Baltimores baseball club (NA), B 128, 388-89
Lord Boswell, O 572
Lord Lonsdale, I 400
Lord Murphy, O 209
Lorenzen, Frances Billerbeck, I 183
Lorenzen, Jill, I 183-84
Lorenzen, Lori, I 183-84
Lorenzen, Lynn F., I *183-85*
Lorenzo, "Rich," I 646
Lorillard, George, S 536
Lorillard, Pierre, O *200-01*, 206
Lorillard Stakes, O 604
Lorimer, Robert, S 544
Los Angeles Angels baseball club (AL), S 24, 57, 68, 171, 246; *See also* California Angels baseball club (AL)
Los Angeles Angels baseball club (CaL, PCL), B 9, 35, 65, 84, 88, 120, 122, 153, 193, 236, 265, 484, 579; S 20, 135, 162
Los Angeles Athletic Club, I 493, 663
Los Angeles Aztecs Soccer Club (NASL), O 305, 307
Los Angeles Buccaneers football club (NFL), F 410
Los Angeles Chargers football club (AFL), F 55, 127, 396, 437; S 432
Los Angeles City College, O 319,

363; **S** 204

Los Angeles Clippers basketball club (NBA), **I** 19, 278; **S** 280, 294, 302, 306, 308, 328

Los Angeles Coliseum, Los Angeles, CA, **B** 159, 427; **F** 95, 153-54, 338, 500, 638; **O** 87, 92, 456, 509; **S** 61

Los Angeles Coliseum Relays, **O** 439, 456; **S** 591

Los Angeles Community College, **I** 521

Los Angeles Dodgers baseball club (NL), **B** 7-9, 13, 44, 57-58, 61, 70, 76, 81, 102, 137-39, 159, 162, 196, 201, 209, 216, 233-34, 256, 258, 264, 277, 284, 305, 315, 338, 364, 372, 379-80, 417, 425, 427, 437, 448, 455, 467, 477-78, 497, 504, 518, 521-22, 540, 543-44, 575, 583, 595, 608, 618-19; **O** 49, 81-82, 92-93; **S** 2-3, 7-8, 24-26, 28, 30, 46, 49, 53, 61, 67, 80, 90, 107, 109, 112, 114, 120, 132-33, 138, 142, 148, 153, 160, 167, 171, 175, 184-85, 204, 244

Los Angeles Dons football club (AAFC), **F** 43, 118, 184, 318, 340, 379, 488; **S** 361, 460

Los Angeles *Examiner,* **F** 154, 472; **O** 81

Los Angeles *Express,* **F** 154

Los Angeles Express football club (USFL), **F** 211, 671; **S** 409

Los Angeles Forum, Inglewood, CA, **O** 92

Los Angeles Harbor College, **B** 594

Los Angeles Jets basketball club (ABL, NBL), **I** 274, 334

Los Angeles Invitation Diving Meet, **I** 490

Los Angeles Invitation Swim Meet, **I** 619

Los Angeles Junior Women's Golf Tournament, **S** 509

Los Angeles Kings hockey club (NHL), **I** 544, 551, 554; **S** 538-39

Los Angeles Lacrosse Club, **O** 240

Los Angeles Lakers basketball club (NBA), **I** 2, 4, 15, 19-20, 26, 33-34, 46-47, 58, 60, 66, 101-02, 121-22, 133, 136, 138, 142, 145-47, 150-51, 154, 165, 184, 189, 230, 241, 243-44, 249, 260, 266, 275, 293, 298, 322-23; **O** 92-93; **S** 251, 253-54, 268-69, 275, 288, 297, 301, 306-08, 319, 328

Los Angeles Mercurettes Track Club, **S** 577

Los Angeles Municipal Tennis Championships, **S** 553

Los Angeles Olympic Organizing Committee, **S** 597

Los Angeles Open Bowling Tournament, **I** 351

Los Angeles Open Golf Tournament, **O** 116, 131, 144, 147, 154, 158, 172; **S** 507, 512, 521

Los Angeles Outdoor Track and Field Meet, **O** 430, 432, 543, 545

Los Angeles Raiders football club (NFL), **F** 8-9, 43, 62, 105, 179-80, 196, 206, 229-30, 236, 258, 286, 321, 335, 352, 384, 388, 399, 473, 481, 494, 502, 517, 593; **S** 374, 379, 495

Los Angeles Rams football club (NFL), **F** 7, 24-25, 30, 32, 39, 59, 71, 91, 93, 112, 129-30, 135, 140, 143, 152, 161, 169, 182, 186, 190, 197, 199, 203, 205, 207, 210, 215-16, 224, 238, 244, 268-69, 272, 285, 296-97, 320, 326, 332, 348, 363-64, 367, 372, 387, 389-90, 394, 409, 419, 421, 432, 462-64, 488-89, 492-93, 496, 500, 503,

510, 516, 519, 536, 538, 542, 548, 553, 555-56, 575, 590, 602, 608, 617, 619, 637-40, 649, 656-57, 667; **I** 150, 261; **O** 62, 444; **S** 364-65, 408-09, 419, 452-53, 468-69, 475, 489, 493, 504

Los Angeles State University, **O** 561; **S** 577

Los Angeles Strings Tennis Club (WTT), **O** 336, 352

Los Angeles Summer Olympic Games, *See* Olympic Summer Games, 1932, 1984

Los Angeles Tennis Club, **O** 365; **S** 553

Los Angeles *Times,* **F** 100, 130-31; **O** 81

Los Angeles *Times* GTE Indoor Track and Field Meet, **O** 481

Los Angeles *Times* Woman of the Year, **O** 338

Los Angeles Toros bowling club (NBL), **I** 348

Los Angeles Track Club, **O** 425, 429

Los Angeles Turnverein Society, **I** 521, 537

Los Angeles Valley College, **I** 526

Los Angeles White Sox baseball club (CWL), **B** 482; **S** 43

Los Angeles Wildcats football club (AFL), **F** 178

Loscalzo, Joseph R., *See* Midget Wolgast

Losee, Albert, **O** 230

Lotowhite, **O** 178

Lott, George M., Jr., **O** 347, 360, *367-69,* 395, 404, 408, 410, 417-18

Lott, Ronald M. "Ronnie," **S** 427

Lotus Ford Racing Car, **O** 11

Lotz, Edwin L. "Ed," **O** *241*

Lotz, Phillip L. "Phil," **O** *241-42*

Lou Gehrig All-Star Basketball Team,

I 305

Lou Gehrig Award, **B** 422

Loubet, Nathaniel "Nat," **I** 382

Louganis, Gregory E. "Greg," **I** 486, 490, *491-93*

Loughery, Kevin M., **I** 309

Loughran, Beatrix, **S** 601; *See also* Beatrix Loughran Harvey

Loughran, Thomas "Tommy," **I** 360, 372, *428-29,* 463, 475; **S** 610

Louis, Joe, **F** 602; **I** 361, 365, 367-68, 382, 385, 395, 405-06, 409-10, 415, 426, *429-30,* 437, 462, 472; **S** 343

Louis Le Grand, **O** 218

Louisiana Downs, New Orleans, LA, **O** 204, 206, 227

Louisiana Handicap, **O** 615

Louisiana Sports Hall of Fame, **F** 121, 588; **S** 110

Louisiana State Athletic Commission, **I** 400

Louisiana State University, **B** 3, 133; **F** 30, 47, 81, 91, 101, 209, 284, 293, 296, 301, 308, 407, 518, 522, 534, 539, 576, 587, 598-600, 618-19, 621, 632, 641; **I** 41, 113, 124, 193, 204, 237, 636; **O** 465; **S** 109-10, 276, 421, 424, 461, 465, 469-70

Louisiana State University Athletic Hall of Fame, **F** 588

Louisiana Superdome, New Orleans, LA, **I** 466; **S** 255

Louisiana Tech University, **F** 59; **I** 214-15, 285, 291; **S** 428

Louisville baseball club (AA), **B** 2, 44, 56-57, 72, 105-06, 115, 126, 167, 169, 229, 250, 281, 345, 393, 407, 421, 446, 454, 467, 536, 559, 571, 577; **S** 58, 66, 163, 195, 223

Louisville baseball club (IL), **B** 182; **S** 51

Louisville Black Caps baseball club (NSL), **B** 343
Louisville Colonels baseball club (NL), **B** 52, 90-91, 94-95, 104, 157-58, 217, 265, 271, 281, 326, 447, 457, 579, 581, 600; **S** 37, 169, 225, 233
Louisville Colonels basketball club (ABA), **I** 98
Louisville Colonels Black baseball club, **S** 9
Louisville Colonels football club (NFL), **I** 264
Louisville *Commercial,* **B** 456
Louisville Eclipse baseball club (AA), **B** 82, 168
Louisville 500 Auto Race, **O** 16
Louisville Track and Field Meet, **O** 457
Louisville White Sox baseball club (Negro Leagues), **B** 269
Love, Robert "Bob," **F** 480
Lovellette, Clyde E., **I** 5, 109, 180, *184-85,* 199, 281, 319; **S** 302
Lovelock, "Jack," **O** 431-32, 445-46
Lovely, Leonard, **I** 269
Lovetere, John, **F** 224
Lovett, James D., **B** 122
Lowe, A. H., **O** 372
Lowe, Paul E., **F** *442-43*
Lowe, Robert L. "Bobby," **B** 550; **S** *115-16*
Lowell, MA baseball club (EL, NEL), **B** 64, 110, 301, 357, 550
Lowell of Boston baseball club, **B** 122
Lowery, Dominic G. "Nick," **S** 486
Lowry, "Ted", **I** 437
Loyola University, Baltimore, MD, **I** 206
Loyola University, Chicago, IL, **F** 48, 264, 302, 650; **S** 333
Loyola University, Los Angeles, CA,

I 231
Loyola University, New Orleans, LA, **I** 74; **F** 532, 538
Lozier Company, **O** 24
Lucadello, Anthony "Tony," **B** 502
Lucas, Charles F. "Red," **S** *116-17*
Lucas, Harold, **F** 642
Lucas, Jerry R., **I** 23, 67, 117, 161, 184, *185-87,* 220, 231, 296
Lucas, John H., Jr., **S** *298-99*
Lucas, Richard "Richie," **F** 164
Lucayan Club, The Bahamas, **O** 169
Lucci, Gustave, **I** 502, 504, 514
Luchine, Canada hockey club, **I** 555
Lucien Appleby, **S** 526
Luckenbill, Theodore "Ted," **I** 174
Luckman, Sidney "Sid," **F** 39, 55, 66, 308, 350, *356-57,* 609; **S** 404, 460
Lucky Debonair, **O** 218
Lucky International Golf Tournament, **O** 113
Lucullete, **S** 527
Lucy, **O** 586
Luderus, Frederick W. "Fred," **S** 144
Luding, Christa, **S** 603
Ludington, Ronald E. "Ron," **I** 515
Lugano, Switzerland hockey club, **I** 567
Luisetti, Angelo H. "Hank," **I** 22, 37, 99, 113, 139, 141, 157, *187-88;* **S** 270
Lujack, John C., Jr. "Johnny," **F** 26, 55, 176, 249, 341, 345, *357-59,* 606-07; **S** 491
Lukas, Darrell Wayne, **S** *529-30*
Luke Blackburn, **O** 206; **S** 533
Lumpp, Raymond G. "Ray," **S** 323
Lunardoni, Ada, **I** 525
Lund, Francis L. "Pug," **F** 49; **S** *443-44*
Lundquist, Carl, **B** 561
Lundquist, Stephen K. "Steve," **I**

604-06
Lundy, Lamar, F 224, 297-98, 441
Lundy, Richard "Dick," B *338-39,*
378, 620
Luque, Adolfo "Dolf," B 553; S
117-18
Luppino, Arthur "Art," F 663
Lurie, Robert A. "Bob," B 540
Luro, Horatio, O 228
Lusitania Recreation Soccer Club,
East Cambridge, MA, O 299
Luther College, B 316
Lutz, Robert C. "Bob," O 400
Luxembourg National Soccer Team, O
305
Luzinski, Gregory M. "Greg," B 168;
S *118-19*
Luzinski, Richard, S 118
Luzinski, Ryan, S 119
Luzinski, William, S 118
Lyle, Albert W. "Sparky," B *339-40;*
S 123
Lyle, "Ron," I 383
Lyman, William R. "Link," F *359-
60;* S 412
Lynch, James R. "Jim," F 277, 334
Lynch, "Joe," I 400, *430-32*
Lynch, Thomas J. "Tom," B *340-41*
Lynchburg, VA baseball club (Pil,
VL), B 179, 430
Lynchburg, VA *News,* B 430
Lynn, Fredric M. "Fred," B *341-42,*
471; S 214
Lynn, Janet, *See* Janet Lynn Nowicki
Salomon
Lynn, Robert "Bob," I 521
Lynn, MA baseball club (NEL), 117,
195, 208, 239
Lyon, "Bill," S 96
Lyons, Dennis P. A. "Denny," S
199-20
Lyons, James "Jimmie," B *342-43*
Lyons, Stephen J. "Steve," B 505

Lyons, Theodore A. "Ted," B *343-
44,* 565
Lysistrata, O 51
Lytle, Robert W. "Rob," F 527

Maccabee of Israel Soccer Club, O
294
McAdoo, Robert A. "Bob," I 60,
188-89, 204
McAfee, George A., F *361-62,* 608,
626
McAfee, Kenneth "Ken," F 138
McAleer, James R. "Jimmy," B 400
McAlester, OK baseball club (SSL),
S 87
McAllister, "Bud," S 607
McAllister, "Jimmy," I 450
McAnally, Ronald "Ron," O 591
MacArthur, Douglas, F 440; I 84,
254; S 568
MacArthur Bowl football game, F
277
McAtee, John L., O 193, *201-02*
McAteer, Myrtle, O 325
Macauley, Charles E., Jr. "Ed," I 12,
126-27, 166, *188-89,* 212, 238,
262; S 331
McAvoy, "Jock," I 426
McBean, Alvin O. "Al," S 243
McBride, Arnold R. "Bake," S 34
McCabe, Frank, O 588, 593, 597
Maccabiah Games, I 617, 665-66; S
563, 574
McCallum, John D., F 606; S 376,
431, 489
McCann, James D., O 583
McCann, Terrence J. "Terry," I *649-
50*
McCarnes, Robert, I 182
McCarney, "Billy," I 389
McCarron, Christopher "Chris," O
202-04, 218
McCarron, Gregg, O 203

McCartan, John W. "Jack," I 568-69
McCarter, "Jim," I 427
McCarthy, Charles L. "Clem," O 99
McCarthy, "Connie," I 477
McCarthy, Elizabeth L., O 367
McCarthy, Joseph V. "Joe," B 129, 146, 155, 258, *345-46*, 446, 490, 536, 596; S 163, 181
McCarthy, Thomas F. "Tommy," B *347-48*
McCarthy, William I. "Billy," O 373
McCarty, "Downy," O 237
McCarver, James Timothy "Tim," B 51; S *354-55*, 356
McCauley, Donald F., Jr. "Don," F 296
McCauliff, Eugene "Gene," O 418
McChesney, S 526-27
McClanahan, "Rob," I 568
McClary, David, S 534
McCleester, John, I 402
McClellan, "Bill," I 377-78
McClellan, Daniel "Dan," B 255
McClelland, Kevin W. , S 538
McClendon, Charles "Charlie," F 199
McClung, Thomas L. "Tom," S *444-45*
McCluskey, Joseph P. "Joe," S *587*
McColl, Duncan, S 446
McColl, Milt, S 446
McColl, William, Jr. "Bill," F 533; O 493; S *445-46*
McCombs, M. J., O 171
McCook, NE baseball club (NeSL), B 421
McCool, Frank, I 560
McCormack, Mark, O 149
McCormack, Mike, F *362-63*
McCormick, Frank A., B 29, *348-49*
McCormick, Glenn, I 493
McCormick, Harry E. "Moose," B 255

McCormick, James "Jim," B 11, *349-50*, 496
McCormick, Kelly, I 493
McCormick, Patricia Keller "Pat," I *493-94*
McCormick, Vincent C. "Vince," F 469
McCosky, William Barney, B 119, 300
McCovey, Willie L., B *350-51*, 514
McCoy, "Al," I 376
McCoy, Charles "Kid," I 366, *432-33*, 457, 460-61, 464
McCoy, Kathy Rigby, I *531-32*
McCoy, Michael C. "Mike," F 458
McCoy, "Tom," I 402
McCracken, Emmett Branch, I *191-92*, 310-11; S 317
McCracken, Herbert "Herb," F 40
McCracken, Jack D., I 106, *192-93*
McCreary, Conn, O *204-05*
McCreary, Jay, I 192
McCrocklin, "Will," I 67
McCuskey, David "Dave," I 646, 649, 659
McCutchan, Arad, I *193-94*
McCutchen, Mario, I 528
McCutcheon, Floretta Doty, I *345-46*
McCutcheon, Lawrence "Larry," F *363-64*
McCutcheon School of Bowling, I 345
McDaniel, David, S 530-32
McDaniel, Henry, O 582; S *530-31*
McDaniel, Kerry, B 352
McDaniel, Lyndall D. "Lindy," B *351-52*
McDaniel, Max Von, B 352
McDaniel, Mildred, *See* Mildred McDaniel Singleton
McDaniel, "Will," O 582
McDermott, Hugh, I 69

McDermott, John J., Jr., **O** *140-41,* 155

McDermott, Maurice J. "Mickey," **S** 95

McDermott, Robert "Bobby," **I** *194-95;* **S** 270

MacDonald, Daniel, **I** 662

McDonald, "Arch," **O** 45; **S** 349

McDonald, David "Dave," **O** 38

McDonald, "Ed," **I** 373

McDonald, Henry, **F** 183

McDonald, Patrick J. "Pat," **O** *489-90,* 524

McDonald, "Scotty," **I** 231

McDonald, Thomas F. "Tommy," **F** *364-65,* 485, 618, 653; **S** 427

McDonald's American Cup Gymnastic Championships, **I** 523, 526, 533, 535-36

McDonald's Golf Classic, **O** 152; **S** 518

McDonald's International Diving Meet, **I** 492

McDonough, "Will," **S** 346, 357

McDougald, Gilbert J. "Gil", **S** 192

McDowell, Samuel E. T. "Sam," **S** *120-21*

McDowell, Thomas "Tom," **S** 120

McElhenny, Hugh E., Jr., **F** 294, *365-66,* 653

McElhenny, Lance, **F** 366

McElreath, James, **O** 19

McElreath, Jimmy E., **O** *18-19*

McEnroe, John P., Sr., **O** 369

McEnroe, John P., Jr., **O** 341-42, *369-71,* 381

McEver, Eugene T. "Gene," **S** *446-47*

McEwan, John J., **F** 200, 30, 440; **S** *447-48*

McFadin, Lewis P. "Bud," **F** *366-68*

McFarland, "Packy," **I** 390

McGann, "Gene," **S** 127

McGee, **O** 582

McGee, James "Jim," **O** 3

McGee, Michael "Mike," **S** 456

McGee, Pamela "Pam," **I** 214

McGee, Paula, **I** 214

McGee, Shannon, **S** 320

McGeehan, W. O., **O** 64

McGill, Bill, **I** 94

McGill, "Eddie," **I** 474

McGill, Ralph, **F** 231

McGill University, **I** 228

MacGilvary, Ronnie, **I** 198

McGinnis, George F., **I** 78, 82, 130, *195-96,* 313

McGinnity, Joseph J. "Joe," **B** 45-46, *352-54*

McGinty, "Ed," **S** 331

McGlocklin, Jon P., **I** 192; **S** 9

McGoorty, "Eddie," **I** 376, 390, 465

McGovern, John F., **F** 38, 655

McGovern, Joseph Terrance "Terry," **I** 357, 387-88, *433-35*

McGowan, Alexander, **S** 626

McGowan, William A. "Bill," **S** *121-22*

McGrath, Matthew J. "Matt," **O** 489, *490-91*

McGrath, Vivian B., **O** 322, 410, 418

McGrathiana Stud Farm, **O** 589

McGraw, Frank E. "Tug," **S** *122-23*

McGraw, John J., **B** 21, 45-46, 48, 52, 64, 66, 105, 148, 153, 155, 157, 173, 202, 226, 230, 239-41, 245, 261, 267, 278, 281-82, 298, 301-02, 332, 353, *354-55,* 359, 361, 363, 384, 390, 416, 431-32, 457, 481, 488, 492-94, 524, 534, 539, 551-52, 562, 569, 582, 599, 638; **F** 428; **I** 14; **O** 54, 208, **S** 19, 43, 48, 55, 143, 187, 194, 216, 218, 223, 240

McGreehy, "Pat," **B** 90

McGregor, Kenneth "Ken," **O** 349,

390

McGugin, Daniel E. "Dan," **F** 109-10, 150, *368-69,* 406-07, 422, 522, 669

McGuire, Alfred J., Sr. "Al," **I** 56, *196-98,* 200; **O** 63; **S** 425

McGuire, Alfred J., Jr., **I** 197

McGuire, Edith, **S** 577; *See also* Edith M. McGuire Duvall

McGuire, Frank J., **I** 23, 58, 78, *198-200,* 282; **S** 266, 304, 316

McGuire, James T. "Deacon," **S** *123-24,* 194

McGuire, Richard J. "Dick," **I** 93, 197, *200-01,* 239

McGwire, Mark D., **S** 38

McHale, John J., **B** 175, *356;* **I** 250

McHale, Kevin E., **S** *299-300*

McHale, Martin J. "Marty," **B** 208

McIlwain, David "Dave," **S** 545

McInnis, John P. "Stuffy," **B** 19, 65, 103, *357-58*

McIver, Helene Madison, *See* Helene Madison Kapphahu

Mack, Connie, **B** 19, 28, 34, 46, 74, 99, 101, 103, 105, 112, 119, 126, 154, 160-61, 163, 196-97, 208, 232, 245, 254, 275, 287, 299-300, 321, 333-34, 345, 352, 355, *358-59,* 401, 443, 450, 453, 459, 483, 493, 510-13, 579; **F** 41, 428; **I** 75; **S** 21, 37, 59, 81, 127, 181, 189, 196, 200, 231

Mack, Earl T., **B** 163, 358, 443

Mack, Roy, **B** 358

Mack Lee Hill Trophy, **S** 407

Mack Truck Award, **F** 237

McKale, J. F. "Pop," **I** 79

McKay, James K. "Jim," **O** *75-77*

McKay, John H., Sr., **F** 201, 206, *369-70,* 545

McKay, John H., Jr., **F** 369

McKean, Edward J. "Ed," **B** 93, *359-60;* **S** 36

McKechnie, William B., Sr. "Bill," **B** 3, 215-16, *360-61,* 614; **S** 228

McKechnie, William B., Jr., **B** 360

McKee, Evelyn Rawls, **I** 488

McKeesport, PA baseball club (PSA), **B** 114

McKelvin Award, **S** 282

Mackenzie, Alister, **O** 136

McKenzie, Gordon "Gordy," **O** 12

McKenzie, Reginald "Reggie," **F** 527

McKeon, John A. "Jack," **S** 241-42

McKernan, John L., *See* Jack Kearns

McKerr, Travis, **S** 531

Mackey Arena, West Lafayette, IN, **I** 225

Mackey, John, **F** *370-71*

Mackey, Raleigh, **B** *362-63,* 543

McKim, Josephine E., **I** 599

McKinley, Adeline, **O** 337

McKinley, Charles R. "Chuck," **S** *555-56,* 561

McKinley, Robert, **S** 555

McKinney, Frank, **I** 584

McKinney, Horace A. "Bones," **I** 12

McKinney, "Jack," **I** 178-79

McKinney, Oran, **I** 67

McKnight, Felix R., **F** 317

McKnight, W. L., **O** 581

McLain, Dennis D. "Denny," **B** 41; **S** 57, *124-25,* 186

McLane, James P., Jr. "Jimmy," **I** *606-07*

McLaren, "Don," **I** 350

McLaren Race Car, **O** 28

McLarnin, James A. "Jimmy," **I** 370, 421, *435,* 436, 451, 459

McLaughlin, Frederic, **I** 553

McLaughlin, James, **O** *205-07*

Maclay Trophy, **O** 267

McLendon, Gordon B., **O** *77-78,* 82, 92, 100

McLendon, John B., **I** *201-02*

McLennon Stakes, **O** 223

McLeod, Frederick R. "Fred," **O** 134

MacLeod, John M., **I** 145, 224, 310; **S** *300-01*

McLoughlin, Maurice E., **O** 332, 356, 361-62, 366, *371-73*, 416-17

McMahon football club, St. Louis, MO, **O** 301

McMahon, James R. "Jim," **F** 182, *371-73*, 517, 671; **S** 39

McMahon, John J. "Jack," **I** 198-99; **S** 268

McMahon, John J. "Sadie," **B** 176, *363-64*

McMahon, "Red," **I** 39

McManus, James K., *See* James K. McKay

McManus, Martin "Marty," **S** *125-26*

McMillan, "Terry," **S** 381

McMillen, Charles Thomas "Tom," **I** 71; **S** 280, 298

McMillin, Alvin N. "Bo," **F** 35, 277, *373-74*, 393, 403, 434, 471; **I** 67

McNab, "Alec," **O** 300

McNair, Donald "Don," **I** 665

McNally, David A. "Dave," **B** *364-65*, 403

McNally, John V., **F** 315, 329, *374-75*, 392; *See also* Johnny Blood

McNally, Morris, **I** 419

McNamara, Joanne, **I** 535

McNamara, Julianne L., **I** *532-34*

McNamee, Graham, **O** 77, *78-80*, 98

McNamee Award, **F** 132

McNaughton, Duncan, **O** 476

McNaughton Trophy, **I** 555

McNeese State University, **I** 74; **S** 478

McNeil, Lori, **O** 351

McNeill, William Donald "Don," **O** 386; **S** 552, *556-57*

McNichols Sports Arena, Denver, CO, **I** 78

McPartland, "Kid," **I** 420

MacPhail, Leland S., Sr. "Larry," **B** 26, 84, 125, 346, *365-67*, 558, 561; **S** 23, 45-46, 106, 127, 228

MacPhail, Leland S., Jr. "Lee," **B** 48, *367-68;* **S** 29

McPhee, John A. "Bid," **B** 117, *368-69*

McPherson College, **I** 181

McQuade, Francis, **B** 539

McQuinn, George, **S** *126-28*

McRae, Harold A. "Hal," **B** 47, *369-70*

MacRobert, Ethelda Bleibtrey, *See* Ethelda Bleibtrey MacRobert Schlafke

McSpaden, Harold "Jug," **O** 145

McTigue, Michael F. "Mike," **I** 359, 428, 462, 475

McVey, Calvin A. "Cal," **B** 270, *370-71*, 603, 628

McVey, "Sam," **I** 419

Macon, Mark L., **S** 268

Macon, GA Acmes baseball club (Negro Leagues), **B** 333

Macon, GA baseball club (SAL, SL), **B** 337, 392, 425, 459, 571; **S** 20, 162, 207

Macy, "Ike," **O** 358

Mad Hatter, **O** 199, 609; **S** 526-27

Mad Play, **S** 527

Madame Temple, **O** 583

Madamoiselle Award, **I** 611

Madden, Bartley, **I** 424

Madden, John E., **F** 179-80, *375-77;* **S** 335, 468

Madden, John E., **O** 600, 608; **S** 531

Madden, Preston, **O** 614

Madigan, Edward P. "Ed," **F** *377-79*

Madison, Helene E., *See* Helene Madison Kapphahu

Madison A&M University, **F** 81

Madison Square Boxing Club, New York, NY, I 445

Madison Square Garden, New York, NY, F 563; I 14, 21, 27, 32, 67, 132, 141, 157-58, 180, 187, 241, 258, 282, 289, 305, 363, 372, 386, 400, 404-05, 434, 441, 446, 453, 509, 546, 566; O 88, 105, 264, 269, 391, 440, 446, 454, 467, 505, 520, 522, 527, 560; S 261-62, 297, 325, 343, 433, 585, 610

Madison Square Garden Hall of Fame, I 87, 134

Madison Square Garden Network, S 353-54

Madison Stars baseball club (Negro Leagues), B 290

Madison, WI baseball club (ML), B 284

Madlock, Bill, Jr., B *371-73;* S 94, 142

Madrid, Spain Track and Field Meet, O 504

Magadan, David J. "Dave," S 170

Magee, Sherwood R. "Sherry," B *373-74*

Magic Lanes Bowling Team, I 351

Magic Valley, ID baseball club (PrL), S 24

Maglie, Salvatore A. "Sal," B 9, 132; S 118, *128-29*

Magomadev, Tara, I 658

Mahan, Edward W. "Eddie," F 65, 238, *379-80*

Mahan, "Larry," O *265-66*

Mahan, Lyle E., O 356

Maher, Peter "Pete," I 366

Mahnken, John E., I 250

Mahoney, Christopher J."Chris," B 208

Mahoney, Harold S., O 413

Mahre, "Phil," O *285-86*

Mahre, "Steve," O 285-86

Mahubah, O 595

Maid of Flight, O 591

Maiden, Stewart, O 135; S 512

Maier, Enrique, O 343

Mainichi Marathon, Otsu, Japan, O 536

Mains, Willard E., S 197

Maisel, Frederick C. "Fred," B 456

Majestic Prince, O 190, 599

Major Indoor Soccer League, O 295, 298, 302, 304-06, 308, 311

Major Indoor Soccer League All-Star Game, O 304

Major Indoor Soccer League Championships, O 295, 304, 311

Major Indoor Soccer League Most Valuable Player, O 304

Major League All-Star Baseball Team, I 332

Major League Baseball Championships, O 63, 82-83, 93, 272

Major League Players Association, S 80, 133, 149

Majors, John "Johnny," S *448-49,* 480

Majors, Shirley, S 448

Make Sail, O 222

Mako, C. Gene, O 330-31, 374

Malarcher, David J. "Dave," B 190, 339, 342, 533, 548-49; S *129-30*

Malavasi, Raymondo G. "Ray," F 590

Malevich, "Jack," I 565

Malibu Stakes, O 218

Mallon, Margaret "Meg," S 508-09

Mallory, Molla Bjurstedt, O 329, 332, 361, *373-74,* 388, 391, 411, 415

Malme, Sweden Track and Field Meet, O 504

Malone, Moses E., I *202-03;* S 257-58, 269

Malone, Perce L. "Pat," **B** 183
Malone, Ralph, **I** 18
Maloney, James W. "Jim," **S** 76, *130-31*
Maloney, "Tommy," **I** 390
Mambrino, **O** 587
Man in Motion, **S** 344
Man of the Year Award, **S** 78, 88, 399, 414, 418, 529
Man o'War, **O** 194-97, 199-200, 211, 215, 577-79, 582, *595-96,* 597, 605, 607-09, 613; **S** 533
The Man Stan Musial: Then and Now, **S** 338
Manager of the Year Award, **S** 58, 78, 88, 107-08, 135, 150, 181, 230
Mancha, Vaughn, **F** 595
Manchester College, **S** 256
Manchester, CT Recreation Club, **S** 587
Manchester, NH baseball club (EL, NEL), **B** 35, 575
Manchester United Soccer Club, **O** 291
Mandell, "Sammy," **I** 392, 411, *435-36*
Mandella, Samuel, *See* "Sammy" Mandell
Mandic, John J., **I** 97
Mandich, James M. "Jim," **F** 527
Mandlikova, Hana, **O** 379
Manero, Anthony "Tony," **O** 116
Mangin, Gregory S. "Greg," **O** 368, 595
Mangrum, James "Jim," **O** 141
Mangrum, Lloyd E., **O** *141-42,* 145; **S** 513
Manhattan Athletic Club, **O** 505
Manhattan Beach-Brighton Beach, CA Swim, **I** 589
Manhattan Brewery football club, Chicago, IL, **O** 299
Manhattan Chess Club, **I** 671

Manhattan College, **I** 33, 141, 252, 261; **S** 342-43
Manhattan College Athletic Hall of Fame, **S** 343
Manhattan Field, New York, **B** 198
Manhattan Handicap, **O** 192, 603
Manley, Effa, **B** 362
Manley, Elizabeth, **S** 626
Mann, Carol Ann, **S** 509; *See also* Carol Mann Hardy
Mann, Gerald, **F** 407
Mann, Louis, **O** 129
Mann Act, **I** 409
Manning, "Archie," **F** 622
Manning, Daniel R. "Danny," **I** 35; **S** *301-03*
Manning, "Ed," **S** 301
Manning, "Greg," **I** 71
Manning, Harold W., **O** 423
Mannion, Father Thomas, **I** 327
Mansfield, OH baseball club (ISL, OSL), **B** 268, 581
Mansfield State Normal School, **S** 502
Mantell, Frank, **I** 377, 390, 416, 448
Mantle, Mickey C., **B** 278, 296, 318, *374-75,* 382, 385, 388, 411, 515, 518, 597; **O** 272; **S** 22, 86, 147-48, 340
Manuel, **O** 224; **S** 436
Manufacturers World Auto Championship, **O** 12
Manush, Henry E. "Heinie," **B** 219, *375-77;* **S** 13
Maple, "Eddie," **O** 611
Maple Stakes, **O** 604
Mara, "Jack," **F** 381; **O** 60
Mara, Timothy J. "Tim," **F** 4, 278, *380-82,* 447-48; **O** 87
Mara, Wellington T., **F** 346, 353, 381
Maranatha Baptist Bible College, **I** 654
Maranville, Walter J. "Rabbit," **B** 14,

170, *377;* S 70

Maravich, Peter P. "Pete," I 41, 169, *203-05,* 226; S 298, 330

Maravich, Press, I 43, 203-04

Marberry, Fredrick "Fred," B 226, 606; S *131-32*

Marble, Alice, O 327, 331, 338, 343-44, 348, 357, 359, 363, *374-75,* 415

Marble Girl, O 173

Marburger, "Sam," I 376

Marcelle, Everett, B 378

Marcelle, Oliver H., B 339, *378,* 620

Marchegiano, Rocco F., *See* "Rocky" Marciano

Marchetti, Gino J., F 146, 165, 297-98, 348, *382,* 519, 521

Marciano, "Rocky," I 366, 395, 401, *436-38,* 442, 472, 645; O 60

Mare Island Marines football club, F 46, 112, 233

Margolin, Stacy, O 371

Margrave, O 188

Maria (horse), O 101

Maria (yacht), O 101

Marichal, Juan A., B 97, *378-80;* S 30, 118, 221

Marietta College, B 285; F 456, 558; S 216

Marilynn Smith Founders Golf Classic, O 168

Marin, John W. "Jack," I 119

Marino, Daniel C., Jr. "Dan," F 149, *383-85*

Marino, "Hank," I 341

Marino, "Young," I 378

Marion, Martin W. "Marty," B *380-81*

Marion, NC baseball club (ApL, WCL), B 179, 497

Marion, OH baseball club (OPL, OSL), B 113, 134

Marion, OH Oorang Indians football

club (NFL), F 183, 232

Maris, Roger E., B 201, 277, *381-83,* 597

Mariucci, John P., I 547, 554, *564-65,* 572; S 543

Marks, Joseph "Jack," F 504

Marks, Leo, O 196

Marlboro Award, O 364, 414

Marlboro Cup, O 584, 606-07, 610

Marlboro 500 CART Race, S 619

Marlboro Grand Prix CART Race, S 619

Marlboro Race Track, Upper Marlboro, MD, O 28

Marlboro Sportswriter of the Year, O 69

Marlboro 300 Auto Race, O 18, 39

Marlet Stables, O 180

Marolt, William C., O 280

Marquard, Richard W. "Rube," B 208, *383-84,* 612

Marquette, "Bud," I 531

Marquette University, F 3, 6, 30, 142, 152, 457, 504; I 72, 127, 197, 200, 269, 280, 282, 299, 302, 312; O 496, 552; S 325

Marquez, Luis A., B 453

Marquis of Queensbury Rules, I 369, 467

Marr, C. A. "Runt," B 43

Marr, Charles "Charlie," F 281

Mars, "Kayo," I 365

Marsans, Armando, B 227

Marshall, George P., F 28-29, 178, 290, 329, *385-86;* I 223; S 287, 437

Marshall, James L. "Jim," F 25, 451; S *449-50*

Marshall, John B., I 606

Marshall, John Thomas "Tom," I 68

Marshall, "Marty," I 427

Marshall, Michael G. "Mike," S *132-34*

Marshall, Pamela "Pam," O 558
Marshall Field, Chicago, IL, F 159
Marshall Junior College, S 424
Marshall University, F 202; I 103; S 290-91
Marshalltown Community College, I 8
Marta, O 222
Martain, William "Bill," I 271
Martell, "Wendy," S 320
Martin, Abraham "Abe," F 347
Martin, Alastair, O 396
Martin, Alfred M. "Billy," B 181, 185, 329, 375, *384-86,* 442; S 73, 230
Martin, Charles M., F 517
Martin, "Denver Ed," I 408
Martin, Dorothy Hamill, *See* Dorothy Hamill Forsythe
Martin, George, O 430
Martin, Harvey B., F 650
Martin, "Jack," S 324
Martin, James "Jim," F 176, 249
Martin, Johnny L. "Pepper," B 143, *386-87;* I 365
Martin, Leon, I 665
Martin, Leotis, I 428
Martin, Royce, O 204, 222
Martin, Slater "Dugie," I 110-11, 165, *205-06*
Martin, "Terry," I 431
Martin, Townsend, O 105
Martin Award, F 390
Martin Trophy, F 275
Martina, Joseph "Joe," S 197
Martinez, Emilio, I 426
Martinez, Horacio, B 379
Martini and Rossi Auto Race Driver of the Year, O 39
Martini and Rossi Sportswriter of the Year, O 69
Martinsburg, WV baseball club (BRL), B 119, 232, 620; S 12

Martinsville, VA Auto Race, O 1
Martinsville, VA baseball club (BSL, CrL), B 376, 517
Martinsville, VA Speedway, O 41; S 605
Martter, Perry F., I 663
Marty, Walter, O 476
Marullo, "Tony," I 465
Marx, Gregory A. "Greg," F 458
Maryland Association for the Improvement of the Breed of Horses, O 94
Maryland Athletic Club, O 233
Maryland Athletic Hall of Fame, O 238, 240, 250
Maryland Board of Football Officials, O 238
Maryland Jockey Club, O 95
Maryland Lacrosse Club, O 235, 245
Maryland Lacrosse Hero's Award, O 236
Maryland Lacrosse Officials Association, O 237
Maryland Racing Commission, I 407; S 525
Maryland Sports Hall of Fame, O 245
Maryland State Amateur Boxing Championships, I 406
Maryland State Athletic Commission, I 478
Maryland State Badminton Championships, O 244
Maryland State Soccer Association, O 303
Maryland Thanksgiving Basketball Tournament, I 215
Marysville, CA baseball club (FWL), S 79
Maryville College, F 150; I 139; S 211
Mascia, John "Johnny," O 192
Maseroti Auto Race Car, O 28, 35
Masher, O 177

Masi, Philip S. "Phil," I 572; S 186

Maskette, O 211-12; S 533

Maslow, Jonathan, S 132

Mason, Donald "Don," F 126

Mason, Kathy Rigby, *See* Kathy Rigby McCoy

Mason, Robert "Bob," S 545

Mason, Thomas C. "Tommy," I 532

Mason, Weldon, F 407

Mason City Junior College, I 85

Mason-Dixon Conference, I 277

Mason-Dixon 500 Auto Race, O 1

Massachusetts Amateur Golf Tournament, O 148

Massachusetts Greatest Woman Athlete, O 343

Massachusetts Handicap, O 605

Massachusetts Institute of Technology, I 572, 669

Massachusetts Open Golf Tournament, O 112

Massey, "Lew," I 469

Massillon, OH Tigers football club (Ind.), F 66, 183, 262, 402, 456, 464, 505; S 178, 387

Masters Golf Tournament, Augusta, GA, O 1934, 153, 156-57; 1935, 138, 153; 1936, 156; 1937, 116, 145; 1938, 127, 150; 1939, 127, 138; 1940, 118-19, 141; 1941, 169; 1942, 145, 153; 1947, 118, 153; 1949, 113, 158-59; 1950, 118; 1951, 131, 138; 1952, 113, 159; 1953, 131; 1954, 159; 1955, 142; 1956, 113; 1957, 125; 1958, 149; 1960, 149; 1962, 149; 1963, 157; 1964, 149; 1966, 139; 1967, 132; 1970, 115, 139; 1974, 159; 1976, 124; 1977, 166; 1981, 144, 166; 1986, 147; S 510, 519, 522-23

Masters Gold Tournament, I 403

Masters Track and Field Meet, O 522, 553

Masterson, Walter E. "Walt," S 196

Matchefts, John P., I 572

Mate, O 198, 613

Matei, Ilie, I 641

Mathes, Joseph J. "Joe," B 503

Mathes, Roland, I 609

Mathews, Edwin L., Jr. "Eddie," B 4, *387-88,* 502

Mathews, Robert T. "Bobby," B *388-90*

Mathewson, Christopher "Christy," B 3, 5, 46, 54, 66, 89, 112-13, 154, 173, 227, 328, 352, 384, *390-91,* 408, 420, 450, 488, 493, 550, 556, 569, 638; O 89; S 137, 161, 187, 223, 241

Mathewson, Henry, B 390

Mathias, Robert B. "Bob," O 477, *492-93;* S 572

Mathis, "Buster," I 385-86

Matisi, Anthony F. "Tony," F 353

Matlack, Jonathan T. "Jon," S 90-91

Matron Stakes, O 224-25, 578

Matson, James Randel "Randy," O *493-94;* S 586

Matson, Oliver G. "Ollie," F 382, *387-88,* 521, 557; S 586

Matte, Bruce, F 526

Matte, Thomas R. "Tom," F 614

Matter, "Andy," I 646

Matthews, Gary N., S *194*

Matthews, "Matty," I 464

Matthews, Raymond "Ray," F 35

Matthews, Vincent E. "Vince," O 458

Mattick, Robert J. "Bobby," S 71, 130

Mattingly, Donald A. "Don," B 623

Mattoon, IL baseball club (KL), B 157

Mauch, Gene W., B 71, 614; S 16, 58, 133, *134-35,* 180, 204

Maud Adams, **O** 206
Maude S., **O** 174
Maureen Connolly Brinker Award, **O** 328
Maurer, John, **I** 256
Maurice Stokes Memorial Benefit Basketball Game, **I** 53, 308
Mauriello, "Tami," **I** 424
Max Hirsch Memorial Fund, **S** 528
Max Ritter Award, **I** 585
Maxim, "Joey," **I** 413, 424, 441-42, 455
Maxwell, Cedric B. "Cornbread," **I** 318
Maxwell, Susan *See* Susan Maxwell Berning
Maxwell, Vernon, **I** 281
Maxwell Club, **F** 226, 462
Maxwell Memorial Award, **F** 8, 24, 32, 51, 53, 100, 130, 132, 138, 149, 154, 191, 197, 221, 226, 243, 248, 310, 337, 344, 350, 356, 364-65, 431, 437, 473, 490, 515, 545, 568, 604, 622, 629; **S** 366, 406, 473, 480, 487, 494
Maxwell Race Car, **O** 26
May, Carlos, **B** 391
May, Lee A., **B** *391-92*
May, Mark, **F** *388;* **S** 480
May, Milton S. "Milt," **S** 174
May, Scott G., **I** 162; **S** 263, *303-04*
May, William L. "Willie," **O** 437-38
May Berry, **O** 215
May Hempstead, **S** 527
Mayasich, John E., **I** *565-66,* 568, 572
Mayberry, John C., **S** *136-37*
Mayer, Alan, **O** *303-04*
Mayer, Alvin Richard "Dick," **O** 143
Mayflower Golf Classic, **S** 505, 518-19
Mayhood, "Charley," **I** 433

Maynard, Donald R. "Don," **F** 253, 295, *388-89*
Mays, Carl W., **B** 285-86, *392-93*, 492, 500, 508; **S** 28-29
Mays, Gerald A. "Jerry," **S** *450-51*
Mays, "Rex," **O** 4, *19-20*
Mays, Willie H., **B** 2, 72, 97, 133, 185, 274, 318, 350-51, 374, 388, *393-95*, 502, 514, 540, 618; **O** 272; **S** 22, 25, 30, 234, 347
Maysville, KY baseball club (BGL), **B** 534
Mayweather, Floyd, **I** 422
Mazda Golf Tournament, **O** 137
Mazda LPGA Golf Classic, **S** 505, 508, 519
Mazeroski, William D. "Bill," **B** *395-96;* **S** 271
MBS LPGA Golf Classic, **S** 508-09
Mead, Andrea, *See* Andrea Mead Lawrence
Mead, Bradford, **O** 283
Mead, "Eddie," **I** 477
Mead, Janet, **O** 283
Mead, Peter, **O** 283
Meador, Edward D. "Ed," **F** *390-91*
Meadow Brook Hunt Club, **O** 261
Meadow Stable, **O** 607
Meadowbrook Country Club, Birmingham, MI, **O** 125
Meadowlands Farm, **O** 207
Meadowlands Indy Auto Race, **O** 3
Meadowlands Pace, **O** 600
Meadowlands Sports Complex, East Rutherford, NJ, **O** 105, 203, 481, 600; **S** 401, 619
Meadowlands Turf, **O** 591
Meadows, Earle E., **O** 444, 556; **S** *587-88*
Meadows Track, **O** 207
Meagher, Mary T., **I** *607-08*
Meanwell, Walter E. "Doc," **I** 85, 167, *206-07,* 234

Meany, Helen, I 494
Mears, Rick R., O 17, *20-21*, 28-29; S 619-20
Mears, Roger, O 20
Mears, William "Bill," O 20
Mecklenburg, Karl B., S *451-52*
Medal of Honor, Western Conference, S 392
Medalie, Gladys Vivian, *See* Gladys Medalie Heldman
Medford, OR baseball club (NWL), B 191
Medica, Jack C., I 608
Medoc, O 571
Medved, Alexander, S 624
Medwick, Joseph M. "Joe," B 45, 323, 366, *396-97*, 403, 582; S 143, 201
Meehan, John F., F 627
Meehan, "Willie," I 391
Meely, Cliff, I 230, 304
Meggysey, David M. "Dave," S 387
Meharry Medical College, S 168
Mehl, Walter, O 446, 520-21
Mehnert, George N., I *650-51*, 665
Mehre, "Harry," F 595
Mehring, Robert "Bob," F 646
Mehrtens, Warren, O 572
Melbourne, Australia Summer Olympic Games, *See* Olympic Summer Games, 1956
Melbourne, FL baseball club (CRL), B 70
Mellody, "Honey," I 425, 474
Melnyk, "Steve," S 524
Melton, Nancy Lopez, *See* Nancy Lopez Melton Knight
Melton, Timothy "Tim," O 137
Membrino, O 596
Memmott, A. James, S 336
Memorial Golf Journalism Award, O 70
Memorial Golf Tournament, O 135, 147; S 520
Memorial Gymnasium, West Lafayette, IN, I 227
Memorial Stadium, Ann Arbor, MI, F 669
Memorial Stadium, Baltimore, MD, S 48
Memorial Stadium, Berkeley, CA, F 411
Memorial Stadium, Lawrence, KS, I 182
Memphis State University, I 280, 303, 317; S 259, 354
Memphis, TN Americans Soccer Club, O 308
Memphis, TN baseball club (IL, SL, TL), B 76, 419, 515, 601; S 202, 233, 246
Memphis, TN baseball club (SA), B 12, 14, 134, 154, 249, 266, 312, 400, 525, 551; F 288; S 202, 233, 246
Memphis, TN City Golf Tournament, O 142
Memphis, TN Open Golf Classic, O 142, 163; S 507
Memphis, TN Red Sox baseball club (NAL), B 32, 192, 599
Memphis, TN Sounds basketball club (ABA), I 226; S 274
Memphis, TN Southmen football club (WFL), F 122, 277, 420, 634
Mendez, Jose, S *137-38*
Menke, Frank G., F 415
Mentor, I 276
Mentor, S 531
Menze, Louis, I 5, 256
Mercedes, Hector, S 625
Mercer, E. L. "Roy," F 552
Mercer Race Car, O 26
Mercer University, F 81, 110, 576
Mercur, Frederick "Fritz," O 322
Meredith, James E. "Ted," O *494-96,*

512, 534; **S** 575

Meredith, Joe Don, **F** 331; **O** 47-48, 59, *80-81;* **S** 455

Merestead Hockey and Lacrosse Camps, **O** 270

Meriden, CT baseball club (CtL, EL), **B** 221, 358, 586

Merillat, Louis A. "Lou," **F** 126

Merion Country Club, **O** 270

Merion Cricket Club, Haverford, PA, **O** 394, 406

Meriweather, "Willie," **I** 95

Merkle, Frederick C. "Fred," **B** 53, 170, 354, 457, 557; **S** 156

Mermaid, **O** 597

Mernik, Joseph "Joe," **F** 555

Merrell, Grady, Sr., **I** 674

Merrell, Grady, Jr., **I** 674

Merrell, Mary Brennan, **I** *674-75*

Merrick, James, **S** 252

Merrihew, Stephen W., **O** *375-76*

Merrill, Gretchen van Zandt, **I** 515

Merrill-Lynch Shootout Golf Championship, **S** 524

Merrimack College, **B** 634

Merritt, "Ed," **O** 505

Merritt, Robert "Bobby," **O** 180

Merritt Junior College, **F** 411

Merriwell, Frank, **O** 54

Merry Monarch, **O** 589

Mesa Junior College, **I** 653; **S** 17-18

Meservey-Thornton, IA High School, **I** 183

Messenger, **O** 587, *596-97*

Messersmith, John Alexander "Andy," **B** 365, 403; **S** *138-39*

Messner, Daniel, Jr. "Dan," **O** 580

Met A Wrestling Tournament, **I** 650-51

Metacomel Golf Club, Providence, RI, **O** 164

Metairie Race Course, New Orleans, LA, **O** 594

Metcalf, Terrance R. "Terry," **F** 399

Metcalfe, Ralph H., **O** *496-97,* 515, 552, 568

Metheny, Linda Jo, *See* Linda Jo Metheny Mulvihill

Metro Conference, **I** 56; **S** 263, 310

Metrodome, Minneapolis, MN, **S** 146

Metropolis Country Club, White Plains, NY, **O** 113

Metropolitan Amateur Athletic Union Track and Field Championships, **O** 470, 490

Metropolitan Amateur Golf Tournament, **O** 160, 162

Metropolitan Association Boxing Championships, **I** 389

Metropolitan Baseball Writers Association of New York, **I** 141

Metropolitan Golf Association Distinguished Service Award, **O** 117

Metropolitan Golf Championships, **S** 512

Metropolitan Handicap, **O** 199, 211, 224, 592; **S** 533

Metropolitan Junior Hockey Association of New York, **I** 566

Metropolitan League, **I** 14, 32, 65, 223, 233, 260

Metropolitan League Championships and Playoffs, **I** 32, 223

Metropolitan Mile Race, **O** 202, 222

Metropolitan New York Junior Swim Championships, **I** 588

Metropolitan Open Golf Championships, **O** 112-13, 128, 158, 169

Metropolitan Reserves of Newark baseball club, **B** 429

Metropolitan Sports Center, Bloomington, MN, **I** 548

Metropolitan Tennis Championships, **O** 354, 377

Metropolitan Track Writers
Association, **O** 436
Metropolitan Track Writers
Association Outstanding Female
Athlete, **O** 436
Meusel, Emil F., **B** 66, *397-98*
Meusel, Robert W. "Bob," **B** 106,
397-98, 399
Mexia, TX baseball club (TL), **S** 131
Mexican, "Jim," **I** 425
Mexican Baseball Hall of Fame, **B**
148
Mexican Davis Cup Team, **S** 561
Mexican Grand Prix, **O** 11
Mexican League, **B** 6, 32, 55, 85,
132, 141, 148, 213, 262, 270, 273,
288, 290, 435, 526, 599-600, 619;
S 9-10, 128, 194
Mexican National Soccer Team, **O**
296, 300-01, 305
Mexican National Tennis
Championships, **O** 343, 409
Mexican Olympic Weightlifting Team,
I 630
Mexican Olympic Wrestling Team, **I**
662
Mexican 1,000 USAC Auto Race, **S**
614
Mexican Professional Soccer League,
O 294
Mexico City, Mexico Summer
Olympic Games, *See* Olympic
Summer Games, 1968
Meyer, Alvah T., **O** 443
Meyer, Deborah E., *See* Deborah
Meyer Reyes
Meyer, Edward, **O** 21
Meyer, "Joey," **I** 209
Meyer, Leo R., **F** 3, 29, *391-92*
Meyer, Louis, Sr., **O** 14, *21-22,* 33-
35
Meyer, Louis, Jr., **O** 22
Meyer, Raymond J. "Ray," **I** 116,

164, *207-09,* 210; **S** 252-53, 309
Meyer, Ronald S. "Ron," **F** 42; **I**
492
Meyer, Russell C. "Russ," **B** 375
Meyer, William A. "Billy," **B** 306
Meyer Morton Award, **S** 500
Meyer Stadium, Fort Worth, TX, **F**
391
Meyerhoof, "Harry," **O** 610
Meyerle, Levi S., **B** *399-400*
Meyers, Ann E., *See* Ann Meyers
Drysdale
Meyers, David W. "Dave," **I** 72, 331
Meyers, Mary M., **O** 314
Meyers, Robert "Bob," **I** 72
Miami Beach, FL baseball club (FSL),
B 396, 410
Miami Beach, FL Bath and Tennis
Club, **I** 487
Miami, FL baseball club (FECL, FIL,
IL, FSL), **B** 72, 387, 436, 574,
591, 618; **S** 69, 92, 140, 228
Miami, FL *Daily News,* **F** 241, 249;
S 558
Miami, FL Dolphins football club
(AFL), **F** 18, 122, 225, 253, 465,
609-10, 633; **O** 67, 472, 538; **S**
379, 441
Miami, FL Dolphins football club
(NFL), **F** 7, 18, 43, 73, 119, 122,
191, 196, 206, 219, 222, 225-26,
246, 274, 295-96, 304, 321, 323-
24, 331, 333-34, 384-85, 388, 397,
404, 412, 423, 428, 432, 535, 543-
44, 561, 568, 590, 593, 609-10,
632-33, 659; **I** 250; **O** 67, 472,
538; **S** 373, 375, 386-87, 410,
441, 455
Miami, FL Floridians basketball club
(ABA), **S** 292
Miami, FL Four Ball Title, **O** 127
Miami, FL Heat basketball club
(NBA), **I** 58, 289

Miami, FL Open Golf Tournament, **S** 507, 515

Miami, FL Seahawks football club (AAFL), **S** 430

Miami, FL Touchdown Club, **F** 185, 236

Miami University of Ohio, **B** 8, 30, 485; **F** 51, 69, 164, 210, 251-52, 457-58, 525-26; **S** 345, 592-93

Miami-Biltmore Golf Tournament, **O** 120, 127

Miceli, "Joe," **I** 477

Michael, Eugene R. "Gene," **B** 329, 618

Michael, William, **S** 370

Michaels, Alan "Al," **S** 350, 355, *355-56*

Michaels, Edward "Ed," **S** 452

Michaels, Louis A. "Lou," **S** *452*

Michaels, Matthew, **S** 452

Michaels, Walter "Walt," **S** 452

Michalske, August "Mike," **F** *392-93*

Michen, Wallace, **I** 52

Michigan College of Mines, **I** 177

Michigan 400 Auto Race, **O** 30

Michigan Hall of Honor, **S** 500

Michigan Intercollegiate Athletic Association, **F** 136, 244, 292

Michigan International Speedway, Brooklyn, MI, **O** 9, 21, 28-29; **S** 606, 619

Michigan Marlboro 500 Auto Race, **O** 3, 16-17, 21, 38

Michigan-Ontario League, **S** 79

Michigan Panthers football club (USFL), 97, 671; **S** 454

Michigan Professional Golf Association Tournament, **O** 157

Michigan Sports Hall of Fame, **F** 106, 193, 341, 405, 413, 629; **I** 344; **O** 157; **S** 57, 228

Michigan Stadium, Ann Arbor, MI, **F** 194, 526

Michigan State University, **B** 209, 476; **F** 1, 32, 136-37, 188, 249, 261, 324, 338, 344-45, 404, 407, 413, 458, 523, 531, 556, 594, 642; **I** 146, 199, 230, 488, 569, 639; **O** 240; **S** 133, 167, 316, 391-92, 402, 435, 472, 494, 547, 616

Michigan Tech University, **I** 571

Michigan 200 Auto Race, **O** 18

Michigan 250 CART Race, **S** 619

Michigan Wrestling Club, Ann Arbor, MI, **I** 640, 650

Michigan City, IN baseball club (ML), **B** 379

Mickal, Abraham "Abe," **F** 599

Mid-American Conference, **F** 251-52, 288, 330, 457, 525-26; **I** 7, 302; **S** 281, 362, 592

Mid-American Conference Championships, **I** 7

Mid-Atlantic Conference, **S** 452, 456

Mid-Pines Country Club, Southern Pines, NC, **O** 111

Mid-Southern Open Golf Tournament, **O** 165

Mid-State Open Golf Tournament, **S** 522

Mid-West Conference, **S** 616

Mid-West Conference Championships, **S** 616

Middle Atlantic Amateur Athletic Union, **F** 579

Middle Atlantic League, **S** 83, 86, 127, 149, 163, 200, 207, 228

Middle Atlantic PGA Tournament, **S** 522

Middle Atlantic States Figure Skating Championships, **I** 502

Middle Atlantic States Gymnastic Championships, **I** 530-31

Middle Atlantic States Weightlifting Championships, **I** 633

Middle Distance Track and Field
Championships, O 505
Middle States Association, O 406
Middle States League, S 82, 238, 246
Middle States Sears Cup Field Hockey
Team, O 270
Middle States Tennis Championships,
O 325, 333, 338, 366, 377, 392
Middlecoff, Emmett Cary, O 125,
142-43
Middletown, OH Mansfield baseball
club (NA), B 428
Middleground, S 527
Middleweight Boxing Championships,
I 356, 359, 370, 372-73, 376-78,
386-87, 390, 393-94, 396-98, 414-
16, 418-19, 422-23, 426, 432, 445,
448-49, 455-56, 460-61, 464-66,
474-75, 481-83
Midland, TX baseball club (SpL, TL),
B 279, 542; S 205
Midlands Wrestling Tournament, I
641, 655
Midlothian Golf Club, Blue Island, IL,
O 128
Midwest Junior Hockey League, I 557
Midwest League, S 8, 83-84, 134,
152, 174, 242, 354, 357
Midwest Roadster and Stock Car
Association Championships, S
620
Midwest Sprint Car Championships,
S 614
Midwestern Athletic Association, I
202
Midwestern Conference, F 279
Midwestern State Figure Skating
Championships, I 512-13
Midwestern States Golden Gloves
Tournament, I 427
Mieuli, Franklin J., I 8, 303
Migay, Rudolph J. "Rudy," S 541-42
Mihalik, Zigmund J. "Red," I *209-
10*
Mikan, George L., Jr., I 7, 10, 92,
113, 134, 165, 188, 190, 194, 205,
209, *210-12*, 213, 241, 334; S
277, 286, 317
Mike Bossy Trophy, S 539
MIkkelsen, Srvid Verner "Vern," I
165, *212-13*
Mikkelson, Peter J. "Pete," S 243
Milan, J. "Cal," O 582
Milan, Jesse Clyde, B 289, *400*
Milburn, Rodney, Jr. "Rod," O 447,
497-98
Milde, Lothar, O 511
Miler, Johnny, I 429
Miles College, B 391-92; O 485
Milford, DE baseball club (ESL), S
68
Milkmaid, O 215; S 525-26
Miller, "Alvie," I 415
Miller, "Candy," I 167
Miller, Cheryl D., I *213-16*
Miller, Cleophus, Jr. "Cleo," F 482
Miller, Creighton E., F 344
Miller, Daniel "Dan," F 576
Miller, Darrell, I 213
Miller, Delvin G. "Del," O *207-08*
Miller, Donald "Don," F *187-90*,
200, 393; *See also* Four Horsemen
Miller, Edmund J. "Bing," B *401-02*
Miller, Edward "Stretch," I 223
Miller, Freddie, I *438-39*
Miller, Harry, O 25
Miller, Henry J. "Heinie," F 350
Miller, James E. "Hack," B 621
Miller, John B. "Dots," B 590
Miller, John L. "Johnny," O *143-44*
Miller, Larry, I 282
Miller, Laurence, O 143
Miller, Lennox, O 472, 531
Miller, Marvin J., B 186, *402-03*
Miller, Ralph H., I 5, *216-17*
Miller, Ray, I 459

Miller, Reginald "Reggie," I 213
Miller, Saul, I 213
Miller, Stuart L. "Stu," S *139*
Miller, Walter, I 663; O *208,* 211, 217; S 527
Miller High Life 400 NASCAR Race, O 28, 44; S 606
Miller High Life 500 NASCAR Race, O 1
Miller Race Car, O 7
Miller Stakes, O 596
Miller's Damsel, O 570
Milligan, Bowman, I 403-04
Milligan, Tommy, I 475
Milliken, Joseph "Joe," S 604
Milliken University, F 414
Millner, Wayne V., F 385, *393-94*
Millrose Athletic Association, New York, O 535; S 589, 596
Millrose Track and Field Games, O 424, 486, 507, 522, 528, 539-40
Mills, Arthur G., B 637
Mills, Curtis, O 458
Mills, Freddie, I 424
Mills, James B., O 222
Mills, Leroy, F 94, 571
Mills, Ogden, O 184
Mills, William M. "Billy," O *498-99*
Millsaps College, S 164
Milstead, Century A., F 302
Milton, Thomas W. "Tommy," O 8, 22-23, 25
Milwaukee Athletic Association, O 464, 483
Milwaukee Auto Race, O 16, 20, 37, 42
Milwaukee Badgers football club (NFL), F 4, 98, 113, 142, 373-74, 477, 498, 551; I 264
Milwaukee baseball club (WL), B 28, 161, 225, 358
Milwaukee Bears baseball club (NNL), B 255
Milwaukee Braves baseball club (NL), B 1, 3-4, 9, 30, 62, 133, 163, 216, 230, 251, 278, 291, 356, 380, 385, 387-88, 393, 421-22, 485, 503, 517, 525, 559, 575, 583, 591; I 312, 333; O 46; S 33, 39, 46, 69, 75-76, 112, 130, 135, 162-63, 219-21
Milwaukee Brewers baseball club (AA), B 133, 161, 230, 288, 373, 388, 501, 512, 534-35, 573; F 402; S 81, 86, 102, 150, 197, 207, 245
Milwaukee Brewers baseball club (AL), B 2, 115, 161, 180, 264, 316, 342, 388, 441, 514, 543-44, 579, 639; S 6, 9, 12, 84, 87, 106, 141, 175, 193, 213, 215, 244
Milwaukee Bucks basketball club (NBA), I 3-4, 9, 50, 53, 78, 124, 169, 219, 251-52, 278; S 9, 263, 272, 283, 294, 299, 302, 304, 307, 603
Milwaukee Does basketball club (WBL), I 50
Milwaukee Four Ball Golf Tournament, O 127
Milwaukee Hawks basketball club (NBA), I 110, 133-34, 238, 335; S 318
Milwaukee Heil Products Bowling Team, I 341
Milwaukee 100 USAC Race, S 614
Milwaukee 150 USAC Race, O 17-18
Milwaukee Race Track, O 586
Milwaukee *Sentinel,* O 96
Milwaukee Shooting Stars basketball club, I 72
Milwaukee Sports Hall of Fame, I 341
Milwaukee 200 USAC Race, O 39; S 614, 620

Mims, Madeline Manning Jackson, O
499-500
Mina, Mauro, I 384
Mincher, Donald R. "Don," S 202
Minds, Jack H., S 502
Mineo, O 571
Minneapolis Athletic Club, F 561
Minneapolis Auto Race, O 6
Minneapolis baseball club (WA, WL),
  B 45, 78, 447; S 215, 233
Minneapolis Flour City hockey club,
  I 553
Minneapolis football club (AFL), F
  445
Minneapolis Lakers basketball club
  (NBL, BAA, NBA), F 218, 591; I
  19, 44, 86, 92, 109, 120, 133,
  165, 184, 190, 205, 209, 211-13,
  240-41, 270, 319; S 286, 318-19
Minneapolis Millers baseball club
  (AA), B 21, 81, 85-86, 105, 120,
  132, 146, 173, 197, 251, 274, 328,
  361, 373, 393, 400, 540, 547, 577,
  580, 601, 615, 633; F 293; S 5,
  14, 45, 79, 81, 135, 197-98, 208,
  239
Minneapolis Millers hockey club
  (CeHL, AHA), I 553; S 537
Minneapolis Red Jackets football club
  (NFL), S 425
Minneapolis-St. Paul baseball club
  (Negro Leagues), I 293-94
Minneapolis-St. Paul hockey club
  (USHL), I 564
Minneapolis *Tribune,* F 374
Minnesota Amateur Hockey
  Association, I 559, 563
Minnesota Athletic Club, S 444
Minnesota Boxing Commission, I
  390
Minnesota College Conference, S
  309-10
Minnesota Fats, *See* Rudolf W.

Wanderone, Jr.
Minnesota Fighting Saints hockey
  club (WHA), I 557
Minnesota Intercollegiate Athletic
  Association, F 315
Minnesota Junior Stars hockey club, I
  548
Minnesota Muskies basketball club
  (ABA), S 273, 288
Minnesota North Stars hockey club
  (NHL), I 549-51, 558, 564, 568,
  570, 573; S 403, 544
Minnesota Pipers basketball club
  (ABA), I 213; S 292
Minnesota Sports Hall of Fame, F
  413, 556; I 391, 565
Minnesota State Golf Championships,
  O 110
Minnesota State High School Hockey
  Championships, I 547, 549, 565,
  572
Minnesota Twins baseball club (AL),
  B 14, 70-71, 139, 201, 227-28,
  263, 272, 295, 305, 314, 385, 445,
  497, 518, 631, 633; F 592; S3,
  11-12, 14-15, 25, 31, 53, 120,
  132-33, 135, 145-46, 152, 157-58,
  160, 167, 171, 205, 211, 215, 222,
  234, 402
Minnesota Vikings football club
  (NFL), F 36, 42, 50, 73, 76, 99,
  122, 134, 150, 161, 180, 185, 197,
  202, 218-19, 246, 277, 280, 285-
  86, 333-34, 366, 376, 411, 432,
  451-52, 461, 463, 479, 485-86,
  494, 540, 546, 561, 572-73, 583-
  84, 586, 590-91, 609, 615, 618,
  620, 667; I 532; S 363, 365, 379,
  384, 398-99, 402-03, 449-50, 469,
  482, 486, 490, 495, 497
Minnesota-Wisconsin League, S 6
Minoso, Saturnino Orestes "Minnie,"
  S 106, *139-41,* 247

Minter, Alan, I 396-97
Minter, Anne, O 397
Minto, Harold, I 606
Mintz, Jake, I 366
Mira Costa Junior College, F 76; S
    27
Miske, Billy" I 391
Miss Disco, O 572
Miss Jemima, O 199
Miss Oceana, O 222
Miss Order, O 206
Miss Weesie, O 216
Miss Woodford, O 209, 589, 597-98
Missile Bell, O 222
Mission Hills Golf and Country Club,
    Palm Springs, CA, S 516
Mission Ski Academy, O 280
Mission Viejo, CA Nadadores Swim
    Club, I 491, 575, 582-83, 593
Missions, CA baseball club (PCL), B
    65
Mississippi Agricultural &
    Mechanical University, B 413; F
    49, 83, 292-93
Mississippi College, B 545; F 47
Mississippi Open Golf Tournament, S
    515
Mississippi Sports Hall of Fame, I
    315
Mississippi State Hall of Fame, S
    598
Mississippi State University, F 95,
    186, 514-15, 599; I 135-36; S
    367-68, 448, 480
Mississippi State Women's Basketball
    Championships, I 314
Mississippi Veterans Memorial
    Stadium, Jackson, MS, S 465
Mississippi Vocational College, F
    297
Missoula, MT baseball club (PrL,
    UL), B 295; S 21
Missouri Amateur Athletic Union

League, I 148
Missouri Amateur Athletic Union
    Track and Field Championships, O
    546, 555
Missouri Baptist College, O 311
Missouri Intercollegiate Athletic
    Association, F 167; S 496
Missouri Sports Hall of Fame, B 67;
    I 5, 140; O 547; S 569, 581
Missouri State Amateur Golf
    Championships, O 151
Missouri State Teachers College, O
    156
Missouri State Wrestling
    Championships, S 627
Missouri Track and Cross Country
    Coaches Association Hall of Fame,
    S 569
Missouri Valley College, B 420
Missouri Valley Conference, B 469;
    F 77, 133, 167, 170-71, 222, 253,
    335, 359, 446, 463, 479, 515, 521,
    527, 531, 533, 609, 627, 645; I
    69, 77, 81, 126-27, 139, 206, 216,
    232, 251, 268-69, 271; S 259,
    268, 274, 398, 401, 428, 435, 440,
    488, 580
Missouri Valley League, S 110
Mister Gus, O 228
Mistletoe Shalie, O 182
Misty Mom, O 184
Mitchell, Charley, I 369, 467
Mitchell, Jack, F 78, 581; S 408,
    462
Mitchell, James J., O 460
Mitchell, Lydell D., F 93, 246, 296,
    394-95, 399, 460, 518
Mitchell, Richie, I 469, 476
Mitchell, Robert C. "Bobby," F 386,
    395-96
Mitchell, SD baseball club (SDA), B
    40
Mitri, Tiberco, I 418

Mix, Ronald J. "Ron," F *396-97*

Mize, John R. "Johnny," B 8, 45, *403-04,* 520, 597; S 23, 95

Mobile, AL baseball club (SA, SAL, SL), B 279, 330, 601; F 522

Mobile, AL Black Bears baseball club (Negro Leagues), B 1

Mobile, AL Tigers baseball club (Negro Leagues), B 435-36

Mobley, Rudolph "Rudy," F 663

Modell, Arthur "Art," F 70; S 384

Modesto, CA baseball club (CaL), B 10, 179, 248, 277, 284, 405, 514; S 34, 59

Modesto, CA Junior College, F 294, 382; I 93

Modesto, CA Relays, O 429

Modesty, O 209

Modosian, Vladimir, I 659

Modzelewski, Edward "Ed," F 397

Modzelewski, Richard B. "Dick," F 223, *397,* 503

Modzelewski, Stanley J., *See* Stanley J. Stutz

Moe, Douglas E. "Doug," I 112; S *304-05*

Moegle, Richard "Dick," F 422

Moens, Roger, O 442

Moffitt, Billie Jean, *See* Billie Jean Moffitt King

Mogridge, George A., S 111, 190

Moha, Bob, I 377, 448

Moir, John "Johnny," S 309

Mokatain, O 526-27

Mokray, William G. "Bill," I *217-18*

Molenda, John J. "Bo," F 194

Molina, Louis, I 363

Molina, Tinti, S 224

Moline, IL baseball club (3IL), B 215; S 46

Molinski, E. M. "Ed," F 576

Molitor, Paul L., S *141-42,* 201

Molodet, "Vic," I 43

Molsen Three Star Soccer Player of the Month, O 295

Molter, William "Bill," O 603; S *531-32*

Molyneux, Algernon, I 439

Molyneux, "Tom," I 426, *439-40*

Monarch, O 583

Monarch Bay Canoe Club, I 650

Moncrief, Sidney A., I *218-20*

Monday, "Kenny," I 658

Monday, Robert J. "Rick," B 276; S 88, *142-43,* 241, 355

"Monday Night Football," O 47, 59, 78, 80; *See also* ABC-TV "Monday Night Football"

Mondschein, Irving "Moon," O 492

Monessen, PA baseball club (PSL), S 86

Monitor, O 46, 65

Monitor, S 536

Monmouth College, I 180; O 464

Monmouth Cup, O 595, 605

Monmouth Oaks Stakes, O 597

Monmouth Park Race Track, Long Branch, NJ, O 178, 201, 204, 206, 219, 227, 604; S 529

Monmouth Park Racing Association, O 177

Monmouth Stakes, O 597

Monro-Matic Bowling Tournament, I 343

Monroe, Vernon Earl "The Pearl," I 90, *220-21*

Monroe, William "Bill," B 286; S *142-43,* 189

Monroe, "Willie," I 397

Monroe, LA baseball club (CSL), B 406; S 235

Monroe, LA Monarchs baseball club (Negro Leagues), B 520

Monroe, NC baseball club (WCL), B 439

Monsky, Leroy, F 595

Mont Saint Anne, Canada Alpine Skiing Competition, **O** 274

Montana, Joseph C., Jr. "Joe," **F** *398-99,* 632; **S** 383

Montana, "Small," **I** 447, 480

Montana State University, **I** 138, 301-02, 562; **S** 486, 604

Montanez, Pedro, **I** 354

Montclair, NJ Athletic Club, **O** 241, 248

Montclair State College, **I** 27-28, 157, 316

Monteith, William "Scotty," **I** 378

Monterrey, CA Grand Prix Stock Car Race, **O** 28

Monterrey, Mexico baseball club (MEL), **S** 9

Monterrey Peninsula Junior College, **F** 631

Montgomery, **S** 526-27

Montgomery, Cleotha "Cle," **F** 399

Montgomery, Clifford "Cliff," **F** 350

Montgomery, James P. "Jim," **I** 584

Montgomery, Robert "Bob," **I** 404, *440-41,* 477, 483

Montgomery, Wilbert, **F** *399-400,* 619

Montgomery, AL baseball club (SA, SAL, SEL, SL), **B** 27, 93-94, 353, 455-56, 534, 537, 595; **O** 42; **S** 5, 145, 225, 236

Montgomery, AL Grey Sox baseball club (Negro Leagues), **B** 533; **S** 188

Montilla, Miguel, **I** 452

Montpelier, VT baseball club (GML, NEL), **B** 195, 468

Montreal Alouettes football club (CFL), **F** 50, 478, 508, 656, 662; **S** 448, 572

Montreal baseball club (EL, IL), **B** 8-9, 26, 97, 109, 137, 159, 193, 229, 258, 266, 282-83, 377, 417, 480, 510, 521, 614; **S** 19, 60, 108, 167

Montreal Canadiens hockey club (NHL), **I** 553, 560, 562, 566, 571-72; **S** 93, 352, 538, 543, 547

Montreal Concordes football club (CFL), **F** 209

Montreal Expos baseball club (NL), **B** 75-76, 139-40, 152, 159, 174, 216, 356, 364-65, 425, 486, 515, 522, 532, 575, 614, 618; **I** 250, 261; **S** 25, 53, 89, 92-93, 113, 128, 132-33, 142, 153, 163, 166, 171-72, 230, 242, 354

Montreal Hakoah Soccer Club, **O** 291

Montreal Maroons hockey club (NHL), **I** 537

Montreal Soccer Club (NASL), **O** 307-08

Montreal Sparta Soccer Club, **O** 291

Montreal Summer Olympic Games, *See* Olympic Summer Games, 1976

Monza, Italy 500 Auto Race, **O** 4-5, 7-8; **S** 620

Monzon, Carlos, **I** 396

Moody, Helen Wills, *See* Helen Wills Moody Roark

Mookey, "Jack," **O** 479

Moomaw, Donn, **S** *452-53*

Moore, Archie, **I** 361, 413, 437, *441-42,* 449, 481

Moore, Bernard "Bernie," **F** 81, 599, 618

Moore, Bobby, *See* Ahmad Rashad

Moore, Burton, **O** 546

Moore, Charles H. Jr. "Charley," **O** 466

Moore, Donald M. "Don," **S** 284

Moore, Elisabeth H. "Bessie," **O** 325, 333, 354, *376-77,* 383, 406

Moore, George E., **O** 376

Moore, Kenneth C. "Kenny," **O** 435

Moore, "Kid," I 479
Moore, Leonard E. "Lenny," F 165, 395, *400-01*
Moore, Louis "Lou," O 32
Moore, "Memphis Pal," I 389, 417, 431
Moore, "Philadelphia Pal," I 365
Moore, Roy, I 400
Moore, Terry, S *143-44*
Moore, Walter "Dobie," B 6
Moore, William Wilcy, S 132
Mooresville, NC baseball club (NCSL), B 607
Moorhead, MN baseball club (NoL), B 382
Moose Jaw, Canada baseball club (WCaL), B 193
Mora, James E., Sr. "Jim," S *453-54*
Mora, James E., Jr., S 454
Moran, Charles B. "Charlie," B 376; F 35, *402-03*
Moran, Frank, I 376, 476
Moran, "Gussy," S 554
Moran, James E., *See* Jimmy Goodrich
Moran, Owen, I 357, 480
Moran, "Pal," I 476
Moran, Patrick J. "Pat," B 120, 488; S *144-45*
Moran, Thomas "Tom," F 403
Moreau, Marcel, I 448
Morehouse College, O 503
Moreland, George, O 199
Morello, O 206
Morgan, Edwin W. "Pepper," S 23
Morgan, Emma Leavitt, O 333
Morgan, J. D., I 331; O 324
Morgan, Joe L., B 10, 85, 191, 196, *404-05*, 432, 486; S 52, 72, 240, 244
Morgan, Joseph M. "Joe," I 416
Morgan, Ralph, I *221-22*

Morgan, Robert M. "Bobby," B 168
Morgan, Vernon T. "Vern," B 70
Morgan Cup, O 258
Morgan State University, F 72, 183, 312, 334, 500; I 89
Morgan Strasser Soccer Club, O 295-96
Morgenweck, Frank, I *222-23*
Morgenweck, William "Bill," I 222
Moriarty, Eugene J. "Gene," B 554
Moriarty, George J., B 606; S 13, 126
Morley, William R. "Wild Bill," F 644
Morningside College, F 6-7
Morozova, Olga, O 352
Morrall, Earl E., F 127, *404-05;* S 432
Morrill, William K., Sr., O 242, *243-44*
Morrill, William K., Jr., O *242-43*, 244
Morris, Betty, I *346-47*
Morris, Carl, I 398
Morris, Eugene "Mercury," F 122, 333
Morris, Glenn E., O *500-01*; S 441
Morris, Jay, S 511
Morris, John A., S 527
Morris, John M., S 536
Morris, John S. "Jack," S *145-46*
Morris, Lawrence "Larry," F 187
Morris, Robert "Bob," I 346
Morris, William "Bill," I 481
Morris Golf Club, Morristown, NJ, O 133
Morris Park, O 213; S 536
Morrison, Fred "Curly," F 173
Morrison, Jesse Raymond, F 35, 54, 368, *405-07*
Morrissey, John C., I 399, 403, *442-44*
Morrissey, Thomas P. "Tom," O 467

Morrissey's Fanatorium Lanes, Grand
    Rapids, MI, **I** 355
Morrow, Bobby Joe, **O** 471, *501-02;*
    S 594
Morse, Frank B., **F** 603
Mortimer, Kathleen Harriman, **O** 278
Morton, "Janks," **I** 422
Morton, Kemper, **S** 613
Morton, Larry Craig, **F** 273, 568; **S**
    454-55
Morton, "Molly," **O** 528
Mortson, James A. G. "Gus," **I** 564
Morvich, **O** 194; **S** 533
Mosbacher, Emil, Jr. "Bus," **O** *266*
Mosbacher, Robert A., **O** 266
Mosconi, Joseph, **I** 675
Mosconi, William J. "Willie," **I**
    675-76
Moscow, **O** 593
Moscow, USSR Summer Olympic
    Games, *See* Summer Olympic
    Games, 1980
Moscow, USSR Track and Field Meet,
    O 433, 477
Moses, Edwin C., **O** *502-04*
Moses, Haven C., **F** *408*
Moses, Wallace, Jr. "Wally," **B** *406*
Mossley Hall Challenge Cup, **O** 339
Most Courageous Player Award, NFL,
    S 367
Most Happy Fella, **O** 182
Most Improved Player Award:
    (Baseball), **S** 205; (Golf), **S** 506,
    509
Most Outstanding Swimmer Award,
    Washington DC AAU, **S** 621
Most Popular NASCAR Driver, **S**
    606
Most Valuable Player Award, Baseball:
    (AL), **B** 7, 36-37, 41, 48, 65, 71,
    101, 103, 123, 149, 180, 196, 198,
    210, 212, 222, 232, 249, 272, 277,
    289, 305, 341, 375, 382, 411, 419,
    455, 472, 475, 477-78, 513, 516,
    615-16, 634, 639; (NL), **B** 1, 22,
    33, 40, 43, 69, 80-81, 97-98, 135,
    140, 156, 167, 170, 191, 202, 209,
    215, 246, 252, 258, 260-61, 267,
    274, 308, 315, 335, 348, 350, 381,
    394, 397, 405, 409, 412, 418, 440,
    478, 480, 486, 502, 530, 552, 560,
    567, 569-70, 588, 618; (AL, NL),
    S 9, 12, 23-24, 27, 32, 44, 51, 57-
    58, 67-68, 71, 75, 91-92, 95, 101,
    104, 118, 125, 136, 138, 146-47,
    153, 165-66, 182, 187, 191, 193,
    196, 202, 205, 225, 236, 238, 245
Most Valuable Player Award,
    Basketball: AAU Tournament, **I**
    55, 188, 193, 241, 325; ABA, **I**
    52, 82, 98, 121, 142, 196; ABA
    All-Star Game, **I** 299; ABA
    Playoffs, **I** 82, 98, 196; AIAW
    Tournament, **I** 290, 334; College,
    I 40, 58, 61, 87, 93, 138, 166,
    185, 191, 215, 241, 249, 252, 257,
    260, 266, 294, 300, 304, 310-11,
    328; Holiday Festival Tournament,
    I 252; Maurice Stokes Benefit
    Game, **I** 53; NAIA Tournament, **I**
    15; NBA, **I** 3, 26, 46, 54, 124,
    140, 153, 188, 203, 237-38, 240,
    251, 263, 309, 317, 319; NBA All-
    Star Game, **I** 10-11, 17, 24, 52,
    54, 82, 88, 96, 104, 153, 169,
    237, 247, 266, 274, 298, 323, 328;
    NBA Playoffs, **I** 17, 26, 82, 117,
    119, 144, 146-47, 247, 309, 324;
    NBL, **I** 44, 62, 194-95, 211;
    NCAA Tournament, **I** 85, 100,
    180, 184, 214-15, 249, 291-298-
    99; NIT Tournament, **I** 87, 100,
    127, 155, 180, 190; Pro Team, **I**
    42, 48, 137; Rainbow Classic, **I**
    303; Winston Holiday Classic, **I**
    214; World Pro Tournament, **I** 194;

World Professional Leagues, **I** 73
Most Valuable Player Award,
    Basketball: **S** 251, 255, 261-62,
    267, 273-74, 278, 282-83, 286,
    288, 292, 295, 299, 302, 317, 327,
    329
Most Valuable Player Award, Football:
    College, **F** 11, 18, 26, 56, 59, 67,
    76, 79, 99, 122, 136, 139, 149,
    153, 162, 176, 181, 185, 193, 218,
    221-22, 226, 233, 237, 240, 243,
    248, 258, 261, 263, 265, 267, 269,
    271-72, 274-77, 283, 286, 296,
    302, 305, 308, 310, 312, 320, 322,
    330, 330, 336, 346, 355-57, 367,
    374, 390-91, 397, 412-13, 418,
    423-24, 426-27, 431, 439, 443,
    457, 461, 464, 468, 473, 475, 481-
    82, 490, 492, 495, 497, 501, 509,
    518, 530, 537, 541, 545-49, 553-
    54, 556, 560, 568-69, 571, 574-75,
    577, 586-88, 599, 604, 609, 622,
    630, 634-35, 637, 642, 649-51,
    658, 664, 670-71; Professional, **F**
    2, 9, 20, 25, 33, 50, 56, 59, 67-69,
    87, 101, 113, 122, 133-34, 140,
    154, 185, 191, 197, 203, 207, 215-
    16, 222, 226, 236, 246, 248, 253,
    256, 268, 271, 274, 279, 295-96,
    298, 330, 332, 349, 363, 384, 387,
    394, 397, 401, 405, 412, 419-20,
    430-31, 441, 451-52, 462, 467,
    471, 473, 485, 491, 493, 502-03,
    524, 529, 535, 540, 548-49, 562,
    565-68, 581, 583, 588-89, 593,
    601, 613-15, 618, 630-31, 635,
    639, 641, 650-51, 658, 667;
    Professional or College, **S** 361,
    375, 379-80, 385-86, 398, 402,
    407, 414-15, 425, 430, 432, 441-
    43, 455, 458, 463, 472, 476, 486,
    498, 504; Service, **F** 555
Most Valuable Player, Ice Hockey, **I**
    553-54, 558-59, 561; **S** 541-42,
    544, 548
Most Valuable Player, Volleyball, **I**
    676; **S** 613
Mostil, John A. "Johnny," **S** 54
Mota, Manuel F. G. "Manny," **B** 618;
    S 21, 53
Mothel, Carrol "Dink," **B** 6
Mother Goose, **O** 202
Mother Goose Stakes, **O** 604
Motley, Marion, **F** 70, 215, 294,
    408-10, 656
Motor Cop, **S** 525-26
Motor Trend 500 Auto Race, **O** 11
Motta, John Richard "Dick," **I** *223-
    25;* **S** 253, 313
Mount, Peter "Pete," **I** 225
Mount, Rick C., Sr., **I** 169, *225-26,*
    272
Mount, Rick C., Jr., **I** 225
Mt. Carmel College Seminary, **S** 219
Mt. Carmel, PA baseball club (PSL),
    B 266
Mt. Holyoke College, **O** 253; **S** 64
Mt. Hood, OR Ski Competition, **O**
    280
Mt. Moosilauke, NH Alpine Ski
    Competition, **O** 286
Mt. Ranier, WA Ski Competition, **O**
    277
Mt. San Antonio Relays, Walnut, CA,
    O 438, 486
Mt. San Jacinto Junior College, **O**
    558
Mt. Spokane, WA Ski Competition,
    O 277
Mt. Washington, NH Auto Race, **O**
    24
Mt. Washington, NH Ski
    Competition, **O** 276
Mt. Washington Wolfpack Lacrosse
    Club, **O** 233, 235, 237-40, 242-
    47, 249-51, 303

Mt. Washington Wolfpack Lacrosse Club Trophy, **O** 245

Mountain Elk, **O** 200

Mountain States Athletic Conference, **F** 136, 466, 647, 657; **S** 396, 424

Mouzon, Wesley, **I** 441

Moyer, "Denny," **I** 396

Moyers, Carol F., **O** 304

Moyers, Roy, **O** 304

Moyers, Steven C. "Steve," **O** *304-05*

Mr. Werner Alpine Ski Competition, **O** 289

Mrs. Warren, **O** 222

Mugabi, John, **I** 397

Muha, Joseph "Joe," **F** 661

Muhammad, Eddie Mustafa, **S** 623

Muhammad Ali: The Champion, **S** 347

Muhlenberg College, **F** 534; **I** 30, 154, 306

Muirfield Village Golf Course, Dublin, OH, **O** 147

Muldoon, William A. "Billy," **I** 462

Mulford, Ralph, **O** *23-24*

Mullane, Anthony J. "Tony," **B** *406-07;* **S** 82

Mullaney, Joseph A. "Joe," **I** 154; **S** 325

Mullen, Brian, **I** 567

Mullen, "Ironfoot," **O** 470

Mullen, "Joe," **I** 549, 554, *566-67*

Mullen, "Tom," **I** 567

Muller, Harold P. "Brick," **F** 142, *410-11,* 552

Mullin, Christopher P. "Chris," **S** *305-06*

Mullin, George J., **B** 282, *408-09*

Mullins, Lawrence "Moon," **F** 95

Mulloy, Gardnar, **O** 355, 390, 401; **S** 551, *557-58*

Mulloy, Robin, **S** 557-58

Multnomah Athletic Club, Portland, OR, **I** 495, 614, 655

Mulvihill, Linda Jo Metheny, **I** 532, *534-35*

Mulvihill, Richard M. "Dick," **I** 532, 534

Muncie, George, **F** 411

Muncie, Harry V. "Chuck," **F** *411-12,* 620

Muncie, Nelson, **F** 411

Muncie, William "Bill," **F** 411

Muncrief, Robert C. "Bob," **S** 126

Munger, Louis, **O** 269

Munger Bicycle Manufacturing Company, **O** 269

Munich, Germany Summer Olympic Games, *See* Olympic Summer Games, 1972

Municipal Stadium, Baltimore, MD, **F** 200

Municipal Stadium, Cleveland, OH, **B** 241

Municipal Stadium, Kansas City, MO, **S** 237

Municipal Stadium, Philadelphia, PA, **O** 512

Muniz, Armando, **I** 422

Munn, Clarence L. "Biggie," **F** 126, 136-37, 404, *412-14*

Munroe, "Jack," **I** 408

Munsingwear Bowling Team, **I** 339

Munson, Thurman L., **B** 277; **S** 136, *146-47,* 152

Murcer, Bobby R., **S** *147-48*

Murchison, Ira J., **O** 502; **S** *588-89*

Murnane, Timothy H. "Tim," **B** 325, 347

Murphy, Calvin J., **I** 169, *226-27,* 230

Murphy, Charles C. "Stretch," **I** 168, *227-28*

Murphy, Charles W., **B** 83-84, 416, 457; **S** 161

Murphy, Dale B., **B** *409-10*

Murphy, Dennis, O 262

Murphy, Dwayne K., B 249

Murphy, "Harlem Tommy," I 434, 454

Murphy, Isaac, O 183, 205, *208-10*

Murphy, James A. "Jimmy," O *24-25*

Murphy, "Jimmy," I 460

Murphy, John J. "Johnny," S *148-49*

Murphy, Joseph "Joe," S 538

Murphy, "Kid," I 370

Murphy, Michael "Mike," O 483

Murphy, Robert "Bob," S 195

Murphy, Thomas W. "Tom," O 613

Murray, Eddie C., B *410-11;* S 206

Murray, Fay, S 45

Murray, Francis K., O 377

Murray, Frank, F 155; I 269

Murray, Frederick S., O 377

Murray, "Jack," S 314

Murray, James P., Jr. "Jim," O 69, *81-82*

Murray, Richard D. "Rich," B 410

Murray, Robert Lindley, O 362, *377-78,* 403

Murray, William D. "Bill," F 453; S *455-56*

Murray State University, I 88-89

Murray State University Hall of Fame, I 89

Murren Alpine Ski Competition, O 286

Murtaugh, Daniel E. "Danny," B 206; S *149-50,* 230

Musburger, Brent W., S 356, *356-57*

Musial, Stanley F. "Stan," B 51, 342, *411-13,* 486, 503, 530, 583; O 57; S 52, 72, 106, 143, 196, 347

Muskegon Junior College, S 624

Muskegon, MI baseball club (CL, MISL), B 244, 356

Muskegon, OK baseball club (SWL, WA), B 146, 586

Muskingum College, S 290

Muskogee, OK baseball club (WA), F 522; S 190, 235

Musso, George F., F *414,* 417

Mutrie, James J. "Jim," B 429; S *150-51*

Mutual Broadcasting Company, I 423; S 343

Mutual of New York Tournament of Champions, O 163

Mutuals of New York baseball club, B 115

Muybridge, Edward, O 609

My Charmer, O 606

My Giants, S 350

My Life With the Pros, S 339

Myer, Charles S. "Buddy," B *413-14,* 577; S 14

Myers, A. Wallis, O 362; S 559

Myers, Dennis E. "Denny," F 569

Myers, Edwin E. "Ed," O 462

Myers, Elmer G., B 280

Myers, Kenneth "Ken," B 138

Myers, Laurence E. "Lon," O *504-06,* 559; S 571

Myers, Robert L. "Chief," F 35, 402-03

Myers, Thomas "Tommy," F 458

Myopia Golf Course, South Hamilton, MA, O 107

Myrick, Julian S., O 418; S *558-59*

Myricks, Larry E., O 485

Myrtle Harkness, S 531

Myshkin, Vladimir, I 567

Naber, John P., I 578, 593, *608-09*

Nabisco Dinah Shore Golf Tournament, O 166; S 505-06, 510, 520

Nagashima, Hideyuke, I 659

Nagurski, Bronislaw "Bronko," F 54, 68, 161, 170, 267, 360, *415-18,* 472, 638; S 378, 425, 484

Nagy, Helen, I 348

Nagy, Steve J., I *347-48*

Nahant, MA Tennis Championships,
O 250, 391-92

Naismith, James, F 563; I 4, 36, 77,
88, 107, 125, 201, *228-30,* 256,
306, 497

Naismith Award, I 184, 214-15, 266;
S 280, 295, 302-03

Naismith Memorial Basketball Hall of
Fame, F 564; I 2, 5, 7, 11-12,
14, 16, 18-23, 29-31, 33, 36-40,
42, 45, 48, 52, 58, 62-68, 70, 73,
75, 77, 81, 84-85, 87-89, 92, 94,
97, 101, 103-04, 106, 108, 112-13,
115-16, 118, 123, 125, 127-32,
134-35, 137, 139-40, 142, 144,
149, 152, 154, 156-57, 159, 164,
166, 168, 171-72, 176, 178-79,
182, 185, 188, 190-91, 193-95,
198, 200, 204-05, 207-09, 211,
217-18, 221-22, 228, 230-33, 235-
36, 239-41, 245, 247-48, 250-51,
254, 256, 261, 263-65, 268-71,
273, 275-77, 284, 286-88, 290-91,
295-97, 302-03, 305-07, 311, 313-
16, 319, 321-23, 326, 332-33; O
68; S 278-79, 284, 287, 289, 314

Naismith Memorial Basketball Hall of
Fame Committee, I 218, 326

Namath, Joseph W. "Joe," F 75, 134,
165, 191, 341, 389, 405, *418-19,*
431-32, 493; O 105; S 359, 479

Nance, James S. "Jim," F 122, *419-
20*

Nance, Larry D., I 328

Nancy Hanks, I 328

Nanev, Alexander, I 659

Nanne, Louis V. "Lou," I 564

Nanticoke, PA basketball club (PSL),
I 21

Nantura, O 594

Nantura Stock Farm, O 594-95

Napa, CA Golf Tournament, O 166

Naples, FL Open Golf Tournament, O
129

Napoles, Jose, I 396

Naptha, O 220

Nardin, Arthur, O 267

Narragansett Pier, RI Tennis
Tournament, S 562

Narragansett Race Track, Pawtucket,
RI, O 605

NASCAR Circuit, *See* National
Association for Stock Car Auto
Racing or Winston Cup Circuit

Nash, Charles F. "Cotton," S 286

Nash, William M. "Billy," B 238; S
151-52

Nashua, O 176, 184-85, 217, 228,
573, 576, *598-99,* 603, 612; S
532

Nashua, NH baseball club (NEL), B
8, 417

Nashville, O 228

Nashville Aquatics Club, I 579

Nashville *Banner,* F 90, 109, 249, 416

Nashville Business College, I 54,
123, 283-84, 324-25

Nashville *Daily News,* O 89

Nashville Elite Giants baseball club
(NNL, NSL), B 269, 436; S 9

Nashville Goldblumes basketball club,
I 123, 253, 283-84

Nashville *Tennesseean,* O 69, 89

Nashville Track and Field Meet, O
457

Nashville Vultce Aircraft basketball
club (AAU), I 283-84

Nashville Vols baseball club (SA,
SL), B 128, 134, 266, 537; S 20,
45, 116-17, 130, 160, 228

Nasrullah, O 572, 598, 607

Nassau, S 531

Nassau Coliseum, Uniondale, NY, I
82

Nassau County Country Club, Glen
Cove, NY, O 136, 160
Nassau Invitation Tennis
Championships, O 378
Nassau Trophy, O 28
Nassek, O 216
Nastase, Ilie, O 324, 335, 399
Natchez, O 572
Nathan, Tony C., F 384
Nathan Mallison Award, I 596
The Nation, O 54
The National, S 341
National Academy of Artistic
Gymnastics, I 535
National Academy of Sports, I 611
National Agricultural College, F 46
National Amateur Athletic Federation,
F 563
National Amateur Basketball
Association, I 277
National Amateur Cup, O 301, 305,
309
National American Athletic
Association Gymnastic
Championships, I 529
National Association for Girls and
Women in Sports, I 2
National Association for Stock Car
Racing Circuit, O 1-3, 27-28, 30,
41, 43-44
National Association of Amateur
Athletes of America, O 268
National Association of Amateur
Athletes of America Track and Field
Championships, O 504
National Association of Athletic
Directors, S 279
National Association of Basketball
Coaches, I 7, 26, 37, 39-40, 85,
91, 97, 116, 127-31, 154, 182,
207, 209, 235, 256, 269, 276, 281,
287-88, 296, 321-22; S 255, 259,
279, 283, 295, 303

National Association of Basketball
Coaches Merit Award, I 38, 94,
125, 235
National Association of Basketball
Coaches Metropolitan Award, I 37,
85, 130, 140-41, 155, 235, 276,
287
National Association of Basketball
Coaches Research Committee, I
287
National Association of Basketball
Coaches Rules Committee, I 269
National Association of College
Basketball Coaches, S 312
National Association of Collegiate
Athletic Directors Hall of Fame, F
406
National Association of Collegiate
Directors of Athletics, I 40
National Association of Intercollegiate
Athletics, B 460; F 75, 131, 390,
499, 615; I 15, 20, 74-75, 88,
116, 177-78, 202, 246-47, 330,
486; O 428, 437, 497; S 114,
133, 267, 311, 327, 389, 415
National Association of Intercollegiate
Athletics Basketball Tournament, I
15, 20, 74, 16, 178, 202, 246-47,
330; S 267, 290, 311, 327
National Association of Intercollegiate
Athletics Diving Championships, I
486
National Association of Intercollegiate
Athletics Executive Committee, I
74
National Association of Intercollegiate
Athletics Football Championships,
F 399; S 389
National Association of Intercollegiate
Athletics Golf Championships, I
74
National Association of Intercollegiate
Athletics Hall of Fame, B 460; F

76, 89, 390, 414, 499, 503; I 20, 75, 89, 92, 128, 152, 193, 202, 213, 218, 247

National Association of Intercollegiate Athletics Tennis Championships, I 74

National Association of Intercollegiate Athletics Track and Field Championships, I 74; O 428, 437, 497

National Association of Intercollegiate Athletics Wrestling Championships, I 655

National Association of Intercollegiate Basketball, *See* National Association of Intercollegiate Athletics

National Association of Professional Base Ball Players, B 82, 270-71, 527, 603, 627-28, 637; S 49, 97

National Association of Professional Base Ball Players All-Star Game, S 81

National Association of Sportscasters and Sportswriters, O 45, 58, 63, 68-69, 82-83; S 341-42, 345, 347, 351, 357-58

National Association of Sportscasters and Sportswriters Hall of Fame, O 46, 58; S 343

National Association of Sportscasters and Sportwriters Sportscaster of the Year, O 63, 68; S 351, 357-58

National Association of Sportscasters and Sportswriters Sportswriter of the Year, O 69, 82-83; S 341, 345, 347

National Baseball Congress, S 204

National Baseball Hall of Fame, B 2, 6, 9, 12-15, 17-18, 20-22, 26, 29, 32-34, 36, 40, 42, 46, 52-54, 60, 64, 70, 72, 78-79, 83-85, 89-90, 92-93, 95-96, 98, 100, 102, 104-05, 107-10, 112, 118-19, 122, 124, 128-29, 141, 143, 147-51, 153, 159-60, 169-71, 174, 177-78, 182, 185, 188, 190, 198, 201, 203, 207, 211-12, 214-16, 218-19, 223, 229, 232, 237-38, 243-47, 251, 253, 259, 261, 266-67, 269, 272, 274-75, 279, 282, 286, 289, 291, 293, 297-301, 303-06, 309-10, 315, 321, 324-25, 329-30, 333-34, 336, 338, 344, 346-47, 351-52, 355, 359, 361, 366, 375-77, 380, 384, 388, 391, 394, 396, 404, 409, 412, 420, 428, 431-32, 435, 443, 451, 464, 467, 471, 473-74, 477-81, 484, 489-90, 493, 495, 501, 507-08, 513, 516-17, 521, 526, 528-29, 535, 542-43, 549, 552, 556-57, 562, 568, 570, 580-81, 586-87, 589-92, 598-99, 602, 604, 608, 612, 616, 619, 621, 629, 631, 635-36, 639; F 278; I 102, 371; O 45-46, 50, 53-54, 56, 65, 68, 72-73, 75, 90-91, 93, 96, 98; S 2, 6, 13, 16, 19, 29, 39, 43, 56, 72, 74, 81, 83, 91, 94-95, 99, 101, 103, 107-08, 112, 122, 125, 137, 150-51, 159, 199, 210, 226, 233, 235, 264, 338, 342, 344, 346, 349-50, 358-59

National Baseball Hall of Fame Veterans Committee, S 338

National Basketball Association, F 15, 218, 280, 591; I 2-3, 8-12, 14-20, 23-27, 31, 33-36, 41, 44-47, 49-54, 58, 60-61, 64, 70-73, 77-84, 86-87, 89-90, 92-96, 98, 100-13, 117-24, 133, 135-38, 141-54, 156, 158-61, 165, 169, 171-72, 178, 184-86, 189-90, 193, 195-98, 200-01, 203-05, 209-13, 217-21, 224-27, 230-34, 237-39, 241, 243-45, 247, 249, 251-53, 258, 260,

262-63, 266, 268, 270-71, 274-75,
277-79, 282-83, 288-90, 293-94,
298-300, 302-04, 306, 308-11,
315, 317-19, 322-23, 326-27, 333-
35; **O** 52, 70, 93, 102, 105, 429;
S 181, 240, 251, 253-56, 259,
261, 263-65, 268-70, 272-74, 276,
278-85, 288, 291-94, 297-302,
304-08, 312-13, 315-19, 321-23,
325-31, 351, 603
National Basketball Association All-
Rookie Team, **I** 42, 46, 54, 83,
87,118, 137, 160, 169, 226, 260,
266, 303, 309-11, 324
National Basketball Association All-
Star Game, **I** 4, 10-12, 15, 17, 19,
24, 27, 33, 42, 44, 46, 50-52, 54,
58, 62, 64, 78, 82, 86-87, 92, 96,
100, 102, 104, 108, 117-19, 121,
124, 136-37, 143, 145, 147-49,
151, 153, 160, 169, 185-86, 188,
190, 197, 203, 211, 213, 221, 237,
239, 241, 247, 263, 266, 274, 278-
79, 288, 298, 303, 308-11, 315,
319, 323-24, 328, 334-35; **S** 251-
53, 257-58, 265, 269, 272, 275-76,
286, 288, 294, 300, 306, 308-09,
319, 322, 326-29
National Basketball Association All-
Time Team, **I** 3, 11-12, 19, 45,
52, 62, 82, 89, 118, 152, 211,
237, 251, 263, 275, 323
National Basketball Association Board
of Governors, **I** 289
National Basketball Association Coach
of the Year Award, **I** 12, 44, 93,
107, 111, 124, 133, 160, 224, 278
National Basketball Association
Comeback Player of the Year
Award, **I** 160
National Basketball Association
Defensive Player of the Year Award,
I 153

National Basketball Association
Game of the Week, **I** 263
National Basketball Association
Players Association, **I** 52, 234; **S**
299
National Basketball Association
Playoffs and Championships: **I**
110, 138, 213, 303, 315, 335; **S**
253-55, 257, 269, 272, 281-82,
285-86, 288, 294, 300-01, 304-07,
313, 326-29; 1950, **I** 44-45, 133,
165, 205, 211-12, 241, 270; 1951,
I 44-45, 62, 114, 133, 165, 171,
319; 1952, **I** 44-45, 133, 165,
171, 205, 211-12, 241, 319; 1953,
I 133, 165, 171, 205, 211-12, 241;
1954, **I** 44-45, 165, 184, 205,
211-12, 241, 270, 319; 1955, **I**
44-45, 159, 211-12, 270; 1956, **I**
11, 100, 103, 149; 1957, **I** 12, 36,
52, 109, 111, 123-24, 165, 238-39,
245, 262; 1958, **I** 108-09, 111,
123-24, 190, 205, 237-38, 245,
262, 319; 1959, **I** 12, 36, 52, 109,
123-24, 150-51, 238, 245, 262,
327; 1960, **I** 12, 36, 52, 109, 123-
24, 150-51, 238, 245, 262, 327;
1961, **I** 12, 36, 52, 109, 123-24,
150-51, 184, 190, 238, 245, 262;
1962, **I** 12, 36, 52, 109, 123-24,
150-51, 199, 245, 262; 1963, **I**
12, 36, 52, 109, 117, 123-24, 150-
51, 184, 245, 262; 1964, **I** 12,
109, 111, 117, 123-24, 150-51,
184, 245, 262; 1965, **I** 12, 109,
117, 123-24, 150-51, 262, 300;
1966, **I** 12, 109, 117, 150-51,
262, 271, 300; 1967, **I** 47, 50, 58,
104, 111, 117, 160, 262, 275, 315;
1968, **I** 107, 117, 133, 136, 151,
160, 220, 243, 262; 1969, **I** 53,
117, 133, 136, 151, 220, 262, 278;
1970, **I** 15, 31, 64-65, 87, 133,

148, 220, 247, 260; 1971, I 50, 133, 220, 251, 278; 1972, I 19, 47, 101, 132, 186, 249, 275, 322; 1973, I 15, 31, 47, 65, 82, 87, 124, 133, 186, 221, 247, 278; 1974, I 54, 117, 124, 133, 244, 278-79, 324; 1975, I 17, 34, 119, 133, 150, 224, 244, 263; 1976, I 54, 82, 124, 244, 263, 279, 310, 324; 1977, I 82, 244, 300, 309, 317, 323; 1978, I 82, 119, 224, 247, 300, 323, 328; 1979, I 82, 119, 144, 224, 300, 323, 328; 1980, I 52, 82, 122, 146, 219; 1981, I 9, 12, 26, 82, 146, 219, 249; 1982, I 26, 58, 82, 146, 189, 219; 1983, I 58, 82, 146, 161, 203, 219; 1984, I 12, 26, 82, 145-46, 150, 203, 219; 1985, I 2, 26, 82, 142, 146-47, 150, 189, 203, 249, 266, 323; 1986, I 12, 26, 82, 145, 147, 150, 153, 219, 266, 318; 1987, I 2, 26, 61, 82, 147, 150-51, 203, 249, 298, 304, 323; 1988, I 2, 61, 79, 83, 98, 147, 151, 153, 161, 203, 244, 249, 298, 309, 323, 328

National Basketball Association Rookie of the Year, I 17, 23-24, 26, 46, 51, 53, 60, 83, 124, 185, 188, 220, 237, 247, 266, 298, 309

National Basketball Association Rules Committee, I 103, 115

National Basketball Coaches Association, I 5, 140, 198

National Basketball Coaches of the U. S., I 222, 242, 265

National Basketball Federation, I 37

National Basketball League, F 215; I 44, 61-62, 66, 99, 110, 114-15, 132-33, 165-66, 168, 194-95, 203, 209, 219, 270, 335; S 269-70, 277, 283-84, 289, 293, 333

National Basketball League All-Star Game, I 194-95

National Basketball League Coach of the Year, I 44

National Basketball League Playoffs and Championships, I 44, 62, 66, 99, 114, 132-33, 165, 194-95, 241, 318-19; S 277, 293, 309

National Basketball Officials Committee, I 125

National Basketball Rules Committee, I 125, 128, 130-31, 207, 221, 242, 306, 321; S 279, 321

National Black Sports Hall of Fame, S 416

National Bowling Council, I 536

National Bowling League, I 348

National Boxing Association, I 381, 387, 389, 423-24, 438, 450, 456, 463, 466, 468, 470, 477, 482

National Broadcasting Company, F 67, 134, 226, 349, 442, 486; I 162, 176,197, 200, 217, 503, 511, 523, 533, 536, 541, 638; O 46-49, 55, 63, 65, 67-68, 83, 93, 99-100, 105, 130, 164, 216, 308, 501, 537; S 339, 341, 354, 471, 493

National Broadcasting Company "Baseball Game of the Week," O 65, 68, 93

National Broadcasting Hall of Fame, S 343

National Challenge Cup Soccer Championships, O 291, 294, 296, 299, 301, 303, 305-06, 309-10

National Collegiate Athletic Association, B 504, 623; F 8-9, 11, 15, 39, 47, 62, 66, 86, 98, 104, 147, 149, 151, 162, 164, 190, 201, 210, 213, 227, 230, 276, 286, 305, 323, 336, 352, 372, 387, 392, 394, 419, 444, 448, 453, 460-61, 481, 499, 501, 508-09, 518, 539,

544, 546-47, 549, 563-64, 576-77, 581, 609, 630, 658, 663-65, 671; I 37, 41, 43, 47, 56, 60, 72, 90, 94-95, 98, 100, 104, 109, 116, 127, 132, 139-40, 146, 150, 154, 172, 174, 177-78, 184, 204, 214-17, 222, 225, 230, 235, 237, 248, 251, 266, 276, 278-79, 281, 293, 302-04, 320-21, 326, 329, 331, 521-22, 541-42, 576, 617, 642, 644, 652, 664, 671; O 47, 63, 67, 80, 83, 143, 146, 449, 469; S 18, 56, 255, 262-63, 267-68, 274-75, 278-80, 282-83, 285-86, 291-92, 294-97, 301-03, 305-06, 309-12, 317-18, 320-21, 323-28, 330, 370, 378-79, 385, 400, 405, 408, 410, 415-16, 427, 431, 473, 478, 480, 486, 547

National Collegiate Athletic Association Annual Basketball Guide, I 222

National Collegiate Athletic Association Baseball Championships, B 341, 623; I 16; S 8, 18, 37-38, 54, 56, 74, 94, 103, 133, 142, 201, 204, 208, 213, 241, 320

National Collegiate Athletic Association Basketball Rules Committee, I 70

National Collegiate Athletic Association Basketball Tournament, F 24; I 5, 40, 66-67, 130, 162, 174, 208-10, 231-32, 276-77, 280-82, 287, 292; O 63; S 251-53, 255, 259, 261-63, 266-69, 274-75, 278, 280, 282-83, 285-86, 291-92, 294-97, 301-03, 305, 310-12, 316-17, 321, 323-25, 327-28, 362; 1939, I 70, 91, 131, 191, 235; 1940, I 67, 129; 1941, I 85, 99, 126; 1942, I 63, 241; 1943, I 70,

76, 250, 276; 1944, I 235; 1945, I 139-40, 235; 1946, I 40, 140, 166, 235; 1947, I 51, 70, 85, 97, 154, 166, 205; 1948, I 51, 94, 154, 166, 205, 256; 1949, I 97, 140, 256; 1950, I 42-43, 51, 132, 295; 1951, I 43, 80, 94, 108-09, 244, 256; 1952, I 43, 81, 109, 180, 182, 184, 198-99, 281; 1953, I 81, 134, 191, 237-38, 281; 1954, I 43, 81, 100, 109, 179-80, 237-38, 244; 1955, I 97, 150, 179-80, 262; 1956, I 43, 124, 150, 178, 210, 252, 262; 1957, I 46, 172, 198-99; 1958, I 19, 135, 178, 252, 256; 1959, I 127, 199, 231, 322; 1960, I 67, 117, 161, 186, 231, 295; 1961, I 94, 127, 161, 186, 295; 1962, I 67, 161, 186, 276, 295; 1963, I 97; 1964, I 52, 101, 210, 216, 259, 331; 1965, I 31, 43, 52, 97, 101, 193, 210, 259, 331; 1966, I 25, 52, 94, 249, 256, 259; 1967, I 3, 52, 89-90, 118, 220, 331; 1968, I 3, 52, 118, 331; 1969, I 3, 52, 55, 225, 331; 1970, I 55, 97, 169, 216, 226, 280, 331; 1971, I 55, 97, 199, 331; 1972, I 56, 189, 199, 317, 331; 1973, I 199, 280, 299, 317, 331; 1974, I 71, 199, 280, 299; 1975, I 56, 256, 300, 331; 1976, I 115, 162; 1977, I 197, 200, 282, 293; 1978, I 72, 146, 219; 1979, I 26, 146, 219; 1980, I 41, 56; 1981, I 162, 216, 266, 282, 298; 1982, I 56, 152, 216, 281-83, 291, 300; 1983, I 152-53, 174, 214, 216, 283, 285, 291, 300, 303; 1984, I 83, 115-16, 152-53, 174, 214, 216, 283, 291, 300-01, 303; 1985, I 71, 83, 110, 115-16, 214, 216, 283, 285, 291, 301, 303;

1986, I 56, 214-15, 283, 291;
1987, I 56, 281, 283, 291, 293;
1988, I 35, 283, 291
National Collegiate Athletic
   Association Basketball Tournament
   Committee, I 40, 182, 235, 287,
   321
National Collegiate Athletic
   Association Cross Country
   Championships, I 182; O 518,
   527-28, 566
National Collegiate Athletic
   Association Diving
   Championships, I 485, 491
National Collegiate Athletic
   Association Football
   Championships, F 3, 5, 14, 40,
   43, 49, 51-53, 64, 69, 73, 75, 91,
   94, 100, 112, 116, 120, 127, 129,
   136-37, 145, 147, 149, 153, 176,
   182, 187-88, 190, 194-95, 198,
   204, 209, 213, 230-31, 243, 249;
   1, 261-62, 272-73, 277, 298-300,
   302, 316-17, 342-44, 349, 351,
   357, 364, 367, 369, 377-78, 383,
   391, 402, 407, 413, 418, 425, 431,
   433-34, 437, 439-40, 442-44, 454,
   457-58, 460, 463, 465, 468-69,
   471-75, 504-05, 507-09, 512, 514,
   516, 518, 523, 526, 531-32, 534,
   537, 544-45, 550-52, 555, 570,
   579, 581, 585, 594-95, 603, 605,
   621, 625, 636-37, 641-42, 651,
   653, 668; I 562; S 370, 379, 396,
   400, 403-04, 411, 419, 428-31,
   443, 448-49, 458, 468-69, 476,
   479-80, 487, 491, 495, 500
National Collegiate Athletic
   Association Football Rules
   Committee, F 47, 81, 85-86, 251,
   257, 407, 429, 460, 563, 603, 626
National Collegiate Athletic
   Association Golf Championships,

I 70, 79, 93, 642; O 134; S 510,
   514, 519
National Collegiate Athletic
   Association Ice Hockey
   Tournament, I 548-50, 561-66; S
   541, 543, 547
National Collegiate Athletic
   Association Indoor Track and Field
   Championships, O 428, 461, 485,
   506, 564, 566; S 581, 584
National Collegiate Athletic
   Association Lacrosse
   Championships, O 233-34, 237,
   239-46, 249, 302-03
National Collegiate Athletic
   Association Lacrosse Rules
   Committee, O 236, 240, 243
National Collegiate Athletic
   Association Men's Gymnastic
   Championships, I 521-22, 527-28,
   537, 539-40
National Collegiate Athletic
   Association Men's Swimming
   Championships, I 70, 578, 584,
   591, 593-95, 601-02, 604-05, 608,
   614, 618; S 602
National Collegiate Athletic
   Association Olympic Committee, I
   287
National Collegiate Athletic
   Association Outdoor Track and
   Field Championships, F 630; I
   76, 182, 642; O 423-24, 428, 432,
   434-35, 437-38, 442, 444-45, 450,
   456, 458, 461, 464-65, 468-70,
   477-78, 480-81, 485, 494, 496-97,
   502, 506, 510, 518, 520, 528, 532-
   33, 536-37, 542-43, 545, 549, 563,
   566-68; S 427, 467, 566, 568,
   570, 572, 576, 578-81, 584, 586-
   87, 589-90, 594
National Collegiate Athletic
   Association Rules Committee, I

287, 486

National Collegiate Athletic
Association Ski Championships,
O 281

National Collegiate Athletic
Association Soccer
Championships, O 240, 292, 302,
310

National Collegiate Athletic
Association Tennis
Championships, O 320, 322, 324,
335, 338-39, 341, 345, 366, 369,
377, 393, 398-99, 407, 409, 413,
416, 419; S 554, 556, 561

National Collegiate Athletic
Association Women's Golf
Championships, O 114

National Collegiate Athletic
Association Women's Gymnastic
Championships, I 534

National Collegiate Athletic
Association Women's Swimming
Championships, I 580, 583, 608;
S 607-08

National Collegiate Athletic
Association Wrestling
Championships, I 635-40, 642,
644-47, 649-54, 656-59, 662, 664-
66; S 608-09, 611, 616

National Collegiate Athletic
Association Wrestling Rules
Committee, I 648

National Collegiate Athletic
Association Wrestling Tournament
Outstanding Wrestler, I 646, 656,
659

National Collegiate Basketball
Association of America, I 131,
218

National Cowboy Hall of Fame, O
265

National Cycling Association, O 269

National Federation of State High

School Athletic Associations, I
222, 242-43, 287; S 279

National Figure Skating Association,
S 601

National Football Coaches
Association, S 461

National Football Foundation College
Football Hall of Fame, F 3, 5-6,
10-12, 14, 21, 25, 27-28, 31, 33,
35, 37-39, 43, 45-47, 49, 52, 54,
57, 63-64, 67, 74-75, 80-81, 84,
86, 93-94, 100, 102-03, 107, 109,
112, 114-15, 117, 120-21, 126-27,
131, 133, 144-45, 148, 150, 153-
54, 158, 160, 164, 168, 170, 172,
175-76, 186-88, 193, 198-99, 201-
02, 204, 207, 212, 214, 216, 218,
221, 226, 230, 239-42, 244, 249,
254, 256-59, 261, 265, 267, 271-
72, 277-79, 282, 284, 290, 292,
297-98, 301-03, 310, 313, 318-20,
323, 337, 341-42, 344, 347, 352-
53, 357, 359, 362, 365-67, 369,
374, 377, 380, 387, 392-93, 406,
411, 413, 415, 421-23, 425-26,
429, 431, 434-35, 437-41, 443,
446, 452, 454, 457, 459, 464-65,
468, 471-72, 476, 491-92, 499,
504, 512, 514, 525, 528, 530, 532,
535, 538-40, 545, 549-51, 554,
559, 564, 574-75, 580, 584, 594,
598, 604, 618, 622-23, 626-27,
629, 636-37, 644, 646-48, 651-53,
655, 657, 659-60, 662, 668, 670,
674; I 112-13, 127; O 61; S 361-
62, 365-66, 368, 371, 376, 378,
382, 386, 388, 392, 397, 402, 405,
410, 414, 416-19, 421, 423-24,
431, 434, 436, 438, 443-44, 446-
48, 450, 452-53, 455-56, 458-60,
464-65, 467-68, 470-71, 475-77,
481-83, 485, 492, 494-96, 498-
502, 504

National Football Foundation Gold
Medal Award, **F** 52
National Football Foundation Scholar-
Athlete Award, **F** 24
National Football League, **F** 1, 3-4,
7-12, 14-20, 23-26, 28-31, 33-37,
39-43, 45-46, 48, 50, 55-56, 59,
62-63, 67-73, 75-80, 83, 87-89,
91-92, 96-98, 100-01, 103-07, 111-
13, 115, 118-19, 121-22, 127-38,
140, 142-43, 146, 148-50, 152,
155, 157-58, 160-63, 165, 169-70,
176, 178-80, 182, 184-91, 193-99,
202-03, 205-08, 210, 214-22, 224-
30, 232-38, 241, 243-50, 254, 256,
258-60, 263-64, 267-69, 271-85,
288, 290-98, 303-05, 307-08, 311-
12, 314-16, 319-25, 328-36, 339-
41, 344, 346-57, 360, 362-67, 370-
76, 378, 380-82, 384-90, 392-401,
403-05, 408-12, 414-15, 417-21,
423-25, 427-28, 430-33, 437, 440-
43, 445, 447-49, 453-56, 461-64,
466-67, 470-73, 477-83, 485-96,
499-500, 502-03, 508-11, 516-19,
521-22, 524, 528-29, 535-40, 542-
43, 545-51, 553-62, 565-81, 583-
91, 593-94, 596-602, 604-05, 607-
10, 613-15, 617-20, 622-23, 627-
29, 631-35, 637-43, 645-47, 649-
54, 656-62, 665, 667-68, 670-72; **I**
22, 80, 117, 150, 154, 249-50,
261, 264, 272, 378, 532, 660-61;
O 43, 49, 52, 56, 60, 62, 68, 80,
87, 104-05, 296, 308, 427, 436,
439, 444, 450, 468, 472, 501, 506-
07, 538, 543, 554; **S** 45, 268,
335, 344, 348, 352, 358, 361-68,
370, 372-74, 377-79, 381, 383-87,
389-91, 395, 398-99, 401-15, 419-
20, 422, 425-32, 436-42, 445-46,
448-49, 451-64, 466-72, 474-75,
478, 481-97, 499-500, 503-04,
572, 610-11
National Football League Alumni
Association, **F** 249, 332, 340,
650, 661; **S** 492
National Football League
Championship Games and Playoffs,
F 1-2, 4, 7, 9, 11-12, 20, 23, 28,
31, 39-40, 42, 48, 67-68, 70, 72,
93, 98, 103-04, 106-07, 111, 113,
119, 128-31, 140, 142-43, 146,
150-52, 165, 169-70, 178-79, 184,
186-87, 196-99, 203, 205-07, 214-
17, 219, 223-24, 229, 232, 234,
237-38, 245, 249, 259-60, 263,
267, 271, 278-80, 282-83, 285,
294, 303, 308-09, 321-23, 328,
336, 340-41, 346, 348, 352-54,
357, 359, 362-64, 367, 370, 372,
375-76, 381-82, 386, 388, 392-93,
395, 397, 399-400, 405, 409, 414-
15, 417, 421, 430, 432, 447, 454-
55, 462-64, 466, 471, 480, 487,
489, 491, 493, 495, 502-03, 510,
519, 521, 529, 536-39, 542-43,
548, 558-59, 566-67, 573-75, 578,
588-89, 604, 608-09, 614, 617-19,
629, 632-33, 639, 641, 646, 649-
50, 656-67, 660-62; **I** 660; **O** 49,
80; **S** 368, 370, 373, 378-79, 383,
383-86, 390, 399, 409-12, 414-15,
419, 427, 429-30, 436, 438-41,
445, 451-52, 454-55, 458, 460,
466-67, 471, 474, 478, 481, 486,
488-90, 492, 497, 500, 503-04
National Football League Gladiator
Award, **F** 568
National Football League Management
Council, **S** 399, 475
National Football League Players
Association, **F** 19, 25, 248-49,
296, 352, 371, 491, 537, 589, 615,
635; **S** 387, 471
National Football League Rules

Committee, F 6, 34, 234
National Foundation of High School
    Athletic Associations, F 486
National Gymnastics Judges
    Association, I 524
National Gymnastics Judges
    Association Hall of Fame, I 525
National High School Athletic
    Coaches Association, I 297
National Hockey League, I 36, 453,
    544-45, 557-64, 566-73; O 105; S
    93, 344, 352-53, 403, 537-48
National Hockey League All-Rookie
    Team, I 544
National Hockey League All-Star First
    Team, I 544-45, 547, 559
National Hockey League All-Star
    Game, I 545, 547, 550, 559, 562-
    63; S 542, 545, 548
National Hockey League
    Championships, See Stanley Cup
    Championships and Playoffs
National Hockey League All-Star
    Second Team, I 545, 547, 560-61
National Hockey League Rendezvous
    Team, S 542, 548
National Hockey League Rookie of the
    Year, See Calder Trophy
National Hockey League's Pinnacle
    Award, I 547, 560
National Horse Show, O 267, 391
National Industrial Basketball League,
    I 70, 202, 326
National Industrial Basketball League
    Championships and Playoffs, I 70,
    202
National Intercollegiate Athletic
    Association of America, S 279
National Invitation Basketball
    Tournament, F 607; I 6-7, 56, 61,
    67, 94, 100, 127, 132, 154-55,
    162, 209, 217, 232, 277, 280, 282,
    292; S 255, 259, 261, 266-67,

284, 292, 295, 312, 321-22, 325;
    1939, I 22, 264; 1941, I 22-23;
    1942, I 67; 1973, I 67, 126, 171;
    1944, I 171; 1945, I 6-7, 208,
    211, 257, 305; 1946, I 80; 1947,
    I 42, 155; 1948, I 43, 67, 86,
    126-27, 190, 270; 1949, I 67,
    230-31; 1950, I 67, 80, 132, 180,
    198; 1951, I 80, 180, 196, 198,
    320; 1952, I 67, 179-80; 1953, I
    50, 67, 10, 179-80, 261; 1954, I
    67, 124, 216; 1955, I 124; 1959,
    I 7, 171; 1962, I 7, 216, 300;
    1963, I 7, 216, 300; 1964, I 24-
    25, 300; 1965, I 171; 1966, I
    320; 1967, I 87, 162; 1968, I
    162; 1969, I 162, 178; 1970, I
    162, 197; 1971, I 162, 282; 1972,
    I 71; 1976, I 300; 1977, I 174;
    1978, I 26; 1980, I 115; 1982, I
    115; 1984, I 247
National Invitation Bicycle
    Championships, O 407
National Invitation Track and Field
    Meet, O 488
National Jaycees Junior Golf
    Tournament, O 124; S 516
National Jewish Hospital Open Golf
    Tournament, S 513-14
National Junior College Athletic
    Association Soccer
    Championships, O 301
National Lacrosse Hall of Fame, F 69
National Lawn Tennis Hall of Fame,
    See International Tennis Hall of
    Fame
National League of New England
    Soccer, O 309
National League of Professional Base
    Ball Clubs, B 60, 83, 109-10,
    175, 201, 216, 226, 242, 253, 271,
    285, 298, 306, 308-10, 318, 321,
    336, 340-41, 356, 374, 380, 390,

428, 430, 432, 441, 457, 463, 502, 504, 514, 523-24, 526-27, 541, 550-52, 567, 570, 576, 581, 594, 628, 630, 636-38; **I** 6, 14, 30, 93, 105, 149, 165, 236, 261, 274, 312, 333, 572; **O** 45-46, 48-49, 52-57, 59-60, 65, 74-75, 81-83, 89, 92-93, 102, 137, 208, 293, 299; **S** 2-8, 10-11, 13-17, 19-27, 30-39, 41-43, 45-51, 53, 55, 58-65, 67-80, 83-90, 92-100, 103-20, 122-28, 130-36, 138-40, 142-44, 146, 148-57, 159-80, 182-91, 193-96, 198-99, 210-10, 212-13, 215-16, 218-23, 225, 227-30, 232-34, 237, 239-45, 247-48, 335, 342-43, 346-52, 354-56, 358-59, 399, 402, 424, 440, 494-95

National League of Professional Base Ball Clubs All-Star Team, **I** 105

National League of Professional Base Ball Clubs Championship Series, **S** 1969, 122, 149; 1970, 73, 80, 150, 166; 1971, 103; 1972, 73, 80, 166; 1973, 166; 1974, 27, 114, 150, 185, 244; 1975, 24, 73, 150, 166, 217; 1976, 73, 80, 166; 1977, 8, 27, 109, 114, 118, 185; 1978, 8, 27, 109, 114, 118, 185; 1979, 15, 217; 1980, 16, 80, 118, 123, 355; 1981, 8, 27, 109, 114, 142, 174-75, 185; 1982, 84, 207; 1983, 8, 80, 109, 134, 166-67, 175, 185; 1984, 27, 49, 80, 114, 134, 153, 174, 205, 218, 399; 1985, 30, 109, 167, 175, 207, 355; 1986, 80, 114; 1987, 30-31, 174, 182, 207; 1988, 96, 109; 1989, 80, 174, 182; 1991, 80, 109

National League of Professional Base Ball Clubs Playoff Game (1951), **S** 46, 162, 221, 349

National League Select Soccer Club, **O** 299-300

National Museum of Racing's Hall of Fame, **O** 173, 176, 178-79, 184-90, 193-94, 196-98, 200, 202, 206, 208-10, 212-14, 216, 218, 220-24, 226-27, 229, 231, 571-74, 576-82, 585, 589, 593-96, 598-99, 601-02, 605-09, 612, 614-15; **S** 525-29, 531-32, 534-36

National Polish-American Sports Hall of Fame, **F** 397

National Pro-Am Bowling Tournament, **I** 351

National Professional Basketball League, **I** 222

National Professional Soccer League, **O** 292

National Public Parks Women's Tennis Championships, **S** 549

National Public Radio, **O** 49; **S** 337, 341

National Recreation Association, **I** 108

National Rodeo Championships, **O** 265

National Round Robin Tennis Championships, **O** 419

National Ski Association, **O** 278-79

National Ski Hall of Fame, **O** 276, 278-79, 284, 287, 289

National Softball Hall of Fame, **O** 262

National Sports Festival, **I** 501, 526, 585, 640; **S** 296, 321, 597

National Sports Hall of Fame, **I** 654

National Sportscaster of the Year Award, **O** 63, 93

National Sportscasters Hall of Fame, **O** 84

National Stallion Stakes, **O** 213, 225, 578

National Track and Field Hall of Fame, **O** 269, 424, 427, 429, 433,

435, 438, 443, 445-46, 448-50,
453, 459, 461, 464, 466, 468, 471-
74, 478-79, 484, 493-96, 499-500,
502, 506, 509-10, 513, 516-17,
519-22, 524, 526-27, 531, 533,
535, 538-39, 543, 545, 547, 551-
54, 556-57, 561, 566-68; S 566,
568-69, 572-74, 577-78, 581-82,
585, 591, 593-95, 598
National Turf Digest, O 186
National Turf Writers Association, O
181, 193, 198
National Turnfest, I 525
National Turnverein Club, Newark,
NJ, I 650-51
National Velvet, O 214
National Women's Basketball
Association, I 215
National Women's Invitation
Basketball Tournament, I 175,
246, 285
National Wrestling Coaches
Association, I 635, 648, 652; S
609
National Wrestling Hall of Fame, I
639-40, 645, 647-48, 650-54, 656,
660, 662-64, 666
Nationwide 500 Auto Race, O 44
Native Dancer, O 189, *599-600*
Naturalist, O 196
Naulls, William D. "Willie," I 106;
S 251
Navin, Frank J., B 50, 156, *415-16,*
554
Navin Field, Detroit, MI, B 50, 211,
606
Navratil, Miroslav, O 379
Navratilova, Martina, I 176; O 326,
351-52, 363, 370, *379-82,* 387,
397
Navy, *See* United States Naval
Academy
Nazareth, PA Auto Race, O 37

Nazareth, PA Race Track, S 620
NBA, *See* National Basketball
Association
NBC, *See* National Broadcasting
Company
NCAA, *See* National Collegiate
Athletic Association
NCAA News, F 506
Neale, Alfred E. "Greasy," F 259,
282, 315, *420-22,* 480, 536, 576,
619, 660-61; S 488
Neale, William H., F 302
Nealon, O 196
Neave, Oliver, I 590
Nebraska basketball club (WPBL), I
175
Nebraska College Conference, F 443
Nebraska Football Hall of Fame, F
360, 480
Nebraska Sports Hall of Fame, F
360, 646; O 179
Nebraska State League, S 79, 246
Nebraska Wesleyan University, F 102
Nedana, S 526-27
Needham, "Danny," I 460, 464
Needles, James R., I 231
Neely, Carrie, O 325, 354, 377, 420
Neely, Jess C., F 275, 368, *422-23,*
525; S 421
Neely, Ralph E., F *423-24*
Neeskins, Johan, O 298
Neff, Arle, O 78
Negro American League, B 483, 608
Negro League All-Star baseball game,
I 143
Negro National League, B 189, 224,
255, 548-49, 608; I 102, 143,
268, 332, 426; S 9-10, 19, 99,
129-30, 168, 188-89, 223-24, 238
Negro National League
Championships, S 19, 99, 129,
137, 224
Negro Southern Conference, B 520

Negro Southern League, **S** 129
Negro Southern League
  Championships, **S** 129
Negus, Frederick "Fred," **S** 476
Nehemiah, Renaldo, **O** *506-07*
Nehf, Arthur N. "Art," **B** 291, *416-17;* **S** 226
Neily, Harry, **B** 346
Nellie Flag, **O** 175, 601
Nelson, "Battling," **I** 357, 388, *444, 453,* 479
Nelson, "Battling Dick," **I** 377
Nelson, Darrin M., **F** 426
Nelson, Donald A. "Don," **I** 124; **S** 294, *306-07*
Nelson, Eddie, **O** 575
Nelson, Hubert "Hub," **I** 547
Nelson, John Byron, **O** 129, 131, 134, 141, *144-46,* 150, 155, 166, 169; **S** 511-13
Nelson, Kevin, **F** 426
Nelson, Larry G., **S** 552
Nelson, Lindsey, **F** 271; **O** 77, *82-84*
Nepala, Ondrej, **I** 519
Nerud, John A., **O** 581
Nesbit, Harold A., **O** 413
Nesser, Alfred "Al," **F** 97; **S** *456-57*
Nesser, Charles, **F** 97; **O** 457
Nesser, Frank, **F** 97; **O** 456-57
Nesser, Fred, **F** 97; **O** 456-57
Nesser, John, **F** 97; **O** 456-57
Nesser, Philip "Phil," **F** 97; **O** 456-57
Nesser, "Ted," **F** 97; **O** 456-57
Nesty, Anthony, **S** 603
Nettles, Graig, **S** *152-53*
Nettles, James W. "Jim," **S** 152
Neun, John H. "Johnny," **S** 13
Neva, Norvall, **I** 232
Nevada Athletic Commission, **I** 381
Nevada State Amateur Golf
  Tournament, **S** 517

Nevele Pride, **O** 182, 587
Never Bend, **O** 222
Never Say Die, **O** 201
Nevers, Ernest A. "Ernie," **F** 117, 315, 392, *424-25,* 524, 638; **S** 436
Neves, Ralph, **O** *210*
New Bedford, MA baseball club
  (NEL), **B** 117, 297, 377, 541; **S** 69
New Bedford, MA Clam-Eaters
  baseball club, **B** 541
New Bedford, MA Whalers football
  club (ASL), **O** 299
New Britain, CT basketball club, **I** 30
New Castle, PA baseball club (MSL),
  S 246
New England Amateur Athletic Union
  Track and Field Championships, **O** 454
New England Badminton
  Championships, **O** 415
New England Basketball Association,
  I 313
New England Basketball Coaches
  Association, **I** 37, 287
New England College Hockey
  Tournament, **I** 561
New England Junior Wightman Cup
  Team, **O** 416
New England Lacrosse
  Championships, **O** 245
New England League, **B** 110; **I** 65; **S** 29, 37, 111
New England Patriots football club
  (NFL), **F** 42-43, 143, 157, 163, 185, 195-96, 222, 236-37, 285-86, 316, 372, 376, 385, 420, 462, 473, 488, 496, 547-48, 586, 620, 642-43, 665; **S** 429, 454, 464, 475
New England Soccer Club (NASL), **O** 294
New England Steamrollers football

club (ArFL), S 464
New England Tennis Championships,
O 368, 377
New England Whalers hockey club,
See Hartford Whalers hockey club
New England Women's Amateur Golf
Tournament, S 508
New England Women's Junior Golf
Tournament, S 506
New Hampshire Ladies Amateur Golf
Tournament, S 506, 508
New Hampshire Ladies Junior Golf
Tournament, S 506
New Hampshire Sweepstakes, O 581
New Haven Arena, New Haven, CT, I
240
New Haven, CT baseball club (EL), B
34, 123, 156, 400; F 573; S 127,
165
New Haven, CT hockey club (CAHL),
I 240
New Haven, CT Nighthawks hockey
club (AHL), I 554, 573
New Haven, CT Skyhawks basketball
club (USBL), I 176
New Haven, CT Track and Field Meet,
O 460
New Haven Register, O 81
New Jersey Americans basketball club
(ABA), I 335
New Jersey Athletic Association, I
316
New Jersey Devils hockey club
(NHL), I 544, 550; S 544
New Jersey Gems basketball club
(WBL, WPBL), I 28, 73, 175
New Jersey Generals football club
(USFL), F 182, 589, 630-31, 633;
S 411
New Jersey Golden Gloves
Tournament, I 401, 477
New Jersey Golf Association, O 161
New Jersey Jammers basketball club

(USBL), I 10
New Jersey Nets basketball club
(ABA, NBA), I 9, 35, 153, 160-
61, 189, 247, 279; S 282, 292,
313
New Jersey Open Golf Tournament, O
109
New Jersey Rockets Soccer Club
(MISL), O 304
New Jersey Soccer Hall of Fame, O
293, 297
New Jersey Sports Hall of Fame, I
254
New Jersey State Athletic
Commission, I 472
New Jersey State High School
Basketball Championships, I 29,
316
New Jersey State Soccer
Championships, O 294, 300, 306
New Jersey Tennis Championships, O
333
New Jersey's Old Timers Athletic
Association, I 30
New Mexico Highlands College, F
589, 663-64
New Mexico Military Institute, F 568
New Mexico State University, F 253,
608, 663-64; S 291, 425-26
New Mexico Women's State Amateur
Golf Championships, O 137
New Orleans Buccaneers basketball
club (ABA), I 34; S 304-05
New Orleans Fair Grounds, O 215
New Orleans Jazz basketball club
(NBA), I 19, 96, 102, 121, 204,
290
New Orleans Nets Tennis Team
(WTT), S 298
New Orleans Open Golf Tournament,
O 126
New Orleans Pelicans baseball club
(SA), B 174, 241, 413, 508, 524,

537, 595; **S** 5, 86, 150, 163, 219, 233

New Orleans Race Track, **O** 580

New Orleans Saints football club (NFL), **F** 20, 76-77, 88, 104, 135, 169, 271, 351, 412, 509, 562, 566, 572, 587, 665; **S** 399, 426, 454, 487

New Providence, **O** 225

The New Republic, **O** 54

New South Wales Open Tennis Championships, **O** 397

New York *American,* **F** 192; **O** 90; **S** 342

New York Americans football club (AFL), **F** 243; **S** 394

New York Americans hockey club (NHL), **I** 453, 553, 571

New York Americans Soccer Club, **O** 294, 296, 300

New York Arrows Soccer Club (MISL), **O** 311

New York Athletic Club, **I** 84, 377-78, 424, 429, 588, 670, **O** 64, 424, 442-43, 454, 459-60, 470, 489, 491, 495, 510, 521, 531, 558-59; **S** 565, 571, 587-88, 591, 598

New York Athletic Club Election Day Track and Field Games, **O** 505

New York Athletic Club-London Athletic Club Dual Track and Field Meet, **O** 559

New York Athletic Club Track and Field Games, **O** 424, 440; **S** 566, 591

New York Bacharach Giants baseball club (Negro Leagues), **B** 338; **I** 143

New York baseball club (PL), **B** 111-12, 171, 297-98, 428; **S** 70, 155

New York Basketball Writers Association, **S** 295

New York Bay Swim, **I** 589

New York Big Gorhams baseball club, **B** 238

New York Black Yankees baseball club (NNL), **B** 30, 334, 339, 543, 599; **I** 143, 332; **S** 188

New York Boxing Commission, **I** 450

New York Boxing Writers Association, **I** 367, 387, 398, 423-24

New York Bulldogs football club, **F** 341

New York Busy Izzies basketball club, **I** 87-88

New York Chuckles basketball club (AAU), **I** 175

New York, City College of, **F** 4, 195; *See also* City College of New York

New York City Golden Gloves Team, **I** 423, 482

New York City Golden Gloves Tournament, **I** 395, 423, 445, 449, 455

New York *Clipper,* **B** 82; **S** 82, 178

New York Coliseum, **S** 342-43

New York Cosmos Soccer Club (MISL), **O** 295, 298, 305

New York Cosmos Soccer Club (NASL), **O** 105, 294-95, 297-98, 307-08

New York Cricket Club, **O** 86

New York Cuban baseball club (NNL), **B** 132, 147, 290, 338, 548; **S** 222

New York *Daily News,* **F** 457; **O** 59, 63-64, 85; **S** 347, 358-59

New York Downtown Athletic Club, **F** 257, 501

New York *Evening Mail,* **I** 670; **O** 89

New York *Evening World,* **F** 115, 406, 426; **S** 345, 444

New York Express Soccer Club (MISL), **O** 295

New York Fencing Club, I 669
New York Giants baseball club (NL),
   B 3, 10-11, 19-21, 27, 29, 34-35,
   45-46, 52-53, 63-64, 66, 72, 81,
   89, 95, 108, 111-12, 116-17, 123,
   131-33, 136, 145, 148, 153-57,
   162, 170-71, 173, 175, 177, 183-
   84, 198-99, 202-03, 208, 216-17,
   228, 230-31, 245-46, 259-61, 266-
   68, 273-74, 278, 282, 291, 297-98,
   301-03, 307-08, 323, 325-26, 329,
   332, 335-36, 338, 340, 348, 353-
   55, 357, 361, 363, 366, 368, 374,
   376, 383-84, 390-91, 393-94, 396-
   97, 403, 408, 416-17, 427-29, 432,
   447, 450, 452, 457, 468, 481, 483,
   488, 492-94, 501, 503, 509, 514,
   524-25, 531, 534, 539-40, 550-52,
   555-57, 565, 568-69, 571-72, 582-
   83, 588, 592, 597-99, 606-07, 612,
   620, 624-25, 627, 638; F 301,
   403, 563, 597, 638; I 14; O 45,
   54, 74, 78-79, 82, 89, 91, 93, 208;
   S 3-5, 19, 21-22, 24, 33, 36-37,
   43, 45-48, 55, 60-61, 64-65, 68-
   71, 86, 100, 105, 113, 116-19,
   128, 131, 139, 143, 149-51, 153-
   57, 162, 165, 169, 173, 177-78,
   184, 187-88, 191, 194, 198, 202,
   207, 218-19, 221, 223, 232, 234,
   239-40, 248, 342-43, 347-50, 402
New York Giants football club (NFL),
   F 4, 9, 11, 17, 23, 33, 42, 68, 72,
   78, 83, 98, 104, 107, 112, 122,
   141, 143, 152, 163, 178, 187, 194-
   95, 206-07, 215-16, 220-21, 224,
   232, 236, 256, 259-60, 267, 271,
   277-79, 282-83, 309, 321, 331,
   346, 348, 352-54, 357, 362, 364-
   66, 372, 378, 381, 388-89, 397,
   404-05, 417, 430, 447-48, 462,
   480, 488, 503, 510, 521, 542, 548,
   567, 573-74, 578, 583, 589, 593,
   597, 600-01, 607-08, 614, 645,
   651, 665, 667; O 60, 65, 87, 105,
   308, 439; S 348, 362, 365, 368,
   385, 390, 404-05, 414-15, 426,
   429, 436, 440-41, 445, 455, 457-
   58, 461, 465-66, 471, 482-83, 494-
   95, 497, 503
New York Gorhams baseball club, S
   238
New York Gothams baseball club
   (NL), See New York Giants
   baseball club (NL)
New York Gothams basketball club, I
   273
New York Hakoah Soccer Club, O
   299
New York Herald, I 371
New York Herald-Tribune, F 110,
   125, 468, 551; O 50-51, 72, 96,
   565; S 351
New York Highlanders baseball club
   (AL), See New York Yankees
   baseball club (AL)
New York Islanders hockey club
   (NHL), I 550, 557, 563, 568; S
   544-45
New York Jets football club (AFL), F
   50, 72, 134, 165, 253, 277, 320,
   389, 405, 418, 432, 483, 543, 591;
   O 105; S 335, 363, 452, 463,
   475; See also New York Titans
   football club (AFL)
New York Jets football club (NFL), F
   25, 43, 96, 140, 180, 196, 296,
   371, 385, 394, 418-20, 427-28,
   493, 496, 566; O 105; S 335,
   420, 459, 475
New York Jockey Club, O 101, 177;
   S 525
New York Journal, B 201
New York Journal-American, S 335
New York Knickerbocker Club, O
   470

New York Knickerbockers baseball club (Ind.), **B** 77-78, 627

New York Knickerbockers basketball club (NBL, BAA, NBA), **I** 15, 18, 23, 31, 44, 46, 51, 64-65, 82-83, 87, 92-93, 100, 106-07, 114, 121, 133, 141-42, 148, 161, 171, 186, 189-90, 195-97, 200-01, 204-05, 220-21, 240, 247, 249, 260-61, 270, 277, 305, 310, 319, 323, 335; **O** 105; **S** 264-65, 269, 292, 298, 301, 319, 322-23, 327, 330

New York Lawn Tennis Club Championships, **O** 334

New York Lincoln Giants baseball club (ANL, ECL), **B** 30, 286-87, 334, 342, 378, 451-53, 465, 500, 519, 533, 553, 612; **I** 143, 332; **S** 19-20, 188, 238, 242

New York Lincoln Stars baseball club (Negro Leagues), **B** 333, 549

New York *Mail,* **S** 345

New York Marathon, **O** 523, 528, 536-37

New York Maroons baseball club (NL), *See* New York Giants baseball club (NL)

New York Metropolitan League, **I** 552

New York Metropolitans baseball club (AA), **B** 297, 429, 464; **S** 97, 150-51

New York Mets baseball club (NL), **B** 15, 30, 36, 42-43, 49, 58, 61, 73, 76, 80, 138, 191, 201, 215-16, 242, 250, 252, 257-58, 261, 264, 274, 277, 306, 311, 313-14, 335, 351, 394, 431, 438, 441, 472, 490, 497-98, 504-05, 508, 515, 521, 525, 532, 535, 559-60, 582-83, 598, 614; **O** 60, 83, 93, 137; **S** 25-26, 35, 52-53, 58, 60, 73, 76, 79, 84, 87, 96, 103-04, 122-23, 130, 132, 146, 149, 160, 170, 208, 212-13, 218-20, 230, 247, 355, 359

New York Military Academy, **I** 23

New York *Morning and Sunday Telegram,* **O** 74

New York *Morning Telegraph,* **O** 53

New York Mutuals baseball club (NA, NL), **B** 60, 128, 271, 388-89, 399, 442, 531

New York Nationals basketball club, **I** 131

New York Nationals Soccer Club, **O** 306

New York Nets basketball club (ABA), **I** 3, 17, 65, 82, 196, 335; **S** 266, 274

New York-New Jersey League, **S** 117

New York Original Celtics basketball club (EL, MeL, ABL), **I** 14, 20-21, 29-30, 32-33, 49, 65-66, 69, 88, 102, 131, 143, 157-58, 170-71, 194, 223, 250, 305; **S** 260, 287, 313-14

New York-Pennsylvania League, **B** 109, 373, 483; **I** 194-95; **S** 6, 51, 95, 127, 143, 154, 166, 193, 200, 207, 216, 228, 240

New York Pioneer Athletic Club, **I** 69; **S** 594-95

New York Pioneer Club Invitation Track and Field Meet, **O** 443

New York Police Athletic Association, **I** 665

New York Police Athletic League, **S** 595

New York *Post,* **F** 266; **O** 74, 600; **S** 359

New York *Post* Athlete of the Year, **O** 600

New York *Press,* **I** 382; **O** 74; **S** 359

New York Quaker Giants baseball club, **S** 143

New York Racing Association, O 180, 197

New York Rangers hockey club (NHL), I 453, 546, 548, 551-52, 554, 567-68; O 105; S 537-38, 546-47

New York Renaissance basketball club, I 48-49, 68-69, 143-44, 333; S 260, 277, 283

New York Roosevelts basketball club, I 88

New York Rovers hockey club (EAHL), I 552

New York Soccer Club, O 310

New York Spartans basketball club, I 68

New York *Sporting Times,* O 268

New York Stars football club (WFL), S 463-64

New York State Athletic Commission, I 360, 380, 393, 421, 423, 442, 449; O 268

New York State Boxing Association, O 71

New York State Boxing Championships, I 389, 417, 447, 466, 480

New York State League, B 117, 309; I 14, 20, 29, 32, 65, 88, 170, 222-23, 273, 313; S 3, 19, 43, 45, 121, 159, 198, 240, 260, 287

New York State League Basketball Championships, S 287

New York State Soccer Championships, O 306

New York State Tennis Championships, O 333

New York State Wrestling Championships, I 635-37

New York Stock Exchange hockey club (NYML), I 552

New York *Sun,* F 169, 270, 415, 479, 605; I 116, 382; O 72; S 434

New York *Telegram,* I 382

New York Tennis Club, O 383

New York Tennis Club (WTT), O 364

New York *Times,* B 107, 140, 194, 389, 443, 528; F 66, 289, 346, 351, 354, 571; I 516; O 60-62, 69, 71-72, 96, 121, 200, 220, 407, 456; S 64, 335-36, 350, 460, 499, 511-12, 560, 562-63, 569

New York *Times* "Sports of the Times," S 335

New York Titans football club (AFL), F 26, 31, 165, 367, 389, 479; S 474-75; *See also* New York Jets football club (AFL)

New York Touchdown Club, F 351

New York *Tribune,* O 54, 89

New York Turf Writers Association, S 528

New York Turf Writers Training Award, O 216

New York Unions of Morrisania baseball club, B 122, 627

New York University, B 222, 402; F 58, 339, 350, 353, 571, 573; I 25, 38, 40, 107, 141, 156, 200, 260, 270, 305, 512, 524; O 60, 307, 374, 431, 446, 566; S 246, 309, 311, 322-23, 413, 486

New York University Hall of Fame, I 40

New York University Settlement House Whirlwinds basketball club, I 32, 87-88, 131, 170, 273, 305

New York *World,* F 270; I 382; O 54, 91

New York *World-Telegram,* F 5; I 141, 371, 382

New York *World-Telegram & Sun,* I 371

New York World's Fair Aquacade, I 589

New York Writers Association, **I** 198
New York Writers Distinguished
    Service Award, **I** 38
New York Yacht Club, **O** 50-51, 101-
    02, 266
New York Yankees baseball club (AL),
    B 1, 4-5, 10, 13, 19, 24-26, 33,
    36, 39, 43, 48-49, 54-55, 62, 65,
    75, 84, 86-87, 89-92, 101-02, 106,
    118, 137-39, 143, 146-49, 156,
    159, 161, 163, 174-75, 181, 183,
    187-88, 193, 201, 206, 210, 217-
    18, 220, 222, 226, 229, 233, 245,
    249-50, 257-58, 260, 263-64, 266-
    69, 271-72, 274, 277, 279, 284,
    286, 288-89, 291-92, 295-96, 298,
    301, 308, 311, 325, 337, 339-41,
    345-46, 349, 351-52, 360-61, 366-
    67, 374-75, 377, 379, 381-82, 385-
    86, 392-93, 395, 397-98, 403, 406,
    408, 416-17, 421-22, 430, 438,
    441, 443-45, 449, 451, 454, 456,
    459-60, 469-70, 472, 475-76, 489-
    90, 492, 494-95, 500, 505, 508,
    510, 517-18, 520-21, 524-25, 534-
    35, 537, 544, 547, 552, 554, 558-
    59, 565, 567, 570-72, 575, 588-91,
    593, 595, 597-98, 602, 606, 608,
    612-13, 622-24, 633, 635-36, 638;
    F 9, 84, 100, 162, 209, 233, 287,
    573; **I** 113, 333; **O** 45-46, 49, 60,
    67, 74, 79, 82, 89; **S** 2, 8, 11-12,
    21-22, 24-25, 27-28, 31-35, 38-39,
    41, 46, 51, 55, 60, 65, 67, 70, 73-
    74, 76-78, 80, 83, 86-87, 89-92,
    94-95, 98, 101-02, 104-07, 111-13,
    120, 124, 127-28, 130, 132, 136,
    138, 142-43, 146-50, 152-53, 155-
    57, 159, 165, 167, 170-75, 181-82,
    184-86, 189-93, 196, 199-200,
    203-05, 208, 211-12, 216, 222,
    227-30, 237, 239-40, 243-44, 264-
    65, 297, 353-55, 462

New York Yankees football club
    (AAFC), **F** 26, 179, 369, 381,
    453, 549, 645, 656, 670; **S** 440,
    465
New York Yankees football club
    (AFL), **F** 23, 146, 178, 217, 309,
    331, 362, 392, 618, 670; **O** 87,
    93; **S** 440, 465
New York Yankees Soccer Club
    (ACSL), **O** 299
New York to San Francisco, CA Long
    Distance Walk, **O** 560
New York to Seattle, WA Auto Race,
    O 10
New Yorker, **O** 62, 64, 85; **S** 336
Newark, NJ Athletic Club, **S** 588
Newark, NJ Athletic Track and Field
    Committee, **S** 565
Newark, NJ baseball club (AA), **B** 11
Newark, NJ baseball club (EL), **B**
    103, 353, 363, 580, 584, 586; **S**
    13
Newark, NJ Bears baseball club (IL),
    B 36, 54, 66, 85-86, 109, 155,
    257-58, 266, 289, 346, 348, 483,
    509-10, 529, 550; **S** 21, 67, 86,
    101, 127, 149, 172, 181
Newark, NJ Browns baseball club, **S**
    242
Newark, NJ Dodgers baseball club
    (NNL), **B** 132, 338-39
Newark, NJ Eagles baseball club
    (NNL), **B** 127, 132, 141, 151,
    273, 338-39, 362-63, 417, 436,
    543, 599-600, 609
Newark, NJ *Evening News,* **O** 347
Newark, NJ football club, **O** 293, 310
Newark, NJ German Soccer Club, **O**
    300
Newark, NJ Mules basketball club, **I**
    30
Newark, NJ Peps baseball club (FL),
    B 361, 409, 468

Newark, NJ Soccer Club, O 292
Newark, NJ Stars baseball club (ECL), S 238
Newark, NJ *Sunday Call,* F 109
Newark, NJ Turners basketball club (ISL), I 223
Newark, NJ Veladrome, O 264
Newark, NY baseball club (NYPL), B 639
Newberry College, S 318-19
Newburgh, NY basketball club (HRL), I 273
Newcomb College, I 13
Newcombe, Donald "Don," B 9, 70, 362, *417-18,* 467, 469; S 86
Newcombe, John, O 324, 341
Newcomer of the Year Award, BEC, S 302
Newell, Marshall, F 64, *425-26*
Newell, Peter "Pete," I *230-31,* 232
Newhouse, Jean Shiley, O 448, *507-08*
Newhouser, Harold "Hal," B *418-19,* 438
Newlin, Michael F. "Mike," I 94
Newman, Harry L., Sr., F 23; S 390, *458-59*
Newman, Harry L., Jr., S 458
Newman, Neil, S 534
Newman, Wallace, F 470
Newmarket Handicap, O 201
Newmarket Race Track, O 219, 596, 609
Newnan, GA baseball club (GAL), B 551
Newport, AR baseball club (NEAL), B 299
Newport, RI Casino, O 51, 398; S 560
Newport, RI Invitation Tennis Tournament, O 368, 396, 410, 416, 420-21; S 556
Newport Cup, O 420

Newport News, VA baseball club (Pil, VL), B 34, 256, 521
Newport News, VA Shipbuilding Apprentice School, S 413
Newport Royals Soccer Club, O 306
The News Balladium, Benton Harbor, MI, I 80
Newsom, Norman L. "Bobo," B 590; S 60, *153-54*
Newsome, Ozzie, F *426-28*
Newspaper Enterprises Association, B 169; F 18, 50, 90, 221, 497, 551; S 386
Newstetter, Wilber, O 462
Newsweek, I 536; S 338, 351
Neyland, Robert R., Jr. "Bob," F 20, 126, 151, *301-02,* 428-29, 440, 523, 576, 621; S 354, 413, 446-47, 460
NFL, *See* National Football League
NHL, *See* National Hockey League
Niagara Acres, O 100
Niagara Dream, O 600
Niagara International Tennis Championships, O 354
Niagara Medal, I 50
Niagara University, B 345; I 49-50, 113, 226; S 289
Niagaras of Brooklyn baseball club, B 122
Niagara's Sports Hall of Fame, I 50
Niarhos, Constantine G. "Gus," S 112
Niatross, O *600*
Nice, France Track and Field Meet, O 532
Nichols, Charles A. "Kid," B 96, *419-20,* 506, 538, 556, 617; S 36, 76, 115
Nichols, Harold J., I *651-52,* 654; I 624
Nichols, Robert, O 242
Nicholson, Glenda, I 255

Nicholson, John P., **O** 520

Nicholson, William B. "Bill," **S** *154-55*

Nickerson, Victor "Lefty," **O** 591

Nicklaus, Jack W., **O** 124, 132, 234, *146-47,* 166-67; **S** 510, 514, 516-17

Nieder, William H. "Bill," **O** 509; **S** 586, *589-90*

Niehaus, Albert B. "Al," **B** 114

Niekro, Joseph F. "Joe," **B** *420-21,* 422

Niekro, Philip H. "Phil," **B** 420, *421-23*

Nielsen, Gifford, **F** 562; **S** 396

Nielsen, Kurt, **O** 394, 407

Nielson, Oscar, *See* "Battling" Nelson

Niles, Nathaniel W., **I** 499; **O** 378

Nimbus, **O** 214

999 Racing Car, **O** 10, 26

Ninowski, James "Jim," **F** 395

Nissan Cup Golf Team, **S** 520

Nissan Indy Auto Race Challenge, **O** 38

Nissen, Inge, **I** 285

Nissen Award, **I** 528, 540

Nitschke, Raymond E. "Ray," **F** 354, 430

Nixon, Norman E. "Norm," **S** *308-09*

Nixon, Richard M., **O** 274; **S** 202, 417

Nobis, Thomas H., Jr. "Tommy," **F** *431,* 515

Noble Victory, **O** 182

Nodarske, Vincenzio, **O** 175

Nolan, Richard C. "Dick," **F** 566, 578

Noll, Charles H. "Chuck," **F** 59, 211, *432-33,* 511, 590

Nomellini, Leo J., **F** 49, *433-34,* 521

Noor, **O** 577

Norelius, Charles, **I** 623

Norelius, Martha, *See* Martha Norelius Wright

Noren, Irving A. "Irv," **S** 95

Norfolk, **O** 594

Norfolk, "Kid," **I** 391, 394

Norfolk, VA baseball club (Pil, VL, VSL), **B** 36, 62, 187, 244, 257, 390; **S** 19, 87, 204, 230

Norfolk, VA Golf Tournament, **S** 522

Norfolk, VA Naval Training Station basketball team, **I** 132

Norfolk State University, **S** 272

Norman, **O** 174

Norman, Greg, **O** 147; **S** 523-24

Norman, "Jerry," **I** 331

Norman, Kenneth D. "Ken," **S** 292

Norman, Roger, **O** 541

Norpoint Royals Soccer Club, **O** 297

Norris, James D., Jr., **I** 430

Norris, Walter O. "Kid," **O** *244-45*

Norris Trophy, **I** 561

Norristown, PA baseball club (Ind.), **B** 363

North, John, **S** 384

North American Alpine Ski Championships, **O** 280

North American Boxing Federation, **I** 422

North American Figure Skating Pairs Championships, **I** 499, 509, 515, 519

North American Gymnastic Championships, **I** 529

North American Ladies Figure Skating Championships, **I** 499, 507, 509-10, 512, 515; **S** 601

North American Men's Figure Skating Championships, **I** 502-03, 512-14; **S** 601

North American Outdoor Speed Skating Championships, **O** 316-18

North American Soccer League, **O**

294-95, 297-98, 301, 303-08, 311
North American Soccer League All-
Star Team, O 298, 304, 307-08,
311
North American Soccer League
Championships, O 295, 298, 301,
307-08
North American Soccer League Rookie
of the Year, O 298, 308
North American Soccer Player of the
Year, O 294, 304, 306
North American Yacht
Championships, O 103
North Atlantic Road Racing
Championships, O 13
North basketball team, S 321
North California Amateur Golf
Tournament, O 138
North Carolina Agricultural &
Technical University, I 90, 152; O
428; S 256
North Carolina College, I 151, 201;
O 427
North Carolina Intercollegiate
Conference, F 170
North Carolina League, S 182
North Carolina Pre-Flight Training
Center, F 480, 621
North Carolina Sports Hall of Fame,
F 304; I 152; S 67, 27, 456
North Carolina State League, S 108
North Carolina State University, F
14, 78, 170, 175, 197, 262, 453,
495-97, 515, 539, 576; I 42-43,
51, 60, 174, 180, 198, 226, 280-
81, 295, 299; O 529; S 263, 413,
419-20, 459
North Central Conference, F 7, 333;
I 269, 646, 654; S 281, 321, 451
North Dakota Agricultural &
Mechanical College, F 108
North Dakota State University, F
144; I 614, 637

North East Conference, S 313
North Hempstead, NY Golf Club, O
109
North Medford, MA Club 20-Mile
Race, S 582
North Platte, NE baseball club
(NeSL), B 444; S 79, 246
North Sides, S 530
North-South Amateur Golf
Tournament, S 518
North-South Football bowl game, S
391
North-South lacrosse game, See All-
Star College (North-South) lacrosse
game
North-South Match Horse Race, O
571. 583, 602, 609
North-South Open Golf Tournament,
O 112, 128, 131, 133, 142, 145;
S 507, 512
North-South Shrine football game, F
33, 127, 132-33, 185, 207, 277,
321, 330, 364, 523, 528, 558
North-South Women's Golf
Championships, O 159, 165
North State Conference, F 403
North State Intercollegiate Conference,
S 304
North Texas Junior College, F 455
North Texas State University, F 186,
199, 222, 253; I 246, 251; S 324,
401
North Wilkesboro, NC Speedway, O
41; S 605
Northeast Arkansas League, B 22; S
185
Northeast Louisiana University, F
121; S 296
Northeast Missouri State University,
F 167; I 92; S 258
Northeastern University, I 561
Northern California Gymnastic
Championships, I 658

204

Northern California Seniors Track
Club, O 472
Northern Colorado University, S 319
Northern Dancer, O *599*
Northern Illinois Track and Field
Association Hall of Fame, S 598
Northern League, S 57, 73, 81, 162,
173, 233
Northern Lights Basketball
Tournament, I 215
Northern Teachers College Athletic
Conference, F 137
Northern Tennis Championships, O
350
Northrop Field, Minneapolis, MN, F
262
Northwest League, B 569; S 2, 88,
105, 115, 155, 160, 165, 206
Northwest Missouri State University,
I 192; S 496, 528
Northwestern Conference, F 148
Northwestern Louisiana State
University, F 557; I 304
Northwestern Oklahoma University, S
77-78, 397
Northwestern Tennis Championships,
O 362
Northwestern University, B 333, 573;
F 13, 44-45, 49, 94-95, 149, 152,
173, 188-89, 194, 215, 227, 241,
249, 355, 438, 442, 457-58, 506,
526, 532, 551, 554, 602, 627, 651,
673; I 5, 55, 181-82, 193, 208,
235, 325, 514, 646, 649; O 122,
549; S 357, 362, 417, 461, 593
Northwood Institute, I 25
Norton, "Al," I 376
Norton, Brian I. C. "Babe," O 362
Norton, "Ken," I 383, 401
Norton, Raymond "Ray," O 538
Norton Spirit, O 36
Norwalk, CT basketball club (CtL), S
314

Norwegian Crown Prince Olaf Award,
O 278
Norwegian National Ice Hockey Team,
I 548
Norwegian National Tennis
Championships, O 373
Norwich University, B 357
Norwood, E. M., O 592
Norwood Park Tennis Championships,
O 420
Nose Dive, S 528
Notter, Joseph A. "Joe," O 208,
210-12
Nova, "Lou," I 358, 458
Nova Scotia Voyageurs hockey club
(AHL), I 562
Novak, Gregori, I 631
Novak, Michael D. "Mike," I 264
Novelty, O 593; S 526-27
Now What, O 231
Nowak, Paul, S *309*
Nowell, Melvyn P. "Mel," I 67
Nowicki, Janet Lynn, *See* Janet Lynn
Nowicki Salomon
Nucatola, John P. "Johnny," I *231-32*
Nugent, Thomas "Tom," F 111
Number, O 222
Numbered Account, O 576
Nunamaker, Leslie G. "Les," B 456
Nurmi, Paavo, O 519, 548
The Nursery Farm, O 177
Nursery Stud, Lexington, KY, O 595
Nusslein, Hans, O 404
The Nut, O 211
Nuthall, Betty M., O 343
Nutra-Sweet Men's Figure Skating Pro
World Championships, I 508
Nutra-Sweet Women's Figure Skating
Pro World Championships, I 504
Nuxhall, Joseph H. "Joe," B 216

Oak Hills Country Club, Rochester,

NY, **O** 163; **S** 520

Oak Hills Country Club, San Antonio, TX, **O** 166

Oak Park Country Club, **O** 156

Oakford, Barbara Worth, **O** 267

Oakland Athletics baseball club (AL), **B** 7, 14, 37-38, 58, 134, 138, 149, 179, 181, 248-49, 251, 262, 271-72, 277, 284, 305, 318, 342, 351, 369, 385-86, 394, 405, 437, 445, 503, 532, 543-44, 595, 610, 614; **I** 30; **O** 57; **S** 7-9, 11-12, 27, 48-49, 51, 53, 77, 83-84, 88-89, 104, 107-09, 112, 114, 123, 125, 138, 142, 158, 160, 166-67, 182, 185, 213, 217, 241-42, 344

Oakland Bittners basketball club, **I** 92, 172

Oakland Golf Club, **O** 161

Oakland Invaders football club (USFL), **F** 99, 553, 561; **S** 454

Oakland Oaks baseball club (PCL), **B** 86, 114, 132, 225-26, 251, 302, 335, 385, 397, 433, 535, 569; **O** 208; **S** 4, 24, 46, 67, 94, 105-06, 111, 157

Oakland Oaks basketball club (ABA), **I** 17, 33-34, 111; **S** 305

Oakland Raiders football club (AFL), **F** 50, 55, 72-73, 91, 128, 179, 253, 354, 376, 479, 539, 561, 590-91, 615, 631; **S** 363, 366, 377, 389, 463

Oakland Raiders football club (NFL), **F** 1, 50, 59, 62, 71, 73, 77, 128, 180, 219, 229, 235, 246, 258, 280, 295, 312, 333-34, 376, 396, 408, 427, 432, 445, 473, 502, 517, 539-40, 550, 556-57, 561-62, 565, 580, 585-86, 590, 615, 620, 659; **S** 379, 441, 446, 468

Oakland *Tribune*, **F** 294

Oakland City Baptist College, **B** 488

Oakland Hills Country Club, Detroit, MI, **O** 112

Oakmont Country Club, Pittsburgh, PA, **O** 158; **S** 522-23

Oates, Johnny L., **S** 16

Obelmejias, Fulgencio, **I** 397

Oberlin College, **B** 584; **F** 257; **O** 543

O'Brien, "Coley," **F** 592

O'Brien, John J., Sr., **I** *232-33,* 273

O'Brien, John J., Jr., **I** 233

O'Brien, Lawrence F., Jr. "Larry," **I** 103, 156, *233-34,* 289

O'Brien, "Pat," **F** 433

O'Brien, "Philadelphia Jack," **I** 419, *445*

O'Brien, Robert David "Davey," **F** 3, 356, 372, 391, *437-38;* **S** 374

O'Brien, "Ron," **I** 491

O'Brien, "Tommy," **I** 365

O'Brien, William Parry, Jr., **O** 504, *509;* **S** 586, 589

O'Brien National Quarterback Award, **F** 356, 372

Occidental College, **I** 490; **O** 444; **S** 397, 432, 453-54

Occupation, **O** 579

Ochiltree, **S** 535

Ochowicz, James L. "Jim," **O** 317

Ochowicz, Sheila Grace Young, **O** *316-17*

O'Connell, Daniel F. "Danny," **B** 503

O'Connell, "Ed," **I** 663

O'Connell, James J. "Jimmy," **B** 323

O'Connell, Michael T. "Mike," **I** 563

O'Connor, Edward G., **O** 548

O'Connor, John J. "Jack," **B** 322, 454

O'Connor, Paul "Bucky," **F** 532

O'Connor, Peter, **O** 463; **S** 592

O'Connor, Winfield S. "Winnie," **O** *212-13*

O'Day, Henry F. "Hank," **B** 310, 377, 389; **S** *155-56,* 179

O'Dea, Patrick J. "Pat," F *438-39;* S 434

Odom, George M., O *213-14*

Odom, George P., O 214

Odom, Johnny L. "Blue Moon," B 179

Odoms, Riley M., F 408

O'Donnell, Charles L., F 507

O'Donnell, "Chuck," I 340

O'Doul, Francis J. "Lefty," S *156-57*

O'Dowd, "Mike," I 390

Oerter, Alfred A., Jr. "Al," O *510-11;* S 578

Oeschger, Joseph C. "Joe," B 302

Offenhauser Midget Race Cars, O 3

Offensive Rookie of the Year Award, S 414, 474

Official National Basketball Association Guide, I 218

Oftring, Frank, I 154

Ogden, UT baseball club (PCL, PrL, UIL), B 58, 200, 209, 248, 335, 478; S 90, 109

Oglesby, Frank, S 616

Oglethorpe College, B 14

Oh, Sadaharu, S 96

Oh, Baby I Love It, S 355

O'Hara, Frank, I 180

Ohe, Sueo, S 588

Ohio Amateur Golf Tournament, O 149, 154

Ohio Basketball Coaches Association, S 272

Ohio Conference, F 51, 210, 251, 257, 457, 469, 558, 607; I 6; S 270, 290, 484

Ohio Medical University, B 23

Ohio Northern University, F 668; S 78

Ohio Open Golf Tournament, O 146, 154, 329

Ohio-Pennsylvania League, B 169, 322; S 3, 42

Ohio Stadium, Columbus, OH, F 100

Ohio Stakes, O 595

Ohio State Athletic Board, F 174

Ohio State Baseball Hall of Fame, S 103

Ohio *State Journal,* F 97, 232

Ohio State Junior Golf Tournament, O 146

Ohio State League, B 547; S 4, 238

Ohio State Quarterback Club Trophy, F 100

Ohio State University, B 205-06, 264, 560-61; F 13, 44, 69, 93, 99-100, 133, 152, 164, 167-68, 172-73, 188-90, 210, 217, 226-29, 241, 251-52, 261, 272, 289-90, 297, 299, 339, 368, 393, 410, 427, 454, 457-58, 473, 492, 526, 528, 530-31, 552, 555, 585, 610, 627, 633, 642, 648, 656, 668; I 22, 67, 91, 117, 149, 161, 184-86, 216, 228, 231, 234-35, 264, 295, 485, 584, 603-04, 628, 663; O 55, 146, 167, 449, 514, 552, 560; S 171, 263, 345, 362, 380, 393, 397-400, 402, 405-06, 414, 420, 435, 449, 491, 493, 566

Ohio State University Sports Hall of Fame, F 172, 241, 290; S 362, 398, 414, 449

Ohio State Weightlifting Championships, I 627

Ohio University, B 502

Ohio Valley Conference, F 480; I 66

Ohio Valley Dapper Dan Hall of Fame, S 272

Ohio Wesleyan University, B 472; F 183, 213, 668; I 128, 265

Ohmylove, O 203

Ohta, Akia, I 635

Oil Capitol, O 205

Oil City, PA baseball club (MSL), S

82, 246

Oil City, PA football club, **F** 61

Okamoto, Ayako, **O** 114; **S** 508

O'Keefe, "Eddie," **I** 415

Okker, Thomas "Tom," **O** 324

Oklahoma Agricultural & Mechanical University, *See* Oklahoma State University

Oklahoma Amateur Athletic Union Association, **I** 326

Oklahoma Athletic Hall of Fame, **I** 70, 140, 208, 297; **S** 397

Oklahoma Baptist College, **F** 627

Oklahoma City, OK baseball club (AA, TL, PCL), **B** 261, 577, 594; **S** 25, 78, 83, 111, 136, 148, 154

Oklahoma City, OK Race Track, **O** 195

Oklahoma City, OK Sterling Milk basketball club (AAU), **I** 139, 276

Oklahoma City, OK University, **F** 627; **S** 506

Oklahoma City, OK Women's Amateur Golf Tournament, **S** 506

Oklahoma Coaches Hall of Fame, **S** 609

Oklahoma Hall of Fame, **S** 11

Oklahoma High School Girls Basketball Coaches Association, **I** 297

Oklahoma Outlaws football club (USFL), **F** 220

Oklahoma State High School Girls Basketball Tournament, **I** 296-97

Oklahoma State Teachers College, **B** 589-90

Oklahoma State University, **F** 78, 170-71, 508, 515, 52, 627, 664; **I** 40, 69-70, 116, 139-41, 162, 166, 257, 296, 638-39, 642, 652-53, 657-59, 662, 664; **O** 308; **S** 302, 323, 397, 428, 473, 496, 608-09, 616

Oklahoma State Wrestling Championships, **I** 638, 644, 653, 662-63

Oklahoma Women's Amateur Golf Tournament, **S** 506

Okun, Yale, **I** 426

Olajide, Michael, **S** 613

Olajuwon, Hakeem A., **I** 174, 266

Olathe, KS Naval Base basketball club, **I** 93

Olberding, Mark A., **I** 98

Old Dominion Tennis Championships, **O** 377

Old Dominion University, **I** 175, 284-85

Old Guttenberg Race Track, **O** 188

Old Intercollegiate Lacrosse Association, **O** 233

Old Mizzou: A Story of Missouri Football, **S** 338

Old Point Breeze Race Track, **O** 7

Old Rosebud, **O** 196, *600-01,* 613

Older Horse of the Year, **S** 530

Oldfield, Berna E. "Barney," **O** 7, 10, *25-27,* 31

Oldham, John O. "Johnny," **I** 68

Olds, William H. "Bill," **F** 296

Oldsmobile Golf Classic, **S** 508

Ole Bob Bowers, **O** 590

Ole Miss Hall of Fame, **S** 465

Olean, NY baseball club (NYPL), **B** 354; **S** 193

O'Leary, Daniel "Dan," **B** 553

Olin, "Bob," **I** 423, 426, 458

Oliphant, Elmer Q. "Ollie," **F** 126, *439-41,* 552

Oliphant, Thomas "Tommy," **O** 225

Oliva, Antonio P. "Tony," **B** 97, 228; **S** *157-58*

Oliveira, Joao, **O** 424-25

Oliver, Albert J. "Al," **B** *425-26*

Oliver, Edward S. "Porky," **O** 112

Olivera, "Tony," **I** 447

Olmedo, Alejandro "Alex," **S** 554

Olmstead, Susan Christina von Saltza "Chris," **I** *609-10,* 619

O"Loughlin, Frank H, "Silk," **B** 110; **S** 41

Olsen, Harold G., **I** 206, *234-35*

Olsen, Merlin J., **F** 224, 298, *441-42,* 640; **O** 63; **S** 504

Olsen, Philip V. "Phil," **F** 442

Olsen's All-American Red Heads basketball club, **I** 57

Olson, Carl, **O** 565

Olson, Carl "Bobo," **I** 442, 455

Olson, "Eddie," **I** 547

Olson, Jeannette, **I** 8

Olson, Robert Luther "Lute," **S** 278, *309-11*

Olsonite Auto Driver of the Year, **O** 2, 41, 44

Olympia Academy, Paris, France, **I** 673

The Olympia, London, England, **I** 454

Olympic Arena, Detroit, MI, **I** 569; **S** 539

Olympic Auditorium, Los Angeles, CA, **O** 62

Olympic Basketball Tournament, **I** 269

Olympic Club, San Francisco, CA, **F** 378, 552; **I** 660

Olympic Festival, **S** 584

Olympic Games, Summer: 1896, **S** 571; 1900, **F** 240; **O**, 354, 459-60, 482-83, 512; **S** 567, 591-92, 595-96, 622; 1904, **F** 262; **I** 525, 529-30, 587-88, 650-51, 669; **O** 421, 423, 459-60, 464, 470-71, 487, 535; **S** 592; 1906, **I** 108, 588, 623; **O** 459, 464, 471, 488, 524, 535; **S** 592; 1908, **I** 108, 588, 651, 665; **O** 459-60, 467, 470-71, 488, 491, 524, 534-35; **S** 565; 1912, **F** 66, 597; **I** 76, 598, 671; **O** 255, 268, 373, 443-44, 451, 455, 459, 462-63, 467, 479, 483, 490-91, 495, 498, 520, 524, 534-35, 548; **S** 565, 585; 1920, **F** 410; **I** 38, 380, 389, 486, 494, 499, 598, 600, 620, 669, 671; **O** 263, 377, 444, 451, 461-62, 490-91, 495, 517, 519, 530; **S** 498, 580, 589, 622; 1924, **F** 563; **I** 380-81, 417, 459, 486, 494, 497-98, 555, 589, 598, 600-01, 669, 671; **O** 263, 297, 385, 387, 415, 417, 439-40, 444, 452, 465, 471-73, 491, 513, 517, 519, 530, 549, 552; **S** 580, 589; 1928, **I** 486, 494-95, 586, 598-99, 620-23, 653, 669, 671; **O** 234, 246, 426, 440, 444, 452, 465, 471-73, 484, 491, 508, 513, 517, 530, 549, 551, 567-68; **S** 568, 574, 581, 593; 1932, **I** 486-87, 490, 496, 524, 586, 598-99, 610, 621-22, 632, 653, 662, 669, 671; **O** 62, 71, 171, 239, 246, 250, 302, 427, 441, 444-45, 464-66, 470-71, 476, 496, 508, 514, 546, 549, 551-52, 555, 568; **S** 574-75, 587; 1936, **F** 478; **I** 5, 76, 129, 140, 229, 265, 447, 487, 496, 524-25, 580, 621-22, 633, 639, 670-71; **O** 60, 64, 84, 250, 423, 432, 444-45, 452, 465, 476, 485-86, 496, 501, 514-15, 545-47, 552, 554-55, 563, 566, 568; **S** 566, 569, 582, 587-88, 593-94, 608; 1948, **I** 92, 166, 256, 326, 490, 524, 531, 541, 587, 606, 626, 628-29, 631, 639, 646-47, 665, 671; **O** 62, 291, 309, 443-44, 448-49, 453-54, 492, 521, 552, 557, 560; **S** 266, 268, 577-78, 582, 590-91, 595; 1952, **F** 294, 387; **I** 5, 166, 180, 184, 449, 485, 490,

493, 521, 531, 542, 604, 606, 626, 628-31, 644, 659-60, 665, 671; O 62, 69, 267, 301, 309, 423, 453, 492-93, 509, 521-22, 557, 560-61; S 572, 578, 594-95, 598; 1956, I 70, 150, 190, 250, 262, 485, 493, 521, 528-29, 542, 604, 625, 628-30, 644-45, 660, 671; O 62, 69, 267, 301, 424, 429, 437, 442, 449, 453, 456, 471, 477, 501-02, 509-10, 516, 522, 525, 537-39, 557, 561; S 567-68, 570, 572-73, 578, 581, 583, 589, 594-95, 597; 1960, I 23, 182, 186, 202, 231, 250-51, 277, 322, 326, 353, 490, 496-97, 521, 528-29, 610-11, 629-31, 639, 649-50, 664, 671; O 60, 62, 69, 267, 429, 432-33, 435-36, 438, 449-51, 456-57, 477-78, 502, 509-10, 525, 538, 546, 552; S 259, 568-69, 571, 573, 583, 586, 590, 596-97; 1964, I 31, 34, 94, 97, 140, 209, 287, 326, 385, 490, 497, 522, 528-29, 534, 537, 582, 584, 611, 614-15, 619, 629, 631, 671; O 47, 60, 69, 267, 430, 432-33, 438-39, 447, 457, 466-68, 478, 494, 509-10, 526, 550, 553; S 38, 569, 571, 573, 586, 592, 597-98; 1968, I 121, 140, 209, 287, 323-24, 383, 386, 489, 522, 528, 531, 534, 537, 542, 584, 586, 594, 601, 610, 612-15, 617-19, 630, 650, 657, 663, 666, 671; O 47, 60, 69, 267, 428, 432-33, 435, 447, 458, 460-61, 471-72, 486, 498-99, 510-11, 516, 527, 533, 541, 543, 550-51, 553; S 573, 577, 597; 1972, F 62; I 140, 210, 287, 489, 524, 528, 532, 534, 537, 575-77, 584, 594-95, 601-02, 613, 617-18, 630, 642, 650, 654-57, 663, 666, 671; O 47-48, 60, 69, 76, 307, 311,

429, 435, 447, 458, 475, 488, 497, 499-500, 518, 523, 526-27, 533, 536, 564, 566-67; S 259, 573, 577, 597, 621, 624; 1976, I 27, 60, 72, 175, 259, 283, 287, 290-91, 300, 422, 452, 466, 490-91, 522, 524, 529, 534-35, 539, 575, 577-79, 584-85, 593-95, 608-09, 616, 630, 637, 654-55, 671; O 47-48, 69, 76, 96, 309, 425, 438, 447, 474-75, 489, 500, 502-03, 523, 532, 536, 540, 557, 562, 564; S 621, 623; 1980, F 352; I 27, 59, 73, 175, 287, 291, 329, 491, 529, 532-33, 535, 540, 573, 577-78, 584, 591-93, 596, 605, 607, 637, 642, 654; O 63, 69, 97, 314, 425, 480, 500, 503, 506, 511, 523, 528, 532, 540, 557, 562; S 253, 617; 1984, I 63, 73, 162, 214, 287, 291, 296, 304, 329, 332, 491-93, 523, 526-28, 530, 532-33, 535-38, 540-41, 578, 580, 582-83, 585-87, 592, 596-97, 605-09, 617, 635-38, 640-42, 658-59; O 68, 76, 259, 271, 425, 435-36, 481, 485-87, 502-03, 508, 528-29, 532, 540, 542, 557, 562; S 255, 296, 306, 579, 583-85, 602, 613; 1988, I 176, 215, 309, 492, 523, 536, 608, 638, 666; O 482, 498, 504, 507, 541-42; S 579-80, 583-84, 602, 607; 1992, S 56, 258, 306, 315, 608

Olympic Games, Winter, 1924, I 499, 509, 555; S 537; 1928, I 499, 509, 515; O 258, 286, 315; S 546; 1932, I 380, 499, 509; O 258, 279, 316-18; S 601; 1936, I 499, 509, 515; O 276; 1948, I 502, 569; O 277, 284; S 614-15; 1952, I 503, 506, 514; O 278, 284; S 614-15; 1956, I 507, 511-

12, 514, 564-65; **O** 287-88; **S** 539; 1960, **I** 326, 504, 512-13, 515, 548, 565, 568-69, 573; **O** 287-88; **S** 539-41; 1964, **I** 26, 510, 548; **O** 281, 287-88; **S** 543; 1968, **I** 510, 516, 518-19, 548; **O** 69, 281, 314, 318; 1972, **I** 516, 519, 554, 558, 566; **O** 69, 274-75, 282, 314-16; 1976, **I** 500, 504-05, 564; **O** 69, 76, 275, 282, 285, 313, 315-17; 1980, **I** 505-06, 508, 519, 548, 550, 567; **O** 69, 280, 283, 285, 313-15, 317-18, 447; **S** 356, 539, 547-48; 1984, **I** 500, 508, 517, 544; **O** 273, 280, 283, 285; **S** 544, 603, 628-29; 1988, **I** 215, 501; **O** 273, 280; **S** 603, 626; 1992, **S** 604

Olympic Marathon, **O** 519, 529

Olympic Organizing Committee, **I** 586, 609, 611; **O** 271, 508; **S** 596

The Olympic Pageant, **S** 498

Olympic Stadium, Berlin, Germany, **O** 520; **S** 569

Olympic Stadium, St. Louis, MO, **S** 568

Olympic Torch Award, **I** 75

Omaha, **O** 183, 585, *601-02*

Omaha Cup, **O** 226

Omaha, NE baseball club (AA, WA, WL), **B** 43, 47, 53, 214, 241, 249, 337, 356, 376, 397, 419, 460, 506, 595, 622; **S** 70, 120, 215, 237

Omaha, NE Fairgrounds, **I** 648

Omaha, NE *World-Herald,* **F** 495

O'Malley, Peter, **B** 426-27

O'Malley, Walter F., **B** 201, *426-27,* 473, 540; **O** 81, 92

Omar Khayyam, **O** 196; **S** 527

Omnibus Stakes, **O** 604

Omondale, **O** 211

On Trust, **S** 532

Once Double, **O** 590

One Count, **O** 196, 599

One-Eyed King, **O** 222

111th Cavalry Club, **F** 175

100-Mile-An-Hour-Club, **O** 15

One I Love, **S** 533

O'Neil, John "Buck," **B** 6

O'Neill, James E. "Tip," **B** 57, 298; **S** 158

O'Neill, John J. "Jack," **S** 158

O'Neill, Michael J. "Mike," **S** 158

O'Neill, Stephen F. "Steve," **S** *158-59*

Oneonta, NY baseball club (NYPL), **B** 431; **F** 162

Ongais, "Danny," **O** 37

Onion Creek Golf Club, **O** 119

Onkotz, Dennis "Denny," **F** 460; **S** *459*

Onofrio, "Al," **F** 138

Onondaga Indians Lacrosse Club, **O** 249

Ontabye, **O** 101

Ontario, CA 500 Auto Race, **O** 18-19, 37, 39, 43

Ontario, CA Motor Speedway, **O** 13, 18; **S** 614

Ontario, CA 200 Mile Auto Race, **O** 34

Ontario Rugby Football Union, **F** 92

Onwentsia Golf Club, Lake Forest, IL, 107

Onysko, "Rick," **I** 528

Oosterbaan, Benjamin G. "Bennie," **F** 98, 193-94, 322, *442-43,* 668; **S** 500

Ophthalmics, College of, **B** 604

Oppenheim, Baron, **O** 196

Optimist Bowl football game, **F** 390

Optner Trophy, **F** 288

Oral Roberts University, **O** 500

Orange Athletic Club, **F** 343

Orange Blossom Classic, **F** 312, 331

Orange Blossom Golf Classic, **S** 505

Orange Bowl football game, **F** 5-6, 37, 71, 81, 138, 151, 167, 195, 198, 208-09, 219, 235-36, 246, 289, 302, 319, 338, 364, 418, 422, 427, 431, 434, 444, 489, 495, 507-08, 518, 534, 537, 546, 549, 560, 567, 570, 575-76, 581-83, 594, 619, 622, 632, 653; **O** 49, 52, 70; **S** 368-69, 381-82, 394-95, 403-04, 418-21, 428-29, 456, 459, 466, 474, 479

Orange Bowl Sports Hall of Fame, **F** 575; **S** 419

Orange Coast College, **B** 460

Orange County, CA Hall of Fame, **I** 73

Orange Lawn Invitation Tennis Championships, **O** 412

Orange Lawn Tennis Club, Mountain Station, NJ, **O** 412

Orange Lionettes of California softball club, **O** 262

Orange, NJ Tornadoes football club, **S** 610

Orange Tennis Championships, **O** 418

Orantes, Manuel, **O** 34

Order of the Black Eagle, **S** 613

Ordinate, **O** 206

Oregon Agricultural College, *See* Oregon State University

Oregon High School Coaches Association, **O** 434

Oregon League, **S** 98

Oregon Sports Hall of Fame, **F** 25, 536; **I** 92, 616; **O** 461, 545

Oregon Sportswriters and Sportscasters Association, **I** 97

Oregon State Tennis Championships, **O** 361

Oregon State University, **F** 2, 24, 157, 501, 513, 536, 626; **I** 5, 96-97, 172, 216-17, 646, 655-56; **O** 461; **S** 303, 442, 503

Oregon State University Wrestling Hall of Fame, **I** 656

Oregon State Wrestling Championships, **I** 656

Orengo, Joseph C. "Joe," **S** 24

Original Celtics basketball club, *See* New York Original Celtics basketball club

Oriole Park, Baltimore, MD, **S** 48

Oriole Stakes, **O** 593

Orlando, FL baseball club (FSL), **B** 70, 557, 631; **S** 15

Orlando, FL Juice baseball club (SPBA), **S** 35

Orlando, FL Renegades football club (USFL), **F** 519

Ormsby, Emmett T. "Red," **B** 109

O'Rourke, Charles "Charlie," **F** 344; **S** *459-60*

O'Rourke, Francis J. "Frank," **B** 212

O'Rourke, James H. "Jim," **B** 428, 604

O'Rourke, John, **B** 428

Orr, David L. "Dave," **B** 78, *428-29*

Orr, Robert G. "Bobby," **I** 563; **S** 542

Orser, Brian, **I** 501

Ortega, Gaspar, **I** 395

Orth, Albert L. "Al," **B** 430

Ortiz, Carlos J., **I** 363, 368, *444-45*

Ortiz, Manuel, **I** *447-48*

Orton, George W., **F** 231; **O** *511-12*

Osborn, Harold M., **O** 482, *512-14*

Osborne, Margaret, *See* Margaret Osborne duPont

Osborne, Thomas W. "Tom," **F** *443-44,* 507, 582

Osburn, Ruth, **S** 574

Oshkosh, WI All-Stars basketball club (NBL), **I** 85, 110; **S** 277, 283, 293, 309, 333

Oshkosh, WI baseball club (NWL, WSL), **B** 230, 265, 347, 506

Osipowich, Albina, **I** 599

Oslo, Norway Track and Field Meet, **O** 430, 442, 450, 528, 532, 554, 564

Osmanski, William T. "Bill," **F** 12-13; **O** 554; **S** *460-61*

Osteen, Claude W., **B** 544; **S** *159-61,* 244

Osteen, David "Dave," **S** 160

Osteen, Gavin, **S** 160

O'Sullivan, Marius, **O** 533

Osuna, Rafael H., **S** 555-56, 561

Oswego, NY Indians basketball club, **S** 260

Otapolik, Hugo, **I** 639, 652

Otis, Amos J., **B** *430-31*

Ott, Melvin T. "Mel," **B** 160, 267, *431-33,* 552, 611, 638

Ottawa, Canada baseball club, **B** 55; **S** 199

Ottawa, Canada Capitols Lacrosse Club, **O** 469

Ottawa, Canada Roughriders football club (CFL), **F** 199; **S** 463

Ottawa University, **I** 268

Otten, Donald F. "Don," **I** 7

Otten, Mac W., **I** 7

Otterbein College, **B** 23; **I** 6; **S** 397

Ottey, Marlene, **S** 579

Otto, James E. "Jim," **F** 334, *445*

Ottumwa, IA baseball club (CA), **B** 65, 228

Ouachita Baptist College, **B** 278; **F** 245, 295

Ouachita Junior College, **S** 388

Ouimet, Francis de Sales, **O** 112, 121, 128, *147-48*

Ouimet, Wilfred, **O** 148

Our Boots, **O** 204

Outerbridge, Augustus, **S** 559

Outerbridge, Emilius, **O** 382

Outerbridge, Eugenius, **O** 382; **S** *559-60*

Outerbridge, Laura, **S** 560

Outerbridge, Mary E., **O** *382-83;* **S** *559-60*

Outing, **F** 231; **O** 122, 383

Outing Club, **O** 279

Outing Weekly Tennis Record, **O** 383

Outland Award, **F** 36, 51, 112, 136, 138, 176, 198, 222, 297, 307, 344, 388, 397, 431, 441, 444, 454, 490, 495, 497, 515, 537, 546, 570, 582, 585, 606, 641, 650, 667; **S** 374, 395-96, 404, 414, 431, 456, 480

Outrigger Canoe Club Water Race, **I** 495

Outstanding Athlete Award, Penn Relays, **S** 568

Outstanding Back and Passer Award, SEC, **S** 463

Outstanding Lifter Award, **O** 631

Outstanding Lineman Award, Orange Bowl, **S** 403-04

Outstanding Umpire Award, *The Sporting News,* **S** 121

Overall, Orval, **S** *161-62*

Overlin, "Ken," **I** 466, 481

Overseas Crusade basketball club, **I** 8

Ovett, "Steve," **O** 532

Owen, Arnold M. "Mickey," **B** 366; **S** 86

Owen, Benjamin G. "Bennie," **F** *445-46*

Owen, George, Jr., **I** 563; **S** *546-47*

Owen, Guy, **I** 515

Owen, Laurence L., **I** 515

Owen, Maribel Vinson, **I** *515-16*

Owen, Maribel Y., **I** 515

Owen, Marvin J. "Marv," **B** 396

Owen, Spike D., **S** 74

Owen, Stephen J. "Steve," **F** 4, 78, 103, 178, 215, 278, 346, *447-48,* 645

Owen, "Ted," I 324

Owen, William "Bill," F 448

Owen Field, Norman, OK, F 446

Owens, Brigman "Brig," F 480

Owens, "Eddie," I 293

Owens, James "Jim," F 78, 288, 515;
S *461-62*

Owens, James C. "Jesse," I 612, 615,
662; O 432-33, 452-53, 466, 473,
476, 486, 496, 501-02, *514-16,*
546, 552, 561, 563, 568; S 566,
568, 591, 594

Owens, "Lem," S 127

Owens, Loren E. "Steve," F *448-49,*
546; S 405

Owens, Marvin D. "Marv," F 480

Owens, Raleigh C., F 600

Owens, Thomas W. "Tom," I 142

Owensboro, KY baseball club (KL), B
279; S 163, 190

Oxford-Cambridge Lacrosse Club, O
245, 249

Oxford-Cambridge Tennis Tournament,
S 501

Oxford-Cambridge Track and Field
club, O 431-32, 439

Oxford University, I 380, 590; O
260-61, 548

Ozark Amateur Athletic Union Boxing
Tournament, I 427

Ozark Amateur Athletic Union District
Track and Field Championships, O
546, 555

Ozarks, College of the, F 390

Pabst Women's Open Golf
Tournament, O 129

Pacheco, "Tony," S 25

Pacific Association, I 498, 619

Pacific Association Track and Field
Championships, S 575

Pacific Coast Athletic Association, F
115; I 292-93, 616

Pacific Coast Athletic Conference, S
310

Pacific Coast Conference, F 2, 23,
66, 113-14, 127, 153, 160, 169,
207, 220-21, 256, 299-300, 313,
321, 335, 365, 369, 378, 410, 424,
471, 491-92, 512-15, 523, 528,
533, 536, 538-39, 552, 595, 617,
627, 636-39, 645, 662; I 37, 55,
63, 76, 91, 93, 96, 101, 131, 134,
172, 187, 274, 330, 497; O 493,
545; S 423, 445, 453, 468, 484,
495-96, 503, 574, 580, 586-88,
590

Pacific Coast Conference
Championships, S 38, 197-98,
588

Pacific Coast Conference Coaches
Association, F 523

Pacific Coast Golf
Interchampionships, O 138

Pacific Coast League, B 16, 90, 122,
360, 569, 594, 612; O 208; S 2,
4-6, 8, 12, 16, 20-21, 23-24, 46,
52-53, 59, 61-62, 67-68, 78-80,
90, 93-94, 101, 103, 105-07, 109-
12, 114, 116, 118, 134-36, 138,
156-57, 160-63, 166, 177, 184-85,
195, 197-98, 232, 243, 247, 355-
56

Pacific Coast League's Hall of Fame,
S 197

Pacific Coast Professional Football
League, F 638

Pacific Coast Professional Football
League Championship Game, F
638

Pacific Coast States Diving
Championships, I 490

Pacific Coast States Figure Skating
Championships, I 510

Pacific Coast States Tennis
Championships, O 353, 361-62,

368, 371
Pacific Coast States Wrestling
    Championships, I 655-56
Pacific Eight Conference, F 32, 190,
    206, 288-89, 351, 369, 411, 472-
    73, 485, 501, 544, 580, 648, 667;
    I 331; O 461, 518; S 251, 326-
    28, 409, 427, 442, 454, 479-80,
    493
Pacific Eight Conference
    Championships, O 424, 518; S
    251, 259, 285
Pacific International League, S 70, 79
Pacific Lutheran University, I 115-16
Pacific North-West Alpine Ski
    Competition, O 277
Pacific Northwest Amateur Wrestling
    Championships, I 656
Pacific Northwest League, S 209
Pacific Northwest Open Golf
    Tournament, O 109, 114
Pacific Northwest Ski Association, O
    278
Pacific Side baseball club, I 332
Pacific Southwest Tennis
    Championships, O 347, 409; S
    549-50, 553
Pacific Southwestern Conference, F
    135
Pacific Ten Conference, B 16; F 157,
    161-62, 227, 324; I 116, 216-17;
    O 528; S 251-52, 259, 278, 285,
    310, 392, 468, 579
Pacific Ten Conference
    Championships, S 252, 310, 468
Pacific University, O 464, 469
Paciorek, Thomas M. "Tom," S 244
Packard Motor Company, O 7- 8, 23
Packer, "Billy," I 197
Paddock, Charles W. "Charlie," O
    444, 455, *516-17*, 531, 558, 567;
    S 589
Paddock's Club, Hialeah Park, O 205

Paducah, KY baseball club (KL), I
    165
Pafko, Andrew "Andy," S 142, *162-
    63*
Page, Alan C., F 277, *451-52*, 458;
    S 450
Page, Estelle Lawson, O 110-11
Page, Harlan O. "Pat," I 129, *235-
    37*
Page, Joseph F. "Joe," B 469
Page, Theodore "Ted," B 31, 88
Page Fence Giants baseball club,
    Adrian, MI, B 195, 286
Pagna, Thomas "Tom," F 458
Paige, Leroy R. "Satchel," B 31-32,
    127, 192, 213, 223-24, 269, 271-
    72, 290, 331, *435-37*, 453, 466,
    520, 574, 609, 613; S 9, 83, 99,
    189
Pails, "Dinny," O 390
Paines, Ralph, F 373
Pairbypair, O 196
Pakermo, "Frankie," I 477
Palace, Fred, B 482
Palafax, Anthony "Tony," O 369
Palau, Andrew "Andy," F 353
Palestinian, O 178
Palfrey, Sarah, *See* Sarah Palfrey
    Fabyan Cooke Danzig
Palin, "Sep," O 586-87
Palm, Wiking, I 665
Palm Beach County Hall of Fame, S
    266
Palm Beach Gardens Golf Club, O
    117
Palm Beach Handicap, O 205
Palm Festival, F 188
Palmberg, "Wally," I 97
Palmer, Arnold D. "Arnie," O 60,
    112, 114-15, 120, 143, 146-47,
    148-50, 167; S 519
Palmer, James A. "Jim," B *437-38*;
    S 355-56

Palmer, Leonard, **I** 273

Palmer, Milfred J. "Deacon," **O** 148-49

Palmer, Pedlar, **I** 434

Palmer, Pete, **S** 82

Palmer Stadium, Princeton, NJ, **F** 309

Palomer Junior College, **F** 135

Pan American Exposition, Buffalo, NY, **S** 289

Pan-American Federation of Basketball, **I** 326; **S** 279

Pan-American Games, **S** 259, 296, 302, 320, 568, 570-71, 577-78, 583-84, 595, 597; 1947, **O** 309; 1951, **I** 626; **O** 255; 1955, **I** 253, 485, 528, 606, 638-39, 676; **O** 477, 509, 538; 1959, **I** 182, 246, 277, 326, 528-29, 610, 613, 638; **S** 435, 456, 478, 509; 1963, **I** 55, 123, 247, 497, 528-29, 613-14, 650; **O** 433, 457; 1967, **I** 165, 323, 489, 534, 576, 612, 617, 619, 650; **S** 428, 458, 494, 499, 533, 550, 553; 1971, **I** 193, 246, 489, 497, 534, 639, 642, 650, 663; **S** 497, 536; 1975, **I** 72, 116, 175, 258, 290-91, 609, 654; **S** 475; 1979, **I** 59, 72-73, 162, 291, 296, 298, 491, 591, 593, 605, 607; **O** 425, 436, 480, 485, 506; 1983, **I** 153, 214, 304, 329; 1987, **I** 56, 215, 492, 523, 658-59; **O** 425, 482, 487, 532-33

Pan-American Games Committee, **I** 307

Pan Pacific Games, **I** 583, 592

Pan Pacific Swim Championships, **S** 603, 607

Panasonic-Las Vegas Invitation Golf Tournament, **S** 519

Pancho Segura's Championship Strategy, **S** 551-52

Panhandle-Pecos Valley League, **S** 235

Panhandle Sports Hall of Fame, **I** 246

Panteleo, "Joe," **I** 645

Panty Raid, **O** 182

Papaleo, Guglielmo, *See* Willie Pep

Papke, William H., Sr. "Billy," **I** 414, 416, *448*

Papke, William H., Jr., **I** 448

Papp, **S** 527

Pappas, Milton S. "Milt," **B** *438-39;* **S** 175

Papyrus, **S** 527

Parade, **F** 8, 139, 149, 547, 629; **I** 183, 214; **O** 493; **S** 280

Paraguay National Soccer Team, **O** 29

Paramount News, **F** 515

Pardee, John P. "Jack," **F** 74, 593

Parent, Frederick A. "Fred," **B** 91

Paret, Benny "Kid," **I** 395

Paret, Jahail Parmly, **O** 325, *383-84,* 413

Parham, "Joe," **I** 395

Parilli, Vito "Babe," **F** 74, 198-99; **S** *462-64*

Paris, France Track and Field Meet, **O** 432, 504, 516

Parke, James C. "J. C.," **O** 362, 366

Parke H. Davis Poll, **S** 477

Parker, "Charley," **I** 342

Parker, Clarence M. "Ace," **F** *452-53,* 626

Parker, David G. "Dave," **B** *439-40*

Parker, Frank A., **O** 324, 355, 365, *384,* 389; **S** 553, 557

Parker, James T. "Jim," **F** 26, 165, *453-54*

Parker, Raymond K. "Buddy," **F** 341, *454-56,* 528; **S** 438, 467

Parker, Robert, **F** 455

Parkville Lacrosse Club, **O** 303

Parma, George, **O** 379

Parmalee, LeRoy E. "Roy," **B** 593; **S**

116

Parnell, Melvin L. "Mel," S *163-64*
Parnell Ranch, S 529
Parnelli Jones Enterprises, S 614
Parole, O 201
Parratt, George W. "Peggy," F *456-57*
Parrish, Lance M., S 225
Parseghian, Ara R., F 74, 211, 276, *457-59*, 526, 572; S 311, 379
Parshall, "Doc," O 207
Parsons College, S 319
Parsons, KS baseball club (MVL), B 2
Partilla, "Ray," I 363
Partlow, Roy, B 453
Partners of the Americas Sports Exchange, I 95
Pasadena, CA Athletic Association, O 509
Pasadena, CA Athletic Club, S 574
Pasadena City College, I 292
Pasadena Junior College, S 50, 475
Pasadena *Star-News,* O 517; S 500
Pasarell, Charles, O 356
Pasek, John P., B 101
Pasha, O 200
Paskert, George H. "Dode," B 611
Passaic, NJ High School, I 28-29, 253-54, 316
Passeau, Claude W., B 616; S *164*
Pasteurized, O 223
Pastime Athletic Club, O 268
Pastor, "Bob," I 367, 424, 458
Pastorella, O 578
Pastorini, Dante A., Jr. "Dan," F 180, 473, 562
Patek, Frederick J. "Freddie," S 237
Patenaude, Bertram "Bert," O *305-06*
Patera, John A. "Jack," F 363
Paterno, Joseph V. "Joe," F 93, 164, 394, *457-59*, 526, 572; S 459
Paterson, NJ baseball club (AtL), B

25

Paterson, NJ basketball club (ABL, ISL), I 30, 222-23, 261
Paterson, NJ football club, O 293, 306
Paterson, NJ Olympics baseball club, B 303
Pathe News, O 49
Patrick, Gilbert "Gil," O 187, 594
Patrick, Lester "Les," I 537
Patten, Case L. "Casey," B 547
Patten, "Chuck," I 646
Patterson, Floyd, I 427, 442, *448-49;* O 59; S 625
Patterson, Gerald L., O 362
Patterson, "Pat," I 340, 350
Patterson, Scott, B 595
Patterson, William "Billy," F 293
Patton, Melvin E. "Mel," O 444, 453, 558-59; S 577, *590-91*, 594
Patty, J. Edward "Budge," S 558
Patty Berg Golf Classic, O 118
Patucci, "Pat," I 440
Patulski, Walter G. "Walt," F 458
Paul, "Don," F 640
Paul, Gabriel H., Sr. "Gabe," B 125, 134, 215, *441-42*
Paul, Gabriel H., Jr., B 441
Paul, Lee, O 589
Paul, Robert "Bob," I 504
Paul, "Tommy," I 417, 438
Paul Jones, O 596
Paulen, Adrian, O 533
Paulette, Eugene E., B 323
Pauley, Edwin, F 493
Pauley Pavilion, Los Angeles, CA, I 331
Paulk, Charles "Charlie," I 251
Pavelich, Mark, I *567-68*
Pavot, O 175
Pawson, Leslie, S 582
Pawtucket, RI baseball club (EL, IL), B 115, 182, 341, 471; S 37

Paxton, Claude, O 497
Payne, Cecil, I 438
Payton, Walter J., F 9, 62, 68, 246-47, 395, *461-62*, 494; S 379
PDM Dutch Cycling Team, S 617
Peabody Award, S 336
Peabody College, S 368
Peabody Institute, O 250
Peach Blossom Golf Tournament, O 152
Peach Bowl football game, F 324, 355, 650; S 369, 402
Peak Performance 500 NASCAR Race, S 606
Peale, Norman Vincent, S 508
Pearce, Richard J. "Dickey," B *442-43*
Pearce, Robert E. "Bob," I 653
Pearl Harbor Navy All-Stars, F 305
Pearless Green Dragon Racing Car, O 26
Pearson, Charles M., F 609; S 489
Pearson, David G., O 1, *27-28*, 30, 41, 44
Pearson, Drew, F *462-63*, 592
Pearson, "Larry," O 27
Pearson, Leonard "Len," B 141
Pebble Beach, CA National Pro-Am Golf Tournament, O 144
Peck, Robert D., Jr. "Bob," F 200, *463-64*
Peckington, John, B 576
Peckinpaugh, Roger T., B 179; S 14, *164-65*
Pedestrian, O 559
Pedroso, Eusaquio, S 224
Pedroso, Fernando, S 10
Peekskill, NY basketball club, I 305
Pegler, James Westbrook, F 378; O 64, *84-85*
Peile, S. C. F., O 392
Pelham, NY Golf Club, O 109
Pell, Charles, S 399-400

Pell, Theodore R. "Teddy," O 378
Pellegrini, Robert "Bob," F *464-65*
Pellington, William "Bill," F 165
Pen-Del Lacrosse Coaches Association, O 236
Pena, "Johnny," I 438
Pender, Melvin "Mel," O 472
Pender, Paul, I 359, 456
Pendleton, OR softball club, O 257
Penick, Daniel, O 322
Peninger, Grady, I 664
Peninsula baseball club (CrL, IL), B 33, 76, 369; S 51, 170
Penn Athletic Sporting Goods, S 293
Penn Bicycle Club basketball club (NPBL, HRL), I 222-23
Penn National Race Track, Harrisburg, PA, O 203, 223
Penn Relays, F 171, 413; O 441, 462-63, 466, 489, 506, 512, 532; S 343, 568, 581, 591-92, 596
Penn State University, B 452, 591; F 35, 46, 65, 93, 164, 181, 200, 204, 209, 224, 235, 242, 245-46, 379, 383, 392, 394, 399-400, 407, 427, 459-61, 469, 489-90, 502, 504, 552, 556, 581, 627, 634-35; I 179-80, 184, 209-10, 238, 302, 541-42, 636, 642, 646; O 292, 423; S 358, 369, 414, 418, 459, 487, 576, 610
Pennant, S 533
Pennick, Harvey, S 510
Pennock, Herbert J. "Herb," B 74-75, 269, *443-44;* S 203
Pennsylvania-Delaware League, O 235-36
Pennsylvania-Delaware League Lacrosse Championships, O 235-36
Pennsylvania Grass Tennis Championships, O 394
Pennsylvania Military College, O 98

Pennsylvania Open Golf
Championships, **O** 141
Pennsylvania Sports Hall of Fame, **B**
396; **F** 39, 259, 341; **I** 11, 62,
179; **O** 270, 296; **S** 29, 358, 418-
19, 482
Pennsylvania State Association, **S**
113
Pennsylvania State Boxing
Commission, **O** 481
Pennsylvania State League, **I** 14, 21,
65, 88, 250; **S** 86, 240
Pennsylvania State Squash
Championships, **O** 270
Pennsylvania State Tennis
Championships, **O** 270, 417
Pennsylvania Wrestling Hall of Fame,
I 647-48
Pensacola, FL baseball club, **F** 522
Pensacola, FL Naval Air Station, **F**
568
Pensacola, FL Open Golf Tournament,
S 516, 519
Pensive, **O** 195, 205
Penske, Roger, **O** *28-29,* 37; **S** 606
Penske Auto Racing Team, **O** 29, 36
People to People Basketball Tour, **I**
321
People to People Sports Committee, **I**
380
Peoples, Robert "Bob," **I** 625
People's Republic of China Volleyball
Team, **S** 613
Peoria, IL baseball club (CA, CL,
3IL, WL), **B** 80, 353, 401, 572; **S**
13, 45
Peoria, IL Caterpillar Diesels
basketball club (AAU), **I** 172, 210
Peoria, IL Reds baseball club (Ind.), **B**
463
Peoria, IL Sportswriters Association,
O 53
Pep, "Willie," **I** 447, *449-51,* 461-62

Peppe, Michael "Mike," **I** 603
Pepperdine College, **I** 74-75, 144
Pepperdine College Athletic Hall of
Fame, **I** 75
Pepsi 400 NASCAR Race, **S** 606
Pepsi Invitation Track and Field Meet,
O 482, 486
Perez, Atanasio R. "Tony," **B** 486; **S**
157, *165-66*
Perez, Victor "Young," **I** 389
Perfection, **O** 201
Performance of the Year Award,
LPGA, **S** 517
Perkins, Donald A. "Don," **F** 331,
466
Perkins, Ralph F. "Cy," **B** 101, 119
Perkins, Samuel B. "Sam," **I** 282
Perkins, Walter Ray, **F** 75
Pernfors, Michael, **O** 342
Perranoski, Ronald P. "Ron," **S** *166-
67*
Perranoski, Stanley "Stan," **S** 166-67
Perreault, **O** 229
Perry, Curtis R., **I** 230
Perry, "Doyt," **F** 526
Perry, Fletcher Joseph "Joe," **F** 294,
467-68, 600
Perry, Frederick J. "Fred," **O** 322,
330-31, 343, 395-96, 410, 418
Perry, Gaylord I., **B** *444-46,* 505; **S**
30, 120
Perry, Herbert Scott, **B** 550
Perry, James E. "Jim," **B** *444-46;* **S**
145
Perry, Timothy D. "Tim," **S** 268
Perry, William, **I** 403
Perry Medal, **O** 278
Personality, **O** 192-93
Peru National Tennis Championships,
O 343
Perzanowski, Ronald, *See* Ronald
Perranoski
Pesgrave, William, **O** 201

Pesky, John M. "Johnny," **B** *446-47*
Pete Rose: My Story, **S** 352
Peter Jackson Golf Classic, **S** 518-19
Peter Pan, **O** 196, 211; **S** 533
Peter Quince, **S** 533
Peter the Great, **O** 185, 586
Peters, Donald "Don," **I** 533
Petersburg, VA baseball club (VL), **B** 92, 326, 470
Peterson, Benjamin L. "Ben," **I** 652, *653-54,* 655
Peterson, Douglas "Doug," **O** 606
Peterson, Henry, **O** 461
Peterson, John A., **I** 654, *655*
Peterson, Mark, **O** *306*
Peterson, William "Bill," **F** 206, 210
Petillo, Kelly, **O** 9, 35
Petoskey, "Ted," **S** 458
Petrarca of Padua basketball club (ItL), **S** 304
Petrie, Geoffrey M. "Geoff," **I** 53
Petrolle, "Frankie," **I** 451
Petrolle, "Pete," **I** 451
Petrolle, William M. "Billy," **I** 392, 435, *451-52*
Petronelli, "Goody," **I** 397
Petroskey, George, **I** 416
Pettenghill, E. H., **O** 199
Pettengill's Stable, **O** 219
Pettis, Gary G., **S** 215
Pettit, Robert L., Jr. "Bob," **I** 109, 111, 113, 124, 133, 190, *237-38*
Petty, Jesse L., **B** 553, 626
Petty, Kyle, **O** 30, **S** 605
Petty, Lee, **O** 27, 29
Petty, Maurice, **O** 30
Petty, Richard, **O** 1-2, 27, *29-31,* 41, 44; **S** 605
Petway, Bruce, **B** 255, 286, 333, 533, 553; **S** 143, *167-68*
Peyton, Baillie, **O** 602
Peytona, **O** 583, *602*
Pfann, George R., **F** *468-69;* **S** 431

Pfeffer, Nathaniel Frederick "Fred," **S** *168-69*
Pfeiffers Bowling Team, Detroit, MI, **I** 348
Phagan, "Johnny," **I** 482
Pharmer, Arthur "Art," **F** 415
Phelan, James J. "Jim," **I** 180
Phelps, Richard "Digger," **S** *311-12*
Phelps, William Lyon, **O** 71, 376
Philadelphia Athletics baseball club (AA), **B** 117, 126, 363, 389, 481, 541; **S** 119
Philadelphia Athletics baseball club (AL), **B** 19, 34, 46, 65, 99, 101-05, 112-13, 118-19, 126, 145, 156-57, 162-63, 170, 181, 195-97, 208, 211, 228-29, 231-33, 254-55, 266, 275, 279-80, 287-88, 290-91, 299-300, 302, 311, 322, 333, 343, 348, 353, 357-59, 377, 383, 387, 390, 401, 406, 408, 443-44, 450, 452, 459, 483-84, 500, 509-12, 523, 529, 537, 550, 553, 574, 579-80, 601, 621, 634-36; **F** 40-41, 453; **I** 332, 340; **S** 1, 13, 21, 37, 52, 59, 66, 72, 79, 81, 127, 154, 161, 171, 177, 189-90, 196, 200, 207, 209, 231, 240-41, 247, 342
Philadelphia Athletics baseball club (NA), **B** 11, 128, 270, 399, 465
Philadelphia Athletics baseball club (NL), **B** 60, 271, 399, 465, 481
Philadelphia Atoms Soccer Club (NASL), **O** 307-08
Philadelphia baseball club (PL), **B** 59, 126, 224, 507
Philadelphia basketball club (EL), **I** 32, 333
Philadelphia Bell football club (WFL), **F** 2, 662
Philadelphia College of Osteopathy, **O** 513
Philadelphia Cricket Club, **O** 108,

321, 405; **S** 418, 562

Philadelphia Cricket Team, **S** 616

Philadelphia Cuban X-Giants baseball club (Negro Leagues), **B** 189, 286, 333

Philadelphia Eagles football club (NFL), **F** 2, 12, 33-34, 45, 48, 70-71, 96, 100, 118, 131, 135, 143, 152, 180, 197, 207, 210, 218, 220, 243, 249, 263, 277, 279-80, 282, 285, 303-05, 314-16, 320, 323, 331, 354, 363-65, 373, 375-76, 387, 393, 399-400, 421, 437, 448, 462, 464, 470-71, 473, 478-79, 496, 502, 511, 536, 538-40, 550, 566-67, 576, 580, 591, 615, 617-20, 631-33, 642, 656, 660-61, 670; **O** 436; **S** 364-65, 427, 437-38, 462, 466-67, 478, 482, 488-89, 491

Philadelphia *Evening Telegraph*, **F** 350

Philadelphia Fever Soccer Club (MISL), **O** 308

Philadelphia Flyers hockey club (NHL), **I** 551, 557-59, 570

Philadelphia Freedoms Tennis Club (WTT), **O** 364

Philadelphia Fury Soccer Club (NASL), **O** 307-08

Philadelphia Giants baseball club (Negro Leagues), **B** 189, 255, 286, 333, 451, 465, 500, 519; **I** 332; **S** 142-43, 168, 238

Philadelphia Giants basketball club, **I** 49

Philadelphia Half-Marathon, **O** 529

Philadelphia Hilldale baseball club (ANL, ECL), **B** 88, 147, 290, 334, 338, 362, 482, 500, 553, 609; **I** 332; **S** 137, 242

Philadelphia Hockey Association, **O** 270

Philadelphia *Inquirer,* **F** 309; **O** 270

Philadelphia Jaspers basketball club, **I** 273

Philadelphia Keystones baseball club (UA), **B** 399

Philadelphia Lacrosse Club, **O** 235

Philadelphia League, **I** 20

Philadelphia Nationals Soccer Club (ASL), **O** 291

Philadelphia *North-American,* **O** 406; **S** 342

Philadelphia Open Golf Tournament, **O** 140

Philadelphia Panthers basketball club, **I** 49

Philadelphia Passions Soccer Club, **O** 306

Philadelphia Phillies baseball club (NL), **B** 4-9, 15, 20-21, 27, 34-35, 42, 48, 52, 59, 61-62, 66, 73-75, 87, 92, 106, 111, 113, 120, 125-26, 133, 143, 154, 156, 159, 161, 168, 174, 183-84, 186-87, 197, 206, 215, 238, 245, 250, 281, 291, 295-96, 298, 301, 308-09, 313-14, 316, 321-23, 329-30, 337, 340, 347-48, 357-58, 373, 379, 405-06, 420, 425, 430-31, 444, 452, 460-61, 465, 468, 474-77, 486, 502, 507, 526, 534, 544, 554, 556, 559, 562, 567, 588, 590-91, 600, 602, 607, 611-12, 621-22, 628; **F** 111, 403, 420; **I** 105, 149; **S** 4-5, 15-16, 20, 22-23, 32, 39, 42, 47, 55, 58, 60, 63, 65-66, 75-76, 78, 83, 92-93, 95-96, 104-05, 108, 110-11, 118-19, 123, 128, 132, 134-35, 139, 144, 152, 155-57, 159-60, 164, 166, 171, 173, 179, 183, 185, 191, 196-97, 202-03, 209, 216, 218-20, 232, 237, 239-40, 354-55

Philadelphia *Record,* **F** 204, 269; **O** 96

Philadelphia 76ers basketball club (NBA), **I** 17, 26, 33, 46-47, 50, 58, 82, 89, 103-04, 111, 122, 136, 146, 159, 165, 189, 196, 203, 219, 224, 243-44, 249, 262, 271, 278, 302, 311, 315, 317; **S** 257, 268-69, 291-92

Philadelphia Soccer Club (ASL), **O** 305

Philadelphia Spartans Soccer Club (ASL, NPSL), **O** 292

Philadelphia SPHAS basketball club (EBL, ABL), **I** 14, 102, 178; **S** 309

Philadelphia Sportswriters Association, **B** 20

Philadelphia Stars baseball club (NNL), **B** 88, 141, 150, 338-39, 362, 533, 543, 620; **S** 99

Philadelphia Stars basketball club, **I** 143, 332

Philadelphia Stars football club (USFL), **F** 7, 99; **S** 254

Philadelphia Tigers baseball club, **I** 332

Philadelphia Track and Field Classic, **O** 488

Philadelphia Turnverein Society, **I** 529-30

Philadelphia Ukrainians Soccer Club (ASL), **O** 291

Philadelphia Urik Truckers Soccer Club (ASL), **O** 291, 293

Philadelphia Warriors basketball club (BAA, NBA), **I** 10-11, 14, 45-46, 50-51, 89, 100, 102-03, 120, 149, 178-79, 198-99, 235, 239, 252, 268, 277, 282; **S** 256, 316

Philadelphias Independent baseball club, **S** 177

Philadelphia's Olympics baseball club, **B** 627

Philippine Baseball League, **B** 87

Philippine National Soccer Team, **O** 301

Phillip, Andrew M. "Andy," **I** 51, *238-39*

Phillippe, Charles L. "Deacon," **B** 90, 95, 158, 327, *447-48*

Phillips, O. A., **F** 63, 87-88

Phillips 66ers/Oilers basketball club (AAU), **I** 77, 160, 138-39, 166, 172, 180, 188, 192-93, 326-27

Phillips University, **F** 447; **I** 275-76, 325-26

Phipps, Michael E. "Mike," **F** 633

Phipps, Mrs. Henry Carnegie, **O** 184, 572

Phipps, Ogden, **O** 181, 575-76

Phoenician Swim Club, Phoenix, AZ, **S** 621

Phoenix, AZ Auto Race, **O** 37

Phoenix, AZ baseball club (ArTL, ASL, PCL), **B** 39, 191, 351, 385; **S** 59, 103, 134

Phoenix, AZ Hotel Stakes, **O** 209

Phoenix, AZ 100 USAC Race, **S** 614

Phoenix, AZ 150 Auto Race, **O** 18

Phoenix, AZ Open Golf Tournament, **O** 127, 143-44; **S** 520, 523

Phoenix, AZ Racquets Tennis Club (WTT), **O** 352

Phoenix, AZ Road Race, **O** 528

Phoenix, AZ Roadrunners hockey club (WHA), **I** 553-54

Phoenix, AZ Stadium, **B** 277

Phoenix, AZ Suns basketball club (NBA), **I** 101, 124, 144-45, 147-48, 160, 249, 279, 310-11; **O** 429; **S** 275, 288, 301, 326-27, 331

Phoenix, AZ Valvoline 200 Cart Race, **S** 620

Physical Education, **I** 1, 108

Pian, "Sam," **I** 459

Pic, **F** 77

Picard, Henry B., **O** *150;* **S** 515

Piccolo, **O** 223

Piccolo, Louis Brian, **F** 248, 349, 524, 548

Piccolo Award, **B** 422; **F** 248, 349, 548

Pickering Hunt Club, **O** 340

Pico Peak Ski Competition, **O** 283-84

Piedmont College, **B** 403

Piedmont League, **S** 3, 6, 17, 20, 33, 87, 135, 153, 195, 204, 207, 228, 230, 234

Pierce, Bemus, **F** *469-70*

Pierce, Walter William "Billy," **B** *448-49;* **S** 106

Pierce Junior College, **I** 55

Piersall, James A. "Jimmy," **S** 95

Pietri, Dorando, **O** 467

Pihos, Peter "Pete," **F** *470-71*

Pike, Milo, **O** 68

Pike's Peak Auto Race, **O** 23, 37-38

Pike's Peak Climb, **S** 614

Pilgrim, Paul H., **O** 471, 488

Pilot, James "Jim," **F** 663

Pilot, Jr., **O** 174

The Pilot Light and the Gas House Gang, **S** 338

Pim, Joshua, **O** 366, 414

Pimlico Cup, **O** 582

Pimlico Futurity Stakes, **O** 194, 198, 216, 231, 576

Pimlico Invitation Stakes, **O** 577

Pimlico Race Track, Baltimore, MD, **I** 407; **O** 173, 176, 179, 184, 186-87, 193-94, 200-03, 206, 208-09, 212, 216, 218, 221, 231, 571, 592, 605; **S** 535-36; *See also* The Preakness

Pimlico Special Stakes, **O** 614-15

Pimlico Stakes, **O** 201, 597

Pincay, La Fitt, Jr., **O** 203, 570, 611

Pinckert, Erny, **F** 299, *471-72*, 512

Pinckney, Edward L. "Ed," **S** 254

Pine Bluff Judges baseball club, **F** 281

Pine Hollow Stud Farm, **O** 600

Pine Needle Golf Club, **O** 165

Pine Valley Golf Club, **S** 418

Pineapple Bowl football game, **F** 637

Piniella, Louis V. "Lou," **B** 386; **S** *169-70*

Pinkston, Clarence E., **I** 486, 498

Pinson, Vada E., Jr., **B** 185, *449-50*

Pinto, Donna de Varona, **I** *610-12*

Pioneer football club, Fall River, MA, **O** 299

Pioneer in Pro Football, **S** 387

Pioneer League, **B** 22; **S** 24, 30, 88, 90, 109, 128

Pipp, Walter C. "Wally," **B** 156, 193

Pirrone, Paul, **I** 481

Pit Crew Championship, **S** 605

Pitcher of the Year Award, **S** 63, 90, 93, 132, 180, 211, 214, 243

Pitts, Elijah E., **F** 354; **S** 414

Pitts, Frank, **S** 414

Pittsburg State Teachers College, **S** 112

Pittsburgh Athletic Club, **F** 177

Pittsburgh baseball club (AA), **S** 82, 155

Pittsburgh baseball club (PL), **B** 29, 117, 207, 240, 549

Pittsburgh City Hall of Fame, **O** 296

Pittsburgh Colored Giants baseball club (Negro Leagues), **B** 287

Pittsburgh Condors basketball club (ABA), **I** 20, 149-50; **S** 292

Pittsburgh *Courier,* **B** 363, 378, 453, 600, 613; **F** 539; **S** 10, 189

Pittsburgh Crawfords baseball club (NNL), **B** 31, 88, 127, 147, 150, 213, 223-24, 244, 289-91, 436, 453, 543, 620; **I** 426; **S** 9-10

Pittsburgh Dapper Dan Club, **F** 198

Pittsburgh Feds baseball club (FL), **B**

313; **S** 85
Pittsburgh hockey club (AHAUS, AHL), **I** 421; **S** 537
Pittsburgh Keystones baseball club (Negro Leagues), **B** 453; **S** 238
Pittsburgh Maulers football club (USFL), **F** 519
Pittsburgh Penguins hockey club (NHL), **I** 551; **S** 540, 544
Pittsburgh Pipers basketball club (ABA), **S** 288, 292-93
Pittsburgh Pirates baseball club (NL), **B** 2-3, 25, 27-30, 61, 72, 90-91, 94-95, 97-98, 105, 110, 113-14, 118, 123, 128, 140, 154, 156, 158, 163, 167, 173-74, 200, 203, 206-07, 210, 215, 217, 220, 222, 228-29, 231, 240, 246, 250, 256, 266, 268-69, 283, 289, 301, 303, 306-07, 309, 312-13, 326-28, 332, 337, 350-51, 357-58, 360-61, 372-73, 376-77, 379, 384, 395, 401, 408, 417, 425, 431, 439-40, 444, 447, 453, 457, 460, 473, 476, 482, 484, 510, 515-16, 524, 530-31, 534, 544, 547, 550, 559, 562, 567-70, 575-76, 579-82, 589-91, 595, 600, 604, 617-18, 626, 636; **F** 9, 46, 202, 290, 314, 358, 374, 453; **I** 105; **O** 65, 83; **S** 6, 15, 19-21, 24-25, 33, 35, 37, 39, 41, 47, 58-60, 62-63, 69-71, 73, 75-76, 84-85, 105-06, 110-11, 115-16, 119-21, 131, 135, 150, 164-65, 174-75, 179-80, 184, 189, 191, 195-97, 209-10, 216-20, 222, 228, 230, 243, 358, 401, 440
Pittsburgh Pirates football club (NFL), **F** 278, 315, 374-75, 511, 647; **S** 481, 488
Pittsburgh *Post-Gazette,* **F** 383
Pittsburgh *Press,* **F** 200, 556
Pittsburgh Rens basketball club (ABL), **S** 288
Pittsburgh Stars football club (NFL), **F** 41
Pittsburgh Steelers football club (NFL), **F** 25, 34, 56, 63, 73, 79-80, 105, 133, 150, 155, 180, 218-19, 221-23, 235-36, 246, 263, 292-94, 303, 315, 327, 330, 333, 339, 341, 348, 363, 375-76, 384, 397, 404-05, 408-09, 421, 432-33, 454, 461, 510-11, 528, 536, 553, 558, 565, 568-70, 580-81, 590, 613, 642-43, 657; **O** 296; **S** 285, 358, 366-67, 385, 398-99, 407, 414-15, 426, 432, 437-38, 463, 467, 481, 488, 611
Pitsburgh Yellowjackets hockey club, **I** 547
Pittsfield, MA baseball club (EL), **B** 182, 339, 372, 518; **S** 193, 213
Pittsfield, MA Country Club, **O** 107
Pizarro, Juan R., **S** 243
Pizza Hut College All-Star basketball game, **S** 268
Pladner, Emile "Spider," **I** 389
Plainfield Country Club, Edison Township, NH, **O** 164
Plank, Edward S. "Eddie," **B** 112, 255, 287, 333, 359, *450-51,* 456, 579-80; **S** 137, 161, 199, 241
Platon, **O** 173
Plattsburg, NY baseball club (Ind.), **B** 509
Plaudit, **O** 220
Playboy, **S** 337
Player, Gary J., **O** 135, 159
Player of the Month Award, **S** 34, 44, 136, 331
Player of the Year Award, **S** 11, 52, 71, 78, 89, 142, 192, 204, 212, 225, 228, 236, 253-54, 257-58, 261-63, 271, 274, 278, 280, 282, 292, 294-95, 303, 315-17, 322,

327, 366, 373, 383, 389, 395, 402, 404, 406, 414-16, 433-34, 442-44, 458, 465, 473, 480, 487, 494, 505, 508, 513-14, 517, 519-20, 522, 613

Player's Challenge Tennis Championships, **O** 397

Players League, **B** 83, 303, 528, 592, 604; **S** 100, 151, 155, 178, 198, 215

Players League Championships, **S** 151, 178

Playfour Track, Spokane, WA, **O** 193

Playground and Recreation Association of America, **I** 108

Playoff Bowl football game, **S** 426

Pleasant Colony, **O** 183

Pleasant Valley Golf Classic, **O** 124

Plimpton, George A., **F** 405

Plough, the Loom, and the Anvil, **O** 95

Plunkett, James W. "Jim," **F** 180, *472-73,* 577, 592

Pocahontas Stakes, **O** 597

Pocamoke City, MD baseball club (ESL), **S** 60

Pocatello, ID baseball club (UIL), **B** 35

Pocono 500 Auto Race, **O** 3, 10, 18, 21, 37, 39, 43

Podoloff, Maurice, **I** 156, *239-40;* **S** 261, 286

Podoloff Cup, **I** 240

Podres, John J. "Johnny," **S** 167

Poe, Arthur, **F** *475-76*

Poe, Edgar A. "Pete," **F** *474*

Poe, Gresham H., **F** *476*

Poe, Neilson "Net," **F** *475*

Poe, Samuel J., **F** *474*

Poe Brothers, **F** *473-76*

Poe Field, Princeton, NJ, 475

Poile, David "Dave," **S** 540

Poinsette Basketball Classic, **I** 209

Poker, **O** 606

Poland National Soccer Team, **O** 297

Poland National Track and Field Team, **O** 43, 475, 550, 555

Poland National Wrestling Team, **I** 666

Poles, Spottswood "Spot," **B** 286, 342, *451-52,* 466

Polhad, Carl, **B** 228

Police Athletic League, **I** 445

The Police Gazette, **I** 399, 475

Policowski, Daniel "Dan," **F** 456

Polish-American Hall of Fame, **B** 118; **S** 296

Polish Falcon Athletic Club Track and Field Games, **O** 555

Polk, Stuart, **O** 183

Pollard, Frederick D., Sr. "Fritz," **F** *476-78,* 498, 647

Pollard, Frederick D., Jr., **F** 478

Pollard, J. "Red," **O** 605

Pollard, James C. "Jim," **I** 63, 165, 205, 213, *240-41*

Pollard, La Taunya, **I** 315

Pollock, Andrea, **I** 579

Polo Grounds, New York, NY, **B** 3, 66, 70, 157, 310, 492, 494, 540, 551, 598-99; **F** 357, 378, 381, 386, 403, 407, 421, 651; **I** 405, 459; **O** 87, 306, 505; **S** 60, 208, 234, 342, 347, 440-41

Polynesian, **O** 599

Pomona College, **O** 357

Pompano Beach, FL baseball club (FSL), **S** 205

Pompey, **O** 183

Pompey, Yolande, **I** 442

Pompez, Allesandro, **B** 379

Pompoon, **O** 200, 614

Ponca City, OK baseball club (SSL), **B** 609

Ponce, PR baseball club (PRWL), **S** 188

Pond, Raymond W. "Ducky," F 30
Ponder, O 179, 195
Pont, John, F 526
Ponta Del Gada Soccer Club (NSL), O 309
Pontiac, O 201
Pontiac Excitement 500 NASCAR Race, S 605
Pontiac, MI Chaparrels basketball club, I 96
Pony League, S 20, 29, 32
Poock, Glenda, S 320
Pool, Robert B., O 245
Poole, G. Barney, F 621; S 385, 464-65
Poole, James "Jim," F 447, 621; S 464
Poole, Oliver, S 465
Poole, Raymond "Ray," F 621; S 464
Pop Warner Award, S 455
Popovich, Paul E., B 618
Popular Mechanics, O 122
Popular Science, S 338
Popular Sports, O 531
Poquette, Jean, O 506
Porsche Race Cars, O 11-12, 28
Port Townsend, WA baseball club (Ind.), B 324
Portage Country Club, Akron, OH, O 155
Portage Lake, MI hockey club (IL), S 546
Porter, Charles, O 456
Porter, Henry V. "H. V.," I 242-43
Porter, Kevin, I 298; S 312-13
Porter, William T., O 85-86
Porterhouse, O 189, 228-29
Portillo, Chile Ski Competition, O 281
Portland, Rene Muth, I 258
Portland, ME baseball club (NEL), B 161; S 111

Portland, ME to Chicago, IL Long Distance Walk, O 559-60
Portland, OR baseball club (NWL, PNL), B 246, 392, 507, 556; S 165, 209
Portland, OR baseball club (PCL), B 20, 49, 65, 86, 101, 200, 254, 258, 262, 284, 288, 334, 393, 436, 524, 612-13, 621; F 40; S 12, 21, 59, 70, 79, 116
Portland State University, I 656; S 330
Portland Trail Blazers basketball club (NBA), I 53, 203, 244, 278, 317-18, 327; S 254, 275-76, 304, 315, 328
Portland 200 Auto Race, O 3
Portsmouth, OH baseball club (MAL, OSL), B 8, 291, 524; S 207
Portsmouth, OH Spartans football club (NFL), F 107, 417, 480, 573; S 436
Portsmouth, VA baseball club (Pil, VL, VSL), B 197, 326, 331, 511, 547, 562, 620; F 453; S 17, 19-20, 207
Portugal National Soccer Team, O 305
Portuguese-Americans Soccer Club, Fall River, MA, O 309
Posey, Cumberland W., Jr. "Cum," B 88, 132, 147, 244, 452-54, 612; S 189
Posse, Nils, I 13
Posse Normal School of Physical Education, I 13
Post, Richard M. "Dickie," S 442
Post, Walter C. "Wally," B 125
Post Stakes, O 595
Potomac, O 177, 597; S 533
Potomac Handicap, O 595-96
Potsdam State University, F 116; I 28

Potsdam State University Hall of Fame, **I** 29

Potter, Nelson T., **B** 475

Potter Runmaker Cup, **F** 172

Pottsville, PA Club football club (AnL), **F** 259

Pottsville, PA Maroons football club (NFL), **F** 40, 98, 259, 315, 374; **S** 439

Potvin, Denis C., **I** 563

Potzsch, Annet, **I** 505-06

Pouch, Helena Hellwig, *See* Helena Hellwig

Poughkeepsie, NY baseball club (HRL), **B** 53

Poughkeepsie, NY basketball club (NYSL), **I** 223

Powell, Arthur L. "Art," **F** 179, *478-79*

Powell, Charles "Charlie," **F** 479

Powell, James "Jim," **B** 454

Powell, John Joseph "Jack," **B** *454-55;* **S** 60

Powell, John Wesley "Boog," **B** *455*

Powels, George, **B** 185

Power, Victor P. "Vic," **S** *170-71*

Powers, Michael R. "Doc," **B** 522

Powers, "Tom," **I** 473

Poynton, Dorothy, *See* Dorothy Poynton Teuber

Prairie View Agricultural & Mechanical College, **B** 114, 520; **F** 273, 499, 591; **I** 19; **S** 389

Pralle, Fred, **I** 106; **S** 302

Prasse, Erwin, **F** 13

Pratt, Derrill B. "Del," **B** *455-56;* **S** 190, 199

Pre-Olympic Figure Skating Invitational Meet, **I** 504

Preakness Stakes, **O** 173, 175-76, 185, 189-90, 197-99, 201, 203-06, 216, 218, 220, 222-27, 229, 231, 570, 572-73, 575, 577, 579, 585, 596, 598-99, 601, 606-08, 610-15; **S** 345, 527, 529-30, 534-35

Prefontaine, Linda, **O** 517

Prefontaine, Steve R., **O** 435, *517-19, 528*

Prefontaine Track and Field Classic, **O** 519

Premier, **O** 206

Prenn, Daniel, **O** 395

Prentice Cup Tennis, **S** 501

Presbyterian College, **F** 526; **I** 280

Presbyterian Theological College, Montreal, Canada, **I** 228-29

Presidential Medal of Freedom, **S** 417

President's Commission on Olympic Sports, **F** 280; **O** 497; **S** 597

President's Council on Physical Fitness and Sport, **F** 310; **I** 74, 611; **O** 83, 282; **S** 597

Presidio, CA Golf Club, **O** 138

Presnell, Glenn, **F** *479-80*

Press, William J., **I** 651

Preston North End Soccer Club, England, **O** 296

Prestwick Golf Club, **O** 158

Pretty Pose, **O** 211

Price, "Andy," **I** 422

Price, Clarence M. "Nibs," **I** 16

Price, Edward J. "Eddie," **F** 515; **S** *465-66*

Price, Ernest C., *See* Jack Dillon

Price, Peter, **S** 341

Price, William, **S** 555

Priceless Gem, **O** 192

Prichard, Vernon E. "Vern," **F** 126

Priddy, Gerald E. "Jerry," **B** 475

Priestner, "Cathy," **S** 603

Primonetta, **O** 612

Prince, John, **S** 259

Prince, Robert "Bob," **S** 349, *357-58*

Prince Charlie, **O** 604

Prince of Wales, **I** 400

Prince of Wales Conference All-Stars, I 545
Prince Royal, S 533
Prince S., O 215
Princess of Wales Stakes, O 602
Princess Rooney, O 183
Princeton Field, Princeton, NJ, F 84
Princeton University, B 113, 259, 298, 318-19; F 58, 64-65, 84-85, 108, 115-16, 119-20, 173, 176, 188, 192, 204, 238, 250, 255, 265-66, 269-70, 298-99, 309-11, 342-43, 379-80, 469, 473-76, 505, 540-41, 571, 602-03; I 31, 137, 178, 222, 259-60, 485, 497, 543-44, 556; O 61, 99, 238, 259, 320, 408, 431-32, 445, 464, 469, 550; S 297, 340, 371, 397, 433-34, 444, 453, 575
Princeton University-Cornell University Track Club, O 431-32
Princeton University Invitation Track and Field Meet, O 445
Prinstein, Meyer, O 463; S 591-92
Priscillian, O 526-27
Prize of Nations Equestrian Event, O 267
Pro Bowl football game, F 1, 3, 9, 16-17, 20, 25, 33, 36, 42, 50, 56, 59, 63, 68, 72-73, 76, 79-80, 88, 96, 101, 105-06, 111-12, 119, 121-22, 131, 135, 140-41, 143, 146, 150-51, 161, 169, 184-85, 187, 191, 198, 205, 207, 220, 222-23, 226, 229, 235-38, 245, 247, 264, 271, 274, 279, 286, 291-92, 294-95, 303-04, 312, 322, 324, 330-32, 334, 336, 339-41, 347, 351, 362-64, 367, 370, 382, 384-85, 387, 390, 394-95, 398-400, 412, 419, 423, 427, 430-31, 434, 441, 448, 451, 454, 462-63, 466, 470, 481, 483, 490-91, 493, 496, 499, 502, 509, 519, 524, 529, 539, 542, 546, 548, 550, 557, 565-66, 569, 581, 583, 585, 587-88, 593, 601, 605, 608, 610, 618, 633-35, 641, 643, 652, 658-60, 662, 667; O 468; S 364-65, 373-75, 377, 379, 383, 386, 399, 406-07, 410, 413, 415, 427, 429-30, 449, 451-52, 467-68, 474, 483, 485-86, 490, 492-93, 495, 497, 499-500, 504
Pro Football Digest, F 193; S 437
Pro Football for the Fan, S 471
Pro Football Hall of Fame, F 2, 10, 18, 21, 24, 26, 28-29, 31, 33, 36, 42, 48, 56, 59, 61, 69-70, 72-73, 79-80, 89, 97, 103-04, 106-07, 112-13, 123, 132, 134, 146, 151, 154, 160, 169, 179, 184, 186, 203, 205, 208, 210, 216, 218, 223-24, 229-30, 235, 237, 254, 256, 258, 261, 263, 267, 269, 271, 273, 278-80, 282, 298, 304, 315, 319, 329-30, 332, 334-35, 337, 340-41, 346-47, 352, 355, 360-63, 366, 371, 375, 382, 384, 386-87, 389, 392-93, 396-97, 401, 408, 414-15, 419, 421, 425, 430, 434, 441, 445, 448, 452, 454, 462-63, 467, 471, 487, 489, 496, 499, 503, 512, 517, 525, 529, 545, 566, 568-70, 574-75, 581, 584, 587-88, 598, 600, 602, 604, 607-10, 614-15, 618-19, 629, 634, 639, 645, 657-58, 660, 662, 668; O 61; I 378; S 375, 379, 391, 412, 429, 457, 475, 487, 497, 503
Pro Football Hall of Fame All-Time AFL Team, S 375, 450
Pro Football Hall of Fame All-Time NFL Team, S 379, 391, 410, 440, 467, 497, 504
Pro Football Illustrated, F 193
Pro Football Weekly, F 99; S 414

Proctor, Charles N., O *286-87*

Proctor, Mary Miller, O 286

Proctor Knott, O 604

Produce Stakes, O 196, 578, 595, 602

Professional (All-American) Red Heads basketball club, O 547

Professional Athletes Career Enterprises, B 210; S 263

Professional Basketball Writers Association, I 170, 263

Professional Bowlers Association, I 339-40, 342-44, 347-51

Professional Bowlers Association Championship, I 337, 340, 343, 349, 351

Professional Bowlers Association Hall of Fame, I 339, 343, 349-51

Professional Bowlers Association Player of the Year Award, I 343, 349

Professional Bowlers Association Tournament of Champions, I 351

Professional Figure Skating Championships, I 517

Professional Football Writers Association of America, F 137, 583, 589; S 414

Professional Golfers Association, O 135, 138, 147, 149, 152, 154, 156-57, 166; S 507-08, 510, 516, 519-23

Professional Golfers Association Hall of Fame, O 108-13, 116-17, 119-20, 122, 126-28, 130, 132, 134, 136, 138, 140, 142-43, 146, 148, 150, 153-58, 161-62, 169, 172; S 508, 513, 516

Professional Golfers Association Player of the Year Award, O 112, 115, 125, 132, 143, 147, 150, 158, 163, 166-67

Professional Golfers Association

Rookie of the Year Award, O 126, 163

Professional Golfers Association Seniors Classic, O 112, 133, 140, 149, 153-54

Professional Golfers Association Seniors Tour, O 126, 139, 157-59; S 507-08, 516

Professional Golfers Association Tour, O 108-09, 113, 116, 118-19, 124-26, 128, 134-35, 139, 141-42, 146-47, 149, 158-59, 163-64, 166-68; S 507-08, 510, 516, 519-23

Professional Golfers Association Tournament, S 512-13, 515, 521; 1916, O 109, 133; 1919, O 109; 1920, O 133; 1921, O 128; 1922, O 153; 1923, O 153; 1924, O 128; 1925, O 128; 1926, O 128; 1927, O 128; 1928, O 119; 1929, O 119; 1930, O 108; 1933, O 127, 153; 1934, O 120, 153; 1935, O 120, 128; 1936, O 155; 1937, O 155; 1938, O 153; 1939, O 145, 150; 1940, O 145; 1942, O 159; 1945, O 145; 1946, O 131; 1948, O 131; 1949, O 113, 158-59; 1951, O 125; 1955, O 125; 1956, O 113; 1959, O 159; 1968, O 112; 1969, O 124; 1974, O 163; 1977, O 139; 1982, O 124-25; 1984, O 163-64; 1985, O 126, 164

Professional Golfers Association West Stadium Course, La Quinta, CA, O 164

Professional International Track Association, O 429, 468, 543, 551

Professional Lawn Tennis Association, O 352

Professional Rodeo Cowboy Association, O 265

Professional Rodeo Cowboy

Association All-Around Cowboy
    Championships, O 265
Professional Women's Bowler
    Association, I 346
Professional Women's Bowler
    Association Showboat Classic, I
    347
Professional Women's Bowler
    Association Tournament, I 342
Prosaic, O 206
Prothro, James Thompson, Jr.
    "Tommy," F 190, 361
Proud Clarion, O 183, 225, 579
Providence College, I 128, 300, 327;
    S 325-26
Providence *Journal-Bulletin,* I 217
Providence, RI baseball club (EL, IL,
    NEL), B 105, 155, 161, 197, 240,
    347, 360, 384, 392, 468; S 19,
    37, 48, 81, 194, 197
Providence, RI Grays baseball club
    (NL), B 96, 116, 207, 256, 350,
    389, 428, 463-64, 531, 555, 592,
    628
Providence, RI Reds hockey club
    (AHL), I 546-47, 560, 564
Providence, RI Soccer Club (ASL), O
    293
Providence, RI Steamrollers basketball
    club (BAA), I 179
Providence, RI Steamrollers football
    club (NFL), F 113, 188-89, 477-
    78; I 660-61
Providence, RI 100-Mile Auto Race,
    O 23
Provincial League, S 9, 128, 190
Provo, UT *Daily Herald,* S 396
Proximity Award, O 182, 191
Prudery, S 533
Pruitt, Gregory D. "Greg," F *480-
    82,* 546
Pruitt, Michael "Mike," F *482-83*
Pryor, Aaron, I *452-53*

Public Broadcasting System, O 68; S
    339
Public School Athletic League, I 108,
    115, 176, 206; O 268, 300, 302,
    307
Public School Athletic League Hall of
    Fame, I 176
Pueblo *Chieftain,* O 90
Pueblo, CO baseball club (CdL, WL),
    B 8-9, 173-74, 195, 288, 507,
    609, 618
Puentes Grandis Soccer Club, Cuba,
    O 294
Puerto Rican Grand Prix Auto Race,
    O 28
Puerto Rican National Basketball
    Team, S 259
Puerto Rican Olympic Basketball
    Team, S 24
Puerto Rican Olympic Volleyball
    Team, I 774
Puerto Rican Winter Baseball League,
    B 6, 56, 97, 132, 141, 148, 150,
    213, 244, 273, 331, 370, 599, 620;
    S 10, 99, 113, 188
Puerto Rican Winter League
    Championships, S 188
Pugel, "Rudy," I 341
Puggins, S 526-27
Pugh, Gordon S., O *245-46*
Pugh, Jethro, Jr., F 322
Pulaski, VA baseball club (ApL), B
    40
Pulitzer Prize, O 61, 84, 96; S 336
Pulliam, Harry C., B 158, 253, *456-
    57;* S 179
Punch Imlach Memorial Award, S
    548
Purcell, James Mark, F 213; S 590
Purchase, O 196, 199; S 526-27
Purdue University, B 501; F 13, 26,
    44-45, 95, 133, 162, 212, 225,
    243, 283, 307, 314, 338, 353, 369,

404, 432, 439, 482, 551-52, 555, 572, 667, 673; I 130, 146, 162, 167, 169, 225, 227-28, 264, 272, 281-82, 302, 312, 329; O 459; S 59-60, 203-04, 271, 276, 303, 333, 361-62, 381, 491
Purdy, Clair J., F 477
Purdy, Samuel, O 609
Puritan, O 185
Puy Saint Vincent, France Supergiant Slalom Competition, O 273
Pyform, Arnaud, O 358
Pyle, Charles C. "Cash and Carry," F 217, 381, 392; O *86-88,* 329, 385

Qawi Dwight Muhammad, *See* Dwight Braxton
Quack, O 228
Quad Cities baseball club (ML), B 279; S 174
Quailey, "Les," O 70
Quaker State Open Bowling Tournament, I 349
The Quality of Courage, S 340
Quarry, "Jerry," I 386
The Quarterback, F 606
Quashed, O 602
Quax, Richard "Dick," O 540
Quebec baseball club (Pro L), S 128
Quebec Junior Major Hockey League, S 539, 544
Quebec Nordiques hockey club (WHA, NHL), I 554
Quebec City, Canada baseball club (EL), B 76, 140
Queen, Melvin J. "Mel," S 61
Queen Hopeful, O 173
Queens College, I 27
Queen's Plate, Woodbine, O 225
Queensborough Club, O 192
Quencherve, Gilles, O 542
Questad, Larry R., O 438
Quick, Richard, I 591; S 607

Quickly, O 578
Quickstep Stakes, O 224
Quigg, Joseph "Joe," I 199
Quigley, Martin, O 65
Quincy, IL baseball club (CA, ML), B 64, 420, 542
Quincy, IL baseball club (3IL), B 62, 279, 330, 563; S 87
Quinn, John P., B 75, *459-60*
Quinn, Robert "Bob," S 200
Quisenberry, Daniel R. "Dan," B *460-61;* S 63
Quist, Adrian K., O 322, 390; S 552

Rabb, Warren, S 469
Race of Two Worlds, Monza, Italy, S 620
Raceland, O 177
Racine, WI Horlick Legion football club (NFL), S 45
Racing Soccer Club, Madrid, Spain, O 293
The Racquet, See American Lawn Tennis
Racquet Club, New York, NY, O 396
Racquet Club, Philadelphia, PA, S 418
The Racquet and Tennis Club of New York, S 372, 490
Radatz, Richard R. "Dick," S 22, 167
Radbourne, Charles G. "Hoss," B 57, 207, 227, 420, *463-64*
Radcliff, Raymond A. "Rip," B 119, 582
Radcliffe, Theodore "Double Duty," B 88
Radcliffe College, I 506, 515, 539; O 253
Radio Daily, O 46
Radio Digest, O 79
Radix Trophy, O 153
Rafaloski, Gary, I 535
Raging Bull, I 418

Rahal, Robert "Bobby," S *619-20*

Raiders Soccer Club, St. Louis, MO, O 301

Rail Charity Golf Classic, S 508-09, 518-19

Rainbow Basketball Classic, Honolulu, HI, I 303

Raines, Timothy "Tim," S *171-72*

Raleigh, NC baseball club (CrL, Pil), B 222, 396, 425, 515, 518, 633; S 15, 118, 153, 195, 242

Ralph Lowe Stable, O 173

Ralston, John, F 631

Ralston, Richard Dennis, S 553-54, 556, *560-61*

Ralston, Robert, S 560

Ramage, Lee, S 610

Ramopo, O 224

Ramos, "Sugar," I 368

Ramsay, John T. "Jack," I *243-44*, 327

Ramsey, Floyd, S 431

Ramsey, Frank V., Jr., I 109, 113, 124, *244-45*, 257

Ramsey, Garrard S., F 528; S *466-67*

Ramsey, Michael A. "Mike," S 542, *547-48*

Ramsey, Stephen W. "Steve," F 577

Rancho Del Paso, Del Paso, CA, O 597-98

Rand, Mary, O 553

Randall, James "Jim," B 373

Randalls Island, NY Track and Field Meet, O 521

Randle, Ulmo S., Jr. "Sonny," F 220; S 426

Randolph, Archibald, O 608

Randolph, William L. "Willie," B 441

Randolph Award, F 615

Randolph Field, TX football club, F 154-55

Rankin, Judith Torluemke, O *150-51*

Ranzany, "Pete," I 422

Ranzino, Samuel S. "Sam," I 43

Rapacz, John, F 78

Rapee, Audrey Peppe, I 509

Rapid Water, S 526-27

Rapp, Vernon F. "Vern," B 44

Rappaport, Dennis, S 613

Raritan Stakes, O 588

Raschi, Victor J. A. "Vic," S 104, *172-73*

Rascoe, Robert B., I 68

Rashad, Ahmad, F *485-86*

Rasmussen, Eric R., S 84

Rassas, Nicholas "Nick," F 277

Rathman, Richard "Jim," O 42; S *620-21*

Ratleff, William Edward "Ed," I 292; S 296

Ratner, "Augie," I 372

Ratterman, George, F 216, 249

Rattler, O 230, 608

Rawlings Sports Goods Company, S 42

Rawls, Elizabeth E. "Betsy," O *151-52*

Rawls, Katherine L., See Katherine Rawls Green

Rawls, W. J. C. "Sonny," I 488

Ray, Buford "Baby," F 407

Ray, De Witt, S 169

Ray, Donald L. "Don," I 67

Ray, Edward "Ted," O 128, 148, 169

Ray, Hugh L. "Shorty," F *486-87*

Ray, "Johnny," I 367

Ray, Joie W., O *519-20*

Raybestos Brakettes softball club, O 261

Raycroft, Joseph E., I 236

Rayl, James R. "Jimmie," I 192

Raymond, Louise R., O 373, 391

Raymond, Mrs. Edward, See Louise R. Raymond

Reach, Alfred J. "Al," **B** 399, *464-65*

Reach, Milton, **I** 269

Reach & Company, **B** 465, 511-12

Reach's Official Base Ball Guide, **B** 465; **S** 189

Reader's Digest, **O** 69; **S** 336, 349

Reading, PA baseball club (EL), **B** 42, 102, 382, 477, 502, 518; **S** 16, 118

Reading, PA baseball club (IL, ISL, NYPL, NYSL, TSL), **B** 19, 34, 80, 244, 249, 367, 593; **I** 154; **S** 60, 159, 240

Reading, PA Bears basketball club (EL), **I** 20-21; **S** 287, 314

Reading, PA Country Club, **O** 144

Reagan, "Johnny," **I** 373

Reagan, Ronald W., **F** 52, 414, 433; **I** 393; **O** 52; **S** 453

Real Delight, **S** 529

The Real McKay, **O** 76

Reber, **O** 583

Reber-Kutz Farm, Lancaster, OH, **O** 583

Recreation Park, Detroit, MI, **B** 554

Red Barber Award, **O** 49

Red Cloud Athletic Foundation, **F** 7

Red Cloud, NE baseball club (NeSL), **B** 567

Red Mile, Lexington, KY, **O** 580, 587, 600

Red Rain, **O** 231

Red River Valley League, **B** 84

Red Rolfe Field, Hanover, NH, **S** 181

Red Springs, NC baseball club, **I** 340

Redbirds: A Century of Cardinal Baseball, **S** 338

Redding, Richard "Cannonball Dick," **B** 286, 451, *465-66,* 500, 612

Redin, Harley J., **I** *245-47*

Redlands Field, Cincinnati, OH, **B** 30; **S** 117, 210

Redlands University, **I** 292

Reece, Beasley, **F** 480

Reed, Howard D. "Howie," **S** 54

Reed, Robin L., **I** *655-56*

Reed, Sykes, **I** 39

Reed, Willis, Jr., **F** 591; **I** 31, 64, 121, 133, 220, *247-48;* **S** 322

Reedy, William, **O** 401

Reese, "Bonesetter," **S** 141

Reese, David "Dave," **F** 53, 550

Reese, "Eddie," **I** 578

Reese, Harold H. "Pee Wee," **B** 9, 169, 366, *466-67;* **S** 46

Reeves, Daniel E. "Dan," **F** *487-88*

Reeves, Daniel F. "Dan," **F** *488-89*

Reeves, George, **O** 217

Reeves, Robert E. "Bobby," **B** 123

Refund, **S** 536

Regal Gleam, **O** 192

Regan, Richard J. "Richie," **I** 261

Regina, Canada baseball club (WCaL), **B** 613

Regina, Canada football club (CFL), **F** 560

Regis College, **F** 260

Regner, Thomas "Tom," **F** 277

Regret, **O** 196, 199, 211; **S** 533

Rehm, Fred, **I** 85

Reich, "Al," **S** 314

Reich, Ernest "Ernie," **I** 21; **S** 287, *313-14*

Reichler, Joseph L. "Joe," **O** 62

Reid, Herman, Jr. "J. R.," **I** 283

Reid, Michael B. "Mike," **F** 460, *489-90*

Reid, William A. "Bill," **I** *248*

Reid, William T., **S** 376

Reiff, Joseph "Joe," **I** 182

Reigh Count, **O** 578; **S** 531

Reilley, "Pete," **I** 372

Reinbeck, IA High School, **I** 182

Reiser, Harold P. "Pete," **B** 467, 582; **S** 61

Remagen, O 215
Renault French Cycling Team, S 617
Renfro, Melvin L. "Mel," F 331; S
    467-68, 499
Renko, Steven "Steve," S 214
Reno, NV baseball club (CaL), B 80,
    138; S 48
Renos baseball club, S 198
Renshaw twins, O 338
Rensselaer Polytechnic Institute, I
    313, 564-65
Renzulli, Peter, O 306-07
Repulski, Eldon J. "Rip," B 168
Requittal, O 188; S 533
Restigauche, S 526-27
Reticule, O 225
Retton, Mary Lou, I 533, 535-36
Retzlaff, Palmer E. "Pete," F 490-
    91, 618
Reulbach, Edward M. "Ed," B 467-
    69, 507; S 161
Reuschel, Paul R., S 174
Reuschel, Ricky E., S 173-74
Reuss, Jerry, B 67; S 174-75
Reveillon, O 192
Reveiz, Fuad, S 447
Revenge, O 583
Reviewer, O 603
Revolta, John "Johnny," O 141; S
    515-16
Rey Del Carreres, S 531
Rey El Santa Anita, S 531
Reyes, Deborah Meyer, I 612-13
Reynolds, Allie P., B 469-70; S 86,
    173
Reynolds, Carl N., B 146
Reynolds, Jerry, I 263
Reynolds, Lester "Les," I 227
Reynolds, Robert O. "Bob," F 491-
    92
Reynolds, W. N., O 207
Rheingens, Bradley B. "Brad," I 637-
    38

Rhode Island State College, I 67,
    217; See also University of Rhode
    Island
Rhode Island State Hall of Fame, S
    322
Rhoden, Richard A. "Rick," S 175
Rhubarb in the Catbird Seat, S 340
Rice, Edgar C. "Sam," B 470-71; S
    179
Rice, Henry Grantland, B 355; F 29-
    30, 44, 66, 83, 90, 145, 150, 159,
    172, 187, 200, 239, 261-62, 310,
    406, 415, 506, 530, 575, 605, 621;
    I 112-13; O 54, 64, 73-74, 88-
    90, 96, 159; S 422, 460
Rice, James E. "Jim," B 471-72, 635
Rice, Joseph Gregory "Greg," O
    520-21
Rice, Kenneth "Ken," S 479
Rice, Larry, O 20-21
Rice Institute/University, B 490; F
    139, 245, 257, 275, 318, 389, 422,
    519-20, 567, 599, 647; S 408
Rice Trophy, F 132, 621
Rice University Relays, I 69
Riceville High School, I 183
Richard, James Rodney, S 175-76
Richards, A. Keene, O 602
Richards, Brandon, O 522
Richards, Dudley S., I 515
Richards, Elvin "Kink," F 447
Richards, Paul R., B 438, 441, 608;
    S 112, 176-77
Richards, Renee, O 381; S 298
Richards, Richard "Dick," F 492
Richards, Robert E. "Bob," O 477,
    521-23, 533; S 570
Richards, Vincent "Vince," O 63, 68,
    362, 368, 385-86, 387, 404-05,
    417
Richardson, Abram Harding "Hardy,"
    B 52, 604; S 177-78
Richardson, Jerome, Jr. "Pooh," S

278

Richardson, Michael Ray, I 161

Richardson, Robert C. "Bobby," B 351

Richeson, W. Lyle, F 302

Richey, George Clifford, Sr., I 550

Richey, George Clifford, Jr. "Cliff," I 550

Richey, Nancy, *See* Nancy Richey Gunter

Richfield Coliseum, Cleveland, OH, S 281

Richmond, "Link," I 80

Richmond, Rose, O 212

Richmond, Timothy "Tim," O 42

Richmond, William, "Bill," I 439-40

Richmond, IN baseball club (OIL), B 61

Richmond, VA baseball club (AA, IL), B 14, 329, 409, 421, 575; S 7, 48, 51, 113, 151, 212

Richmond, VA baseball club (AtL, Pil), B 87, 90, 251, 327, 483

Richmond, VA baseball club (VL), B 34, 228, 459, 600

Richmond, VA Raceway, O 28, 41

Richmond, VA Rebels football club (ConFL), F 471

Richmond, VA Robins hockey club (AHL), I 557

Richter, John, I 43

Richter, Leslie A. "Les," F *492-93*

Rickard, George L. "Tex," I 375, 388, 405, 412, *453-54*, 479; O 519

Rickenbacker, Edward V. "Eddie," O 7, 15, 23, *31*

Rickenbacker Car Company, O 31

Ricketts, Richard J. "Dick," I 180; S 284

Rickey, Wesley Branch, B 8, 36, 44-46, 69, 88, 97, 193, 206, 215, 224, 236-37, 260, 268-69, 301, 426, *472-73*, 480, 515-16, 562,

583, 597, 602; F 183, 498; S 23-24, 42, 46, 110

Ricks, James "Pappy," I 49, 68

Riddle, Chase, B 73; S 34

Riddle, Glen, O 199

Riddle, Samuel D. "Sam," O 178, 198, 595-96, 613-14

Rider College, I 14, 22; O 308; S 311

Rider Moore-Stewart Business School, *See* Rider College

Ridgewood, NJ Country Club, O 144

Ridon, O 228

Riegels, Roy, F 5-6

Riel, "Bert," I 182

Riesen, Louis, I 338

Riessen, Martin C. "Marty," O 326

Rigby, Kathy, *See* Kathy Rigby McCoy

Rigby, Paul "Bob," O *307*

Riggin, Aileen M., *See* Aileen Riggin Soule

Riggins, Frank, F 493

Riggins, John, F 206, 395, *493-94;* S 373

Riggs, Robert L. "Bobby," O 331, 355, 364-65, 374, 380, *386-87,* 389, 397; S 552-53, 556

Righetti, David A. "Dave," B 460; S 123

Rigler, Charles "Cy," S *178-80*

Rikes, Thomas "Tom," I 199

Riley, O 183, 595

Riley, Charles, O 514

Riley, John "Jack," F 472

Riley, John P. "Jack," I 565, *568-69*

Riley, Lee, I 249

Riley, Leon F., I 248

Riley, Patrick J. "Pat," I *248-50*

Rimington, Dave B., F 444, *494-95*

Rimmer of Lancashire, I 440

Ring, James J. "Jimmy," B 202, 260

The Ring, I 353, 366-67, 369, 371-

72, 375, 381-83, 386, 402, 410, 423, 430, 435, 437, 450, 461, 471, 473, 477; **S** 613

The Ring Record Book and Boxing Encyclopedia, **I** 382, 441

The Ring's Boxing Hall of Fame, **I** 354-62, 364-65, 367-69, 371-73, 375-76, 378-79, 381, 385-91, 393, 395, 399-40, 402, 404, 407-08, 410, 413-17, 419-20, 422, 424-25, 428-29, 433-35, 440, 442, 444-45, 448-50, 452-54, 456, 458, 460-62, 467, 469, 474-75, 477-80, 483-84

The Ring's Boxing Museum, **I** 382

The Ring's Fight of the Year Award, **I** 423

The Ring's Fighter of the Year Award, **I** 367, 423, 477, 482

Ringo, James S. "Jim," **F** *495-96*

Rio Grande Valley Open Golf Tournament, **O** 113

Riordan, Michael W. "Mike," **I** 220; **O** 341, 365

Ripken, Calvin E., Jr. "Cal," **B** 411

Ripley, Elmer "Rip," **I** *250*

Ripley, Melissa Belote Hamlin, **S** *621*

Ripon College, **I** 234

Rippy, Benjamin, *See* Charles W. Jones

Risen, Arnold D. "Arnie," **I** 114

Riskiev, Rufat, **S** 623

Risko, Eddie "Babe," **I** 367, 372, 426, 462, 466, 475, 481

Risque, **O** 196

Ritcher, James A. "Jim," **F** 495, *496-97*

Ritchey, Claude C., **B** 28

Ritchie, "Willie," **I** *454-55,* 475, 480

Ritger, Richard "Dick," **I** 351

Riva Ridge, **O** 183

Rivas, Ramon, **S** 268

River Downs, **O** 186

River Oaks Country Club, Houston, TX, **O** 113

Riverfront Stadium, Cincinnati, OH, **B** 191

Rivers, Joe "Mexican Joe," **I** 454, 480

Rivers, John M. "Mickey," **B** 441

Riverside City College, **I** 292

Riverside Grand Prix Stock Car Race, **O** 11, 28

Riverside Junior College, **O** 11

Riverside Park, Kansas City, MO, **O** 173

Riverside Raceway, Riverside, CA, **F** 494; **O** 41

Riverside 250 Auto Race, **O** 28

Rives, Nathaniel, **O** 573

Riviera Golf Course, Los Angeles, CA, **O** 118

Riviera Lanes, Akron, OH, **I** 344

Rixey, Eppa, Jr., **B** 336, *374;* **S** 179

Rizzuto, Philip F. "Phil," **B** 346, *374-75;* **S** 67, 148, 239

Roanoke College, **I** 95

Roanoke, VA baseball club (Pil, VL), **B** 90, 376; **F** 276; **S** 19

Roark, Aidan, **O** 388

Roark, Helen Wills Moody, **O** 327, 329, 332, 360-61, 380, *387-88,* 389, 415

Robbie, Joseph "Joe," **F** 226

Robbins Drydock Soccer Club, **O** 306

Roberson, Irvin "Bo," **O** 433, 553

Roberson, Rudolph, **I** 201

Robert B. Hermann Trophy, **O** 301, 310

Robert Dunbar New England Writing Award, **S** 339

Robert E. Lee Award, **S** 455-56

Robert L. Douglas Basketball League, **I** 69

Roberto Clemente Award, **B** 52, 115,

422

Roberto Clemente: Batting King, **S** 347

Roberts, Augusta, **S** 562

Roberts, Clifford "Cliff," **O** 136

Roberts, David "Dave," **I** 569

Roberts, David A. "Dave," **B** 595

Roberts, Douglas W. "Doug," **I** 545, 569

Roberts, Floyd, **O** 35

Roberts, Gordon "Gordie," **I** *569-70*

Roberts, Gregory L. "Greg," **F** 546, 582

Roberts, J. D., **F** 653

Roberts, James B. "Jim," **F** 403

Roberts, James B. "Red," **I** 67

Roberts, Robin E., **B** 74, 351, *475-77*

Roberts, Yvette, **S** 320

Robertson, Bailey, **I** 251

Robertson, Charles C. "Charley," **B** 501

Robertson, James, **B** 225

Robertson, Lawson N., **O** 440-41, 471, 508

Robertson, Oscar P., **I** 23, 130, 195, 225, 231, 234, *250-52*, 259, 278, 288, 313, 322; **S** 268, 282

Robertson, Ronald F., **I** 514

Robertson, Sherrard A. "Sherry," **B** 225

Robertson, William, **B** 225

Robeson, Paul B., **F** *497-99;* **S** 416

Robey, Fredrick R. "Rick," **I** 145

Robinson, Aaron A., **B** 448

Robinson, Adeline King, **O** 405; **S** *561-62*

Robinson, Bradley "Brad," **F** 108

Robinson, Brooks C., Jr., **B** 300, *477-78*, 502; **S** 14, 103, 153

Robinson, David M., **S** 278, *314-15*

Robinson, Edward G. "Eddie," **F** 75, *499-501*

Robinson, Edward N., **F** 477, 625

Robinson, Elizabeth, *See* Elizabeth Robinson Schwartz

Robinson, Flynn J., **I** 251

Robinson, Frank, **B** 35, 125, 185, 438, 441, 449, *478-79*, 619; **S** 44, 335

Robinson, Frederic H. "Fred," **B** 481

Robinson, Jack R. "Jackie," **B** 9, 17, 84-85, 190, 210, 467, 473, *479-81*, 520, 583, 609; **F** 183, 248, 498, 637-38; **O** 272; **S** 140, 189, 196

Robinson, Jerry D., **F** *501-02;* **S** 393

Robinson, John A., **F** 8; **S** *468-69*

Robinson, Johnny Nolan, **S** *469-70*

Robinson, Larry C., **I** 562

Robinson, Ray, **S** 355

Robinson, Richard David "Dave," **F** 430, *502-03*

Robinson, "Sugar Ray," **I** 359, 386, 393, 418, *455-56*, 483; **S** 335

Robinson, Wilbert, **B** 193, 240-41, 249, 281, 353, 363, *481-82*, 567

Robinson, Wilbert, Jr. "Will," **I** 120-21; **S** 273

Robinson, William "Bill," **O** 552

Robinson, William Edward "Eddie," **S** 171

Robinson, William H. "Bill," **B** 117

Robisch, David G. "Dave," **I** 142

Robison, Frank D., **B** 64, 92, 576

Robison, M. Stanley, **B** 92, 576

Robnett, Marshall F., **F** 434

Robson, "Tommy," **I** 372

Robustelli, Andrew R. "Andy," **F** 397, *503-04*, 542

Rocha, Ephraim "Red," **I** 45, 98, 159

Roche, Anthony D. "Tony," **O** 324

Roche, Clifford "Cliff," **O** 365, 389

Roche, John M., **I** 199

Roche Cup, **O** 281

Rochester, NY Americans hockey club
(AHL), **I** 545
Rochester, NY Athletic Club, **I** 206
Rochester, NY baseball club (AA,
NYSL), **S** 123-24, 198
Rochester, NY baseball club (EL,
NA), **B** 52, 171, 240
Rochester, NY baseball club (IL), **B**
8, 44, 109, 145, 214-15, 229, 326,
360-61, 377, 380, 387, 403, 411-
12, 441, 455, 459, 478-79, 503,
516, 524-25, 583, 595, 638; **S** 71,
149, 191, 230, 354
Rochester, NY Centrals basketball
club (ABL), **I** 222-23, 261
Rochester, NY Country Club, **O** 128
Rochester, NY *Democrat &*
Chronicle, **B** 441
Rochester, NY *Democrat &*
Chronicle Press Club, **I** 45
Rochester, NY Eber Brothers
basketball club, **I** 114
Rochester, NY football club (Ind.), **F**
183
Rochester, NY International Golf
Tournament, **O** 168
Rochester, NY Invitation Golf
Tournament, **S** 505, 518
Rochester, NY Jefferson football club
(NFL), **F** 4, 12
Rochester, NY Press Radio Club, **I**
45
Rochester, NY Pros basketball club
(NBL), **I** 114-15
Rochester, NY Royals basketball club
(NBL, BAA, NBA), **F** 215; **I** 23,
44, 61-62, 99, 110-11, 114-15,
132-33, 149, 241, 308, 318-19; **S**
265, 283-84, 309
Rochester, NY Sports Hall of Fame, **I**
45
Rock Hill, SC baseball club (WCL),
B 10, 73, 179

Rock Island, IL *Argus,* **F** 476
Rock Island, Il baseball club (SML),
B 279
Rock Island, IL Independents football
club (NFL), **F** 12, 113, 232, 254,
601-02
Rockford College, **I** 517
Rockford, IL baseball club (3IL), **B**
310
Rockford, IL Forest City baseball club
(NA), **B** 11, 527
Rockford, IL *Morning Star,* **O** 104
Rockingham Race Track, Salem
Depot, NH, **O** 203
Rockingham Special Stakes, **O** 581
Rockne, Knute K., **F** 12-14, 43, 90,
94, 126, 148, 188-90, 211-12, 245,
254, 259, 29, 328, 343-45, 359,
374, 377, 391, 415, 433, 439, 456,
464-65, 468, *504-07,* 532, 538-39,
595, 601, 645-46; **I** 207; **O** 60-
61, 89, 104; **S** 448, 483
Rockne Club, Kansas City, MO, **I**
81, 127
Rockne Trophy/Award, **F** 51, 79,
129, 248, 308, 344, 397, 515, 575,
585, 667; **S** 443
Rockton Arena, Rockford, IL, **I** 516
Rockwell, Dean, **I** 640
Rocky Marciano Memorial Award, **I**
442
Rocky Mount, NC baseball club
(BRL, CRL, Pil), **B** 331, 376,
392, 446; **F** 597; **S** 221
Rocky Mountain Amateur Athletic
Union Association, **I** 326
Rocky Mountain College, **S** 330
Rocky Mountain Conference, **F** 105-
07, 339, 559; **I** 301, 320; **S** 331
Rocky Mountain Conference
Championships, **S** 331
Rod Laver's Tennis Digest, **S** 339
Rodgers, Guy W., Jr., **I** 103, 178,

238

199, *252-53*
Rodgers, John S. "Johnny," F 136, 44, *507-09*
Rodgers, "Pepper," F 618
Rodgers, "Terry," F 508
Rodgers, William H. "Bill," O *523-24*
Rodriguez, Luis, I 396
Rodriguez, Rafael, I 422
Roe, Elwin C. "Preacher," B 467; S *180*
Roe, Seely, O 587
Roebuck Invitation Golf Tournament, O 135
Roettger, Oscar F., B 481
Rogan, Wilbur "Bullet," B 290, *482-83*
Roger Penske Racing Enterprise, O 28
Rogers, Annette J., S 593
Rogers, Doris, I 123
Rogers, George W., Jr., F 8, 412, *509-10*
Rogers, Lurlyne Greer, I *25*
Rogers, Marie, I 123
Rogers, "Nat," B 533
Rogers, William C. "Bill," S 510
Rohm, C. "Pinky," F 599
Rojas, Octavio R. "Cookie," B 431; S 237
Roland, Johnny E., S 496
Roldan, Juan Domingo, I 397; S 612
Rolex Award, S 508, 517
Rolfe, Robert A. "Red," B 346, 356; S *180-81,* 297
Rolla Vollstedt Lightning Race Car, O 13
Roller, Benjamin, I 648
Roller Skating Coach of the Year, I 674
Rollins, Kenneth H. "Kenny," S 261, 287
Rollins College, O 49, 319, 336,

359, 365; S 506, 518
Roman, Edward "Ed," I 132
Roman, Jose "King," I 383
Roman Soldier, O 601
Romani, Archive San, O 446
Romanian International Gymnastic Invitation Meet, I 539
Romanian National Hockey Team, I 548
Romanian National Wrestling Team, I 639, 641
Romanowski, Walter "Walt," S 616
Rome, Italy Summer Olympic Games, *See* Olympic Summer Games, 1960
Rome, Italy Track and Field Meet, O 504
Romig, Joseph "Joe," S *470*
Rommel, Edwin A. "Ed," B *483-84,* 553
Romnes, Elwin N. "Doc," I *570-71*
Romney, G. Ott, I 301
Ronald Basketball Encyclopedia, I 218
Ronald Press, I 131
Ronald Reagan Award, S 341
Roncocas Stable, O 183, 201, 215, 219; S 527
Rondon, Vincente, I 384
Rooker, James P. "Jim," S 63
Rookie of the Month Award, S 315
Rookie of the Year Award, F 11, 17-18, 63, 68, 77, 87, 143, 150-51, 158, 185, 222, 253, 264, 279, 305, 330, 351, 366, 384, 387, 401, 418, 431, 451, 473, 508-09, 524, 546, 586, 589, 600, 632, 642-43; S 3, 15, 26-27, 32, 48, 66, 77, 89, 134, 140, 146, 157, 170-71, 201, 214, 230, 236, 272-73, 275-76, 278, 282, 304, 315, 327-29, 353, 365, 373, 385, 414-15, 474, 497, 506-07, 514, 517, 538, 542, 604, 614,

619

Rooney, Arthur J., Sr. "Art," F 80, 315, 375, 460, *510-12,* 580

Rooney, Arthur J., Jr., F 511

Rooney, Daniel M., Sr. "Dan," F 510-11

Rooney, Daniel M. , Jr., F 511

Rooney Award, F 460

Roosevelt, Ellen C., O 321, 333, 405; S 562

Roosevelt, Franklin D., F 178

Roosevelt, Grace W., O 321, 333, 405

Roosevelt, Theodore, F 108; I 378, 644; O 268; S 376

Roosevelt Raceway, Westbury, NY, O 19, 105, 181, 191, 575

Roosevelt Raceway's Founders Plate, O 575

Roosma, John S., I *253-54*

Root, Charles H. "Charlie," B *484-85*

Root, "Jack," I 398, 432, *456-58*

Roper, Marion Dale, I 496

Roper, Robert "Bob," I 391

Roper, William W. "Bill," F 84, 475

Ropes, "Patty," I 535

Rosalind, O 587

Rosburg, Robert "Bob," O 115

Rose, "Charley," I 389

Rose, Eleanor Holm, *See* Eleanor Holm Whalen

Rose, Leonard "Len," I 458

Rose, Mauri, O *31-32,* 34, 37

Rose, Mervyn G., O 363, 390

Rose, Peter E. "Pete," B 10, 39, 258, 298, 314, 412, 440, *485-87,* 516; S 64-65, 72, 92, 352

Rose, Ralph W., O 490, *524-25,* 535-36

Rose Bowl football game, F 2, 506, 11, 32, 34-35, 45-46, 49, 74, 79, 81, 100, 112, 114, 120, 127, 141, 152, 160, 172-73, 175, 184, 201, 213, 220-21, 225, 227-28, 233, 244, 256, 261-62, 281, 289, 300-01, 307, 313, 327, 350, 356, 361, 368-69, 377, 402, 404, 407, 410, 413, 421, 424, 442-43, 471-73, 477, 491-92, 504-05, 512, 523, 526, 533, 538, 544, 549, 551-52, 575-76, 579-80, 585, 594-95, 604, 625-27, 636, 638-39, 648, 658, 667-68, 670; O 49, 52, 63, 67-68, 70, 79, 493; S 94, 361, 380, 388, 392-93, 402, 414, 421-22, 439, 445, 449, 462, 468, 480-81, 486, 493, 495

Rose Bowl Hall of Fame, F 575

Rose Polytechnic Institute, B 416-17; F 437

Rose Room Gymnasium, St. Paul, MN, I 390

Rose Tree Fox Hunting Club, O 512

Rosen, Albert L. "Flip," S 69, *181-82;* S 495

Rosenberg, Aaron D., F 299, *512-13*

Rosenberg, Charley "Phil," I 389, 468

Rosenbloom, Carroll D., F 292

Rosenbloom, Leonard "Len," I 458

Rosenbloom, Maxie, I 426, *458-59,* 463, 475

Rosenblum, "Max," I 170

Rosenbluth, James, S 315

Rosenbluth, Leonard R. "Lenny," I 199; S *315-17*

Rosewall, Kenneth R. "Ken," O 324, 341, 349, 394, 407; S 554

Rosofsky, Barnet D., *See* Barney Ross

Ross, Barney, I 355, 364, 435, 451, *459-60*

Ross, Daniel R. "Dan," F 15

Ross, J. K. L., O 201, 215, 608; S

525, 531
Ross, James, I 312
Ross, Samuel, O 79
Rossides, Eugene "Gene," F 350; O 426
Rossman, Claude R., B 156
Roswell, NM baseball club (PPVL, SpL), B 530; S 235
Rote, Tobin C., F 422
Rote, William Kyle, Sr., F 35, 431, 448, 578; O 308; S 470-72
Rote, William Kyle, Jr., O 307, 308; S 471
Roth, Braggo, S 511
Roth, Mark S., I 337, 348-49
Roth, Robert F. "Bobby," B 280
Rothstein, Arnold, I 357
Rothwell, "Billy," See Young Corbett
Rotterdam, The Netherlands Marathon, O 528
Rouillard, Nancy, I 515
Round Table, O 576, 603; S 532
The Roundup, S 551
Roush, Edd J. "Ed," B 302, 488-89
Routis, Andre, I 353
Routt, Joseph E. "Joe," F 434, 514
Rowe, Curtis, Jr., I 331
Rowe, Harmon, F 608
Rowe, James G., Sr. "Jimmy," O 211, 578, 589, 597; S 532-34
Rowe, James G., Jr., O 613; S 533-34
Rowe, John C. "Jack," B 52, 604; S 178
Rowe, Lynwood T. "Schoolboy," S 62, 182-84
Rowing Hall of Fame, O 61
Rowing Writers Association of America, O 62
Rowland, Clarence H. "Pants," B 606; S 110
Rowswell, Albert K., S 358
Roxborough, John, I 429

Royal, Darrell K., F 514-16, 550; S 462
Royal Albert Hall, London, England, I 400
Royal and Ancient Golf Club, St. Andrews, Scotland, O 148
Royal Central Institute of Gymnastics, I 1
Royal Clint, O 229
Royal Lytham Golf Course, O 135
Royal Yacht Squadron, O 101
Royals Stadium, Kansas City, MO, S 136
Royden, Norris, O 202
Roys, Earl, I 461
Royster, Jeron K. "Jerry," S 244
Rozelle, Alvin R. "Pete," F 91, 307, 412, 419, 488, 516-18; S 374, 399
Rozelle Rule, F 371, 517
Rozier, Mike, F 182, 209, 444, 518-19, 570
Rubber City Open Golf Tournament, O 146
Ruble, Olan G., I 254-55
Rubin, Barbara Jo, O, 214-15
Rubin, Dorothy, O 571
Rubin, Samuel "Sam," O 591
Ruby, Lloyd, O 32-33
Rucker, George Napoleon "Nap," B 155
Ruddock, "Razor," S 626
Rudi, Joseph O. "Joe," S 84, 214
Rudolph, Wilma G, O 435-36, 457, 525-26, 546
Ruel, Claude, I 562
Ruel, Herold D. "Muddy," B 212, 356, 456; S 190
Ruether, Walter H. "Dutch," S 184
Ruffian, O 603-04
Ruffing, Charles H. "Red," B 470, 489-90
Rugby Union Rules, F 85

Ruhe, **O** 173

Ruhlin, "Gus," **I** 407

Rules Demonstration Committee, **I** 313

Rum Customer, **O** 191

Runnels, James E. "Pete," **B** *490-91*

Runner's World, **O** 529

Runner's World Runner of the Year, **O** 529

Runnymede Farm, Paris, KY, **O** 588-89, 597

Runyan, Paul S., **O** *152-53*

Runyon, Alfred Damon, **I** 375, 405; **O** 54, 64, 74, *90-92*

Rupp, Adolph F., **I** 5, 31, 53, 77, 94, 108-09, 116, 132, 139, 142, 244, 249, *255-58,* 293; **S** 261, 277, 287, 318, 384

Rupp Arena, Lexington, KY, **I** 110, 257

Rupp Trophy, **I** 266

Ruppert, Jacob, Jr. "Colonel," **B** 26, 366, *491-93,* 558, 597

Rush, Catherine Cowan "Cathy," **I** *258-59,* 284

Rush, "Ed," **I** 258

Rush Medical School, Chicago, IL, **S** 436, 484

Rusie, Amos W., **B** 199, 217, *492-94,* 556; **S** 36

Russell, Allan E., **B** 226

Russell, Cazzie L., Jr., **I** 31, 132, 186, *259-60*

Russell, Charles Andrew "Andy," **F** 236

Russell, Fred, **I** 457

Russell, Jack E., **S** 45

Russell, Jo Anne, **O** 335

Russell, John D. "Honey," **I** *260-61*

Russell, William E. "Bill," **B** 209; **S** 26, 114, *184-85*

Russell, William F. "Bill," **I** 12, 36, 47-48, 52-53, 111, 121, 124, 136, 150, 160, 180, 184, 190, 210, 231, 238, 245, *261-63,* 300, 302; **S** 307, 315, 331

Russell Sage College, **I** 507

Russian National Tennis Championships, **O** 389

Russo, Paul, **O** 4

Rustle, **S** 531

Rutgers University, **F** 40, 348, 403, 497-98; **I** 22, 38, 128, 157, 288; **O** 104; **S** 19, 29, 477

Ruth, George H. "Babe," **B** 1, 18-19, 25-26, 49, 65, 87-88, 94, 106, 120-21, 155, 197, 201, 208, 210, 213, 223, 259, 267, 269, 275, 277, 279, 305-06, 331, 346, 376, 382, 388, 394, 414, 432, 471, 482, 484, 492, *494-95,* 500, 510, 516, 535, 554-55, 565-66, 611, 613, 616; **I** 33, 364; **O** 59-60, 74-75, 82, 89-90, 99, 202, 299, 310; **S** 10, 41, 47, 54, 81, 85, 112, 155, 189, 231, 233, 235, 340

Ruthali, Janoe, *See* Jack Root

Rutherford, John S. III "Johnny," **O** 16, *33-34*

Ruthven, Richard D. "Dick," **S** 63

Ruttman, Troy, **S** 620

Ruuska, Sylvia, **I** 610

Ryan, Allen, **O** 198

Ryan, Elizabeth "Bunny," **O** 329, 354, 373, 387, *388-89*

Ryan, Frank B., **F** *519-20*

Ryan, George, **I** 456

Ryan, James D. "Buddy," **F** 548

Ryan, James E. "Jimmy," **B** *495-96,* 568

Ryan, "Jim," **I** 490

Ryan, "Jimmy," **I** 456

Ryan, John B. "Jack," **B** 145

Ryan, Lynn Nolan, **B** 176, *497-98;* **S** 44, 58, 91, 138

Ryan, "Paddy," **I** 467

Ryan, Patrick J. "Pat," O 491
Ryan, "Tommy" (boxer), I 373, 432, 460-61, 464
Ryan, "Tommy," (boxing manager), I 398
Ryba, Domenic J. "Mike," S 16
Ryba, James "Jim," F 595
Ryder Cup, O 112-13, 116, 118-120, 124-28, 130, 132, 139, 141-42, 145, 147, 150, 153-56, 158, 163, 169; S 507, 511, 514-16, 519-20, 522-24
Rydzewski, Francis X. "Frank," F 377
Rye, NY Tennis Championships, O 418
Rysdyk, William, O 587-88
Ryskamp, Wyllis, I 344
Ryun, James R. "Jim," O 458, 488, 526-27, 532, 564, 567

Saari, Roy A., I 608, 613-14
Saari, Urho, I 613
Saban, Louis H. "Lou," F 16, 409, 445; S 478
Sacahuista, S 530
Sachs, Edward "Eddie," O 38
Sachs, Leonard D., I 263-64
Sackler, Howard, I 410
Sacks, Gregory "Greg," S 605
Sacramento, CA Auto Race, O 5, 37, 42
Sacramento, CA baseball club (CaSL), B 259
Sacramento, CA City College, B 42
Sacramento, CA Kings basketball club (NBA), I 247, 263; S 254
Sacramento, CA Solons baseball club (PCL), B 27, 167, 235, 329, 336, 387, 397; S 23-24, 52, 59, 68, 101, 197
Sacramento, CA State College, I 276
Sacred Heart College, B 246

Saddler, "Sandy," I 362, 450, 461-62
Safeco Golf Classic, O 164, 168; S 508-09, 518
The Saga of American Football, S 498
Sagamore Farm, O 599
Sagawa, Yoshito, I 603
Saggy, O 577
Saginaw, MI baseball club (NWL, SML), B 96, 237
Sagittarius, O 178
Sahara Invitation Golf Tournament, O 521
Saigh, Fred M., B 45
Sailer, Toni, O 288
Saimes, George T., F 472-73
Sain, John F. "Johnny," B 62, 526; S 185-86
St. Andrews Golf Course, O 155, 169; S 516
St. Anton, Austria Ski Competition, O 280
St. Bartholomew's Club, New York, NY, O 466
St. Benedict's Prep School, Newark, NJ, I 29
St. Bonaventure University, F 80, 534; I 67, 169, 174
St. Clair, James W., I 70
St. Clair, Robert B. "Bob," F 521-22
St. Cloud, MN baseball club (NoL), B 21, 51, 81, 445
St. Cloud, MN State Teachers College, I 546-49
St. Francis College of Pennsylvania, I 33; S 312-13
St. Gabriels basketball club, S 314
St. George football club, O 306
St. Germans, O 613
St. Ignatius College, S 184
St. John, Lynn W., I 242, 264-65
St. John Arena, Columbus, OH, I

265

St. John's College, Baltimore, MD, **O**
241-42, 244-45, 248

St. John's University, Collegeville,
MN, **F** 374-75

St. John's University, Jamaica, NY,
F 607; **I** 43, 67, 70, 109, 129,
141, 157-58, 171, 180, 196-200,
232, 247, 264, 281, 305, 334; **S**
262, 266, 305-06

St. Joseph, MO baseball club (WA,
WL), **B** 2, 94, 142, 215, 307, 310,
330, 373, 547, 595; **S** 120, 215

St. Joseph, MO Boosters Club
basketball club (AAU), **I** 276

St. Joseph, MO Hillyard Chemical
Company basketball club, **I** 63,
139, 181

St. Joseph's College, **B** 173, 256; **I**
178-79, 243; **O** 104

St. Lawrence University, **S** 191, 431,
541

St. Leger Stakes, **O** 201

St. Leo College, **S** 133

St. Louis All-American Born All-Stars
Soccer Club, **O** 293

St. Louis baseball club (NA, UL,
WA), **B** 29, 206; **S** 47

St. Louis Blues hockey club (NHL), **I**
546, 549, 558, 566, 570; **S** 352-
53, 540

St. Louis Bombers basketball club
(BAA, NBA), **I** 179, 190

St. Louis Brown Stockings baseball
club (AA), **B** 11, 78-79, 107, 171,
194, 225, 265, 297, 307, 347, 407,
442, 496, 537, 576, 598; **S** 119,
178

St. Louis Browns baseball club (AL),
B 32, 36, 40-41, 44, 49, 55, 64,
106, 109, 137, 142, 161, 167, 177-
78, 193, 219, 221, 231, 243, 261,
279, 292, 322, 330, 343, 347, 376,
381, 401, 408, 436, 451, 454, 456,
472, 475, 484, 508, 516, 525, 535,
538, 572, 574, 577, 580, 582, 585-
86, 613, 624; **F** 23, 241, 424,
430; **I** 268; **O** 75, 78, 234; **S** 13,
17, 21, 31-33, 54-55, 98, 100,
110-12, 125-27, 153-54, 159, 189-
90, 198-202, 218, 227, 231, 234-
35

St. Louis Browns baseball club (NL),
S 19, 47, 65, 70, 118, 382

St. Louis Browns Hall of Fame, **S**
32, 202

St. Louis Cardinals baseball club
(NL), **B** 2, 5, 7-8, 29, 36, 39-40,
43-46, 48, 51, 53-54, 62, 64, 67,
73, 78-79, 81, 86, 88, 92, 101,
111-13, 123, 126, 133, 139, 142-
43, 145-46, 152-55, 161-62, 168,
177, 185-86, 193, 201-03, 207,
214-15, 217, 224, 228-29, 236-38,
251-52, 260-62, 267-69, 271, 295-
96, 313, 323, 325, 335, 346, 352,
354-55, 360-61, 365, 370, 372,
377, 380-81, 387, 396, 401, 403-
04, 406, 412-13, 419-20, 441, 443,
445, 449, 454, 461, 473, 481, 490,
492, 503-05, 507, 511, 513-14,
517-18, 524-26, 530, 540, 542,
544, 559-61, 567, 575-76, 583,
585-86, 591, 593, 595, 597, 600,
608, 614, 617, 622, 633, 636, 639;
F 29, 173, 308, 402; **I** 6, 30, 105,
312; **O** 55-57, 65, 71, 75, 82-83,
293, 299; **S** 4, 12, 15-17, 23-24,
26, 30-36, 38-39, 42, 53, 57, 61,
75, 84, 87, 90, 92, 99, 105-06,
109-10, 116, 125, 127-28, 131,
135, 139-41, 143-44, 149, 158,
160, 172-74, 180, 183, 186-90,
193, 196-97, 201-03, 206-08, 210,
212-13, 215-18, 223, 230, 233,
237, 239, 338, 352, 354-55, 424,

494-95

St. Louis Cardinals football club (NFL), **F** 16-17, 25, 48, 115, 121, 140-41, 219-20, 248, 341, 363, 389, 418, 453, 485, 557, 654, 657-58; **S** 352, 370, 425-26, 468, 496-97

St. Louis Central Breweries Soccer Club, **O** 305

St. Louis Country Club, **S** 522

St. Louis Exposition (1904), **I** 108

St. Louis Giants baseball club (NNL), **B** 88, 343, 548; **S** 188

St. Louis *Globe-Democrat*, **O** 150

St. Louis Golden Gloves Tournament, **I** 427

St. Louis Hawks basketball club (NBA), **I** 20, 33, 86, 92-93, 107, 109-11, 133, 137, 184-85, 190, 205, 237-38, 245, 279, 327; **S** 280, 284, 318, 320

St. Louis hockey club (AHA, USHL), **I** 560, 564

St. Louis Major Soccer League, **O** 301

St. Louis Maroons baseball club (UA), **B** 407; **S** 233

St. Louis Open Golf Tournament, **O** 163

St. Louis *Post Dispatch,* **B** 593; **O** 55; **S** 338

St. Louis Quarterback Club, **S** 497

St. Louis Red Stockings baseball club (Ind.), **B** 206

St. Louis Shamrocks Soccer Club, **O** 299

St. Louis Spirits basketball club (ABA), **I** 202-03

St. Louis Sports Hall of Fame, **I** 350; **O** 302; **S** 569

St. Louis *Star,* **O** 96

St. Louis Stars baseball club (NNL), **B** 31, 533, 543, 599, 612

St. Louis Stars Soccer Club (NASL), **O** 305, 311

St. Louis Steamers Soccer Club (MISL), **O** 295, 311

St. Louis Summer Olympic Games, *See* Olympic Summer Games, 1904

St. Louis Terriers baseball club (FL), **B** 54, 450, 557-58; **S** 98

St. Louis *Times,* **S** 338

St. Louis Turnverein Society, **I** 525

St. Louis University, **B** 396; **F** 108-09, 112; **I** 67, 126-27, 158, 166, 180, 184, 190; **O** 301-02, 310; **S** 331, 353

St. Louis University Hall of Fame, **I** 127

St. Louis Whites baseball club (Ind.), **B** 347

St. Louis World's Fair Basketball Tournament, **I** 4; **S** 289

St. Mary's College, Notre Dame, IN, **B** 107; **I** 607

St. Mary's College of California, **B** 259; **F** 171, 294, 353, 377-79, 512; **S** 23, 111

St. Mary's College of Minnesota, **I** 163

St. Mary's College of Wisconsin, **B** 292

St. Mary's Pre-Flight School basketball club, **I** 188

St. Mary's Pre-Flight School football club, **F** 533, 555

St. Mary's University, **I** 553

St. Michael's College, **I** 30

St. Michael's Soccer Club, Fall River, MA (FRDSL), **O** 309

St. Moritz, Switzerland Alpine Ski Competition, **O** 288

St. Moritz, Switzerland Ice Skating Club, **I** 515

St. Moritz, Switzerland Winter

Olympic Games, *See* Winter
Olympic Games, 1924, 1948
St. Nicholas Arena, New York, NY, **I**
404, 421, 556
St. Nicholas hockey club, New York,
I 543-44; **O** 367, 399, 420
St. Nicholas Magazine, **F** 118
St. Norbert College, **F** 392
St. Patrick's College of Canada, **S**
352
St. Paul, MN Athletic Club hockey
club (AHAUS), **S** 537
St. Paul, MN baseball club (AA), **B**
8, 28, 86, 107, 136, 161, 217,
268, 360, 521, 614; **O** 233; **S** 12,
45, 53, 59, 110-11, 126, 149, 167
St. Paul, MN baseball club (WL), **B**
217, 407, 496
St. Paul, MN Open Golf Tournament,
O 113, 124
St. Paul, MN Saints hockey club
(AHA), **I** 553, 555, 557, 570
St. Paul, MN Vulcans hockey club
(MJHL), **I** 557
St. Paul's School, Concord, NH, **I**
556
St. Petersburg, FL baseball club (FIL,
FSL), **B** 10, 197, 251, 327; **S** 34,
217
St. Petersburg, FL Open Golf
Tournament, **O** 113, 124
St. Petersburg *Times,* **O** 75, 359
St. Simon, **O** 605
St. Thomas College, **F** 314; **I** 158,
165, 570, **S** 29
Sailors, Kenneth L. "Kenny," **I** 157
Saitch, Eyre "Bruiser," **I** 49, 68
Sakamoto, Isamu, **I** 537, 540
Sakamoto, Makato D., **I** 522, 526,
537-38, 540
Sakhalan, Victor, **I** 528
Salad Bowl football game, **F** 526
Salas, "Joe," **I** 381

Salazar, Alberto B., **O** *527-29*
Salazar, Richard, **O** 527
Salem College, **S** 290
Salem, MA baseball club (NEL), **B**
160, 164, 238, 357
Salem State College, **I** 606
Salem, VA baseball club (ApL, CrL),
B 81, 425, 439; **S** 24, 216
Salica, "Lou," **I** 406, 447
Salina, **O** 604
Salinas, CA baseball club (CaL), **B**
80
Salisbury, NC baseball club (WCL),
B 594
Sallee, Harry F. "Slim," **S** *186-87*
Sallie McClelland, **O** 589
Sally's Alley, **O** 194
Salomon, Janet Lynn Nowicki, **I** 504,
516-17
Salow, Morris, **I** 384
Salsinger, H. G., **F** 194
Salt Lake City, UT baseball club
(PCL, UIL), **B** 120, 184, 217,
236, 325, 558; **S** 23, 105, 157
Salt Lake City, UT *Deseret Times*
basketball club, **I** 92
Salt Lake City, UT Golden Eagles
hockey club (CeHL), **I** 554, 566
Salt Lake City, UT Race Track, **O** 26
Salvator, **O** 209, *604-05*
Sam Houston College, **B** 599
Sam Snead Award, **O** 117
Samford University, **S** 368-69
Sampson, Ralph L., Jr., **I** *265-67*
Samuels, Dale, **F** 572
Samuelson, Joan Benoit, **O** *529-30*
San Antonio, TX baseball club (TL),
B 55, 66, 114, 249, 254, 405,
477, 499, 609; **S** 31, 48, 116,
126, 173, 201, 244
San Antonio, TX Black Aces baseball
club (Negro Leagues), **B** 362
San Antonio, TX Broncos baseball

club (Negro Leagues), **B** 612

San Antonio, TX Handicap, **O** 606

San Antonio, TX Open Golf Tournament, **S** 515

San Antonio, TX Spurs basketball club (ABA, NBA), **I** 35, 96, 98, 224; **S** 269, 278, 285, 299, 305, 315

San Bernardino Valley College, **I** 676; **S** 578

San Diego Bay Swim, **I** 580

San Diego Chargers football club (AFL, NFL), **F** 9-10, 77, 92-93, 104-05, 115, 121, 135, 157, 180, 190-91, 202, 210, 223-24, 230, 273, 285, 291-92, 295-96, 298, 371, 394, 412, 432, 508, 553-64, 614, 632, 659-60, 662; **S** 398, 407-08, 425, 432, 441-42

San Diego Clippers basketball club (NBA), **I** 278-79, 317-18; **S** 308, 328, 330-31

San Diego Conquistadors basketball club (ABA), **I** 47, 111, 150-51; **O** 429; **S** 286-87

San Diego football club (USFL), **F** 210

San Diego Golf Club, **O** 115

San Diego Grand Prix Auto Race, **O** 42

San Diego Hall of Champions, **I** 581

San Diego Hall of Fame, **O** 153

San Diego Indoor Track and Field Meet, **O** 436, 458

San Diego Jaws Soccer Club (NASL), **O** 303

San Diego Junior College, **F** 478

San Diego Marines Basketball Team, **I** 89

San Diego Open Golf Tournament, **O** 115, 144, 166-67; **S** 507, 523

San Diego Padres baseball club (NL), **B** 10, 43, 134, 139, 180, 209, 216, 220, 251, 264, 335, 351, 392, 420-22, 439, 522, 614-15, 623; **S** 27, 31, 49-50, 77, 84, 104, 106, 134, 142, 146, 153, 206, 218, 225

San Diego Padres baseball club (PCL), **B** 42, 102, 151-52, 167, 306, 392, 615; **S** 79, 157, 166, 197

San Diego Rockets basketball club (NBA), **I** 118, 226, 230, 249

San Diego Sails basketball club (ABA), **S** 296

San Diego Sockers Soccer Club (MISL, NASL), **O** 303-04, 308

San Diego State University, 76, 115, 206, 376, 408; **I** 580; **O** 139, 429; **S** 80, 152, 405

San Diego Track and Field Meet, **O** 498, 526-27

San Felipe Handicap, **O** 569

San Francisco Athletic Club, **I** 366, 663

San Francisco City College, **F** 387, 544

San Francisco Clippers football club (AFL), **F** 638

San Francisco *Examiner,* **F** 90; **S** 342

San Francisco 49ers football club (AAFC, NFL), **F** 2-3, 16-17, 104-06, 121, 143, 180, 203, 215, 224, 293-95, 366, 384, 398-99, 404, 433, 443, 453, 467, 473, 485, 521-22, 524, 539, 545, 548, 560, 577, 589, 600, 605, 656; **O** 104, 468, 506-07; **S** 374, 383, 389-90, 411, 415, 427, 446, 452, 481, 483, 493, 499-500

San Francisco Giants baseball club (NL), **B** 9, 38-39, 74, 81, 133, 175, 191, 216, 250, 268, 316, 350-52, 372, 379-80, 394, 405, 410, 425, 445, 448, 479, 518, 521, 525-26, 540, 618; **I** 105; **O** 83; **S** 2,

8, 30-31, 49-50, 83, 103, 108,
114, 120, 134, 139, 148, 174-76,
182, 188, 198, 241, 347, 349-50,
356, 402
San Francisco Golf Club, **O** 143
San Francisco *News,* **F** 118
San Francisco Olympic Club, **I** 498;
O 545
San Francisco *Post,* **O** 90
San Francisco Seals baseball club
(PCL), **B** 42, 102, 151-52, 167,
306, 392, 615; **S** 23, 31, 52, 61,
68, 101, 105, 110, 156-57, 161-62,
232
San Francisco Track and Field Meet,
O 529
San Francisco Stewart Chevrolet
basketball club (AAU), **I** 188, 334
San Francisco Warriors basketball club
(NBA), *See* Golden State Warriors
(NBA)
San Jose, CA Auto Race, **O** 17
San Jose, CA baseball club (CaL), **B**
47; **S** 237
San Jose, CA City College, **S** 210
San Jose, CA Club football club
(ConFL), **F** 631
San Jose, CA State University, **F**
161-62, 220, 261-62, 478, 631,
636, 668; **O** 271, 458, 543; **S**
392
San Jose, CA Track and Field Meet,
O 532
San Jose, CA Weightlifting Meet, **I**
630
San Leandro, CA Beavers Swim Club,
I 619
San Luis Obispo, CA Handicap, **O**
218
San Luis Rey Stakes, **O** 229
San Marino, CA Lacrosse Club, **O**
235
San Mateo, CA Junior College, **F**

631; **O** 545, 563
Sanatory Gymnasium, Cambridge,
MA, **I** 539
Sanchez, Salvador, **I** 414
Sand & Sea Club Volleyball Team, **I**
676
Sandberg, Carl, **I** 39
Sandberg, Ryne D., **B** 42
Sande, Earle H., **O** 183, 193, *215-
16, 585,* 596
Sanders, Barry D., **S** *473-74*
Sanders, George Douglas "Doug," **S**
. *516-17*
Sanders, Henry R. "Red," **F** 74, 368,
522-24; **S** 453
Sanders, Richard J. "Rick," **I** *656-57*
Sanders, Summer, **S** 607-08
Sanders, Thomas E. "Satch," **I** 12,
124
Sandersville, GA baseball club (GSL),
B 351
Sandusky, OH baseball club (Ind.), **B**
126
Sandy Koufax: Strikeout King, **S** 347
Sanford, George F., **F** 265, 644
Sanford, FL baseball club (FSL), **B**
630; **S** 1
Sanford Memorial Stakes, **O** 195-96,
199, 569, 595
Santa Ana, CA Track and Field Meet,
O 522
Santa Ana Junior College, **I** 496
Santa Anita Derby, **O** 173, 569
Santa Anita Handicap, **O** 218, 591,
603, 605-06; **S** 530
Santa Anita Maturity Stakes, **O** 603
Santa Anita Race Track, Arcadia, CA,
O 204, 210, 218, 229, 606; **S** 532
Santa Barbara, CA baseball club
(CaL), **B** 9, 543-44, 614; **S** 90
Santa Clara, CA baseball club (CWL),
S 20
Santa Clara, CA Hall of Fame, **I** 619

Santa Clara, CA Swim Club, I 610-11, 614-15, 617, 619
Santa Clara University, B 89; F 78, 169, 198, 275, 378, 539, 599, 638; I 16; O 294, 493; S 7, 197, 382, 463
Santa Clara University Lacrosse Club, O 235
Santa Cruz, CA baseball club (CaL), B 153
Santa Monica, CA City College, I 676; O 543; S 251, 327, 427, 549
Santa Monica, CA Golf Tournament, O 120
Santa Monica, CA Track Club, O 485
Santee, David N., I 508
Santee, David Wesley "Wes," I 670-71; O 526
Santo, Ronald E. "Ron," B 499, 609
Santop, Louis L. "Lou," B 286, 451, 466, 500
Santry, "Eddie," I 411
Santurce, PR baseball club (PRWL), S 188
Saperstein, Abraham M. "Abe," I 33, 68, 173, 267-68, 293-94
Sapporo, Japan Winter Olympic Games, See Olympic Winter Games, 1972
Saraceni, Eugene, See Eugene Sarazen
Saracheck, Bernice, S 267
Sarajevo, Yugoslavia Winter Olympic Games, See Winter Olympic Games, 1984
Sarasota, FL baseball club (GCL), B 30, 44, 220, 514, 622; S 15, 174, 217, 237
Sarasota, FL Golf Classic, O 137
Saratoga Cup, O 198, 209, 582, 595, 613; S 533
Saratoga Grand Prize, O 209

Saratoga Handicap, O 198, 215, 614
Saratoga Race Track, Saratoga Springs, NY, I 442; O 180, 196, 204, 206, 211, 216, 219, 227, 229, 231, 570, 592, 600-01; S 533-34
Saratoga Special Stakes, O 189, 225, 578, 611, 614
Saratoga Springs, NY basketball club, I 66
Sarazen, S 527
Sarazen, Eugene "Gene," O 63, 108, 120, 138, 153-54, 172; S 515, 523
Sargent, Dudley A., I 538-39; O 253
Sargent, N. C., O 133
Sargent Normal School of Physical Education, Cambridge, MA, I 107, 316
Sarles, Roscoe, O 23
Sarnia, Canada Imperials (Ontario Rugby Football Union), F 92
Sarron, "Petey," I 355, 417, 438-39
Saskatchewan, Canada Roughriders football club (CFL), S 449
Satchel Paige All-Stars, S 9, 188-89
Sather, Glenn C., S 538
Saturday Evening Post, I 611; O 62, 64, 69, 72-73, 517; S 349, 351
Saudi Arabian National Sports Program, S 591
Sauer, George H., Sr., F 541; S 474-75
Sauer, George H., Jr., S 475
Sauer, Henry J. "Hank," S 162, 187-88
Sauer, Richard, S 403
Saunders, "Rusty," I 32, 223
Saunders, "Willie," O 601
Saunteres, S 536
Sauve, Robert "Bob," I 544
Sava, Charles, I 586-87
Savage, M. W., O 580-81
Savage School of Physical Education,

New York, NY, **I** 131, 305; **O** 307

Savannah, GA baseball club (SAL, SL), **B** 34, 94, 167, 185, 409

Savard, Serge A., **I** 562

Saveliev, Sergei, **O** 282

Savitt, Richard D. "Dick," **S** 554, *562-63*

Sawgrass Golf Course, Ponte Vedra, FL, **S** 521-22

Sawyer, Edwin M. "Eddie," **B** 15, 75; **S** 105

Saxton, "Johnny," **I** 359

Sayers, Gale E., **F** 17, 298, 312, 366, 493, 507, *524-25;* **S** 409

Sayers, Roger, **F** 507

Sayers, "Tom," **I** 399

Sayles, William N., **S** 24

Saylor, "Jack," **F** 528-29

Scafide, John, **S** 388

Scales, George, **B** 453; **S** *188-89*

Scapa Flow, **O** 183

Scarce, Guerrant M. "Mac," **S** 123

Scarry, Michael "Mo," **F** 203

Sceneshifter, **O** 216

Schaaf, "Ernie," **I** 358, 429

Schabinger, Arthur A. "Art," **I** *268-70*

Schact, Alexander "Al," **B** 227

Schaefer, Herman H. "Herm," **I** 165

Schaefer, Jacob, Sr., **I** 673

Schaefer 500 Auto Race, **O** 18

Schaefer Trophy, **O** 294

Schaknov, Mikhail, **I** 650

Schalk, Raymond W. "Ray," **B** 108, *501;* **S** 159

Schang, Robert M. "Bobby," **S** 189

Schang, Walter H. "Wally," **B** 456; **S** 62, *189-90*

Schauer, Alexander J. "Rube," **O** 54

Schayes, Adolph "Dolph," **I** 44, 159, *270-71*

Schayes, Daniel L. "Dan," **I** 270

Schectman, Oscar B. "Ossie," **I** 23

Scheffing, Robert B. "Bob," **B** 334

Schemansky, Dennis, **I** 631

Schemansky, Jerome, **I** 631

Schemansky, Norbert, **I** *631-32*

Schembechler, Glenn E., Jr. "Bo," **F** *525-27;* **S** 344, 435

Schenectady, NY baseball club (CAL), **S** 108

Schenectady, NY Company E basketball club, **I** 313

Schenkel, "Chris," **S** 350

Schenley Award, **F** 622

Schick Award, **S** 258, 315

Schiefelbein, "Al," **S** 102

Schiffer, Frank, **F** 182-83

Schiller, William, **I** 398

Schilling, Carol, **S** 525

Schlafke, "Al," **S** 622

Schlafke, Ethelda Bleibtrey MacRobert, **S** *621-22*

Schlichenmaier, "Terry," **I** 596

Schlichter, Walter, **S** 238

Schlundt, Donald "Don," **I** 192, 272, **S** 303, *317-18*

Schmeisser, William C. "Father Bill," **O** 233, *246-47,* 249

Schmeling, Max, **I** 358, 429-30, 462, 475; **S** 610

Schmelz, Gustavus H. "Gus," **S** 194

Schmid, Harald, **O** 502-04

Schmidt, Charles "Charlie," **B** 155-56

Schmidt, Ernest J. "Ernie," **I** *271-72*

Schmidt, Francis A., **F** 272, 391, *527-28*

Schmidt, John, **F** 528

Schmidt, Joseph P. "Joe," **F** *528-30*

Schmidt, Michael J. "Mike," **B** 168, *502-03;* **S** 89

Schmitz, Mark, **I** 666

Schneider, William C. "Buzz," **I** 567

Schnellbacher, Otto, **F** 608

Schnellenberger, Howard, **S** 384

Schniebs, Otto, **O** 276

Schoendienst, Albert F. "Red," **B** 44, 51, *503-04*

Schoendienst, Kevin, **B** 504

Schoenfeld, James G. "Jim," **S** 542

Scholar-Athlete Award, NFF, **S** 450

Scholastic Coach, **F** 648; **I** 276, 305

Scholastic Magazine, **F** 149

Scholastic Medal, BTC, **S** 402

Scholdam, Edith, **I** 512, 514

Schollander, Donald A. "Don," **I** 588, *614-15*

Schollander, Martha P., **I** 614

Schollander, Wendell, Sr., **I** 614

Schollander, Wendell, Jr., **I** 614

Scholz, Jackson V., **O** *530-31;* **S** 589

Schommer, John J., **I** 236, *272-73*

School of Gymnastics, Milford, CT, **I** 529

School of Kurt Thomas Gymnastics, Scottsdale, AZ, **I** 540

Schorling, John M., **B** 189

Schotting, Peter, **O** 316

Schrader, "Ken," **S** 605

Schramm, Texas E., Jr. "Tex," **S** *475-76*

Schreck, "Mike," **I** 398

Schreibauer, Herman, **I** 427

Schreiner, David N. "Dave," **S** *476-77*

Schreiner Institute, **F** 42

Schrempf, Detlef, **I** 116

Schroeder, Frederick R., Jr. "Ted," **O** 337, 355, 365, *389-90,* 418; **S** 553-54

Schroeder, John L., **O** 389

Schroth, Clara M., *See* Clara Schroth Lomady

Schubert, Mark, **I** 575, 583, 593

Schul, Robert K. "Bob," **S** *592-93*

Schuler, Frank, **I** 426

Schulte, Frank M. "Wildfire," **B** 507; **S** *477*

Schulte football club, St. Louis, MO, **O** 301

Schultz, Augusta, **O** 333

Schultz, David L. "Dave," **I** *657-58*

Schultz, Mark P., **I** 635, 657-58, *658-59*

Schultze, Henry F., **O** 530

Schulz, Adolph G. "Germany," **F** 200, *530-31,* 668

Schumacher, Harold L. "Prince Hal," **B** 267; **S** *191-92*

Schumacher Undertakers Soccer Club, **O** 300

Schupp, Ferdinand M. "Ferdie," **O** 54

Schwab, Frank J., **S** *477*

Schwall, Donald B. "Don," **S** 243

Schwartz, Elizabeth Robinson, **S** *593-94*

Schwartz, Marchmont H. "Marchy," **F** 95, *532-34*

Schwartzwalder, Floyd B. "Ben," **F** 122, *534-35*

Schwarz, Wolfgang, **I** 519

Schwed, Peter, **O** 62

Schwimmhalle, Munich, Germany, **I** 618

Scientific Ball, **S** 169

Scioto Country Club, **O** 146

Scoggin, "Matt," **I** 492

Score, Herbert J. "Herb," **B** 635; **S** 83, *192-93*

Scotland National Soccer Team, **O** 291, 294, 296, 300-01, 309

Scotland Olympic Swim Team, **I** 595

Scotland Rangers Soccer Club, **O** 300

Scots-Americans Soccer Club, Kearny, NJ, **O** 309

Scott, Barbara, **I** 502

Scott, Burke, **S** 317

Scott, Charles T. "Charlie," **I** 121, 279, 282; **S** 327

Scott, Daniel "Dan," **O** 599

Scott, George C., Jr., **B** 115; **S**

193-94

Scott, Howard, I 356

Scott, Jacob E. III "Jake," F 18, *535-36*

Scott, James "Jim," B 101

Scott, Paul, S 616

Scott, Steven M. "Steve," O *531-33*

Scott, W. L., O 219

Scott's Farm, Lexington, KY, O 599

Scottdale, PA baseball club (MAL), B 396; S 149

Scottsbluff Junior College, F 332

Scozza, "Lou," I 426, 458, 463

Scranton, PA baseball club (CL, EL, NYPL, NYSL, PSL), B 63, 93, 141, 376, 510; S 127, 163, 228, 240

Scranton, PA basketball club (EL), S 314

Scranton, PA Miners basketball club (EBL), I 250; S 284

Scripps-Howard Newspapers, O 55

Scullions Steel of St. Louis Soccer Club, O 306

Scully, Vincent E. "Vin," O 49, 65, *92-94;* S 348, 353-54

Scypion, Wilford, I 397

Sea O'Erin, O 173

Sea Pine Handicap Golf Tournament, O 126

Seabiscuit, O 184, 198, *605-06,* 614-15; S 525

Seabright Invitation Tennis Championships, O 329, 348, 366, 395-96, 416, 418

Seabright Lawn Tennis Club, O 413

Seagate Stakes, O 196

Seagrams basketball club, I 114

Seagrams Seven Sports Award, F 105; I 153; O 118, 203; S 505

Seagren, Robert L. "Bob," O 458, *533-34*

Seales, "Sugar Ray," I 397-98

Seals Stadium, San Francisco, CA, I 370

Searching, O 192

Sears, Eleonora R., O 329, *390-92,* 393

Sears, Evelyn, S 511

Sears, Frederic R. "Fred," O 349-50, 390-93

Sears, Herbert M., O 391, 393

Sears, Philip S., O 391, 393

Sears, Richard D. "Dick," O 334, 338, 350, 368, 391, *392-93,* 398, 402

Sears, Victor "Vic," F *536*

Sears Open Golf Tournament, O 129

Sears Roebuck Track and Field Meet, Chicago, IL, O 462

A Season in the Sun, S 352

Season of Glory: The Amazing Saga of the 1961 Yankees, S 340

Season Ticket, S 336

Seattle Slew, O 573, *606-07,* 610-11

Seattle Song, O 606

Seattle, WA Auto Race, O 37

Seattle, WA baseball club (NWL), B 193

Seattle, WA baseball club (PCL), B 4, 49, 63, 65, 120, 249-50, 261, 288, 324, 329, 446, 449, 569, 618; S 6, 79, 116, 138, 157, 160, 163, 177, 195, 243

Seattle, WA Golf Club, O 152

Seattle, WA Mariners baseball club (AL), B 262, 395, 445, 449, 505, 615, 619; S 7, 16, 57, 73, 134, 212

Seattle, WA Open Bowling Tournament, I 351

Seattle, WA Pilots baseball club (AL), B 138; S 128, 132, 170, 228

Seattle, WA *Post Intelligencer,* I 16

Seattle, WA Seahawks football club (NFL), F 157, 161, 180, 190-91,

247, 285-86, 295, 321, 335, 363-64, 384, 483, 485, 635; **S** 387, 454

Seattle, WA SuperSonics basketball club (NBA), **I** 119, 121-22, 135, 144, 224, 263, 279, 300, 327-28; **S** 251, 327

Seattle, WA Sounders Soccer Club (NASL), **O** 298, 306, 311

Seattle, WA Track and Field Meet, **O** 545

Seattle, WA University, **I** 18

Seattle's Sportsman of the Year, **I** 116

Seaver, George Thomas "Tom," **B** 314, *504-05;* **S** 38, 146

Sebring, FL Auto Race, **O** 475

Sebring, FL Grand Prix Auto Race, **O** 13, 28, 33; **S** 620

Sebring Reye Dreyfus Twin Cup, **O** 13

Second Air Force Football Team, **F** 155

Second International Congress on School Hygiene, **I** 108

Secory, Frank E., **O** 93

Secreteriat, **O** 183-84, 573, 577, 579, 584, *607,* 610

Sedalia, KS baseball club (MVL), **B** 468

Sedgman, Frank, **O** 358-59, 390; **S** 554, 558

Sedran, Bernard "Barney," **I** 87-88, *273-74*

Seehonk, MA Golf Course, **O** 114

Seeley, Jonas, **O** 587

Sefton, William H. "Bill," **O** 444, 556; **S** 587

Seghi, Phillip "Phil," **B** 485

Segura, Francisco "Pancho," **O** 340, 401; **S** 551-52

Seikaly, Rony F. "Ron," **S** 264

Seitz, Peter, **B** 402

Seivold, Joseph, Jr. "Joe," **O** *247-48*

Seixas, Elias Victor, Jr. "Vic," **O** 359, *393-95,* 407; **S** 554

Sejdi, Sadan, **I** 658

Selbach, Albert K. "Kip," **S** *194-95*

Selby, Norman, *See* Charles McCoy

Select Stakes, **O** 592

Selee, Frank G., **B** 83, 154, 160, *506-07,* 557; **S** 36, 115, 151

Seligson, Julius, **O** 395

Selinger, Arie, **S** 613

Sellers, Ronald "Ron," **F** 206

Selma, Richard J. "Dick," **O** 22

Selma, AL baseball club (AlFL), **S** 170

Selmon, Dewey W., **F** 537

Selmon, Lee Roy, **F** *537,* 582

Selmon, Lucious, **F** 537

Selvy, Franklin D. "Frank," **I** 113; **S** *318-19*

Selznick, Eugene, **I** *676-77*

Semanska, Agnes, **O** 379

Seminole Handicap, **O** 576, 584

Seminole Junior College, **S** 11

Semple, John "Jock," **S** 583

Sencio, Clever, **I** 468

Senior Bowl football game, **F** 18, 59, 63, 76, 118, 133, 185, 274, 279, 303, 372, 430, 461, 464, 482, 528, 542, 550, 553, 556, 565, 577, 587, 643; **S** 391, 395, 462, 493, 504

Senior Intercollegiate Basketball League, **I** 232

Senior Olympics Program, **O** 547

Senior Professional Baseball Association, **S** 26, 35, 79, 84-85, 94, 104, 153

Senior Scholastic, **F** 24

Sensation, **S** 536

Sensational, **O** 222

Sensitive Prince, **O** 569

Seoul, South Korea Summer Olympic Games, *See* Olympic Summer Games, 1988

Sepora, Joseph "Joe," I 664
September Stakes, O 605
Sergeant Edmund Buckley Trophy, I 33
Serrel, William "Bonnie," B 6
Servo, "Marty," I 393, 455
Sesquicentennial Independent Celebration Track and Field Games, O 512
Sestak, Thomas J. "Tom," S 477
Seth Lowe Junior College, I 11
Seton Hall University, I 23, 43, 61-62, 180, 260-61, 318-19; S 594
Seton Hall University Hall of Fame, I 62
Settle, "Al," I 360
Seven Blocks of Granite, F 102, 188, 214, 344, 353, 651, 661; S 400
7-11 Cycling Team, O 317
Seven Hills Club, Nashville, TN, I 579
Seven Veils, O 197
The Seventh Game, S 352
Seventh Regiment Tennis Club, New York, NY, O 411
Severn, Daniel "Dan," I 636
Sewanee College, F 109, 293, 576
Sewell, James Luther "Luke," B 508, 535; S 14, 195
Sewell, Joseph W. "Joe," B 508, 536; S 195
Sewell, Thomas W. "Tommy," B 508
Sewell, Truett B. "Rip," B 616; S 195-96
Seymour, James B. "Cy," B 301, 509
Seymour, Paul N., F 527; I 44
Shade, "Dave," I 361, 458, 463
Shaffer, "Doug," I 492
Shafter V, O 217
Shakespeare, William F., F 393
Sham, O 607
Shamokin, PA baseball club (AtL, CPL), B 92, 118
Shannon, Howard P., I 94
Shannon, Thomas Michael "Mike," O 56
Shannon II, S 532
Shantz, Robert C. "Bobby," B 51; S 196-97
Shantz, Wilmer E. "Billy," S 196
Share, Charles E. "Charlie," I 7
Sharkey, Jack, I 372, 428-29, 431, 438, 462-63, 475, 479; O 469
Sharkey, Thomas J. "Tom," I 366, 407, 462
Sharkey Athletic Club, New York, NY, I 378
Sharman, William W. "Bill," I 12, 16, 110, 124, 190, 262, 274-75, 278, 322
Sharp, Linda, I 214
Sharpe, Albert Howard, I 321
Sharples, "Jeff," S 538
Shaughnessy, Clark D., F 2, 38, 44, 49, 102, 205, 231, 234, 301, 415, 532-33, 537-38, 638
Shaughnessy, "Mike," I 461
Shaver, "Gus," F 512
Shavers, "Earnie," I 401
Shavlakadze, Robert, S 596
Shavlik, Ronald D. "Ron," I 43
Shaw, Dennis W., F 485
Shaw, George, F 24, 613
Shaw, Lawrence T. "Buck," F 12, 33, 491, 538-39, 618
Shaw, Quincy A., Jr., O 334, 398
Shaw, Robert L. "Bob," F 285
Shaw, Timothy A. "Tim," I 616-17
Shaw, Warren Wilbur, O 15, 17, 22-23, 34-35, 37
Shaw, William L. "Billy," S 478-79
Shawkey, James R. "Bob," B 345, 509-10
Shawnee Open Golf Tournament, O 140

Shea, Frank J., **O** 495

Shea, James "Jim," **O** 318

Shea, John A., **O** *317-18*

Shea, William, **I** 250

Shea Stadium, Flushing, NY, **B** 505; **O** 105

Sheboygan, WI baseball club (WSL), **S** 81

Sheboygan, WI Redskins basketball club (NBL), **I** 66, 132-33; **S** 277, 293

Sheckard, Samuel J. "Jimmy," **B** *510-11*

Sheehan, "Bobo," **S** 517

Sheehan, Patricia L. "Patty," **S** *517-18*

Sheepshead Bay Five basketball club, Brooklyn, NY, **S** 314

Sheepshead Bay Race Course, Brooklyn, NY, **O** 23, 184, 208-09, 219-20

Sheide, Gary, **S** 396

Shelby, Carroll, **O** 12

Shelby Blues Athletic Club, **F** 182-83, 456

Shelby, NC baseball club (WCL), **B** 179

Shelbyville, KY baseball club (BGL), **B** 534

Shell, Arthur "Art," **F** *539-40*

Shellenback, Frank V., **S** *197-98*

Shelton, Ernest "Ernie," **O** 456

Shelton, Everett F. "Ev," **I** 106, 158, *275-76*

Shenanigans, **O** 603

Shepard, Lawrence W. "Larry," **S** 230

Shepard, Robert E. "Bob," **B** 227

Shepherd, Sharon, **S** 571

Sheppard, David J. "Dave," **I** 628

Sheppard, Melvin W. "Mel," **O** 495, 531, *534-35*

Sher, "Jack," **F** 358

Sherbrooke, Canada baseball club (EL), **S** 216

Sheridan, John F., **S** *198-99*

Sheridan, Martin J. "Marty," **O** 489, *535-36*

Sherman, "Allie," **F** 206, 218, 279

Sherman Institute, **F** 470

Sherman, TX baseball club (WA), **B** 638

Sherrill, "Jackie," **F** 383, 388; **S** *479-80*

Sherry, Norman B. "Norm," **B** 76

Shevlin, Thomas L. "Tom," **F** 117, 266, 298, *540-41;* **S** 433

Shibe, Benjamin F. "Ben," **B** 358, *511-12;* **F** 41

Shibe, Thomas S., **B** 512

Shibe Park, Philadelphia, PA, **B** 110, 119, 500, 512; **S** 23

Shields, Francis X. "Frank," **O** 322, 347, 386, *395-96,* 409, 418

Shields, James, **O** 188

Shields, "Will," **O** 582

Shiley, Jean, *See* Jean Shiley Newhouse

Shimizu, Zenzo, **O** 362

Shimmer, **S** 531

Shine, Michael L., **O** 503

Shinnecock Hills Golf Club, Southampton, NY, **O** 125, 132-33

Shipley, Beryl, **S** 296

Shipp, Charles W., **S** 279

Shires, Abraham "Abe," **F** 576

Shires, Chester Arthur "Art," **F** 602

Shirley, James Dallas, **I** *276-77*

Shively Sports Center, Lexington, KY, **I** 110

Shoal Creek Golf Course, Birmingham, AL, **O** 164

Shoate, Roderick "Rod," **F** 582

Shockcor, Urban, *See* Urban Shocker

Shocker, Urban J., **B** 456; **S** *199-200*

Shoemaker, William L. "Bill," **O**

176, 178, 189-90, 203, *216-19,* 225, 229, 598, 610, 612

Shofner, Delbert M. "Del," **F** *541-42*

Shooting for the Gold: A Portrait of America's Olympic Athletes, **O** 335

Shore, Edward W. "Eddie," **S** 546

Shore, Ernest G. "Ernie," **S** 111

Short, Robert E. "Bob," **I** 19

Shorter, Frank C., **O** 523, *536-37*

Shotton, Burton E. "Burt," **B** 456

Show, Eric V., **B** 487

Shreveport, LA baseball club (EDL, TL), **B** 114, 326, 512, 516, 551, 601; **S** 50, 79, 218, 245

Shreveport, LA *Journal,* **I** 291

Shreveport, LA Steamers football club (WFL), **F** 389; **S** 404

Shrine All-Star Game, *See* East-West Shrine All-Star Game

Shriver, Pamela H. "Pam," **O** 280-81, 287, *396-97*

Shue, Eugene W. "Gene," **I** 113, *277-78*

Shugart, Frank H., **B** 217

Shula, David D., **F** 543-44

Shula, Donald F. "Don," **F** 122, 219, 225, 333, 370-71, 384, 405, 432, 454, *542-44,* 609; **I** 250; **S** 384

Shula, Michael "Mike," **F** 543-44

Shurlock, Arthur D. "Art," **I** 526

Shut Out, **O** 175

Shute, Herman Bryce, **O** 154

Shute, Herman Densmore "Denny," **O** 154

Shuttle Jet, **O** 611

Sibson, "Tony," **I** 397

Siddons, George, **I** 420

Sidwell, William "Billy," **O** 390

Siebern, Norman L. "Norm," **B** 382

Siebert, Richard W. "Dick," **S** 127, 141, *200-01,* 402

Siegfried, Larry, **I** 161, 186

Sievers, Roy E., **S** *201-02*

Sievers, William, **S** 201

Sievert-Hans, Heinrich, **O** 501

Sigula, **O** 598

Sikma, Jack W., **S** 603

Silas, Paul T., **I** 101, 124, *278-80*

Siler, George, **I** 388

Silk, David "Dave," **I** 568

Silver Skates Competition, **O** 104, 315

Silver Skis Competition, **O** 277

Silver Slugger Award, *TSN,* **S** 35, 51, 85, 158, 236

Silverdome, Pontiac, MI, **F** 546

Silvester, L. Jay, **O** 511

Sime, David W. "Dave," **O** 502, *537-38*

Simmons, Aloysius H. "Al," **B** 50, 101, 106, 163, 232, 247, 267, 359, 401, *512-13*

Simmons, Curtis T. "Curt," **B** 75; **S** 183, 188, *202-03*

Simmons, John E., **S** 320

Simmons, "Lon," **S** 349

Simmons, Ted L., **B** *513-14*

Simms, "Eddie," **I** 426

Simms, William "Willie," **O** *219-20*

Simon, Richard "Dick," **O** 13

Simpson, George S., **O** 496, 552

Simpson, James "Jim," **S** 353

Simpson, Orenthal J. "O. J.," **F** 16, 19-20, 32, 140, 314, 431, 496, 518, *544-45,* 667; **S** 458

Simpson, Robert "Bob," **O** 155

Simpson, Scott W., **O** 166

Simpson College, **I** 254

Sims, Billy Ray, **F** 481, *546-47,* 582, 660

Sinclair, Harry, **O** 215; **S** 527

Singapore National Soccer Team, **O** 301

Singer, "Al," **I** 363, 436

Singletary, Michael "Mike," F 548
Singleton, Kenneth W. "Ken," B
514-15
Singleton, Mildred Louise McDaniel,
O 538-39
Singley, Charles, I 180
Sington, Fred W., F 625
Sinjon, O 267
Sinkwich, Francis "Frank," F 81,
549; S 405
Sinyarski, Vladimir, I 664
Sioux City, IA baseball club (WL), B
21, 40, 65, 107, 217, 416; S 239
Sioux City, IA Open Golf
Tournament, O 113
Sioux Falls, SD baseball club (NoL),
S 73
Sipes, Barbara, I 255
Sir Archy, O 573-74, 608, 609
Sir Barton, O 199-200, 215, 596,
608-09; S 525-26
Sir Galahad III, O 585
Sir Henry, O 101, 571, 609-10
Sires and Dams Book, O 227
Sisemore, Jerald G. "Jerry," F 550
Sisler, David M. "Dave," B 516
Sisler, George H., Sr., B 100, 275,
293, 331, 456, 515-17; S 13, 126-
27
Sisler, George H., Jr., B 516
Sisler, Richard A. "Dick," B 516
Sitko, Emil M., F 176, 249; S 480
Six-Day Bicycle Races, Madison
Square Garden, New York, NY, O
264, 269
Sixty, William "Billy," I 341
Sixty-One: The Game, The Record,
The Men, S 353
Skate America, S 628
Skate Canada, I 501
Skate Ranch, Santa Ana, CA, I 674
Skate Show for Peace, I 502
Skating, I 499

The Skating Club of Boston, I 499,
506
The Skating Club of New York, I 509
Skeen, Richard, O 337, 365
Skiddy Award, I 45
Skinner, John Stuart, O 86, 94-96
Skinner, Jonty, I 591
Skins Golf Game, O 164; S 524
Skladany, Joseph O. "Joe," S 481-82
Skowron, William J. "Bill," B 143;
S 56, 203-04
Skyline Conference, I 94
Skywalker, O 183
Slam Dunk Championship, NBA, S
329
Slaney, Mary Decker Tabb, O 539-
41
Slaney, Richard, O 539
Slapnicka, Cyril C. "Cy," B 176,
563, 605
Slater, Frederick W. "Duke," F 299,
550-52
Slattery, James R. "Jimmy," I 360,
428, 458, 463-64
Slaughter, Enos B. "Country," B 143,
485, 517-18, 597; S 17, 143
Slaughter, "Sammy," I 481
Slavin, "Jack," I 464
Sleepy Hollow Tennis
Championships, O 377
Slew o' Gold, O 606
Slewpy, O 606
Slider, Chester, I 356
Slippery Rock Teachers College, B
509
Sloan, Cassius, O 220
Sloan, Gerald E. "Jerry," I 193-94
Sloan, James F. "Tod," O 187, 220-
21; S 527
Sloan, Norm L., I 280-81
Sloan, Stephen "Steve," F 561; S
479
Sloane, Mrs. Dodge, O 198

Slocum, Henry W., Jr., **O** 334, 338, 351, 392, *398-99,* 420

Slow Poke, **O** 206

Sly Fox, **O** 220

Smalley, Roy F., Jr., **S** 135, 204

Smalley, Roy F. III, **S** 38, 135, *204-05*

Smallwood, "Ed," **I** 193

Smart Angle, **O** 222

Smarten, **O** 222

Smathers, E. E., **S** 526

Smid, Thomas, **O** 379

Smiley, "Gene," **I** 90

Smilgoff, James "Jim," **B** 316

Smith, Adrian H., **I** 231

Smith, Alexander "Alex," **O** 107, 140, *155-56,* 157-58, 160, 164

Smith, Amos "Mysterious Billy," **I** 460, *464,* 473

Smith, Andrew L. "Andy," **F** 299, 410, 439, *552-53*

Smith, Billy Ray, Sr., **F** 553

Smith, Billy Ray, Jr., **F** *553-54*

Smith, Bruce P., **F** 49, *554-56*

Smith, Calvin, **O** 472, 487, *541-42*

Smith, Carl Reginald "Reggie," **B** 411, *518-19;* **S** 7

Smith, Charles, **S** 202

Smith, Charles "Chino," **B** *519*

Smith, Charles A. "Bubba," **F** 127, *556-57,* 642

Smith, Charles K., **O** 399

Smith, Charles W. "Charley," **B** 43

Smith, Dean E., **I** 58, 189, *281-83;* **S** 275, 282, 304

Smith, "Denver Ed," **I** 366

Smith, "Don," **F** 29, **I** 427

Smith, Douglas A. "Doug," **F** 287

Smith, Earl S., **S** 179

Smith, Ed W., **I** 444

Smith, "Eddie," **I** 479

Smith, Elmer J., **B** 65; **S** 5

Smith, Ernest F. "Ernie," **F** 299, 512; **S** 495

Smith, Everett W., Jr., **O** *248*

Smith, Frank, **I** 368

Smith, Gene, **I** 300

Smith, George, **O** 155

Smith, "Gunboat," **I** 424-25

Smith, Harold, **S** 613

Smith, Harry B., **F** 299

Smith, Hilton L., **B** *520-21*

Smith, Horton, **O** 141, *156-57*

Smith, Jackie L., **F** 220, 427, *557-58;* **S** 426, 497

Smith, James, **S** 625

Smith, James "Jim," **O** 155

Smith, James L. "Jimmy," **I** 367

Smith, Jeff, **I** *464-65*

Smith, Jimmy (bowling), **I** 345

Smith, Jimmy (boxing), **I** 414, 481

Smith, John I., **O** 582

Smith, John W., **O** 458

Smith, Kenny, **I** 283

Smith, Larry, **I** 452

Smith, Lawrence E. "Tody," **F** 556

Smith, Lee A., Jr., **S** *205-06*

Smith, Lee Roy, **I** 642

Smith, Lucius A., **F** 554

Smith, MacDonald, **O** 155, *157-58*

Smith, Margaret, **S** 563

Smith, Maurice, **F** 594

Smith, Osborne E. "Ozzie," **B** 410; **S** 31, *206-07,* 218

Smith, Pete, **I** 341

Smith, "Ren," **O** 156

Smith, Rhoda W., **O** 399

Smith, Richard "Dick," **F** 651

Smith, Riley, **F** 281; **S** 439

Smith, Robert, **F** 356

Smith, Robert "Bobby," **O** *308-09*

Smith, Robert W., **F** 40

Smith, Russell "Rusty," **I** 493

Smith, "Solly," **I** 420

Smith, Stanley R. "Stan," **O** 324, *399-400*

Smith, Thomas, S 259

Smith, Thomas "Silent Tom," O 605; S 525

Smith, "Tiger," I 419

Smith, Tommie C., O 458, 486, 516, 542-44, 551

Smith, Walker, Jr., See "Sugar Ray" Robinson

Smith, Wallace "Bud," I 366

Smith, Walter W. "Red," B 598; F 110; O 61, 69, 96-97; S 86, 245, 335, 337-38

Smith, William T. "Bill," I 659-60

Smith, William "Wee Willie," I 49, 69, 439

Smith, William "Willie," O 155, 157

Smith, Willie Ray, Sr., F 556

Smith, Willie Ray, Jr., F 556

Smith, Zeke, F 495; S 431

Smokin Yankee, O 182

Smolnik, Michael "Mike," I 21; S 287, 314

SMU/Dr. Pepper Hall of Fame, F 659

Smuggler, O 586

Snavely, Carl G., F 305, 558-59, 584; S 391, 416

Snead, Norman B. "Norm," S 482-83

Snead, Samuel J. "Sammy," F 248; O 113, 118, 125-26, 131, 141, 143, 145, 153, 158-59, 160, 163; S 507, 522

Snedecker, E. V., O 592

Sneed, Edgar M. "Ed," S 523

Snell, Mathews "Matt," F 165

Snell, Peter, O 526

Sneva, Thomas E. "Tom," O 35-36

Snider, Albert, O 176, 576

Snider, Edwin D. "Duke," B 9, 521-22; S 162

Snow, Jack T., F 276-77, 458

Snowbound, O 267

Snowden, Hal, Jr., O 591

Snyder, Jimmy "The Greek," S 357

Snyder, "Larry," O 449, 514

Snyder, Robert "Bob," F 638

So You Think You're a Die Hard Tiger Fan," S 344

Soar, Albert Henry "Hank," F 447; S 390

Sobers, Ricky B., I 293

Soccer Coach of the Year, O 292

Society of Directors of Physical Education, F 563

Sockalexis, Lewis M. "Lew," B 522-23

Soden, Arthur, S 97

Sol, O 206

Soldier Field, Chicago, IL, F 94, 153, 194, 275, 500, 554; O 104

Soldiers Field, Cambridge, MA, F 64

Solem, Ossie M., F 413, 653

Solicitor, O 207

Solotar, "Ed," S 621

Solotar Swim Club, Washington, DC, S 621

Somers, Charles W., B 523-24

Somethingroyal, O 607

Sonnenberg, Gustave A. "Gus," I 660-61

Sooner State League, S 11, 87

Sophie, Ronald "Ron," I 277

Sophomore Athlete of the Year, University of Illinois, S 88

Sophomore League, S 163

Sorority Stakes, O 604

Sosa, Elias M., B 277

Souchak, Michael "Mike," O 144

Soule, Aileen Riggin, O 494-95

South African National Swim Team, I 591

South African Sun City Golf Classic, O 114

South Atlantic Golf Tournament, S 521

South Atlantic League, B 552, 589;

S 3, 5, 20, 57, 108, 162, 207,
219, 231
South Bend, IN baseball club (CL), B
72, 136, 547
South Bend, IN *Times,* O 72
South Bend, IN *Tribune,* I 156; O
104
South Carolina Athletic Hall of Fame,
F 488, 641, 643; O 117
South Carolina State College, F 297
South Dakota Conference, F 490
South Dakota State University, F 27,
333, 490; I 79
South Florida Golf Tournament, O
162
South Korea National Soccer Team, O
301
South Texas League, S 120
Southampton Invitation Tennis
Championships, O 366, 368, 377-
78, 396, 418; S 556
Southampton Soccer Club, O 303
Southeast Missouri State University,
F 390
Southeast Polk, IA High School, I
183
Southeastern Conference, B 608; F
5, 19-20, 54, 73-75, 81, 91, 95,
101, 104, 110, 121, 145-47, 150,
170, 186, 198-99, 202, 236, 281,
284, 286-88, 296, 301-03, 308,
319-20, 405-07, 418, 422, 425,
429, 470, 514-15, 522-23, 535,
543-44, 549, 560-61, 567, 575,
577, 583, 587, 594-95, 598-600,
603-04, 606, 618, 621, 630, 632; I
67, 109, 135, 204, 237, 245, 249,
256, 281, 497, 591-92; O 465-66;
S 257, 259-61, 271, 276-77, 286,
309, 318, 329, 349, 365-66, 368,
378, 382-85, 394-95, 399, 412,
421-22, 424, 430-31, 439, 448-49,
452, 460, 462-66, 469-70, 478-80,
498, 504
Southeastern Conference
Championships, O 465-66; S
261, 276, 329, 385, 394-95, 422,
430, 449, 463-64
Southeastern Intercollegiate Wrestling
Association Championships, S
617
Southern Amateur Women's Golf
Tournament, O 159
Southern Association, B 169; S 1, 5,
19-20, 45, 116-17, 121, 130-31,
150, 163, 177, 219, 225, 228, 230,
245-47
Southern California Athletic
Conference, F 7, 114; S 432,
453-54
Southern California Golden Gloves
Tournament, I 447
Southern California Junior College
Player of the Year, I 55
Southern California Pro Golf
Tournament, O 120
Southern California Tennis
Association, S 553
Southern California Tennis
Championships, O 327, 332, 353;
S 549-50
Southern California Women's Golf
Tournament, O 329
Southern Colorado State College, B
220
Southern Conference, F 5, 14, 53,
74, 109-10, 118, 127, 145, 150,
170, 175, 188-89, 205, 274, 278,
299, 305, 327, 345-46, 361, 397,
405-07, 421-22, 428, 452, 515,
522, 531, 534, 538-39, 558-59,
574, 576, 584, 587, 595, 621, 625-
26; I 40, 42, 67, 99, 277, 280-81,
322; S 106, 282, 399, 413, 419-
22, 424, 430, 446-47, 455-56, 464,
484

Southern Conference Championships, S 271, 388, 420-21, 430, 456
Southern Connecticut Gymnastic Club, I 529
Southern Connecticut State University, I 528
Southern Division Lacrosse Intercollegiate Championships, O 249
Southern 500 NASCAR Race, O 1, 44; S 606
Southern Hills Country Club, Tulsa, OK, S 507
Southern Illinois University, Carbondale, IL, F 247-48, 524; S 210
Southern Illinois University, Edwardsville, IL, I 93
Southern Illinois University Hall of Fame, F 248
Southern Intercollegiate Athletic Association, F 47, 108-09, 150, 175, 230, 257, 293, 368, 402, 406, 422, 475-76, 530, 537, 565, 594-95, 603, 635, 669
Southern Intercollegiate Athletic Conference, B 508, 536; O 468; S 441
Southern Kansas basketball club (AAU), I 148
Southern Lacrosse Officials Association, O 237, 243
Southern Ladies Roller Skating Championship, I 674
Southern League, S 3, 6, 51, 66, 84, 86, 93, 119, 128, 135, 152, 154, 160, 194, 198, 202, 225, 233, 235-37
Southern Men's Amateur Golf Tournament, O 521
Southern Methodist University, B 254; 30, 35, 42, 94, 139, 171, 174, 221, 223, 265, 275, 280, 317-18, 340, 345, 353, 366, 369, 378, 383, 405-07, 491, 506, 532, 541, 572, 617, 628-29, 637, 658-59; I 605; O 80, 170; S 373, 401, 450, 471, 499, 550, 561
Southern Methodist University/Dr. Pepper Hall of Fame, S 450
Southern Ocean Racing Conference, O 103
Southern Open Golf Tournament, O 126, 143, 153
Southern Oregon State College, I 131; S 330
Southern Pacific Track and Field Championships, O 492; S 574
Southern States Tennis Championships, O 354
Southern University, B 51; F 56, 96; O 447, 497
Southern Women's Amateur Golf Tournament, S 512
Southgate Open Golf Tournament, O 129
Southland Conference, F 663-64; S 324, 401
Southland Conference Championships, S 324, 401
Southland Olympic Award, I 553, 579
Southwest Bell Invitation Golf Tournament, S 510
Southwest Conference, F 3-4, 9, 29-30, 35, 39, 42, 47, 73-74, 87, 121, 139, 170, 206, 223, 257, 278, 280, 293, 316-18, 331, 336, 340-41, 346-47, 367, 378, 389, 391-92, 403, 405-07, 422, 431, 434, 437, 446, 448, 514-16, 519, 527, 541-42, 547-48, 550-53, 578, 581, 621, 628-29, 658, 663; I 174, 583, 605; O 69, 83, 323, 485; S 54, 74, 96, 145, 382, 401, 419-20, 423-24, 428, 438, 448, 450, 462, 471, 474, 477-80, 489, 494

Southwest Conference
Championships, O 485; S 54, 74,
420, 423, 480
Southwest Football Officials
Association, S 494
Southwest International League, B 16
Southwest Missouri State University,
I 90
Southwest Open Golf Tournament, O
120
Southwest Pacific Intermediate Ladies
Roller Skating Championships, I
674
Southwest Texas State University, I
174
Southwest Women's Amateur Golf
Tournament, O 164
Southwestern Athletic Conference, F
56, 62-63, 72, 75, 96, 131, 273,
285, 295, 499-501, 590-91; S
364, 389, 415
Southwestern Athletic Conference
Championships, S 389
Southwestern Baptist Theological
Seminary, I 664
Southwestern Bible College, S 327
Southwestern College, F 422, 576
Southwestern Louisiana Institute, B
133; F 83
Southwestern Louisiana University, S
296, 388-89
Southwestern University, I 580; S
324
Southworth, William H. "Billy," B
215, 258, 524-25
Souza, John, O 309, 310
Soviet Union National Gymnastic
Team, I 542
Soviet Union National Ice Hockey
Team, I 548, 559, 562, 565, 567-
69, 573; S 548
Soviet Union National Men's
Basketball Team, I 27, 70, 72,
140, 162 S 310
Soviet Union National Swim Team, I
579, 583, 592
Soviet Union National Track and Field
Team, O 438, 457, 475, 479, 518,
542
Soviet Union National Women's
Basketball Team, I 55, 123, 215,
246, 255, 285, 325
Soviet Union National Wrestling
Team, I 639, 645, 650, 654, 658-
59, 666
Soviet Union Olympic Ice Hockey
Team, S 541
Soviet Union Olympic Track and Field
Team, S 581, 596-97
Spahn, Warren E., B 14, 62, 380,
420, 451, 525-26; S 17, 60, 103,
186
Spain, Truman, F 407
Spain National Soccer Team, O 291
Spalding, Albert G. "Al," B 77, 79,
270-71, 496, 527-28, 603, 628,
637; S 69
Spalding Basketball Rules, I 13
Spalding Sporting Goods Company, B
465, 527, 607; I 125, 139, 269; O
157, 320, 512
Spalding's Official Base Ball Guide,
B 82, 194, 430, 527
Spalding's Official Intercollegiate
Football Guide, F 86, 158, 415,
440, 477, 531; S 494
Sparling, Raymond "Ray," F 512
Sparta College, I 286
Spartakiade Games, I 329
Spartan, O 201
Spartan Valor, O 223
Spartanburg, SC baseball club (CrA,
TSL), B 42, 102; S 230-31
Spartanburg, SC Country Club, O
152, 170
Spassky, Boris, I 672

Spaulding, William H. "Doc," **F** 27, 637

Speaker, Tristram E. "Tris," **B** 110, 151, 247, 259, 275, 286, 291, 400, 488, *528-30,* 536, 625; **I** 53; **S** 111-12, 143, 231, 235

Spear, Robert, **I** 282

Spears, Clarence W. "Doc," **F** 254, 416; **S** 424, *483-84*

Spears, Marion O. "Odie," **I** 67

Special Olympics, **I** 523; **S** 205, 301, 312, 517, 597

Spectacular, **O** 610

Spectacular Bid, **O** 570, 592, *610-11*

Spectrum, Philadelphia, PA, **I** 104

Speed Bowl, **O** 191

Speedie, Mac C., **F** 215, 409, *559-60*

Speedy Count, **O** 191

Speight, Robert "Bob," **I** 43

Spellman, John F., **I** 661

Spencer, H. O., **I** 651

Spencer, Robert L. "Bob," **S** *319-20*

Spencer Haywood Foundation, **I** 122

Spencer Penrose Award, **I** 561

Spendthrift, **O** 592

Spendthrift Farm, Lexington, KY, **O** 612

Spengler, Louis "Lou," **O** 508

Sperry & Hutchinson Open Golf Tournament, **O** 129; **S** 518

Speyrer, Charles W. "Cotton," **F** 516

Spiedel, Charles "Charlie," **I** 646

Spinaway, **S** 536

Spinaway Stakes, **O** 604

Spink, Alfred H., **B** 325, 399, 576

Spink, Charles C., **O** 73, 97

Spink, J. G. Taylor, **O** *97-98*

Spinks, Leon, **I** 401, 407, *465-66;* **S** 622-23

Spinks, Michael, **I** 401, 466; **S** *622-24,* 625

Spirit of the Times and Life in New York, **O** 85-86

Spitz, George B., **O** 476

Spitz, Mark A., **I** 584, 588, 593, 615, *617-18;* **O** 269, 535; **S** 602-03

Spivey, William "Bill," **I** 109, 233, 257

Spoelstra, Arthur C. "Art," **I** 68

Spohn, Gerald, **I** 181

Spokane, WA baseball club (NWL, PCL, PNL), **B** 58, 139, 264, 372, 522, 544, 613, 618-19; **S** 2, 24, 53, 90, 109, 114, 185, 209

Spokane, WA Shockers football club (ConFL), **F** 561

Spooner, Karl B., **S** 176

Sport, **B** 48; **F** 2, 33, 59, 132, 248, 271, 333, 415, 504, 545, 575; **I** 617; **O** 69, 307; **S** 347, 350

Sport's Performer of the Year, **I** 617; **O** 474

Sporting Life, **I** 670; **O** 97

The Sporting News, **B** 1, 9, 13, 18, 23, 35, 37-38, 40-42, 44, 48, 50, 69-71, 73, 76, 103, 115, 123, 133, 139-40, 146, 149, 153, 159, 168-69, 180, 191, 198, 212, 232-33, 245, 251-52, 254, 272, 277, 284, 295, 306, 308, 313, 316, 322, 325, 341, 352, 364, 367, 370, 379, 394-95, 397, 405, 409, 412-13, 421, 444, 471, 477, 486-87, 490, 503, 505, 514, 517, 521, 525-26, 540, 542, 544, 569-70, 573, 583, 610, 618, 625, 639-40; **F** 9, 16-17, 25, 55, 59, 63, 72-73, 77, 79, 99, 106, 130, 140, 149-50, 181, 195, 219-21, 226, 237, 248, 279, 286, 296, 321, 334, 337, 384, 401, 462, 473, 487, 497, 525, 537, 539, 546, 557, 562, 583, 585, 591, 667; **I** 10, 25-26, 56, 86-87, 89, 147, 153, 160, 212, 234, 298, 315, 331, 343, 349,

548; O 49, 55, 73-75, 97-98, 272;
S 6, 15, 19, 26, 35, 48, 51-52, 56,
71, 73, 77, 85, 88, 93, 107, 121,
132, 135, 140, 158, 166, 171, 175,
180, 192-93, 204, 208, 211-12,
214, 228, 236, 243-44, 253, 274,
282, 294, 303, 315, 327, 330, 337-
38, 344, 346, 348, 353-54, 363,
369-70, 382, 389, 399, 402, 414,
419, 427, 442, 448, 475, 496-97
The Sporting News Broadcaster of the
Year, O 78
The Sporting News Hockey Coach of
the Year, I 548
The Sporting News Sportsman of the
Year, I 26, 234, 331; O 272
Sportlife, F 269
Sports Broadcasters Association, O 46
Sports Broadcasters Hall of Fame, O
68
Sports Car Club of America Circuit,
O 28, 37; S 614, 619
Sports Car Club of America Top
Amateur Driver, S 619
Sports Car Club of America Trans-Am
Championship, S 614
Sports Channel, S 68
Sports Illustrated, B 185, 634; F 24,
29, 59, 90, 101, 132, 140, 213,
358, 413, 415, 425, 431, 437, 460,
517, 572, 575, 598, 606, 629, 638,
641; I 2, 17, 225, 536, 550, 611,
645; O 81, 125, 150-51, 163, 176,
326; S 180, 336, 340, 346, 351,
357, 383, 413-14, 417, 517, 618
Sports Illustrated Silver Anniversary
Football Team, S 413-14, 417
Sports Illustrated Sportsman of the
Year, O 150, 163, 352, 364, 502-
03; S 517, 618
Sports Illustrated Sportswoman of the
Year, I 536
Sports of Our Times: Columns and

Commentaries, S 335
Sports of the Times, O 60-61, 71
Sports Teams for the Prevention of
Drug Abuse, F 548
Sportscaster of the Year Award, O 83
Sportsman Park, St. Louis, MO, B
45, 67, 229, 576; O 57; S 201
Sportsman's Show, Minneapolis, MN,
I 572
Sportsmen's World Award, I 77
Sportswoman, I 499; O 254, 335
Sportswoman of the Year Award, O
457, 529
Sportswriter of the Year Award, O 61
Sportswriters Association of
Connecticut, O 262
Sportswriters Hall of Fame, O 53
Spradling, George, I 167
Sprague, Kenneth "Ken," F 477
Spring Lake Invitation Tennis
Championships, O 368
Spring Mill Golf Course,
Philadelphia, PA, O 159
Springbok, S 530-33
Springfield College, F 563-64, 663; I
37, 128-29, 268, 287-88, 524, 534,
637; S 279
Springfield College Hall of Fame, I
288
Springfield, IL baseball club (3IL), B
157, 330, 535; S 187, 201
Springfield, IL basketball club, S 287
Springfield, IL Race Track, O 35, 42
Springfield, MA baseball club (EL,
IA, IL, NA), B 52, 66, 85, 90,
111, 116, 155, 160, 236, 239, 377,
379, 509, 574, 630; S 20, 98, 104
Springfield, MA Flame basketball
club (USBL), I 176
Springfield, MO baseball club (WA),
B 116, 236
Springfield, MO baseball club (CL,
MAL), B 8, 237, 328, 469; S 82-

83
Sprinkle, Edward "Ed," F 26, 609; S 484-85
Sprinter of the Year, O 584
Sproul, Dennis, F 291
Sprouse, Alline Banks, I 123, 283-84
Sprowl, Robert J., Jr. "Bob," B 594
Spur, O 196
Spurrier, Graham, F 560
Spurrier, Stephen O. "Steve," F 225, 560-61
Spy Song, O 572
Squaw Valley, CA Ski Competition, O 282
Squaw Valley, CA Winter Olympic Games, See Olympic Winter Games, 1960
Stabler, Ken M. "Snake," F 55, 75, 180, 341, 561-62; S 479
Stack, Frank, O 318
Stacy, Hollis, S 518-19
Stacy, Tillie, S 518
Stadio Olympico, Rome, Italy, O 433
Stadium Club, Rochester, NY, I 45
Stagecoach, O 216
Stagehand, O 223
Stagg, Amos Alonzo, F 44-45, 75, 119, 159, 244, 422, 429, 501, 562-65, 654, 665-66; I 236, 272
Stagg Award, F 6, 164, 242, 313, 422, 429, 564
Stagg Bowl football game, F 564
Stagg Field, Chicago, IL, F 564
Stagg Track and Field Meet, O 549
Stahl, Charles S. "Chick," B 161
Stahl, Garland "Jake," B 255
Stalcup, Thomas Virgil "Red," S 320
Stallard, Evan Tracy, B 382
Stallings, George T., B 89
Stallings, Harry, S 426
Stallworth, David "Dave," I 220
Stallworth, Johnny L. "John," F

565-66, 581, 590
Stamford, CT basketball club (EL), S 314
Stamina, O 196
Stamm, Michael E. "Mike," I 584
Stan, O 173
Standard-Register Turquoise Golf Classic, S 508
Stander, "Ron," I 386
Stanfel, Richard "Dick," F 26, 521, 566-67
Stanfield, Andrew W. "Andy," O 451; S 594-95
Stanford, Leland, O 185
Stanford University, B 54, 324; F 2, 24, 35, 66-67, 74, 102, 106, 113-14, 153, 161-62, 187-88, 220-21, 261-62, 281, 299-301, 313, 350-52, 368, 377, 411, 424-25, 438, 472-73, 491, 504-05, 512-13, 533, 538, 564, 585, 592, 595, 631-32, 636, 658, 668; I 5, 22, 37, 39, 63, 91, 139, 141, 157, 172, 187, 241, 333, 417, 486, 496-98, 582, 595, 609, 658-59; O 79, 138, 165-66, 170, 314, 347, 369, 377, 389, 438, 440, 444, 493, 544, 552, 556, 568; S 15, 266, 325, 422, 439, 445-46, 454, 467, 495-96, 551, 553, 575-76, 588, 607-08, 626-27
Stanford University Hall of Fame, F 425; I 188
Stanko, Steve, I 626, 629
Stanky, Edward R. "Eddie," B 133; O 57; S 139, 207-08
Stanley, Marianne Crawford, I 175, 258, 284-85
Stanley Cup Hockey Playoffs and Championships, I 453, 546-47, 550-51, 553, 557, 560, 562-63, 566, 570-71; S 537-38, 540, 543-44, 546-47
Stannard, Henry, O 544

Stansbury, Terence R., **S** 268
Star of Brooklyn baseball club, **B** 128
Star of Stars Trophy, **S** 542
Star Shoot, **O** 608
Stargell, Wilver D. "Willie," **B** 503, *530-31;* **F** 59
Stark, Albert D. "Dolly," **S** *208-09*
Stark, Archibald "Archie," **O** *309-10*
Stark, Monroe R. "Dolly," **S** 209
Starr, Bryan Bartlett "Bart," **F** 322, 353, 355, *567-68;* **S** 364
Starr, Heriwentha Faggs, **I** *595*
Start, Joseph "Joe," **B** *531-32*
State University of New York College at Cortland, **I** 584
State University of New York College at Potsdam, *See* Potsdam State University
Staten Island Athletic Club Tennis Team, **S** 562
Staten Island Cricket and Baseball Club, **O** 350, 382, 392; **S** 559-60, 562
Staten Island Cricket and Baseball Club Tennis Championships, **O** 350, 382, 392; **S** 560
Staten Island Indians baseball club (Ind.), **B** 429
Staten Island Stapletons football club (NFL), **F** 573
Stats, Dwayne, **S** 354
Staub, Daniel J. "Rusty," **B** *532-33;* **S** 244
Staubach, Roger T., **F** 37, 331, 431, *568-69;* **S** 455
Stautner, Ernest "Ernie," **F** 146, *569-70*
Stayfree Division II Coach of the Year, **S** 320
Steady Star, **O** 600
Steamboat Springs, CO Ski Competition, **O** 282
Stearns, John H., **S** 123

Stearns, Norman "Turkey," **B** 519, *533-34*
Stebbins, Harold, **F** 214
"Steel Curtain," **S** 407
Steele, "Freddie," **I** *466-67*
Steele, Richard, **S** 626
Steers, George, **O** 101
Steers, Lester L. "Les," **O** 470, *544-45*
Stefanich, James "Jim," **I** 342
Steffen, Gerhardt A., *See* Willie Ritchie
Steffen, Walter P., **F** 159; **I** 272; **S** 397, *485-86*
Stegeman, Herman J., **F** 109-10
Steinbrenner, George M. III, **B** 277, 318, 340, 386, 441-42; **S** 65, 73, 170
Steiner, "Ray," **I** 127
Steinkraus, William C. "Bill," **O** *266-68*
Steinkuhler, Dean E., **F** 444, 495, *570-71*
Steinmetz, Alan, **I** 286
Steinmetz, Christian, **I** *285-86*
Steinmetz, Christian, Jr., **I** 286
Steinmetz, Donald "Don," **I** 286
Steinseifer, Carrie, **I** 596-97
Steitz, Edward S., **I** *286-88*
Stelzle, Jacob, *See* Jacob Stenzel
Stenerud, Jan, **F** 25; **S** *486-87*
Stengel, Charles D. "Casey," **B** 143, 147, 245, 251, 290-92, 385, 404, 432, 469, 475, 482, 490, *534-35,* 549, 597-98; **O** 60, 83; **S** 37-38, 91, 95, 107, 117, 340
Stengel: His Life and Times, **S** 340
Stenmark, Ingemar, **O** 285
Stenographer, **O** 207
Stenroos, Albin, **O** 452
Stenzel, Jacob C. "Jake," **S** 19, *209-10*
Stephen P. Austin University, **S** 324

Stephens, H. W. "Brodie," F 410, 552
Stephens, Helen H., O 545-47, 555; S 569, 593
Stephens, John, O 597
Stephens, Vernon D. "Vern," B 535-36; S 126
Stephens, Woodford C. "Woody," O 221-22, 611; S 528
Stephenson, Jackson Riggs, B 508, 536-37
Stephenson, Janet, S 509
Sterling College, S 453
Sterling, IL baseball club (3IL), B 195
Stern, David J., I 234, 288-89
Stern, William "Bill," O 77, 82, 98-100; S 348
Sternaman, Ed C. "Dutch," F 234
Stetcher, Joseph "Joe," I 648
Stetson, John, O 430
Steubenville, OH baseball club (ISL), B 581
Steuber, Robert "Bob," F 168
Stevens, Edwin, O 101
Stevens, Father Alois J., I 427
Stevens, John, I 233
Stevens, John C., O 100-02
Stevens, Marvin A. "Mal," F 57, 302
Stevens, Richard, O 419
Stevens, Robert L., O 101, 609
Stevens Institute of Technology, O 7, 101, 402
Stevens Point Teachers College, B 512
Steward, Emanuel, S 612-13
Stewart, Alexander M. "Alex," F 60; S 626
Stewart, Eddie, I 440
Stewart, Ernest D. "Ernie," B 243
Stewart, Lusia Harris, I 289-90, 314
Stewart, "Moose," F 599
Stewart, Norman "Norm," S 320-21
Stewart, Robert "Bobby," S 625

Stewart, William J. "Bill," I 553, 570, 571-72; S 186, 544
Stieb, David A. "Dave," S 210-11
Stieber, Fred, O 244
Stift, "Billy," I 457
Stiles, Maxwell, F 417
Still, Arthur B. "Art," F 104
Stinchcomb, Gaylord Peter "Pete," F 241
Stingley, Darryl F., F 586
Stipanovich, Stephen S. "Steve," I 304
Stirling, Alexa, See Alexa Stirling Fraser
Stivetts, John E. "Jack," B 537-38
Stix, Baer, and Fuller Soccer Club, St. Louis, MO, O 294, 299, 305
Stock, Milton J. "Milt," S 207
Stockholm, Sweden Summer Olympic Games, See Olympic Summer Games, 1912
Stockholm, Sweden Track and Field Meet, O 465-66, 489, 528, 530, 548
Stockli, Fritz, I 665
Stockton, Dick, O 335
Stockton, CA baseball club (CaL), S 59, 96
Stockton, CA Junior College, F 564
Stockwell, Mark, I 592
Stockwood Farm, O 589
Stoefen, Lester R. "Les," O 331, 368, 410, 418
Stokes, Maurice, I 308, 319
Stollenwerck, Logan, F 406
Stoller, Samuel "Sam," O 515
Stoltz, Martin, O 288
Stolz, Allie, I 441
Stone, George R., B 64
Stone, Jonathan T., S 211-12
Stonebraker, Homer, I 130, 312-13
Stoneham, Charles A., B 539
Stoneham, Horace C., B 175, 427,

432, *539-40*
Stoneland, O 215
Stoner Creek Stud, O 578-79
Stones, Dwight E., S 566-67
Storey, Edward J., F *571-72*
Storm Damage, O 191
Stottlemyre, Melvin L., Sr. "Mel," S *212-13*
Stottlemyre, Melvin L., Jr., S 213
Stottlemyre, Todd V., S 213
Stouder, Sharon M., *See* Sharon Stouder Clark
Stouffer, Vernon, B 441
Stout, James "Jimmy," O *222-23*
Stove, Betty, O 363
Stovey, George, B 11
Stovey, Harry D., B *540-41*
Stow, Thomas "Tom," O 330, 343, 348; S 551
Stowe, VT Alpine Ski Competition, O 288
Stoyanova, Boriana, I 535
STP Turbocar, O 18
Strachan, John R., O 418
Straight Deal, O 192
Strain, Ted, I 85
Strait of Gibraltar Swim, I 581
Strakhov, Gennady, I 654
Stram, Henry L. "Hank," F 36, 76, 133-34, *572-73;* S 203
Strange, Allan, S 519
Strange, Curtis N., S 514, *519-20*
Strange, Thomas W., Jr., S 519
Stratton, David Michael, S 478
Stratton, Monty F., S 126
Stratton Mountain, VT Golf Classic, S 518
Strauss, Astrid, I 583
Strauss, Isador, I 445
Street, James, F 515
Street and Smith's, I 214
Streeter, Samuel "Sam," B 453
Streit, Saul, I 257

Strength and Health, I 628-29
Stribling, Young, I 360, 428
Strickler, George, F 187
Stricklett, Elmer G. "Spitball," B 586
Stripp, Joseph V. "Joe," B 250
Strobar Division Lacrosse Championships, O 240
Strode, Woodrow "Woody," F 637, 656
Strohs Bowling Team, Detroit, MI, I 348
Strokes of Genius, S 337
Stromboli, S 526-27
Stromsund, Sweden Speed Skating Competition, O 316
Strong, Elmer Kenneth, Jr. "Ken," F *573-74;* S 390, 458
Strong, Frank, F 174
Strong, Nat C., B 189
Strong, T. R. "Ted," B 6
Strunk, Amos A., S 190
Strupper, G. Everett, F 231
Studebaker Motor Company, O 8
Stuhldreher, Harry A., F 172, *187-90,* 574; S 476; *See also* Four Horsemen
Stuhldreher, Walter, F 189
Stumpf, "Eddie," B 561
Sturdy, Denise Long, *See* Denise Long Andre
Sturgess, Eric W., O 337-38, 355, 390
Sturgis, M. E., O 580
Stutz, Stanley J. "Stan," I 155; S *321-22*
Stutz Race Car, O 6, 26
Stuyvesant Handicap, O 595-96
Stydahar, Joseph L. "Joe," F *574-75*
Stymie, O 192, 205, 571
Stymie Manor, Monkton, MD, O 192
Su Mac Lad, O 182
Suarez, Justo, I 451

Suburban Handicap, **O** 178, 185-87,
199, 211, 220, 222, 224-25, 580-
81, 584, 592, 605; **S** 533
Suburban Stakes, **O** 177
Successor, **O** 581
Suffolk College, **S** 375
Suffolk Downs, **O** 203
Suffridge, Robert L. "Bob," **F** 575-
77
Sugar Bowl Basketball Tournament,
New Orleans, LA, **I** 124, 127
Sugar Bowl football game, **F** 3, 5-6,
12, 30, 74, 77-78, 81, 91, 138,
147, 149, 168, 170-71, 198, 286-
87, 302, 305, 308, 316-17, 331,
336, 344, 383, 391, 397, 407, 418,
422, 427, 434, 437, 444, 458, 460,
515, 534, 539, 542, 553, 558, 560-
61, 575-76, 594-95, 598-99, 604,
621-22, 630, 636, 641; **O** 49, 52,
100; **S** 366, 379, 401, 412, 418,
421, 428, 448, 460-61, 463, 479,
487, 498
Sugar Bowl Hall of Fame, **F** 575
Sugar Ray Robinson Youth
Foundation, **S** 579
Suggs, John B., **O** 159
Suggs, Louise, **O** *159-60;* **S** 509
Suhey, Matthew J. "Matt," **F** 93
Sukeforth, Clyde L., **B** 250, 480
Sukova, Helena, **O** 379-80
Sukova, Vera, **O** 379
Sul Ross State College, **B** 79
Sullivan, Danny, **O** 29
Sullivan, "Ed," **I** 379; **O** 310
Sullivan, Jack "Twin," **I** 414, 448
Sullivan, James E., **I** 670; **O** *268-
69,* 455
Sullivan, John L. "The Great John
L.," **I** 369, 377, *467-68,* 474
Sullivan, "Kid," **I** 379
Sullivan, Mike "Twin," **I** 377
Sullivan, Patrick J. "Pat," **F** *577-78;*

S 431
Sullivan, Theodore P. "Ted," **B** 107
Sullivan, "Tommy," **I** 357
Sullivan, "Yankee," **I** 402-03, 443
Sullivan Award, **F** 54, 605; *See also*
James E. Sullivan Memorial
Trophy
Sulphur Springs, TX baseball club
(ETL), **S** 235
The Summer Game, **S** 336
Summer Handicap, **O** 209
Summer Solstice, **O** 173
Summer Tan, **O** 598
Summerall, George "Pat," **F** 376,
378-79
Summerhays, "Johnny," **I** 452
Summertime Promise, **O** 226
Summitt, Patricia Head "Pat," **I** *290-
92*
Sumners, Rosalynn D., **I** *517-18;* **S**
628
Sumter, SC baseball club (WCL), **B**
30
Sun Beau, **O** 586, 606; **S** 531
Sun Belt Conference, **I** 285; **S** 208,
259
Sun Belt Conference Championships,
S 208
Sun Bowl football game, **F** 147, 149,
210, 253, 289, 296, 389, 444, 457,
582, 608, 632, 663; **S** 382, 401,
423, 425, 499
Sun Briar, **O** 196, 200, 582; **S** 531
Sun Briar Court, Binghamton, NY, **O**
582
Sunbury, PA basketball club (EBL), **I**
243
Sun City Challenge Golf Tournament,
O 124
Sundberg, James H. "Jim," **S** *213-
14*
The Sun Field, **O** 54
Sunkist Invitation Track and Field

Meet, Los Angeles, CA, O 507, 532, 540
Sunny's Halo, O 183
Sunnyvale Ice Palace, I 500
Sunoco Ferrari Race Car, O 28
Sunset Fields Golf Tournament, O 120
Sunset Handicap, O 591
Sun Valley, ID Ski Club, O 278
Sun Valley, ID Ski Competition, O 277-78, 284, 287
Super Bowl football game, F 1, 7, 9-10, 15-18, 36, 43, 50, 55-56, 59, 62, 73, 76, 104, 122, 128, 131, 133-34, 143, 150-51, 161, 163, 165, 180, 196, 202, 206, 219, 223-24, 226, 230, 236-37, 246, 258, 264, 274, 280, 286, 292, 296, 303-04, 322-24, 330-31, 333-34, 347, 352, 354-55, 363, 371-72, 376, 384, 388-89, 398, 400, 405, 408, 419, 423-24, 430, 432, 451, 462, 473, 481, 487-88, 490, 502, 511, 517, 529, 535, 540, 543, 545, 547-48, 557-58, 561, 565, 567-69, 572-73, 579-81, 583-84, 596-91, 593, 610, 614-15, 620, 632, 634, 640, 643, 650, 662, 667; O 56, 63, 67, 69, 105, 468; S 363, 366-67, 373-75, 379, 383, 386, 399, 410-11, 413, 419, 430, 432, 441, 449-52, 455, 463, 469, 475, 486, 490, 504
Super Bowl Harness Racing, O 182
Super Derby, O 204, 227
Superior, NE baseball club (NeSL), B 296
Superior, WI baseball club (MWL, NoL), B 20, 262
Superior State College, I 158
Superman, S 533
Super Middleweight Boxing Championships, I 423

The Superstars, I 503
Superstars Competition, O 47, 307-08
The Superteams, I 503
Supper Date, S 525
Suriname Olympic Team, S 602
Surrender, O 206
Susman, Karen Hantze, O 363; S 550, 563-64
Susman, Rod, S 563
Susquehanna College, F 564
Sutherland, John B. "Doc," F 39, 259, 300, 421, 511, 579-80, 627, 636; S 477, 481
Sutphin, "Al," I 240
Sutter, Clifford S. "Cliff," O 410
Sutter, Howard Bruce, B 542; S 206
Suttles, George "Mule," B 269, 542-43, 612
Sutton, Donald H. "Don," B 543-45; S 80, 160
Sutton, "Eddie," I 219
Sutton, Ezra B., B 270
Sutton, Florence, O 336, 352, 391, 411
Sutton, May, See May Sutton Bundy
Suzy Q Ranch, Puente, CA, O 217
Swale, O 222, 606, 611-12
Swann, Lynn C., F 370, 565, 580-81, 590
Swaps, O 176, 185, 217, 228, 598, 612-13
Swarthmore College, B 367; F 468; I 306; O 235-36, 291, 339
Sweden National Gymnastic Team, I 542
Sweden National Ice Hockey Team, I 545, 548, 568; S 543
Sweden National Soccer Team, O 310
Sweden Olympic Swim Team, I 620, 623
Sweden Olympic Wrestling Team, I 638, 641, 665

Sweeney, Charles J. "Charlie," **B** 463
Sweep, **O** 211; **S** 533
Sweet Slew, **O** 606
Sweetser, Jess W., **O** 162
Sweikert, Robert "Bob," **O** 4
Swiaki, William "Bill," **O** 426
Swift Stakes, **O** 224-25, 588
Swigert, **O** 589
Swigert, Daniel, **O** 604
Swigert Stakes, **O** 209
Swimmer of the Year, **I** 576, 579,
 584, 592, 594, 605, 612, 614, 617,
 619; **S** 602, 607
Swimming and Diving Hall of Fame,
 I 497, 603
Swimming World, **I** 576, 579, 584,
 592, 594, 596, 603, 612, 617, 619
Swindell, Forrest Gregory "Greg," **S**
 74
Swing On, **O** 605
Swiss Gymnastic Society, *See* Swiss
 Turnverein Society
Swiss Turnverein Society, Hudson
 County, NJ, **I** 524
Switzer, Barry, **F** *581-82;* **S** 369-70
Switzerland Olympic Wrestling Team,
 I 665
Swope, Herbert B. "Herb," **O** 196
Sword Dancer, **O** 218, 579
Swymmer, Anthony L., **O** 589
Sylphide, **O** 583
Sylvestri, Lowe, **O** 192
Syracuse, NY Athlete of the Year, **I**
 45, 50
Syracuse, NY Auto Race Track, **O**
 25, 42
Syracuse, NY baseball club (EL, IL,
 NYSL), **B** 4, 40, 85, 92-93, 155,
 215, 233, 236, 262, 334, 387, 584,
 617; **S** 5, 104, 146, 190
Syracuse, NY basketball club (ABL),
 I 131
Syracuse, NY Hardwood Club, **I** 113

Syracuse, NY Nationals basketball
 club (NBL, NBA), **I** 15, 44, 50,
 103-04, 110-11, 113, 149, 159,
 199, 270, 315, 334; **S** 317, 319
Syracuse, NY Stormers football club
 (USFL), **F** 448
Syracuse University, **F** 4, 68, 122,
 126-28, 200, 231, 298, 302, 349-
 50, 359, 370, 407, 413, 419-20,
 469, 477, 495, 497, 531, 534, 567,
 627, 646-47, 653, 669; **I** 24-25,
 50, 112-14, 270, 281, 306; **O** 426;
 S 104, 255, 263, 339-40, 398,
 418, 459, 591-92
Syria Olympic Wrestling Team, **I** 636
Sysonby, **S** 533
Sysonby Mile Handicap, **O** 579, 598
Szabo, Ecaterina, **I** 536
Szabo, Miklos, **O** 520

Tabb, Mary Decker, *See* Mary Decker
 Tabb Slaney
Tabb, Ronald "Ron," **O** 539
Taber, Norman S. "Norm," **O** 479,
 547-48
Tabitha, **O** 212
Tacoma, WA baseball club (NWL,
 PCL, PNL, WIL), **B** 225, 288,
 351, 353, 379; **S** 70, 79, 161
Tacoma, WA Stars Soccer Club
 (MISL), **O** 295, 306
Tacoma, WA 250 Auto Race, **O** 23
Tacony, **O** 230, 584
Taft, William Howard, **O** 162, 268; **S**
 445
Tagstad, Steffen, **S** 623
Taikeiyo Club Motor Golf
 Tournament, **O** 166
Taiwan National Soccer Team, **O** 301
Take Back, **O** 206
Talbert, William F. "Billy," **O** 349,
 384, 390, *400-01,* 406-07; **S** 553,
 556, 558

Taliaferro, Myron E. "Mike," **F** 17
Talladega, AL Superspeedway, **S** 605
Tallahassee, FL baseball club (GFL),
  B 510; **S** 219
Tallahassee, FL Open Golf
  Tournament, **O** 126, 163
Tam O'Shanter Golf Tournament, **S**
  523; *See also* Ladies World
  Championship Golf Tournament
Tamburo, Samuel "Sam," **F** 126
Tamiami Auto Race Track, **O** 38
Tammany, **O** 187
Tampa, FL baseball club (FIL, FSL),
  B 33, 87, 179, 279, 326-27, 337,
  369, 392, 396; **S** 244
Tampa, FL Golf Club, **O** 109
Tampa Bay, FL Bandits football club
  (USFL), **F** 561
Tampa Bay, FL Buccaneers football
  club (NFL), **F** 152, 222, 288, 370,
  537, 560, 671-72
Tanana, Frank D., **S** *214-15*
Tanana, Frank R., **S** 214
Tanforan Handicap, **O** 577
Tangerine Bowl football game, **F** 181,
  221, 286-88, 330; **S** 291, 382
Tank's Prospect, **S** 530
Tannehill, Jesse N., **B** 91, 95, 327,
  547-48
Tannehill, Lee F., **B** 547; **S** 232
Tanner, Charles W. "Chuck," **S** 243
Tanner, Robert, **F** 415
Tapani, Kevin R., **S** 145
Tappan, George, **O** 605
Tar Heel, **O** 207, 574
Tara, **O** 586
Taral, Fred, **O** *223-24;* **S** 527
Tarasovic, George, **F** 599
Taris, Jean, **I** 586
Tarkanian, "Danny," **I** 293
Tarkanian, Jerry, **I** 56, *292-93*
Tarkenton, Francis A. "Fran," **F** 81,
  161, 185, 248, 304, 404, *583-84,*

618, 667; **S** 482
Tarleton, "Nel," **I** 438
Tarleton State Junior College, **I** 245-
  46
Tarpley, Roy J., Jr., **S** 301
Tarport Hap, **O** 207
Tartan Farm, **O** 581
Tass, **I** 612
Tatum, James M. "Jim," **F** 78, 168,
  584-85, 653; **S** 428
Tatum, John D. "Jack," **F** *585-86*
Tatum, Reece "Goose," **I** 119, 173,
  267, *293-94*
Taube, "Mel," **I** 168
Taunton, MA baseball club (NEL), **B**
  390
Tavern Pale Bowling Team, Chicago,
  IL, **I** 338, 341
Tayloe, John, **O** 608
Taylor, Arthur "Art," **O** 608-09
Taylor, Benjamin H. "Ben," **B** 331,
  362, *548,* 549; **S** 143
Taylor, Charles A. "Chuck," **F** 533
Taylor, Charles B. "Bud," **I** 417, 435,
  468-69
Taylor, Charles H. "Chuck," **I** *294-
  95*
Taylor, Charles I. "C. I.," **B** 144,
  342, 362, *548-49;* **S** 43, 129
Taylor, Charles R. "Charley," **F** 96,
  290, 292, 295, 325, *586-87*
Taylor, Chris J., **I** 652; **S** *624-25*
Taylor, E. P., **O** 225
Taylor, Frederick Morgan, Sr., **O** 550
Taylor, Frederick Morgan, Jr., **O** 465,
  548-50
Taylor, Frederick W., **O** *402-03*
Taylor, Fredrick R. "Fred," **I** 161-62,
  186, *295-96*
Taylor, Herbert B. "Herb," **O** 318
Taylor, Howard A., **O** 338, 392, 398-
  99
Taylor, James "Candy Jim," **B** 132,

141, 244, *548-49*
Taylor, James C. "Jim," **F** 33, 69, 247, 354, 395, *587-88*
Taylor, John I. "Johnny," **B** 259, 548-49
Taylor, Lawrence "LT," **F** *588-89*
Taylor, Lionel T., **F** *589-90*
Taylor, Luther H. "Dummy," **B** 46
Taylor, Margaret T., **O** 411
Taylor, Marshall W., **O** 264, *269-70*
Taylor, "Mickey," **O** 606
Taylor, Mrs. "Mickey," **O** 606
Taylor, Oliver H. "Ollie," **I** 174
Taylor, Otis, Jr. "Slug," **F** *590-91*
Taylor, Robert, **F** 61
Taylor, Roosevelt "Rosey," **F** 500
Taylor, Theodore "Ted," **B** 140
Taylor, William H. "Bill," **B** 321
Taylorville, IL baseball club (IML), **B** 501
Tbilisi, USSR Wrestling Tournament, **I** 657-58
Teague, Bertha Frank, **I** *296-97*
Teague Award, **F** 327
Team America Soccer Club, Washington, DC, **O** 295, 298, 307
Team USA-Canada Cup Hockey Series, **I** 545, 550, 559; **S** 540, 543, 545
Tebbetts, George R. "Birdie," **B** 441; **S** 120
Tebeau, George E. "White Wings," **S** 215
Tebeau, Oliver W. "Patsy," **B** 63, 92, 523; **S** 36, *215-16*
Tebell, "Gus," **I** 207
Tecumseh, **O** 206
Tediashvili, Levan, **I** 654-55
Tekulve, Kenton C. "Ken," **B** 460; **S** *216-17*
Telavera, Tracee, **I** 535
Telemark Turn, **O** 279
Tellez, Thomas "Tom," **O** 485

Temesvari, Andrea, **O** 381
Tempe, AZ Track and Field Meet, **O** 438
Temperate Sil, **O** 218, 229
Temple, "Ed," **O** 457, 525, 550
Temple Cup Baseball Series, **B** 301, 307, 360, 363, 493, 592; **S** 152, 178, 210, 215
Temple, TX baseball club (TL), **B** 570-71
Temple University, **F** 2, 110, 316, 405-07, 636; **I** 178, 252, 531, 646; **O** 291-92, 508; **S** 267-68
Temple University Hall of Fame, **F** 316; **I** 179, 252
Templeton, Garry L., **S** 206, *217-18*
Templeton, Kenneth, **S** 217
Templeton, Robert L. "Dink," **O** 444; **S** 575
Templeton, Spiavia, **S** 217
Ten Broeck, **O** 201
Ten Broeck, Richard, **O** 594
Tendler, "Lew," **I** 421, *469*, 475
Tener, John K., **B** *549-50*
Tennant, Eleanor, **O** 327, 374
Tennessee Agricultural & Industrial State University, **I** 201-02; **S** 416
Tennessee Athletic Council, **F** 151
Tennessee Derby, **S** 531
Tennessee Rats baseball club, **S** 43
Tennessee Sports Hall of Fame, **F** 145, 406; **I** 284, 325
Tennessee State Golf Tournament, **O** 142
Tennessee State University, **F** 279; **I** 15; **O** 432, 457, 499, 525, 550; **S** 595, 597-98
Tennessee State University Hall of Fame, **S** 598
Tennessee State Weightlifting Championships, **I** 625
Tennessee Tech University, **I** 289
Tenney, Frederick C. "Fred," **B** 160,

506, *550-51;* S 115
Tennis, O 342, 394, 400, 407-08
Tennis Players League, O 419
Tennis Yearbook, O 400
Tenny, O 209, 605
Tenny, Meshach, O 612
Ter-Ovanesyan, Igor, O 428, 433
Terlazzo, Anthony "Tony," I 627, 629, *632-33*
Terlazzo, John, I 633
Terpak, John B., I 629, 633
Terrain, "Sam," I 426
Terranova, "Phil," I 406, 461
Terre Haute, IN Athletic Club, I 127
Terre Haute, IN baseball club (CL, CIL, 3IL), B 53-54, 178, 195, 416, 472, 484, 577, 584; I 149; S 226
Terre Haute, IN Track and Field Meet, O 526
Terrell, "Ernie," I 384
Terris, "Sid," I 392, 435
Terry, Aline M., O 376
Terry, Chuck, I 292
Terry, Ralph W., B 351
Terry, William H. "Bill," B 40, 106, 249, 267, 302, 332, 355, 540, *551-52;* S 45
Terry, Wyllys, F 116
Terry, Zebulon A. "Zeke," S 232
Tesreau, Charles M. "Jeff," S 181, *218-19,* 265
Testa, Tuesdee, O 215
Testaverde, Vincent F. "Vince," S *487-88*
Teuber, Dorothy Poynton, I *495-96*
Teufel, Timothy S. "Tim," S 218
Tevis, Walter, I 675, 677
Tewanima, Lewis, O 498
Tewksbury, John Walter, S *595-96*
Texaco Star Race Car, O 13
Texarkana, TX baseball club (BStL), B 490

Texarkana, TX Bicentennial Hall of Fame, I 57
Texarkana, TX Country Club, O 144
Texarkana, TX Junior College, F 663
Texas Agricultural & Industrial (A&I) College, F 615
Texas Agricultural & Mechanical (A&M) University, F 35, 47, 74, 121, 138-39, 278, 287, 316-18, 336-37, 392, 402-03, 428, 434-35, 514, 561, 619, 641; I 180; O 494; S 96, 373, 382, 399-401, 423-24, 462, 477-80, 494, 498, 585
Texas Agricultural & Mechanical (A&M) University Athletic Hall of Fame, F 402, 435; S 424
Texas All-Star football game, F 653
Texas Amateur Golf Tournament, O 152
Texas Baseball Hall of Fame, S 79
Texas Christian University, F 3, 17, 29, 35, 68, 171, 317, 341, 346-47, 386, 391, 401, 403, 437, 527, 534, 541, 549, 598-99, 621, 628-29, 637; I 205; O 67; S 385, 408, 449, 463-64
Texas High School Coaches Association, F 547
Texas High School Football Hall of Fame, F 659
Texas Intercollegiate Athletic Association, F 402
Texas League, B 601; S 2, 10, 17, 30-32, 34, 38, 48, 50, 55, 58, 71, 79, 83, 87, 90, 103, 111, 116, 126, 131, 134, 149, 154, 159, 173-74, 183, 195, 201, 205, 214, 217-18, 226-27, 239, 244-45, 422
Texas Mines University, F 608
Texas-Oklahoma League, S 131
Texas Open Golf Tournament, O 113, 116, 118, 130, 144, 154, 163; S

510, 515
Texas Rangers baseball club (AL), **B**
31, 39, 139, 159, 262, 340, 372,
385, 425, 445, 532, 545, 616, 619,
624; **S** 2, 7, 15, 29, 44, 58, 77-
78, 90-91, 94, 106, 115, 132, 136,
148, 177, 205, 208, 213-15, 237
Texas Relays, **F** 62
Texas Southern University, **F** 590; **O**
471
Texas Sports Hall of Fame, **B** 22,
491; **F** 3, 42, 224, 332, 347, 367,
389, 406, 423, 434, 437, 514, 587,
601, 629, 659; **I** 205; **O** 164; **S**
424
Texas Sportswriters Association, **F**
280
Texas Stadium, Irving, TX, **F** 274
Texas State Bowling Tournament, **I**
338
Texas State Technical Institute, **S** 475
Texas State Women's Golf
Tournament, **O** 172
Texas Tech University, **F** 91, 170,
293, 378, 457
Texas Tennis Hall of Fame, **S** 551
Texas Wesleyan University, **S** 78
Texas Western University, **F** 389; **I**
249, 257
Texas Women's Amateur Golf
Championships, **S** 513
Texas Women's State Public Links
Golf Tournament, **S** 513
Texas World Speedway, **O** 16, 39
Thames River Swim, **I** 590
Thanksgiving Day Handicap, **O** 225
Thayer, Abbot, **B** 637
Theismann, Joseph R. "Joe," **F** 462,
591-94
Theodore Roosevelt Award, **S** 410
Theus, Reggie W., **I** 293
Thevenot, **I** 590
Third Air Force football club, Tampa,

FL, **F** 515, 604
Thirty-first Separate National Guard
Company basketball club,
Herkimer, NY, **S** 260
Thoeni, Gustavo, **O** 285
Thomas, Bobby Clendon, **F** 653
Thomas, Claudia Kolb "Golden Girl,"
I 603, 619
Thomas, Clinton "Clint," **B** 519,
552-53
Thomas, Dale O., **I** 665
Thomas, Debra, *See* Debra Thomas
Vanden Hogen
Thomas, Frank J., Jr., **S** *219-20*
Thomas, Frank W., **F** *594-96*
Thomas, Frederick H. "Fred," **B** 291
Thomas, George, **F** 78, 515; **S** 462
Thomas, Isiah L. III, **I** 162, *297-99*
Thomas, James T. "J. T.," **F** 222
Thomas, "Joe," **I** 414
Thomas, John C., **S** *596-97*
Thomas, Joseph "Joe," **F** 296
Thomas, Kurt B., **I** 526, *539-40*
Thomas, M. Carey, **O** 253
Thomas, Marcel, **I** 377
Thomas, Paul, **S** 597
Thomas, "Ronnie," **S** 415
Thomas, Roy A., **S** *220-21*
Thomas, Thurman L., **S** 473
Thomas, William "Bill," **S** 197
Thomas Field, Tuscaloosa, AL, **F**
596
Thomason, James "Jim," **F** 434
Thomasville, NC baseball club (CrL,
NCL, NCSL), **B** 185, 388; **S** 182
Thomlinson, David "Dave," **S** 540
Thompson, Alexis "Lex," **F** 421, 511
Thompson, Aundra, **F** 105
Thompson, Cecil L. "Young Jack," **I**
381, *469-70*
Thompson, Cecil R. "Tiny," **I** 546
Thompson, Charles "Charley," **O** 215
Thompson, David O., **I** 60, 96, 280,

299-300
Thompson, Fred, I 497
Thompson, George, I 443
Thompson, Henry C. "Hank," B 55, 609
Thompson, Herbert "Herb," S *534-35*
Thompson, "Jack," I 470
Thompson, Janet, I 255
Thompson, John A. "Cat," I *301-02*
Thompson, John R., Jr., I 83, *300-01*
Thompson, Katherine Rawls, *See* Katherine Rawls Green
Thompson, L. P., S 533
Thompson, Lloyd, O 476
Thompson, Lurtis T. "Tommy," S *488-89*
Thompson, Robert "Bob," (boxer), I 470
Thompson, Robert "Bob," (swimmer), I 596
Thompson, Samuel L. "Sam," B 143, 184, 238, *553-55*
Thompson, W. P., S 533
Thompson, W. S., S 533
Thompson, William "Bill," S 410
Thompson Trophy, F 568
Thomsen, Leo, S 616
Thomson, Robert B. "Bobby," B 133, 274, 503; S 46, 162, *221*, 349
Thora, O 595
Thorn, John, S 82
Thornhill, Charles "Charlie," F 642
Thornhill, Claude E. "Tiny," F 114
Thornton, North, S 602
Thoroughbred Club of America, S 528
Thoroughbred Racing Association, O 180, 612; S 528
Thorpe, James F. "Jim," F 4, 68, 97, 197, 231, 360, 498, 505, 510, 588, *596-98*, 635, 638; I 543, 662; O

90, 268, 493, 535; S 387, 397, 411-12, 585
Thorpe, Thomas J., F 231
Thorpe Trophy, F 462, 588, 601, 613
Three-I League, B 79; I 149; O 293, S 13, 28, 45, 68, 87, 187, 201, 217, 219, 226
Three Rings, O 197
Three Rivers, Canada baseball club (ProL), S 190
Three Rivers Stadium, Pittsburgh, PA, B 97, 530; F 510
Thrilling Sports, O 531
Throckmorton, Harold A., O 320
Throneberry, Marvin E. "Marv," B 382; O 60
Thunderer, O 212
Thurber, Delos P., O 476
Thurman, Robert B. "Bob," B 453
Thurmond, Nathaniel "Nate," I 7, 112, 147, *302-03*
Thurston, Fred C. "Fuzzy," F 321
Tiant, Luis C., Sr., S 222
Tiant, Luis C., Jr., S 118, *221-23*
Tick On, S 527
Tickey, Bertha Regan, O 261-62
Tickner, Charles, I *518-19*
Ticknor, Benjamin A. II "Ben," F 57; S *489-90*
Ticknor, William, Jr., S 489
Tidal Stakes, O 578, 588, 604
Tidball, "Jack," O 320
Tidewater, VA baseball club (IL), B 421, 431, 515
Tiernan, Michael J. "Mike," B *555-56*
Tiger, "Dick," I 384, 387, 396
Tiger Stadium, Baton Rouge, LA, F 598
Tilden, William T. II "Bill," O 89, 121, 325, 329, 331, 347, 356, 360-62, 365-66, 368, 373, 375, 378, 385, 392, *403-05*, 410, 412, 417;

S 341, 559
Tillman, Henry, S 625-26
Tillman, Wyomia Tyus, O 457, *550-51*
Tim Tam, O 195; S 529
Timberlake, Robert W. "Bob," F 104
Time, F 278, 564; I 168, 536, 606, 611; O 81, 272; S 346, 351, 473, 563
Time Man of the Year, O 272
Timmons, Robert "Bob," O 526
Timoleon, O 573, 608
Tingelhoff, Henry Michael "Mick," F 25; S *490-91*
Tinker, Joseph B. "Joe," B 84, 170, 311, 507, 509, *556-57*, 611
Tinker Field, Orlando, FL, B 557
Tinsley, Gaynell C. "Gus," F *598-600*
Tipton, Eric G., F 361, 452, 626
Tisdale, Wayman L., I *303-04;* S 325
Tisdall, Robert "Bob," O 465
Titan Stakes, O 604
Titleholder's Golf Championship, O 160
Tittle, Yelberton A., Jr. "Y. A.," F 3, 67, 69, 187, 294, 384, 404, 542, *600-01*
Toano, S 526
Tobacco Bowl football game, F 534
Tobey, David, I *304-05*
Tobian, Gary M., I 496-97
Tobin, "Abe," I 379
Tobin, John T. "Jack," B 279, *557-58*
Todd, Pat Canning, O 358; S 550
Tokyo, Japan Giants baseball club, S 157
Tokyo, Japan Summer Olympic Games, *See* Olympic Summer Games, 1964
Tolan, Robert "Bobby," B 594

Tolan, Thomas Edward "Eddie," O 453, 455, 496, 515-16, *551-52*, 568
Toledo, OH baseball club (AA), B 11, 46, 109, 114, 184, 193, 250, 258, 283, 332, 337, 345, 393, 397, 407, 432, 524, 534, 551, 563, 565, 572, 584, 621; S 21, 28, 54, 123, 131, 155, 159, 195, 226
Toledo, OH baseball club (IA, IL, ISL, WA), B 45, 92, 292, 421; S 147, 233
Toledo, OH basketball club (ABL), I 170-71
Toledo, OH Crawfords baseball club (Negro Leagues), B 88
Toledo, OH Jim White Chevrolets basketball club (NBL), S 270
Toledo, OH *News Bee*, B 292
Toledo, OH Open Bowling Tournament, I 351
Toledo, OH White Huts basketball club, S 270
Tolson, John C., O *248-49*
Tom Fool, O 575, 599
Tome, Maurice, I 22
Tomjanovich, Rudolph "Rudy," I 230
Tomy Lee, O 218
Toney, Andrew, S 269
Toney, Fred A., S *223*
Tonnemaker, Frank Clayton "Clay," S *491-92*
Tony Hinkle Memorial Fieldhouse, Indianapolis, IN, I 130
Toomey, William A. "Bill," O 475, *552-53*
Top Flight, O 231
Topeka, KS baseball club (SWL, WL), B 29, 55, 195, 237, 547; S 233
Topeka, KS Giants baseball club (Negro Leagues), B 144
Topeka, KS Sizzlers basketball club (CBA), I 324

Topgallant, O 229
Topping, Daniel R., Sr. "Dan," B 26, 366, *558-59;* S 46
Topsoil, S 526-27
Torgeson, Lavern, F 528
Torgoff, Irving "Irv," I 23
Torluemke, Judith, *See* Judith Torluemke Rankin
Toronto, Canada Argonauts football club (CFL), F 224, 448, 478, 593; S 457
Toronto, Canada baseball club (EL, IA), B 25, 52, 407; S 41, 123
Toronto, Canada baseball club (IL), B 10, 87, 141, 161, 167, 211-12, 229, 283, 292, 299, 301, 306, 321-22, 326, 339, 367, 376, 518, 583, 614; S 1, 46, 91, 105, 127, 159, 195, 199, 211, 218
Toronto, Canada Blue Jays baseball club (AL), B 48, 152-53, 262, 370, 422, 425, 461, 622, 631; S 2, 25, 49, 53, 136-37, 146, 210-11, 213, 215, 254, 353-54
Toronto, Canada Huskies basketball club (BAA, NBA), I 240; S 181
Toronto, Canada Maple Leafs hockey club (NHL), I 547, 553, 555, 560, 564, 570-71
Toronto, Canada Marlboros hockey club, I 558
Toronto, Canada Soccer Club (NASL), O 308
Toronto, Canada Track and Field Meet, O 496
Toronto, Canada University Grads hockey club, S 546
Torre, Frank J., B 559
Torre, Joseph P., Sr., B 559
Torre, Joseph P., Jr. "Joe," B 410, *559-60;* I 261; S 53
Torres, Jose, S 625
Torrez, Michael A. "Mike," S 89

Torrienti, Christobal, B 189; S *233-34*
Tortenson, O 206
Tortorick, Dominick, I 399
Toscani, Francis "Bud," F 378
Tose, Leonard H. "Len," S 437
Toski, Robert "Bob," S 507
Tosmah, O 178
Total Baseball, S 82
Touchdown Club of New York, F 6, 52, 84, 564
Touchdown Club of New York Award, F 6
Touching Second, S 345
Toulmin, Bertha Townsend, O 321, 324-25, *405-06*
Toulmin, Frances Biddle, O 406
Toulmin, Marion P., O 406
Tour de France Cycling Race, S 617-18
Tour de Trump Cycling Race, S 618
Tour of Champions Golf Tournament, O 129
Tour of Italy Cycling Race, S 618
Tour of Switzerland Cycling Race, S 618
Tournament of Champions Players Golf Championships, O 124, 139, 143, 166; S 514, 521
Tournament Park, Pasadena, CA, F 477
The Tours basketball club, I 88
Tovar, Cesar L., B 502
Toweel, "Vic," I 447
Tower, Oswald, I *306-07*
Towery, William Carlisle, I 67
Towler, Daniel L. "Dan," F 363, 608
Town Tennis Club, New York, NY, O 419
Towns, Forrest G. "Spec," O *554*
Towns, "Reggie," S 584
Townsend, Anne B., O *270-71*
Townsend, Bertha, S 562; *See also*

Bertha Townsend Toulmin

Townsend, H. C. II, **O** 406

Towson, MD Post 22 Lacrosse Club, **O** 303

Towson, MD State University, **B** 437; **I** 71; **O** 239

Toy Bowl football game, **F** 53

Tozzo, Rocco, *See* Rocky Kansas

Trabert, Marion A. "Tony," **O** 394, *406-08*

Tracer-Milan European basketball club, **I** 189

Tracey, "Tom," **I** 420

Track and Field News, **I** 671; **O** 432, 437, 461, 518, 528, 536, 542; **S** 579, 584

Track and Field News Athlete of the Year, **O** 425, 481, 497, 536, 557, 564; **S** 584

Track and Field News Coach of the Year, **O** 435

Track Athletic Congress Track and Field Championships, **O** 424-25, 436, 480-81, 485-86, 498-99, 506; *See also* Amateur Athletic Union Championships entries

Tracy, "Kid," **I** 441

Trader Bedford, **O** 267

Traffic Judge, **O** 222

Trafford, Bernard W. "Bernie," **F** 63-64

Trafton, George, **F** 14, 377, *601-02*

Traicoff, "Chris," **I** 664-65

Trainor, "Mike," **I** 422

Trammell, Alan S., **S** *224-25*, 236

Trance, **O** 214

Transamerica University of Southern California Basketball Classic, **I** 215

Trans-American, **O** 28

Trans-Mississippi Women's Golf Tournament, **O** 111, 146; **S** 513

Trans-National Golf Tournament, **O** 152

Transouth 500 Auto Race, **O** 27

Transylvania College, **B** 84; **F** 150

Trautman, George M., **B** *560-61*

Traveller, **O** 85

Travers, Jerome D. "Jerry," **O** 121-22, 156, *160-61*

Travers Stakes, **O** 198-99, 204, 223-24, 227, 229, 569, 575, 579, 585, 596, 599, 602, 613

Travis, Cecil H., **S** 14, *225-26*, 246

Travis, Walter J., **O** 160, *161-62*

Traynor, Harold T. "Pie," **B** *561-63*, 581

Treasure Valley, ID baseball club (PrL), **B** 420; **S** 88

Tregoning, "Larry," **I** 259

Tremaine, Carl, **I** 389

Tremont, **O** 588

Tremont Stakes, **O** 187, 595

Trenchard, Thomas G. "Doggie," **F** 61, 342, *602-03*

Trenton, **O** 583

Trenton, NJ Auto Race Track, **O** 42

Trenton, NJ baseball club (EL, ISL, MSL), **B** 8, 168, 219, 221, 393, 555; **S** 238

Trenton, NJ basketball club (MeL), **I** 32

Trenton, NJ 500 Auto Race, **O** 13, 16

Trenton, NJ Handicap, **O** 178, 573

Trenton, NJ 100 Auto Race, **O** 4

Trenton, NJ 300 Auto Race, **O** 18, 39

Trenton, NJ Tigers basketball club (ABL), **I** 14, 261

Trenton, NJ 200 Auto Race, **O** 18; **S** 614

Trester, Arthur L., **I** *307*

Trevino, Lee B., **O** 126, 159, *162-64*

Trevira-Twosome 10 Mile Race, **O** 530

Trevor, George, **F** 5, 38, 90, 109,

153, 172, 193, 240, 261, 270, 415, 439, 452, 468, 550, 598; S 388, 424, 434

Tri-Cities Blackhawks basketball club (NBL, NBA), I 11, 194-95; S 283

Tri-City baseball club (NWL), B 251; S 2

Tri-County League, I 273

Tri-State Conference, F 40

Tri-State League, I 340; S 18-20, 187, 209

Tri-State Tennis Championships, O 325

Trinidad National Soccer Team, O 305

Trinidad State Junior College, I 121

Trinity College, B 60; F 299, 440; O 81; S 566; *See also* Duke University

Trinity University of Texas, F 663-64; S 96, 555, 563

Trinycaral, O 592

Triple Crown of Horse Racing, O 175-76, 178, 184, 190, 194-95, 198-200, 203-04, 216, 218, 223, 226, 229, 569, 572-73, 575-77, 579, 585, 592, 596, 598-99, 601-02, 604-05, 607-08, 610-11, 613-15; S 525, 527, 529

Trippe, "Joe," I 21

Trippi, Charles L. "Charley," F 48, 81, 113, 305, 549, *603-04;* S 381, 438, 491

Troon Golf Club, O 154, 167

Tropical Park, Miami, FL, O 178, 205, 214; S 531

Trosky, Harold A., Sr. "Hal," B 169, *563*

Trosky, Harold A., Jr., B 563

Trost, Alan P. "Al," O *310-11*

Trost, Walter, O 310

Trost's West County Soccer Club, O 311

Trotting Triple Crown, O 182, 191

Trouble, O 101

Trout, Paul H. "Dizzy," B 86; S *226-27*

Trout, Steven R. "Steve," S 226

Troy, Michael F. "Mike," I 584

Troy, NY baseball club (NYSL), B 170, 507, 599; S 240

Troy, NY Haymakers baseball club (NL), B 52, 111, 171, 297, 303, 598; S 150, 168-69

Troy, NY Trojans basketball club (NYSL), I 21, 32, 170, 313; S 260, 287

Troye, Edward, O 86

Trucks, Virgil O. "Fire," S *227-28*

True Temper Golf Tournament, O 120

Truex, Max E., S 592

Trujillo, Rafael, S 189

Trull, Donald D. "Don," F 55

Truman, Harry S., I 339, 341, 393

Trumpy, Robert T., Jr. "Bob," F 15; S *492-93*

Trustee, O 583

Tsioropolous, Louis "Lou," I 109, 257

Tsunamai Slew, O 606

Tubbs, Billy, S *323-25*

Tubbs, Gerald "Jerry," F *604-05,* 653

Tubbs, "Tommy," S 325

Tuckahoe Stakes, O 604

Tucker, Anthony "Tony," S 625

Tucker, "Fronnie," O 457

Tucker, Gerald M., I 70

Tucker, James D. "Jim," I 180

Tucker, William "Bill," I 344

Tucker, Young Arnold, F 130, *605-07*

Tuckerman Alpine Ski Competition, O 287

Tuckerman Inferno Ski Competition, O 276

Tucson, AZ baseball club (ArTL, PCL), B 577; S 112

Tucson, AZ Open Golf Tournament, O 134, 143-44, 163, 166; S 507

Tudor, John T., S 84

Tuerta, O 611

Tufts, Nathan A., F 350

Tufts University, B 298

Tuite, James, O 61

Tulane University, B 54; F 49, 52-53, 243, 293, 296, 300, 317, 434, 470-71, 512, 526, 531, 537-38, 553, 598-600, 664; I 204, 321; S 163, 388, 465-66

Tulsa, OK baseball club (AA, PCL, TL, WL), B 3, 44, 55, 73, 109, 237, 251, 382, 387, 478, 514, 526, 601; F 23; S 34, 125-26, 174, 217

Tulsa, OK Business College Stenos basketball club, I 5

Tulsa, OK hockey club (AHA), I 559-60

Tulsa, OK University, F 6, 77-78, 171, 335, 463, 515, 521, 527, 609; O 137

Tuned to Baseball, S 349

Tunkhannock, PA baseball club (NYPL), I 194

Tunnell, Emlen "Em," F 331-32, 521, *607-08*

Tunney, James J. "Gene," I 372, 374, 380, 391, 394-95, 428, 453, 462, 465, *471-72;* O 60, 89, 263

Tupelo, MS Redwaves basketball club, I 314

Tupper, Fred, O 69

Turcotte, Ronald "Ron," O 183, 607

Turf, O 596

Turf Classic, O 591

The Turf Foundation, O 180

Turgeon, Pierre, S 545

Turk, Frank, B 77

Turkish Dardanelles Swim, I 581

Turkish National Soccer Team, O 301

Turkish Olympic Wrestling Team, I 655, 659, 665-66

Turkish Trousers, O 229

Turku, Finland Track and Field Meet, O 430

Turley, Robert L. "Bob," B 597

Turmore, Mrs. Arthur, O 133

Turnberry Golf Tournament, O 126

Turnbull, Douglas C., Jr. "Doug," O *249-50*

Turnbull, Jack, O 239, 249

Turnbull, Wendy, O 335, 380

Turnbull Lacrosse Trophy, O 236, 238, 240, 251

Turnbull-Reynolds Lacrosse Trophy, O 251

Turner, Clay, I 425

Turner, Clyde "Bulldog," F *608-09;* S 484

Turner, "Gil," I 404, 477

Turner, James B. "Jim," F 25

Turner, Lesley, O 358

Turner, Nash, O *224-25*

Turner, Robert Edward III "Ted," B 318; O 83, *102-03;* S 90

Turner, Rubin, F 500

Turner, "Terry," S 623

Turner, William "Billy," O 606

Turner Broadcasting System (TBS), F 271, 452, 618; O 57, 83, 102; *See also* WTBS-Television, Atlanta, GA

Turnverein Hall of Fame, I 651

Turpin, "Randy," I 455

Tuskegee Athletic Hall of Fame, O 449

Tuskegee Institute, O 448, 485, 538-39, 563

Tuttle, Henry "King Tut," I 451

T. V. Lark, S 532

Twentieth Century Athletic Club, San Francisco, CA, I 434

Twentieth Century Sporting Club, I

405
Twenty Grand, O 198, 202, 230-31, 601, *613*
Twiggs, "Eddie," O 138
Twilight Tear, S 529
Twilley, Howard J., Jr., F *609-10*
Twin City Speedway, O 6
Twin Falls, ID baseball club (PrL), B 7
Twin Hills Country Club, Oklahoma City, OK, O 150
Two Fisted Jeff, S 345
Two Lea, S 529
Two World Cup, O 5
Twyman, John K. "Jack," I *307-08,* 319
Tyler, Dorothy, O 448-49
Tyler, Wendell A., S *493-94*
Tyler B, O 207
Tyler, TX baseball club (TL), B 406, 516
Tyrer, James E. "Jim," F *610-11*
Tyson, Mike G., I 383, 401; S 623, *625-26*
Tyson Holly Farms 400 NASCAR Race, S 605
Tyus, Wyomia, S 577; *See also* Wyomia Tyus Tillman

Udall, Morris K. "Mo," I 80
Udall, Stewart L., I 80
Ueberroth, Peter V., B 252, 318, 375, 394, 440; O *271-72,* 525
Ueker, Robert G. "Bob," S 239
Uetake, Yojiro, I 662
Uhle, George E., B *565-66*
Ulinski, Harry, F 199
Umphlett, Thomas M. "Tommy," S 95
Umpire of the Year Award, S 29
Uncle, O 600; S 526-27
Uncle Byrn, O 201
Unglaub, Robert A. "Bob," B 547

Union and Racquet and Tennis Clubs, O 335
Union Association, B 628, 637; S 233
Union City, TN baseball club (KL), B 503; S 81, 246
Union City, TN Reds basketball club, I 32
Union College, F 256, 441
Union Course Race Track, O 101, 230, 544, 570-71, 583-84, 587, 602, 609
Union League, S 21, 47
Union-Whitten, IA High School, I 7-8
Uniontown, PA Auto Race, O 23, 25
Uniontown, PA baseball club (POML), B 117
Unitas, John C. "Johnny," F 165, 190-91, 248, 273, 292, 296, 304, 370-71, 401, 405, 454, *613-15;* S 398-99
United Nations Handicap, O 581, 603
United Press, *See* United Press International
United Press International (UPI), F 8, 18, 30, 36, 59, 72, 80, 90, 99, 106, 121, 127, 132, 137, 140, 143, 146, 169, 184, 210, 222, 226, 248, 258, 276-77, 286, 310, 331, 338, 363, 367, 462, 467, 482-83, 497, 508, 528, 545, 548-49, 554, 560, 570-71, 576, 609, 622, 634-35, 641, 650, 671; I 10, 26, 41, 90, 109, 134, 209, 266, 293, 296, 301, 611, 615; O 80, 84; S 6, 88, 252, 257, 273, 284, 295, 297, 312, 316, 321, 391, 402, 414, 419, 443, 448, 453, 461
United Press International Female Athlete of the Year, I 611
United Press International Poll, S 268, 291, 428-29

United Press International Sportsman of the Year, I 615

United States Achievement Academy Hall of Fame, I 652

United States Age 45 Clay Court Singles Tennis Championships, S 558

United States Age 45 Grass Court Singles Tennis Championships, S 558

United States Age 45 Hard Court Singles Tennis Championships, S 558

United States Age 45 Wood Singles Tennis Championships, S 558

United States Air Force Academy, F 346, 539; I 282, 489, 513

United States Air Force All-Star Basketball Team, I 70, 295

United States All-Star Bowling Tournament, I 340

United States Alpine Skiing Championships, O 273, 275, 279-81, 284-86, 288

United States Amateur Bicycle Sprint Championships, O 264

United States Amateur Golf Tournament, O 111, 121-22, 125, 135-36, 138-39, 146, 148-49, 160-61; S 514, 521

United States Amateur Soccer Championships, O 296

United States Armed Forces Basketball Championships, I 130, 248

United States Armed Forces Basketball Tours, I 272

United States Army 86th Regiment Basketball Team, I 50

United States Army Football All-Stars, F 514

United States Auto Club Championships, S 614, 620

United States Auto Club Circuit, O 3-5, 10-12, 16-17, 19, 21, 32-33, 36-39, 42-43; S 614

United States Auto Club Driver of the Year, O 1, 3-5, 10, 16, 19, 21, 27-30, 33-34, 36-39, 42, 44

United States Auto Club Rookie of the Year, O 2-3, 13, 19-20, 27, 29, 36, 39-41, 43

United States Basketball Association, I 74

United States Basketball League, I 10, 176

United States Basketball Writers Association, I 81, 209, 215, 266, 281, 296; S 267, 282, 304

United States Bicycle Sprint Championships, O 316-17

United States Billiards Championships, I 673, 675

United States Bobsled Championships, O 258

United States Boxing Association, I 397

United States Boys Doubles Tennis Championships, O 365, 400

United States Boys Singles Tennis Championships, O 365, 385, 396, 400; S 501, 552

United States-Bulgaria Wrestling Meet, I 640, 666

United States-Canada Cup Hockey Tournament, I 545-46, 550-51, 554, 557-59, 562-63; S 540, 542-43, 545

United States Canoeing Championships, I 629

United States Chess Championships, I 671-72

United States-China Gymnastic Meet, I 527

United States Clay Court Doubles Tennis Championships, O 364, 386, 401; S 550

United States Clay Court Mixed Doubles Championships, O 415

United States Clay Court Singles Tennis Championships, O 329, 331, 336, 344, 347, 352, 355-56, 362, 364, 368, 401, 416; S 550, 554, 556

United States Club Lacrosse Association, O 237

United States Club Lacrosse Open Championships, O 239-40, 242-44, 247, 250

United States Club Lacrosse Player of the Year, O 237

United States Coast Guard Academy, F 216, 267

United States Coast Guard Basketball Team, I 241

United States Coast Guard Clippers hockey club, I 547, 564

United States College Baseball All-Stars, S 205

United States Collegiate Hall of Fame, O 400, 408

United States Committee for Sports for Israel, I 132

United States Department of State Basketball Tour, I 180, 192, 210, 213, 246, 255, 287

United States Department of State Diving Tour, I 497

United States Department of State Gymnastic Tour, I 529

United States Department of State Swim Tour, I 609-10

United States Diving-American Cup II Championships, I 492

United States Eastern Amateur Ski Association, O 279

United States Equestrian Team, O 267, 391

United States Father and Son Doubles Tennis Championships, O 339, 418; S 557, 560

United States Fencing Championships, I 669

United States Field Hockey Association, O 254, 259-60, 270-71

United States Field Hockey Association Hall of Fame, O 254

United States Field Hockey Team, O 270

United States Figure Skating Association, I 499-500, 504, 509, 513, 516

United States Figure Skating Dance Championships, I 499

United States Figure Skating Pairs Championships, I 499, 509, 515

United States Football League, F 7, 99, 182, 195, 198, 209-10, 217, 220, 228, 325, 517-19, 553, 561, 589, 630-31, 633, 671; S 375, 409, 411, 451, 454-55, 464

United States Football League Championship Games and Playoffs, F 99; S 409, 454

United States-Germany Swim Meet, I 579

United States Girls Amateur Golf Championships, O 170

United States Girls Doubles Tennis Championships, O 326, 337, 348, 352, 387; S 563

United States Girls Singles Tennis Championships, O 326, 337, 348, 352, 358, 360, 387; S 549, 563

United States Golf Association Tour, O 133, 148, 151, 162, 339; S 505, 511-12

United States Grass Court Singles Championships, O 401

United States Gymnastic Federation, I 522-24, 529, 531, 533, 535, 541

United States Gymnastic Federation American Cup Classic, I 533, 535

United States Gymnastic Federation Female Gymnast of the Year, I 533

United States Gymnastic Federation Hall of Fame, I 528

United States Gymnastic Federation International Invitation Meet, I 526

United States Gymnastic Federation Male Gymnast of the Year, I 540

United States Gymnastic Federation Master Sports Award, I 525

United States Gymnastic Federation Men's Championships, I 523, 540

United States Gymnastic Federation Women's Championships, I 532

United States Hard Court Doubles Tennis Championships, O 336, 364

United States Hard Court Mixed Doubles Tennis Championships, O 336, 364

United States Hard Court Singles Tennis Championships, S 550, 554

United States Hawaiian Open Golf Tournament, S 522

United States Hockey Hall of Fame, I 544, 547, 552-53, 555, 560-61, 564-69, 571-74; S 538-39, 541, 546-47

United States Hockey League, I 564, 576

United States Hockey League Championships and Playoffs, I 571

United States Hotel Stakes, O 588, 595

United States Indoor Doubles Tennis Championships, O 336, 364-65, 383, 401, 411, 415; S 500

United States Indoor Junior Singles Tennis Championships, S 555

United States Indoor Mixed Doubles Tennis Championships, O 415; S 339

United States Indoor Singles Tennis Championships, O 355, 364-65, 373, 377-78, 393, 401, 411, 415; S 550, 554, 557, 563

United States Intercollegiate Lacrosse Association, O 233, 235-36, 243, 247, 250

United States Intercollegiate Lacrosse Association Championships, O 233-37, 239-42

United States Intercollegiate Lacrosse Association Man of the Year Award, O 236-37

United States International Polo Team, O 261

United States International University, F 210; I 292; O 429

United States-Japan Swim Meet, I 603

United States Junior Alpine Ski Championships, O 274, 281, 288

United States Junior Chess Championships, I 671

United States Junior Figure Skating Pairs Championships, I 509, 512, 515

United States Junior Golf Championships, O 139, 143; S 505, 518

United States Junior Hockey Team, I 544, 550-51

United States Junior Ladies Figure Skating Championships, I 506, 509, 511, 515-16

United States Junior Men's Figure Skating Championships, I 500, 502, 513, 519

United States Junior Polo Championships, O 260

United States Junior Roller Skating Championships, I 674
United States Junior Ski Team, O 273-74
United States Junior Tennis Championships, O 330, 343, 352, 359, 368, 385, 389, 393, 395, 39-400, 408-09; S 551-52, 560
United States Junior Weightlifting Championships, I 626, 631
United States Junior Women's Basketball Team, I 175, 291
United States Lacrosse Coaches Association, O 236-38, 244-45
United States Lacrosse Team, O 237, 239, 244, 246-47, 250-51, 259
United States Lawn Tennis Association, O 61, 319, 326, 335-36, 338-39, 343-44, 346-47, 349-50, 352, 356, 361, 363-64, 367, 375, 383, 385, 392-93, 399, 404, 410-12, 415, 420; S 558-60
United States Lawn Tennis Championships, S 560
United States Lawn Tennis Association Service Bowl Award, O 327-28, 336, 338, 343, 349, 352, 359, 364, 414
United States Lawn Tennis Writers Association of America, O 62
United States League, B 224
United States Long Course Swim Championships, S 602, 607-08
United States Marine Corps S. O. S. Football Team, I 275
United States Men's Basketball Team, I 56, 116, 153, 165, 202, 251, 262, 269, 283, 296, 322-23, 326
United States Men' Figure Skating Singles Championships, I 500-04, 508, 512-14, 518-19
United States Men's Outdoor Doubles Tennis Championships, S 556, 558, 561; 1881, O 402; 1882, O 350, 392; 1883, O 350, 392; 1884, O 350, 392, 402; 1885, O 338, 392, 402; 1886, O 350, 392, 402; 1887, O 350, 392; 1889, O 398; 1891, O 335; 1892, O 335; 1895, O 420; 1898, O 345; 1900, O 345, 412; 1902, O 345; 1904, O 412, 421; 1905, O 320, 356, 412, 421; 1906, O 320, 356, 412, 421; 1907, O 320, 356; 1908, O 320, 356; 1909, O 320, 356; 1910, O 320, 356; 1912, O 332, 336, 372; 1914, O 322, 336; 1915, O 362; 1916, O 362; 1918, O 385; 1920, O 362; 1925, O 417; 1926, O 417; 1928, O 368; 1929, O 347, 368; 1930, O 347, 368, 395; 1931, O 322, 408-09; 1932, O 395, 409-10; 1933, O 368; 1934, O 368, 396; 1935, O 322, 408; 1937, O 331; 1939, O 389; 1940, O 365; 1941, O 365, 389; 1942, O 401; 1943, O 365; 1945, O 385, 401; 1946, O 401; 1947, O 389; 1948, O 401; 1968, O 400; 1974, O 400; 1978, O 400; 1980, O 400
United States Men's Outdoor Singles Tennis Championships, S 339, 501, 552-56, 558, 561; 1881, O 392; 1882, O 392; 1883, O 392; 1884, O 392; 1885, O 338, 392; 1886, O 334, 338, 392; 1887, O 338, 392, 398; 1888, O 398; 1889, O 334, 398; 1890, O 334, 398; 1892, O 419; 1893, O 419; 1894, O 419; 1895, O 420; 1896, O 419-20; 1897, O 413, 419; 1898, O 345, 413; 1899, O 383, 413; 1900, O 413-14, 420-21; 1901, O 366; 1902, O 366, 383, 414; 1903, O 340; 1904, O 340,

412; 1905, O 412, 421; 1906, O
339, 421; 1907, O 339, 366;
1908, O 339, 366, 421; 1909, O
339, 366, 371; 1910, O 366, 410;
1911, O 366, 372; 1912, O 339,
372; 1913, O 339, 362; 1914, O
339, 362, 372, 378, 416; 1915, O
361-62, 372; 1916, O 362, 378,
416; 1918, O 378; 1919, O 361-
62, 378; 1920, O 362, 404; 1921,
O 362, 404; 1922, O 362, 404;
1923, O 362, 404; 1924, O 362,
368, 404; 1925, O 362, 404;
1927, O 362, 418; 1928, O 404;
1929, O 322, 347, 404, 418;
1930, O 322, 347, 404, 417-18;
1931, O 322, 347, 368, 410;
1932, O 322, 410, 418; 1933, O
322, 410; 1934, O 322, 418;
1935, O 322, 418; 1936, O 331;
1937, O 331; 1938, O 330-31,
418; 1939, O 386; 1940, O 331,
386; 1941, O 331, 386, 389;
1942, O 389; 1944, O 384, 401;
1945, O 384, 401, 418; 1946, O
365; 1947, O 355, 365; 1948, O
355; 1949, O 390; 1953, O 394,
407; 1954, O 394; 1955, O 407;
1968, O 323-24; 1971, O 399;
1974, O 341; 1975, O 341; 1976,
O 341; 1977, O 341; 1978, O
341; 1979, O 369-70; 1980, O
370; 1981, O 370; 1982, O 342,
370; 1983, O 342; 1984, O 342,
370; 1985, O 342, 370; 1986, O
370; 1987, O 342, 370
United States Men's Roller Skating
Championships, I 674
United States Men's Singles Figure
Skating Championships, S 601
United States Men's Track and Field
Team, I 272
United States Men's Volleyball
Championships, I 676
United States Merchant Marine
Academy, F 357
United States Military Academy, F
14, 37, 51-54, 57-58, 78, 83, 90,
94, 125-26, 129-30, 132, 148, 158-
59, 176, 178, 187, 189, 192, 199-
201, 210, 212, 231, 245, 269, 300-
01, 342, 345, 350, 353, 358, 407,
428, 439-40, 504-06, 532-33, 540-
41, 552, 605-07, 654; I 29, 84,
161-62, 232, 250, 254, 305, 485,
568-69, 602, 636; O 49, 70, 90,
99, 234, 242, 250, 426, 512; S
295, 297, 376-77, 409, 413, 447-
48, 464, 481, 497-98, 501
United States Military Academy
Wrestling Championships, S 498
United States Mixed Outdoor Doubles
Championships, 1890, O 321;
1891, O 333; 1892, O 333; 1894,
O 324-25; 1895, O 325; 1901, O
353-54; 1902, O 377; 1904, O
377; 1906, O 406; 1909, O 415;
1910, O 415; 1911, O 425; 1912,
O 329, 416; 1913, O 329, 403;
1914, O 329, 403; 1915, O 415;
1916, O 391; 1917, O 373; 1921,
O 362; 1924, O 387; 1926, O
389; 1928, O 387; 1929, O 368;
1931, O 368; 1932, O 343; 1933,
O 389; 1934, O 360, 368; 1935,
O 343; 1936, O 374; 1937, O
331, 343; 1938, O 331, 374;
1939, O 374; 1940, O 374; 1941,
O 343; 1942, O 337, 389; 1943,
O 349, 401; 1944, O 349, 401;
1945, O 349, 401; 1946, O 349,
401; 1947, O 337, 401; 1948, O
337, 401; 1949, O 337-38; 1950,
O 349; 1951, O 359; 1952, O
359; 1953, O 359; 1954, O 359;
1955, O 369; 1956, O 349; 1958,

O 349; 1959, O 349; 1960, O 349; 1967, O 363; 1971, O 363; 1973, O 363; 1975, O 335; 1987, O 381

United States Mother-Daughter Grass Doubles Tennis Championships, O 336

United States National Alpine Ski Team, O 273-74, 281, 284-85, 287-88

United States National Basketball Team, S 310

United States National Cricket Team, S 615

United States National Field Hockey Team, O 250, 254, 259

United States National/Olympic Ice Hockey Team, I 548, 554-55, 561, 564-65, 569, 572-73; S 541, 543, 545

United States National/Olympic Swim Team, I 577, 579-80, 584, 593, 596, 598, 603, 605, 611-12, 614-15, 620, 622; O 621

United States National/Olympic Water Polo Team, I 598, 613-14, 617, 620-21

United States National Soccer Team, O 295-98, 301, 304-05, 307-08, 310

United States National Squash Team, O 391

United States National Track and Field Team, O 457, 479, 543

United States National Wrestling Team, S 616

United States Naval Academy, B 34, 365; F 13, 37, 53, 83, 94, 126, 130, 138, 144, 155, 159, 173, 192, 194, 200, 204, 249, 275, 350, 370, 403, 410, 422, 428, 431, 440, 475, 506, 516, 519, 552, 568, 654; I 40, 180, 199, 232, 280, 305, 670;

O 49, 70, 233, 240, 246-47, 512, 527; S 19, 315, 366, 409, 464, 474, 484, 498-99, 552-53

United States Navy Pre-Flight Wrestling Team, I 649

United States Novice Figure Skating Championships, I 502, 504, 506, 510-11, 517; S 626, 628

United States Olympic Basketball Committee, I 40, 74-75, 182, 207, 287, 326

United States Olympic Basketball Officials Committee, I 277, 287, 326

United States Olympic Basketball Team, S 253, 255, 257, 261, 263, 275-76, 280, 286, 302-03, 306

United States Olympic Bobsled Team, I 380

United States Olympic Boxing Team, I 380-81, 385, 449; S 623, 625

United States Olympic Committee, I 74-75, 108, 125, 131, 235, 246, 265, 287, 321; O 258, 317, 439, 447, 497-98; S 133, 279, 568, 597

United States Olympic Committee Sportsman of the Year, I 492; O 425, 502

United States Olympic Committee Sportswoman of the Year, O 317, 481, 541

United States Olympic Cycling Team, O 314

United States Olympic Diving Team, I 485, 490-93, 495-96

United States Olympic Equestrian Jumping Team, O 267

United States Olympic Fencing Team, I 669

United States Olympic Festival, I 492, 638, 658-59

United States Olympic Field Hockey

Team, O 244
United States Olympic Figure Skating Team, I 505, 509, 515-16, 518; S 601, 614-15
United States Olympic Gymnastic Committee, I 493, 507, 523, 529, 532-33
United States Olympic Gymnastic Team, I 521-24, 526-29, 531-33, 535, 537, 540
United States Olympic Hall of Fame, I 449, 491, 536, 575, 611, 616-17, 620; O 453, 474, 484, 502, 510; S 276
United States Olympic Ice Hockey Team, S 537, 539-41, 543-48
United States Olympic Lacrosse Team, O 302
United States Olympic Men's Basketball Team, See United States Men's Basketball Team
United States Olympic Polo Team, O 260, 271
United States Olympic Ski Team, O 274-75, 277-78, 282, 284-88, 318
United States Olympic Soccer Team, O 291, 294-95, 297, 301, 307, 309
United States Olympic Speed Skating Team, O 313-18; S 603
United States Olympic Sports Festival, O 425, 436, 481, 485, 507, 541, 558; S 320, 547
United States Olympic Swimming Team, S 602, 607-08, 621-22
United States Olympic Track and Field Team, S 565-98
United States Olympic Training Center, Colorado Springs, CO, O 493
United States Olympic Trials, S 296, 302, 566, 569-73, 575-77, 579, 581, 584-90, 593-94, 596, 598-99, 607

United States Olympic Volleyball Team, I 676; S 613
United States Olympic Weightlifting Team, I 630
United States Olympic Women's Basketball Team, See United States Women's Basketball Team
United States Olympic Wrestling Committee, I 648, 652, 657, 660, 666
United States Olympic Wrestling Team, I 635-36, 642, 646, 658, 660, 665-66; S 608-09, 624
United States Open Golf Tournament, S 507, 513-16, 519-20, 522-24; 1897, O 107; 1898, O 107; 1899, O 107; 1901, O 107; 1902, O 107; 1903, O 107; 1904, O 107; 1905, O 107; 1906, O 108; 1909, O 108; 1910, O 140, 155, 157; 1911, O 112, 133, 140; 1912, O 140; 1913, O 128, 140, 148; 1914, O 128, 140, 148; 1915, O 160; 1916, O 121, 133; 1919, O 112, 133; 1920, O 119, 133; 1921, O 109; 1922, O 153; 1923, O 133, 136; 1925, O 112; 1927, O 108, 116; 1928, O 119; 1929, O 169; 1930, O 136, 158; 1932, O 153; 1933, O 155; 1934, O 120; 1936, O 116; 1937, O 127, 155; 1938, O 127; 1939, O 145, 155, 159; 1940, O 138, 141, 154; 1941, O 155, 169; 1946, O 141, 145; 1947, O 159; 1948, O 118, 131; 1949, O 142; 1950, O 112, 141; 1951, O 131, 153; 1952, O 112; 1953, O 118, 122, 131; 1954, O 139; 1956, O 142; 1957, O 118, 146; 1958, O 146; 1959, O 115; 1960, O 130, 146, 149; 1961, O 139; 1962, O 147; 1963,

O 112; 1966, O 115, 143, 163; 1968, O 163; 1969, O 119; 1971, O 163; 1973, O 143; 1974, O 134; 1975, O 166; 1977, O 126; 1979, O 134-35; 1982, O 166; 1986, O 125; 1987, O 166

United States Pairs Figure Skating Championships, S 601, 615

United States Pee Wee Golf Tournament, O 151

United States-Poland Wrestling Meet, I 666

United States Polo Association, O 260-61

United States Powerlifting Championships, I 629

United States Pro Tennis Championships, O 331, 365, 368, 386, 399, 404-05, 407-08, 410

United States Pro Wrestling Championships, I 643

United States Professional Bicycle Sprint Championships, O 264, 269

United States Professional Gymnastic Classic, I 540

United States-Romania Wrestling Meet, I 639

United States-Scotland All-Star Soccer Game, O 296

United States Senior Ladies Figure Skating Singles Championships, I 499, 503-05, 507, 509-10, 512, 515-17

United States Senior Ladies Roller Skating Championships, I 674

United States Senior Polo Championships, O 280

United States Seniors Doubles Tennis Championships, O 336

United States Seniors Mixed Doubles Tennis Championships, O 336

United States Seniors Open Golf Tournament, O 116, 130

United States Seniors Singles Tennis Championships, O 386

United States Short-Course Swim Championships, S 603, 607

United States Soccer Federation Hall of Fame, O 292-94, 296-97, 300, 302-03, 307, 309-10

United States-Soviet Union Gymnastic Meet, I 528

United States-Soviet Union Swim Meet, I 579, 583, 592

United States-Soviet Union Track and Field Meet, I 670; S 570, 573

United States-Soviet Union Weightlifting Meet, I 625

United States-Soviet Union Wrestling Meet, I 666

United States Speed Skating Championships, O 316-17; S 603

United States Sports Academy, I 215; S 341

United States Squash Racquets Championships, O 415

United States Swimming, I 596, 605, 614

United States Swimming Federation International Invitation Swim Meet, I 583, 592, 598

United States Track and Field Championships, O 255

United States Track and Field Federation, S 279

United States Track and Field Hall of Fame, O 446, 450, 478, 496, 522, 545; S 279

United States Trotting Association, O 182, 191, 207

United States-Turkey Wrestling Meet, I 666

United States Veterans Doubles Tennis Championships, O 339, 412, 415; S 559

United States Volleyball Association, I 676

United States Weightlifting Championships, I 625-27, 629-32

United States Women's Amateur Golf Tournament, O 110-11, 114, 117, 132-33, 159, 329, 406; S 511-12, 520-21

United States Women's Basketball Team, I 55, 59, 72, 214-15, 253, 258, 290-91, 325, 329

United States Women's Figure Skating Championships, S 626, 628

United States Women's Golf Association Tour, S 511, 518

United States Women's Junior Tennis Championships, O 327, 347

United States Women's Lacrosse Association, S 270

United States Women's Open Golf Tournament, O 111, 114, 129, 151-52, 160, 168, 170, 172, 321; S 505-06, 508-10, 513-14, 518

United States Women's Outdoor Doubles Tennis Championships, S 511, 550; 1890, O 405; 1891, O 333; 1892, O 333; 1894, O 324-25; 1895, O 325; 1896, O 377; 1897, O 325; 1898, O 325; 1901, O 325; 1902, O 325, 353; 1903, O 377; 1904, O 332; 1905, O 336; 1906, O 336, 406; 1909, O 415; 1910, O 415; 1911, O 391, 415; 1912, O 329; 1913, O 329; 1914, O 329; 1915, O 391, 415; 1916, O 373, 391; 1917, O 373, 391; 1922, O 387; 1924, O 387; 1925, O 329, 387; 1926, O 389; 1928, O 387; 1930, O 343; 1932, O 343, 360; 1934, O 343, 360; 1935, O 343, 360; 1937, O 343, 374; 1938, O 343, 374; 1939, O 343, 360, 374; 1940, O 343, 374; 1941, O 337, 343, 348; 1942, O 337, 348; 1943, O 337, 348; 1944, O 337, 348; 1945, O 337, 348; 1946, O 337, 348; 1947, O 337, 348; 1948, O 337, 348; 1949, O 337, 348; 1950, O 337, 348-49; 1951, O 358, 360; 1952, O 358, 360; 1953, O 358, 360; 1954, O 358-60; 1955, O 337, 348; 1956, O 337, 348; 1957, O 338, 348; 1958, O 357; 1959, O 357; 1960, O 357; 1961, O 357; 1962, O 357; 1964, O 363; 1967, O 335, 363; 1969, O 357-58; 1971, O 335; 1974, O 363; 1977, O 335; 1978, O 363; 1979, O 335; 1982, O 335; 1983, O 397; 1984, O 397; 1986, O 381, 397; 1987, O 381, 397

United States Women's Outdoor Singles Championships, S 549, 551, 562; 1887, O 321, 405; 1888, O 321, 405; 1889, O 405; 1890, O 333, 405; 1891, O 333; 1892, O 376; 1893, O 376; 1894, O 324, 406; 1895, O 325, 376; 1896, O 325, 376; 1897, O 325, 376; 1898, O 325, 354; 1899, O 353, 383; 1901, O 325, 354, 376; 1902, O 325, 353-54, 376-77; 1903, O 354, 376; 1904, O 332, 377; 1905, O 336, 376-77; 1906, O 377, 406; 1907, O 336; 1909, O 411, 415; 1912, O 329, 391; 1913, O 329; 1914, O 329, 411; 1915, O 373, 415; 1916, O 373, 391; 1917, O 373, 406; 1918, O 373, 403; 1919, O 403, 415; 1920, O 373; 1921, O 329, 361, 373; 1922, O 373, 387; 1923, O 387; 1924, O 329, 387; 1925, O 387; 1926, O 373, 388; 1927, O 387; 1928, O 387; 1929, O 387;

1930, O 387; 1931, O 387; 1932, O 360, 380, 387; 1933, O 360-61, 387; 1934, O 360; 1935, O 360, 387; 1936, O 360, 374; 1938, O 374; 1939, O 374; 1940, O 374; 1941, O 359; 1942, O 319, 337; 1943, O 319, 337; 1944, O 319, 337; 1945, O 337; 1946, O 319, 337; 1947, O 337; 1948, O 349; 1949, O 349; 1950, O 344, 349; 1951, O 327; 1952, O 327; 1953, O 328; 1954, O 328, 358-59; 1955, O 358; 1956, O 360; 1957, O 344; 1960, O 357; 1961, O 357; 1969, O 364; 1971, O 352, 364; 1972, O 363; 1974, O 364; 1975, O 351; 1976, O 351; 1977, O 351; 1978, O 326, 351, 396; 1979, O 326, 351; 1980, O 351; 1981, O 326, 380; 1982, O 351; 1983, O 351, 380; 1984, O 351, 380; 1985, O 380; 1986, O 380; 1987, O 352-53, 380-81, 397

United States Women's Squash Championships, O 270, 391

United States Women's Squash Racquets Association, O 391

United States Women's Veterans Doubles Tennis Championships, O 391

United States Women's Volleyball Championships, I 676

United States World Cup Golf Team, O 117

United States World Roller Skating Team, I 674

United States Wrestling Federation, I 639, 650, 652, 663

United States Wrestling Federation Championships, I 663

United States Wrestling Federation National Wrestling Hall of Fame, S 609, 617

United States Yacht Championships, O 103

United States Young Master's Billiards Championships, I 673

United States-Yugoslavia Wrestling Meet, I 639

Universal Gymnasium, Boston, MA, I 634

University Club of Boston Hockey Team, S 546

University of Akron, F 257, 457; I 90, 147

University of Alabama, B 455, 508, 536; F 74-75, 109, 121, 160, 236, 281, 287, 302, 331, 407, 418, 422, 427-28, 431, 458, 481, 491, 501, 508, 534, 544, 553, 561, 567, 576, 594-95, 600, 625-27; I 204, 249, 314, 497; O 45-46, 79, 105, 542; S 365, 368, 379, 382, 395, 399, 403-04, 418-19, 421-22, 436, 439, 446-47, 465, 479, 498

University of Alabama-Birmingham, S 259

University of Arizona, F 43, 98, 291, 663; I 79, 184, 215, 283, 617; O 418; S 278, 310

University of Arizona Sports Hall of Fame, I 80

University of Arkansas, F 9, 39, 42, 46, 73, 118, 171, 206, 275, 287, 302, 317, 336, 501, 516, 527, 553, 578, 581; I 218-19; S 401, 419-20, 428, 448, 456, 480, 489

University of Arkansas at Little Rock, I 304

University of Arkansas at Pine Bluffs, S 407

University of Baltimore, I 132; S 239, 250

University of Bridgeport, F 503; O 111

University of British Columbia, F
114
University of Buffalo, F 261, 469; S
289
University of California at Berkeley, B
83, 200, 249; F 5-6, 45, 61, 113,
142, 153, 172-73, 255, 299, 377-
78, 410-12, 421, 492, 512, 533,
539, 552, 566, 595, 627, 631, 637-
38; I 16, 91, 96, 172, 230-31,
235, 586-87, 607-08, 610; O 212,
330, 371, 388, 415, 469, 563; S
83, 94-95, 130, 138, 161, 380,
445, 454-55, 496, 551, 580-81,
588-89, 602
University of California at Irvine, I
491-92; O 531, 533; S 347
University of California at Long
Beach, F 667
University of California at Los
Angeles (UCLA), F 31-32, 114,
127, 157, 169, 228, 244, 317, 356,
377-78, 404, 413, 501-02, 523,
533, 549, 604, 637-39, 667, 670; I
3, 35, 55-56, 59, 72, 97, 101, 116,
118, 152, 172, 210, 213, 225, 228,
231, 246, 257, 260, 280, 282, 292,
299, 317-18, 330-31, 526-27, 533,
537, 540-41, 575-76, 584, 593,
611, 657-59; O 62, 324, 341, 365,
424-25, 456, 472, 477-78, 480-81,
493, 557, 563; S 27, 71, 251-52,
259, 278, 285, 291, 294, 312, 325-
28, 333, 361, 392-93, 402, 427,
453-54, 493, 506, 572, 579, 591
University of California at Los
Angeles Gymnastic Invitation
Meet, I 527
University of California at Riverside,
O 563
University of California at San Diego,
O 314
University of California at Santa

Barbara, I 582
University of Chattanooga, F 576,
594-95; S 436
University of Chicago, F 13, 44-45,
58, 84, 119, 152, 155, 158, 240,
244, 261-62, 438-39, 530, 532,
538, 551, 563-64, 665-66, 668,
673; I 129, 228, 235-36, 272,
333, 646; O 324, 368, 488, 524;
S 276-77, 397, 445, 485
University of Cincinnati, B 124, 268,
285, 314; F 14, 101, 210, 457,
526, 558, 664; I 216, 231, 251,
259, 307-08, 594; O 400-01, 406-
07; S 106, 251
University of Colorado, F 18, 61-62,
151, 258, 288, 481, 508, 647; I 5,
39, 139, 304, 664; O 134, 281,
288, 539, 552-53; S 241, 382,
399, 420, 454, 470, 473, 627
University of Connecticut, S 420
University of Dayton, F 80, 432; I
198, 282; S 284
University of Delaware, S 452, 456
University of Delaware Hall of Fame,
S 456
University of Denver, I 179, 380; S
392
University of Detroit, F 107, 148,
212, 531; I 64, 121, 248, 251,
660; S 308, 324
University of Edinburgh, O 108
University of Florida, F 104, 110,
138, 287, 355, 522, 553, 560-61,
606; I 280-81, 579-80; O 48-49,
536; S 182, 378, 399-400, 504,
516
University of Georgia, B 85; F 57-
58, 81, 109-10, 138, 150, 188,
287, 294, 305, 331, 353, 367, 383,
460, 509, 512, 535, 549, 583, 595,
599, 603-04, 630, 632, 635; I 10,
210, 285; O 554; S 329, 394-95,

405, 424, 430, 449

University of Hawaii, **F** 637; **S** 445

University of Houston, **F** 99, 138-39, 181, 331, 397, 481, 664-65; **I** 83, 118, 173-74, 300; **O** 485; **S** 523, 613

University of Idaho, **F** 321, 528, 664; **I** 76, 148; **S** 423

University of Illinois at Chicago, **I** 649

University of Illinois at Urbana-Champaign, **B** 41-42; **F** 27, 44, 74, 79, 158-59, 172-74, 217, 233, 241, 272, 299, 358, 381, 395, 430, 438-39, 458, 469, 475, 486, 551, 555, 627, 646, 669-70, 673-74; **I** 43, 109, 159, 238-39, 242, 267, 272, 286, 527-29, 534, 584, 651, 664; **O** 87, 255, 493, 513, 521-22; **S** 88, 259, 291-92, 296-97, 361, 397, 402, 424, 445, 480, 492, 502

University of Iowa, **B** 11; **F** 12-13, 27, 44, 95, 100, 152, 194, 227, 243, 249, 261, 289, 297, 299, 301, 307, 319-20, 338, 345, 355-56, 377, 379, 415-16, 425, 482, 506, 550-51, 555, 607, 673; **I** 16, 93, 146, 150, 184, 193, 201, 210, 215-17, 225, 254, 269, 542, 584, 635-36, 641-42, 646-47, 649, 659, 666; **O** 446; **S** 213, 288, 306, 310, 392, 401-02, 420, 476

University of Jacksonville, **S** 327

University of Kansas, **F** 78, 116, 288, 362, 422, 446, 480, 493, 524, 627, 688; **I** 4-5, 33, 35-37, 39, 45-47, 63, 69, 77, 86, 116, 148, 172, 180-82, 184, 198-99, 206, 216, 229, 251, 256, 281-82, 323-24, 328-29; **O** 427, 431, 445-46, 498, 510, 518; **S** 3, 295, 301, 316-17, 325, 392-93, 408-09, 474, 580, 586, 589

University of Kansas Hall of Fame, **I** 217, 329

University of Kansas Relays, **I** 69

University of Kentucky, **B** 84; **F** 15, 54-55, 74, 198-99, 271, 320, 373, 543, 576, 641; **I** 19, 23, 31, 42, 53, 94, 108-10, 113, 116, 142, 146, 154-55, 166, 180, 198-99, 204, 225, 237-38, 244-45, 249, 256-57, 260, 265, 308, 648; **S** 257, 259-61, 276-77, 286, 303, 309, 318, 349, 382-84, 446, 452, 462-63

University of Kentucky Invitational Basketball Tournament, **I** 180, 209

University of Louisville, **F** 613; **I** 56, 79, 109, 189, 308-09, 330, 606; **S** 263, 295

University of Maine, **F** 58, 65, 192, 440; **O** 463

University of Maryland at College Park, **F** 57-58, 61, 74, 111, 155, 168, 338, 364, 397, 464, 538, 585, 632, 650, 653; **I** 71-72, 113, 160, 202, 206, 277, 636-37, 642; **O** 234, 237, 242, 246-47, 249, 506; **S** 101, 122, 298, 382, 428-29, 484

University of Maryland Eastern Shore, **F** 539

University of Massachusetts, **I** 81; **S** 460, 581

University of Miami (FL), **F** 16, 50, 71, 93, 136, 182, 184, 188, 195, 209, 258, 288, 370, 405, 445, 460, 518, 534, 570, 572, 606-07, 609; **I** 16, 179, 225, 491; **O** 358; **S** 56, 182, 428, 487, 557

University of Michigan, **B** 211, 273, 365, 472, 476, 513, 515, 584; **F** 6, 14, 34, 38, 45, 98-99, 109, 120, 130, 141, 158-59, 172-74, 176, 184, 193-94, 200, 212, 217, 227-28, 239-41, 243-44, 261-63, 267,

272, 287-89, 298-99, 322, 343, 345, 368-69, 413-14, 422, 432, 446, 458, 477, 492, 512, 525-27, 530, 537, 554-55, 594, 627, 655, 660, 668-69; I 6, 31, 101, 210, 259-60, 312, 488, 496, 547, 572, 639-41, 645, 651, 661; O 12, 443, 464, 473, 483, 514, 524, 551; S 56, 136, 219, 292, 303, 362, 380, 397, 402, 424, 435, 444, 458, 494, 500-01, 547

University of Michigan Hall of Honor, F 660; I 652

University of Minnesota, Duluth, F 137; I 567

University of Minnesota, Morris, B 313

University of Minnesota, Twin Cities, B 623; F 11, 13, 27, 36, 38, 44, 48-49, 92, 119, 144, 158-59, 161, 174, 194, 218, 227, 255, 261-62, 413, 415-17, 433, 458, 469, 506, 537, 550, 554, 627, 650-55, 660, 669, 673; I 79, 137, 158, 164-65, 167, 241, 330, 497, 547-50, 557, 561-65, 568, 571-73, 640, 666; O 110; S 141, 200-01, 281, 299, 309, 333, 361, 397, 402-03, 419-20, 424, 443-44, 447, 451, 462, 484, 491, 539, 541, 543, 547, 578

University of Mississippi, B 583; F 230, 293, 319, 422, 577, 598-600, 621-22; O 142; S 366, 385, 412, 428, 464-65, 479

University of Missouri at Columbia, B 626; F 6, 37, 73, 91, 95, 136-38, 147, 167-68, 219, 324, 341, 438, 659; I 77, 206-07, 304, 536; O 67, 530-31; S 320-21, 338, 352, 381-82, 394-95, 399-401, 406-08, 418, 435, 459, 496, 580

University of Missouri at St. Louis, O 305

University of Montana, F 49

University of Nebraska-Lincoln, F 2, 47, 71, 102, 135-36, 159, 189, 195-96, 208-09, 214, 217, 245, 263, 291, 296, 301, 325, 359-60, 443-44, 477, 479-80, 487, 494-95, 506-08, 518, 524, 527, 538, 551, 554-55, 561, 570-71, 582, 592, 627, 645-46, 655, 668; I 140, 269, 302, 660; S 331, 370, 403-04, 410-11, 428, 440, 456, 474-75, 479, 490, 579

University of Nevada, Las Vegas, I 292-93, 519; S 95, 295

University of Nevada, Reno, F 409, 539; I 181

University of New Hampshire, B 182; F 181, 571; I 561-62; S 474, 507

University of New Hampshire Pro-Am Golf Classic, S 507

University of New Mexico, F 466; I 384, 646; O 536; S 273

University of Nigeria, O 561

University of North Alabama, S 415

University of North Carolina, F 53, 78, 109, 155, 227, 275, 305, 324, 422, 453, 553, 558-59, 584, 588, 599, 603-04, 606, 621; I 34, 40, 46, 58, 99, 130, 152-53, 172, 188-89, 198-99, 265, 281-83, 285, 298, 645; O 124, 248, 393, 429; S 259, 270-71, 274-75, 280, 282-83, 304-05, 310, 316, 346, 410, 447, 464

University of North Dakota, F 27, 199, 478; S 281, 539, 543

University of Northern Iowa, I 8, 646-47, 659-60, 665; S 321, 616

University of Notre Dame, B 11, 356, 396, 468, 522, 587, 610, 633; F 12-14, 16, 43, 53, 74, 89-90, 94-95, 112, 126-27, 132, 136, 138, 145, 148-49, 153, 159, 175-76,

181, 187-90, 200, 211-14, 221,
225, 244-45, 248, 254, 271, 276-
77, 297, 299-300, 314, 316, 323,
327-28, 337-39, 344, 349, 357-59,
371, 374, 377, 379, 381, 385, 393,
399, 407, 409, 416, 424, 427, 433,
438, 440, 451, 456-58, 472, 495,
504-08, 512-13, 516, 528, 530,
532-33, 539, 551, 566, 572, 577,
592, 594-95, 601, 606, 613, 627,
630, 645-46, 648; I 40-41, 60,
138, 141, 151, 156, 158, 163-64,
193, 208, 250, 257, 269, 312, 317,
607; O 52, 70, 81, 83, 90, 96,
104, 115, 520-21, 564; S 271,
301, 309, 311-12, 317, 333, 366,
373-75, 379-80, 399-400, 404,
418, 424, 428, 437, 440, 448, 471-
72, 476, 480-81, 486, 495-96, 498
University of Oklahoma, B 351; F
16, 50, 77-78, 136, 168, 171, 198,
208, 289, 301-02, 338, 345, 364,
367, 407, 423, 445-46, 448, 481-
82, 508, 515-16, 527, 534; 537,
546, 576, 581-82, 584-85, 599,
604-07, 622, 641, 653; I 35, 69-
70, 91, 166, 303-04, 338, 522-23,
635-36, 644, 650, 652, 658-59,
663; O 67; S 278, 301-02, 324-
25, 358, 369-70, 403, 408, 419-20,
428-29, 461-63, 496
University of Oregon, B 304; F 34-
35, 46, 190, 350, 369, 378, 485,
617; I 59, 70, 91, 131, 172, 235;
O 418, 434, 450, 469-70, 518,
527-28, 545, 562; S 67, 276, 448-
49, 467-68, 484, 498
University of Paris, O 516
University of Pennsylvania, B 426,
558; F 32, 34, 38, 40, 46, 61, 64,
71, 85, 94, 116, 192, 204, 231,
239-40, 243, 256-57, 265-66, 309,
342-43, 350, 426, 468-69, 474,

506, 530-32, 552, 597, 607, 668-
69; I 141, 189, 221-22, 236, 243,
272, 285, 574, 614; O 70, 235-36,
256, 270, 338, 403, 440-41, 483,
495, 508, 511-12, 599; S 220,
265, 311, 371, 376, 394, 416-18,
431, 502, 566-67, 575, 595-96
University of Pittsburgh, B 411, 452;
F 40, 113, 139, 142, 173, 175,
200, 213-14, 221-22, 231, 242,
249, 272, 300, 313, 350, 353, 359,
383, 388, 463-64, 459, 472, 504,
509, 512, 528, 532, 538, 574, 579,
592, 603, 613, 627, 636, 651, 661,
665; I 38-39, 85, 99, 138, 179,
209, 302; O 395, 565-66; S 120,
271-72, 278, 357-58, 406, 409,
428, 444, 448-49, 459, 477, 479-
81, 495, 584
University of Pittsburgh at
Johnstown, S 611
University of Pittsburgh Hall of
Fame, S 272
University of Puget Sound, O 277-78
University of Rhode Island, I 99, 128,
155, 257, 305; S 322
University of Richmond, B 62
University of Rochester, I 114, 154;
S 351
University of Rochester Basketball
Classic, I 115
University of San Francisco, F 378,
382, 387, 409, 516, 521, 566; I 8,
150, 180, 190, 210, 216, 230-31,
262; S 184, 299, 331, 437, 554
University of Scranton, S 29
University of Seattle, I 257
University of South Alabama, S 208
University of South Alabama Athletic
Hall of Fame, S 208
University of South Carolina, F 110,
383, 487, 509; I 78, 189, 198-99,
280; S 420

University of South Florida, **B** 477; **S** 108

University of Southern California, **B** 57, 120, 248, 341, 504, 545; **F** 8, 11, 23, 32, 46, 49, 94-95, 114, 127, 129, 138, 141, 153-54, 176, 201-02, 206-07, 220-21, 225, 227-28, 249, 256, 277, 299-301, 338, 345, 361, 369-70, 377, 396, 408, 458, 471, 491, 506, 512-13, 526, 532-33, 544-45, 576, 580, 585, 592, 595, 626, 637-39, 648-49, 662, 667; **I** 15-16, 39, 73, 93, 110, 140, 172, 264-65, 274, 490, 521-22, 537, 586, 608-09, 613-14, 642; **O** 337, 358, 399, 440, 444, 455-56, 472-73, 493, 496, 509, 516, 533, 568; **S** 18, 38, 54, 56, 71, 103, 201, 204, 241, 326, 338, 347, 370, 388, 392, 453, 468, 473, 481, 495-96, 500, 518, 552, 561, 574-75, 577-78, 586-90, 594

University of Southern Mississippi, **F** 230; **S** 465

University of Southwest Louisiana, **B** 233

University of Tampa, **F** 288, 549; **S** 108, 169-70

University of Tennessee at Martin, **I** 290

University of Tennessee, Knoxville, **B** 48-49; **F** 20, 74, 109, 126, 145, 150, 169-70, 281, 287, 293, 300-01, 344, 355, 367, 397, 407, 421, 428-29, 452, 523, 534, 542, 575-76, 621; **I** 120-21, 160, 290-91, 372; **O** 82, 142, 437; **S** 211, 354, 413-14, 418, 428, 446-49, 460, 487, 584, 598

University of Tennessee, Memphis, **S** 276

University of Texas at Arlington, **S** 74-75

University of Texas at Austin, **B** 254; **F** 6, 35, 47, 78, 87-88, 159, 245, 287, 302, 318, 336, 338, 340-41, 356, 366-67, 369, 392, 394, 398, 402, 418, 431, 444, 446, 455, 458, 504, 514-16, 534, 547, 550, 568, 592, 600, 628, 632, 641; **I** 91, 205, 215, 536, 578, 583; **O** 322-23; **S** 54, 74-75, 320, 412, 438, 475, 510, 514-15

University of Texas at El Paso, **F** 139; **I** 9-10; **O** 428; **S** 303

University of Texas at San Antonio, **I** 304

University of the Pacific, **F** 179-80, 564

University of Toledo, **F** 607; **I** 6; **S** 270, 484

University of Toronto, **O** 511

University of Tulsa, **I** 139, 326; **S** 398, 488

University of Utah, **F** 292, 559, 657; **I** 94-95; **S** 331, 396, 492

University of Vermont, **B** 208, 468; **O** 274-75, 451, 463

University of Virginia, **B** 318, 456, 474; **F** 37, 109, 154-55, 380, 421, 475-76, 543; **I** 152, 265-66, 646; **O** 239, 247, 464; **S** 179, 255, 265, 366, 429

University of Washington, **F** 23, 79, 114, 144, 152, 213, 221, 249, 288, 325, 335, 355, 365, 512-15, 533, 554-55, 579, 625, 645; **I** 75-76, 115-16, 134-35, 172; **S** 402, 454, 461-62, 495

University of Wisconsin Club Award, **F** 643

University of Wisconsin-Eau Claire, **I** 486

University of Wisconsin-Madison, **B** 316; **F** 10-11, 13, 25, 27, 51, 94, 108, 158-59, 189, 194, 214, 237,

241, 260-61, 268-69, 355, 416, 438-39, 469, 482, 506, 530-31, 643, 654-55, 673; **I** 15, 85, 206, 234, 286, 312, 658, 666; **O** 314-15, 483, 520; **S** 266, 434, 462, 476, 484, 530, 543, 547

University of Wisconsin-Milwaukee, **O** 317

University of Wisconsin-Stout, **I** 655

University of Wyoming, **F** 136, 151, 664; **I** 70, 157-58, 250, 276, 646; **S** 252, 331, 395, 424, 473

Unseld, Westley S. "Wes," **I** 121, 220, 224, 278, *308-09;* **S** 313

Unser, Alfred, Sr. "Al," **O** 10, 29, 34, *36-38,* 39; **S** 614

Unser, Alfred, Jr. "Al," **O** 36-38; **S** 619-20

Unser, Delbert B. "Del," **S** 123

Unser, Jerry, **O** 36, 38

Unser, Jerry H., **O** 36, 38

Unser, Robert W., Sr. "Bobby," **O** 3, 11, 28-29, 34, 36-37, *38-39*

Unser, Robert W., Jr. "Bobby," **O** 39

Unser-Gorza Auto Racing Team, **O** 39

Upset, **O** 195-96, 199-200, 595; **S** 533

Upset Lad, **O** 196

Upshaw, Eugene "Gene," **F** *615*

Upton, Charles, **I** 456

Upton, Jill, **I** 123

Ursinus College, **O** 259

Uruguay National Soccer Team, **O** 299

USA Aquatics Club, **I** 585

USA-Mobil Outdoor Track and Field Championships, **O** 425, 436, 482, 486, 504, 532

USA-Network, **I** 234, 288; **O** 308; **S** 353

USA Olympic Federation, **I** 540

USA-Poland Track and Field Meet, **O** 457

USA-USSR Track and Field Meet, **O** 457

USI Golf Classic, **S** 521

USSA Ronald Reagan Award, **S** 341

Ussery, Robert "Bob," **O** 183, *225-26*

Utah-Idaho League, **S** 23

Utah Jazz basketball club (NBA), **I** 60-61, 95, 160, 204; **S** 263, 329, 331

Utah Sports Hall of Fame, **I** 94

Utah Stars basketball club (ABA, NBA), **I** 20, 202, 226, 275

Utah State University, **F** 230, 441, 663; **I** 224, 301; **S** 396

Utay, Joseph "Joe," **S** *494*

Utica College, **I** 50

Utica, NY baseball club (EL, IL, Ind., NYSL), **B** 15, 66, 224, 297; **S** 178

Utica, NY basketball club (NYSL), **I** 88, 273

Uzcudun, Paolino, **I** 372, 429, 475

Vagrancy, **O** 184

Vairo, "Lou," **I** 551

Val d'Isere, France Alpine Ski Competition, **O** 273, 288

Valdiserri, Roger, **F** 592

Valenciennes, **O** 196

Valentine, Thomas "Tom," **O** 400

Valenzuela, Fernando, **S** 171

Valgar, "Benny," **I** 392

Valkenberg, James, **S** 330

Valley Junior College, **S** 392

Valleydale 400 Auto Race, **O** 44

Valparaiso University, **I** 158; **S** 259

Van Arsdale, Richard A. "Dick," **I** 192, *309-10,* 310-11

Van Arsdale, Thomas A. "Tom," **I** 192, 309, *310-11*

Van Bebber, Jack F., **I** *662*

Van Berg, John C. "Jack," **O** *226-27*

Van Berg, Marion, **O** 226
Van Brocklin, Norman "Norm," **F** 303, 369, 491, *617-18*
Van Buren, Stephen "Steve," **F** 400, *618-20*, 660; **S** 488
Van Eeghan, Mark, **F** 620
Van Every, Harold, **F** 554
van Halmay, Zoltan, **I** 587-88
Van Haltren, George E., **B** 301, *568-69*
Van Hellemond, Andrew "Andy," **I** 557
Van Lennep, Frances, **O** 575
Van Lennep, Frederick, **O** 575
Van Loan, Charles, **O** 90
van Osdel, Robert L., **O** 476
Van Pelt, Brad A., **S** *494-95*
Van Ranst, Cornelius, **O** 570-71, 597, 609
Van Ryn, John W., Jr., **O** 322-23, 347, 368, 395, *408-09*, 410
Van Wie, Virginia, **S** *520-21*
Vanatta, Robert "Bob," **S** 321
Vance, Arthur C. "Dazzy," **B** *567-68*
Vancouver, Canada baseball club (PCL), **B** 353, 477, 575; **S** 9, 107, 157, 184
Vancouver, Canada Soccer Club (NASL), **O** 303
Vancouver, Canada Tigercats football club (CFL), **F** 535, 560
Vancouver, WA baseball club (NWL), **S** 105
Vanden Hogen, Debra Thomas "Debbie," **S** *626-27*
Vander Meer, John S. "Johnny," **B** 168, 336, 470; **S** *228-29*
Vanderbilt, Alfred G., **O** 599
Vanderbilt, William K., **O** 51
Vanderbilt Cup Auto Races, **O** 7, 31
Vanderbilt University, **F** 35, 74, 109-10, 147, 150, 231, 368-69, 405-07, 422, 522-23, 530-31, 541, 576,

625, 669; **I** 204; **O** 88-89; **S** 195, 470
Vandeweghe, Ernest M., Jr. "Ernie," **I** 212
Vandeweghe, Ernest M. III "Kiki," **I** 143
Vandivier, Robert F. "Fuzzy," **I** 130, *311-13*
Vangilder, Elam R., **S** 13
Vanguard, **S** 536
Vanity, **O** 608
Vardon, Harry, **O** 128-29, 132, 148
Vardon Trophy, **O** 115-16, 119, 125, 130-31, 141-42, 145, 153, 158-59, 163, 166; **S** 514
Vare, Glenna Collett, **O** 110, 133, 156, *164-65*, 329; **S** 512, 520-21
Vare Trophy, **O** 110, 137, 151-52, 165, 170; **S** 508, 517
Varipapa, "Andy," **I** 338
Varner, Margaret, **O** 349
Varnoff, George, **S** 588
Varrichione, Frank, **S** 452
Vasquez, Jacinto, **O** 604
Vasser College, **O** 253
Vaughan, Joseph F. "Arky," **B** *569-70*
Vaughn, James L. "Hippo," **B** 291, *570-72;* **S** 223
Vaught, John H. "Johnny," **F** *621-22;* **S** 385, 412
Veach, Robert H. "Bobby," **B** 211, 247, *572-73*
Vecsey, George S., **I** 93; **O** 381
Veeck, William L., Sr., **B** 573
Veeck, William L., Jr. "Bill," **B** 13, 32, 41, 151, 181, 201-02, 222, 230, 243, 435-36, 534, *573-74*, 576; **O** 57; **S** 6, 177, 227
Veee, Julie, **O** 304
Vega, Jose Armando, **I** 542
Velez Sarsfield Soccer Club, Buenos Aires, Argentina, **O** 299

Venezuelan Baseball League, **B** 6, 12-13, 132, 148, 213, 331, 485
Venice, CA baseball club (PCL), **B** 454, 602
Venice, CA Swim Club, **I** 582
Ventura, IA High School, **I** 183
Ventura Junior College, **F** 23
Venturi, Kenneth "Ken," **O** 113
Venzke, Eugene G. "Gene," **O** 446, 519
Verdun, Canada hockey club (QJMHL), **S** 539, 544
Vergez, John L. "Johnny," **B** 588; **S** 45
Vernon, James B. "Mickey," **B** *574-75;* **S** 182
Vernon, CA baseball club (PCL), **B** 397, 459, 602; **S** 162, 197
Vernon Castle, **O** 183
Vertex, **O** 178
Vessels, Billy D., **F** 546, *622-23,* 653
Veterans Stadium, Philadelphia, PA, **S** 118
Vetoyanis, Theodore, *See* George Zaharias
Vezina Trophy, **I** 544, 546-47, 561
Vicksburg, MS baseball club (CSL), **B** 250; **S** 233
Victor Award, **O** 151, 326
Victor Hanson Medal of Excellence, **I** 113
Victoria, Canada baseball club (PNL), **B** 302
Victoria, Canada Cougars Canadian Junior B hockey club, **I** 569
Victoria, TX baseball club (TL), **B** 137, 264, 364, 446
Victorian, **O** 231
Victorias of Winnepeg, Canada hockey club, **S** 546
Victors of Bridgeport baseball club, **B** 428

Victory After the Game, **S** 415
Vidmar, Peter, **I** 537-38, *540-41*
Vienna, Austria Hakoah Soccer Club, **O** 293, 306
Vignaux, Maurice, **I** 673
Vilecco, "Jerry," **I** 646
Villa, "Pancho," **I** 389, 435, 468
Villanova University, **B** 574; **F** 24, 189, 198, 309, 440; **I** 10, 83, 128, 169, 301, 659; **O** 236, 488; **S** 570, 581
Vince, Ralph, **F** 103
Vince Lombardi Award, **S** 370, 373, 414
Vincennes Junior College, **I** 189
Vincent, Francis T., Jr. "Fay," **S** 56, 140
Vines, "Ed," **O** 409
Vines, Henry Ellsworth, **O** 331, 347, 365, 368, 404, *409-11,* 418; **S** 501, 553-54
Viney, Robert "Bob," **F** 642
Vingo, Carmine, **I** 437
Vinson, Maribel Y., *See* Maribel Vinson Owen
Virdon, William C. "Bill," **S** *229-30*
Virgil, **O** 589
Virginia Closed Golf Tournament, **O** 158
Virginia League, **B** 179, 430; **S** 121
Virginia Military Institute, **B** 430; **F** 155, 186
Virginia, MN baseball club (NoL), **B** 580
Virginia Polytechnic Institute, *See* Virginia Tech University
Virginia Slims of Houston, TX Tennis Tournament, **O** 353
Virginia Slims of New England Tennis Tournament, **O** 397
Virginia Slims of New Orleans, LA Tennis Tournament, **O** 353
Virginia Slims of New York, NY

Tennis Tournament, O 353
Virginia Slims Tennis Tournaments,
    O 336, 351, 353, 381; S 552
Virginia Sports Hall of Fame, F 145
Virginia Squires basketball club
    (ABA), I 17, 34, 81-82, 96, 279;
    S 305
Virginia State League, S 19
Virginia State Tennis Championships,
    O 377
Virginia Tech University, F 93, 146,
    154-55, 258; I 265; O 513; S
    382, 399, 447
Virginia Union University, B 151
Virginia Wings hockey club (AHL), I
    554
Viruet, Adolfo, I 422
Vis, Russell J., I 662-63
Visalia, CA baseball club (CaL), B
    449, 515
Viskari, Antti, S 583
Vislocky, John, S 566
Vitalis Award, F 547; O 558
Vitalis/USA Olympic Invitation
    Indoor Track and Field Meet, O
    481, 540-41, 557
Vito, O 197; S 527
Vitt, Oscar J. "Ossie," B 563; S 232
Voice of the Hawkeyes, I 636
Voices from the Great Black Baseball
    Leagues, S 129
Voigt, David Quentin, B 637; O 75
Voit Memorial Trophy, F 472-73,
    501
Vollstedt, Rolla, O 13
Volpe, Raymond "Ray," O 130
Von Boeckman, Ramona, I 314
von Cramm, Baron Gottfried, O 322,
    331, 395
Von der Ahe, Christian F. "Chris," B
    194, 407, 575-76; S 36
von Saltza, Susan Christina, See
    Susan Christina von Saltza

Olmstead
Voorhees, Louise D. "Lida," O 405
Vorbrock, Ernst, I 584
Vosburgh Handicap, O 584
Voshell, S. Howard, O 378
Vosmik, Joseph F. "Joe," B 576-77
Vow Boys, Stanford University, F
    220-21, 491, 513; See also
    Stanford University
Vucerovich, William, Sr., See
    William Vuckovich, Sr.
Vuckovich, William, Sr. "Bill," O 37,
    39-40, 42
Vuckovich, William, Jr. "Bill," O 40
Vulcain, O 593; S 526-27

Wabash College, F 244; I 167
WABC Radio-Television, New York,
    NY, F 208; O 59
Wachter, Edward A. "Eddie," I 21,
    313-14
Wachter, Lew W., I 313; S 260
Waco, TX baseball club (BStL, TL),
    B 456, 602; S 219
Waddell, George E. "Rube," B 90,
    155, 359, 383, 450, 579-80, 636;
    S 203
Waddell, Robert "Bob," S 485
Wade, Lily Margaret, I 289, 314-15
Wade, William "Billy," F 146, 617
Wade, William Wallace, F 300, 327,
    452-53, 477, 595, 625-26, 627; S
    421, 456
Wade Stadium, Durham, NC, F 626
Wade Trophy, I 28, 175, 315, 328
Wadkins, Jerry Lanston "Lanny," O
    124, 139; S 514-15, 521-22
Wagner, Ernest B. "Griz," I 312
Wagner, John Peter "Honus," B 25,
    28, 90, 95, 139, 158, 334, 342,
    507, 509, 569, 581-82; O 75
Wagner, Marie E., O 329, 411-12
Wagner College, I 250

Wagon Wheel Skate Center, Rockton, IL, I 516

Wagonhurst, E. O., F 116

Waigma, Wilson, O 532

Wainwright, Helen E., I 494

Wait a Bit, O 223

Waitz, Greta, O 529

Wake Forest University, F 63, 170, 205, 320, 509; I 42-43; O 149; S 413, 482, 519, 521

Wakefield, Richard C. "Dick," B 50

Walberg, George E. "Rube," B 232

Walcott, O 206

Walcott, "Jersey Joe," I 365-66, 429, 437, *472-73;* O 52

Walcott, Joseph "Joe," I 366, 377, 388, 420, 464, *473-74*

Walden, George C., S 535

Walden, Robert J., S 536

Walden, Robert Wyndham, S 527, *535-36*

Waldhelm, Donald "Don," I 383

Waldorf, Lynn O. "Pappy," F 215, *626-28*

Waldorp, Anthony "Tony," O 489

Walker, Charles, B 453

Walker, Chester "Chet," I 58, 104, 153, *315-16*

Walker, Clarence W. "Tillie," S *230-32*

Walker, Clyde, O 363

Walker, Edward P. "Mickey," I 361, 370, 394, 413, 428, 469, *474-75*

Walker, Ernest R. "Ernie," B 582

Walker, Ewart G. "Dixie," B 582

Walker, Ewell Doak, Jr., F 33, 35, 139, 340, *628-29;* S 471

Walker, Fred "Dixie," B 366, 467, *582-83,* 584; S 180

Walker, Gerald H. "Gee," B *583-84*

Walker, Harry W. "Harry The Hat," B 582-83

Walker, Harvey W. "Hub," B 583

Walker, Herschel J., F 182, 518-19, *629-31*

Walker, James J. "Jimmy," I 141; S *325-26*

Walker, James V., F 655

Walker, John, O 532

Walker, Moses Fleetwood "Fleet," B *584-85*

Walker, "Paulie," I 481

Walker, Sidney, *See* Beau Jack

Walker, "Sonny," I 429

Walker, Wade, F 78, 515; S 462

Walker, Welday W., B 585

Walker Cup Golf Team, O 138, 142, 148; S 514, 519

Walla Walla, WA baseball club (NWL), S 206

Wallace, "Eddie," I 415

Wallace, Francis, F 505

Wallace, John H., O 227-28

Wallace, Roderick J. "Bobby," B 92, 348, *585-86;* S 36

Wallace, "Rusty," S 605-06

Wallace's Kid, I 444

Wallach, Harry, I 380

Wallach, Maud Berger, O 406, 411

Walsh, Adam J., F 638

Walsh, "Christy," F 33, 504; S 490

Walsh, David H., I *316-17*

Walsh, Donald, S 305

Walsh, Edward Arthur, B 586-87

Walsh, Edward Augustin "Ed," B 292, 468, *586-88;* S 342

Walsh, "Jimmy," I 415

Walsh, "Red," I 399

Walsh, Stella, O 448, 546, *555-56*

Walsh, William E. "Bill," F 15, 295, *631-32;* S 383

Walston, Robert H. "Bobby," F *632-33*

Walt Disney Golf Classic, O 125

Walter Brown Award, I 36, 288

Walter Camp Trophy, S 373

Walter Kennedy NBA Citizenship Award, I 42, 169, 309; S 263

Walters, William H. "Bucky," B 74, 125, 216, 336, *588-89;* S 228

Waltham, MA baseball club (MasL), B 506

Walton, William T., Jr. "Bill," I 56, 59, 189, 244, 278, *317-18,* 331; O 269; S 302

Waltrip, Darrell L., O *40-42;* S 605

Wambsganss, William A. "Billy," B 65, 208, 536; S 5, 156

Wanamaker Award, F 33

Wanamaker Mile, O 454

Wanda, O 201

Wanderone, Rudolf W., Jr. "Minnesota Fats," I *677-78*

Waner, Lloyd J. "Little Poison," B 127, *589-90,* 591

Waner, Paul G. "Big Poison," B 32, 589, *590-91*

Wanzer, Robert F. "Bobby," I 114, *318-19*

War Admiral, O 198, 575, 596, *613-14*

War Cloud, O 199

War Jeep, O 614

War Relic, O 596

Warburton, Irvine Cotton, F 299-300, 513; S *495-96*

Ward, Aaron L., B 302

Ward, Arch, O *103-04*

Ward, Cornelia, I 314

Ward, Holcombe, O 345-46, *412-13,* 414, 421-22

Ward, John Montgomery "Monte," B 117, 137, 429, 463, *591-93;* S 151

Ward, John S., O 198

Ward, Rodger M., O 4, *42-43;* S 620

Ward, Sherrill, O 584

Ward's Malt, O 198

Ware, Leonard E., O 413

Ware Award, F 495

Warfield, Elisha, O 594

Warfield, Frank, B 269, 339, 620

Warfield, Paul D., F 122, *633-34*

Warmerdam, Cornelius "Dutch," O 521, *556-57;* S 588

Warneke, Lonnie "Lon," B *593-94*

Warner, Curtis E. "Curt," F 93, 394, 460, *634-35*

Warner, Edward "Ed," I 132

Warner, Glenn S. "Pop," F 90, 113-14, 230-32, 240, 259, 261, 265-66, 299, 313, 319, 342, 359, 402, 424, 425, 463, 469, 504, 513, 550, 575, 579, 596-98, *635-37;* S 397, 477

Warner, H. M., O 198

Warner, John R. "Jack," B 245

Warner, William "Bill," O 564

Warning, S 526

Warren, "Mike, " I 331

Warren, OH baseball club (IOL), B 581

Warren, PA Penns basketball club (NBL), S 293

Washburn, Watson M., O 417-18; S 559

Washburn University, F 446; I 181-82; S 114

Washburn University Hall of Fame, I 182

Washer, "Jan," O 362

Washington, Earl, S 264

Washington, Eugene "Gene," F 127

Washington, Evelyn Ashford, O *557-58*

Washington, Joe D., F 582

Washington, Katherine, I 123

Washington, Kenneth S. "Kenny," F 489, *637-38,* 656; S 251

Washington, Mark H., F 245

Washington, "Pat," F 287

Washington, Raymond "Ray," O 558

Washington, Richard L., I 331

Washington Amateur Athletic Union, S 64

Washington Athletic Club, Seattle, WA, I 598-99

Washington City Hunt, O 95

Washington College, B 83; O 240, 247; S 154, 230

Washington, DC All-Star Hall of Fame, F 396

Washington, DC baseball club (AA, NA) B 256; S 47, 124

Washington, DC Bears basketball club, I 49; S 283

Washington, DC Black Senators baseball club (NNL), B 548

Washington, DC Bullets basketball club (NBA), I 25, 119, 121-22, 150, 161, 203, 221, 224, 278, 309, 328; S 256, 269, 272, 280, 299, 313, 331

Washington, DC Capitols basketball club (ABA, NBA), I 11-12, 17, 34, 274

Washington, DC Capitols hockey club (NHL), I 550-51, 562, 573; S 540, 545

Washington, DC Elite Giants baseball club (NNL), B 269, 362

Washington, DC Generals basketball club, I 176

Washington, DC Grays baseball club (NAL), B 6, 56, 453, 609, 620

Washington, DC Palace Five basketball club (ABL), I 250; S 287

Washington, DC Pigskin Club, See Washington, DC Touchdown Club

Washington, DC Pilots baseball club (EWL), B 269, 543

Washington, DC Post, F 520; O 275; S 337

Washington, DC Potomacs baseball club (ECL), B 548

Washington, DC Redskins football club (NFL), F 4, 7, 9, 17, 26, 28-32, 37, 39, 42, 68, 80, 122, 129, 140, 143, 152, 155, 160, 179-80, 182, 206-07, 215-16, 229, 234, 248, 264, 273, 279, 283, 290, 292, 298, 304-05, 316, 324, 329, 333, 352, 354, 357, 362, 384, 386-88, 395, 397, 399, 414, 417, 437, 443, 463-64, 472-73, 481, 493-94, 502-03, 510, 519, 535, 538, 542-43, 548, 566, 574, 577, 586-87, 589, 593-94, 601, 608, 610, 639, 642, 660; O 43; S 364-65, 372-73, 379, 385, 387, 401, 410, 422, 429, 437, 441, 446, 460-61, 472, 482, 497, 503

Washington, DC Senators baseball club (AL), B 18, 49, 72, 87, 92, 112, 118-20, 123-24, 126, 128, 144, 146, 155, 177-78, 183, 186, 188, 196, 217-19, 225-27, 244-45, 257, 264, 270, 280, 288-89, 292-93, 295, 304-05, 317-18, 330-32, 343, 348, 361, 372, 376, 398, 400-01, 408-09, 413, 417, 430, 446, 448, 456, 470, 490-91, 496, 513, 516, 529, 547, 552, 558, 566, 571-72, 574, 577, 582, 584, 600, 606, 616-17, 630, 635; I 295; O 45, 90; S 3, 12-14, 21, 24, 31, 45-46, 64, 78-79, 87, 95, 102, 105, 111, 117, 127, 131-32, 140, 149, 153-54, 158, 160, 165, 170, 179, 184, 191, 194, 196, 202, 204, 208, 212-13, 225-27, 231, 235, 246-47, 342, 349

Washington, DC Senators baseball club (NL), B 45, 116, 155, 217, 265, 308, 358, 428, 531, 538, 627; S 37, 41, 70, 100, 124, 155, 178, 194

Washington, DC Tapers basketball

club (ABL), I 250

Washington, DC *Times,* F 117

Washington, DC Touchdown Club, F 52, 71, 121, 236, 258, 308, 332, 337, 354, 376, 396, 413, 437, 457, 491, 547, 553, 583; S 395-96, 467-68

Washington, DC Touchdown Club Award, F 121, 437

Washington, DC Touchdown Club Hall of Fame, F 396

Washington, PA baseball club (POML), B 360

Washington Park, Brooklyn, NY, B 429

Washington Park, Chicago, IL, O 175-76, 185, 217, 224, 598, 612, 615

Washington Park Futurity Stakes, O 575-76

Washington Park Golf Club, Chicago, IL, O 156

Washington Park Handicap, O 198, 581, 603

Washington Park International Stakes, O 222, 580

Washington Ski Club, O 277

Washington Sports Hall of Fame, F 366

Washington State Hall of Fame, F 366

Washington State Junior College Conference, F 114

Washington State Tennis Championships, O 361

Washington State University, F 160, 256, 477, 625; I 85, 115-17, 172; S 26, 350-51, 397, 404, 421, 479-80, 495-96

Washington University, St. Louis, MO, F 113, 165, 559; I 109; O 346; S 258, 426, 502, 586

Washington and Jefferson College, F 40, 60, 199-200, 239, 257, 259-60, 313, 410, 421, 552; I 39; S 293

Washington and Lee University, B 215, 430; F 154-55, 324, 498, 603; O 242

Wassaja, Mustapha, I 385

Wassberg, Thomas, O 283

Watch Hill Claiming Race, O 605

Water Girl, O 206

Waterbury, CT baseball club (EL), B 39, 80, 111-12, 238, 439, 584; S 216

Waterfield, Robert "Bob," F 39, 216, 617, *639-40*

Waterford Park, O 189

Waterloo, IA baseball club (IoSL, 3IL), B 12, 79, 383

Waterloo, IA baseball club (ML), B 182, 460, 518, 622; F 209; S 242

Waters, B. G. "Bert," F 64

Waters, Charles T. "Charlie," F 245, *640-41,* 650

Watertown, NY baseball club (BL), B 510

Watkins, Thomas "Tom," B 551

Watkins, William H. "Bill," B 554

Watkins Glen, NY Six Hour Auto Race, O 13

Watson, Donald "Don," I 601

Watson, James, O 505

Watson, Lillian D. "Pokey," I 582

Watson, Louis "Lou," I 192

Watson, Robert J. "Bob," B *594-95*

Watson, Stephen R. "Steve," F 408

Watson, Thomas S. "Tom," O 134, *165-67;* S 510, 514, 521, 523

Watson, Walter, I 377

Watts, Robert "Bobby," I 397

Watts, Stanley H. "Stan," I *319-21*

Waupun, WI baseball club, S 81

Wausau, WI baseball club (NoL), B 449

Wave, O 101

Waxahachie, **O** 217
Waxahachie, TX *Light,* **S** 177
Waycross, GA baseball club (GFL), **S** 247
Wayland, Eugene, **O** 582
Wayland Baptist College, **I** 54-55, 246, 284-85, 325
Wayne Larkin Memorial Award, **S** 548
Wayne State University, **B** 513
Waynesboro, PA baseball club (BRL), **S** 200
Waynesburg College, **I** 22
WBBM Radio-Television, Chicago, IL, **S** 357
WBKB-Radio, Chicago, IL, **O** 52
WBNX-Radio, New York, NY, **S** 343
WCBH-Television, Boston, MA, **S** 339
WCCM-Radio, Lawrence, MA, **O** 68
WCCO Radio-Television, Minneapolis, MN, **F** 486; **S** 402-03
WDGY-Radio, Minneapolis, MN, **F** 174
WEAF-Radio, New York, NY, **O** 79
Weatherall, James P. "Jim," **F** *641-42,* 654
Weatherly, **O** 266
Weaver, Earl S., **B** 438, *595-97;* **S** 356
Weaver, George D. "Buck," **S** *232-33*
Weaver, James, **O** 330
Weaver, James R. "Red," **F** 35, 403; **I** 67
Webb, Del E., **B** 26, 366, 558
Webb, James "Skeeter," **S** 159
Weber, Richard A. "Dick," **I** 340, *349-51*
Weber State Junior College, **I** 224, 320
Webster, Alexander "Alex," **S** 466

Webster, F. A. M., **O** 465
Webster, George D., **F** *642-43*
Webster, Michael L. "Mike," **F** 565, *643-44*
Webster, Robert D. "Bob," **I** 490, *496-97*
Wedgeworth, Raymond, **S** 415
Wedgworth, Peggy Rawls, **I** 488
Weekes, Harold H., **F** *644-45*
Weems, Doris, **I** 123
Wefers, Bernard J. "Bernie," **O** *558-59*
Wehrli, Roger R., **S** *496-97*
Weick, William "Bill," **I** 646
Weidenborner, "Cy," **I** 555
Weightlifting Hall of Fame, **I** 629
Weiland, Ralph C. "Cooney," **S** 541
Weill, "Al," **I** 354, 437
Weimer, Jacob "Jake," **B** 332
Weiner, Herman, **I** 425
Weinmeister, Arnold "Arnie," **F** *645*
Weir, Edward S. "Ed," **F** *645-46*
Weir, Frank D., **O** 600-01
Weiser, ID baseball club (IdSL, IOSL), **B** 288; **S** 92
Weiskopf, Thomas D. "Tom," **O** *167-68*
Weiss, George M., **B** 26, 535, 559, *597-98;* **S** 91, 127, 173
Weiss, Robert W. "Bob," **I** 35
Weiss Park, New Haven, CT, **B** 597
Weissmuller, Peter John "Johnny," **I** 486-87, 586, 601, 614, *620-21,* 623; **O** 63, 501; **S** 569
Welch, Aristides, **O** 585
Welch, Michael F. "Mickey," **B** 297, *598-99;* **S** 150
Welch, Samuel, **O** 583
Welch, W. Ralph, **F** 645
Welch's Farm, Philadelphia, PA, **O** 584
Weld, Theresa, *See* Theresa Weld Blanchard

Weldon, L. D., **O** 474

Wellesley College, **O** 253

Welling, "Joe," **I** 469

Wells, Lloyd, **F** 591

Wells, Stanfield M., **F** 299

Wells, Wayne A., **I** *663-64*

Wells, Willie, **B** 6, 148, 273, 543, *599-600*, 612

Wells, W. R. "Clifford," **I** *321-22*

Wellsville, NY baseball club (NYPL), **B** 421; **S** 193

Wellwood Hanover, **O** 191

Welp, Christian A., **I** 116, 134

Welsh, "Freddy," **I** 411, 421, 444, 454, 475-76, 480

Welsh, George T., **S** 366

Welsh, "Jack," **I** 480

Welsh, "Spider," **I** 444

Welter Stakes, **O** 209

Welterweight Boxing Championships, **I** 355-56, 359, 361, 366, 369-70, 373, 376-77, 381, 388, 393-96, 412-13, 418, 421-23, 425, 432, 435, 455-56, 459-61, 464, 469-70, 473-74, 483

Welu, "Billy," **I** 350

Wembley Stadium, London, England, **O** 492

Wenatchee Junior College, **F** 114

Wenatchee, WA baseball club (NWL, WIL), **B** 626; **S** 88, 160

Wentz, Barney, **S** 439

Wepner, "Chuck," **I** 428

Werblin, David A. "Sonny," **I** 247; **O** *104-06*

Werden, Percival W. "Perry," **S** *233-34*

Werden's All-Stars baseball club, **S** 233

Wergeles, "Chick," **I** 404

Wernberg, **O** 206

Werner, "Ed," **O** 287

Werner, Wallace J. "Buddy," **O** *287-89*

Wertz, Douglas G., **F** 318

Wertz, Victor W. "Vic," **B** 394; **S** *234-35*

Wesleyan University, **F** 173, 475; **I** 177; **O** 71, 523

West, David Belford, **F** *646-47*

West, Jerry A., **I** 19, 23, 101, 147, 231, *322-23;* **S** 319

West, Samuel F. "Sammy," **S** *235-36*

West, Stanley "Stan," **F** 515; **S** 462

West, "Tommy," **I** 464, 473

West Baden, IN Sprudels baseball club (Negro Leagues), **B** 549

West Berlin, Germany Speed Skating Competition, **O** 317

West Chester State College, **I** 258; **O** 259

West Coast Relays, **O** 440, 484, 492

West Coast Wildcats football club (AFL), **S** 457

West Cornwall Club, **O** 109

West End Hotel Stakes, **O** 597

West Frankfurt, IL baseball club (ISL), **B** 595

West Germany National Soccer Team, **O** 300-01

West Germany National Ice Hockey Team, **I** 548

West Germany Olympic Ice Hockey Team, **S** 476

West Germany Olympic Weightlifting Team, **I** 630

West Germany Olympic Wrestling Team, **I** 658

West Haven, CT baseball club (EL), **B** 233

West Hudson Soccer Club, **O** 292-93, 309

West Liberty State College, **B** 420

West Orange, NJ Golf Club, **O** 109

West Palm Beach, FL baseball club

(FSL), **B** 76

West Palm Beach, FL Tropics baseball club (SPBA), **S** 79, 104

West Penn Amateur Golf Tournament, **O** 149

West Side Tennis Club, Flushing, NY, **O** 320, 356, 367, 415, 420; **S** 558-59

West Side Victory Club, Nashville, TN, **I** 579

West Texas State University, **O** 494; **S** 268

West Virginia Amateur Golf Tournament, **O** 154

West Virginia Association of Sportscasters, **F** 574

West Virginia Golf Classic, **S** 518

West Virginia Sports Hall of Fame, **F** 198, 203, 575

West Virginia Sportswriters Hall of Fame, **O** 450; **S** 291

West Virginia University, **F** 60-61, 200, 261, 274, 278, 350, 403, 407, 534, 574, 603, 668; **I** 39, 42-43, 67, 154, 322; **S** 369, 420

West Virginia Wesleyan University, **F** 28, 420-21

West of England Tennis Championships, **O** 350

Westchester Country Club, Rye, NY, **O** 117, 156

Westchester Cup, **O** 261, 299

Westchester Golf Classic, **O** 112, 124, 143; **S** 519

Westchester League Soccer Championships, **O** 299

Westchester Polo Club, **O** 51

Western Amateur Golf Tournament, **O** 121; **S** 521

Western Association, **S** 10-11, 17, 87, 190, 215

Western Athletic Conference, **F** 290-92, 324, 363, 371-72, 586, 663,

671; **I** 94, 320-21; **S** 254, 273, 395-96, 406-07, 492

Western Baptist College, **B** 6

Western Carolinas League, **B** 179; **S** 24, 51

Western Collegiate Athletic Association, **I** 59, 214-15, 292

Western Collegiate Athletic Conference, **O** 271, 481

Western Collegiate Hockey Association, **I** 548, 550, 563, 565, 567; **S** 543

Western Conference, **F** 12-14, 26-27, 38, 44-45, 49, 69, 94-95, 108, 119-20, 144, 152, 158, 172-73, 188-89, 193-94, 210, 217, 229, 233, 237, 240-41, 243-44, 255, 260-63, 267, 272, 283, 299, 319, 339, 343, 358, 369, 373, 377, 379, 413, 415-17, 425, 433, 438-39, 442, 446, 470, 475, 486, 528, 530-31, 533, 537-38, 550-52, 554, 563-64, 572, 602, 627, 650-51, 653-56, 660, 665, 668-70, 673; **S** 201, 333, 381, 392, 424-25, 434-35, 443, 447, 458, 480, 484-85, 566, 593, 598; *See also* Big Ten Conference

Western Conference Championships, **S** 201, 333, 424, 434-35, 458, 480, 485, 502

Western Golf Association, **O** 53

Western Illinois University, **S** 173

Western Intercollegiate Conference, **O** 464, 483, 524, 551

Western International League, **B** 16; **S** 79, 238

Western Junior Golf Tournament, **S** 521

Western Junior Singles Tennis Championships, **S** 556

Western Kentucky Teachers College, *See* Western Kentucky University

Western Kentucky University, I 66-67, 97-98, 116

Western League, B 79, 107, 285, 535, 547; S 32, 53, 82, 100, 110, 120, 123, 156, 196, 198, 215, 233, 239, 241

Western Maryland College, F 163, 242

Western Michigan Golf Tournament, S 521

Western Michigan University, F 358, 594; S 362

Western Open Golf Tournament, O 107-09, 112, 121, 127-28, 130-31, 133, 135, 140-42, 155, 158, 162, 166-67; S 515

Western Pennsylvania Amateur Soccer Championships, O 295

Western Pennsylvania Open Golf Tournament, O 133

Western Pennsylvania Open Soccer Championships, O 295

Western Pennsylvania Sports Hall of Fame, S 358

Western Reserve University, F 469, 543; O 154; S 339, 436; See also Case Western Reserve University

Western States Tennis Championships, O 325, 409

Western Union International Golf Tournament, O 151

Western Union Weightlifting Invitation Meet, I 626

Western Women's Amateur Golf Tournament, O 114, 159

Western Women's Junior Golf Tournament, O 129

Western Women's Open Golf Tournament, O 111, 129

Westfall, Robert B. "Bob," F 120

Westhead, Paul W., I 249; S 305

Westinghouse Broadcasting Company, S 358

Westminster College (MO), I 63-64, 139-40; S 580

Westminster College (PA), I 74, 141; S 261-62

Westmoreland County, PA Sports Hall of Fame, F 177; S 272

Weston, Edward Payson, O 559-60

Weston, Harold, S 612

Westphal, Paul D., I 144; S 326-27

Westphal, William "Bill," S 326

Westrope, "Jackie," O 210

Wethered, Joyce, O 165; S 521

Wethered, Roger H., O 133

Wetmore, Maud, O 133

Wetsel Junior College, F 407

Wettig, Pamela "Pam," I 184

Wettstone, Eugene "Gene," I 541-42

Weyand, Alexander M. "Babe," F 440; I 76; S 497-98

Weyhing, August "Gus," B 600-01

Weyhing, John, B 600

WGN Radio-Televison, Chicago, IL, O 52-53, 57, 272; S 343

Whalen, Eleanor Holm, I 487, 580, 621-22, 670; O 501

Wharton County Junior College, F 61

WHDH Radio-Television, Boston, MA, O 67

Wheat, Zachariah D. "Zack," B 488, 601-02

Wheaties Sports Federation, I 650

Wheatley Stables, O 184, 572, 605

Wheaton College, O 454

Wheelan, Jay, I 528

Wheeler, John, B 391

Wheeler, Samuel "Sam," I 173

Wheeling, WV baseball club (CL, IOL, ISL, MAL, TSL), B 25, 49, 217, 360; S 18-19, 42, 120, 127, 209, 238

Wheeling, WV Hall of Fame, F 274

Wheeling, WV Stogies baseball club, F 510-11

Whichone, O 585; S 533

Whimsical, O 211

Whirlaway, O 175, 195, 198, 204, 613, *614-15;* S 529

Whirlpool Golf Championship of Deer Creek, S 518

Whisk Broom II, O 211, 605; S 533

Whiskaway, S 533

Whiskery, O 202

Whitaker, Louis R., Jr. "Lou," S 225, *236*

White, Albert C. "Al," I 486, *497-98*

White, Arthur P. "Tarzan," F 447

White, Byron R. "Whizzer," F 248, 511, 568, 615, *647-48;* S 473

White, Charles R., F 8, *648-49;* S 468

White, "Charley," I *475-76*

White, Donald S. "Don," I 167

White, Dwight L., S 407

White, "Eddie," I 21

White, Frank, Jr., S *236-37*

White, George, F 30

White, Guy H. "Doc," B *602-03*

White, Harwood, O 374

White, James L. "Deacon," B 52, 270, 371, *603-04*, 628; S 178

White, Joseph H. "Jo Jo," I 121, 124, *323-24*

White, King Solomon "Sol," B 286, 333, 451, 500; S 143, *238-39*

White, "Larry," I 426

White, Major Andrew, O 70

White, Marilyn E., O 457

White, Michael "Mike," F 411

White, Nera D., I 123, *324-25*

White, Randy L., F *649-50*

White, Roy H., S 44

White, Sammy, F 485

White, Sherman, I 233

White, Wilford D."Danny," F 325

White, William D. "Bill," S 148, *239-40*

White, William H. "Will," B 463, 603, *604-05*

White, Willye B., S *597-98*

White Award, F 132, 248, 568, 615

White Horse Acres, Lexington, KY, O 606

White Mountain Alpine Ski Competition, O 297

White Plains, NY basketball club (HRL), I 314

White Plains, NY Golf Club, O 152

White Rat, S 88

White Sands Country Club, Virginia Beach, VA, S 519

Whitefish Mountain Alpine Ski Competition, O 284

Whitehill, Earl O., B *605-07*

Whiteley, Frank Y., Jr., O 579, 584, 603

Whitestag Trophy, O 284

Whitfield, Malvin G. "Mal," O 443, 458, *560-62*

Whitman, Hendricks H., O 413

Whitman, Malcolm D. "Mac," O 345, 383, *413-14*, 421

Whitman College, O 464

Whitmire, Donald B. "Don," S *498-99*

Whitmore, James A., O 77

Whitney, Casper, F 115, 158, 204, 343, 469

Whitney, Cornelius V., O 231

Whitney, Harry Payne, O 196, 201, 230-31; S 533-34

Whitney, John Hay, O 216

Whitney, Lawrence A., O 490

Whitney, Mrs. Harry Payne, O 198, 613; S 533-34

Whitney, William C., O 221

Whitney, W. U. C., S 526

Whitney Handicap, Saratoga Springs, NY, O 592
Whitney Stakes, O 570, 584, 614
Whittier College, B 545; F 7, 114
Whittingham, Charles E. "Charlie," O 228-29
Whittingham, Joseph, O 228
Whittingham, Michael C., O 229
Whitworth, Kathrynne A. "Kathy," O 152, 168-69, 170; S 509
Whitworth, Norman, O 579
Whizzer White Humanitarian Award, S 367
WHOM-Radio, New York, NY, S 343
Why Time Begins on Opening Day, S 337
Wichita, KS baseball club (AA, WA), B 30, 400, 542; S 173, 205
Wichita, KS baseball club (WL), B 288, 384, 569, 586
Wichita, KS Henrys basketball club (AAU), I 192, 326
Wichita, KS Vickers basketball club (NIBL), I 70
Wichita State University, I 31, 216; O 427; S 428
Wichita Falls-Longview, TX baseball club (TL), F 23; S 31
Wicker, Robert K. "Bob," S 161
Wicks, Sidney, I 331; S 285, 327-28
Wickware, Frank, B 255, 286; S 143, 168
Widdoes, Carroll C., F 272
Wide World of Sports, I 8; O 47, 59, 76
Widener, George D., O 201
Widener, Joseph E., O 186, 215; S 531
Widener Cup, O 198, 614
Widener Handicap, O 205, 223, 584
Widseth, Edwin C. "Ed," F 49, 447, 650-51

Wiggins, Mitchell, I 289
Wightman, Hazel Hotchkiss, O 329, 343, 354, 359-60, 364, 373-74, 387, 391, 414-16, 417
Wightman Cup Tennis Team, O 326-27, 329, 332, 335-36, 338, 343-44, 349, 352, 357, 359-60, 364, 373-74, 387, 389, 396-97, 414-15; S 550-51, 559, 564
Wilberforce University, S 238
Wilcox, David "Dave," S 499-500
Wilcutt, D. C., I 127
Wildair, S 533
Wilde, "Jimmy," I 40, 431, 481
Wildfire, S 191
Wilding, Anthony F., O 366, 372, 421
Wildung, Richard K. "Dick," F 49, 555, 651-52
Wilhelm, James Hoyt, B 352, 607-08; S 90, 216, 243
Wilke, Louis G. "Lou," I 325-27
Wilkens, Leonard R. "Lenny," I 107, 327-28
Wilkerson, Robert L. "Bobby," I 162; S 303
Wilkes, "Jack," I 461
Wilkes, Jackson Keith, See Jamaal Wilkes
Wilkes, Jamaal, I 56, 189, 331; S 328-29
Wilkes-Barre, PA baseball club (CL, EL, NYSL, NYPL, PSL), B 117, 326, 345, 496, 586; F 573; S 83, 248
Wilkes-Barre, PA Barons basketball club (EL), I 32, 195
Wilkes Spirit of the Times, O 583
Wilkie, David, I 595
Wilkins, Gerald B., S 330
Wilkins, Jacques Dominique, I 79, 153; S 329-30
Wilkins, Mac Maurice, O 562

Wilkins, Richard "Dick," **O** 562

Wilkinson, Charles B. "Bud," **F** 78, 168, 345, 515-16, 641, *652-54;* **S** 461

Wilkinson, James L. "J. L.," **B** 482, *608-09;* **S** 43, 137, 224

Will Be There, **O** 216

Willard, Jess, **I** 374, 376, 409, 412, 453, *476-77;* **O** 91; **S** 457

Willett, Robert Edgar "Ed," **B** 255

William Appleton's, Nahant, MA, **O** 349

William Johnston Trophy, **O** 401

William P. Kyne Handicap, **S** 532

William Penn College, **S** 319

William R. Jones Cup Games, **I** 291

William Schmeisser Memorial Trophy, **O** 247

William Smith College, **I** 45

William Woods College, **O** 546-47

William and Mary College, *See* College of William and Mary

William and Mary Hall of Fame, **F** 119

Williams, Archibald F. "Archie," **O** *563-64,* 566

Williams, Barney, *See* Battling Levinsky

Williams, Billy L., **B** 58, *609-10*

Williams, Carl, **S** 625

Williams, Charles D., **O** 416

Williams, Charles L. "Buck," **I** 71

Williams, "Christy," **I** 444

Williams, Claude P. "Lefty," **B** 108

Williams, Dorothy Rawls, **I** 488

Williams, Douglas L. "Doug," **F** 500

Williams, "Duke," **I** 384

Williams, Fred C. "Cy," **B** *610-11*

Williams, Freeman, Jr., **S** 329, *330-31*

Williams, Harry P., **B** 432

Williams, Henry L., Sr., **F** 27, 48-49, 144, 262, 537, *654-55*

Williams, Henry L., Jr., **F** 654

Williams, Irish "Ike," **I** 404, 441, *477*

Williams, James A. "Froggie," **F** 275, 422

Williams, Jerome R. "Jerry," **F** 566

Williams, Jesse, **B** 6

Williams, Joe "Smoky Joe," **B** 88, 286, 290, 331, 451, 453, 466, 500, *611-12;* **S** 137, 143

Williams, Kenneth R. "Ken," **B** 279, 558, *613-14;* **S** 202, 231

Williams, "Kid," **I** 370, 389, 399-400, 415, *477-78*

Williams, Lori, **I** 255

Williams, Mrs. F. Churchill, *See* Frances Biddle Toulmin

Williams, Mrs. Louise, **O** 329

Williams, Percy, **O** 465

Williams, R. F. "Rollie," **I** 206

Williams, Reggie, **I** 301

Williams, Richard H. "Dick," **B** 140, *614-15,* 633; **S** 89, 241

Williams, Richard N. II "Dick," **O** 329, 362, 368, 372, *416-17*

Williams, Robert "Bob," **F** 249

Williams, Theodore S. "Ted," **B** 41, 264, 300, 339, 342, 350, 491, 536, 570, 608, 611, *615-17,* 633, 635; **O** 60; **S** 40, 67, 79, 95, 195, 198, 338

Williams, Thomas M. "Tommy," **I** 545, 562-63, 569, *573-74*

Williams, Ulis, **O** 438

Williams, Victor, **S** 575

Williams, Warren, Jr., **I** 573

Williams, Wayne, **O** 542

Williams College, **B** 354; **F** 64, 84; **I** 177, 306, 313; **S** 297

Williams Grove Auto Race, **O** 5

Williamson, Edward N. "Ed," **B** 11, 541

Williamson, Ivan B. "Ivy," **F** 11

Williamson, "Jimmy," S 260

Williamson, Paul, F 338, 598

Williamson System, F 595

Williamsport, PA baseball club (EL), B 7, 61, 313, 395, 497; S 126, 150, 183, 187, 202, 230

Williamsport, PA baseball club (NYPL), B 66, 471; S 154, 207

Williamston, WV baseball club (MtnSL), B 413

Willie Mays: The Say-Hey Kid, S 347

Willis, John, O 590

Willis, Victor G. "Vic," B 95, *617-18*

Willis, William K. "Bill," F 70, 409, *656-57*

Willis L. Kilmer Stable, O 196

Willow Park Women's Invitation Open Golf Tournament, O 129

Wills, Elliott T. "Bump," B 619

Wills, Harry, I 419, 462, *478-79*

Wills, Helen, *See* Helen Wills Moody Roark

Wills, Maurice M. "Maury," B 9, 51, 131, *618;* S 53, 220

Wilmington, DE baseball club (ISL, TSL), B 34, 74, 345, 476; F 40; S 202

Wilmington, DE basketball club (EBL), I 150

Wilmington, DE Bombers basketball club (ABL), I 273

Wilmington, DE Wheelmen, O 375

Wilmington, NC baseball club (ECL), S 19

Wilson, "Alex," O 564

Wilson, Brenda Ann, O 215

Wilson, David C. "Dave," F 562

Wilson, Enid, S 521

Wilson, Ernest Judson "Jud," B 339, *619-20*

Wilson, George, S 457

Wilson, "Jackie," I 406

Wilson, James "Jimmie," B 588

Wilson, "Johnny," I 394, 428

Wilson, Lawrence F. "Larry," F *657-58;* S 497

Wilson, Lewis R. "Hack," B 40, 536, *620-22*

Wilson, Marc D., F 473; S 396

Wilson, Robert E., Jr. "Bobby," F 407, *658-59*

Wilson, Shelby A., I *664*

Wilson, Thomas "Tom," B 362

Wilson, Wendell S., F 674

Wilson, Willie J., B *622-23*

Wilson, NC baseball club (CrL), B 70

Wilson Sporting Goods Company, B 218; O 111, 129; S 424, 513

Wilson Teachers College, B 603

Wilt, Frederick L. "Fred," O 424, 521; S *598-99*

Wiltse, George L. "Hooks," B 46; S *240-41*

Wimbledon Junior Girls Tennis Championships, S 563

Wimbledon Men's Doubles Tennis Championships, S 558, 561; 1913, O 372; 1915, O 372; 1920, O 417; 1929, O 322, 408; 1930, O 322, 347, 408; 1931, O 368, 408; 1934, O 368; 1937, O 311; 1938, O 331; 1939, O 386; 1946, O 365; 1947, O 365

Wimbledon Men's Seniors Tennis Championships, O 400

Wimbledon Men's Singles Tennis Championships, S 555, 557, 559, 561, 563; 1892, O 334; 1896, O 366; 1905, O 366; 1910, O 421; 1913, O 372; 1920, O 404; 1921, O 404; 1923, O 362; 1927, O 418; 1929, O 418; 1930, O 322, 347, 395, 404; 1931, O 395, 409,

418; 1932, O 395, 410, 418; 1933, O 410; 1934, O 396, 418; 1935, O 418; 1936, O 331; 1937, O 331; 1938, O 330-31; 1939, O 386; 1947, O 365; 1949, O 355, 390; 1953, O 394, 407; 1955, O 407; 1969, O 356; 1972, O 399; 1974, O 341; 1975, O 323-24, 341; 1977, O 369; 1980, O 370; 1981, O 370; 1982, O 342, 370; 1983, O 370; 1984, O 342, 370; 1985, O 342; 1987, O 342

Wimbledon Mixed Doubles Tennis Championships, 1929, O 387; 1937, O 374; 1938, O 331; 1939, O 374, 386; 1947, O 338; 1948, O 338; 1949, O 338; 1950, O 338; 1951, O 359; 1952, O 359; 1953, O 369; 1954, O 359; 1955, O 359; 1956, O 359; 1962, O 349; 1967, O 363; 1970, O 335; 1971, O 363; 1972, O 335; 1973, O 363; 1974, O 363; 1980, O 326

Wimbledon Women's Doubles Tennis Championships, S 563; 1914, O 389; 1924, O 387; 1927, O 387; 1930, O 387; 1934, O 389; 1938, O 343, 374; 1939, O 343, 374; 1946, O 337, 348; 1947, O 358; 1948, O 337, 348; 1949, O 337, 348; 1950, O 337, 348; 1951, O 358-60; 1952, O 358, 360; 1953, O 358, 360; 1954, O 337, 348; 1957, O 358; 1959, O 358; 1960, O 358; 1961, O 363; 1962, O 363; 1965, O 363; 1966, O 358; 1967, O 335, 363; 1968, O 335, 363; 1970, O 335, 363; 1971, O 335, 363; 1972, O 363; 1973, O 335, 363; 1975, O 352; 1979, O 363; 1981, O 397; 1982, O 397; 1983, O 397; 1984, O 397; 1986,

O 381, 397

Wimbledon Women's Singles Tennis Championships, S 549-51; 1900, O 354; 1905, O 332; 1906, O 332; 1907, O 332; 1922, O 373; 1924, O 415; 1926, O 329; 1927, O 387; 1928, O 387; 1929, O 332, 387; 1930, O 387; 1932, O 387; 1933, O 387; 1935, O 387; 1936, O 360; 1938, O 361, 387-88; 1939, O 374; 1946, O 319; 1947, O 349; 1948, O 337; 1949, O 337; 1950, O 337; 1951, O 358-59; 1952, O 327; 1953, O 328; 1954, O 328; 1955, O 337; 1956, O 359-60; 1957, O 344, 357; 1961, O 357; 1966, O 363; 1967, O 363; 1968, O 363; 1972, O 363; 1973, O 363; 1974, O 351, 363; 1976, O 351; 1978, O 326, 379; 1979, O 379; 1981, O 351; 1982, O 363, 379; 1983, O 379-80; 1984, O 351, 379; 1985, O 351, 379; 1986, O 379; 1987, 379-80

Winch, "Art," I 459

Winchester, KY Hustlers baseball club (BGL), S 223

WIND-Radio, Chicago, IL, S 349

Wind, Herbert Warren, I 51; O 134; S 511

Windham, Rhonda, I 214

Windship, George B., I 633-34

Windsor, Canada baseball club (BL), S 199

Windsor Race Track, O 596

Windy City Speedway, S 191

Winfield, David M. "Dave," B 623-24; S 201

Winfrey, W. C., O 575, 599

Wingate, David, I 300

Wingate, Wilson, O 242

Winged Foot Country Club,

Mamaroneck, NY, **O** 113, 115, 134, 169; **S** 523-24
Wingfield, Walter Clopton, **S** 559
Winklefield, "Jimmy," **O** 183
Winkles, Bobby B., **S** 18, *241-42*
Winner, Charles H. "Charley," **F** 165; **S** 426, 497
Winning Colors, **S** 530
Winnipeg, Canada baseball club (NoL), **B** 73
Winnipeg, Canada Blue Bombers (CFL), **F** 218, 297
Winnipeg, Canada Jets hockey club (WHA, NHL), **I** 554; **S** 539-40, 542
WINS-Radio, New York, NY, **S** 343
Winslett, Hoyt "Wu," **F** 625
Winslow, F. B., **O** 419
Winslow, Kellen B., **F** 191, 291, *659-60*
Winston, Alexander, **O** 9
Winston Cup NASCAR Circuit, **O** 2, 27, 30, 41, 43-44; **S** 604-05
Winston Cup NASCAR Driving Championships, **O** 1-2, 30, 41, 43-44; **S** 604-06
Winston 500 NASCAR Race, Talledega, AL, **O** 1-2; **S** 605-06
Winston Holiday Basketball Classic, **I** 214
Winston-Salem, NC baseball club (CrL, Pil), **B** 115, 339, 356, 490, 595; **S** 51, 75, 193, 234, 242
Winston-Salem, NC Hanes Hosiery basketball club, **I** 253
Winston-Salem State University, **I** 89-91, 220
Winter, Fred "Tex," **I** 16, 94
Winter Haven, FL baseball club (FSL), **B** 471, 497, 515
Winter Haven, FL Super Sox baseball club (SPBA), **S** 94
Winter Park, CO Ski Competition, **O** 281, 288
Winterbottom, Thomas, **S** 311
Wintermute, Urgel "Slim," **I** 70, 91-92
Winters, Brian J., **I** 219
Winters, Frank J. "Coddy," **I** *574*
Winters, Jesse, **S** *242*
Winton Bullet Race Car, **O** 26
Wisconsin Athletic Hall of Fame, **F** 89, 269, 282; **S** 81, 103, 476
Wisconsin Bowlers Association Doubles Tournament, **I** 351
Wisconsin Caddie Championships, **S** 515
Wisconsin High School Football Coaches Hall of Fame, **S** 279
Wisconsin Interscholastic Athletic Association, **S** 279
Wisconsin Open Golf Tournament, **S** 515
Wisconsin Sports Hall of Fame, **I** 286
Wisconsin State League, **S** 63, 81, 162
Wisconsin Wrestling Hall of Fame, **I** 654
Wisconsin Wrestling Tournament, **I** 654
Wisconsin Rapids, WI baseball club (ML), **B** 631
Wise, Richard C. "Rick," **B** 73
Wise Counselor, **S** 531
Wiseman, James "Jim," **I** 162
Wismer, Harry, **F** 243
Wissahickon Challenge Cup, **O** 321, 325, 377, 405
Wistert, Albert A. "Al," **F** *660-61;* **S** 500
Wistert, Alvin L., **F** 660; **S** *500-01*
Wistert, Francis M., **F** 660; **S** 458, 500
Wistful, **S** 526-27, 529
Witasek, Herman, **S** 277

Withers Stakes, O 187, 199, 211, 222, 224-25, 578-79, 588, 596, 601; S 534
Witherspoon, Mark, O 486
Witt, Katarina, S 626
Witt, Lawton W. "Whitey," B 106
Witte, John "Johnny," I 21; S 287, 314
Witte, Leslie "Les," S *331-32*
Witte, Willard "Dutch," S 331
Wittenberg, Henry, I 662, *664-66*
WIXI-Radio, Pittsburgh, PA, S 358
WJAS-Radio, Pittsburgh, PA, S 358
WJR-Radio, Detroit, MI, S 348-49
WJZ-Radio, New York, NY, O 70
WKN-Radio, Knoxville, TN, O 82
W. L. Ranch, O 198
WLW-Radio, Cincinnati, OH, S 356, 493
WMAR-Radio, Baltimore, MD, O 75
WMBD-Radio, Peoria, IL, O 52
WMCA-Radio, New York, NY, O 52
WNEW Radio-Television, New York, NY, S 471
Wohlhuter, Richard C. "Rick," O *564-65*
Wojciechowicz, Alexander F. "Alex," F 188, 353, *661-62;* S 400
Wolf, Raymond, F 584, 621
Wolfe, Jack "Kid," I 431
Wolfe, Joseph, S 628
Wolfe, Mildred Burke Younker, S *627-28*
Wolfe, Violet, S 628
Wolfe, William "Billy," S 627
Wolfson, Louis "Lou," O 569
Wolgast, Adolph "Ad," I 411, 420, 444, 454, 476, *479-80*
Wolgast, "Midget," I 389, *480-81*
Wolman, Jerry, S 437
Wolverine, O 223
The Woman Bowler, I 346-47
The Women Superstars, I 28, 73, 176, 503
Women's American Basketball Association, I 176
Women's Basketball Committee, I 255
Women's Basketball League, I 28, 50, 73, 175
Women's Basketball League First Team, I 28, 175
Women's Basketball Rules Committee, I 246
Women's Home Companion, O 72, 359
Women's International Bowling Congress, I 342, 346-47
Women's International Bowling Congress All-Events Tournament, I 342, 344, 347
Women's International Bowling Congress Doubles Tournament, I 344
Women's International Bowling Congress Hall of Fame, I 342, 344, 346-47
Women's International Bowling Congress Match Game Tournament, I 344
Women's International Bowling Congress Queen's Tournament, I 342, 347
Women's International Bowling Congress Singles Tournament, I 342, 347
Women's International Bowling Congress Team Championships, I 342, 344, 347
Women's Lob, O 336
Women's National Rules Committee, I 297
Women's Olympic Track and Field Committee, S 569
Women's Professional Basketball League, I 8, 73, 175, 259, 290

Women's Professional Basketball
League Rookie of the Year, **I** 175
Women's Sports, **O** 260, 364
Women's Sports Association of New
York, **I** 494, 588, 622; **S** 622
Women's Sports Club of Tidewater, **I**
285
Women's Sports Foundation, **I** 291,
511, 579, 597, 611, 613; **O** 114,
160, 326, 328, 364, 482, 500; **S**
597-98
Women's Sports Foundation Amateur
Athlete of the Year, **I** 579; **O** 482
Women's Sports Foundation Hall of
Fame, **I** 613; **O** 114, 160, 328,
364, 500; **S** 598
Women's Sports Foundation
Professional Sportswoman of the
Year, **O** 326
Women's Sports Hall of Fame, **I** 580,
611
Women's Tennis Association, **O** 326,
364
Women's Tennis Association Player of
the Year, **O** 326
Women's Tennis Classic, Brisbane,
Australia, **O** 397
Women's Western Derby Golf
Tournament, **O** 111
Women's World Wrestling
Championships, **S** 628
Won't Tell You, **O** 569
Wood, Craig R., **O** 152-53, 155,
169
Wood, Gar, **O** 64
Wood, Howard E. "Smoky Joe," **B**
624-25; **S** 183
Wood, Joseph P., **B** 624
Wood, Marvin, **I** 130
Wood, "Randy," **S** 545
Wood, Richard, **F** 370
Wood, Sidney B., Jr., **O** 322, 331,
347, 395-96, *418-19;* **S** 559

Wood, Sidney B. III, **O** 418-19
Wood, Timothy L. "Tim," **I** 518,
519-20
Wood, Wilbur F., Jr., **S** *242-44*
Wood, William Barry, Jr., **O** 70; **S**
501-02
Wood, William V. "Willie," **F** *662-
63*
Wood Memorial Stakes, **O** 185, 192,
198, 569, 572-73, 579, 585, 598,
601, 606-07
Woodard, Lynette, **I** 315, *328-29*
Woodbine Track, Toronto, Canada, **O**
225
Woodburn Farm, Lexington, KY, **O**
174
Woodchopper, **O** 183
Wooden, John R., **I** 3, 55-56, 94,
101, 113, 116, 134, 168, 227-28,
257, 275, 293, 299, 312-14, *329-
32,* 584; **O** 477; **S** 251, 259,
271, 303, 326-28
Woodford, Catesby, **O** 588-89, 597
Woodford Farm, **O** 222
Woodford Town football club, **O** 306
Woodhouse, O. E., **S** 560
Woodley, David E., **F** 384
Woodling, Eugene R. "Gene," **S** 146
Woodman, "Joe," **I** 477
Woodrow Wilson Pace, **O** 600
Woodruff, George W., **F** 204, 240,
595; **S** *502-03*
Woodruff, Harvey T., **F** 533
Woodruff, Hiram W., **O** *229-30,* 583
Woodruff, John "Colonel Ogden," **O**
229
Woodruff, John Y., **O** *565-66*
Woodruff, Robert "Bob," **F** 73
Woods, Barry, **O** 71
Woods, "Cockey," **I** 467
Woodson, Michael D. "Mike," **I** 162
Woodson, Warren B., **F** 525, *663-64;*
S 425

Woodstock Farm, Chesapeake, MD, O 592

Woodstock Plate, O 201

Woodstock Stakes, O 192, 219, 576, 579, 581, 592, 610

Woodward, William F., Sr., O 184, 585, 598, 601

Woodward, William F., Jr., O 598

Woodwind Handicap, O 584

Woody, Ronald "Ron," I 557

Woody Stephens Stable, O 222

Woolf, George, O 605

Woolf, Herbert M., O 175, 195; S 528

Woolford Farm, O 195

Woolpert, Phil D., I 231

Woolvine, William "Bill," I 591

Woolworth, Norman, O 182

Wooster Athletic Association, F 183

WOR-Radio, New York, NY, O 272

Worcester, MA baseball club (AtA, NEL), B 63-64, 96, 238-39, 246, 326, 534

Worcester, MA baseball club (NL), B 64, 96, 238, 326

Worden, Neil, F 338

Work, Milton, O 405

Work, Mrs. Milton, O 406

Workman, Raymond "Sonny," O 193, *230-31*

World All-Tournament Basketball Team, I 59, 194

World Amateur Golf Cup, S 519

World Amateur Hockey Championship, I 35

World Aquatics Championships, I 491

World Balkline Billiards Championships, I 673

World Baseball Hall of Fame and Museum, S 140

World Basketball Association, S 316

World Basketball Championships, S 296, 310, 330

World Basketball Tournament, I 14, 28, 48-49, 55, 59, 66, 68, 88, 123, 175, 194, 211, 215, 223, 246, 258, 267, 291, 296, 325-26, 329; S 320

World Boxing Association, I 383-86, 396-97, 422, 452; S 612-13, 623, 625-26

World Boxing Association Heavyweight Championships, S 623, 625-26

World Boxing Association Light-Heavyweight Championships, S 613, 623

World Boxing Association Welterweight Championships, S 612

World Boxing Council, I 383, 385, 397, 401, 422-23, 466; S 612, 623, 625-26

World Boxing Council Heavyweight Championships, S 623, 625-26

World Boxing Council Light-Heavyweight Championships, S 612, 623

World Boxing Council Middleweight Championships, S 612

World Boxing Council Super Welterweight Championships, S 612

World Boxing Council Welterweight Championships, S 612

World Boxing Hall of Fame, S 343

World Boxing Organization Super Middleweight Championships, S 612-13

World Canoeing Championships, I 629

World Championship Golf Tournament, O 112, 131

World Championship of Women's Golf, O 164

World Championship Tennis Group, F

280; **O** 324, 341; **S** 561

World Chess Championships, **I** 672

World Class Track Club, **O** 436-37, 480

World Cross Country Championships, **O** 528

World Cup Alpine Skiing Championships, **O** 273-75, 280-85, 288

World Cup Alpine Skiing Circuit, **O** 273-75, 280-86, 288

World Cup Field Hockey Championships, **O** 259

World Cup Golf Tournament, **O** 69, 119, 144, 159, 163; **S** 511, 519

World Cup Ice Hockey Team, **S** 542

World Cup Men's Gymnastic Championships, **I** 522-23, 537, 539-40

World Cup Soccer Championships, **O** 291-92, 296-99, 301, 305, 309, 311

World Cup Speed Skating Championships, **S** 603

World Cup Track and Field Championships, **O** 425, 432, 485, 500, 506, 518, 557, 567; **S** 579, 584, 597

World Cup Volleyball Tournament, **S** 613

World Cup Women's Gymnastic Championships, **I** 529, 531, 533, 535

World Cup Wrestling Championships, **I** 637-39, 641-42, 654-60, 663

World Cycling Championships, **O** 316-17

World Drivers Championships, **O** 11

World Endurance Championships, **S** 619

World Festival, **S** 320

World Football League, **F** 2, 122, 258, 264, 277, 389, 419-20, 634,

662; **S** 404, 463-64

World Games Swimming Championships, **I** 575, 578-79, 591-92, 595-96, 605, 608-09, 611, 616

World Golf Hall of Fame, **O** 108-09, 119, 132, 136, 146-47, 150, 154, 164-65, 170

World Hard Court Tennis Championships, **O** 362, 404

World Hockey Association, **I** 553-54, 557-58, 562, 569-70, 573; **O** 63

World Hockey Association All-Star First Team, **I** 554, 558

World Hockey Association Championships and Playoffs, **I** 573

World Hockey Association Rookie of the Year, **I** 558

World Hockey Tournament, **I** 548, 563, 569

World Junior Cycling Championships, **S** 617

World Junior Hockey Tournament, **I** 511

World Junior Ladies Figure Skating Singles Championships, **I** 517

World Junior Speed Skating Championships, **O** 313

World Junior Wrestling Championships, **I** 657

World Lacrosse Games, **O** 237

World League of American Football, **S** 475

World Match Play Golf Tournament, **O** 135

World Men's Figure Skating Singles Championships, **I** 500-03, 508, 512-14, 518-19

World Open Golf Tournament, **O** 124, 143; **S** 510

World Pairs Figure Skating Championships, **S** 615

World Physique Title, I 630
World Powerlifting Championships, I 629
World Pro Wrestling Championships, I 643, 648, 661
World Professional Basketball Tournament, S 270, 277, 283, 293
World Professional Bicycle Sprint Championships, O 264, 269
World Professional Figure Skating Championships, I 503
World Professional Road Racing Championships, S 617-18
World Professional Seniors Golf Championships, O 112
World Professional Ski Championships, O 282-83
World Professional Swimming Championships, I 602
World Professional Tennis Championships, O 355
World Rodeo Championships, O 265
World Senior Ladies Figure Skating Singles Championships, I 504-07, 509-12, 515-17
World Senior Speed Skating Sprints, O 313-14, 316
World Senior Track and Field Championships, O 509
World Series, Black: 1915, B 500; 1916, B 549; 1921, B 500; 1924, B 6, 290, 362, 482, 500, 553, 609; 1925, B 6, 290, 362, 482, 500, 553, 609; 1926, B 192, 338-39; 1927, B 338-39; 1942, B 1, 56, 436, 520, 609, 620; 1943, B 453, 620; 1944, B 453, 620; 1945, B 282, 620; 1946, B 55, 151, 273, 362, 520, 609; 1948, B 244; 1954, B 88; See also Black World Series
World Series, College, B 341, 623; See also College World Series

World Series, Major League Baseball: F 40, 402, 420; I 105, 357, 572; O 45-46, 49, 56, 58, 63, 65, 67, 69-71, 74, 77, 79, 82-83, 89, 93, 98; S 61, 66, 68, 92, 94, 96, 155, 191, 204, 218, 235, 344, 348, 351, 356; 1903, B 27, 91, 95, 105, 110, 158, 328, 447, 581, 636; S 41, 156; 1905, B 46, 126, 154, 353, 390, 450, 580; S 3, 156, 198, 342; 1906, B 108, 137, 311, 468, 511, 587, 602; S 98, 161, 191; 1907, B 83, 156, 170, 282, 292, 311, 511; S 156, 161, 191, 198; 1908, B 83, 156, 170, 282, 292, 311, 457, 511, 557; S 156, 161, 191, 198; 1909, B 2, 95, 158, 282, 292, 327, 408, 581, 617; 1910, B 19, 103, 112, 287, 311, 340, 357, 359, 450, 511-12; S 156, 161, 179, 191, 198; 1911, B 19, 34, 103, 113, 157, 340, 357, 408, 450, 512; S 4, 41; 1912, B 208, 259, 340, 529, 624-25; S 111, 179, 218; 1913, B 19, 34, 103, 340, 357, 359, 450, 512; S 21, 179, 189-90, 218, 240-41; 1914, B 19, 103, 170, 357, 377, 450, 510; S 21, 41, 190; 1915, B 21, 93, 259, 474, 494, 529, 625; S 111, 144, 179; 1916, B 135, 208, 259, 392, 494, 534; S 41, 111, 156; 1917, B 103, 108, 173, 501; S 179, 232, 248; 1918, B 26, 259, 291, 357, 392, 571; S 21, 85, 156, 190; 1919, B 90, 93-94, 103, 108, 135, 173, 275-76, 323, 412, 501; S 66, 117, 126, 144, 179, 184, 187, 232, 345; 1920, B 24, 65, 118, 208, 228, 280, 456, 529, 565, 625; S 5, 41, 156; 1921, B 10, 19, 21, 66, 202, 266, 282, 302, 393, 397, 416, 459,

638; S 179, 190, 223; 1922, B 10, 19, 21, 202, 231, 282, 302, 393, 397, 416-17, 534, 638; S 21-22, 190; 1923, B 21, 282, 291, 302, 397, 417, 444, 494, 534, 638; S 21, 156, 190; 1924, B 219, 245, 282, 289, 293, 302, 332, 417, 471, 638; S 41, 131, 165; 1925, B 72, 118, 128, 158, 219, 245, 289, 293, 357, 361, 471, 562, 572; S 70, 105, 131, 165, 179, 184; 1926, B 5, 40, 238, 260, 325, 444, 473, 524; S 41, 156; 1927, B 129, 210, 269, 444, 494, 562, 589, 591; S 70, 105, 184; 1928, B 238, 361, 377, 494; S 122, 179; 1929, B 65, 101, 197, 229, 232, 345, 359, 401, 417, 483-84, 513, 537, 621; S 41; 1930, B 101, 197, 228, 232, 238, 254, 359, 401, 459, 513; S 179; 1931, B 40, 101, 145, 197, 203, 228, 387, 473, 483, 513; S 122, 208; 1932, B 87, 228-29, 235, 325, 346, 484, 489, 494, 537, 593, 630; S 41; 1933, B 123, 183, 219, 267, 376, 471, 552, 606; S 45, 117, 191; 1934, B 49, 101, 142, 203, 212, 238, 323, 387, 396, 473, 567; S 131, 183; 1935, B 49, 101, 200, 212, 219, 235, 309, 584, 593, 630; S 62, 110, 122, 183, 208, 343; 1936, B 27, 183, 267-68, 325, 552; S 149, 181, 191; 1937, B 27, 267-68, 325, 489, 552; S 10, 149, 181; 1938, B 80, 200, 235, 489, 630; S 62, 110, 181; 1939, B 145, 489, 513, 588; S 102, 122, 149, 181; 1940, B 17, 27, 49, 125, 145, 212, 216, 254, 335, 348, 361, 588; S 154, 183, 227, 245; 1941, B 86, 183, 200, 396, 582; S 24, 62, 68, 86, 102, 122,

149, 181; 1942, B 86, 146, 380-81, 412, 473, 525; S 10, 32-34, 86, 102, 143, 149, 181; 1943, B 86, 346, 525; S 33-34, 102, 141; 1944, B 381, 412, 525; S 33-34, 122, 127, 343; 1945, B 49-50, 80, 119, 230, 235, 356, 419, 630; S 155, 159, 164, 177, 225, 228, 245; 1946, B 123, 152, 381, 406, 412, 517, 635; S 17, 39, 143; 1947, B 36, 55, 86, 145, 366, 469, 521, 570, 582; S 86, 122, 127-28, 207; 1948, B 41, 151, 163, 167, 176, 258, 329, 525, 573; S 10-11, 108, 182, 186, 207; 1949, B 55, 70, 367, 418, 469, 535, 559, 597; S 10, 86, 113, 122, 173, 180; 1950, B 6, 55, 75, 187, 367, 469, 476, 535, 559, 597; S 95, 104, 113, 155, 173; 1951, B 55, 133, 274, 367, 374, 394, 469, 535, 559, 597; S 113, 173, 186, 207, 349; 1952, B 70, 367, 385, 404, 469, 521, 535, 559, 597; S 46, 113, 173, 180, 186; 1953, B 70, 367, 375, 385, 469, 535, 559, 597; S 46, 113, 173, 180, 186, 203; 1954, B 133, 162, 177, 274, 329, 394, 540, 594; S 64, 128, 182, 234, 347, 349; 1955, B 1, 70, 418, 426, 480, 521; 1956, B 36, 70, 367, 418, 517, 535, 559, 597; S 80; 1957, B 1, 4, 62, 388, 526; S 29, 353; 1958, B 1, 4, 62, 367, 388, 535, 559, 597; S 39, 353; 1959, B 9, 13, 79, 196, 312, 338, 448, 619; S 67, 112, 344; 1960, B 97, 174, 206, 383, 395, 473, 559; S 20, 29, 60, 75-76, 150, 230, 353; 1961, B 263, 383, 449; S 130, 353; 1962, B 263, 316, 351, 379, 383, 394, 448; S 349, 353; 1963, B 9, 138-39, 159, 264, 315, 383,

619; **S** 167, 204, 353; <u>1964,</u> **B** 26, 43-44, 187, 214, 383; **S** 203, 212, 354-55; <u>1965,</u> **B** 9, 139, 305, 315, 619; **S** 3, 53, 120, 160, 167; <u>1966,</u> **B** 13, 138-39, 364, 367, 437, 477-78, 544, 619; **S** 29, 167; <u>1967,</u> **B** 51, 67, 73, 187, 214, 339, 383, 503, 518, 614, 633, 635; **S** 193, 354; <u>1968,</u> **B** 51, 67, 73, 79, 214, 262, 296, 335, 383, 388, 503; **S** 57, 80, 125, 186, 354; <u>1969,</u> **B** 257, 314, 364, 498, 504-05, 598; **S** 35, 122, 146, 149; <u>1970,</u> **B** 16, 364, 392, 477-78, 486, 596; **S** 35, 71, 166; <u>1971,</u> **B** 97-98, 206, 364, 395, 425, 530; **S** 29, 150; <u>1972,</u> **B** 272, 277, 369, 486, 614; **S** 9, 84, 88-89, 166; <u>1973,</u> **B** 36, 272, 277, 394, 532, 614; **S** 9, 88-89, 123; <u>1974,</u> **B** 58, 134, 180, 272, 277, 544; **S** 9, 27, 80, 88-90, 114, 138, 185, 244; <u>1975,</u> **B** 10, 33, 115, 134, 182, 342, 486, 634-35; **S** 52, 72-73, 88-89, 166, 222; <u>1976,</u> **B** 10, 33, 191, 272, 340, 386, 486; **S** 28, 72-73, 89, 146-47, 153, 166, 346; <u>1977,</u> **B** 233, 272, 277, 284, 340, 386, 442, 518, 544; **S** 8, 27-29, 89-90, 114, 142, 147, 153, 185; <u>1978,</u> **B** 220, 233, 278, 320, 442, 518, 544; **S** 8, 27, 90, 114, 142, 147, 153, 185; <u>1979,</u> **B** 206, 372, 411, 440, 515, 530; **S** 15, 25, 76, 217, 357; <u>1980,</u> **B** 42, 48, 73, 75, 370, 431, 461, 486, 502, 622; **S** 16, 123, 237, 357; <u>1981,</u> **B** 220, 234, 284, 518, 595, 624; **S** 8, 27, 80, 109, 114, 142, 148, 153, 167, 174-75, 185, 357; <u>1982,</u> **B** 67, 115, 180, 252, 295, 514, 542, 544, 639; **S** 84, 87, 141, 207, 357; <u>1983,</u> **B** 73, 411, 486, 502, 515; **S** 166, 213; <u>1984,</u> **B** 10, 220, 614; **S** 50, 80, 146, 153, 218, 225, 236; <u>1985,</u> **B** 48, 370, 461, 622; **S** 207, 237, 355-56; <u>1986,</u> **B** 58, 76, 252, 472, 505; **S** 52, 96; <u>1987,</u> **S** 12, 15, 31, 158, 207; <u>1988,</u> **S** 49, 80, 107, 109, 167, 185; <u>1989,</u> **S** 49, 108, 174, 182, 356; <u>1990,</u> **S** 7, 49, 108, 166, 170; <u>1991,</u> **S** 146, 158

World Series of Golf, **O** 135, 139, 166; **S** 519, 521

World Series of Women's Golf, **O** 118

World 600 Auto Race, **O** 1, 27

World Sprint Bicycle Championships, **O** 317

World Sprint Speedskating Championships, **O** 313-14, 316-17; **S** 603-04

The World Superstars, **I** 503

World Swim Championships, **S** 603, 607-08

World Team Tennis, **O** 336, 341, 352, 364-65; **S** 298

World Team Tennis Championships, **O** 352

World Team Tennis Rookie of the Year, **O** 352

World Tennis, **O** 326, 343, 354, 364; **S** 551, 553, 558

World Track and Field Games: **S** 579, 584; <u>1983,</u> **O** 425, 486, 503, 528, 532, 540, 542; <u>1987,</u> **O** 425, 436-37, 482, 487, 504, 533, 541-42, 558

World Trophy, **O** 319, 374

World University Games, **I** 27, 72, 165, 195, 290, 310-11, 323, 329, 489, 497, 521, 523, 526, 537, 539; **O** 499; **S** 296, 320-21, 330, 587

World Volleyball Championships, **I** 676; **S** 613

World Weightlifting Championships, **I**

625-31, 633

World Women's Figure Skating
Championships, S 626, 628-29

World's Fair Derby, O 187

World's Invitation Bowling
Tournament, See Brunswick
World's Invitation Bowling
Tournament

World's Playground Stakes, O 610

*The World's Tallest Midget: The Best
of Frank Deford,* S 340

Worsham, Lewis E., Jr. "Lew," O
159; S *522-23*

Worsham, Richard, S 523

Worster, "Steve," F 516

Worth, IL Race Track, O 196

Worthe, Jorg, I 592

Worthington, Harry T., O 463

Worthy, James A., I 283-84

Wottle, David J. "Dave," I 564, *566-
67*

WPIX-Television, New York, NY, S
239

WPVI-Television, Philadelphia, PA, S
123

Wrangler Sanforest 400 Auto Race,
Richmond, VA, O 1, 41

Wrenn, Everts, O 420

Wrenn, George L., Jr., O 420

Wrenn, Robert D. "Bob," O 350,
413, *419-21*

Wrestling Coach of the Year, I 639,
642, 652

Wrestling Rules Committee, I 652

Wrestling's Man of the Year, I 652

Wright, Alfred, F 638

Wright, Archibald L., See Archie
Moore

Wright, Arthur, O 169-70

Wright, Beals C., O 339, 345, 372,
412-14, *421-22*

Wright, "Chalky," I 406, 450

Wright, Elmo, F 98, *664-65*

Wright, "Empie," O 335

Wright, Forrest Glenn, B 27, *625-
26;* S 206

Wright, George, B *626-29;* O 421

Wright, "Hoo," F 273

Wright, Irving C., O 373, 421

Wright, John R. "Johnny," B 453

Wright, Joseph "Joe," I 623

Wright, Marc S., O 462

Wright, Marion, O 333, 405

Wright, Martha Norelius, I *623*

Wright, Mary K. "Mickey," O 152,
168, *169-71;* S 509

Wright, Nathaniel "Nate," S 497

Wright, Richard, I 430

Wright, "Ted," I 396

Wright, Warren, Sr., O 195, 571,
576-77, 614-15; S 528-29

Wright, William Henry "Harry," B
370-71, *626-29;* S 65

Wright & Ditson Sporting Goods
Company, B 628; O 421

Wrightington, Edgar N., F 64

Wrigley, Philip K. "Phil," B 593,
629-30; S 142

Wrigley, William, Sr., B 417, 629

Wrigley, William, Jr., B 345, 629

Wrigley Field, Chicago, IL, F 31,
234, 415; O 53, 87; S 62, 84,
155, 162, 164, 175

Wrigley Swim Marathon, Toronto,
Canada, I 623

Wrobleski, Stanley "Stan," I 39

WSB-Radio, Atlanta, GA, S 348

WTBS Radio-Television, Atlanta, GA,
I 18, 263, 288-89; O 57, 83, 102,
272

WTCG-Radio, Atlanta, GA, See
WTBS Radio-Television, Atlanta,
GA

WTCN-Radio, Minneapolis, MN, S
201

Wuensch, Robert "Bobby," F 516

Wunderlick, "Jerry," I 39
Wyant, Adam M., F *665-66*
Wyant, Andrew, F 666
Wyatt, Bowden, F 576; S 448
Wyatt, John Whitlow "Whit," B 366;
    S 32
Wyckoff, Clinton R., F 426
Wykagel Country Club, New
    Rochelle, NY, S 322
Wykoff, Frank C., O 496, 516, 558,
    567-68
Wyllie, W. F., O 191
Wyman, Arnold "Pudge," F 27
Wynn, Early G. "Gus," B 242, 295,
    630-32; S 64, 83
Wynn, James S."Jimmie," S *244-45*
Wysocki, Ruth, O 540
Wytheville, VA baseball club (ApL),
    B 518; S 158

Xavier College of Australia, F 438
Xavier University (LA), O 496
Xavier University (OH), B 30-31, 61-
    62
Xerceise, O 198

Yachtman of the Year Award, O 103
Yackel, Kenneth J. "Ken," I 545
Yager, Abraham "Abe," B 299
Yagla, Charles E. "Chuck," I 657
Yakima, WA baseball club (WeIL), S
    79
Yakima, WA Browns baseball club
    (Negro Leagues), B 192
Yakult, Japan Swallows baseball club
    (JCL), S 90
Yale Bowl, New Haven, CT, F 57-58,
    86, 192, 239, 302, 380
Yale University, B 60, 597, 625, 634;
    F 38, 51, 57-58, 63-66, 84-86,
    116-18, 125, 155, 159, 177, 191-
    93, 195, 200, 238-39, 245, 250,
    255, 261, 264-66, 269-70, 298-99,
    301-02, 310-11, 342-43, 368, 379-
    80, 406-07, 421, 425-26, 469, 473-
    77, 504, 520, 530, 540-41, 563,
    603, 644, 647-48, 654; I 128,
    131, 156, 179, 199, 222, 239, 250,
    380, 472, 538, 543, 590, 602-03,
    606, 615, 642, 663; O 15, 61, 77,
    91, 256, 267, 356, 398, 419, 438-
    39, 536; S 56, 64, 181, 297-98,
    371-72, 376, 413, 433-34, 444-45,
    489, 501-02
Yale University Athletic Committee,
    F 117, 299
Yale University Football Association,
    F 58
Yancey, William J. "Bill," I 49, 68,
    144, *332-33*
Yang, C. K., O 478
Yankee, O 589
Yankee Conference, S 420, 460, 474
Yankee Stadium, New York, NY, B
    48, 110, 131, 149-50, 211, 213,
    291, 334, 366, 374, 382, 492, 495,
    510, 519, 545; F 98, 331, 500,
    532, 578; I 102, 359, 368, 405,
    421, 436, 455, 462; O 46, 74; S
    99
The Yankees: The Four Fabulous
    Eras of Baseball's Most Famous
    Team, S 335, 340
Yarborough, William Caleb "Cale," O
    1, 41, *43-44*
Yardley, George H., I *333-34*
Yarosz, "Eddie," I 481
Yarosz, Thaddeus "Teddy," I 367,
    481-82
Yarosz, "Tommy," I 481
Yarrow Brae Farm, Savage, MD, S
    525-26
Yary, Anthony Ronald "Ron," F 370,
    667-68
Yastrzemski, Carl M., B *633-34*, 635
Yastrzemski, Michael "Mike," B 634

Yates, Jilson, **O** 571

Yawkey, Thomas A. "Tom," **B** 124, *634-35; S 40*

Yawkey, William H., **B** 50, 408, 415-16, 634

Yeshiva University, **I** 665-66

Yomiuri Giants baseball club, **S** 96

Yonkers, NY Bantams basketball club, **I** 170

Yonkers, NY baseball club (EL), **B** 304

Yonkers, NY Marathon, **O** 466; **S** 583

Yonkers, NY Raceway, **I** 195; **S** 191

York, Preston Rudolph "Rudy," **S** *246-47*

York, PA baseball club (CL, EL, EIL, NYPL, Pil), **B** 330, 477, 537; **S** 6, 163, 200, 238, 242-43

Yorke, Billie, **O** 360

Yost, Edward F. "Eddie," **B** 304; **S** *246-47*

Yost, Fielding H. "Hurry Up," **F** 45, 47, 120, 158, 194, 240, 261-62, 343, 368, 439, 442, 446, 530-31, 603, *668-70;* **O** 464; **S** 435

Yost Fieldhouse, Ann Arbor, MI, **F** 669

You, Richard, **I** 630

You Know Me Al, **S** 248

Younce, Leonard "Len," **S** *503-04*

Young, Bobby Joe, **I** 452

Young, Claude H. "Buddy," **F** 56, 358, *670-71*

Young, Denton T. "Cy," **B** 4, 63-64, 92, 207, 360, 420, 439, 493, 538, 580, *635-37;* **S** 36, 49, 63, 216

Young, Dick, **S** *358-59*

Young, Donna, *See* Donna Young Caponi

Young, Jewell, **I** 167; **S** *353*

Young, "Jimmy," **I** 383

Young, John Steven "Steve," **F** *671-*

72; **S** 396

Young, Le Grande, **F** 671

Young, Milton, **O** 589

Young, Nicholas E., **B** 110, 457, *637-38*

Young, Sheila, *See* Sheila Young Ochowitz

Young, Walter, **S** 582

Young, William "Bull," **I** 476

Young America Cricket Club, Philadelphia, PA, **O** 338-39

Young America Cricket Club Invitation Tennis Championships, **O** 339

Young America Stakes, **O** 610-11

Young Corbett, *See* Corbett, Young

Young Corbett III, *See* Corbett III, Young

Young Fashion, **O** 583

Young Griffo, *See* Griffo, Young

Young Kid Kearns, *See* Kearns, Jack

Young Marino, *See* Marino, Young

Young Men's Christian Association, **F** 563; **I** 28, 77, 107-08, 122, 125, 222, 228-29, 232, 251, 254-55, 272, 486, 488, 522, 527, 534, 584, 602-03, 610, 620, 629, 634, 640, 653, 665, 676; **S** 315, 555, 566

Young Montreal, **I** 417

Young Stribling, *See* Stribling, Young

Youngblood, Herbert Jackson III "Jack," **S** 469, *503-04*

Younger, Paul "Tank," **F** 363, 500

Youngs, Joseph, *See* "Tommy" Ryan

Youngs, Ross M. "Pep," **B** 66, *638-39*

Youngstown, OH baseball club (IOL, ISL, MSL), **B** 184, 326, 359; **S** 246

Youngstown, OH *Vindicator,* **B** 169

Youngstrom, Adolph F. "Swede," **F**

4; **S** 483

Younker, Mildred Burke, *See* Mildred Burke Younker Wolfe

Yount, Lawrence K., **B** 639

Yount, Robin R., **B** 411, *639-40*

Your Host, **O** 189, 591

Youthful Stakes, **O** 569, 595

Yowarsky, Walter "Walt," **F** 199, 503

Yucatan Stakes, **O** 601

Yugoslavia National Basketball Team, **I** 60, 121

Yugoslavia National Soccer Team, **O** 301, 310

Yugoslavia National Wrestling Team, **I** 639, 658

Yuma, AZ baseball club (IVL), **S** 111

Z Belgian Cycling Team, **S** 618

Zachary, Jonathan Thomas "Tom," **B** 558

Zaharias, George, **I** 170, 172

Zaharias, Mildred Didrikson "Babe," **F** 308; **O** 90, 109-11, 159, 164, 170, *171-72*, 508; **S** 509

Zahn, Wayne, **I** *351*

Zale, "Tony," **I** 368, 393, *482-83*

Zaleski, Anthony F., *See* "Tony" Zale

Zalesky, James G. "Jim," **I** *666-67*

Zalesky, "Lenny," **I** 666

Zanesville, OH baseball club (MAL, OPL, TSL), **B** 291

Zaslofsky, Max "Slats," **I** 51, *333-34*

Zawoluk, Robert M. "Zeke," **I** 180, 198-99

Zayak, Elaine, **I** 505-06; **S** *628-29*

Zbyszko, Stanislaus, **I** 644

Zelica, **O** 580

Zenthoefer Fur Soccer Club, St. Louis, MO, **O** 301

Zernial, Gus E., **S** *247-48*

Zeus, **S** 526-27

Zev, **O** 215, 582; **S** 526-27

Ziegenfus, Valerie J., **S** 550

Ziegfeld, Florenz, **I** 622

Ziegler, William, Jr., **O** 198

Ziert, Paul, **I** 522-24

Zilly, John "Jack," **F** 249

Zimmer, Charles L. "Chief," **S** 36

Zimmer, Donald W. "Don," **S** 167

Zimmerman, Arthur, **O** 375

Zimmerman, Donald "Don," **S** 38

Zimmerman, Henry "Heinie," **S** *248-49*

Zivic, "Eddie," **I** 483

Zivic, "Fritzie," **I** 356, 367, 404, 455, *483-84*

Zivic, "Jack," **I** 483

Zivic, "Pete," **I** 483

Zivojinovic, Slobodan, **O** 370

Zoeller, Frank U., Jr. "Fuzzy," **S** *523-24*

Zombori, Oden, **S** 608

Zoo Zoo, **O** 201

Zorich, "Chris," **S** 420

Zorn, James A. "Jim," **F** 335

Zouski, "Steve," **I** 383

Zuk, Robert, **S** 50

Zukauskas, Joseph P., *See* Jack Sharkey

Zulueta, Orlando, **I** 461

Zuppke, Robert C. "Bob," **F** 38, 44, 218, 233, 669, *673-74;* **I** 286

Zurich, Switzerland Track and Field Meet, **O** 447, 480-81, 506, 541-42, 557-58; **S** 584

Zurita, Juan, **I** 477

Zwick, "Phil," **I** 439

About the Compiler

DAVID L. PORTER is Louis Tuttle Shangle Professor of History at William Penn College in Oskaloosa, Iowa. He is the editor of *Biographical Dictionary of American Sports: Baseball, Biographical Dictionary of American Sports: Football, Biographical Dictionary of American Sports: Outdoor Sports, Biographical Dictionary of American Sports: Basketball and Other Indoor Sports*, and *Biographical Dictionary of American Sports: 1989-1992 Supplement for Baseball, Football, Basketball, and Other Sports* (Greenwood Press, 1987-1992), a comprehensive multivolume reference work devoted to all major American sports. He is the author of *The Seventy-Sixth Congress and World War II, 1939-1940* and *Congress and the Waning of the New Deal*, and an associate editor of *American National Biography*. His articles have appeared in such books as *The Dictionary of American Biography, Directory of Teaching Innovations in History, The Book of Lists 3, The Hero in Transition, Biographical Dictionary of Internationalists, Herbert Hoover and the Republican Era, Franklin D. Roosevelt: His Life and Times, The Rating Game in American Politics, Sport History, Sports Encyclopedia North America, Book of Days 1988, The Harry S. Truman Encyclopedia, The Encyclopedia of Baseball Team Histories, Statesmen Who Changed the World*, and *Twentieth Century Sports Champions*. He has published articles in *American Heritage, Senate History, Aerospace Historian, The Palimpsest, American Historical Association Perspectives, Midwest Review, The North American Society for Sport History Proceedings, The Society for American Baseball Research Review of Books*, and numerous other state or topical historical journals. His articles also have appeared in the *Washington Post, Chicago Tribune, Des Moines Register*, and other newspapers. He is currently writing books on the San Diego Padres baseball club, on how historians rate America's greatest figures, and on the role of the U.S. Congress on foreign policy issues in 1941. He and his wife, Marilyn, a public school teacher, have two children, Kevin and Andrea.